T0211645

Lecture Notes in Computer Science 12208

More information about this series at http://www.springer.com/series/7409

Qin Gao · Jia Zhou (Eds.)

Human Aspects of IT for the Aged Population

Healthy and Active Aging

6th International Conference, ITAP 2020
Held as Part of the 22nd HCI International Conference, HCII 2020
Copenhagen, Denmark, July 19–24, 2020
Proceedings, Part II

 Springer

Editors
Qin Gao
Tsinghua University
Beijing, China

Jia Zhou
Chongqing University
Chongqing, China

ISSN 0302-9743   ISSN 1611-3349 (electronic)
Lecture Notes in Computer Science
ISBN 978-3-030-50248-5   ISBN 978-3-030-50249-2 (eBook)
https://doi.org/10.1007/978-3-030-50249-2

LNCS Sublibrary: SL3 – Information Systems and Applications, incl. Internet/Web, and HCI

Foreword

The 22nd International Conference on Human-Computer Interaction, HCI International 2020 (HCII 2020), was planned to be held at the AC Bella Sky Hotel and Bella Center, Copenhagen, Denmark, during July 19–24, 2020. Due to the COVID-19 coronavirus pandemic and the resolution of the Danish government not to allow events larger than 500 people to be hosted until September 1, 2020, HCII 2020 had to be held virtually. It incorporated the 21 thematic areas and affiliated conferences listed on the following page.

A total of 6,326 individuals from academia, research institutes, industry, and governmental agencies from 97 countries submitted contributions, and 1,439 papers and 238 posters were included in the conference proceedings. These contributions address the latest research and development efforts and highlight the human aspects of design and use of computing systems. The contributions thoroughly cover the entire field of human-computer interaction, addressing major advances in knowledge and effective use of computers in a variety of application areas. The volumes constituting the full set of the conference proceedings are listed in the following pages.

The HCI International (HCII) conference also offers the option of "late-breaking work" which applies both for papers and posters and the corresponding volume(s) of the proceedings will be published just after the conference. Full papers will be included in the "HCII 2020 - Late Breaking Papers" volume of the proceedings to be published in the Springer LNCS series, while poster extended abstracts will be included as short papers in the "HCII 2020 - Late Breaking Posters" volume to be published in the Springer CCIS series.

I would like to thank the program board chairs and the members of the program boards of all thematic areas and affiliated conferences for their contribution to the highest scientific quality and the overall success of the HCI International 2020 conference.

This conference would not have been possible without the continuous and unwavering support and advice of the founder, Conference General Chair Emeritus and Conference Scientific Advisor Prof. Gavriel Salvendy. For his outstanding efforts, I would like to express my appreciation to the communications chair and editor of HCI International News, Dr. Abbas Moallem.

July 2020   Constantine Stephanidis

HCI International 2020 Thematic Areas and Affiliated Conferences

Thematic areas:

- HCI 2020: Human-Computer Interaction
- HIMI 2020: Human Interface and the Management of Information

Affiliated conferences:

- EPCE: 17th International Conference on Engineering Psychology and Cognitive Ergonomics
- UAHCI: 14th International Conference on Universal Access in Human-Computer Interaction
- VAMR: 12th International Conference on Virtual, Augmented and Mixed Reality
- CCD: 12th International Conference on Cross-Cultural Design
- SCSM: 12th International Conference on Social Computing and Social Media
- AC: 14th International Conference on Augmented Cognition
- DHM: 11th International Conference on Digital Human Modeling and Applications in Health, Safety, Ergonomics and Risk Management
- DUXU: 9th International Conference on Design, User Experience and Usability
- DAPI: 8th International Conference on Distributed, Ambient and Pervasive Interactions
- HCIBGO: 7th International Conference on HCI in Business, Government and Organizations
- LCT: 7th International Conference on Learning and Collaboration Technologies
- ITAP: 6th International Conference on Human Aspects of IT for the Aged Population
- HCI-CPT: Second International Conference on HCI for Cybersecurity, Privacy and Trust
- HCI-Games: Second International Conference on HCI in Games
- MobiTAS: Second International Conference on HCI in Mobility, Transport and Automotive Systems
- AIS: Second International Conference on Adaptive Instructional Systems
- C&C: 8th International Conference on Culture and Computing
- MOBILE: First International Conference on Design, Operation and Evaluation of Mobile Communications
- AI-HCI: First International Conference on Artificial Intelligence in HCI

Conference Proceedings Volumes Full List

1. LNCS 12181, Human-Computer Interaction: Design and User Experience (Part I), edited by Masaaki Kurosu
2. LNCS 12182, Human-Computer Interaction: Multimodal and Natural Interaction (Part II), edited by Masaaki Kurosu
3. LNCS 12183, Human-Computer Interaction: Human Values and Quality of Life (Part III), edited by Masaaki Kurosu
4. LNCS 12184, Human Interface and the Management of Information: Designing Information (Part I), edited by Sakae Yamamoto and Hirohiko Mori
5. LNCS 12185, Human Interface and the Management of Information: Interacting with Information (Part II), edited by Sakae Yamamoto and Hirohiko Mori
6. LNAI 12186, Engineering Psychology and Cognitive Ergonomics: Mental Workload, Human Physiology, and Human Energy (Part I), edited by Don Harris and Wen-Chin Li
7. LNAI 12187, Engineering Psychology and Cognitive Ergonomics: Cognition and Design (Part II), edited by Don Harris and Wen-Chin Li
8. LNCS 12188, Universal Access in Human-Computer Interaction: Design Approaches and Supporting Technologies (Part I), edited by Margherita Antona and Constantine Stephanidis
9. LNCS 12189, Universal Access in Human-Computer Interaction: Applications and Practice (Part II), edited by Margherita Antona and Constantine Stephanidis
10. LNCS 12190, Virtual, Augmented and Mixed Reality: Design and Interaction (Part I), edited by Jessie Y. C. Chen and Gino Fragomeni
11. LNCS 12191, Virtual, Augmented and Mixed Reality: Industrial and Everyday Life Applications (Part II), edited by Jessie Y. C. Chen and Gino Fragomeni
12. LNCS 12192, Cross-Cultural Design: User Experience of Products, Services, and Intelligent Environments (Part I), edited by P. L. Patrick Rau
13. LNCS 12193, Cross-Cultural Design: Applications in Health, Learning, Communication, and Creativity (Part II), edited by P. L. Patrick Rau
14. LNCS 12194, Social Computing and Social Media: Design, Ethics, User Behavior, and Social Network Analysis (Part I), edited by Gabriele Meiselwitz
15. LNCS 12195, Social Computing and Social Media: Participation, User Experience, Consumer Experience, and Applications of Social Computing (Part II), edited by Gabriele Meiselwitz
16. LNAI 12196, Augmented Cognition: Theoretical and Technological Approaches (Part I), edited by Dylan D. Schmorrow and Cali M. Fidopiastis
17. LNAI 12197, Augmented Cognition: Human Cognition and Behaviour (Part II), edited by Dylan D. Schmorrow and Cali M. Fidopiastis

38. CCIS 1224, HCI International 2020 Posters - Part I, edited by Constantine Stephanidis and Margherita Antona
39. CCIS 1225, HCI International 2020 Posters - Part II, edited by Constantine Stephanidis and Margherita Antona
40. CCIS 1226, HCI International 2020 Posters - Part III, edited by Constantine Stephanidis and Margherita Antona

http://2020.hci.international/proceedings

6th International Conference on Human Aspects of IT for the Aged Population (ITAP 2020)

Program Board Chairs: Qin Gao, Tsinghua University, China, and Jia Zhou, Chongqing University, China

- Inês Amaral, Portugal
- Ning An, China
- Venkatesh Balasubramanian, India
- Alex Chaparro, USA
- Honglin Chen, China
- Jessie Chin, USA
- José Coelho, Portugal
- Francesca Comunello, Italy
- Hua Dong, UK
- Katharine Hunter-Zaworski, USA
- Hirokazu Kato, Japan
- Jiunn-Woei Lian, Taiwan
- Chi-Hung Lo, Taiwan
- Eugène Loos, The Netherlands
- Brandon Pitts, USA
- Jing Qiu, China
- Peter Rasche, Germany
- Marie Sjölinder, Sweden
- Wang-Chin Tsai, Taiwan
- Ana Isabel Veloso, Portugal
- Konstantinos Votis, Greece
- Yuxiang (Chris) Zhao, China
- Junhong Zhou, USA
- Martina Ziefle, Germany

The full list with the Program Board Chairs and the members of the Program Boards of all thematic areas and affiliated conferences is available online at:

http://www.hci.international/board-members-2020.php

HCI International 2021

The 23rd International Conference on Human-Computer Interaction, HCI International 2021 (HCII 2021), will be held jointly with the affiliated conferences in Washington DC, USA, at the Washington Hilton Hotel, July 24–29, 2021. It will cover a broad spectrum of themes related to Human-Computer Interaction (HCI), including theoretical issues, methods, tools, processes, and case studies in HCI design, as well as novel interaction techniques, interfaces, and applications. The proceedings will be published by Springer. More information will be available on the conference website: http://2021.hci.international/.

General Chair
Prof. Constantine Stephanidis
University of Crete and ICS-FORTH
Heraklion, Crete, Greece
Email: general_chair@hcii2021.org

http://2021.hci.international/

Contents – Part II

Well-Being, Persuasion, Health Education and Cognitive Support

Aging in Place

Cultural and Entertainment Experiences for Older Adults

Health and Rehabilitation Technologies

Agent-Based Simulation of Medical Care Processes in Rural Areas with the Aid of Current Data on ICT Usage Readiness Among Elderly Patients

Christina Büsing[1]([⊠]), Sabrina Schmitz[1], Mariia Anapolska[1],
Sabine Theis[2], Matthias Wille[2], Christopher Brandl[2], Verena Nitsch[2],
and Alexander Mertens[2]([⊠])

[1] Lehrstuhl II für Mathematik, Junior Professor for Robust Planning in Health Care, RWTH Aachen University, Pontdriesch 10-12, 52062 Aachen, Germany
buesing@math2.rwth-aachen.de
[2] Institute of Industrial Engineering and Ergonomics, RWTH Aachen University, Bergdriesch 27, 52062 Aachen, Germany
a.mertens@iaw.rwth-aachen.de

Abstract. Sustainable health care in rural areas is confronted with enormous challenges as a result of numerous social trends. From a technical perspective, promising digital approaches are being advocated for patient-physician interaction in particular, which aim to facilitate medical care. However, a broad implementation of such systems has hardly been achieved so far and there is a lack of suitable methods to prospectively evaluate the medical, social and financial implications. Simulations represent a promising approach to quantify health care systems and the influence of system changes. In this study, an agent-based simulation is used to model patients and physicians as individual agents. This enables a detailed representation of the interactions taking place in the health care system within a given period of time. This approach allows the comparison of key performance indicators regarding the effects of different system changes. The use of information and communication technologies (ICT) is not a matter of course, especially for older people, for whom an increasing need for care must be assumed. To reflect this in the digitization of the health care system, the patients of the simulation are extended in this study by a factor involving ICT usage readiness, which was collected within the framework of a nationwide trend study. In addition, two appointment systems are developed that support digital ICT. An evaluation has revealed that senior citizens with the currently known ICT usage behavior are placed at a disadvantage with the introduction of digital appointment scheduling systems.

Keywords: Simulation · Health care · Agent systems · ICT · Patients · Demographic change

© Springer Nature Switzerland AG 2020
Q. Gao and J. Zhou (Eds.): HCII 2020, LNCS 12208, pp. 3–12, 2020.
https://doi.org/10.1007/978-3-030-50249-2_1

1 Introduction and Motivation

Health is one of the most important factors for the well-being and prosperity of a society. For this reason, all member states of the World Health Organization (WHO) commit to ensure each person access to health services [1]. In general, people with medical concerns get access to health services by contacting their general practitioners (GPs). GPs provide first examinations, and if necessary, ensure continued medical care, for instance by referring patients to a specialist or to a hospital. Due to this important job of managing patients' access to medical care, GPs are regarded as gatekeepers in health care systems.

However, due to the demographic change the demand for health care services increases while the number of operating GPs decreases. This problem is increasingly observed in rural areas where fewer medical students are willing to open a practice [2]. Consequently, an aging population combined with mainly elderly GPs, who retire swiftly, threaten the guarantee of timely medical care. In addition, access to medical care becomes even more difficult in rural areas due to spatial distances, different age and health structures of the population and constantly increasing cost pressure.

For this reason, the management of a GP's practice is indispensable in order to at least use the available resources optimally. Promising solutions refer to modern, digital and technology-supported forms of patient-physician interaction.

The success of introducing new digital solutions in health care services depends heavily on patients' information and communication technologies (ICT) usage readiness. The usage of ICT is not self-evident, in particular for elderly patients, who have an increasing demand of health care. A widespread introduction of new ICT-based systems such as digital appointment scheduling systems, is virtually non-existent. Furthermore, the influence is unknown and difficult to predict. So far, the empirical added value of digital systems in health care services can be only determined based on pilot studies. Consequently, suitable approaches are sought to investigate the social but also the financial impact of digital supply systems - for health care services in general and in particular for the patient-physician interaction.

A promising approach to quantify supply systems and the influence of system changes are agent-based simulations. Such simulations allow a detailed modeling of the interactions between patients and physicians that take place in the health care system over a given period of time. Individual patient- or physician-specific characteristics and behavior can be modeled using defined probability distributions. Consequently, it is possible to analyze and evaluate specific questions and concrete cause-effect relationships. In particular, age-differentiated disposition characteristics and behavioral patterns can be adequately taken into account. The problem, however, often lies in the lack of representative and encompassing patient- and physician-specific data set.

Our contribution in this study is the analysis of digital communication between physicians and patients with individual ICT usage readiness, which is based on data from the Tech4Age trend study [3], using the agent-based simulation SiM-Care [4]. For this purpose, two appointment systems supporting ICT are conceptualized and integrated into the simulation SiM-Care by Comis et al. [4] (see Sect. 2.1). In addition, to simultaneously imitate the information and communication technology usage behavior

(ICT usage behavior) of patients as realistically as possible, data from the Tech4Age trend study by Mertens et al. [3] are added to the simulation (see Sect. 2.2). This data added to the model allows to approximate the ICT usage behavior of elderly patients in particular and the associated impact of the digitization of care processes on this user group to be addressed. A simulation of the patient-physician interaction yields various key performance indicators (KPIs) that allow for a quantitative evaluation of the system changes taking the ICT usage behavior of the patients into account (see Sect. 3). Finally, a conclusion with prospects for future work is presented, and the study's limitations are pointed out (see Sects. 4 and 5).

1.1 User-Centered Development

Simulation of agents that represent human actors should reflect characteristics of humans if they are to predict human behavior accurately. In order to be able to automatically tailor agents to individual users, information about the respective person is indispensable. In the process of personalization, user-centered development helps to prepare the necessary knowledge about the relevant characteristics of the target group in a structured way. According to DIN EN ISO 9241-11, usability refers to the extent to which a product, system or service can be used by specific users in a specific application context to achieve specific goals effectively, efficiently and satisfactorily. Usability relates to the concepts user friendliness and user experience and can be achieved by placing the user of a product and the user tasks, objectives and characteristics at the center of the development process. The process of usability engineering is iterative and consists of different phases. First phase is the analysis of the usage-context. During the analysis of the usage context, research collects and summarizes information about future users in user profiles or personas. Furthermore, user research activities aim at identifying tasks and objectives of the users, their work processes and corresponding working environment. The second phase within the usability engineering process is the requirements engineering. Here, results of the context analysis lay the ground for the requirement formulation. Finally, prototypes are created that meet the requirements. These prototypes are evaluated together with users, so that the results are incorporated into the improvement and refinement of the prototype. The process ends when the product displays a satisfactory level of usability. The user-centered development process thus demonstrates that sustainable technology design is only possible through participation. Sustainability includes economic, ecological and social aspects. Especially the last two often remain underexposed in technology and product development. Ecological consequences that have not been considered are often only recognized once a product has been realized. Furthermore, many technical products miss the intended target group because there is no clear or a distorted picture of this target group. For example, oftentimes neither gender nor other individual differences are taken into account or only in a stereotypical way. So far, participatory approaches in the field of system modelling are very limited, which is why they are the subject of present investigation.

2 Integration of ICT Usage Readiness into the Agent-Based Simulation

2.1 SiM-Care: Agent-Based Simulation of Patient-Physician Interaction

In this study, the agent-based simulation SiM-Care developed by Comis et al. [4] is used. SiM-Care allows for a detailed modeling of the interactions between patients and physicians occurring in the health care system. Patients and physicians are modeled by simulation agents and represent individuals with personalized characteristics. The characteristics of both physicians and patients can be exchanged and extended in SiM-Care as required. The following is an excerpt of essential characteristics of agents in SiM-Care.

Previously, patients have personal attributes such as an age class and a general health condition. The general health condition of patients particularly includes chronic diseases that need regular check-ups. Further characteristics of patients are, for instance, limited time availabilities due to professional reasons and preferences with regard to physicians. The latter is based on, for example, the distance between the physicians' practices and the patients' homes, as well as positive and negative experiences during the practice visits.

Physicians, on the other hand, have systematic attributes such as appointment scheduling systems and rules, or so-called strategies, pertaining to the admission of patients and the order of treatments. Up to this time, physicians use an appointment scheduling system, the so-called Phone-Call Booking System (PCB), in which the physician's entire working time is divided into time slots of equal length. Each slot can be assigned exactly one appointment, which are only arranged by telephone call. The decision whether patients are admitted for their treatments is also based on physician's predefined strategies. According to the currently implemented strategies, patients who make an appointment in advance are guaranteed treatment. If patients show up at the medical practice unannounced, they may be rejected by the physician due to, for instance, crowded waiting rooms and too many appointments scheduled for that day. However, negative experiences of patients, such as the refusal of treatment or excessively long waiting times, cause a patient to change physicians.

The patient-physician interaction in SiM-Care is triggered by patients who consult their physician because of health concerns. The point in time or frequency at which patients suffer from illnesses are generated from probability distributions that are determined by the patient's age class and general health status. The type and duration of illnesses, as well as the resulting willingness to wait for treatment are also influenced by the patient's age and health condition and determined by probability distributions. As soon as physicians receive a request for an appointment, they respond by proposing an appointment. If this proposal does not satisfy the patient's willingness to wait for treatment, the patient decides to visit the practice without an appointment, i.e. as a walk-in patient.

Simulating with SiM-Care provides both patient- and physician-specific KPIs. Patient-specific indicators are, for instance, waiting times at the practice and the so-called access times, i.e. waiting times up until the actual appointment. Physician-specific indicators include the workload and overtime of physicians. Furthermore, appointment scheduling systems can be evaluated, for example, on the basis of the number of patients who visit the practice with or without an appointment. Overall, the KPIs determined with SiM-Care provide information about the efficiency of medical care processes.

2.2 Tech4Age Trend Study: ICT Usage Readiness Among the Elderly Population

In 2016, the interdisciplinary research team Tech4Age launched a trend study to evaluate the use of information and communication technologies among the elderly (60+) in Germany [3, 5] focused on the information sources preferred for such use, as well as the corresponding media and technical aids to support compliance with medical therapy guidelines in answering questions in everyday life. In addition, data on usage behavior, acceptance and dissemination of technologies were also collected. These aspects were then combined with approaches to quantify individual propensity for technology, perceived usability, health and digital literacy. All data were compiled and evaluated in relation to socio-demographic factors.

The majority of the questions involved close-ended questions, meaning that the participants had to select one or more predefined answers or rate statements on a Likert scale. In addition, open-ended questions were included in order to gain deeper insights into the motivation for specific behavior and to reveal new, unknown aspects. The answers to the open-ended questions were then coded for analysis by two independent researchers.

In October 2018, in the second round of the Tech4Age trend study, a paper-based questionnaire was sent by Deutsche Post AG to 5000 households via Infopost. These were households in which residents aged at least 60 years were registered. The mailing selection represented a random nationwide sample throughout Germany, based on a demographically and socioeconomically representative distribution. With more than 700 answered questionnaires (response rate > 14%), a satisfactory data basis was collected, which constitutes the basis for current estimates of age-differentiated ICT usage readiness. Thus, the ICT usage readiness of senior citizens can be modeled based on socio-geographic and demographic aspects.

2.3 Integration of ICT Usage Readiness in SiM-Care

In this study, the agent-based simulation SiM-Care is used to investigate the effects of digital systems designed for communication between patients and physicians. To increase the validity of SiM-Care, the characteristics of the patients are extended by an individual and age-dependent ICT usage readiness, which is modeled by a value between zero and 100%. Based on the current ARD/ZDF online study 2019 [6], the ICT usage readiness of patients up to and including 49 years of age is set to 100%. To model the ICT usage readiness of patients 60 years of age and older, a multifactorial index is calculated based on data from the Tech4Age trend study. The index takes into account both the basic availability of corresponding technologies as well as the individual frequency of use and readiness to use technology [7] based on the age of the patients. Consequently, factors such as acceptance, competence and assumed control over technologies are represented according to the empirical data basis. As expected, the index shows an overall disproportionate decrease in ICT usage readiness with the increasing age of the respondents. However, it should be noted that this trend is not continuous. Instead, a comparison of the 65–69 age group with 70–74 years reveals that ICT usage readiness is significantly higher in the older age group. This effect can also be observed when comparing the age groups 75–79 years and 80–84 years. Finally, for patients aged 50–59 years, the ICT usage readiness is interpolated.

Furthermore, two appointment systems that support digital and modern ICT are integrated into SiM-Care. These strategies provide, along with the standard telephone-call-based communication, an alternative way to request an appointment – by using ICT. The newly integrated systems, further referred to as digital systems, are the Variable-Slots App Booking System (VSAB) and the Fixed-Slots App Booking System (FSAB). When a physician uses the VSAB system, at the beginning of each day all slots that are not yet assigned and that take place on this day are excluded from the call-based appointment scheduling. These slots are only available for booking exclusively using the ICT. Slots for subsequent days can still be requested by telephone call. In the FSAB system, every day a pre-defined number of slots are reserved for appointment requests solely via ICT and become available to patients for booking on the evening before. All other slots can still be requested by telephone call.

The patient-physician interaction using the new appointment systems and the integrated ICT usage readiness is changed as follows. If patients have a low level of ICT usage readiness, they will contact their physician exclusively by telephone call. In contrast, patients with a high level of ICT usage readiness first use the ICT to request an appointment. If this request is unsuccessful, they follow the same appointment scheduling process as patients with a low level of ICT usage readiness.

3   Case Study

In this case study, the patient-physician interaction in the health care system, which takes place in primary health care, is analyzed for the northern Eifel region by the agent-based simulation SiM-Care. The northern Eifel region is a district of Aachen in which 20 GPs are currently operating. The exact locations of the medical practices as well as the opening hours are modeled in SiM-Care exactly. The population is generated in such a way that both its age distribution and geographical distribution follow the data from the 2011 census [8]. Four acute and three chronic illnesses are chosen among the most frequently diagnosed illnesses to be modeled in SiM-Care [9]. The attributes of the illnesses (average duration, frequency of occurrence and follow-ups) are based on the Barmer GEK Physician Report 2011 [10] and empirical estimates. The proportion of chronically ill patients is also taken from the Barmer GEK Physician Report 2011 [10]. As this study focuses on the northern Eifel region, which is predominantly rural, the ICT usage behavior of patients is based exclusively on data of the Tech4Age study from people who live in rural areas.

The subject of this case study is the impact of new appointment scheduling systems. In particular, the success rate of appointment arrangements is investigated, i.e. how often patients can make an appointment within their willingness to wait. Since all patients in SiM-Care first try to make an appointment by telephone call or, if applicable, additionally by ICT, the number of walk-in patients indicates the number of unsuccessful appointment requests. In the following, the age distribution of walk-in patients is investigated depending on the physicians' appointment scheduling systems and the patients' ICT usage readiness. Furthermore, two different degrees of usability of ICT-based appointment scheduling systems are considered. This allows for modeling different ICT usage readiness depending on the ICT's complexity, i.e. whether the ICT is user-friendly or -unfriendly. The usability of an appointment scheduling system is modeled by a minimal threshold of ICT usage readiness that a patient must have in order to use the ICT for requests.

Figure 1 depicts the percentage of walk-in patients aged up to 50 years, between 50 and 60 years, and over 60 years of age depending on the appointment systems used by physicians. In the following, we focus on the difference between the results for patients aged up to 50 and over 60 years. Generally, the percentage of walk-in patients under 50 years of age decreases when using a digital appointment scheduling system. More precisely, when using a user-friendly FSAB system, the percentage declines from 52% to 51%, while the use of a user-friendly VSAB system results in a percentage of only 48%. Considering user-unfriendly FSAB and VSAB systems, the percentage even declines to 49% and 45%, respectively. In contrast, the percentage of walk-in patients over 60 years of age increases if a digital system is applied, even more significantly in the case of a user-unfriendly appointment scheduling system. More precisely, the use of the FSAB system leads to a share of 31% if the system is user-unfriendly, and a share of 33% if the system is user-friendly. When using the VSAB system the numbers still increases such that a user-friendly system leads to a share of 35% and for a user-unfriendly to a share of 36%. Consequently, patients under 50 years of age are more frequently given an appointment when using a digital appointment system. By contrast, patients over the age of 60 are less likely to make appointments. The performance indicators show that patients with a high level of ICT usage readiness are improving their chances of making appointments. At the same time, it becomes evident that patients whose willingness to use ICT is generally lower are placed at a disadvantage

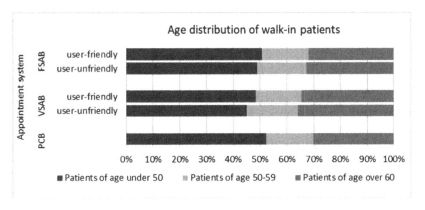

Fig. 1. Age distribution of walk-in patients depending on appointment system and ICT usability.

with regard to arranging appointments. This effect occurs regardless of whether a user-friendly or -unfriendly digital appointment scheduling system is used. If the system is user-unfriendly, patients with a low ICT usage readiness are even more disadvantaged.

4   Conclusion and Future Work

Health care research hopes to be able to respond sustainably to developments in social age structures and geosocial shifts with the help of digitalized processes. The effects and consequences of new integrated systems are often not known. The present study shows that agent-based simulation SiM-Care enables prospective assessments of the implications of technology integration in health care systems. Simulating the individual agents makes it possible to dispense with averages for society as a whole and instead model the individual behavior of patients and physicians. In the case study of the northern Eifel region, the effects of the introduction of digital appointment scheduling systems in medical practices are examined. The results suggest that patients with a low level of ICT usage readiness are at a disadvantage, which particularly affects elderly patients. The evaluation by means of SiM-Care thus enables the prospective assessment of potential impacts of system changes, in particular the early detection of negative effects. Future work on agents considering user and contextual factors are required. Therefore, attributes need to be defined with which users can be characterized with regard to the given context. These might, for example, include personality traits, experience-oriented needs, physiological measures, age and basic attitudes. Such user models would concretize and extend the basic agent models specifically for this specific application area. Existing research and experiences on user and human factors modeling needs to be integrated in a structured way, and where necessary new insights capturing changes and behavior such as, for example, new ICT artifacts or data security aspects over time through representative trend studies need to be generated. In the present case, domain-specific user modelling would make it possible to develop a user-centered model that is precisely tailored to different fields of application. The structures of the basic user model and the consistent modelling principle would allow transferability to other application areas. In addition, by building up a broad database on the variability of user characteristics, it would be possible to draw on existing knowledge when developing future fields of application.

5   Limitations

Prospective simulations always involve limitations for the transferability of the results due to the reduction of the models and with regard to the suitability of the data basis used. This also applies for the statements and evaluations approximated in this study. Factors and influencing variables that are relevant for a valid modeling of patient behavior are inevitably omitted. Despite the large sample size and corresponding filter criteria, the database which is transferred to the northern Eifel region, is restricted. Consequently, certain methodological limitations must be taken into account in data collection, regardless of the basic statements made. The challenge with large-scale trend studies involving questionnaire-based procedures are, for example, that a selective sample bias arises as a result of the individual response behavior (86% of the persons contacted did not respond). This aspect jeopardizes the representativeness of the sample, and further the composition of the samples does not adequately reflect socio-geographic reality with regard to certain variables such as age or educational level. Due to the fact that only information of participants who responded can be taken into consideration when analyzing the data, a systematic shift cannot be ruled out. Therefore, it is possible that specific profile factors in the study are under- or indeed overrepresented and do not accurately reflect the reality of the status quo. However, this restriction can never be excluded in the case of corresponding study designs, where participation takes place voluntarily and requires a certain level of self-initiative. In spite of this constraint, studies with similar limitations have already illustrated their relevance and usefulness to numerous questions in the last decades; it can be assumed that this also applies to the Tech4Age longitudinal study.

In order to depict the reality as precisely as possible, the agent-based simulation SiM-Care requires a big amount of reliable data with respect to various parameters. As it was mentioned in previous sections, some of the data, which is necessary for fine-tuning the simulation, are unavailable, and thus have to be acquired empirically. The validity of these estimations can be augmented by expert knowledge. Moreover, although SiM-Care captures diverse processes on both micro- and macro-level, as well as interrelated influence of events in a health care system, the reality is even more complex. There might be further interactions happening in real-world systems, which are not modeled in SiM-Care but would affect the KPIs evaluated. Therefore, we stress the need for additional model validation prior to taking decisions based on the results of the presented case study.

Finally, the calibration of the model still requires further data describing the status quo of the modeled system. Nevertheless, even if some wrongly chosen parameters cause systematic shifts in SiM-Care's KPI evaluation, the relative qualitative comparison of different input scenarios remains valid and can yield relevant results. This also holds true for the presented case study. The insight of interest is the direction of shift in the age structure of walk-in patients and not its exact quantitative evaluation.

Acknowledgements. The development of the agent-based simulation SiM-Care is part of the Junior Professor for the Robust Planning of Health Care which is supported by the Freigeist-Fellowship of the Volkswagen Stiftung. The work is also supported by the German research council (DFG) Research Training Group 2236 UnRAVeL.

The trend study about ICT usage readiness among the elderly population is part of the research project "TECH4AGE," financed by the Federal Ministry of Education and Research (BMBF, under Grant No. 16SV7111) and promoted by VDI/VDE Innovation + Technik GmbH.

References

1. Dye, C., Reeder, J.C., Terry, R.F.: Research for universal health coverage. Sci. Transl. Med. **5**(199), 199ed13 (2013)
2. Jacob, R., Kopp, J., Schultz, S.: Berufsmonitoring Medizinstudenten 2014. Kassenärztliche Bundesvereinigung (2015)
3. Mertens, A., Rasche, P., Theis, S., Bröhl, C., Wille, M.: Use of information and communication technology in healthcare context by older adults in Germany: initial results of the Tech4Age long-term study. i-com **16**(2), 165–180 (2017)
4. Comis, M., Cleophas, C., Büsing, C.: Patients, primary care, and policy: simulation modeling for health care decision support, pp. 1–30 (2019). arXiv:1910.11027
5. Theis, S., et al.: Predicting technology usage by health information need of older adults: implications for eHealth Technology. Work **62**(3), 443–457 (2019)
6. Bleisch, N., Koch, W., Schäfer, C.: ARD/ZDF-Onlinestudie 2019: Mediale Internetnutzung und Video-onDemand gewinnen weiter an Bedeutung. Media Perspektive **9**, 374–388 (2019)
7. Neyer, F., Felber, J., Gebhardt, C.: Entwicklung und Validierung einer Kurzskala zur Erfassung von Technikbereitschaft. Diagnostica **58**, 87–99 (2012)
8. Information und Technik Nordrhein-Westfalen (IuT-NRW): Zensus 2011: Vielfältiges Deutschland. Statistische Ämter des Bundes und der Länder (2016)
9. Kassenärztliche Vereinigung Nordrhein (K-NRW): Die 100 häufigsten ICD-10-Schlüssel und Kurztexte (nach Fachgruppen) - 4. Quartal 2018 (2018)
10. Grobe, T., Dörning, H., Schwartz, F.: BARMER GEK Arztreport 2011. Asgard-Verlag, St. Augustin (2011)

Research on the Standing Movement of the Elderly

Mengjing Cai[1], Yinxia Li[1(✉)], and Huimin Hu[2,3]

[1] School of Mechanical Engineering, Zhengzhou University, Zhengzhou, Henan, China
Caimengjing001@163.com, liyxmail@126.com
[2] Ergonomics Laboratory, China National Institute of Standardization, Beijing, China
huhm@cnis.ac.cn
[3] AQSIQ Key Laboratory of Human Factors and Ergonomics, Beijing, China

Abstract. With the acceleration of the global aging process, the market for the elderly is getting more and more attention. Standing movement is one of the abilities that must be possessed in daily life, and it is also an important factor affecting the independent life of the elderly. As the elderly increase in age, lower limb strength decreases. In daily standing behavior, many elderly people have difficulty in standing, which may reduce the quality of life of the elderly and is not good for the mental health of the elderly. It can be seen that it is of great practical significance to investigate and design assisted standing products for the elderly. Therefore, this study conducted FTSST (five-times-sit-to-stand test) on the young and elderly groups, and found that the time of FTSST in the two groups was significantly different ($P < 0.05$), but in different genders was not. The method of combining motion capture technology and force plate was used to carry out STS experiments for the elderly. Standing behavior was divided into three phases. The time changes of each phase in the STS process were analyzed. The time spent in phase 3 was the longest. The phase 2 and phase 3 of the STS process need to be focused on. The relationship between GRF (ground reaction forces), joint angles, motion trajectories and assisted standing products was studied. The assistive angle of the assisted standing product was at least 53°. The assistive height of the assisted standing product should ensure that the hip could be lifted at least 250 mm. The standing speed was variable rather than uniform. Changes in GRF and joint angles provided human characteristics data and design references for the design of assisted standing products.

Keywords: The elder · Standing movement · Ground reaction force · Joint angle

1 Introduction

With the development of global economy, population aging may become one of the most important social trends in the 21st century. All citizens of the People's Republic of China who have reached the age of 60 are elderly. According to forecasts by the United Nations Population Fund and the China Aging Committee, by 2025, the proportion of China's elderly population aged 60 and above will exceed 20%, and the

© Springer Nature Switzerland AG 2020
Q. Gao and J. Zhou (Eds.): HCII 2020, LNCS 12208, pp. 13–27, 2020.
https://doi.org/10.1007/978-3-030-50249-2_2

proportion of the elderly population aged 65 and above will reach approximately 14%. China will enter an aging society. Compared with developed countries, the situation of China's aging population is more severe, the problems are more complicated, and the difficulties are more prominent. In view of China's aging situation, the daily life of the elderly has now attracted a lot of attention. Convenience, comfort, safety, and suitability for the elderly have become important topics. The physiological aging of the elderly is a natural law. Generally, the phenomenon of height reduction, hearing loss, visual sensitivity reduction, and power decline will occur [1]. For each individual, daily actions such as standing up from a seat, walking, and going up and down stairs are activities needed for daily life. Standing movement is a necessary action for normal life. People need to perform a large number of standing movement every day. Normal people need to perform 60 ± 22 times a day [2]. Therefore, it is important and necessary for the elderly to complete standing movement [3, 4]. However, with the decline of physiological functions, especially the degradation of lower limb muscle strength, most elderly people often have the ability to walk without standing ability, which may reduce the quality of life of the elderly. Standing instability may lead to falling, which is not only very detrimental to the physical safety of the elderly, but also affects the mental health of the elderly [5, 6].

Standing movement mainly depends on the lower limb muscle strength of the human body to stand up from the sitting process, which has complex biomechanical and dynamic changes. Vander Linden et al. believed that standing movement was a rapid upward transfer of the center of gravity from the sitting to standing position which involves multiple joints and muscle groups of the lower limb muscles of the human body [7]. Blake had shown that about 53% of elderly people's falls were caused by walking or standing instability, and falling was an important cause of injuries and other diseases [8]. Schultz [9] and Alexander [10] had also confirmed in their research conclusions that STS motion can actually be understood as "essentially completing the rising motion of the sagittal plane in a symmetrical manner."

STS (sit-to-stand) movements is a feasible and effective method for evaluating lower limb functional status and balance function in the elderly [11, 12]. Several tests had been proposed to measure lower limb muscle function in the elderly using STS movements. Many scholars at home and abroad have analyzed and studied the biomechanical characteristics of the elderly's standing motion process through the experimental methods of the speed of standing and the number of sitting times within a specified time. Jones et al. proposed that the 30-s chair stand provided a reasonably reliable and valid indicator of lower body strength and the 30-s chair stand, as an indication of lower body strength, had been developed as part of a larger battery of "functional fitness" tests for older adults [13]. Moreover, Lindemann U et al. also reported that there were significant age-related changes in the number of STS movement repetitions [14]. Liming Liu confirmed FTSST had excellent retest reliability in the functional evaluation of the elderly, and can better reflect the lower limb strength, functional activities and other motor functions of the elderly [15]. In addition, Takumi, et al. proved that ground reaction force parameters in the Sit-to-stand test were a reliable and useful method for assessment of lower extremity function in physically frail older adults [16].

There are many products related to assisted standing on the market, mainly seats, sofas, and nursing robots. However, many assisted standing products are not suitable for the elderly due to speed or angle. There are few studies on the relationship between elderly standing behavior analysis and assisted standing products. The research on the relationship between ground reaction force, joint angle and assistive angle in standing movements are also rarely involved. The sofa is one of the essential furniture for the daily life of the elderly. The elderly also have difficulty standing while using the sofa. Therefore, it is necessary to study the standing behavior of the elderly when using the sofa and the interaction between the standing movement and the design of assisted standing products. Reasonable, convenient and pleasant products can be designed to achieve healthy aging and provide safe and comfortable products and services for the elderly.

2 Experiment Method

2.1 Subject

Subject. Subjects were classified into two groups: Young and Elder. Ten elderly persons over 60 years old were selected as the experimental group, 5 males and 5 females. And another 10 young people were selected as the control group for the FTSST, 5 males and 5 males. There were no neuropsychiatric diseases and severe injuries affecting motor system function in both groups. They had no history of lower extremity or spine disorders that affect standing ability. All subjects were required healthy and experimented with good physical and mental condition.

Subject gender, age, height, weight and BMI (Body Mass Index) were noted. The mean age of the Young group was 26.3 years and of the Elder group 65.9 years. Mean ages of the males and females in both the Young and Old groups were similar. Young and Elder Able male subjects tended to be taller and heavier than their female counterparts. Elder group were fatter than the younger ones. Descriptive data for the subjects was included in Table 1.

Table 1. Subject age and anthropometric data

	Young group			Elder group		
	Range	Mean	SD	Range	Mean	SD
Age (years)	21–35	26.3	4.6	60–71	65.9	3.73
Height (m)	1.58–1.83	1.69	0.08	1.5–1.78	1.62	0.1
Weight (kg)	50.3–75	62.11	8.05	50.7–93.8	72.55	13.45
BMI	18.47–25.37	21.77	2.17	22.53–35.43	27.65	4.2

2.2   Main Apparatus

Sofa Device. A sofa device with a sitting height of 420 mm was selected and the softness of the sofa cushion was moderate, as shown in Fig. 1.

Fig. 1. Sofa device

Motion Capture System. The Qualisys 3D motion acquisition and analysis system consists of calibration equipment (see Fig. 2), several digital motion capture cameras (see Fig. 3), analysis software (see Fig. 4), acquisition units, marker balls and equipment fixtures, which can be tested synchronously with external devices such as force plates, electromyography, etc. High-speed cameras were applied to the capture system to accurately capture the movement of measurable objects with active or passive markers. The Qualisys motion capture system is used to accurately capture the standing motion of the human body for quantitative analysis, combined with human biology to make the precise size of human joints. Sagittal joint angle changes was measured and analyzed in this study. The acquisition frequency of the Motion capture system in this study was 100 frames/s.

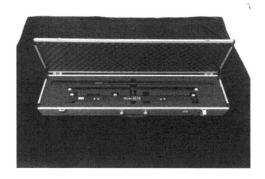

Fig. 2. Calibration equipment

Fig. 3. Motion capture camera

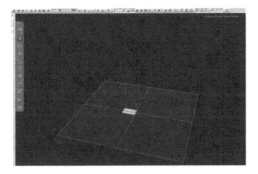

Fig. 4. Analysis software

2.3 Testing Procedure

The elder group was asked to perform 2 functional performance tests as part of their physical performance testing: the FTSST and the STS experiment. The young group was the control group for the FTSST.

- Each subject was informed about the experimental process and signed the experimental informed consent;
- Record the basic information such as the subject's name, gender, age, height, and weight;
- Subjects sat on the sofa device without armrests in accordance with regulations, keeping their upper body upright. At the same time, in order to avoid the impact of the strength of the upper limbs, the subjects were required to keep their arms folded across their chests. Supposed that from standing upright to standing completely was a standing. When the "start" command was issued by the experimenter, the subject started FTSST, and the standing time was recorded with a stopwatch. The timing ended when the fifth hip contacted the seat surface. Repeat the FTSST three times;

- After completing the FTSST, the subject rested for a while. The subject wore tights, and eight markers were placed on the right side of the body to enable tracking of segment movements during the STS experiment. The locations of the markers was shown in Table 2. The sofa cushion for the FTSST was removed and replaced with a sofa cushion with a lower hardness level (the lower the hardness level, the harder the seat surface);

Table 2. The locations of the markers

1	R-SAE
2	R-TRO
3	R-FLE
4	R-FAL
5	R-HAND OUT
6	R-TOE TIP
7	R-ANKLE
8	R-KNEE PAN

- Start the Qualisys Track Manager test software, and the subject sat on the sofa device without armrests and backs in accordance with regulations. The subject's feet were as wide as the shoulders and placed on two side force plates. The subject must complete the standing movement at a normal standing speed in accordance with the principle of comfort. Before the test, subjects were required to practice standing exercises multiple times to achieve the experimental requirement.

3 Data Processing

The average of each subject's FTSST time was used as the result of the FTSST. All statistical analyses were performed using SPSS. A one way ANOVA was used to compare the difference in the time taken for the elder group and the young group to complete the FTSST. Statistical significance of differences was determined at a p 0.05 level using ANOVA for time by group (Young vs Elder) and gender (Male vs Female).

4 Results

4.1 FTSST

The two groups completed the FTSST in accordance with the requirements. One-way analysis of variance was performed on the experimental data of the two groups and different genders. The results were given in Fig. 5 and Fig. 6. The experimental results shown that the time of the FTSST of the young group and the elderly group were different. There was no significant difference in the time of FTSST for different gender, which was consistent with Susan's research [17]. The time of FTSST was shown in Table 3.

The above results shown that the standing time of the elderly group was longer than that of the young group, because the lower limb strength of the elderly decreased with age due to the decline of their physiological functions. There was no such difference between male and female. Regardless of male or female, their lower limb strength decreased with age.

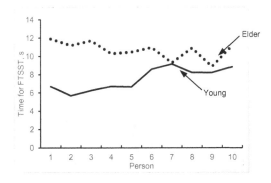

Fig. 5. FTSST time for young and elderly groups

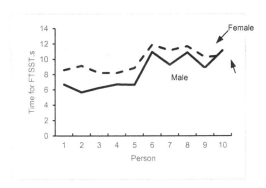

Fig. 6. FTSST time for different genders

Table 3. The results of FTSST

		FTSST	Sig
Age	Young	7.5 ± 1.17	0.000
	Old	10.67 ± 0.92	
Gender	Male	8.31 ± 2.05	0.076
	Female	9.86 ± 1.35	

4.2   Phase Division

The human STS movements process was shown. The human STS movements process was usually divided into three phases. The phase 1: the body's upper body changed from an upright state to a forward tilt (see Fig. 7 and Fig. 8), and the hips started to rise, generating forward and upward momentum. The stress point at phase 1 was mainly the buttocks, which belonged to the preparation phase for STS of the human body. The phase 2: the hips left the seat (see Fig. 9) and the human body moved forward and upward at the same time. The stress point at phase 2 was mainly the lower limbs. The phase 3: the body joints gradually stretched to the maximum until the human body was completely standing (see Fig. 10 and Fig. 11). The time node selection criteria selected in this study were equivalent to reports of Zhonggui Lei [18].

The total standing time and the time spent in each phase were shown in Fig. 12 and Fig. 13. It could be seen from the results that in the STS experiment of the elderly, the time spent in phase 3 was the longest, followed by phase 1, and the time spent in phase 2 was the shortest.

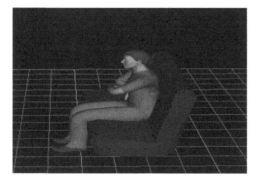

Fig. 7. Sitting position

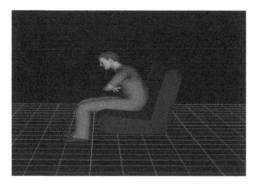

Fig. 8. Lean forward

Fig. 9. Hips away from seat surface

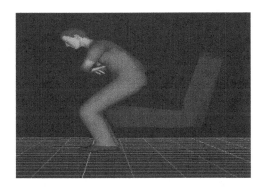

Fig. 10. Body joints stretched

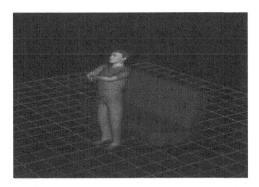

Fig. 11. Standing

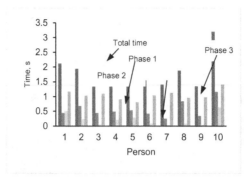

Fig. 12. Result of each phase of STS time

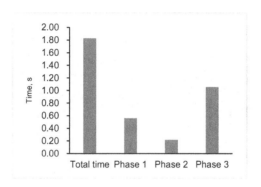

Fig. 13. The time at each phase of the STS process

4.3   Ground Reaction Force (GRF)

As shown in Fig. 14, Data on the GRF of the right foot was analyzed. In the phase 1 of the STS experiment, the subject changed from an upright sitting posture to the upper body leaning forward, GRF gradually increased, and hips slowly lifted upwards. When the hips left the seat, the GRF reached the maximum soon in the phase 2. After entering the phase 3, the joint angle gradually stretched, the body's center of gravity gradually increased, and the GRF gradually decreased and then increases until the body was balanced again. The phase 2 took the least time and GRF was the largest. When entering the phase 3, although the GRF was reduced, it was still greater than the phase 1.

Ground reaction force can better reflect the lower limb strength, functional activities and other motor functions of the elderly. Therefore, for the elderly, GRF is of great research significance, which should be paid attention to when designing auxiliary standing products.

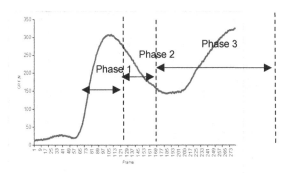

Fig. 14. GRF in the STS movement

4.4 Joint Angle

The definition of joint angles was shown in Fig. 15. In the STS experiment, from the phase 1 to phase 2, the ankle joint angle changed fluctuated slightly. During the STS process, the subjects all leaned forward and left the seat on the hips. And then the body gradually stretched, so the hip joint angle decreased first and then gradually increased. For the knee joint angle, the knee joint angle as a whole gradually increased (see Fig. 16). The change trend of joint angle was consistent with the results of Jianguang Wang [19]. During the STS process, the hip and knee joint angle changes were the most obvious.

According to the joint angle change diagram, in the phase 3, the angle of the hips and knees gradually increased to a maximum value in the process of body stretching. In the phase 3, when the joint angle reached a certain value, the force of the lower limbs was minimal and the body was almost fully extended. When the GRF was minimum in the phase 3, the corresponding angles of the joint was shown in Table 4. At this time, the elder can basically stand completely by relying on inertia. According to the experimental results of this study, on the premise that the seat surface height was 420 mm, the assistive angle of the assisted standing product should ensure that the angle between the seat surface and the horizontal plane was at least 53°.

When designing assisted standing products, it should be ensured that the assistive angle of the seat surface could reach the angle to achieve the purpose of assisting standing.

Fig. 15. Hip (The blue line), knee (The orange line) and ankle (The yellow line) joint angle (Color figure online)

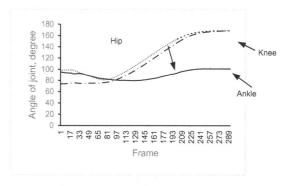

Fig. 16. Joint angle

Table 4. The angles of the joint corresponding to the minimum GRF in phase 3

Hip	Knee	Ankle
136.6°± 17.52	141.51°± 15.22	103.94°± 7

4.5   Motion Trajectory

In the STS experiment, the trajectory of the hip joint was of great importance to the design of the product. The trajectory of the hip joint in space was shown in the Fig. 17. The results of this study was shown that, under the premise of a seat height of 420 mm, the assistive height of the assisted standing product should ensure that the hip could be lifted at least 250 mm from sitting to standing. It was found that in the process of STS, the standing speed increased first and then decreased, which was variable rather than uniform, as shown in the Fig. 18. When designing assisted standing products, it was mainly achieved by increasing the change in hip height and joint angle, so the height difference between the sitting and standing positions and the standing speed must be considered.

Fig. 17. Motion trajectory

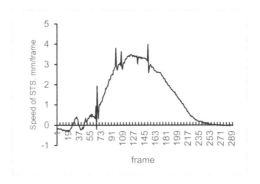

Fig. 18. The speed of STS

5 Conclusion

Studies have shown that in the FTSST, the time used by the elderly is different from the time used by the young. Older people spend more time standing than that of young, which is associated with decreased lower limb strength and balance. Through the analysis of standing behavior of the elderly, with the help of motion capture and analysis of experimental data, it was found that in STS behavior, the human body first leans forward, the GRF gradually increases, and the hip joint decreases. Then, after the hips leave the seat surface, the GRF increases to the maximum. Finally, as the body gradually stretches, the GRF decreases first and then increases, and the angle of each joint increases until it reaches a steady state.

In the design of assisted standing products, the threshold value of the assistive angle of the seat surface should achieve the purpose that the human body is easy to stand, which is related to the change of the GRF and joint angle of the human body in the phase 3. The height difference should be taken into account the height difference between sitting and standing. The assist speed should also be adapted to the normal standing speed. The design of assisted standing products should also take into account the differences among different body types of the elderly.

When designing assisted standing products, designers should consider the interactive relationship between assisted standing products and STS movements, and understand the rules of user behavior, so as to improve user satisfaction. Design changes life, and "design for the elderly" not only expresses the needs of the elderly, but also the needs of social civilization and progress.

Acknowledgments. This research is supported by national key research and development program "research on human-centered design and product user experience evaluation technology standard" (2017YFF0206603).

References

1. Tao, H.: The Research Design of Elderly Lower Limbs Product Based on the Concept of Hospitality Design. Tianjin University of Technology, Tianjin (2015)
2. Dall, P.M., Kerr, A.: Frequency of the sit to stand task: an observational study of free-living adults. Appl. Ergon. **41**(1), 58–61 (2010)
3. Yamada, T., Demura, S.: The relationship of force output characteristics during a sit-to-stand movement with lower limb muscle mass and knee joint extension in the elderly. Arch. Gerontol. Geriatr. **50**(3), e46–e50 (2010)
4. van Lummel, R.C., Walgaard, S., Maier, A.B., et al.: The Instrumented Sit-to-Stand Test (iSTS) has greater clinical relevance than the manually recorded sit-to-stand test in older adults. PLoS ONE **11**(7), e0157968 (2016)
5. Ayelet, D.: The effect of balance and coordination exercises on quality of life in older adults: a mini-review. Front. Aging Neurosci. **11** (2019)
6. Quijoux, F., Vienne-Jumeau, A., Bertin-Hugault, F., et al.: Center of pressure characteristics from quiet standing measures to predict the risk of falling in older adults: a protocol for a systematic review and meta-analysis. Syst. Rev. **8**(1), 232 (2019)
7. Linden, D.W.V., Brunt, D., Mcculloch, M.U.: Variant and invariant characteristics of the sit-to-stand task in healthy elderly adults. Arch. Phys. Med. Rehabil. **75**(6), 653–660 (1994)
8. Blake, A.J., Morgan, K., Bendall, M.J., et al.: Falls by elderly people at home: prevalence and associated factors. Age Ageing **17**(6), 365–372 (1988)
9. Schultz, A.B., Alexander, N.B., Ashton-Miller, J.A.: Biomechanical analyses of rising from a chair. J. Biomech. **25**(12), 1383–1391 (1992)
10. Alexander, N.B., Schultz, A.B., Warwick, D.N.: Rising from a chair: effects of age and functional ability on performance biomechanics. J. Gerontol. **46**(3), M91–M98 (1991)
11. Jones, C.J., Rikli, R.E., Beam, W.C.: A 30-s chair-stand test as a measure of lower body strength in community-residing older adults. Res. Q. Exerc. Sport **70**(2), 113–119 (1999)
12. Ohsugi, H., Murata, S., Kubo, A., et al.: Verification of the correlation between cognitive function and lower limb muscle strength for the community-dwelling elderly. J. Phys. Ther. Sci. **26**(12), 1861–1863 (2014)
13. Jones, C.J., Rikli, R.E., Beam, W.C.: A 30-s chair-stand test as a measure of lower body strength in community-residing older adults. Res. Q. Exerc. Sport **70**(2), 113–119 (1999)
14. Lindemann, U., Claus, H., Stuber, M., et al.: Measuring power during the sit-to-stand transfer. Eur. J. Appl. Physiol. **89**(5), 466–470 (2003)
15. Shen, S., et al.: The relationship between ground reaction force in sit-to-stand movement and lower extremity function in community-dwelling Japanese older adults using long-term care insurance services. J. Phys. Ther. Sci. **29**(9), 1561–1566 (2017)

16. Liu, L., Weng, C., Wang, N., et al.: Five-times sit-to-stand test on physical performance for older people. Chin. J. Rehabil. Theor. Pract. **16**(04), 359–361 (2010)
17. Whitney, S.L., Wrisley, D.M., Marchetti, G.F., et al.: Clinical measurement of sit-to-stand performance in people with balance disorders: validity of data for the five-times-sit-to-stand test. Phys. Ther. **85**(10), 1034–1045 (2005)
18. Lei, Zhonggui, Jiayu, Fu, Zhou, Chuang, Wang, Zhixiong: Study on the safety of the elderly standing chair. Comput. Eng. Softw. **39**(10), 121–125 (2018)
19. Wang, J.: Research on Assistive Chair Design for Elderly People. Zhejiang University, Hangzhou (2008)

Integrating Personal Emergency Response Systems (PERS) into Healthcare Professional Practices: A Scoping Review

Fangyuan Chang$^{(\boxtimes)}$ ⓘ, Sanna Kuoppamäki ⓘ, and Britt Östlund ⓘ

KTH Institute of Technology, Hälsovägen 11, 141 52 Huddinge, Sweden
fancha@kth.se

Abstract. Seeking effective approaches to integrate technology into formal healthcare professionals' daily works has been acknowledged as challenging. The purpose of this article is to provide a comprehensive overview of the recent research concerning the implementation of personal emergency response systems (PERSs), with the focus on the routine use of PERS among formal healthcare professionals, as well as identify current gaps in this area.

The scoping review followed the five-stage framework of Arksey and O'Malley and PRISMA-Extension for Scoping Reviews (PRISMA-ScR). Searches were performed in PubMed, CINAHL, EMBASE, and the Web of Science Core Collection for studies published from 2009 to 2019. Any peer-reviewed studies in English describing strategies, barriers, and facilitators, or assessing the impact of integrating PERS into healthcare professional practices fulfilled the inclusion eligibility. Two reviewers screened the manuscripts and extracted data independently, with a third reviewer resolving discrepancies. Due to a large heterogeneity of included studies, a narrative synthesis was conducted.

In total, 25 studies were included out of 2,319 manuscripts. This study discusses supportive strategies, and enabling and inhibiting factors, as well as integration outcomes. Future studies can contribute to three gaps by examining: 1) how strategies such as training contribute to the effectiveness of technology integration separately and collectively; 2) how working environments affect the effectiveness of realizing operational works; and 3) how technology is shaped by social environments and relationships.

Keywords: Technology implementation · Routine practices · Healthcare professionals · Personal Emergency Response Systems

1 Introduction

Healthcare technology refers to IT devices or software for boosting care productivity and improving overall care quality. It has long been proposed that healthcare technology is likely to counteract the challenges of providing high-quality healthcare to increasing older populations [1]. The actual use of technology in daily lives is essential for realizing the full potential of the adopted technology. However, numerous publications have documented the difficulties associated with the uptake of technologies into actual use [2].

© Springer Nature Switzerland AG 2020
Q. Gao and J. Zhou (Eds.): HCII 2020, LNCS 12208, pp. 28–46, 2020.
https://doi.org/10.1007/978-3-030-50249-2_3

It was found that healthcare technology is uncritically viewed as a way of achieving better efficiencies of care in many technology implementation projects [3, 4], and its implementation is thought of as a standardized process, through which technology packages can 'drop into' routine use [3]. In addition, technology recipients are treated as passive users, whose needs are defined by technology developers instead of themselves [5]. The mismatch between promises of health technology and the reality has been highlighted through various studies [6–8]. This suggests that despite the growing rhetoric supporting the role of technology in care, there remain significant challenges to the uptake of technology into daily practices.

Against this backdrop, plenty of scholars from the field of science and technology studies (STS) have started to explore the processes through which technologies are adopted and integrated into reality [6, 9–11]. A variety of health technologies have been studied, and one concrete example is the personal emergency response system (PERS) [12]. The system usually consists of an alarm button and a telecare system in which a lightweight transmitter wirelessly connects all other telecare devices. Once installed, it will alert emergency response units of an incident that requires immediate attention. The primary aim of PERS are to help older adults be more independent and to facilitate the work efficiency of healthcare professionals in primary care (i.e. private homes or community settings) [13]. Of the voluminous socio-technical studies concerning PERS, however, most have investigated the perceived effectiveness of, the real use of, or the adherence to the system among older adults [14–17]. Healthcare professionals, who occupy a crucial position in delivering high-quality care through PERS, are paid much less attention.

Even though recent socio-technical studies have begun to involve healthcare professionals and emphasize the importance of understanding integrating technology into healthcare professionals' daily practices, studies mostly focus on informal healthcare professionals, such as family members [13, 18]. Little is known about how formal healthcare professionals in primary care settings integrate PERS into their routine practices. Consequently, there is still room for expanding this topic. A broad view of approaches and opportunities to encourage formal healthcare professionals to embed PERS into their daily practices remains largely unexplored. Evidence is required to guide the process of integrating PERS into healthcare professional practices in order to identify approaches that are efficient, effective, and meaningful. Consequently, the purpose of this article is to fulfil these gaps through providing a comprehensive overview of the recent research concerning integration of PERS in formal healthcare professionals' practices, with research questions as follows:

RQ1. What strategies are being used to by implementers or managers or healthcare professionals themselves to integrate PERS into daily practices?

RQ2. What are the enabling or inhibiting factors that influence uptake and embedding of PERS in routine care practices?

RQ3. What are the implementation outcomes of PERS in formal healthcare professional practices?

2 Methods

2.1 Search Process

The scoping review followed the five-stage framework developed by Arksey and O'Malley [19], and the PRISMA-Extension for Scoping Reviews (PRISMA-ScR). The search process included the following steps: in the first phase, major search terms were identified from the search questions. Because the goal is to include as many relevant studies as possible, a broad search strategy focusing on all empirical papers that fully or partly dealt with embedding PERS into care practices amongst formal healthcare professionals was adopted. Hence, broad terms 'PERS', 'formal healthcare professionals' and 'technology integration' were identified. In the second phase, pilot tests were conducted with the broad terms to identify synonymous terms and alternative words that are used in current literature. In the third phase, electronic databases were used to search for our research topic. The principal search was conducted with additional searching, including forward citation and snowballing.

2.2 Selection Strategy

Search Criteria. Despite the fact that implementation of technology has been discussed for a relatively long time, integration of technology to formal healthcare professional practices has been on the research agenda for only ten years [20, 21]. Research published after 2009 in a peer-reviewed journal and written in English is eligible. In addition, selected studies are required to focus on integrating PERS in formal healthcare professionals' practices. Study outcomes could be objective or subjective, reported by healthcare professionals themselves (Table 1).

Table 1. Key search criteria

Inclusion criteria	Exclusion criteria
Studies published from 2009 to 2019	Studies outside these dates
Studies written in English	Non-English studies
Empirical studies in a peer-reviewed journal	No empirical studies, review articles, books
Papers with a concentration on formal healthcare professionals	Papers focusing on other population groups such as older adults
Papers that focus on integrating PERS into practices	Publication has other purposes, such as system development
Studies that analyze the self-report from formal healthcare professionals	Studies where formal healthcare professionals play roles of others such as older adults

Search Terms. Specific Medical Subject Headings (MeSH) and free text terms for PERS (i.e. 'telehealth', 'alarm system', 'social alarm', 'security alarm', 'emergency response system', 'information technology', 'self-managed technology', 'telemedicine') were combined with terms for formal healthcare professionals (i.e. 'carer', 'caregiver', 'assistant nurse', 'routine use', 'nursing homes', 'frontline care worker', 'sheltered housing', 'care homes', 'primary care'). These terms were combined with technology integration terms (i.e. 'embed', 'adoption', 'domestication', 'real world', 'routine care', 'normalization', 'sociotechnical', 'integration', 'dissemination', 'implementation') using Boolean logic operators (AND, OR).

Database. Electronic searches were conducted in multiple databases, including PubMed, CINAHL, EMBASE, Web of Science Core Collection.

Study Screening. Two authors independently screened all titles/abstracts to determine eligibility. The steps for study screening [22] include: 1) merge all references into the Mendeley reference management database and remove duplicates; 2) examine titles and abstracts for obvious irrelevant studies for exclusion; 3) review of full papers to identify eligible papers; 4) make final decisions for study inclusion.

Forward reference searching was conducted through manual searches of reference lists until saturation (no new references are identified). References and literature sources are included in the literature review if they meet eligibility criteria.

2.3 Data Extraction

Data were extracted for each study using a taxonomy, including 1) year of publication, 2) source origin/country of origin, 3) research focus, 4) aims/purpose, 5) research setting, 6) study participants, 7) methodology or study type, 8) duration of the implementation (if applicable), 9) key findings that relate to the review questions. The main author and the second author extracted data together. Discrepancies were resolved by engaging and making consensus with the third author.

2.4 Data Analysis Process

First, we extracted data from studies according to the description in 2.3. Second, we treated extracted data from quantitative studies as qualitative data and combined this with qualitative studies for narrative synthesis. The extracted data were analyzed using directed content analysis methods [23] in Nvivo 12 to identify themes or patterns in the data such as the enabling or inhibiting factors that influence the uptake or embedding of PERS in routine care. This approach avoids reinterpretation of qualitative data, which has been criticized, and ensures the development of patterns or themes grounded in the data. Thirdly, we coded data extracted from these studies and ensured coding definitions were agreed among all members of the research team. The coding taxonomy will be derived from identified variables.

3 Results

The search yielded 2,319 articles (2,235 from the original database search, 84 from forward citation and snowballing), of which 1,694 remained after removing duplicates. A further 1,565 articles were removed after title and abstract screening. Of the remaining 129 full-text articles screened, 104 were excluded, leaving 25 articles (Fig. 1).

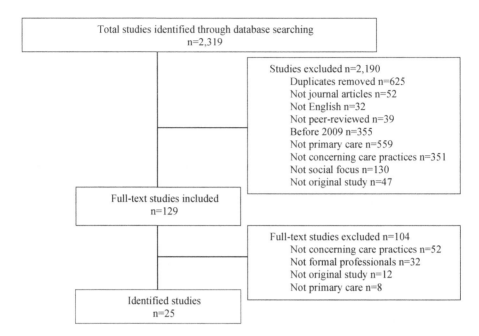

Fig. 1. Flow diagram of search strategy used in the study

3.1   The Characteristics of Selected Papers

Table 2 reports the characteristics of selected papers. The screened literature contains studies primarily from Europe, with a focus on the integration process or outcomes that are assessed or contextualized in the period before, during or after the technology is adopted. Home care was the dominant concern, and most articles involve authors from the same research field. Multiple qualitative and quantitative methods were utilized to study various stakeholders on this topic.

Of the 25 relevant publications concerning integrating PERS into formal healthcare professional practices, around half (n = 14) were published within the last five years, revealing that there was no significant increase in the total number of publications.

Most articles were produced in UK (n = 11). The others were produced in the Netherlands (n = 6), Switzerland (n = 1), Norway (n = 4), Spain (n = 3), Austria (n = 1), Singapore (n = 1), Belgium (n = 1), Sweden (n = 1), Finland (n = 1) and China (n = 1).

A variety of research focus was found, ranging from social science, management, innovation service, psychology, engineering, and health. Of the screened papers, areas relevant to health such as health science, public health, and health service were dominant (n = 13), followed by social science (n = 6), informatics service (n = 4), and engineering (n = 2). In addition, most studies (n = 17) have one author or authors from the same research field, while some studies (n = 7) include authors from two disciplines [24–30] or three [31].

Table 2. Screened paper and characteristics

	Year	Place	Focus	Aims	Domain	Participants	Study type		Duration
[47]	2018	UK	Health and social science	To explore what drove changes during implementation, and identify issues needed to be considered during the process	Home care	181 patients, 109 professionals	Qualitative pilot study	Qualitative interview and focus group data	During implementation
[32]	2018	UK	Primary care health sciences	To explain Non-adoption or Abandonment of technology and difficulties in achieving Scale-up, Spread and Sustainability	Community care	20 care organizations, 10 national-level bodies	Ethnographic study	Observations, semi-structured interviews and documents	After implementation
[24]	2017	UK	Health science, nursing	To explore facilitators and barriers to the implementation of monitoring technologies	Home care	24 staff, 9 relatives and 9 residents	Qualitative study	Interviews, observation, resident care record	All the implementation time
[41]	2017	Switzerland	Applied sciences	To explore the perception of system acceptability for use in daily practice	Community care	17 community nurses	RCT*	Questionnaire, interviews	After implementation
[28]	2017	Austria	Engineering, design	To identify issues and current solutions from a range of people with experience developing systems	Not reported	14 technology developers, carers	Qualitative research	Workshops and an interactive poster	Before implementation
[42]	2017	Spain	Telematics Systems for Information	To assess current satisfaction and future expectations of Telecare professionals when using advanced Telecare solutions	Telecare centre and home	24 telecare experts	Case study	Questionnaire, structured interview	After implementation

(continued)

Table 2. (*continued*)

	Year	Place	Focus	Aims	Domain	Participants	Study type		Duration
[29]	2017	Norway, UK	Health studies, medicine	To identify contextual factors at different organisational levels to guide the implementation in Norwegian primary home care	Home care	Senior managers, nurses and nurse managers	Mixed method study	Document analysis, semi-structured individual interviews and focus group interviews	After implementation
[31]	2017	UK	Information science, health and social care, social science	To examine barriers and facilitators to implementation of digital health at scale	Home care	125 key implementers,7 consumers and patients, 48 health professionals	Case study	Interviews, focus groups, project meetings, observation, survey, document analysis	After implementation
[37]	2017	Norway	Innovation in services	To explore how involved actors relate to, perceive and articulate expectations of the technology in everyday living	Private home	11 patients, 7 relatives, 9 staff	Qualitative study	Observation, in-depth interviews, document analysis	After implementation
[25]	2016	the Netherlands, Singapore	Applied health, social and behavioural sciences	To provide insight into the positions of stakeholder groups involved in the implementation of technology for ageing in place	Not reported	6 older adults, 7 staff, 5 managers, 6 designers, 5 policy makers	Case study	Focus group	Not reported

(*continued*)

Table 2. (*continued*)

	Year	Place	Focus	Aims	Domain	Participants	Study type		Duration
[33]	2016	Belgium	Health and wellbeing	To explore the facilitators and inhibitors for successful implementation among field experts and healthcare providers	Home care	8 field experts	Qualitative study	Semi-structured interviews	After implementation
[38]	2015	Norway	Integrated Care and Telemedicine	To investigate how innovation projects get involved in management work and can be a form of delegated organizational control	Home care	7 project participants, 3 local managers, 3 administration, 2 state health bureaucracy, 4 healthcare professionals, 2 ICT vendors	Qualitative study	Document analysis, semi-structured interviews and group discussions	After implementation
[39]	2015	UK	Health and Society	To understand how social relations mediate the functions of this device and in turn are mediated by them	Home care	47 older people, 9 carers	Case study	Focus group, semi-structured interviews, observation	Before and after implementation
[26]	2015	UK, Netherland, Norway, Spain	Sociology and medicine, social psychology	To develop an ethical framework for telecare systems based on analysis of observations of telecare-in-use and citizens' panel deliberations	Home care	142 older adults and informal carers, 24 carers	Qualitative study	Observation, work shadowing, interviews, older citizens' panels and a participative workshop	After implementation
[34]	2014	UK	Public health	To identify and explore factors that influence adoption, implementation and continued use of telecare technologies	Home care and community care	16 organization participants	Ethnographic study	Semi-structured interviews	During implementation

(*continued*)

Table 2. (continued)

	Year	Place	Focus	Aims	Domain	Participants	Study type		Duration
[45]	2014	Sweden	Psychological health	To understand the needs from several user perspectives	Home care	8-9 alarm users, 4-5 care managers	Ethnographic study	Interviews	During implementation
[40]	2014	the Netherlands	Humanistic studies	To investigate how technology is being used by nurses and support staff in residential care	Residential care	38 staff, 71 clients	Qualitative study	Field observations and informal conversations	After implementation
[27]	2014	Spain, UK	Anthropology, social psychology	To explore the practical effects of technology implementation in different locales	Home care	Not reported	Ethnographic study	Observation, document analysis,	During implementation
[48]	2013	UK	Health science	To assess the impact of telecare on the use of social and health care	Not reported	2,600 people with social care needs	RCT*	Survey	Before and after implementation
[30]	2012	China	Information management, healthcare management	To explore the ease of use and usefulness of a PERS from the perspective of primary caregivers and assess the system benefits in home dementia care	Home care	30 primary caregivers	Qualitative study	Interviews	After implementation
[46]	2012	the Netherlands		To explore the perspectives and care practices of users	Home care		Case study	Questionnaire, interviews	After implementation

(continued)

Table 2. (*continued*)

Year	Place	Focus	Aims	Domain	Participants	Study type		Duration
		Science technology and policy studies	as well as non-users of telecare devices		95 patients (T1), 54 patients (T2), carers and patients		Questionnaire	After the technology is implemented within 3 years
[35]	the Netherlands	Health services research	To gain a better understanding of determinants influencing the success of the introduction of new technologies as perceived by nursing staff	Nursing care	685 nursing staff	Qualitative study		
[36]	2011 UK	Health and society	To identify factors inhibiting the implementation and integration of telecare systems for chronic disease management in the community	Community care	221 health professionals, managers, patients, service suppliers and manufacturers	Comparative study	Semi-structured interviews, task-groups, and workshops	Not reported
[43]	2011 the Netherlands	Occupational health	To obtain an insight into the view of care professionals on system feasibility	Not reported	9 patients, 6 nurses' teams and multidisciplinary teams	Qualitative study	Semi-structured interviews, focus group interviews	After implementation
[44]	2010 Finland	Technology informatics	To contribute to the understanding of technology use in elderly care as a major change in workplaces and for individual care workers	Sheltered accommodation or private home	78 carers	Case study	Questionnaire, follow up interviews	After implementation

*RCT: randomized controlled trials

Of the screened studies, most papers can be divided in to two groups: one group (n = 7) with the purpose of identifying the facilitators or inhibitors for successful integration of PERS in routine care practices [24, 31–36], and the other group (n = 8) with the aim to contextualize how PERS is actually being used in practice [26, 27, 29, 30, 37–40]. In the remaining studies, there are four paper concerning the perspectives from healthcare professionals on targeting variations [41–44], four papers focusing on the differences between stakeholders' reflections during PERS integration [25, 28, 45, 46], and one paper that tried to explore changes during the whole process and the supportive factors [47].

In terms of research settings, most studies (n = 16) are interested in the integration of PERS located within the private homes of older adults, and some studies (n = 7) are interested in the integration in community care. The remaining studies (n = 4) didn't specify the research settings. The total number of investigated settings are 27 as two studies include more than one type of settings [34, 44].

Because of the inclusion criteria, all the studies involve healthcare professionals. The other participants include older adults (n = 17), relatives (n = 3), field experts (n = 5), project managers (n = 7), local nurse managers (n = 6), administrators (n = 2), designers or developers (n = 3), and policy makers (n = 2).

The majority of screened studies are qualitative study (n = 11), case study (n = 6), and ethnographic study (n = 4) [27, 32, 34, 45]. There are also randomized control trials (n = 2) [41, 48], mixed method study (n = 1) [29], and comparative study (n = 1) [36].

The common methods used in these studies are interviews (n = 19), observations (n = 8), focus group interviews (n = 7), surveys (n = 7), document analyses (n = 6), workshops (n = 3), resident care record (n = 1), interactive poster (n = 1), project meeting (n = 1), work shadowing (n = 1), informal conversation (n = 1), and task-groups (n = 1).

Four types of implementation durations were identified, including before imple-mentation (n = 1), during implementation (n = 5), after implementation (n = 15), and before and after implementation (n = 3). The remaining studies have no specified implementation duration (n = 2) [25, 36]. There is only one literature that tracks the entire implementation from before PERS is introduced until it is integrated [24].

3.2 Synthesis of Results

Integration Strategy. Of the screened studies, identified strategies includes training (n = 15) [24–26, 29–31, 33, 35, 37, 38, 40–42, 44], supervision and leadership (n = 13) [24, 28, 29, 32, 34, 37, 40–43, 45, 47, 48], staff involvement (n = 5) [24, 26, 28, 33, 40], and guidelines (n = 5) [29, 31, 33, 35, 36].

Despite a consensus that strategies are important to support healthcare professionals to better integrate PERS into their daily practices, the effectiveness of these strategies was found problematic.

For instance, in terms of the most commonly used strategy 'training', Lennon and his colleagues [31] illustrated that one main concern with respect to the introduction of new technology was a lack of corresponding knowledge and skills. Thus, the importance of training and coaching was highly stressed by healthcare professionals. This finding is greatly supported by other studies [24, 25, 29, 35, 41, 44]. Despite the expectation that training leads to efficient system use and successful implementation [26, 29], most training sessions were pointed out as being insufficient [24, 31, 35, 44]. Melkas [44] argued that a personalized study plan was needed and that formal education should involve everyone. Slightly differently, Hall [24] claimed that current staff training put too much attention on functional instruction while the deeper exploration of anticipated benefits and the underlying rationale for using technologies has been ignored. There is also another viewpoint concerning training. Even though De Veer [35] acknowledged the benefits of training, he illustrated that training alone would not necessarily solve problems of a dysfunctional system,. Instead of merely focusing on the training alone, he suggested that it should be part of multiple implementation strategies.

Aside from training, making guidelines were also greatly considered during implementation. As demonstrated by May [36], some health professionals felt guidelines are important because if the service was clearly effective, then it would be taken up regardless. For some, the translation of policy into official telecare implementation guidelines would facilitate the movement of telecare into mainstream healthcare. However, although guidelines are perceived as good for sharing data, and ensuring the education quality beyond spatial and temporal limits [29], current guidelines were found to be not clear enough, or there is even a great lack of guidelines during the integration process [29, 33, 46].

Enabling or Inhibiting Factors. The screened articles show that integrating PERS into formal healthcare professionals' practices is not simple. The findings were categorized into four themes: 1) system characteristics, 2) operational works, 3) personal readiness, 4) working environment.

System Characteristics. The first prominent theme is the notion that users' assumptions about how they are expected to comply with PERS will influence the integration process. Articles show that the well-designed graphical interface design, high-quality information, good system reliability, flexible feature functionalities, and long device lifecycle are crucial.

As Randi [37] pointed out, PERS is usually designed with expectations that actors with little technological skills will find it easy to use and suitable for themselves. However, how to make the system easy to use and suitable for users requires multiple and further considerations. Melkas [44] explored the information ecology in healthcare organizations, and argued that poor quality of information causes extra stress and additional work, and may weaken or even hinder technology acceptance. Similar findings were supported by others [24, 27, 32, 35–39, 41]. The importance of a well-designed graphical interface [28, 41, 42, 47] and good system usability and reliability [25, 28, 40, 41, 44, 47] were also emphasized as directly affecting the interaction between PERS and its users. In addition, system compatibility was emphasized [24, 35, 42, 44]. This refers to the degree to which PERS is compatible with existing devices or systems, and the social context such as current routines, standards and practices. As such, flexible feature functionalities are required [24, 28, 35, 37]. The length of time that the product lasts was also considered by [27].

Operational Works. Operational works refer to preparatory works, initiation works as well as maintenance works that formal healthcare professionals do to enact a set of practices in relation to PERS.

Preparatory works are highly relevant to making explicit implementation purpose and goals, providing transparent decision-making processes, and offering robust and rigorously planned strategies. Peek and his colleagues [25] explored the necessary processes for successfully implement of PERS, one of which is a changing of attitudes. Through distributing a clear implementation purpose and goals, healthcare professionals can reflect on their existing roles and practices, and thus better promote the integration. Our findings reveal that the low quality of integration is because most healthcare professionals have a poor or incomplete understanding of the implementation goals and purpose [28, 36, 38]. Transparent decision-making processes as well as a robust and rigorously planned strategy were also key subthemes [27, 36, 37, 41] and usually discussed together. For example, Willemse [33] pointed out that financial constraints was one concern of healthcare professionals, as some companies show uncertain financial support strategies according to different implementation phases. Unclear implementation strategies easily confuse healthcare professionals, and thus staff engagement was proposed by many scholars as a way to increase the transparency of the decision-making process [24–26, 28, 29, 31, 33, 36, 37].

In terms of initiation works and maintenance works, they are identified as all the interventions provided by the company or organization in order to facilitate the integration process after the system is adopted. Of the screened paper, mentioned interventions include training staff [24–26, 29–31, 33, 35, 37, 38, 40–42, 44], providing human resources [28, 29, 38], providing research cooperation [30, 33, 38, 44], providing financial resources [25, 28, 30, 31, 33, 35, 36, 41, 42], increasing resource availability [25, 28, 29, 33, 35], staff encouragement [24, 31, 40], collecting feedback [26, 28, 29, 35, 46] and auditing [24, 36, 38].

Personal Readiness. Personal readiness was another theme which influences the technology integration process greatly, including attitudes, knowledge, and skillset.

One significant aspect of personal readiness was healthcare professionals' attitudes towards PERS and its potential. For instance, Cohen and colleagues [41] explored the perceived usefulness and ease of use through questionnaire and interviews, claiming that positive and negative attitudes lead to correspondingly higher and lower usage intentions. Similar findings were reported in other studies such as [24, 28, 33, 35–37, 44], in which other variations in relation to personal attitudes such as privacy, confidence, and patient safety were also emphasized. Aside from personal attitudes, a few studies stressed that more attention should be paid to personal knowledge. Differing from training, personal knowledge here refers to the perceived/learnt knowledge of healthcare professionals. It was believed that healthcare professionals can better manage tasks and time if the system and how it should be used are well learnt [35, 36, 44], with good knowledge about available resources for integrating PERS into daily practices [28, 30, 31, 36, 37, 46]. Skillset was usually discussed together with knowledge, referring to the skills of applying knowledge into practice. For instance, Melkas [44] mentioned how low levels of skill and knowledge can cause feelings of insufficient capability, in turn causing possible fear, distress, and decreased motivation.

Working Environment. Factors in relation to working environment were discussed in almost all screened studies. Subthemes include social environment, material environment, and cultural environment. Oudshoorn [46] argues that even though the introduction of PERS connects practices that were previously separated in time and space, a "place dependency of user-technology relations" exists. This means that the same technology can mean different things in different contexts or situations. Consequently, spaces still matter as the context in which PERS are implemented shape how the system inhibits or facilitates human identities and actions, and redefines the context.

The social environment can be roughly classified into colleague context, patient context, and other stakeholder context. Mort and her colleagues [26] illustrate that telecare has its care limitations and should be perceived as a shift of responsibilities and social relations rather than a solution. De Veer [35] reported that although little evidence could be found to show that group characteristics affect PERS integration, they may be important because colleagues and collective support were mentioned frequently by healthcare professionals. However, May [36] illustrated that healthcare professionals usually work without a shared organizational vision. The same finding was also reported in [24, 35]. In addition, merely promoting cooperation is not the complete solution [33]. It was found that unclear responsibilities and task distribution may inhibit the integration process. In addition, some health professionals expressed concern that regarding professional-patient relations [33], patients' perceptions of PERS [29, 31, 33, 36, 38–41, 47] affect the integration process. Relations with other stakeholders, such as suppliers or managers, can also influence the pace of integration [25, 36].

Studies also emphasized the importance of the material environment, meaning the material resources for supporting PERS need to be workable and adaptive to daily practices. For instance, Lennon [31] reports that factors such as poor internet for device connection significantly affects access to digital resources among healthcare professionals, and thus their readiness to integrate PERS into daily practice. Similar findings are also reported in [35].

Beyond social and material environments, various studies stressed cultural environment as an aspect strongly affecting the integration process. Cultural environment here is defined as the way a work environment is operated from an organizational level. For example, Gjestsen [29] identified three levels of contextual factors, where factors on the meso level (i.e. leadership, workforce, and maturity) were associated with cultural environment. Similarly, May [36] argues that uncertainties found in leadership, ownership, and responsibility disrupt telecare integration, which was also supported by articles [26, 33]. There are also studies that talk about workflow [33, 47] and work structure [28, 31, 33, 35, 37, 38, 42]. In addition, cultural environments are associated with political and societal context as well. Lennon and colleagues [31] argue that current governance regulations are commonly viewed as unfit for purpose" because different healthcare organizations hold different governance rules. Through analyzing the policy documents, Gjestsen [29] claims that project sponsorship as well as external motivators were the primary factors under political context.

Integration Outcomes. The use of PERS can lead to changes in work practices and collaboration among organizations, while at the same time requiring changes in personal knowledge and skills [24–27, 30, 31, 33, 37, 41, 46]. It has an impact on, for instance, sense of privacy, perceived usefulness, perceived ease of use, freedom of managing time and tasks, and patient independency [24–26, 28–30, 33, 36, 37, 41, 42, 44, 46].

However, screened studies sometimes reported different or even opposite findings regarding impacts. For example, the pilot study in [30] showed the adopted system is effective in reducing primary caregiver isolation and uncertainty, and thus gives them 'peace of mind'. Similarly, Vadillo and colleagues [42] assessed perceived usefulness, user satisfaction and expectation among telecare experts, showing a general positive attitude towards their utilized system. However, negative outcomes such as increased work pressure, fatigue, unwillingness to use technology, fear of replacement, loss of work motivation and a sense of dehumanization among healthcare professionals were reported in many other studies [37, 39]. Instead of investigating the impact of PERS, several studies explored the complexity of technology and its use in reality [26, 27, 37]. For instance, Randi [37] categorized the script design of PERS into three clusters: expectation related to the physical artefact, attitudes and values that come into play, and expectation related the technology integration into home care service.

4   Discussion

In response to RQ1, there is a consensus that supportive strategies are necessary for healthcare professionals to understand how to use the technology successfully. However, detailed discussions have largely been sparse. First, the lack of sufficient supportive strategies has been emphasized in many of the studies, with insufficient evidence of how different strategies, such as training, contribute to the effectiveness of technology integration. As articulated by Hall [24], staff stressed the importance of training, which unfortunately appeared mainly informal in reality and thus not sufficient to support staff for a full-understanding of PERS. There are even worse situations in which healthcare professionals didn't receive support when needed [29, 36]. Second, little is known about how different strategies should be combined to maximise potential. In study [35], multifaceted strategies have been recommended because they usually appear to be more effective. In this study, the frequency of strategies mentioned by respondents was calculated. Training was the most frequently mentioned strategy, followed by supervision, opportunities to evaluate the introduction and give feedback, material availability, and encouragement. However, the frequency of mentioned strategies revealed the priority of perceived importance among healthcare professionals, rather than their actual effectiveness in promoting the integration process. Thus, more evidence is required to show the contribution of single and multiple strategies to the effectiveness of technology integration.

Regarding RQ2, multifaceted factors were identified, and this article reveals the importance of the context to integration outcomes. Yet, there is a lack of studies about how working environments impact the effectiveness of realizing operational works. Mort and colleagues [26] claim evaluating technology effectiveness makes little sense without considering the environment where the technology is used. There are more studies starting to look at working environments [26, 29, 37, 46]. All of these provide valuable evidence that shows the complexity of technology integration. However, De Veer [35] acknowledged that training might be good when healthcare professionals have inadequate knowledge of technology use, but it cannot solve problems if the issue is relevant to time constraints. This reveals that the effectiveness of different environmental factors varies. How to ensure the implementation strategies focus on the most important environmental factors remains unknown. Consequently, more studies are needed to explore how working environments impact the effectiveness of realizing operational works.

In terms of RQ3, results are inconsistent regarding the implementation impacts of PERS. Pritchard and colleagues [39] note that: 'a technology can shape and mediate social environments and relationships, which can, in turn, shape the functionalities and usage of the technology.' Despite there being many studies focusing on how the social environment and relationships are shaped and mediated by technology [26, 38], little is known about how technology is shaped by social environments and relationships. There are indeed scholars beginning to explore this gap. For instance, Randi [37] investigated why integration outcomes are different in different contexts by understanding PERS' script design. With the basic idea from Akrinh [49] that each technology has scripts with which people have to comply, Randi argued it is unrealistic to expect technologies such as off-the-shelf and problem-free packages. Nevertheless, there remains a lack of knowledge in this aspect. More studies are needed concerning how technology is reconfigured by social environments and relationships.

5 Conclusion

The article provides an overview of current research concerning the integration of PERS into formal healthcare professionals' practices. It reveals the complexity of integrating PERS, and identifies gaps relevant to implementation strategies, contextual factors, and technology design. The primary limitations of this article are related to the screened articles because only peer-reviewed journal articles written in English were included. Our findings might be useful for technology developers, implementers, and policy makers.

References

1. Howitt, P., et al.: Technologies for global health. Lancet **380**(9840), 507–535 (2012). https://doi.org/10.1016/S0140-6736(12)61127-1
2. Eccles, M.P., et al.: An implementation research agenda. Implement. Sci. **4**(1), 18 (2009). https://doi.org/10.1186/1748-5908-4-18
3. Greenhalgh, T., Procter, R., Wherton, J., Sugarhood, P., Shaw, S.: The organising vision for telehealth and telecare: discourse analysis: Table 1. BMJ Open **2**(4), e001574 (2012). https://doi.org/10.1136/bmjopen-2012-001574

4. Secker, J., Hill, R., Villeneau, L., Parkman, S.: Promoting independence: but promoting what and how? Ageing Soc. **23**(3), 375–391 (2003). https://doi.org/10.1017/S0144686X03001193

5. Mort, M., Roberts, C., Callén, B.: Ageing with telecare: care or coercion in austerity? Sociol. Health Illn. **35**(6), 799–812 (2013). https://doi.org/10.1111/j.1467-9566.2012.01530.x

6. Roberts, C., Mort, M.: Reshaping what counts as care: older people, work and new technologies. Alter **3**(2), 138–158 (2009). https://doi.org/10.1016/j.alter.2009.01.004

7. López Gómez, D.: Little arrangements that matter. Rethinking autonomy-enabling innovations for later life. Technol. Forecast. Soc. Change **93**, 91–101 (2015). https://doi.org/10.1016/j.techfore.2014.02.015

8. Gibson, G., Dickinson, C., Brittain, K., Robinson, L.: Personalisation, customisation and bricolage: how people with dementia and their families make assistive technology work for them. Ageing Soc. **39**(11), 2502–2519 (2019). https://doi.org/10.1017/S0144686X18000661

9. Östlund, B., Olander, E., Jonsson, O., Frennert, S.: STS-inspired design to meet the challenges of modern aging. Welfare technology as a tool to promote user driven innovations or another way to keep older users hostage? Technol. Forecast. Soc. Change **93**, 82–90 (2015). https://doi.org/10.1016/j.techfore.2014.04.012

10. Frennert, S.A., Forsberg, A., Östlund, B.: Elderly people's perceptions of a telehealthcare system: relative advantage, compatibility, complexity and observability. J. Technol. Hum. Serv. **31**(3), 218–237 (2013). https://doi.org/10.1080/15228835.2013.814557

11. Pols, J.: Care at a Distance: on the Closeness of Technology. Amsterdam University Press, Amsterdam (2012)

12. De San Miguel, K., Lewin, G.: Brief report: personal emergency alarms: what impact do they have on older people's lives? Australas. J. Ageing **27**(2), 103–105 (2008). https://doi.org/10.1111/j.1741-6612.2008.00286.x

13. De San Miguel, K., et al.: Personal emergency alarms: do health outcomes differ for purchasers and nonpurchases? Home Health Care Serv. Q. **36**(3–4), 164–177 (2017). https://doi.org/10.1080/01621424.2017.1373718

14. Greenhalgh, T., et al.: What matters to older people with assisted living needs? a phenomenological analysis of the use and non-use of telehealth and telecare. Soc. Sci. Med. **93**, 86–94 (2013). https://doi.org/10.1016/j.socscimed.2013.05.036

15. Bloch, F., Lundy, J.-E., Rigaud, A.-S.: Profile differences of purchasers, non-purchasers, and users and non-users of personal emergency response systems: results of a prospective cohort study. Disabil. Health J. **10**(4), 607–610 (2017). https://doi.org/10.1016/j.dhjo.2017.01.008

16. Mann, W.C., Belchior, P., Tomita, M.R., Kemp, B.J.: Use of personal emergency response systems by older individuals with disabilities. Assist. Technol. **17**(1), 82–88 (2005). https://doi.org/10.1080/10400435.2005.10132098

17. Lai, C.K., Chung, J.C., Leung, N.K., Wong, J.C., Mak, D.P.: A survey of older Hong Kong people's perceptions of telecommunication technologies and telecare devices. J. Telemed. Telecare **16**(8), 441–446 (2010). https://doi.org/10.1258/jtt.2010.090905

18. Chi, N.-C., Demiris, G.: A systematic review of telehealth tools and interventions to support family caregivers. J. Telemed. Telecare **21**(1), 37–44 (2015). https://doi.org/10.1177/1357633X14562734

19. Arksey, H., O'Malley, L.: Scoping studies: towards a methodological framework. Int. J. Soc. Res. Methodol. **8**(1), 19–32 (2005). https://doi.org/10.1080/1364557032000119616

20. Mol, A., Moser, I., Pols, J. (eds.): Care in Practice. Transcript Verlag, Bielefeld (2010). https://doi.org/10.14361/transcript.9783839414477

21. Kuijer, L., De Jong, A., Van Eijk, D.: Practices as a unit of design: an exploration of theoretical guidelines in a study on bathing. ACM Trans. Comput. Interact. **20**(4) (2013). https://doi.org/10.1145/2493382

22. Deeks, J.J., Higgins, J.P., Altman, D.G.: Analysing data and undertaking meta-analyses. In: Cochrane Handbook for Systematic Reviews of Interventions, pp. 243–296. Wiley, Chichester. https://doi.org/10.1002/9780470712184.ch9

23. Hsieh, H.-F., Shannon, S.E.: Three approaches to qualitative content analysis. Qual. Health Res. **15**(9), 1277–1288 (2005). https://doi.org/10.1177/1049732305276687

24. Hall, A., Wilson, C.B., Stanmore, E., Todd, C.: Implementing monitoring technologies in care homes for people with dementia: a qualitative exploration using normalization process theory. Int. J. Nurs. Stud. **72**(April), 60–70 (2017). https://doi.org/10.1016/j.ijnurstu.2017.04.008

25. Peek, S.T.M., Wouters, E.J.M., Luijkx, K.G., Vrijhoef, H.J.M.: What it takes to successfully implement technology for aging in place: focus groups with stakeholders. J. Med. Internet Res. **18**(5) (2016). https://doi.org/10.2196/jmir.5253

26. Mort, M., Roberts, C., Pols, J., Domenech, M., Moser, I.: Ethical implications of home telecare for older people: a framework derived from a multisited participative study. Heal. Expect. **18**(3), 438–449 (2015). https://doi.org/10.1111/hex.12109

27. Sánchez-Criado, T., López, D., Roberts, C., Domènech, M.: Installing telecare, installing users: felicity conditions for the instauration of usership. Sci. Technol. Hum. Values **39**(5), 694–719 (2014). https://doi.org/10.1177/0162243913517011

28. Hallewell Haslwanter, J., Fitzpatrick, G.: The development of assistive systems to support older people: issues that affect success in practice. Technologies **6**(1), 2 (2017). https://doi.org/10.3390/technologies6010002

29. Gjestsen, M.T., Wiig, S., Testad, I.: What are the key contextual factors when preparing for successful implementation of assistive living technology in primary elderly care? a case study from Norway. BMJ Open **7**(9), 12–14 (2017). https://doi.org/10.1136/bmjopen-2016-015455

30. Chou, H.K., et al.: A pilot study of the telecare medical support system as an intervention in dementia care: the views and experiences of primary caregivers. J. Nurs. Res. **20**(3), 169–180 (2012). https://doi.org/10.1097/jnr.0b013e318263d916

31. Lennon, M.R., et al.: Readiness for delivering digital health at scale: lessons from a longitudinal qualitative evaluation of a national digital health innovation program in the United Kingdom. J. Med. Internet Res. **19**(2), 1–37 (2017). https://doi.org/10.2196/jmir.6900

32. Greenhalgh, T., et al.: Analysing the role of complexity in explaining the fortunes of technology programmes: empirical application of the NASSS framework. BMC Med. **16**(1), 66 (2018). https://doi.org/10.1186/s12916-018-1050-6

33. Willemse, E., Roy, R., Jef, A., Tinne, D.: Facilitating and inhibiting factors to implement telemonitoring: a qualitative study. Int. J. Healthc. **2**(1) (2016). https://doi.org/10.5430/ijh.v2n1p111

34. Sugarhood, P., Wherton, J., Procter, R., Hinder, S., Greenhalgh, T.: Technology as system innovation: a key informant interview study of the application of the diffusion of innovation model to telecare. Disabil. Rehabil. Assist. Technol. **9**(1), 79–87 (2014). https://doi.org/10.3109/17483107.2013.823573

35. De Veer, A.J.E., Fleuren, M.A.H., Bekkema, N., Francke, A.L.: Successful implementation of new technologies in nursing care: a questionnaire survey of nurse-users. BMC Med. Inform. Decis. Mak. **11**(1) (2011). https://doi.org/10.1186/1472-6947-11-67

36. May, C.R., et al.: Integrating telecare for chronic disease management in the community: what needs to be done? BMC Health Serv. Res. **11**(1), 131 (2011). https://doi.org/10.1186/1472-6963-11-131

37. Stokke, R.: Maybe we should talk about it anyway: a qualitative study of understanding expectations and use of an established technology innovation in caring practices. BMC Health Serv. Res. **17**(1), 1–13 (2017). https://doi.org/10.1186/s12913-017-2587-3

38. Andreassen, H.K., Kjekshus, L.E., Tjora, A.: Survival of the project: a case study of ICT innovation in health care. Soc. Sci. Med. **132**, 62–69 (2015). https://doi.org/10.1016/j.socscimed.2015.03.016

39. Pritchard, G.W., Brittain, K.: Alarm pendants and the technological shaping of older people's care. Between (intentional) help and (irrational) nuisance. Technol. Forecast. Soc. Change **93**, 124–132 (2015). https://doi.org/10.1016/j.techfore.2014.07.009

40. Niemeijer, A.R., Depla, M., Frederiks, B., Francke, A.L., Hertogh, C.: The use of surveillance technology in residential facilities for people with dementia or intellectual disabilities: a study among nurses and support staff. Am. J. Nurs. **114**(12), 28–37 (2014). https://doi.org/10.1097/01.NAJ.0000457408.38222.d0

41. Cohen, C., Kampel, T., Verloo, H.: Acceptability among community healthcare nurses of intelligent wireless sensor-system technology for the rapid detection of health issues in home-dwelling older adults. Open Nurs. J. **11**(1), 54–63 (2017). https://doi.org/10.2174/1874434601711010054

42. Vadillo, L., Martín-Ruiz, M.L., Pau, I., Conde, R., Valero, M.Á.: A smart telecare system at digital home: perceived usefulness, satisfaction, and expectations for healthcare professionals. J. Sensors **2017** (2017). https://doi.org/10.1155/2017/8972350

43. Zwijsen, S.A., Depla, M.F.I.A., Niemeijer, A.R., Francke, A.L., Hertogh, C.M.P.M.: Surveillance technology: an alternative to physical restraints? a qualitative study among professionals working in nursing homes for people with dementia. Int. J. Nurs. Stud. **49**(2), 212–219 (2012). https://doi.org/10.1016/j.ijnurstu.2011.09.002

44. Melkas, H.: Informational ecology and care workers: safety alarm systems in finnish elderly-care organizations. Work **37**(1), 87–97 (2010). https://doi.org/10.3233/WOR-2010-1060

45. Sjölinder, M., Avatare Nöu, A.: Indoor and outdoor social alarms: understanding users' perspectives. JMIR mhealth uhealth **2**(1), e9 (2014). https://doi.org/10.2196/mhealth.2730

46. Oudshoorn, N.: How places matter: telecare technologies and the changing spatial dimensions of healthcare. Soc. Stud. Sci. **42**(1), 121–142 (2012). https://doi.org/10.1177/0306312711431817

47. Hanley, J., Pinnock, H., Paterson, M., McKinstry, B.: Implementing telemonitoring in primary care: learning from a large qualitative dataset gathered during a series of studies. BMC Fam. Pract. **19**(1), 1–11 (2018). https://doi.org/10.1186/s12875-018-0814-6

48. Steventon, A., et al.: Effect of telecare on use of health and social care services: findings from the Whole Systems Demonstrator cluster randomised trial. Age Ageing **42**(4), 501–508 (2013). https://doi.org/10.1093/ageing/aft008

49. Akrich, M.: The de-scription of technical objects. In: Bijker, W., Law, J. (eds.) Shaping Technology/Building Society. Studies in Sociotechnical Change, pp. 205–224. MIT Press (1992)

Combining Motivating Strategies with Design Concepts for Mobile Apps to Increase Usability for the Elderly and Alzheimer Patients

Christian Eichhorn[1]([✉]), David A. Plecher[1], Martin Lurz[2], Nadja Leipold[2], Markus Böhm[2], Helmut Krcmar[2], Angela Ott[3], Dorothee Volkert[3], Atsushi Hiyama[4], and Gudrun Klinker[1]

[1] Chair for Computer Aided Medical Procedures and Augmented Reality, The Technical University of Munich, Munich, Germany
christian.eichhorn@tum.de, {plecher,klinker}@in.tum.de
[2] Chair for Information Systems, The Technical University of Munich, Munich, Germany
{Martin.Lurz,Nadja.Leipold,Markus.Boehm,Krcmar}@in.tum.de
[3] Institute for Biomedicine of Aging, Friedrich-Alexander-Universität Erlangen-Nürnberg, Erlangen, Germany
{Angela.Ott,Dorothee.Volkert}@fau.de
[4] INAMI.HIYAMA Laboratory, The University of Tokyo, Tokyo, Japan
Hiyama@star.rcast.u-tokyo.ac.jp

Abstract. This work focuses on design concepts, including the goal to motivate interaction with mobile applications for the target group elderly people and with an extended set of guidelines for Alzheimer patients. At the outset, understanding the symptoms of Alzheimer's disease is necessary when focusing on usability issues during interaction with touchscreen-based devices. Improving health via the use of mobile devices is a game changer in many areas. However, an urgent need exists for a fitting theory-based approach, which is missing in many applications, to facilitate the countering of threats such as diseases, age-related decline and situational factors. When assessing various projects, only focusing on how to utilize mobile devices to improve the life quality of the elderly is not adequate. An even more critical aspect is *how to motivate them to actually use mobile devices*, which is inevitable. Therefore, based on our guidance required in the development process, it must include intrinsic and extrinsic motivational strategies to target different user types for mobile applications. With that in mind, we review design strategies when developing for the elderly. Additionally, we offer useful recommendations to form a set of *Design Guidelines* that are structured to address the three major categories of age-related decline: *Cognitive, Perceptual* and *Motor Abilities*. We conclude with an innovative view on application development by introducing *Enabling Applications*, which focus on elderly people, Alzheimer patients and their caregivers alike.

© Springer Nature Switzerland AG 2020
Q. Gao and J. Zhou (Eds.): HCII 2020, LNCS 12208, pp. 47–66, 2020.
https://doi.org/10.1007/978-3-030-50249-2_4

Keywords: Elderly · Alzheimer's Disease · Design · Motivation ·
Guidelines · Gerontechnology · HCI · Serious Games · Nursing Home ·
Aging Society · Gamification

1   Introduction

With an aging society [39], increasing cost in caring and shortage of care personal [29], new approaches are needed to counter a potential care crisis. Aging
people should be encouraged and motivated to live an independent healthy
lifestyle to reduce caring efforts and more importantly enhance their quality
of life. In this field of research, multiple solutions have been tested, including
recent developments focusing on therapeutic robots to encourage elderly people
to adopt a certain healthy behavior and lifestyle [71]. The use of such robots
is limited because of high costs, the need for introduction, and their lack of
upgradability in the future. Therefore, an approach to utilize modern technology that fosters greater independence and is inexpensive is needed [10]. Today's
mobile devices are affordable, accessible for everyone and it is possible to play
and learn everywhere. A plethora of health-related apps e.g. for counting the
user's steps, or calculating the amount of consumed sugar or calories has been
developed. A recently released app, TrackSugAR [57], uses Augmented Reality
(AR) to illustrate the sugar intake. Learning and playing can also be combined
in a so called Serious Game, for example to inform adolescents about healthy
nutrition [60]. These technologies provide a rich opportunity for researchers to
develop solutions specifically for elderly people [16,30,47,70,77]. This arising
opportunity should be capitalized, especially because improvements in touchscreen technology (e.g. size, quality) are simplifying and enhancing the interactions with these devices by elderly people [33,40,70]. Application development
for the elderly demands close attention to its design and functionality. This
demand has already resulted in development issues requiring guidance for both
developers and consumers alike. A good example is the need to collect and structure various factors of age-related decline [42]. Holzinger et al. [33] described four
major challenges of age: Cognitive complexity, motivation, physical ability and
perception. This considered findings by Ownby and Czaja [54] as well as Vasconcelos et al. [70], who proposed *Cognitive, Perceptual* and *Motor Abilities* as
major factors. After grouping recommendations found in the literature, fitting
solutions can be proposed for challenges in terms of a set of recommendations
and guidelines. The approach of collecting and structuring aspects for elderly
people app development will be the underlying theme of this paper and at the
end allows to combine the different sections [53]. In the systematic literature
review [53], the fact that less research was conducted in summarizing guidelines
for the elderly aged 80+ was evident. A combination of general guidelines for the
elderly as well as guidelines for Alzheimer patients can offer a unique view on a
connected group of people. As stated by Nurgalieva et al. [53], generally the view
on guidelines for the elderly targets mostly under 65 years old people, this leaves
out elderly with a higher tendency towards an age-related decline of e.g. cognitive capabilities. After understanding the needs of the elderly and symptoms

of Alzheimer's disease, the focus of this paper shifts towards *how to motivate the elderly to use mobile applications*. The frequently overlooked importance of motivational elements [21] in combination with further research about application design elements closes the circle by incorporating the previous findings into a collection of *Design Guidelines*. These are focused on mobile applications for elderly and structured around *age-related decline* categories. The final conclusion summarizes not only the achievements of this paper, but also introduces the understanding of an *Enabling Application* as a concept to address the elderly and caregivers. This paper does not only identify relevant literature and guidelines, but more importantly follows the goal to solve challenges in mobile app development. This results in a strong foundation of combining existing research with a view on elderly people and Alzheimer's patients.

2   Target Groups

When facing elderly people and Alzheimer's patients in the area of mobile application development, two visible user groups can be identified. First the *active participants*, who are in general open for new experiences and can be easily motivated to use mobile devices. Their motivation arises mostly out of *their* personal needs/interests (*intrinsic motivation*) to use applications. Alzheimer patients in the beginning state could still interact with the device, and they still seemed to be motivated, as Zmily et al. [77] showed in their evaluation. Secondly, *passive participants* in the form of for example hesitating elderly people which have the fear to do something wrong, destroy the device or they are simply disinterested in using modern technology [50]. Another reason could be the missing ability to interact with applications on their own. This user group, e.g. often represented through Alzheimer patients in an advanced state, demands for much more focus on design choices, and besides intrinsic elements, also *extrinsic motivation* elements should be used to get their attention. Of course categorizing elderly people in two groups is difficult as the daily situation can have a major impact on the overall mood of the person. Therefore, this grouping should be considered as an approach to respond to previous development attempts, which didn't focus enough on the highly heterogeneous state of these user groups [24,25,56]. Especially, the essential aspect of motivation is overlooked [5]. Our work tries to focus on finding motivation strategies to incorporate them into design guidelines for future app development.

3   Understanding Alzheimer's Disease

3.1   Problem Statement Behind Alzheimer's

Alzheimer's disease is the most common form of dementia [64] that is a general encompasses memory loss, behavioral changes or the decline of rational thinking [16]. In the NEJM, a study was published which stated the total cost for dementia treatment was between $157 billion and $215 billion in 2010 in the U.S. alone, which even surpasses the cost for heart disease and cancer. In 2040 the cost for Alzheimer's disease is expected to double because of the aging population [35]. Alzheimer can be directly attributed to irreversible changes in the brain, which lead to its destruction [64]. It is incurable and hence the only help for these people is to increase their life quality by mitigating symptoms and assisting their caregivers. Furthermore, different forms of rehabilitation are considered useful, but are often overlooked with the "they're just going to get worse anyway" [76, p. 393] attitude of some clinics. Instead of keeping these people in their darkness, it is important to take out the stress, frustration and isolation to give their life quality by adding "[...] life to the years, not more years to the life" [76, p. 393]. Typical symptoms are the decrease in cognitive thinking, communication, decision making, behavior and memory recall. Understanding the types of syndromes and the corresponding degeneration of a person is important to develop customized strategies, targeting their individual needs [16,76].

3.2 Classification of Alzheimer's Disease Symptoms and Supportive Approaches

One of the most challenging diseases for patients and caregivers alike is Alzheimer's disease. The nature of a neurodegenerative illness with a progressive and irreversible decline in cognition, leading to death, is the missing aspect of an overall general understanding of the disease progress and corresponding symptoms. Therefore, people require intensive support to address the constantly changing and growing needs. *Assistive Technology* in form of smart homes can improve the lifestyle of these people. For example, a smart home application could help with hints, suggestions and reminders in various situations. To convey a message as effectively as possible, five ways of communication with Alzheimer patients are described and recommended as "prompts" by Lapointe et al. [44]: *sound* (e.g. music), *images, text, video* and *light patterns*. Sound messages are the most often used approaches in smart homes, but it is still unclear in the scientific world, which variation of those interaction types works the best due to the many symptoms of Alzheimer's disease [44].

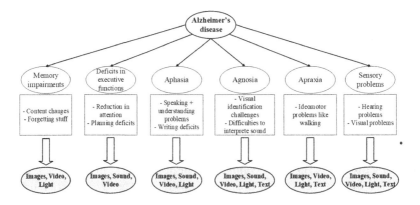

Fig. 1. Alzheimer symptom classification with helpful interaction modalities to reach the patients more specifically [44, p. 4]

In total Alzheimer's disease symptoms can be divided into six major categories, described by Lapointe et al. [44]: Memory impairments, Deficits in executive functions, Aphasia, Agnosia, Apraxia and Sensory problems (see Fig. 1 for more details). To deal with all of the resulting symptoms, several approaches should be taken. A good example would be not to use *sound* messages when an Alzheimer patient has problems with semantic memory (memory impairments), where the usage of *images* or *videos* would yield better results [44]. Often in the field scenario, it is not that simple to choose the correct approach because all categories have to be divided into subsections. For example, for Agnosia, with visual decline occurring as a symptom, *sound* or *music* can work quite well. But there is also the opposite possibility in the case of an auditory decline, the usage of *sound* would be ineffective and *visual* prompts would work better. Even visual difficulties have to be segmented when facing Agnosia. It could be problematic to detect objects, whereas text would be still fine. On the other hand, when facing difficulties to detect and recognize different letters, the usage of images would be beneficial. The same problem of segmentation in different subsections occurs for Apraxia and for Sensory problems. On top of that, as Lapointe et al. [44] are stating, there is a need for more research in the direction of communication with Alzheimer patients with the focus on the different categories of the disease to better address these versatile user groups. Chin et al. [14] already stated the importance of using diverse feedback and interaction schemes for the elderly, which is even more important for Alzheimer patients and their various disease symptoms. Figure 1 is a summary and simplification of the prompt recommendations by Lapointe et al. [44], showcasing a top-level view on the different symptoms.

3.3 Playful Approaches Using Mobile Devices as Chance to Counter Alzheimer's Disease

In the past some applications in the direction of *Assistive Technology* have been developed to address the needs of Alzheimer patients [4]. Stress and delusions are common surrounding circumstances, making life even more stressful for them and their caregivers. Showing pictures or watching videos can calm and stop the feeling of confusion for these people [16]. Also, the exposure to technology, e.g. reminder games, have noticeably improved their cognition even weeks after they played. This so-called *Serious Game* section offers great potential for motivating elderly people with the goal to improve cognitive capabilities [24,70]. A well-known concept in game development tries to keep the player in the flow zone of the game. The flow zone represents the sense of completeness and focus for a player to create the feeling of enjoyment and fulfillment, hence increasing motivation [18]. To achieve these feelings a straightforward and easy to use interface with a well-known environment for *ADLs* is needed. Today *Serious Games* are vastly accessible and therefore also used for home-based rehabilitation [8]. Furthermore, Coppola et al. [16] see a great potential for mobile devices in the form factor of tablets, where still a lot of transition towards accessibility and usability concepts from lessons learned in *Assistive Technology* is needed. Simplicity, mobility and the touchscreen as a more intuitive way to interact with technology even for inexperienced users are the major factors to stimulate people with Dementia [34,51]. Challenges such as a friendly user interface or speech and communication problems can be solved with mobile applications, but even nowadays promising development in the area of Dementia is mostly neglected due to the high difficulty level. Especially projects such as *Alive Inside* [1] have shown what powerful impact technology with the help of music can have. Experiences with media can connect deeply to the person's inner self and remind them of who they are by connecting cultural memories and implicit memory (e.g. habits, skills). Studies have shown that implicit memories are often less effected by the cognitive decline and can be used to enhance the learning success for Serious Games targeting ADLs [69]. This is also known as reminiscence in dementia care activities [4,6]. Other approaches try to get deep connections to their true personality with the help of images as digital photo frames of "familiar people, places and events" [76, p. 394] and on top of that, try to train their memory [4,49]. Busy-boards are apps designed to motivate users to complete different small tasks. When completing the task, a reward is given to motivate further attention. Improvement in cognitive memory (e.g. reduction of the error rate when performing ADLs) by using these applications and *Serious Games* have already been proposed [8]. Combining this approach with a companion (e.g. staff member or another resident) will result in more curiosity. Even Alzheimer people who were totally disinterested, will show a reaction when having a companion around [16]. Imbeault et al. [37] are proposing a technological approach with a *Social/Socially Assistive Robotic (S AR) System*, which combines motivation and *encouragement* with *companionship*, resulting in an active approach to deal with mental disability.

Tziraki et al. [69] recommend the usage of cues in a multisensory approach (visual and auditory) in combination with color/lighting adjustments for Serious Games. Furthermore, they came to the conclusion of involving the framework of *Situated Cognition Learning* through the errorless learning method to extend their cueing approach and to overcome the limitation of low perceived self-efficacy. Thereby commonly errorless learning is combined with active learning of daily situational tasks with the goal to prevent any sorts of negative experiences when performing it. This could be done by showing a positive message (cue) when an error was made [45]. Priming can be utilized for object recognition to connect to other topics or to lead away from a mistake. The reason for choosing such a strategy is to utilize the still intact thinking structures to fill the role of impaired ones. Therefore, learning new content has a higher reminder rate with less mistakes being made [69].

4   The Need for Scientific-Based Mobile App Development

4.1   Limitations in the Current Design Approaches

A common misconception is the belief, that elderly people in general are not interested in mobile devices and cannot adapt to use them [62]. Lorenz and Oppermann [47] see a potential in elderly people because of their variety of abilities learned in their past experiences compared to the younger generation. The social status, life experiences and also impairments lead to rich and versatile backgrounds and identities. Häikö et al. [30] showed the learning potential of elderly people after their first physical contact with the application even when they were not confronted with mobile devices before. Some of them were quite doubtful (*passive participants*), but most elderly people soon saw the benefits of using a mobile phone. On top of that, Coppola et al. [16] achieved great results to reach Alzheimer patients by using iPads with music and pictures. Often the only limiting factor why elderly people will not use new technology, is the fact that there are usability flaws in the design, e.g. too small text [21, 40]. The reason behind such a design is the *One fits all Approach*, which has limitations for certain user groups [42,70]. Seaborn et al. [62] are describing this approach as the narrow focus on the "ideal" average user, which can exclude a substantial percentage of the actual target group from the beginning. A more widely opened design approach, which reflects the diversity of these people (e.g. *active* and *passive participants*), is important to address their needs [14,47]. For Kobayashi et al. [40] and Lorenz and Oppermann [47] stereotypical elderly people phones with big physical buttons are not the right solution because of their lack of health applications, extensibility and often small screens. The advanced interface concept by Lorenz and Oppermann [47] contained more information without overloading the screen. Furthermore, physical buttons cannot change, hence buttons are limiting the versatility [53]. When developing an application for the older generation, it is important to consider the diversity of this user group, e.g. middle-aged or even fitter users. Designs must be adaptable with a *2- or 3 for any* [47, p. 3] design approach. This idea contains a specific interface for elderly and other user groups, if one interface doesn't fit for all, it can be modified or swapped. The interface should have a wide reception with an easy way of interaction for different users [62].

4.2 Evidence-Based Approaches to Motivate the Elderly to Use Modern Technology

Many researchers, such as Sama et al. [59] conclude, that apps have a positive impact and a lot of potential to reach the elderly. Yet, there is still a way to go for application developers and researchers to integrate more aspects of patient engagement and motivational elements. Some papers focuses on designing/motivational elements (e.g. [5,47]). Cowan et al. [17] and Gao et al. [28] suggest a cooperation between developers, change specialists and researchers for more usability and a *theory-based approach* (focus on literature and change models). Dörner et al. [23] recommend a cooperation between several groups of application area specialists for *Serious Games* development to include key principles of the game relevant domains. Sama et al. [59] use the *Transtheoretical Model of Change* to structure individual and social influence, focusing on different types of mobile health apps. They use various categories of engagement to further categorize the different approaches of the apps to change the behavior of the users. These categories include topics such as the change of the personal environment, *goal setting* or social referencing, thereby combining multiple directions of intrinsic or extrinsic elements. Their results are in line with other research, revealing the need for more *theory-based approaches* when developing apps [17,28,65]. Most often app developers choose only *self-monitor* methods, also a part of the *Self-regulation Theories* [12], over other approaches like social referencing because of less programming effort, e.g. a simple step counter app [55]. Marketing interests decide about features, strategies and content of applications, instead of research and literature [55,59]. While often successful models can be reused in other scenarios, some may tend to actually restrict new thinking because of the indirect process of trying to press an approach into the existing model.

5   Boosting Motivation to Interact with Mobile Devices

5.1   The Concept of Motivation

It is important to develop something the elderly really like to use, hence improve their lifestyle and well-being. The need for a motivating background was stated by Andersen et al. [5] as: "The usability of products determines if the product can be used, while the emotional component of it determines if the product will be used" [5, p. 1]. Motivation can be described "[...] as an internal state or as a way to increase the occurrence of certain behaviors (persuasion)" [27, p. 685] and is the topic of research and discussion in the field of elderly people in the last years [33,41]. A mobile device, as something the elderly often think that they are unable to use, can have a positive impact, if they see the potential and their ability to interact with it [73]. Hence the mobile device can be seen as *Persuasive Technology*, changing their view on a healthy lifestyle with an incremental approach, without using coercion [26,58]. Reaching an elderly person who is not interested in modern technology, is a challenge. Therefore, it is an important task to figure out, how to make the device and application more comfortable to use and motivating for them [21,62,73]. For that reason, a first basic understanding of *how to structure the concept of Motivation* is needed. *Motivation* has been categorized into two groups [22]: *intrinsic* (personal incentives, coming from the inside, e.g. pleasure, satisfaction) and *extrinsic* (external benefits given from the outside for achieving something, e.g. money, appreciation). Results have been found in many different scientific fields, where researchers face the problem of motivating elderly people, yet there are not many papers which structure the different approaches and results [41]. This paper will give a short overview on some design-relevant findings. The goal is to structure the results in a useful way to improve design decisions during app development.

5.2   Enabling Factors, Creation of Inner Motivation

When researching the field of motivation in the elderly, a clear side topic seems to be advertisement for elderly people. Advertisement can be separated in factual- and emotional-based advertisement [74]. The elderly can be seen as a "[...] group of individuals, with varied motivations and backgrounds, who are eager to learn about new technology" [52, p. 1] and who simply seem to lack the insight into benefits by using the new technology. In research, it became clear, that the elderly are more open for emotional, "subjective and evaluative" [74, p. 344] advertisement than fact-based one. They are trying to prevent negative emotions and are focusing on positive aspects of their lives instead. Furthermore, elderly people seem to judge information more based on their own experiences and personal values. This, in combination with the decline of cognitive abilities, changes their decision making [14,74]. Naumanen and Tukiainen [52] also mentioned in context of their senior club project with the goal of sustainable learning to use the PC, the advance must be emotionally appealing to motivate the participants. A memorable product or interaction with the elderly must be "related to love and caring" (emotional goals) as Williams and Drolet [74, p. 345] showed in their experiments. The region between too high difficulty and a boring experience is called the flow zone, which creates the feeling of enjoyment and fulfillment, but is hard to achieve for every elderly person [8,18,21]. Therefore, focusing on different cognitive abilities and adapting the difficulty level can increase the enjoyment [14,24]. As an example, the rehabilitation program with adapted difficulty level by Colombo et al. [15] improved motivation and progress. If the elderly have the opportunity to repeat the task (try-and-error [67] and a clear connection to known topics with a positive emotional outcome is established [74], bridges between existing knowledge and new experiences can be build [52]. Castilla et al. [13] are referring to *Psychological Tools* [13, p. 353] and were able to achieve positive feedback by focusing on positive and relaxing experiences. Building up excitement and hence stimulating curiosity *(intrinsic motivation)*, is a driving factor. This is also a main key to convert a *passive participant* into an active one and with good support, learning will work by itself. Early research to counter depression in elderly people focused on *Positive Psychology* (improving positive individual traits). A good example is the experiment from Langer and Rodin [43], where elderly people cared for a plant and the group showed a noticeable improvement in happiness. Another quite new research field is robotics for elderly people. Robots are companions that focus on stimulating *Social Interactions* or a sense of usefulness [27]. The robotic seal PARO showed improvements in feelings and mental stability [71]. The robots have potential, especially because of their physical presence, but they come with trade-offs, as they are costly and need maintenance. The solution for this seems to be a virtual agent in an app for the elderly, which can interact with the person, deliver support for certain situations and can counter their negative feelings [27]. Albaina et al. [3] declared five designing strategies for their virtual coach by focusing on *intrinsic motivation*: 1) Personal focus points (made by experts), 2) *Self-monitoring*, 3) Conditioning, 4) Consistency and 5) Curiosity. Participants in their experiment mentioned the flower as the most motivating element, hence this companion is a good option to keep the game in the mind of the elderly. To prevent false expectations, the flower was chosen instead of e.g. doctor figure, which could lead to a misinterpretation of the application for a diagnoses system. The companion should have a centric role for an application by trying to stimulate positive emotions [3]. A virtual companion can convey positive reinforcement and instructions with the help of multiple interaction patterns, e.g. sound or text and even animations [13,44]. *Self-monitoring* is deeply connected with the *goal setting* approach. Therefore, a *passive participant* can be more easily transformed into an *active participant*. Providing diverse feedback should enable the user to better understand the progress and reminds about the usage of the application. Together *goal setting, self-monitoring* and giving feedback [70] is forming the *Self-Regulation Theory* to create a better focus on a user's independent motivation with intrinsic elements.

5.3   Reinforcing Factors, External Incentives

Rewards are clear incentives for reaching goals. But finding the right rewards seems to be difficult as Albaina et al. [3] stated. Additionally, these rewards have to be directly speaking and appealing for the elderly people to motivate further interaction and interest [5]. As the elderlies are often simply not able to see these benefits, they have to be transformed into perceived needs, showing a positive chance for useful change [67]. Another important factor is simplicity. Smaller and simpler tasks, such as a minimal task list [67], will encourage elderly people to stay at focus and realize the goals [26]. Health improvements as incentives which people need to change their habits, seems to be a one-sided opinion and maybe addresses more *active participants* and excludes *passive participants* from the beginning. Besides *setting goals*, it is also important to show the features of an application as Tang et al. [67] mentioned. Another reinforcing factor can be seen as competitive or collaborative experiences. Such a strategy can be motivating in the area of Serious Game development, where fast performed game actions can lead to fun engagements [51].

5.4   Summary of Motivating Design Concepts

Overall multiple motivating elements where identified and can be categorized into two distinct groups, *intrinsic* and *extrinsic* [22]. Focusing on connection to known experiences means the personal relationship to a specific memory, e.g. pictures or songs which brings old memories back and can even reach an Alzheimer patient [2,4,9,68]. Such emotional concepts have been found helpful to boost self-efficacy and hence improve executive functions performed by Alzheimer patients [69]. *Social* influence through other people around the elderly, e.g. caregivers [34], grandchildren or other elderly people [51,62] can spark more interest, especially for less active people. *Goal setting* as an important learning tool proved to be very powerful [70]. Tang et al. [67] could show, *Social Interaction* can have a huge impact on opinions and *goals* (both connected as extrinsic elements, reinforcing each other). Achieving *Goals* can be quite emotional driven, a person defines *Goals* as important not only because of external incentives, but also through own emotional perspectives [36]. Therefore, *Intrinsic* and *Extrinsic Motivation* is often deeply connected. Often researchers refer to mostly intrinsic concepts, which are enabling and motivating factors for elderly people, but there are proven examples where reinforcing factors are equally important and the combination of both types can have a high chance of mobilizing the elderly [72]. This holds especially true, if talking about Alzheimer patients, where intrinsic elements alone often can't reach a person because their inner self is not fully available [68]. To identify motivators, specific models and questionnaires have been developed. The *Technology Acceptance Model (TAM)* tries to identify evidence *if and why people will use a newly introduced technology* [20].

6   Design Guidelines for Elderly People-Oriented Applications

To address the challenges of age-related changes, the design has to be taken into account. In the area for elderly people development there are numerous principles that describe how to implement an interface [40]. The goal for this work is to have a better understanding of the design concepts for elderly people-oriented mobile applications. Furthermore, to improve the possibility to reach the elderly, motivational elements offer some useful design concepts. The understanding of design for a user group with specific needs should shift away from a general on the average user focused approach to an on the individual abilities of a person focused "accessible and inclusive" [62, p. 5] foundation, e.g. *Ability-based Concept* [75]. To structure all the findings, the three distinctive categories of age-related decline will be used [54]: *Cognitive, Perceptual* and *Motor Abilities*.

6.1   General Design Guidelines Targeting Elderly People

Strategies to Counter Cognitive Decline: When giving instant feedback [14] besides text output, vibration or clear, distinctive and low frequency sound patterns are useful [11,21]. Touchscreen usage is the best interaction option [33] with "finger-based intuitive interactions" [40, p. 84]. Therefore, a touchscreen device is known as direct input device, allowing direct and more natural interactions with new technology and little needed training [40,70]. This even allows simple multitouch gestures with a limitation of two fingers at a time, which are still working without too many problems and were the best approach for an elderly-friendly input method [48]. To overcome reservations by the elderly people, the interface should offer familiar elements and an environment that connects to known experiences. Thus will help elderly people feel more comfortable [31,32,41]. This way of building an application also simplifies the flow of tasks for elderly people and therefore reduces the possibility of forgetting them [66]. A good way to instruct elderly people is a tutorial like approach with continuous advice (e.g. through a companion), as this does not demand from them to remember content from the previous screen and can help if they get lost [9,21,42]. The butler system [13] tries to incorporate a well-known experience, such as a friendly butler as avatar in the system to produce a more familiar feeling which results in more attention.

The butler avatar delivers the basic instructions in text form and communicates further explanations to reinforce the understanding and addresses different preferences/difficulties of the users. Castilla et al. [13] also recommend a virtual autopilot feature to prevent the elderly person from getting stuck in a situation. It will automatically select a destination that fits the current situation. Another use case would be to counter *passive participants*, who don't want to interact with the app by catching their interest with an automatic selection.

Perceptual Design Choices to Overcome Vision and Hearing Limitations: A relevant barrier for elderly people is a too small font size as e.g. Scheibe et al. [61] showed in a study with 48% of the participants facing this issue. Caprani et al. [11] collected their experiences about sizes for elements and structured them. In their findings the minimal size for buttons, as the most optimal solution for touch interactions, should be a square with a size of 20 mm. Other findings suggested over 30 mm in length. Furthermore, when choosing the text font, distinctive advantages of some fonts should be taken into consideration [11]. Sans-serif fonts (e.g. Arial, Helvetica) are a benefitting choice because of their typefaces. Elderly people can more easily recognize characters [7, 66]. For the size, 16 pt (point scale for resolution independent size representation) are recommended [11]. Darroch et al. [19] experimented with font sizes for text and they achieved positive results for a font size between 12 pt and 14 pt on a small device. These results do not differ much from other recent findings, as researchers recommend at least 12 pt for regular text [42, 66]. For the language the mother tongue or the option to change the language reduces complexity [14]. Special interaction elements, e.g. touchable game elements, should be around 12 mm big and the best accuracy was achieved when these elements were located in a corner [46]. Touchable elements must be clearly distinctive from other game elements [61]. Kobayashi et al. [40] suggest a size of at least 8 mm for touchable targets like buttons, icons or interactive text. To achieve better visibility and readability colored text on a colored background and moving text should be avoided [63]. Additionally, to address colorblindness, blue-green tones should be replaced with other colors [42, 66, 69]. When giving feedback, besides standard text output, vibration or distinctive, speech messages can be useful [11]. Hearing or vision limitations can be addressed by offering multiple feedback and input methods, e.g. voice messages [31].

Countering the Decrease of Motor Abilities: Previously, under *perceptual design choices*, size constraints for buttons and other interactive objects have been mentioned with a minimal recommended size of 20 mm [11]. The placement of buttons feels most natural in corners such that positioning can avoid hitting the wrong object [46]. To further boost the usability for touch interactions, button spacing should be at least 3.17 mm and 12.7 mm to compensate for input errors caused e.g. by shaking [11]. Kobayashi et al. [40] suggest a border detection to give feedback when a person misses a button, to prevent confusion.

6.2   Advanced Guidelines for Alzheimer Patients

For the Alzheimer user group additional design approaches should be taken into consideration to address their more demanding needs. Furthermore, in this user group there are many more *passive participants*, as the disease takes away cognitive abilities and is quite often accompanied by depression.

Taking the Limited Cognitive Abilities of a Dementia Patient into Consideration: Zmily and Abu-Saymeh [76] provide five guidelines for instructions and information for mobile application focused on Alzheimer patients:

- Including simple language for interactions
- Repeating instructions multiple times
- Breaking instructions down to straightforward and independent tasks, similar to the short and simple instruction sentences used by Tziraki et al. [69]
- Giving additional time for a response (important to not overstrain Alzheimer patients [8]
- Splitting messages up to avoid information overflow.

Castilla et al. [13] recommended to incorporate playful tools directly into the design to train the memory of the elderly, which is even more important for Alzheimer patients. Another benefitting factor is to remind the Alzheimer patients about the actual usage of the device [76]. The Alzheimer's Society [4] suggests showing the daytime with additional information, such as morning/evening and the weekday to e.g. counter confusion with bright summer evenings. Determining which information should be shown and the approach of the visualization is important, e.g. confronting an Alzheimer patient with a forgotten relative, can result in bad feelings and depression [49]. For Bouchard et al. [8] *Serious Games* lack in-game assistance for cognitive errors and difficulty adjustments especially designed for Alzheimer patients. Helping the patient master a challenge is better than giving them a new one and letting the patient experience a failure [9]. For that reason, Bouchard et al. [8] and Eichhorn et al. [24] implemented dynamic difficulty adjustment systems, that manually improve or decrease the difficulty level of the game and help to keep the player in the flow zone of the application. A *Serious Game* for Alzheimer patients must focus on four cognitive spheres: *memory, planning skills, initiative* and *perseverance* to improve cognitive abilities [8]. To design an interface that feels natural, the Wii gaming console with *ecological interactions* (with simple gestures, less buttons) and a well-known environment creates a lot of motivation and reduces frustration. Similar to the cultural nuances theme implemented by Tziraki et al. [69]. On the other hand, these interactions should not focus on the whole body because of impaired motor skills. Another aspect for an *ecological interaction* design is to reduce configuration or completely avoid the need for preparation. Besides visual and audio feedback, vibro-tactile feedback has been proven as an effective memory aid for people with cognitive disabilities [8].

Scientific Insights Focused on Perception of Alzheimer Patients: Asset creation should take the impairment of vision into consideration by focusing on simple scenes with help and assistance for the player. Additionally, using warm and bright colors like orange and yellow is preferable as they are easier to see and to distinguish than blue or dark colors [38]. Details for nearby images will be blurred and therefore simple images should be used. Combining bright colors, a well-lit display with a high contrast will result in good luminosity, but overdoing it and glaring the user should be avoided [8]. 3D objects or a 3D environment are sometimes beneficial to addresses the need for a familiar world representation. On top of that, problematic for the patients is the ability to distinguish background and objects, thus creating a good depth perception with clear borders is needed. All these visual guidelines can be combined by choosing a clear color system which distinguishes between objects and background, uses a different outline thickness, e.g. with a shader for contrast and shape perception and is continuous throughout the whole application [8]. Furthermore, focusing on multiple feedback patterns can help with specific problems like hearing decline or vision difficulties, as Alzheimer's disease will increase sensory issues, especially in a more advanced state of the disease [14]. That's the reason why Bouchard et al. [8] are recommending multisensory interactions for output and input by using the full potential of mobile devices. This concept has been taken up by Tziraki et al. [69] through written and spoken instructions for each screen.

Addressing Motor Ability Decline of Dementia Patients: Simple input gestures, such as swiping or zooming are still working quite fine, but pinching with panning is generally more difficult. Besides that, tapping should be avoided if possible [40]. However, when designing for Alzheimer patients because of their cognitive decline, the ability to precisely perform these gestures is lost. Therefore, even simple gestures should be used sparsely and only when needed (see Table 1). The touchscreen device should be placed at table height in a comfortable way [69], hence tilting it on a stand could be helpful and allows to keep the device in position when interacting with it.

6.3   Summary Design Guidelines

The findings can be structured into three sections by Ownby and Czaja [54]: *Cognitive* (for mental decline), *Perceptual* (vision and hearing decline) and *Motor Abilities* (physical decline) and are categorized as general and additional advanced guidelines for Alzheimer patients (see Table 1).

7   Enabling Applications, a New View on Application Development for the Elderly People

The first step is gaining a better understanding of Alzheimer's disease via a classification of symptoms into six groups that facilitates a better overview of this disease with "1.000 faces". The unique opportunities to utilize mobile devices to improve quality of life of Alzheimer patients can be identified in many projects. When developing apps for them, a diverse approach is necessary and should be combined with personalized content to improve the possibility of reaching them. To counter threats such as diseases, mobile devices offer a unique opportunity of

Table 1. ▨ Additional Alzheimer recommendations; ▨ excluded in the case of advanced state of Alzheimer's disease; ▨ need for future research.

Summary of Design Guidelines		
Cognitive *working memory, processing speed*	**Perceptual** *vision and hearing decline*	**Motor Abilities** *shaking, decrease in muscle power*
Companion/Avatar	Iconography from their world perspective	Border detection with feedback
Linear navigation (tutorial approach)	Clear design/shapes to differentiate labels/buttons	Border space for buttons: min. 3.17 mm and 12.7 mm ↓
Autopilot	Connection to known experiences	Avoid gestures
Language selection ↓	Button size: min. 20x20mm (square), otherwise min. length: 30mm	
Simple, precise language with repeating instructions	Font size buttons: min. 16 pt	
Extended time information	Font size text: min. between 12 pt and 14 pt	
Avoid the need for a setup by the Alzheimer patient	Gestures (avoid tapping)	
Difficulty settings for the individual user (flow zone)	Special focus on depth perception	
Highlighted keywords for instructions	High contrast between elements	
Busy-boards (small tasks and rewards)	Not all colors are useful e.g. considering colorblindness	
Errorless learning (priming)	Standardized color schema	
	Feedback for a button press	
	Shader for borders	
	Haptic feedback; clear distinctive sound/speech ↓	
	Multisensory cues	

improving health management with applications such as *mHealth* [73]; however an urgent need exists to use a *theory-based approach*, which is missing in many applications. How to motivate elderly people to actually use mobile devices is inevitable. The last chapter focuses on design strategies when developing for the elderly and furthermore picks up elements found in previous chapters to form a set of *Design Guidelines*, structured to counter the three major categories of age-related decline: *Cognitive, Perceptual* and *Motor Abilities*. After the literature overview, our goal for the future is the development of an innovative tablet application for both elderly people and Alzheimer patients. The structural core of this application will be the integration and combination of relevant found motivation elements with a playful design drawing from gamification approaches and a utilization of the identified *Design Guidelines*. Such an application that tries to reach the elderly and changes the view on what mobile devices can do, not only for them, but also for the caregivers, should be seen as an *Enabling Application*.

Enabling thereby is not only heavily connected to motivation, but also focuses on *enabling* effects of the newly introduced technology, changing behaviors and opinions. A concept like that has a high chance of success by combining *intrinsic* and *extrinsic motivation* elements, to break through the thick shell of the Alzheimer's disease and reluctance towards the application or mobile devices. This will be an important strategy for innovative, new application concepts by focusing not only on the elderly, but also on the caregivers. A major goal is to encounter Alzheimer's disease and typical thoughts such as "they're just going to get worse anyway" [76, p. 393]. To tackle the upcoming care crisis, mobile devices can play a key role to solve problems because of their high usability, ubiquitous and mobile nature. It is important to understand, that mobile devices will not replace human interaction, instead this *Assistive Technology* helps to establish connections and moreover can remind the elderly person about important tasks, such as medication taking to maintain or even improve their health and well-being [42,49]. Moreover, we hope to provide support to developers and researchers via the identified *Design Guidelines* to face the challenge of developing apps for the elderly and Alzheimer patients because this user group and its caregivers can considerably benefit from modern technology.

Acknowledgments. The preparation of this paper was supported by the enable cluster and is catalogued by the enable steering committee as enable **54** (http://enable-cluster.de). This work was funded by a grant of the German Ministry for Education and Research (BMBF) **FK 01EA1807A**.

References

1. Alive Inside (2018). http://aliveinside.us. Accessed 22 Dec 2019
2. Music & Memory (2016). http://musicandmemory.org. Accessed 22 Dec 2019
3. Albaina, I., Visser, T., van der Mast, C., Vastenburg, M.F.: A persuasive virtual coach to motivate elderly individuals to walk. In: Proceedings of PervasiveHealth 2009 (2009)
4. Alzheimer's Society: Assistive technology – devices to help with everyday living. https://bit.ly/2spIc9U. Accessed 22 Dec 2019
5. Andersen, C.L., et al.: Challenges and limitations of applying an emotion-driven design approach on elderly users. In: DS 68-7: Proceedings of the 18th International Conference on Engineering Design (ICED 2011), Impacting Society through Engineering Design, vol. 7: Human Behaviour in Design, Lyngby/Copenhagen, Denmark, 15–19 August 2011, pp. 74–84 (2011)
6. Astell, A.J., et al.: Using a touch screen computer to support relationships between people with dementia and caregivers. Interact. Comput. **22**(4), 267–275 (2010)
7. Bernard, M., Liao, C.H., Mills, M.: The effects of font type and size on the legibility and reading time of online text by older adults. In: CHI 2001 Extended Abstracts on Human Factors in Computing Systems, pp. 175–176. ACM (2001)
8. Bouchard, B., Imbeault, F., Bouzouane, A., Menelas, B.-A.J.: Developing serious games specifically adapted to people suffering from Alzheimer. In: Ma, M., Oliveira, M.F., Hauge, J.B., Duin, H., Thoben, K.-D. (eds.) SGDA 2012. LNCS, vol. 7528, pp. 243–254. Springer, Heidelberg (2012). https://doi.org/10.1007/978-3-642-33687-4_21

9. Bull, C.N., et al.: Mobile age: open data mobile apps to support independent living (2017)
10. Cafazzo, J.A., Casselman, M., Hamming, N., Katzman, D.K., Palmert, M.R.: Design of an mhealth app for the self-management of adolescent type 1 diabetes: a pilot study. J. Med. Internet Res. **14**(3), e70 (2012)
11. Caprani, N., O'Connor, N.E., Gurrin, C.: Touch screens for the older user. In: Assistive Technologies. IntechOpen (2012)
12. Carter, M.C., Burley, V., Nykjaer, C., Cade, J.: 'My Meal Mate'(MMM): validation of the diet measures captured on a smartphone application to facilitate weight loss. Br. J. Nutr. **109**(3), 539–546 (2013)
13. Castilla, D., et al.: Process of design and usability evaluation of a telepsychology web and virtual reality system for the elderly: butler. Int. J. Hum. Comput. Stud. **71**(3), 350–362 (2013)
14. Chin, Y.J., Lim, W.N., Lee, C.S.: Mobile game for the elderly: bundled bingo game. In: TENCON 2017-2017 IEEE Region 10, pp. 2262–2267. IEEE (2017)
15. Colombo, R., et al.: Design strategies to improve patient motivation during robot-aided rehabilitation. J. Neuroeng. Rehabil. **4**(1), 3 (2007). https://doi.org/10.1186/1743-0003-4-3
16. Coppola, J.F., Kowtko, M.A., Yamagata, C., Joyce, S.: Applying mobile application development to help dementia and Alzheimer patients. In: Proceedings of Student-Faculty Research Day, CSIS, Pace University (2013)
17. Cowan, L.T., et al.: Apps of steel: are exercise apps providing consumers with realistic expectations? A content analysis of exercise apps for presence of behavior change theory. Health Educ. Behav. **40**(2), 133–139 (2013)
18. Csikszentmihalyi, M.: Toward a psychology of optimal experience. Flow and the Foundations of Positive Psychology, pp. 209–226. Springer, Dordrecht (2014). https://doi.org/10.1007/978-94-017-9088-8_14
19. Darroch, I., Goodman, J., Brewster, S., Gray, P.: The effect of age and font size on reading text on handheld computers. In: Costabile, M.F., Paternò, F. (eds.) INTERACT 2005. LNCS, vol. 3585, pp. 253–266. Springer, Heidelberg (2005). https://doi.org/10.1007/11555261_23
20. Davis, F.D.: A technology acceptance model for empirically testing new end-user information systems: Theory and results. Ph.D. thesis, Massachusetts Institute of Technology (1985)
21. De Carvalho, R.N.S., Ishitani, L., Nogueira Sales De Carvalho, R., et al.: Motivational factors for mobile serious games for elderly users. In: Proceedings of XI SB Games (2012)
22. Deci, E.L., Ryan, R.M.: Intrinsic motivation. The corsini encyclopedia of psychology, pp. 1–2 (2010)
23. Dörner, R., Göbel, S., Effelsberg, W., Wiemeyer, J.: Serious Games (2016)
24. Eichhorn, C., et al.: Innovative game concepts for Alzheimer patients. In: Zhou, J., Salvendy, G. (eds.) ITAP 2018. LNCS, vol. 10927, pp. 526–545. Springer, Cham (2018). https://doi.org/10.1007/978-3-319-92037-5_37
25. Eichhorn, C., et al.: THe innovative reminder in senior-focused technology (THIRST)—evaluation of serious games and gadgets for Alzheimer patients. In: Zhou, J., Salvendy, G. (eds.) HCII 2019. LNCS, vol. 11593, pp. 135–154. Springer, Cham (2019). https://doi.org/10.1007/978-3-030-22015-0_11
26. Fogg, B.J.: Persuasive technology: using computers to change what we think and do. Ubiquity (2002)
27. Gallego-Perez, J., Lohse, M., Evers, V.: Robots to motivate elderly people: present and future challenges. In: 2013 IEEE RO-MAN, pp. 685–690. IEEE (2013)

28. Gao, C., Zhou, L., Liu, Z., Wang, H., Bowers, B.: Mobile application for diabetes self-management in China: do they fit for older adults? Int. J. Med. Inf. **101**, 68–74 (2017)
29. Graham, J.: The disabled and the elderly are facing a big problem: Not enough aides. The Washington Post Health and Science (2017)
30. Häikiö, J., Wallin, A., Isomursu, M., Ailisto, H., Matinmikko, T., Huomo, T.: Touch-based user interface for elderly users. In: Proceedings of the 9th International Conference on Human Computer Interaction with Mobile Devices and Services, pp. 289–296. ACM (2007)
31. Hiyama, A., Nagai, Y., Hirose, M., Kobayashi, M., Takagi, H.: Question first: passive interaction model for gathering experience and knowledge from the elderly. In: 2013 IEEE International Conference on Pervasive Computing and Communications Workshops (PERCOM Workshops), pp. 151–156. IEEE (2013)
32. Holzinger, A., Searle, G., Kleinberger, T., Seffah, A., Javahery, H.: Investigating usability metrics for the design and development of applications for the elderly. In: Miesenberger, K., Klaus, J., Zagler, W., Karshmer, A. (eds.) ICCHP 2008. LNCS, vol. 5105, pp. 98–105. Springer, Heidelberg (2008). https://doi.org/10.1007/978-3-540-70540-6_13
33. Holzinger, A., Searle, G., Nischelwitzer, A.: On some aspects of improving mobile applications for the elderly. In: Stephanidis, C. (ed.) UAHCI 2007. LNCS, vol. 4554, pp. 923–932. Springer, Heidelberg (2007). https://doi.org/10.1007/978-3-540-73279-2_103
34. Hung, L., et al.: Use of touch screen tablets to support social connections and reduce responsive behaviours among people with dementia in care settings: a scoping review protocol. BMJ Open **9**(11), 1–6 (2019)
35. Hurd, M.D., Martorell, P., Delavande, A., Mullen, K.J., Langa, K.M.: Monetary costs of dementia in the united states. N. Engl. J. Med. **368**(14), 1326–1334 (2013)
36. Ijsselsteijn, W., Nap, H.H., de Kort, Y., Poels, K.: Digital game design for elderly users. In: Proceedings of the 2007 Conference on Future Play, pp. 17–22. ACM (2007)
37. Imbeault, F., Bouchard, B., Bouzouane, A.: Serious games in cognitive training for Alzheimer's patients. In: 2011 IEEE 1st International Conference on Serious Games and Applications for Health (SeGAH), pp. 1–8. IEEE (2011)
38. Jones, G.M., van der Eerden, W.J.: Designing care environments for persons with Alzheimer's disease: visuoperceptual considerations. Rev. Clin. Gerontol. **18**(1), 13–37 (2008)
39. Kinsella, K.G., Phillips, D.R.: Global Aging: The Challenge of Success, vol. 60. Population Reference Bureau Washington, DC (2005)
40. Kobayashi, M., Hiyama, A., Miura, T., Asakawa, C., Hirose, M., Ifukube, T.: Elderly user evaluation of mobile touchscreen interactions. In: Campos, P., Graham, N., Jorge, J., Nunes, N., Palanque, P., Winckler, M. (eds.) INTERACT 2011. LNCS, vol. 6946, pp. 83–99. Springer, Heidelberg (2011). https://doi.org/10.1007/978-3-642-23774-4_9
41. Kobayashi, M., Ishihara, T., Kosugi, A., Takagi, H., Asakawa, C.: Question-answer cards for an inclusive micro-tasking framework for the elderly. In: Kotzé, P., Marsden, G., Lindgaard, G., Wesson, J., Winckler, M. (eds.) INTERACT 2013. LNCS, vol. 8119, pp. 590–607. Springer, Heidelberg (2013). https://doi.org/10.1007/978-3-642-40477-1_38
42. Kuerbis, A., Mulliken, A., Muench, F., Moore, A.A., Gardner, D.: Older adults and mobile technology: factors that enhance and inhibit utilization in the context of behavioral health (2017)

43. Langer, E.J., Rodin, J.: The effects of choice and enhanced personal responsibility for the aged: a field experiment in an institutional setting. J. Pers. Soc. Psychol. **34**(2), 191 (1976)
44. Lapointe, J., Bouchard, B., Bouchard, J., Potvin, A., Bouzouane, A.: Smart homes for people with Alzheimer's disease: adapting prompting strategies to the patient's cognitive profile. In: Proceedings of the 5th International Conference on Pervasive Technologies Related to Assistive Environments, p. 30. ACM (2012)
45. Lee, G.Y., Yip, C.C., Yu, E.C., Man, D.W.: Evaluation of a computer-assisted errorless learning-based memory training program for patients with early Alzheimer's disease in hong kong: a pilot study. Clin. Interv. Aging **8**, 623 (2013)
46. Lee, S., Zhai, S.: The performance of touch screen soft buttons. In: Proceedings of the SIGCHI Conference on Human Factors in Computing Systems, pp. 309–318. ACM (2009)
47. Lorenz, A., Oppermann, R.: Mobile health monitoring for the elderly: designing for diversity. Pervasive Mob. Comput. **5**(5), 478–495 (2009)
48. Loureiro, L.D.S.N., Fernandes, M.D.G.M., Nóbrega, M.M.L.D., Rodrigues, R.A.P.: Overburden on elderly's family caregivers: association with characteristics of the elderly and care demand. Revi. Bras. Enferm. **67**(2), 227–232 (2014)
49. Martins, J., et al.: Friend sourcing the unmet needs of people with dementia. In: Proceedings of the 11th Web for All Conference, p. 35. ACM (2014)
50. Massimi, M., Baecker, R.M.: An empirical study of seniors' perceptions of mobile phones as memory aids. In: Technology and Aging—Selected Papers from the 2007 International Conference on Technology and Aging, vol. 21, pp. 59–66 (2008)
51. McCabe, M., et al.: Designing a better visit: touch screen app for people living with dementia and their visitors. Alzheimer's & Dement.: J. Alzheimer's Assoc. **15**(7), P167–P169 (2019)
52. Naumanen, M., Tukiainen, M.: Guided participation in ICT-education for seniors: motivation and social support. In: 2009 39th IEEE Frontiers in Education Conference, pp. 1–7. IEEE (2009)
53. Nurgalieva, L., Laconich, J.J.J., Baez, M., Casati, F., Marchese, M.: A systematic literature review of research-derived touchscreen design guidelines for older adults. IEEE Access **7**, 22035–22058 (2019)
54. Ownby, R.L., Czaja, S.J.: Healthcare website design for the elderly: improving usability. In: AMIA Annual Symposium Proceedings, vol. 2003, p. 960. American Medical Informatics Association (2003)
55. Pagoto, S., Schneider, K., Jojic, M., DeBiasse, M., Mann, D.: Evidence-based strategies in weight-loss mobile apps. Am. J. Prev. Med. **45**(5), 576–582 (2013)
56. Plecher, D.A., et al.: Interactive drinking gadget for the elderly and Alzheimer patients. In: Zhou, J., Salvendy, G. (eds.) HCII 2019. LNCS, vol. 11593, pp. 444–463. Springer, Cham (2019). https://doi.org/10.1007/978-3-030-22015-0_35
57. Plecher, D.A., Eichhorn, C., Steinmetz, C., Klinker, G.: TrackSugAR (2020)
58. Salim, M., Hidir, M., Ali, N.M., Noah, M., Azman, S.: Mobile application on healthy diet for elderly based on persuasive design. Int. J. Adv. Sci. Eng. Inf. Technol. **7**(1), 222–227 (2017)
59. Sama, P.R., Eapen, Z.J., Weinfurt, K.P., Shah, B.R., Schulman, K.A.: An evaluation of mobile health application tools. JMIR mHealth uHealth **2**(2), e19 (2014)
60. Schäfer, H., et al.: Nudge-nutritional, digital games in enable (2017)
61. Scheibe, M., Reichelt, J., Bellmann, M., Kirch, W.: Acceptance factors of mobile apps for diabetes by patients aged 50 or older: a qualitative study. Medicine 2.0 **4**(1), e1 (2015)

62. Seaborn, K., et al.: Accessible play in everyday spaces: mixed reality gaming for adult powered chair users. ACM Trans. Comput.-Hum. Interact. (TOCHI) **23**(2), 12 (2016)
63. Shikder, S.H., Price, A.D., Mourshed, M.: A systematic review on the therapeutic lighting design for the elderly. CIB (2010)
64. Sposaro, F., Danielson, J., Tyson, G.: iwander: an android application for dementia patients. In: 2010 Annual International Conference of the IEEE Engineering in Medicine and Biology, pp. 3875–3878. IEEE (2010)
65. Spring, B.: Evidence-based practice in clinical psychology: what it is, why it matters; what you need to know. J. Clin. Psychol. **63**(7), 611–631 (2007)
66. Strengers, J.: Smartphone interface design requirements for seniors. Inf. Stud. (2012). University of Amsterdam, Amsterdam, The Netherlands
67. Tang, C., Leung, R., Haddad, S., McGrenere, J.: What motivates older adults to learn to use mobile phones. Retrieved December **4**, 2015 (2013)
68. Tyack, C., Camic, P.M.: Touchscreen interventions and the well-being of people with dementia and caregivers: a systematic review. Int. Psychogeriatr. **29**(8), 1261–1280 (2017)
69. Tziraki, C., Berenbaum, R., Gross, D., Abikhzer, J., Ben-David, B.M.: Designing serious computer games for people with moderate and advanced dementia: interdisciplinary theory-driven pilot study. JMIR Serious Games **5**(3), e16 (2017)
70. Vasconcelos, A., Silva, P.A., Caseiro, J., Nunes, F., Teixeira, L.F.: Designing tablet-based games for seniors: the example of cogniplay, a cognitive gaming platform. In: Proceedings of the 4th International Conference on Fun and Games, pp. 1–10. ACM (2012)
71. Wada, K., Shibata, T., Saito, T., Tanie, K.: Effects of robot-assisted activity for elderly people and nurses at a day service center. Proc. IEEE **92**(11), 1780–1788 (2004)
72. West, J.H., Hall, P.C., Hanson, C.L., Barnes, M.D., Giraud-Carrier, C., Barrett, J.: There's an app for that: content analysis of paid health and fitness apps. J. Med. Internet Res. **14**(3), e72 (2012)
73. Wildenbos, G.A., et al.: Mobile health for older adult patients: using an aging barriers framework to classify usability problems. Int. J. Med. Inf. **124**, 68–77 (2019)
74. Williams, P., Drolet, A.: Age-related differences in responses to emotional advertisements. J. Consum. Res. **32**(3), 343–354 (2005)
75. Wobbrock, J.O., Kane, S.K., Gajos, K.Z., Harada, S., Froehlich, J.: Ability-based design: concept, principles and examples. ACM Trans. Access. Comput. (TACCESS) **3**(3), 9 (2011)
76. Zmily, A., Abu-Saymeh, D.: Alzheimer's disease rehabilitation using smartphones to improve patients' quality of life. In: Proceedings of the 7th International Conference on Pervasive Computing Technologies for Healthcare, pp. 393–396. ICST (2013)
77. Zmily, A., et al.: Study of the usability of spaced retrieval exercise using mobile devices for Alzheimer's disease rehabilitation. JMIR mHealth uHealth **2**(3), e31 (2014)

Defining User Requirements of a eHealth Mobile App for Elderly: The HomeCare4All Project Case Study

Roberta Grimaldi[1,2], Eliseo Sciarretta[1(✉)],
and Giovanni Andrea Parente[1,2]

[1] DASIC (Digital Administration and Social Innovation Center),
Link Campus University, via del Casale di San Pio V 44, 00165 Rome, Italy
robertagrim@gmail.com,
{e.sciarretta,g.parente}@unilink.it
[2] CoRiS (Dipartimento di Comunicazione e Ricerca Sociale),
Sapienza University of Rome, via Salaria 113, 00198 Rome, Italy

Abstract. Aging population implies an increase in demand for health care services. This hopefully could be solved by e-health, even if some issues arise about technology acceptance and adoption among the elderly. In this article, the authors illustrate HomeCare4All project as a case study to apply Human Centered Design (HCD) process in the field of digital health services, aiming at designing trustworthy mobile applications for elderly people to book healthcare services at home.

This paper focuses on the early analytic steps of the HCD process and describes the context of use and the definition of user needs through the use of social research techniques and technological studies.

The authors, in fact, show the findings of a state of the art analysis carried out about healthcare services and platforms; then they report the results of a empirical survey, conducted through a questionnaire administered to end users.

Thanks to these studies, the authors can choose the device that suits best to the user needs and they can define the relevant requirements, which will guide the further steps of design process.

Keywords: Elderly · e-Health · User needs · Digital health services

1 Introduction

In the last years, in most of the European Union countries, the elderly population has increased. In 2013, in the EU, the population aged 65 or over is 18.2% [1].

Italy is one of the countries with the highest aging index in the world. According to the ISTAT (Italian Institute of Statistics) forecasts [2], people over 65, who are now about 20% of the Italian population, will increase up to 32% of the total until 2043.

Aging population highlights the problem of increasing demand for health care. Against an average life extension, there will be an increasing growth of less self-sufficient citizens. Increasing costs will be soon unsustainable.

© Springer Nature Switzerland AG 2020
Q. Gao and J. Zhou (Eds.): HCII 2020, LNCS 12208, pp. 67–77, 2020.
https://doi.org/10.1007/978-3-030-50249-2_5

Spending cuts will be achieved also thanks to the use of applied technology in this field. Eventually the elderly will have to face technologies, which will increasingly affect their lives: from the delivery of smart city services [3] to the improvement of home environment, from the health-information services [4] to the support for family carers [5]. In the specific case of elderly using digital health services, it is necessary to consider potential accessibility problems. When older people are not supported by the caregivers in the use of technological devices, there are two main problems: the deterioration of the physical and mental abilities and the technology skills deficit. As time goes by, people become reluctant to change their habits, since this would be perceived as a risk [6].

The elderly are used to human contact in their daily activities, the use of digital devices could demotivate them, causing diffidence to the new type of interaction (for different reasons: fear to make mistakes, difficulty of use, etc.) [7]. In order to optimize older people's acceptance of digital devices, the key factor is to explore their needs and to design a suitable user experience accordingly through a simplified user interface.

The e-health solutions are growing, due to the spreading of the ICT. The literature in this field shows how the new technologies, as expression of Assistive Technologies (ATs) or Information and Communication Technologies (ICTs), may improve the quality of life of older adults in different ways. ATs may provide the elderly the chance to live with an increased sense of safety and independence, allowing them to remain in their homes longer. ICTs improve social support and social well-being in the elderly life [8].

The spread of these technologies highlights the issues about the ICT acceptance and adoption among the elderly. The literature explores the correlation among a number of factors and the use of technology in general, getting more specific about ICT. It was found that the ICT use is affected by age, personal factors and social influence, but also by health, education, and marital status [9, 10]. Another fundamental aspect of the acceptance of the technology by the elderly is a proper design, that takes into account the skills and the physical constraints of this 'special' target [11]. Furthermore, in order to design and develop technologies that meet adequately the elderly needs, a number of studies involve them in the design process [12, 13] despite of their little experiences [14].

2 Aim of the Study

In this article the authors focus on a strategic area of the elderly life: health care, in which the use of technologies has more potential and applications [4, 15]. Ludwig, W., Wolf, K.H., Duwenkamp, C., Gusew, N., Hellrung, N., Marschollek, M., Haux, R. [15] classify the health-enabling technologies based services in six categories: handling adverse conditions, assessing state of health, consultation and education, motivation and feedback, service ordering and social inclusion.

Independently of their category, several types of technologies and devices have been developed or adopted in the health field. The most interesting and innovative regard the use of Smart TVs or mobile devices, since their characteristics, given the specific target, could show some potential. Smart TV is an easy-to-use consumer device or, with other words, the most familiar and common household appliance for the elderly [16]. So many health services exploit these advantages adopting Smart TV sets, while trying to overcome a number of weaknesses about the interaction with these devices.

Concerning mobile devices, several studies explore their use and adoption, with a specific focus on mental and physical diseases [17]. The final goal of these studies is to facilitate the interaction between the elderly and the mobile technologies, stressing the idea that these technologies could be the ideal tool to let this specific target access digital services. Indeed, the touch screen technology, main feature of this type of devices, proved to be the suited interaction method for the elderly, considering the typical cognitive [18] and mobility illness [19]. So it is fundamental to investigate this group's interaction patterns with technologies and devices, in order to identify the effective and efficient modes to meet their needs, ensuring an optimized implementation, adoption and use.

In this article, the authors show the case study of the HomeCare4All project and in particular the results of the early analytic steps of HCD process, with the aim to explore the suitable interaction modes and design to make older people more familiar with mobile applications. The main focus is on the design of interfaces rather than the service itself. In fact, within the project the authors have dealt exclusively with the design of the mobile app, which allows the elderly to access the services offered by the platform.

The authors show the findings of a state of the art analysis carried out about healthcare services and platforms; then they report the results of a empirical survey, conducted through a questionnaire administered to end users.

Thanks to these studies, it is then possible to choose the device that suits best to the user needs and to define the relevant requirements, which will guide the further steps of design process.

3   The Project: HomeCare4All

"HomeCare4All" project was supported by the POR 2007-2013 (Regional Operative Programme) co-founded by the FESR (European funds for the regional districts) and the Italian region of Lazio, Action: VAL (Added Value Lazio) for the companies assembles for Research, Development and Innovation.

The "HomeCare4All" project, from now on also HC4A, meant to rethink and redesign the model to match supply with demand in the health care services at home, through technological innovation.

HC4A aimed to develop a brokerage platform for health and social care services at home. To services providers, HomeCare4All represent a profitable channel to get in touch with the final users, expanding their own business target through an inclusive and always available (24/7) access to their services. On the other hand, for the end users, HC4A could be used as the unique gateway through the health care services galaxy (e.g. diagnostic tests, nursing care, physiotherapist rehabilitation), providing the functionalities of research, consultation, and booking of these services. Furthermore, HC4A provided integrated functionalities of bio-medical data collection, reporting and service rating.

Stated the specific offer of the platform services, the primary target of the project were the elderly, upon which was focused the entire design phase, through a Human Centered Design approach. In this sense, the HC4A platform aimed to provide a consistent user experience with the real interaction skills and resources of the final users. In fact, the first and most important goal of this platform was its accessibility, obtained by following the principles of Design for All [20].

4   Context of Use and User Requirements

The first phase of HC4A project, according to the HCD approach, was focused on the research and analysis about the context of use, including: the market state-of-the-art, the users' characteristics, the devices interface and the interaction modes.

All these collected data were useful in order to define, in detail, the solution to implement for the HC4A project.

4.1   State of the Art

The authors conducted a study about the state-of-the-art of brokerage services already on the health market.

In the Italian contest there isn't a single portal that shows all the services offered by the public providers: each Region has its CUP (single booking service) that allows to book a medical examination. Instead, there are many private intermediation services that allow to start a relationship between private specialist doctors and patients.

Some services exist only in the desktop version, e.g. DoveSalute [21], created directly by the Italian Health Ministry, and Consorzio Assistenza Primaria [22], which conduct the intermediary function applied to the field of pharmacy. DoveSalute [21] doesn't allow the user to book the services they need directly from the website. In terms of interaction, this website doesn't fully exploit the potential of the Web: it lets access a large amount of information but doesn't fulfill the user's need in terms of service booking.

The most popular italian services in the mobile field allow the users to search for a specialist and the direct booking of medical examination. Examples with these type of features are mobile apps such as iDoctors [23] and Dottori.it [24]. For some services, the user can search a health facility by location or by type of service (cardiology, emergency room, etc.). The app allows the users to evaluate the performance of the doctor. The most deserving doctors are shown in a higher position in the search results. Indeed, in many services there is the opportunity to write reviews and to comment the own experience with the services and the doctors. Another interesting mobile app is Med in Action [25] intended for people who are not resident in the town and need a doctor. Through the app the user can localize himself/herself and look for the nearest specialist, with similar methods already described for the two previous apps.

In term of usability, there are some problems in those services that are available both in mobile and desktop versions. For example, in Dottori.it [24] some features are available only in the desktop version (sending and receiving private messages between user and doctor). Other limitations concern the personalization, for example in iDoctors [23] there isn't a clear access to the setting of order results.

4.2   User Needs Analysis

The elderly, defined as those aged 65 or older, composed the primary target of HomeCare4All project. Two other groups are potentially interested in using the services offered by the platform and, thus, have been identified as secondary targets of the project: disabled, both sensory and motor, and stabilized chronic patients, with specific reference to heart patients and diabetics.

Although it is often thought that the elderly do not have a good relationship with technology, it would be a mistake to apply this thought to all the elderly.

Academic literature has shown that the interaction between the elderly and digital technologies is very heterogeneous. As Quan-Haase, Williams, Kicevski, Elueze and Wellman [26] affirm, for example, there are different types of users that can range from those who don't use digital technologies to those who are advanced users. The know-how of the elderly is therefore variable and the variation can be detected based on various factors: age group, social contexts, education, revenue, etc., as already stated in the introduction of this paper. As Hargittai, Piper and Ringel Morris [27] suggest, the differences based on these factors persist online as happens offline and therefore affect the interaction with digital devices.

Even the approach of the elderly towards technology can change: despite the decline of some cognitive abilities, there are in fact among the elderly those who are eager to learn the use of new technologies. As also argued by Selwyn [28], the elderly can see the digital tool more to be used as a recreational activity (games, social relationships, etc.) than as a valuable tool.

Therefore, in consideration of the existing literature, this study of user needs was carried out with the awareness of the heterogeneity of the target audience and its results are limited to the sample taken into consideration, belonging to the potential users of the services offered by the project.

The authors used a questionnaire in order to identify the users, arranging their needs and the technical requirements. Questionnaires were distributed to a sample of potential users, thanks to the collaboration of two health and social care service providers, partners of the project. These companies distributed the questionnaires to their customers, corresponding largely with the project target.

The questionnaire was semi-structured, so the users could answer through a set of predetermined options or through a scale. The questions were administered on paper to 192 users and they were organized in four parts. The first one collected the user personal data, necessary to have a clear picture of the target that potentially would use the HC4A platform. The sample showed a slight majority of women (101) than men (91). The average age was of 71 years (159 users were aged over 65, while 33 of them were less than 65 years old). With regard of the education level (Fig. 1), the sample had a clear majority of users, 71%, with a high educational level, (44% had an high school diploma, and 27% had a university degree). Some questions investigated the user's affection by pathologies: osteoarthritis is the most widespread pathology in this sample. Health factors must be taken into account during the design stage because, given the specificity of the target, they could impact the efficacy of the solution. The collected data showed a prevalence of subjects with issues affecting mobility and daily life gestures. Concerning the self-evaluation of the users' knowledge about the new communication technologies, the results highlighted basically two groups. Indeed, the people having a negative opinion about their knowledge (not at all, little) are in the same amount of the ones more confident (enough, discretely, fine) about it.

Level of education

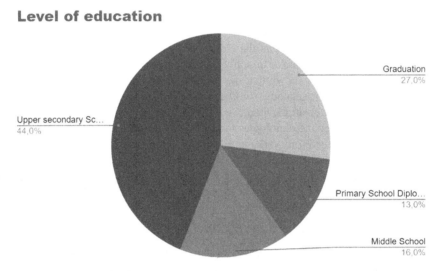

Fig. 1. Level of education for the survey sample.

Another section of the questionnaire was dedicated to the house health and social care services and to the telemedicine services, with the aim to assess the potential target of this type of services and to understand this market trend. The use of house health and social care services was not very common among the target (34% of the sample had used these services at their residence) but the users gave mostly positive reviews about their use experience. Among the reasons that cause the lack of interest was the little trust towards strangers in the house, one of the most common prejudices about the services provided at home.

The third part of the questionnaire was dedicated to the telemedicine services. Through the HC4A platform the user, provided with the appropriate instruments, may in fact have access to a dashboard to monitor his/her vital signs. The majority of the sample had no contact with the telemedicine or not even knew what it was. About the interest in using these services, the results were divided into almost equal groups: 52% was interested and 48% was not. These responses diminished negative impact of the previous question. The interest in trying telemedicine services had, as major motivation (as well as for social and health services and rehabilitation), the saving of time.

Additional motivations that emerge are those concerning the reduction of travel problems or the increase in awareness about own health condition. Closely connected to the latter is also another motivation: by using e-health services, people expect an improvement in monitoring by the doctor. This last consideration represents a first result of the spread of these services, also in terms of better information on the subject. In fact, one of the existing prejudices concerns the mediation of technologies between doctor and patient, in terms of lower quality of care and attention to the patient. On the contrary, thanks to e-health, the patient can be constantly monitored and his medical stats can be evaluated by a multidisciplinary team.

Among people who are not interested in e-health services, the main concerns are excessive responsibility and mistrust of technology. With regard to the first motivation, it's quite natural for users to feel the weight of responsibility in managing their data because at first the doctor's intermediation is missing; in this sense the patient may feel excessively responsible towards the medical care. The second reason, on the other hand, concerns the prejudices regarding the relationship with technologies (Figs. 2 and 3).

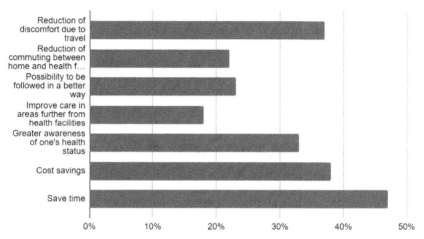

Fig. 2. Motivation of interest towards e-health

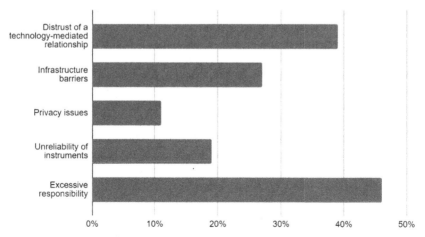

Fig. 3. Reasons for lack of interest towards e-health

The last part of the questionnaire concerned precisely the technological equipment and the usage habits of the sample. This type of information could allow the design of a platform customized for the devices used by the project target. The results of this part showed that a slight majority (54%) of the sample browsed the Internet and they did it mainly through the personal computer (desktop or laptop). These results increase significantly if we consider the sub-target of young adults. But the results about the use of smartphones and tablet were more interesting: 49 users for the first and 32 for the tablet. This was very promising fact, for a target traditionally unaccustomed to new technologies. Practically, a quarter of the analyzed sample as well as had a last generation mobile phone used it for an advanced function as to surf the Internet. The same applied to the tablet. Among the most managed activities there were: to check for emails and to query a search engine. Regarding other technologies, such as smart TVs and webcams, the answers are not as encouraging. For smart TV it's clear that the majority of the sample doesn't have it or, in the most extreme cases, doesn't know what such device is. As for the webcam, only 33% of the sample has one.

So the authors could deduce that these users were comfortable with platforms and services that require a registration and a management of their own profile and related settings. In addition, they seemed to be equally capable of browsing the Internet to explore their topics of interest.

5   Choice of the Device for the Project

The context of use, in the HC4A project, ought to be considered as variable, shiftable, changeable. This characteristic issues from the very aim of the project, that is enabling an inclusive and always available (24/7) access to the health services. For this reason, during the context of use analysis, the authors looked for the most suitable device to achieve this goal and to satisfy the needs of the users, identified in the user need analysis.

Therefore, the most appropriate choice appeared to be the use of a mobile device, specifically the smartphone device.

One of the main reasons behind this choice was the portability of this device, combined with its power in data management. The great success of this technology is due to its versatility: it enables users to be on the Internet, connected to other devices, processing data and having access to information anywhere.

Another important aspect is its interaction modes. Devices such as the smart TVs, for example, have the advantages concerning the size of the screen and the familiarity that the user may have with them. However, the input device is the remote control with buttons that are not very usable, especially for the elderly.

The authors took into account also other interaction modes with the TV, such as a virtual keyboard on the screen or a physical keyboard or the gestures. These indirect interaction systems are the most problematic because they are scarcely intuitive and usable for this type of user [29]. The mouse can be difficult to control because it requires high hand-eye coordination and a consequent cognitive effort [30]. Furthermore aging has an effect on the motor skills of the hands and on their level of precision in movement. The elderly perform a greater number of movements to complete a task than the younger population, increasing duration and errors. Various studies shown that this entails a higher level of fatigue [31]. The keyboards cause the same problems, with the addition of eyesight problems for symbols positioned on the keys [32]. The posture, the positioning of the keys and the pressure of these, can strain forearms and hands [33] compromising the writing skills.

Instead, the touch screen of the mobile device allows a direct interaction with the display and the graphic interface, without the use of intermediary such as the physical buttons. Direct interaction can reduce the learning efforts and therefore improve the performance and the remembrance of the users who use the service [30]. The simplicity and the accessibility through touchscreen make mobile devices easy to use even for the most inexperienced people. Surprisingly, older adults learn how to use the mobile device very quickly. The touchscreen allows great flexibility, enabling a simple functions' design. Furthermore, as emphasized by Yamagata, C., Kowtko, M., Yamagata, C., Joyce, S. [17], mobile devices allow users to change the sensitivity of the touch interface as well as providing a vibration feedback when the screen is touched. The haptic modality is very effective to help the weak such as elderly and visually impaired users. It allows to easily explore, confirm, and select without any assistance [34]. So the touchscreen devices make the interaction more effective, but for the elderly there are still issues related to motor coordination or vision. Since the psycho-physical conditions of the elderly, the service must have short vocal outputs and limited answer options. Only in this way there will be no risk of working memory labors. Moreover, the vocal interface will have to be accompanied by textual support for possible forgetfulness or misunderstanding.

The implementation of natural language as an input/output system can also solve some of the problems arising from using the touchscreen for the elderly. The integration of the two systems, textual and vocal, can therefore represent the most suitable solution to remove the remaining barriers between users and interactive digital devices.

With the integration of natural language recognition, implementable in the mobile devices, several drawbacks may be overcome, obtaining a smaller effort for the elderly. In the design should be considered problems such as hearing impairment or overload of short-term working memory. For this reason it is appropriate to limit the number of significant elements in speech output and transmit the information in a clear and practical way. Through this integration, there is a reduction of the problems related to the hand-eye coordination and to the elderly's lack of familiarity with the technology.

In order to identify the most suitable device, the authors also considered the current diffusion of the different mobile devices. Today, globally 3.8 billion people use mobile devices (penetration of 51%), and in 2017 Internet usage by mobile devices is growing of 40%. In Italy, the Internet penetration is 63% [2]. Furthermore, as noted in the questionnaires, the target of this project already used the smartphone, more than the tablet. This diffusion generates benefits in terms of knowledge of the system and the interaction. This element is even more significant with older users, reluctant to venture into things they do not know.

So the smartphone was identified as the most suitable device for the HC4A project thanks to its main technical features, its direct and intuitive interaction modes and its diffusion in the target of the project.

6 Conclusion and Future Works

After analyzing the users' needs and their interaction with digital devices, the authors concluded that the smartphone is the device that can make it easier to use an e-health service such as HC4A.

In future works, the authors will continue with the definition of the HC4A app, following the phases of the Human Centered Design. So the authors will identify the use cases, the information architecture and design the mobile app's wireframes. In order to verify the validity of the planned solution, the authors will carry out usability tests, with the aim of identifying the critical issues before the final release.

References

1. Publications Office of the European Union: Eurostat Regional Yearbook (2015). http://ec.europa.eu/eurostat/documents/3217494/7018888/KS-HA-15-001-EN-N.pdf. Accessed 09 Dec 2019
2. ISTAT: Annuario statistico italiano (2017). https://www.istat.it/it/archivio/213021. Accessed 17 Jan 2020
3. Grimaldi, R., Opromolla, A., Parente, G.A., Sciarretta, E., Volpi, V.: Rethinking public transport services for the elderly through a transgenerational design approach. In: Zhou, J., Salvendy, G. (eds.) ITAP 2016. LNCS, vol. 9755, pp. 395–406. Springer, Cham (2016). https://doi.org/10.1007/978-3-319-39949-2_38
4. Marschollek, M., Mix, S., Wolf, K.H., Effertz, B., Haux, R., Steinhagen-Thiessen, E.: ICT-based health information services for elderly people: past experiences, current trends, and future strategies. Med. Inf. Internet Med. **32**(4), 251–261 (2007)
5. Magnusson, L., Hanson, E., Borg, M.: A literature review study of information and communication technology as a support for frail older people living at home and their family carers. Technol. Disabil. **16**(4), 223–235 (2004)
6. Atchley, R.C.: A continuity theory of normal aging. Gerontologist **29**(2), 183–190 (1989)
7. Morris, M.G., Venkatesh, V.: Age differences in technology adoption decisions: implications for a changing work force. Pers. Psychol. **53**(2), 375–403 (2000)
8. Blaschke, C.M., Freddolino, P.P., Mullen, E.E.: Ageing and technology: a review of the research literature. Br. J. Soc. Work **39**(4), 641–656 (2009)
9. Heart, T., Kalderon, E.: Older adults: are they ready to adopt health-related ICT. Int. J. Med. Informatics **82**(11), e209–e231 (2013)
10. Venkatesh, V., Morris, M.G., Davis, G.B., Davis, F.D.: User acceptance of information technology: toward a unified view. MIS Q. **27**, 425–478 (2003)
11. Sciarretta, E., Ingrosso, A., Volpi, V., Opromolla, A., Grimaldi, R.: Elderly and tablets: considerations and suggestions about the design of proper applications. In: Zhou, J., Salvendy, G. (eds.) ITAP 2015. LNCS, vol. 9193, pp. 509–518. Springer, Cham (2015). https://doi.org/10.1007/978-3-319-20892-3_49
12. Newell, A. F.: HCI and older people. In: HCI and the Older Population (2004)
13. Massimi, M., Baecker, R.M., Wu, M.: Using participatory activities with seniors to critique, build, and evaluate mobile phones. In: Pontelli, E., Trewin, S. (eds.) 9th International ACM SIGACCESS Conference on Computers and Accessibility, pp. 155–162. ACM, New York (2007)
14. Davidson, J.L., Jensen, C.: Participatory design with older adults: an analysis of creativity in the design of mobile healthcare applications. In: Do, Y.L., Dow, S., Ox, J., et al. (eds.) 9th ACM Conference on Creativity & Cognition, pp. 114–123. ACM, New York (2013)

15. Ludwig, W., et al.: Health-enabling technologies for the elderly–an overview of services based on a literature review. Comput. Methods Programs Biomed. **106**(2), 70–78 (2012)
16. Sciarretta, E., Benedetti, F., Ingrosso, A., Grimaldi, R.: SmarTV care: benefits and implications of Smart TVs in health care. In: Encyclopedia of E-Health and Telemedicine, pp. 1059–1066, IGI Global, Hershey (2016)
17. Yamagata, C., Kowtko, M., Yamagata, C., Joyce, S.: Mobile app development and usability research to help dementia and Alzheimer patients. In: IEEE Long Island Systems, Applications and Technology Conference, pp. 1–6. IEEE, New York (2013)
18. Favilla, S., Pedell, S.: Touch screen ensemble music: collaborative interaction for older people with dementia. In: Shen, H., Smith, R., Paay, G., et al. (eds.) 25th Australian Computer-Human Interaction Conference on Augmentation, Application, Innovation, Collaboration, pp. 481–484. ACM, New York (2013)
19. Williams, D., Ul Alam, M.A., Ahamed, S.I., Chu, W.: Considerations in designing human-computer interfaces for elderly people. In: Gotlieb, H.A., Chen, Z. (eds.) 13th International Conference on Quality Software, pp. 372–377. IEEE, New York (2013)
20. Stephanidis, C. (ed.): User Interfaces for All: Concepts, Methods, and Tools. CRC Press, Boca Raton (2000)
21. Dove Salute. https://www.dovesalute.gov.it/DoveSalute/search/portale. Accessed 09 Dec 2019
22. Consorzio Assistenza Primaria. http://www.consorziocap.it. Accessed 09 Dec 2019
23. iDoctors. https://www.idoctors.it. Accessed 09 Dec 2019
24. Dottori.it. https://www.dottori.it. Accessed 09 Dec 2019
25. Med in Action. http://www.medinaction.com. Accessed 09 Dec 2019
26. Quan-Haase, A., Williams, C., Kicevski, M., Elueze, I., Wellman, B.: Dividing the grey divide: deconstructing myths about older adults' online activities, skills, and attitudes. Am. Behav. Sci. **62**(9), 1207–1228 (2018)
27. Hargittai, E., Piper, A.M., Morris, M.R.: From internet access to internet skills: digital inequality among older adults. Univ. Access Inf. Soc. **18**(4), 881–890 (2019). https://doi.org/10.1007/s10209-018-0617-5
28. Selwyn, N.: The information aged. J. Aging Stud. **18**(4), 369–384 (2004)
29. Wood, E., Willoughby, T., Rushing, A., Bechtel, L., Gilbert, J.: Use of computer input devices by older adults. J. Appl. Gerontol. **24**(5), 419–438 (2005)
30. Vigouroux, N., Rumeau, P., Vella, F., Vellas, B.: Studying point-select-drag interaction techniques for older people with cognitive impairment. In: Stephanidis, C. (ed.) UAHCI 2009. LNCS, vol. 5614, pp. 422–428. Springer, Heidelberg (2009). https://doi.org/10.1007/978-3-642-02707-9_48
31. Sandfeld, J., Jensen, B.R.: Effect of computer mouse gain and visual demand on mouse clicking performance and muscle activation in a young and elderly group of experienced computer users. Appl. Ergon. **36**(5), 547–555 (2005)
32. Czaja, S.J., Lee, C.C.: Designing computer systems for older adults. In: Jacko, J.A., Sears, A. (eds.) The Human-Computer Interaction Handbook, pp. 413–427. L. Erlbaum Associates Inc., Hillsdale (2003)
33. Piper, A.M., Campbell, R., Hollan, J.D.: Exploring the accessibility and appeal of surface computing for older adult health care support. In: Grinter, R., Rodden, T., Aoki, P., et al. (eds.) Proceedings of the SIGCHI Conference on Human Factors in Computing Systems, pp. 907–916. ACM, New York (2010)
34. Nishino, H., Fukakusa, Y., Kagawa, T., Utsumiya, K.: A tangible information explorer using vibratory touch screen. Computing **95**(10–11), 1053–1071 (2013). https://doi.org/10.1007/s00607-012-0226-8

Effect of Display Location on Finger Motor Skill Training with Music-Based Gamification

Naoki Inoue[1], Yuichiro Fujimoto[1(✉)], Alexander Plopski[2],
Sayaka Okahashi[3], Masayuki Kanbara[1], Hsiu-Yun Hsu[4],
Li-Chieh Kuo[4], Fong-Chin Su[4], and Hirokazu Kato[1]

[1] Nara Institute of Science and Technology, Nara, Japan
yfujimoto@is.naist.jp
[2] University of Otago, Dunedin, New Zealand
[3] Kyoto University, Kyoto, Japan
[4] National Cheng Kung University, Tainan, Taiwan

Abstract. The motor control of individual fingers is an important part of daily life, but there are many people who have difficulty with it, such as elderly people and stroke patients. While continuous rehabilitation is necessary for functional recovery of finger mobility and suppression of functional deterioration, it usually requires the assistance of occupational therapists. Furthermore, the rehabilitation process can be monotonous, which makes it difficult for patients to maintain their motivation. Over a series of studies, we have developed a finger movement training system that incorporates gamification and is based on playing music using a Pressing Evaluation Training System that can measure the force exerted by each finger. One remaining problem was that patients had difficulty recognizing the fingering information, and it took some time for them to get used to locating this information quickly. In this study, we applied augmented reality (AR) technology to display each sound element as close as possible to the position of the corresponding finger so that the user could directly perceive the information for each finger while wearing the head mounted display. We conducted a user study with 10 university students to determine if the distance between the sound element display position and the location of each finger had an effect on performance. The results indicated that incorporating AR allowed the users to recognize the correct finger positions more quickly.

Keywords: Finger force training · Gamification · Music play · Augmented reality · Pressing evaluation

1 Introduction

As people age, they often experience a decline in their capability to control different parts of their bodies, and this represents a serious problem for future generations. One major concern for the elderly is a decline in their ability to control their hands, which can appear in the form of reduced finger dexterity, strength, coordination, and sensation [1, 2]. This can significantly affect their ability to perform activities of daily life that require precise finger control, such as grasping and picking up objects.

© Springer Nature Switzerland AG 2020
Q. Gao and J. Zhou (Eds.): HCII 2020, LNCS 12208, pp. 78–90, 2020.
https://doi.org/10.1007/978-3-030-50249-2_6

However, it has also been shown that proper training is effective at helping people to regain the ability to control their hands [3, 4]. Therefore, various programs for training different aspects of hand control have been devised to assist the elderly. One specific type of training is educating for adjusting pinch force precisely during functional task execution. This training usually involves controlling and maintaining the force applied by the fingers over a period of time. When performing any training, continuous rehabilitation is necessary for the functional recovery of finger mobility and the suppression of functional deterioration. However, some types of conventional rehabilitation require the assistance of occupational therapists. Furthermore, the rehabilitation process can often be monotonous, and this leads to difficulty in maintaining motivation.

In previous studies [5, 6], we utilized a pressing evaluation training system (PETS) that can measure the force applied by each finger and automatically evaluate the appropriateness of finger movement to eliminate the need for an occupational therapist. To make the rehabilitation process less monotonous, we also developed a finger movement training system that incorporates music play based gamification [6]. Although this prototype worked well, we found that one of the remaining problems with this system was that users experienced difficulty perceiving the movement information of fingers, and it took some time for each user to get used to locating this information quickly. A usability problem such as this may increase users' frustration and reduce their motivation in the early stages of the rehabilitation process, which could potentially prevent them from continuing their rehabilitation.

In order to alleviate this problem, we applied augmented reality (AR) technology to superimpose information in real space into the music performance gamification scenario. We used an optical-see-through head mounted display (OST-HMD) to give the user the impression that the training guidance was located near his/her finger. The objective of this study was to determine how the distance between the presentation position of the sound element and the position of each finger affected the users' performance. To examine this, we performed a user study with 10 graduate students.

2 Related Work

2.1 Traditional Hand Rehabilitation Methods

Traditional methods for hand motor skills training usually use a device specifically built for hand training and involves a process of motor learning. For example, Olafsdottir et al. [4] used a hand training device that can be set to generate different levels of resistance and found that participants exhibited reduced finger-pinch force variability and improved target control after six weeks of training. Parikh and Cole [7] asked participants to perform tasks that involved picking up a custom-built object and moving it to different positions and orientations.

The custom-built object contained force sensors that measured the force exerted by the participants while grasping the object, and this was used as a way to evaluate hand strength and dexterity. Wu et al. revealed that training improved the finger control in both young and elderly people [3]. Therefore, we can expect that training that is effective for young participants will have a similar effect on the elderly as well.

2.2   Gamification for Rehabilitation

Gamification for rehabilitation has already been put to practical use in various medical settings. There are previous studies that incorporate sound and music play into the rehabilitation of patients' fingers and upper limbs. When training was performed using a keyboard and drum set, it was shown that training using music was more effective at restoring the motor function of fingers [8, 9]. In another study, rehabilitation involved providing sound feedback corresponding to hand position, and it was concluded that participants' ability to recognize their own hand position was improved by sound changes [10]. These results suggest that finger rehabilitation using music and gamification will be effective, but these studies have all been limited to playing simple scales. Furthermore, the continuous use of this technique has not been examined.

2.3   Augmented Reality in Hand Rehabilitation

Recently, AR technology has also been used in rehabilitation programs to enhance the motivation and enjoyment of patients undergoing training. For hand opening rehabilitation, Luo et al. [11] integrated AR with special gloves to display virtual objects for reaching and grasping tasks. They conducted a preliminary study with three participants and found general improvements in patients' performance during standard functional tests. Burke et al. [12] described the design principles for creating AR games for rehabilitation and developed various examples of AR games for rehabilitation using those design principles. Hondori et al. [13] investigated the impact of interface choice on patients' performance during rehabilitation for hand and arm movement. They developed a desktop and projector-based AR version of a popular game, "Fruit Ninja" that could be used for rehabilitation and evaluated patients' performance when using each version. It was found that patients generally exhibited faster reaction times and more targeted movement when using the AR version. They concluded that these results could be attributed to patients' need to consider hand-eye coordination and the higher cognitive ability that was necessary to use the desktop version.

In our previous work [5], we used a haptic device (Phantom Omni [14]) as a substitute for a PETS device to measure finger force and a video-see-through head mounted display (VST-HMD) to display the force visualizations next to the trainees' fingers using AR. We conducted a user study that included 18 students, and while no significant improvement in performance due to AR was found, participants expressed a preferences for AR. Furthermore, in our latest work [6], we enhanced the training system developed in [5] by changing the AR display from a VST-HMD to an OST-HMD (Microsoft HoloLens [15]), and by using a PETS for the training with gamification based on music play. We will refer to this system as AR-PETS hereafter. However, that device was a prototype with a minimal set of functions, and no evaluation was performed. In this study, we refined this prototype by adding the functions described in Sect. 3.2 so that it could be used continuously during actual training. We also conducted a user study with the PETS, the OST-HMD, and the training scenario with gamification to determine the effect of the location of information display on users' performance.

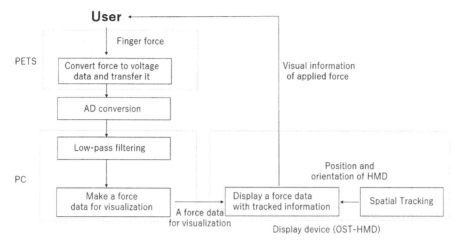

Fig. 1. Process flow of the system.

3 AR-PETS Prototype

The process flow of the system is illustrated in Fig. 1. The system consists of three components: the PETS that measures the finger forces, the PC that process the force data from the PETS, and the display device, which cab be an OST-HMD or a normal PC monitor. At first, a user inputs a force with each of his/her fingers through force sensors on the PETS. The PETS then transfers the raw voltage data to the computer through an AD converter, and the signals are smoothed using a low-pass filter to alleviate the effects of noise. Based on the applied force, the system provides visual and auditory feedback to the user via a normal PC monitor or OST-HMD.

3.1 System Configuration

PETS: Pressing Evaluation and Training System. PETS is a device that uses five load cells (SLB-25, Transducer Techniques, USA) to measure the force input for each finger in real time (Fig. 2). Springs and load cells are located inside each force plate. The user feels a reaction force by pressing down on the force plates with his/her finger, which is important for appropriate finger motor training. The spring can be replaced with ones with different strengths based on the finger status of each user.

PC Data Acquisition and Processing Software. A data acquisition application based on LabWindows/CVI [18] acquires the raw force data that is measured by the PETS. Upon receiving new data from the PETS, the application attempts to reduce noise from the data using a simple moving average filter that takes an average of the last five samples. The resulting filtered data is then delivered via the UDP networking protocol for external programs to use and process. In the case of AR-PETS, the data is sent locally to a separate application in the HoloLens that manages the training program itself.

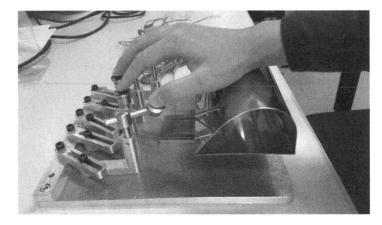

Fig. 2. PETS is a device that can measure the force input by a user's fingers using five load cells.

Display Device. The HoloLens receives the force data for the visualization from the PC software. It is then displayed near the PETS with the position and posture of the HoloLens calculated in the spatial mapping function. We set the location by manually clicking it before the training and assumed the location of the PETS did not change during the training.

3.2   Training with Gamification Based on Music Play

As described in the last section, we applied music play based gamification to finger motor skill training to maintain user motivation and encourage continuous long term training.

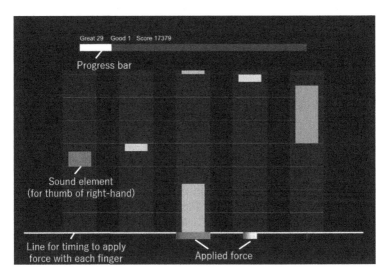

Fig. 3. Screenshot of the training application

Overview. The training application was implemented using Unity [19]. A screen-shot of the application with a PC monitor is shown in Fig. 3. The user can play the music by pressing the five sensors with the corresponding fingers as instructed on the music score. The rectangle object connected to each sound falls vertically along the five lanes corresponding to each finger. We refer to this as the "sound element." When the user moves each finger and applies a force that is above a designed threshold to the PETS, a corresponding sound is played. The original melody is played by applying force to the correct finger sensor at the exact time when the rectangle falling from above overlaps with the line at the bottom of the screen. Therefore, in order to play the correct music, the user should move the specified finger at the specified time for the specified duration. We expect that this method will allow the user to perform finger rehabilitation while enjoying the game.

Change of Finger Training Pattern. Improving the ability to play music correctly does not necessarily correspond to meeting rehabilitation goals. It is necessary to adjust the level of difficulty and training content according to the condition of each user's finger status and his/her rehabilitation goals. Factors to be adjusted include the strength of the pressing force, the tempo of the song, and the finger movement pattern. The strength of the pressing force can be adjusted by changing how much force is needed to produce a sound in the force calibration phase for each finger. The tempo of the song can be adjusted by simply changing both the visual and auditory display speeds. Finger movement patterns include movements for finger independence, finger coordination, finger agility, and the accuracy of the applied force as shown in Fig. 4. It is possible to deal with various patient finger conditions and training goals by combining those movements.

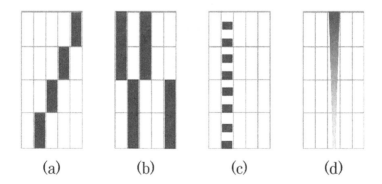

(a)   (b)   (c)   (d)

Fig. 4. Finger motion patterns. (a) Single pressing, (b) Synchronous pressing, (c) Finger agility (interval from moving one finger to the next), (d) Strength variation

Use of User's Favorite Song. We expect that users will be more motivated if their own favorite songs are used for the training, instead of a prepared song. Therefore, we allow the user to select the song used for training. Users can select their favorite songs from a web site [20] that includes thousands of J-pop music data. Because this music data is categorized by instrument, it is easier to create the training content using this data, and then users can also train using the part played by their favorite instrument. Although in the current prototype, developers must manually select a song and create the training from the song, those procedures can be technically automated in the future.

3.3   Feedback from Occupational Therapist

As a preliminary evaluation of the prototype, we asked a professional occupational therapist to use the system with a normal PC display and various difficulty levels and to provide feedback.

First of all, she commented that this system could be expected to be effective in the rehabilitation of patients with mild paralysis or with broken fingers and wrists and also in the prevention of cognitive decline. She also pointed out that she felt pleasure when improving her playing skills by playing the same music score many times and could continue to play without getting bored for more than 30 min.

On the other hand, she pointed out that it would be too difficult for a novice patient to play the actual music even with the simplest music. We presume that one of the reasons for this might be the difficulty of promptly perceiving correspondence between each finger and the sound element. To improve this process, we decided to use HoloLens to incorporate AR into the training and conducted a user study as described in the next section.

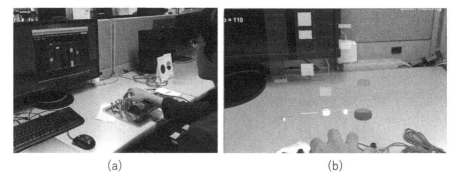

(a)   (b)

Fig. 5. Two display methods: (a) A normal PC monitor. (b) OTS-HMD (HoloLens).

4   User Study

We evaluated whether the aforementioned difficulty with the user's ability to connect each finger and sound element could be alleviated using one of the features of AR, in which the display information can be associated with a real object.

4.1   Experimental Conditions

We compared two methods for displaying visual feedback during training. The first one used a normal PC monitor. Participants completed the experiment while viewing a monitor placed in front of them and operating the PETS on the desk (Fig. 5(a)). The second used with an OST-HMD (Microsoft HoloLens, 23 pixels per 1°). The participants operated the PETS on the desk while directly looking at the scene through the HoloLens. All information, such as the musical score and the sound element was displayed close to each force sensor on the PETS, which means that is was also displayed near each corresponding finger (Fig. 5(b)). The experiment was conducted using a within-subject design where each participant experienced both display methods. The sequence of training condition were randomized to minimize potential order effects. The two different training conditions conducted with the interval of one day.

4.2   Participants

10 graduate students from a local university voluntarily participated in this experiment (22–30 years old, mean: 23.9, standard deviation: 2.3, all right-handed). Only one of them was a person who plays musical instruments and rhythm games on a daily basis. Three of them use AR on a daily basis in their research.

4.3   Procedure

First, the experimenter told each participant the general purpose of this experiment and explained how to use the system. Each participant then played three different practice songs (approximately 3 min per song) using the same display method to get used to the system. After the practice and a 3 min break, he/she played a test song which was different from the three practice songs. While the participant played the test song, the system recorded the time lag between when each sound was actually played and when each sound element should ideally be played (i.e., the time when each rectangle touched the line) as an index indirectly reflecting his/her corresponding finger recognition time. After playing the test song, each participant completed the System Usability Scale (SUS) to assess the basic usability of the system. This procedure was repeated for the other display method on the next day to alleviate the effects of fatigue. To control for effects due to the order that participants used each display method, five participants used the normal PC monitor first, and the other five first used the HoloLens.

4.4   Outcome Measurements

- **Time lag.** The time difference between the exact time when the sound element intersected the line and the time when participants applied the force.
- **Rate of delayed timing.** The rate that the force was applied after the correct timing.
- **System Usability Scale.** The total score for 10 questions that participants ranked based on how much they agree with the usability of the system (from 0 to 100).

4.5   Statistical Analysis

SPSS statistics 26 for Windows (Statistical Package for Social Sciences Inc. Chicago, IL, USA) was used for statistical analysis. Normality in the data distribution was examined with a Shapiro-Wilk test, applying the appropriate parametric and non-parametric statistical tests. The level of significance was set at $p < 0.05$.

4.6   Hypotheses

We tested the following two hypotheses regarding the effect of display location on the participants' recognition of fingering information.

H1. When the HoloLens (AR) is used to display the fingering information near the corresponding finger, the time lag from the appropriate timing is shorter than when the information is displayed away from the finger with a normal PC monitor.
H2. Participants prefer using the HoloLens (AR) over the PC monitor method.

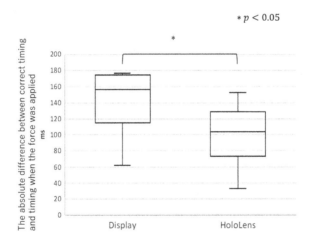

Fig. 6. The absolute time difference between the ideal time and the time when the force was applied for each display method.

4.7   Results

The absolute time differences between the exact time when the rectangle intersected the line and the time at which the user applied a force with his/her finger that exceeded the threshold force are shown in 6. When using the PC monitor, the average time delay was 144 ms. When the HoloLens was used, the average time delay was 101 ms, which was significantly shorter when compared with the PC (Paired t-test, $p < 0.05$).

The ratio of the number of times that a force was applied later than the exact time is shown in Fig. 7. We would expect this value to approach 0.5 if no delay exists. While the average ratio was 0.68 when participants used the PC monitor, it was 0.51 when they used the HoloLens, which was significantly smaller (Paired t-test, $p < 0.05$).

In addition, the results of the SUS questionnaire are shown in 8. The average values were 62.8 and 65.0 for the PC monitor and HoloLens, respectively, and there was no significant difference between the two methods (Wilcoxon signed-rank test, $p = 0.951$).

5   Discussion

5.1   Analysis of the Results

Based the timing results shown in Fig. 6 and 7, H1 was confirmed. It was estimated that a shorter time is needed to recognize the correct fingering when participants used the HoloLens instead of the PC monitor. Furthermore, in the free-form questionnaire, seven participants commented that with AR, they could immediately understand which finger to use because the HoloLens displayed each sound element near the location of the corresponding finger, while they had difficulty understanding it when using a normal PC display. On the other hand, if this is mainly due to the proximity of the information, it might be possible to achieve a similar result without using OST-HMD for AR. For instance, it is possible that just putting a display device, such as a tablet, in front of the user's fingers would have a similar effect as AR because the position of the user's hand did not change during the training in the target situation (Fig. 8).

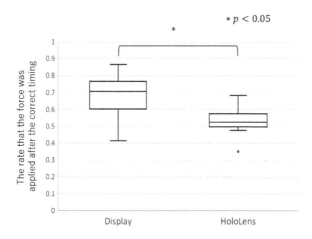

Fig. 7. The rate that the force was applied after the correct timing for each display method. The expected value is 0.5 if there is no perception delay.

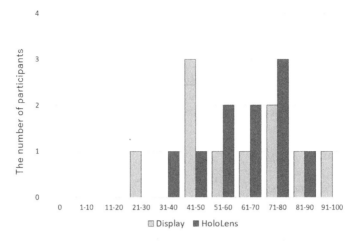

Fig. 8. Histogram of SUS score for each participant for each display method. 0 is the worst. 100 is the best.

The results of the SUS questionnaire indicated that there were no significant differences between the two display methods. Thus, the second hypothesis was not supported in terms of usability. Four participants also provided negative comments related to the narrow field of view of the OST-HMD or the discomfort of wearing it. One plausible explanation for these results is that the negative aspects of the device were offset by the aforementioned positive aspect of recognizing the fingering more easily.

One of the participants pointed out that he had more fun during training when he knew the song and that his prior knowledge of a song had a significant impact on his enjoyment. This supports the usefulness of including a function that allows users to select their own favorite songs.

5.2   Limitation and Future Work

The participants in this experiment were 10 young graduate students who did not exhibit any particular difficulties with hand use while our target users are the elderly and patients with conditions such as mild upper limb paralysis, so it is not clear if these results could be applied more generally. To customize the training for a variety of users and conditions, we have provided functions that allow for flexibility in choosing the finger to be used for the training, fingering pattern, and amount of force to be applied. However, these differences among users are likely to affect the timing and SUS results. In future work, we plan to use the original target users to further evaluate the system.

In this study, we proposed and evaluated a potential method to eliminate one of the obstacles that appeared at the beginning of the training. However, the ultimate goal of this research is to assist the continuation of finger motor skill training. This evaluation is also one of the most important issues in the future. In addition, the current devices (i.e., the PETS and the HoloLens) are heavy and difficult for end users to operate. When performing continuous daily training, it is desirable for users to be able to train at their own homes using devices that are lighter and easier to handle. In the future, we plan to make the PETS more portable and to use a tablet or smartphone as the display devices instead of the PC monitor or HoloLens. This will provide similar finger motor skill training while keeping the user's fingers and the fingering information in close proximity to each other.

6   Conclusion

In this study, we proposed a method of finger motor skill training that uses music play based gamification and incorporated AR technology into this training process to make it easier for users to see the fingering information. We hypothesized that displaying each sound element close to the corresponding finger would reduce the difficulty of using this system and, therefore, make the training process more enjoyable. To test this hypothesis, we conducted a user study with 10 graduate students which demonstrated that the location where the information was displayed affected the time it took users to recognize the correct finger positions. However, some participants pointed out some fundamental problems with the current OST-HMD, including its narrow field of view and the discomfort of wearing it. In future work, we plan to develop a lightweight, portable device that can be used daily by a user at home. In addition, we will determine whether the proposed method enables users who use it continuously to maintain their motivation.

Acknowledgements. This research was supported by the Japan Science and Technology Agency and Ministry of Science and Technology of Taiwan as part of the Japan-Taiwan Collaborative Research Program (106-2923-E-006-005-MY3) and JST CREST (JPMJCR19A).

References

1. Hackel, M., Wolfe, G., Bang, S., Canfield, J.: Changes in hand function in the aging adult as determined by the Jebsen test of hand function. Phys. Ther. **72**(5), 373–377 (1992)
2. Ranganathan, V., Siemionow, V., Sahgal, V., Yue, G.: Effects of aging on hand function. J. Am. Geriatr. Soc. **49**(11), 1478–1484 (2002)
3. Wu, Y., Pazin, N., Zatsiorsky, V., Latash, M.: Improving finger coordination in young and elderly persons. Exp. Brain Res. **226**(2), 273–283 (2013). https://doi.org/10.1007/s00221-013-3433-4
4. Olafsdottir, H., Zatsiorsky, V., Latash, M.: The effects of strength training on finger strength and hand dexterity in healthy elderly individuals. J. Appl. Physiol. **105**(4), 1166–1178 (2008)
5. Plopski, A., Mori, R., Taketomi, T., Sandor, C., Kato, H.: AR-PETS: development of an augmented reality supported pressing evaluation training system. In: Zhou, J., Salvendy, G. (eds.) ITAP 2018. LNCS, vol. 10927, pp. 113–126. Springer, Cham (2018). https://doi.org/10.1007/978-3-319-92037-5_10
6. Ty, J., et al.: Integration of augmented reality with pressing evaluation and training system for finger force training. In: Zhou, J., Salvendy, G. (eds.) HCII 2019. LNCS, vol. 11593, pp. 575–587. Springer, Cham (2019). https://doi.org/10.1007/978-3-030-22015-0_45

7. Parikh, P., Cole, K.: Handling objects in old age: forces and moments acting on the object. J. Appl. Physiol. **112**(7), 1095–1104 (2012)

8. Schneider, S., Schönle, P.W., Altenmüller, E., Münte, T.F.: Using musical instruments to improve motor skill recovery following a stroke. J. Neurol. **254**(10), 1339–1346 (2007). https://doi.org/10.1007/s00415-006-0523-2

9. Villeneuve, M., Penhune, V., Lamontagne, A.: A piano training program to improve manual dexterity and upper extremity function in chronic stroke survivors. Front. Hum. Neurosci. **8**, 662 (2014)

10. Scholz, D.S., Rhode, S., Großbach, M., Rollnik, J., Altenmüller, E.: Moving with music for stroke rehabilitation: a sonification feasibility study. The Neurosciences and Music V. Ann. N. Y. Acad. Sci. **1137**(1), 69–76 (2015)

11. Luo, X., Kline, T., Fischer H., Stubblefield, K., Kenyon, R., Kamper, D.: Integration of augmented reality and assistive devices for post-stroke hand opening rehabilitation. In: Proceedings of the IEEE Engineering in Medicine and Biology Annual Conference, Shanghai, China, pp. 6855–6858. IEEE (2005)

12. Burke, J., McNeil, M., Charles, D., Morrow, P., Crosbie, J., McDonough, S.: Augmented reality games for upper-limb stroke rehabilitation. In: Proceedings of the International Conference on Games and Virtual Worlds for Serious Applications, pp. 75–78 (2010)

13. Hondori, H., Khademi, M., Dodakian, L., McKenzie, A., Lopes, C., Cramer, S.: Choice of human-computer interaction mode in stroke rehabilitation. Neurorehab. Neural Repair. **30**(3), 258–265 (2016)

14. 3D Systems: Phantom Omni. https://www.3dsystems.com/haptics-devices/touch/specifications. Accessed 20 Dec 2019

15. Microsoft: HoloLens. https://www.microsoft.com/en-us/hololens. Accessed 23 Dec 2019

16. Author, F., Author, S.: Title of a proceedings paper. In: Editor, F., Editor, S. (eds.) CONFERENCE 2016, LNCS, vol. 9999, pp. 1–13. Springer, Heidelberg (2016). https://doi.org/10.10007/1234567890

17. Author, F., Author, S., Author, T.: Book title. 2nd edn. Publisher, Location (1999)

18. National Instruments: LabWindowsTM/CVI - National Instruments. http://www.ni.com/lwcvi/. Accessed 16 Jan 2020

19. Unity Technologies: Unity. https://unity3d.com/. Accessed 16 Jan 2020

20. Yamaha Corporation: Yamaha music data shop. https://yamahamusicdata.jp/. Accessed 16 Jan 2020

Comparison of Gaze Skills Between Expert and Novice in Elderly Care

Miyuki Iwamoto$^{(\boxtimes)}$ and Atsushi Nakazawa$^{(\boxtimes)}$

Kyoto University, Yoshida-honmachi, Sakyo, Kyoto, Japan
iwamoto@ii.ist.i.kyoto-u.ac.jp,
nakazawa.atsushi@i.kyoto-u.ac.jp

Abstract. It is known that a person, when ignored by others, causes various negative reactions and enhances aggressive behavior and Self-destructive behavior [1–3]. The same goes for elderly people with dementia, therefore, depending on the care may cause fear and confusion for elderly people with dementia [4].

At the same time, care for the elderly with dementia has a great mental and physical burden on caregivers. For this reason, the turnover rate has increased and it has become difficult to provide adequate care [5–8]. For these problems, as one of the dementia care is gaining attention Humanitude [4, 10]. Humanitude consists of four skills: "see", "touch", "speak", and "stand" [9–11]. So, our research focus on "see", one of the basic skills. A person's gaze is generally directed to an object of interest or attention. The gaze is extremely useful information for estimating the mind of another person [3, 12, 13]. Therefore, we let a caregiver wear the first person camera, and four types of "seeing" behavior patterns during the oral care (care receiver → caregiver, care receiver ← caregiver, mutual gaze, none) measured. We compared the differences between Humanitude experts and novice. There was a large difference in the frequency and time of mutual gaze between expert and novice caregiver for care receiver. The act of matching the sight of eyes is an act of not ignoring the other person, indicating an interest in the care receiver, and it is considered that for the care receiver, the anxiety and fear during care are reduced.

Keywords: Gaze behavior · Annotation · Humanitude · And dementia · Oral care

1 Introduction

According to world population reports, in 2015, it was estimated that there were 46.8 million people with dementia. In developed regions, dementia rates for people over the age of 60 were reported between 4 and 6%. This number increases to 20–33% in people over 85. Estimates suggest that the number of people diagnosed with dementia continues to grow at a rate of 4.6 million people annually, reaching 131.5 million people in 2050 [14, 15].

There are 4.62 million people with dementia over the age of 65 in Japan today, but it is estimated that they will be over 7 million people in the 2030s, approaching 25% of the population over the age of 65. The increased number of people diagnosed with dementia

© Springer Nature Switzerland AG 2020
Q. Gao and J. Zhou (Eds.): HCII 2020, LNCS 12208, pp. 91–100, 2020.
https://doi.org/10.1007/978-3-030-50249-2_7

is a major social problem that will only grow more serious in the future, as life expectancies continue to rise [16].

Due to the damage to higher brain functions such as memory, orientation, knowledge, action, cognition, language, emotion, and personality, people with dementia become antagonistic towards situations in which they've placed themselves. Dementia can be induced by a variety of causes. Its pathology and symptoms are very diverse. Symptoms can be divided into core symptoms and peripheral symptoms. The core symptoms include memory impairment, executive function disorder, apraxia, aphasia, and agnosia. Patients with dementia may exhibit execution dysfunction, difficulty in initiating action, reduction of spontaneity, behavioral conversion dysfunction, impulsive behaviors, and disinhibition. Apraxia is a degradation of motor skills or coordination without any link to sensory impairment. Patients may be unable to put on clothes or use tools properly. Agnosia is an inability to recognize objects through use of the senses, including physical landmarks or other visual stimuli, as in visuospatial agnosia. It may also apply to sounds. "Peripheral symptoms" refers to various behavioral disorders and psychiatric symptoms that appear to be affected by the patient's environment and physical condition. This category includes delusions, hallucinations, anxiety, impatience, depression, wandering, aggressive behavior, sleep disorders, eating disorders, including binge eating and pica, and resistance to care, among others.

The Symptoms of "BPSD". The Behavioral and Psychological Symptoms of Dementia, or BPSD, are the "core symptoms" of dementia. It occurs in conjunction with memory loss, psychiatric symptoms, and a decline in comprehension ability, and was previously referred to as "problematic behavior" or "nuisance behavior". The symptoms are divided into behavioral and psychological symptoms, with more symptoms appearing as the dementia progresses from mild to moderate. Behavioral symptoms may include violence, verbal abuse, wandering, rejection, and unsanitary acts. As the manifestation of symptoms differs from person to person, all symptoms may not always appear. These symptoms appear frequently as dementia progresses from mild to moderate, leading to a rapid decrease in quality of life accordingly [17–20]. It is known that a person, when ignored by others, causes various negative reactions and enhances aggressive behavior and Self-destructive behavior [1–3].

The same goes for the elderly people with dementia who have these symptoms, therefore, depending on the care may cause fear and confusion for elderly people with dementia [4].

At the same time, care for the elderly with dementia has a great mental and physical burden on caregivers. For this reason, the turnover rate has increased and it has become difficult to provide adequate care [5–8].

At the same time, the caregiver requires more time and effort than necessary to care for the elderly with dementia, care for the elderly with dementia has a great mental and physical burden on caregivers. For this reason, the turnover rate has increased and it has become difficult to provide adequate care.

For these problems, as one of the dementia care is gaining attention Humanitide [4, 10].

1.1 What is *Humanitide*

Humanitide is a dementia care technique created by Yves Ginest and Rosette Malle-scotti [11].

Humanitide is a care technique based on comprehensive communication based on perception, sensation, and language, for people who need care, not only for people with dementia and the elderly people. The caregiver always cares for the care receiver by acting on the human characteristics of seeing, speaking, touching, and standing. It is important to keep sending the message "I care about you" to those who need care. It allows people to feel that they are the only beings and that they are respected. *Humanitide* is the philosophy that respects and communicates the humanity of those who need care and consists of more than 150 practical techniques based on it [4, 10, 21–23].

1.2 Purpose

So, our research focus on "see", one of the basic skills.

Although, Gaze is one of the important skill in *Humaniude*. While the difference of the mutual gaze behavior between caregivers and receivers are already reported [24] (Fig. 1), gaze behaviors of the care receivers were not well studied (Fig. 2).

A person's gaze is generally directed to an object of interest or attention. The gaze is extremely useful information for estimating the mind of another person [11, 12].

Therefore, We let a caregiver wear the first person camera, and four types of "seeing" behavior patterns during the oral care (caregiver → caregiver, care-giver ← caregiver, mutual gaze, none) are measured. We compared the differences between humanity experts and beginners.

We examined whether there was a large difference in the frequency and time of gaze matching between novice and expert of *Humanitude*. The act of matching the sight of eyes is an act of not ignoring the other person [1–3], indicating an interest in the care receiver, and it is considered that for the care receiver, the anxiety and fear during care are reduced.

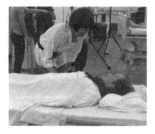

Fig. 1. Mutual gaze

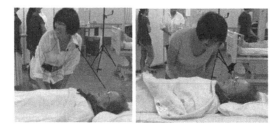

Fig. 2. Left: Line of sight from care receiver to caregiver Right: Line of sight from caregiver to care receiver

2 Experiment

In actual nursing scene at a hospital in Fukuoka, we used three care categories and four types of gaze patterns to measure gaze trends of caregiver and care receiver during oral care.

2.1 Data Collection

We compared the differences between Humanitude experts and Novice. The number of collaborators is 22 nurses (21 Humanitude novice, 1 expert), and the care receiver is 9 elderly people with dementia who are hospitalized.

A total of 29 sessions were given for about 5 min of care per session.

2.2 Classification of Care Categories

Classify the acquired oral care data into 3 categories before care, during care and after care. The three categories were classified under the following conditions (Fig. 3) (Table 1).

Fig. 3. A: Before Care, B: During Care, C: After Care

Table 1. Conditions for care classification

Care stage	Conditions
Before Care	Before a caregiver touches a receiver's mouth
During Care	Performs oral care using a toothbrush
After Care	From the end of the cleaning mouth and leave from the bed

2.3 Gaze Pattern Classification

The conditions for classifying caregivers and care receivers movements of gaze patterns will be described. The movements of gaze patterns were classified into four types.

(a) shows when the mutual gaze. The face of the elderly is located in the center of the frame and the gaze are looking at the camera.

(b) shows the time when the care receiver is looking but the caregiver is not looking.

(c) shows the time when the caregiver is looking but care receiver is not looking. Even if the face of the care receiver is in the center of the frame, when he gaze of care receiver is not looking at the camera, it is considered that only the caregiver is looking.

(d) shows the time when neither is seen. Details are shown in Fig. 4. In the figure, "G" is the caregiver and "R" is the care receiver.

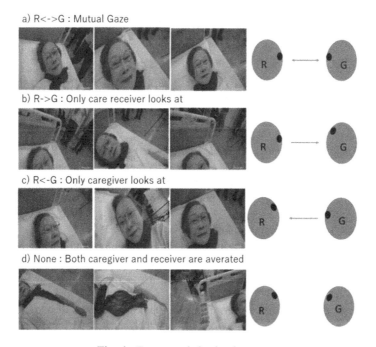

a) R<->G : Mutual Gaze

b) R->G : Only care receiver looks at

c) R<-G : Only caregiver looks at

d) None : Both caregiver and receiver are averated

Fig. 4. Four gaze-behavioral patterns

3   Result

We used three care categories and four types of gaze patterns to measure gaze trends of caregiver and care receiver during oral care.

The time it takes for Novices and expert to take oral care is shown in Fig. 5.

The horizontal axis shows the time taken for Whole care, Before care, During care, and After care. The vertical axis represents care time. Significant differences were found throughout time, Before and After care.

On the other hand, there was no significant difference in time During care between the Novice and the expert. Experts spend about 40% of the time Before Care and After Care. On the other hand, novice accounts for only about 20% of the total time.

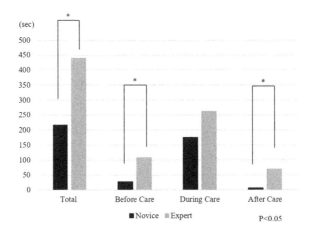

Fig. 5.   The time it takes for Novices and expert to take oral care

We used three care categories and four types of gaze patterns to measure gaze trends of caregiver and care receiver during oral care. Figure 6 shows the results.

The three care receiver shows as A, B, and C

Figure 6 shows the results of *Humanitude* experts and two novice (1 and 2) for each care receiver. The horizontal axis represents the number of frames, and the vertical axis represents each care. R represents a care Receiver and G represents a caregiver. In general, it can be seen that the expert spent a lot of time mutual gaze and the caregiver is seeing care receiver in one session. However, there is almost no difference in the time during care for both expert and novice.

On the other hand, when comparing the gazing time before and after care, it can be seen that the expert spends a certain amount of time, while the novice hardly spends time before and after care. Especially After Care, it was found that Novice hardly saw the care receiver.

During care, the expert has a short time when the caregiver and the care receiver do not look each other, whereas the novice does not look each other for a long time.

The situation that only the care receiver sees was rarely seen by the expert.

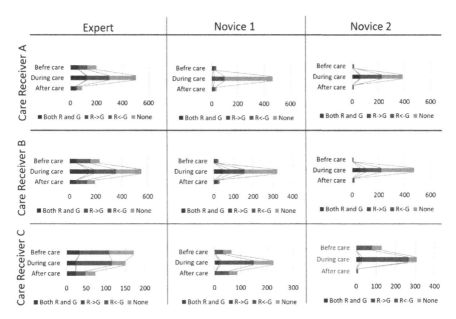

Fig. 6. Gaze behavior analysis results

Figure 7, 8, and 9 show the ratio of Mutual Gaze. The horizontal axis represents three stages, and the vertical axis represents the ratio. Figure 7, 8, and 9 show care receivers A, B, and C, respectively.

Ratio of mutual gaze = Mutual Gaze/caregiver's gaze + care receiver's gaze

Expert was found to have a high percentage of mutual gazes overall.

There was a large difference in gaze ratio between the expert and the novice Before Care and After Care, but the most significant difference was After Care.

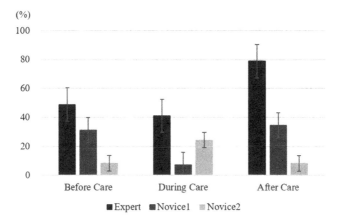

Fig. 7. Percent of mutual gaze (Care Receiver A)

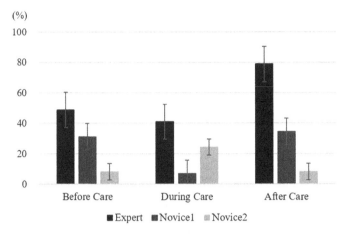

Fig. 8. Percent of mutual gaze (Care Receiver B)

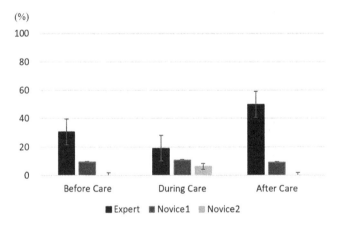

Fig. 9. Percent of mutual gaze (Care Receiver C)

After Care, the two novices accounted for less than 20%, while the expert accounted for a very high percentage of 40–80%.

4   Conclusion

In this study, a first-person camera was worn by a caregiver, and four types of gaze patterns in three stages during oral care were measured (care receiver → caregiver, care receiver ← caregiver, mutual gaze, none). We compared the differences between Expert and Novice in *Humanitide*.

In one session of care, we measured that divided into three stages: Before Care, During Care, and After Care. As a result, it was found that expert spend more time in one session than novices, but there is no significant difference in the time "During

Care". It is considered that there was no difference in the time required for care because the procedure of oral care was decided. On the other hand, significant differences are found in, the duration of Before Care and After care between novices and experts (Experts > Novices).

There are five steps that are important for practice in *Humanitide*. *Humanitide* has the first step, "preparing to meet", and the last step, "promise of resumption". These are items that are not related to direct care but are very important when interacting with people. This is an item that is difficult to practice in a nursing care setting that is usually pressed for time.

Expert perform these two steps, and they spend a certain amount of time Before Care and After Care.

However, novice do not perform this step and immediately perform oral care. It is thought that there was a big difference in time of After Care and Before Care.

The number of mutual gaze between the experts and novices (Experts > Novices).

Considering that the time of Mutual Gaze is longer for the expert than for the novice, it is considered that when the care receiver makes eye contact, the expert notices the care receiver's eye contact and looks at the cared receiver. In this way, it was found that, although both expert and novice intend to see the cared During Care, the novice often do not.

Moreover the ratio of None is smaller in the expert.

The duration of R $\rightarrow$ G is smaller in the expert, which means the care receivers are less ignored in expert's sessions.

Prior literature is known that a person, when ignored by others, causes various negative reactions. Elderly people may feel anxious or fearful about being cared for, in addition if they are ignored by nurses, they may feel more anxious or fearful. Also, I think that it is important for nurses to be aware of elderly gaze, because the act of turning their gaze to the other party may not only be looking but also complaining.

Therefore, the act of "see" is a necessary act for care, and from the contents of the analysis video, taking into account that there were few actions to refuse care that the elderly are removing the expert's hand or turning their face away from the expert during care, the act of "see" was found to be important for care.

5 Future Works

In order to verify whether the same can be said for other cares, we will measure movement of gaze trends in other cares. In addition, even in the same "gaze", the reaction of pleasant or unpleasant is different, so we believe that it is necessary to measure pleasant or unpleasant with physiological data.

Acknowledgement.   This work was supported by JST CREST Grant Number JPMJCR17A5.

References

1. Baumeister, F., Leary, R.: The need to belong: desire for interpersonal attachments as a fundamental human motivation. Psychol. Bull. **117**(3), 497–529 (1995)

2. Twenge, J.M., Baumeister, R.F., DeWall, C.N., Ciarocco, N.J., Bartels, J.M.: Social exclusion decreases prosocial behavior. J. Pers. Soc. Psychol. **92**(1), 56–66 (2007)
3. Matthews, A., Fox, E., Yiend, J., Calder, A.: The face of fear: effects of eye gaze and emotion on attentional engagement. Vis. Cogn. **10**(7), 825–835 (2003)
4. Honda, M.: Introduction to Humanitude, Japan Medical Communication (2014)
5. Etters, L., Goodall, D., Harrison, B.E.: Caregiver burden among dementia patient caregivers: a review of the literature. J. Am. Acad. Nurse. Pract. **20**(8), 423–428 (2008)
6. Meng, S., Brian, M., Tisha, J.O., Gwen, L.S.: Correlates of nursing care burden among institutionalized patients with dementia. Int. Psychogeriatr. **30**(10), 1549–1555 (2018)
7. Cheng, S.-T.: Dementia caregiver burden: a research update and critical analysis. Curr. Psychiatry Rep. **19**(9), 1–8 (2017). https://doi.org/10.1007/s11920-017-0818-2
8. Uribe, F.L., et al.: Caregiver burden assessed in dementia care networks in Germany: findings from the DemNet-D study baseline. Aging Ment. Health Col. **21**(9), 926–937 (2017)
9. Gineste, Y., Marescotti, R., Pellissier, J.: Humanism in nursing. Rech Soins Infirm **94**, 42–55 (2008)
10. Gineste, Y., Marescotti, R.: Interest of the philosophy of humanitude in caring for patients with Alzheimer's disease. Soins. Geronol. **85**, 26–27 (2010)
11. Gineste, Y., Pellissier, J.: Humanitude: Comprendre la vieillesse, prendre soin des Hommes vieux. Armand Colin, Paris (2007)
12. Yarbus, A.L.: Eye Movements and Vision, pp. 171–196. Plenum Press, New York (1967)
13. Turati, C., Simon, F., Milani, L., Umilta, C.: Newborns' preference for faces: What is crucial? Develop. Psychol. **38**, 875–882 (2002)
14. Ferri, C.P., et al.: Global prevalence of dementia: a Delphi consensus study. Lancet **366**, 2112–2117 (2005)
15. International AsD: World Alzheimer report, pp. 25–46 (2009)
16. Ministry of Health, Labour and Welfare: A 2015 year version of annual report on health and welfare, the aging of the world: the Ministry of Health, Labour and Welfare. http://www.mhlw.go.jp/topics/kaigo/kentou/15kourei/3a.html. Accessed 31 Jan 2020
17. Alzheimer, A.: Über einen eigenartigen schweren Er Krankungsprozeb der Hirnrinde. Neurologisches Centralblatt **2**(23), 1129–1136 (1906)
18. Maurer, K., Volk, S., Gerbaldo, H.: Auguste D and Alzheimer's disease. Lancet **349**(9064), 1546–1549 (1997)
19. Biquand, S., Zittel, B.: Care giving and nursing, work conditions and humanitude. Work **41** (Supplement 1), 1828–1831 (2012)
20. McKhann, G.M., et al.: The diagnosis of dementia due to Alzheimer's disease: recommendations from the National Institute on aging-Alzheimer's association workgroups on diagnostic guidelines for Alzheimer's disease. Alzheimer's Dement. **7**(3), 263–269 (2011)
21. Honda, M., Ito, M., Ishikawa, S., Takebayashi, Y., Tierney, L.: Reduction of behavioral psychological symptoms of dementia by multimodal comprehensive care for vulnerable geriatric patients in an acute care hospital a case series. Case Rep. Med. (2016)
22. Ito, M., Honda, M.: An examination of the influence of humanitude caregiving on the behavior of older adults with dementia in Japan, In: Proceedings of the 8th International Association of Gerontology and Geriatrics European Region Congress
23. Honda, M.: Comprehensive Multimodal Care Methodology to Bring Tenderness: Humanitude. Japan. J. Psychosom. Med. **56**(7), 692–697 (2016)
24. Nakazawa, A., Mitsuzumi, Yu., Watanabe, Y., Kurazume, R., Yoshikawa, S., Honda, M.: First-person video analysis for evaluating skill level in the *humanitude* tender-care technique. J. Intell. Robot. Syst. **98**(1), 103–118 (2019). https://doi.org/10.1007/s10846-019-01052-8

Application of Fuzzy Decision Model Selection of Product in Human Factors Design

Hsin-Hung Lin[1]([⊠]) and Jui-Hung Cheng[2]([⊠])

[1] Department of Creative Product Design, Asia University,
No. 500, Lioufeng Rd., Wufeng, Taichung City 41354, Taiwan
hhlin@asia.edu.tw
[2] Department of Mold and Die Engineering,
National Kaohsiung University of Science and Technology,
No. 415, Jiangong Rd., Sanmin Dist., Kaohsiung City 80778, Taiwan
rick.cheng@nkust.edu.tw

Abstract. The use of human-designed products places a greater emphasis on consumer constituents and often affects consumer preferences and purchase preferences for the overall shape of the product. The evaluation model proposed in this paper uses Fuzzy Analytic Hierarchy Process (FAHP) to obtain the degree of emphasis (weight value) of consumers on each evaluation item, and then obtain a more objective overall shape preference. In this paper, the electrotherapy designer is used as a research case. The results show that the evaluation model is indeed feasible, and the research results of this case are also valuable for subsequent designers. This evaluation mode is for products with different shapes, and subsequent researchers or designers can apply this method to different case designs.

Keywords: Product design · Layout strategy · Design method · FAHP

1 Introduction

The low frequency therapy device was used in physical rehabilitation treatment or to relieve pain. It is a non-medicated method to relieve soreness. Electrode pads are used to stimulate the muscles and the sensory receptors of nerve endings in the muscles, so that muscle pain and nerves caused by fatigue or injury Relax and promote local blood circulation to reduce or soothe pain. General home-type low frequency products have two functions: transcutaneous electrical nerve stimulation (TENS) and electrical muscle stimulation (EMS). TENS uses low-frequency shocks to relieve various pains caused by excessive nerve tension, suppresses pain messages from the nerves, and causes the brain to produce endorphin to achieve analgesic effects. EMS can promote muscle movement to increase muscle strength and prevent muscle atrophy. For the elderly over half a year, it can achieve a certain muscle exercise and pain relief function. The "low-frequency therapeutic device" or "transcutaneous electrical nerve stimulator (TENS)" for the elderly belongs to the second-tier medium-risk medical device. The low frequency therapy device can pass the current to the patient's body for stimulation using the adhesive electrode on the patient's skin. When appropriate current parameters are used (such as current intensity, frequency, pulse time, wave pattern, etc.), the current

© Springer Nature Switzerland AG 2020
Q. Gao and J. Zhou (Eds.): HCII 2020, LNCS 12208, pp. 101–112, 2020.
https://doi.org/10.1007/978-3-030-50249-2_8

input into the body will stimulate the nervous system, so that the patient can produce muscle relaxation, soreness, and relieve discomfort. The analgesic principle of the low-frequency therapeutic device is through the "gate control theory", which stimulates the epidermal nerve with current so that it passes through and closes a region called "gate valve" before transmitting to the brain, allowing conduction speed. Slower pain messages are blocked and pain is not felt. In addition to the "gate valve control theory", research has pointed out that low-frequency treatment devices can also cause brain to secrete endorphins, so that patients can achieve pain relief effects. This study is mainly to design a set of TENS to detect acupuncture points. Application of design methods.

Sun et al. [1]. Application triangular fuzzy numbers approach, the past can not be captured by the human senses linear increase assessment of the reliability and authenticity. Conducting a questionnaire survey in a qualitative way, through the consumer's self-subjective judgment, understanding the preferences and needs of the consumer's carts, matching the collected terminology, using the questionnaire to screen out the consumer's shape and function for the self-truss Image vocabulary and expectation psychology. Then, using the method of quantification, the triangle fuzzy is used to calculate the ideal preference of the vocabulary that is most close to the consumer in different self-species. In his research, Tsu-Wu Hu and Yen-Ting Liao used 18- to 38-year-old junior colleges as the research object, and then explored various life attitudes and emotional consumption patterns of the consumer groups, and made appropriate suits with the frame style. Grouping. The consumer group and the frame style give different factors to consider the classification of the facet by evaluating the various attributes of the vocabulary. Through the grouping of the consumer groups, consumers can understand the consumer group and consumption concept of what attributes they are, and clearly understand their own positioning. Through the guidance of the emotional imagery vocabulary, consumers can find the trolleys suitable for their own [2].

Fuzzy theory is a science used to study and deal with fuzzy phenomena. It was first proposed by the cybernetician L.A. Zadeh of the University of California in 1965. It has been more than 40 years. It is used to process inaccurate and ambiguous data, and is operated through rigorous mathematical methods to solve decision problems in a fuzzy environment [3, 4]. There are many evaluation objectives in the design evaluation, such as aesthetics (overall effect, shape, color, decoration, etc.), pleasantness, safety, processability, etc., which are difficult to perform with traditional quantitative analysis methods. To this end, it is necessary to introduce linguistic variables to describe and solve the problem, and then use fuzzy mathematics to quantify the fuzzy information for quantitative evaluation.

S. W. Hsiao uses fuzzy theory and hierarchical analysis to make product decisions [5]. S. W. Hsiao uses fuzzy theory to conduct monochrome color schemes in the automotive design stage for related evaluation. In addition, he uses fuzzy semantics to make automotive design decisions, and uses the description of the word-to-conversion product design to evaluate computer-aided industrial design and imagery.

In addition, some scholars have proposed computer-aided systems to help design engineers shorten development time and reduce file processing time. Moskowitz and Kim proposed a decision support system for optimal product design in 1997 [6]; Temponi et al. The development of an inference structure in the year can infer the relationship between Customer Requirements (CRs) and Design Requirements

(DRs) [7]. However, developing these systems requires expert knowledge and experience to construct rules while facing problems such as whether the system is functioning well. According to the fuzzy set theory, Kim et al. applied the vendor competition analysis in 1998 to construct the relationship function between CRs and DRs, and proposed a fuzzy multi-objective model, but the construction of these relational functions has its difficulties, especially when developing a brand new product, there is no competitor's data available for analysis [8]. Other scholars apply fuzzy sets, fuzzy operations or defuzzification techniques to deal with complex and inaccurate quality functional problems; however, these methods do not consider the relationship between engineering design requirements. Other scholars emphasize that in addition to determining the degree of execution of DRs based on customer satisfaction, we should also consider organizational conditions such as cost factors and technical difficulties to make an optimal decision that is economical, customer-friendly.

2   Theoretical Background

2.1   Fuzzy Synthetic Evaluation

There are many parameters affecting the function of the trolley, so a comprehensive evaluation of multiple relevant indicators should be considered [3]. This method is the so-called FSE method. The fuzzy evaluation includes the following six parts: determining the impact factor set, determining the factor weight set [4], determining the parameter evaluation set, establishing the factor evaluation matrix, and performing fuzzy evaluation and evaluation index processing, respectively explaining as follows:

2.2   Establishing Affecting Factor Set

When conducting the fuzzy evaluation, it is the first thing to confirm the factors affecting the values of evaluation parameters. If it is known that the affecting factors are $u_1, u_2, \ldots, u_m$, then the factor set composed of these parameters is $U = \{u_1, u_2, \ldots, u_m\}$, and this factor set is a common set.

2.3   Determining Factor Weight Set

To reflect the degree of importance of each factor, each factor u_i should be assigned a corresponding weight w_i. Since the degree of importance of each factor may possibly be different, a weight can be assigned to each factor. The aggregation composed of the weights thus becomes the factor weight set, which is represented as $W = \{w_1, w_2, \ldots, w_m\}$. If w_i indicates the weight of the ith factor, then the weight of each factor should satisfy Eq. (1). It can be represented as a fuzzy subset of the factor set, and the weight set is represented by Eq. (2).

$$\sum_{i=1}^{m} w_i = 1, w_i \geq 0 \ (i = 1, 2, 3, \ldots, m) \tag{1}$$

$$\tilde{W} = \frac{w_1}{u_1} + \frac{w_2}{u_2} + \frac{w_3}{u_3} + \cdots + \frac{w_m}{u_m} = (w_1, w_2, w_3, \cdots, w_m) \qquad (2)$$

where the weight of each factor could be determined by means of weighted coefficient method, the analysis by AHP, and paired comparison method or confirmed subjectively based on those required by the real problem. The weights are obtained by the analysis of analytic hierarchy process which was developed by [3], and examined against the consistency to enhance the reliability.

2.4   Determining Parameter Evaluation Set

An evaluation set is the aggregation composed of various kinds of assessment results on the targets of evaluation by the assessor. It is represented by V, which is $V = \{v_1, v_2, \ldots, v_n\}$, and $v_i (i = 1, 2, 3, \ldots, n)$ represents various kinds of possible results of the overall assessment. The purpose of fuzzy evaluation is to obtain the best assessment result from the evaluation set on the basis of considering all affecting factors comprehensively. The relationship between v_i and V is also a relationship in the form of common set. Therefore an evaluation set is also a common set and the evaluation set is V = {completely agree, agree, neither agree nor disagree, disagree, completely disagree}.

2.5   Establishing Factor Evaluation Matrix

The single factor fuzzy evaluation is to judge one factor separately, and to confirm the degree of membership (DOM) for the target of evaluation toward evaluation-set elements. If the target of evaluation in the factor set is the ith factor U_i, the membership grade of the j th element V_i in the evaluation set is r_{ij}, then according to the results of assessments on the ith factor U_i, it can be represented by the fuzzy set as follows:

$$\tilde{R}_i = \frac{r_{i1}}{v_1} + \frac{r_{i2}}{v_2} + \cdots + \frac{r_{in}}{v_n} = (r_{i1}, r_{i2}, \ldots, r_{in}) \qquad (3)$$

where $\tilde{R}_i$ is called the single-factor evaluation set, it is a fuzzy subset of the evaluation set, which can be represented as $\tilde{R}_i = (r_{i1}, r_{i2}, \ldots, r_{in})$. The single-factor evaluation set corresponding to each factor is similarly available as follows:

$$\begin{aligned} \tilde{R}_1 &= r_{11} + r_{12}, \cdots, r_{1n} \\ \tilde{R}_2 &= r_{21} + r_{22}, \cdots, r_{2n} \\ &\vdots \\ \tilde{R}_m &= r_{m1} + r_{m2}, \cdots, r_{mn} \end{aligned} \qquad (4)$$

The fuzzy matrix composed of the membership grade of each single-factor evaluation set is

$$\tilde{R} = (r_{ij})_{m \times n} = \begin{bmatrix} r_{11} & r_{12} & \cdots & r_{1n} \\ r_{21} & r_{22} & \cdots & r_{2n} \\ \vdots & \vdots & \ddots & \vdots \\ r_{m1} & r_{m2} & \cdots & r_{mn} \end{bmatrix} \tag{5}$$

Equation (5) shown above is called the single-factor assessment matrix. Where $\tilde{R}$ is a fuzzy matrix, and can be also viewed as the fuzzy relational matrix from U to V (i.e., fuzzy mapping). However in this study, due to numerous factors to be considered, it is difficult to obtain a reasonable evaluation result if a single-factor fuzzy evaluation is adopted while each factor usually possesses a differing hierarchy. Therefore, the multi-level fuzzy comprehensive evaluation (FCE) is adopted. This is to conduct a FCE on the basis of another FCE [4], and can be conducted over and over again based on demands. Its reason is that there are numerous factors to be considered in complicated selection, and factors are further divided into levels, therefore the multi-factor assessment matrix should be adopted. The factor set should then be divided into several levels according to its characteristics. Firstly the combined evaluation is conducted on each level, and then in-depth combined evaluations on the evaluation results are conducted.

2.6 Conducting Fuzzy Composite Operations

If the fuzzy evaluation matrix of a certain scheme onto the evaluation target is as Eq. (5), considering the weighted comprehensive fuzzy evaluation, the product of fuzzy matrices is then

$$\tilde{B} = \tilde{W} \bullet \tilde{R} = (b_1, b_2, \cdots b_j, \cdots b_n) \tag{6}$$

where symbol "$\bullet$" represents fuzzy composite operations. By means of the weight fuzzy matrix $\tilde{W}$, and factor judgment matrix $\tilde{R}$; there are many kinds of composition methods shown as follows.

【Model 1】When applying the composition by algorithm M $(\wedge, \vee)$, the result is

$$b_j = \bigvee_{i=1}^{m} (w_i \wedge r_{ij}) \quad ; \quad j = 1, 2, \ldots, n \tag{7}$$

【Model 2】When applying the composition by algorithm M $(\bullet, \vee)$, the result is

$$b_j = \bigvee_{i=1}^{m} (w_i r_{ij}) \quad ; \quad j = 1, 2, \ldots, n \tag{8}$$

【Model 3】When applying the composition by algorithm M $(\wedge, +^\circ)$, the result is

$$b_j = \min\{1, \sum_{i=1}^{m} (w_i \wedge r_{ij})\}; j = 1, 2, \ldots, n \tag{9}$$

【Model 4】 When applying the composition by algorithm M $(\bullet, +\,^\circ)$, the result is

$$b_j = \min\{1, \sum_{i=1}^{m} w_i r_{ij}\} \quad ; \quad j = 1, 2, \ldots, n \qquad (10)$$

This model is also called weighted-average (WA) type, and its characteristic is that when w_i is provided with normalization, i.e., $\sum_{i=1}^{m} w_i = 1, \sum_{i=1}^{m} w_i r_{ij} \ll 1$, then said model will be adapted as M $(\bullet, +)$, and then

$$b_j = \sum_{i=1}^{m} w_i r_{ij} \quad ; \quad j = 1, 2, \ldots, n; \quad \sum_{i=1}^{m} w_i = 1 \qquad (11)$$

This model not only considers the influence of all factors, but also keeps the entire message of the single-factor evaluation. When in operation there is no confinement for w_i and r_{ij} on the upper limit, and it is only required to perform normalization on w_i. This is the prominent characteristic and merit of this model.

The principles of Model 1 to 3 are all in search of individual evaluation result under a condition of taking limit values with a certain kind of limitation. Therefore, to varying degrees it will lose a lot of useful information during the evaluation process. This can be used in occasions only concerned with the limit values of things and with an intention to make a certain primary factor stand out. Based on this, Model 4 is adopted as the operational method for composition in this study.

6. Processing of evaluation indices

After obtaining evaluation indices $b_j (j = 1, 2, \ldots, n)$, the concrete results of the target of evaluation can thus be confirmed based on the method of maximum DOM and WA method, and they are explained as follows.

2.7   Maximum DOM

In light of the principle of maximum membership, the corresponding evaluation element v_i to the largest evaluation index b_j is selected as the evaluation result. This method considers only the contribution of the maximum evaluation index, and discards the information provided by other indices. Besides, when the number of the largest evaluation indices is more than one, it is hard to determine any concrete evaluation result by the method of maximum DOM. Therefore the WA method will usually be adopted.

2.8   WA Method

b_j is taken as the weighting factor, and each evaluation element v_j is taken as the result of evaluation by carrying out the weighted average, i.e.,

$$D = \frac{\sum\limits_{j=1}^{n} b_j v_j}{\sum\limits_{j=1}^{n} b_j} \quad (12)$$

if the evaluation index bj is normalized, then

$$D = \sum\limits_{j=1}^{n} b_j v_j \quad (13)$$

If the targets of evaluation are quantitative numbers, then the value of D is calculated by Eq. (13). This value is thus the result of conducting FCE on said quantity. If the targets of evaluation are non-quantitative numbers, for example if the evaluation set is {Excellent, Good, Fair, Bad}, then for the time being it is required to apply quantification on non-quantitative numbers of Excellent, Good, Fair, Bad. Or otherwise the method of maximum DOM must be adopted. Through various evaluation standards mentioned above, the distribution status of the target of evaluation in the characteristic aspect being evaluated can be concretely reflected. The referee can then have an even thorough understanding of the target of evaluation, and can handle this with good flexibility.

2.9   Analytic Hierarchy Process

Hierarchical analysis is a set of decision-making methods proposed by Saaty (1980), which is mainly applied to uncertainties and decision-making problems with multiple multi-criteria [9]. AHP is characterized by a systematic system of complex multi-criteria problems in a concise hierarchical structure. By means of decision makers, the relative importance of the criteria in the same level is compared in pairs, and a pairwise comparison matrix is established to obtain the criteria. Relatively important, the total priority vector of the overall level after the hierarchical string is calculated, that is, the weight of each evaluation criterion. This quantitative result can assist decision makers in the quantitative and comprehensive evaluation of alternatives to identify prioritization of the program and reduce the risk of decision errors. Liu et al. proposed a new weight calculation method, which replaces the pairwise comparison of AHP. Its operation method is called Voting Analytic Hierarchy Process. This method is simpler than AHP, and systematically calculates the weight, and compares the advantages and disadvantages of the supplier with the scores obtained by each supplier.

The operational process of the hierarchical analysis method can be mainly divided into the following five steps:

Step 1: Defining the decision problem.
Step 2: Establish a hierarchical structure.
Step 3: Establish a pairwise comparison matrix. Table 1 is the evaluation scale and relative definition of the hierarchical analysis.
Step 4: Calculate the eigen value.
Step 5: Consistency check.

Table 1. Evaluation scale and relative definition of level analysis

Evaluation scale	Definition
1	Equally important
3	Slightly important
5	Important
7	Extremely important
9	Absolutely important
2, 4, 6, 8	Intermediate insertion value

To calculate the feature vector in step four, there are several algorithms:

(1) Theoretical analysis (Eigenvalue and Eigenvector).
(2) Saaty proposes four approximate solutions: the normalization of the average of the column vectors, also known as the normalization of the Row Average, the normalization of the average of the row vectors, also known as the ANC (Average of Normalized Columns), The normalization of the column vector geometric mean, also known as the normalization of the Geometric Mean of the Rows, and the normalization of the row vector mean.

The consistency check in step 5 is to confirm that the experts are in a pairwise comparison, and the evaluation results are consistent, that is, the expert's preference relationship with the criteria satisfies the recursion. Saaty recommends testing with Consistency Index (*C.I.*) and Consistency Ratio (*C.R.*). If the values of *C.I.* and *C.R.* are both less than 0.1, it means that the paired matrix has consistency. When there is no consistency. The formulas for *C.I.* and *C.R.* are as follows:

$$C.I. = \frac{\lambda_{max} - n}{n - 1} \tag{14}$$

λ_{max} Is the maximum eigenvalue of the matrix
n Matrix order (number of parameters)

$$C.R. = \frac{C.I.}{R.I.} \tag{15}$$

$C.R. < 0.1 \Rightarrow OK$
$C.R. = Consistency\ ratio$
$C.I. = Consistency\ index$
$R.I. = Randan\ index$

3   Case Design

The purpose of this study is to first establish the evaluation indicators for the TENS manual testr the classification and induction of wind turbine grade items. In order to confirm the relevance of the preliminary selection indicators, we used semi-structured interviews to allow experts in related fields to target the computer-integrated TENS manual testr. The expertise of individual judges assesses the importance of each item and corrects or supplements these assessment indicators. Therefore, the establishment of selection indicators, including the first level of the target level (i.e., the final goal); the second layer is the objective layer, with a total of five main aspects; the third level covers 19 evaluation criteria. In order to conduct a system evaluation analysis, the selection factors related to the indicators are summarized and a hierarchical structure is established (as shown in Fig. 1, there are many factors in Fig. 1 that affect the selection of TENS manual testr, so the degree of influence of each factor Using a systematic method to combine and calculate the impact of each factor to obtain quantitative results.

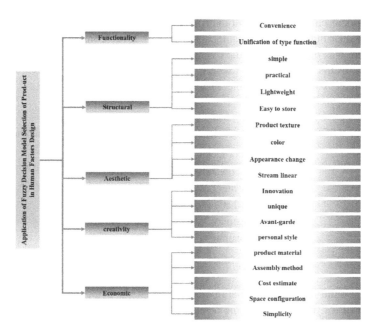

Fig. 1. Factors influence the choice of TENS manual testr

3.1   AHP Weights

The results of the questionnaire have been quantified. Interviewed 21 professionals, including 9 industry-related owners and 12 industry-related employees. The factors that evaluated the TENS manual test index were evaluated and AHP was performed. The fuzzy combination method model 3 is used to calculate the evaluation index, and the final evaluation result is obtained.

In order to reflect the importance of each factor, it was decided to use AHP to find the relative weight. The weight ratio is chosen by experts and scholars. The questionnaire includes research description letters, questionnaire descriptions and examples, importance intensity criteria, indicator levels, explanations and items, and compares the importance of the two factors in each system. The assessment scale can basically be divided into five levels. These five levels are equally important, slightly important, quite important, very important and absolutely important. Their values are 1, 3, 5, 7, and 9, respectively. There are four levels between the scales, which represent 2, 4, 6, and 8. On the left scale, the factors on the left are important to the right. In contrast, the right scale indicates that the right factor is important to the left factor. Ask an expert to review the appropriate assessment items.

According to the analytic hierarchy process, it can be known that the judgment matrix at that time has satisfactory consistency, which indicates that the weight distribution is reasonable. The selection index (function, structure, aesthetics, creativity, economy) has a CR value of 0.01, and the "function" CR value of the lower factor is 0.02; the "structure" CR value is 0.02; the "aesthetic" CR value is 0.02; "creativity" CR value is 0.01; "economic" CR value is 0.02. According to the above C.R value of 0.2, it can be considered that the judgment matrix has satisfactory consistency, indicating that the weight distribution is reasonable. The overall level consistency check of the questionnaire was determined by the overall consistency ratio C.R, C.R was 0.02, and the research results were consistent with C.R. 0.1, indicating that the assessment of the entire hierarchy is acceptable (Table 2).

Table 2. TENS manual test weight set for selecting the upper limit of the indicator

Sort	Upper factor	Weight	C.R.
1	Functionality (U_1)	0.125	0.02
2	Structural (U_2)	0.352	
3	Aesthetic (U_3)	0.241	
4	Creativity (U_4)	0.135	
5	Economic (U_5)	0.147	

It can be found from Table 3 that in the overall scheme evaluation, the design of the TENS manual test is also part of the aesthetic study. We must not only choose some schemes, but also design aesthetic schemes, and finally choose the schemes that the subjects think are the most satisfactory. The value of Option 1 after defuzzification is 0.721, which is a satisfactory level, and then 0.721 (between the normal levels) of Option 1. Therefore, the overall evaluation result is supported by the most decision-making power of Option 1. The solution is not only functional, aesthetic and economical. In terms of sexual considerations, it also has a good performance in designing the function of the TENS handlebar, that is, the program is the best design that can be achieved in the overall design.

When there are multiple design schemes in the product design case, the evaluation system can be used to determine the weight, and the degree of influence of each index on the overall product performance can be judged to further optimize the design process. However, when the raw data of each function is not available or the performance cannot be quantitatively expressed, the qualitative indicators can be set by setting the evaluation value of each element to form a judgment matrix using a fuzzy comprehensive evaluation method, and the fuzzy comprehensive evaluation can be performed to find the most suitable the design of. In this program, this evaluation method is conducive to the quantification of qualitative indicators, thereby reducing the subjectivity of the product development process and facilitating the rapid development of products. Combining the aesthetics of the style, the TENS manual test can increase the aesthetics of the product. In the past, designers and manufacturers mostly considered self-consciousness, and using the basic principles of fuzzy theory can effectively show the weight of various factors.

Table 3. Satisfaction value and defuzzification value of the design case

Design case	Very consistent	Meets the	Ordinary	Incompatible	Very inconsistent	Defuzzication
1	0.302	0.383	0.252	0.063	0.000	0.721
2	0.286	0.254	0.275	0.185	0.000	0.690
3	0.271	0.319	0.221	0.189	0.000	0.661

4   Conclusions

This research proposes a new analytic hierarchy process that combines fuzzy theory with numerical analysis. First, AHP is used to calculate weights that affect the importance of performance parameters. Various parameters are then satisfied. Model 1 has proven to be the best of all designs. The results obtained using the deblurring values to obtain fuzzy weights are also consistent with the results of numerical analysis. The engineering evaluation required for the overall design of any TENS manual test product can be achieved through fuzzy decision methods. This approach focuses on the overall evaluation of the design and the new evaluation of performance. In other words, in addition to improving the outline of the TENS manual test, the entire evaluation method has also been improved as the basis for the overall new aesthetic evaluation model of the TENS manual test. When using fuzzy decision methods in design, this involves complexity associated with different levels. For further research, it is suggested to emphasize the improvement of the TENS manual test function based on cost considerations. When redesigning the TENS manual test product, the evaluation method proposed in this study can be used to study any newly designed concepts and structures, and can reduce the time and effort spent on actual testing.

This study evaluates the weight value of the project and the fuzzy membership weight of each component, which can provide designers with an objective reference when designing the appearance of the design or selecting the priority of parts when performing the TENS manual tester design. Its five evaluation items already include most of the visual area of the overall appearance of the TENS manual measurement handle, which can reduce the disadvantage of only evaluating a single item in the past without considering the integrity of the shape. For subsequent research, this article suggests that the number of styles under each evaluation item can be increased to enrich the database of shapes; in addition, it is recommended to search for styles after a period of time in order to observe the market trend of consumers. In the future, we can refer to the evaluation model of this article to discuss the shape appearance, so that consumers can not only consider the functionality, but also meet the preference for shape appearance.

References

1. Sun, J.H., Tsai, H.C., Chen, S.I.: Using triangles to blur the preferences of different types of consumers. In: The 17th National Conference on Fuzzy Theory and Its Applications, vol. 17, 396–401 (2009)
2. Hu, T.W., Liao, Y.T.: The effects of consumer's visual cognition on the feature composition of bicycle frames. J. Chaoyang Univ. Technol. **15**, 283–300 (2010)
3. Zadeh, L.A.: Fuzzy sets. Inf. Control **8**, 338–353 (1965)
4. Zadeh, L.A.: The concept of a linguistic variable and its application to approximate reasoning I. Inf. Sci. **8**, 199–249 (1975)
5. Hsiao, S.W.: Fuzzy logic based decision model for product design. Int. J. Ind. Ergon. **21**, 103–116 (1998)
6. Moskowitz, H., Kim, K.J.: QFD optimizer: a novice friendly quality function deployment decision support system for optimizing product designs. Comput. Ind. Eng. **32**(3), 641–655 (1997)
7. Temponi, C., Yen, J., Tian, W.A.: House of quality: a fuzzy logic-based requirements analysis. Eur. J. Oper. Res. **117**, 340–354 (1999)
8. Kim, J.K., Han, C.H., Choi, S.H.: A knowledge-base approach to the quality function deployment. Comput. Ind. Eng. **35**(1–2), 233–236 (1998)
9. Saaty, T.L.: The Analytic Hierarchy Process. McGraw-Hill, New York (1980)

Research on Smart Care System
for Elder Sojourners

Feng Liu[(✉)]

Shandong College of Tourism and Hospitality,
Jinan 250200, People's Republic of China
lfstela@163.com

Abstract. The world population is aging, especially in Asia and Europe. Rapid aging poses seriously threats and challenges to elder care service. With the development of economy, seniors are visioning quality life expectation. Sojourning, which means staying in a place outside of one's inhabitant home for some period of time, is getting popular with the growth of seniors' income and education level, the number of senior sojourners are expected to increase in a significant speed in the near future. The paper conducted a detailed analysis and carding on smart care system, from both literature and market perspectives. The paper surveyed the requirements and difficulties standing on the way of quality senior sojourners, and proposed a framework design on the basis of Microsoft IoT platform, to set a smart care system. The purpose is to physically and mentally support those old people living out dependently, if the design is accepted by all sides, it would be a win-win business for senior sojourners, their guardians/children and relatives, IT enterprises and even the local governments.

Keywords: Smart care · Platform · System · Quality senior sojourn life

1 Introduction

Statistics show that most economies are stepping into aging society, especially in Asia and Europe. In Japan, Germany and Italy, over 25% of the population are seniors. Similar thing is happening in China. About 250 million people are aged over 60 at present, which accounts for 17.3% of Chinese population. In 2037, senior Chinese aged 60 or above are expected to take up to 400 million (28.5% out of total). The number of newly retired citizens, who were born from 1950s to 1970s, will increase rapidly in the coming years. China would be a country with the world's largest aging population soon.

Unlike traditional seniors, these people with higher pension are proficient internet and high-tech products users, and they are better-educated, and more energetic and independent in wealth, hobbies and lifestyle. They long for qualify senior life with dignity, self-fulfillment and better experiences. With the development of AI and smart tech, online elderly care service is getting more convenient, long-ranged and accessible, which makes sojourn, at home or abroad, easy and enjoyable. Based on Artificial Intelligence and smart networks, seniors can be served with safer, quicker and more reliable devices to strengthen their poor hearing, touching and eyesight, it is also feasible for them to obtain online health care and psychological and mental comfort,

© Springer Nature Switzerland AG 2020
Q. Gao and J. Zhou (Eds.): HCII 2020, LNCS 12208, pp. 113–127, 2020.
https://doi.org/10.1007/978-3-030-50249-2_9

which is crucial for the old, and a great concern for sojourners' children. At present, smart elderly care is mainly based on GIS, GPS, LBS, SMS, MAS, TTS, database and various APPs to set loop systems and establish O2O community elderly care service platforms. The government in China encourages and supports various sets of smart care system to improve the seniors' life experience with the help of social service workers and local community. Up to now, high-tech devices, like smart bracelet, smart crutch, smart watch, are best sellers in markets, and ALiGenie comes recently with more functions like voice interaction and visual recognition. At the same time, intelligent robots with diverse functions are entering ordinary people's life and getting prevalent with the clients. The old in urban China have easy access at home to comprehensive care service platform that provide first aid, health care, emotional support, living care and further education. All of these need a large technical team to build, maintain and upgrade, which results in keep investing and fixing. The trouble is that the system merely works well at local level, provided that he/she tries a sojourn life in rural areas or at abroad, it is hard to plug into local elderly care platform, and smart sojourn care becomes a daydream. What's more, how to keep tremendous personal data safe is also a substantial issue, and furthermore, it is a cooperative task for all sides, including the government, community, tourism and IT enterprises, social worker and the senior him/herself.

The paper tries to collect documents and analyze the achievements and barriers on domestic senior sojourn or expatriates care, physically and mentally, by means of investigation and documentary research, summarizing studies from the dimensions of paperwork, products, platform and system. The purpose is to testify the possibility to build up an integrate sharing smart care system at a global level. The results illustrate that elder sojourners are more independent and skillful in deciding on tourism products, the majority of them would rather pick DIY Itineraries, pushing travel agencies to advance their products and services. Moreover, social workers in hottest sojourn spots need more training to understand elder sojourners and meet diverse customer needs. It is crucial for the governments to join together and support a global shared elderly care system, with unitary quality controlling standards, close information safety supervision and efficient health care system. If the system proves to be friendly and helpful to the energetic retired seniors, it would benefit all elder people who desire high quality old life, no matter what the race and nationality is. In addition, it would be a significant chance for the travel industry to welcome a boom of gray-haired economy.

The rest parts of the paper are as follows: Sect. 2 is illustrations of works related to the paper, introducing the definitions and technologies concerned; Sect. 3 is about the investigation to the senior sojourners for their requirements and obstacles in sojourn life. In Sect. 4, the detailed implement is proposed and Sect. 5 is the conclusion.

2   Related Work

The idea of smart care system for senior sojourners crosses several borders, including smart care, Internet of things (IoT), smart home, smart health care platform, senior sojourners, etc., all have been deeply researched in recent years.

2.1 Smart Care

Smart care is also called smart elderly care, smart senior care, or intellectual endowment. There is no widely accepted definition for it up to now, and no clear research clue. Generally speaking, smart care means a timely, swift, efficient and low cost service for old people living at home, community, or care center, based on advanced technologies like IoT, Internet and smart devices [1]. According to Meiyu, Zuo, a professor in Renmin University of China, smart care is a set of life service and management based on complex information technology (internet, social net, IoT, mobile computing, cloud computing, big data, etc. Smart care covers automatically monitoring, predicting, hand handling data of the old people, on their daily life, security, health and medical care, entertainment, learning and sharing knowledge. It is friendly and personal interactive, and an efficient way to improve the old people's life quality, for it enlightens their sense of happiness, value and self-esteem [2].

Early to the 1980s, WHO began to promote health care and positive elderly care around the world. Actually the research of smart home care started from the end of 1990s, robots and smart home care devices were practiced and implemented to solve some difficulties that the elders meet in their daily life. The phrase "smart care" was first visioned by National Life Trust in Britain. It tried to provide fully intelligent senior care service for the old, regardless of the time and distance, with the help of network technology and information platform, chips were implanted to home care devices, which worked as sensors to monitor the old to keep them in security and health care in their daily life at home. In December, 2008, IBM introduced "Smart Earth" and "Smart City", and then countries like the U.S, Germany, Japan, Korea and Singapore set out to build "Smart City" and went further for "Smart Care". Chinese government also began to enhance informative elderly care in 2008.

Avinash M, Sathwik Rai M.S and Prof. VIjay Kumar P worked together and developed a 4 System Architecture smart home system based on Wi-Fi, cloud technology and monitoring server, Wireless Sensor Networks (WSNs) and GPS to track and sense the elders and monitor the elder's detailed behavioral status through internet to provide the old safe, sound and secure living through sensors to automatically warn the care taker in emergency, like LPG leakage, and fall detection [3]. In August 2, 2016, Philips released a smart analyzer of the body, a health watch, a thermometer and a blood pressure monitor. These different kinds of Smart health care products can be used with the Philips HealthSuite application, which are compatible with Android and iOS systems. Health and fitness applications (apps) are one of the major app categories in the current mobile app market.

2.2 IoT and Smart Care

The concept of Internet of things (IoT) was created in the late 1990s by Kevin Ashton, a British engineer and a professor in MIT University, who started a research programme and developed key technologies in IoT, like Auto-Id, RFID standard, Electronic Product Code (EPC) and Universal Product Code (UPC). He mentioned in a speech (at POEIPC, 2016 in Beijing) that Internet of Things technology (can be called the 3rd industrial revolution, industry 4.0) is a "world-data-decision-world" system, all the objects in the world can be smart objects through intercommunication and interconnection based on internet technology. It also works at smart care by integrating those networks using sensor technology by giving computer sensors e.g. GPS, blood pressure, heart beat in clients' smart phone, and the smart phone can gather data from the sensors itself automatically without you-creates data-data collected from reports from system, spreadsheet, pie chart, human perception–pattern – decision may be communicate with human beings or with a machine automatic system-leads to some change in the world, especially in wearable devices, smart home and auto-drive car.

Jaimini and Shruti (2017) proposed an E-care system to monitor accurate ECG signal by developing portable sensor device and using IoT, to improve accuracy, EMD empirical mode decomposition is introduced to classify ECG signal, an E-care system is beneficial, it enables people to take care of themselves on a daily basis, the system works well and the real time ECG data send to the IoT cloud, the measured data provide to hospitals or relatives in emergency [4].

Ramachandran Manikandan et al. [5] Proposed Hash Polynomial Two-factor Decision Tree (HP-TDT), which is an IoT-based scheduling method of three stages (including registration, data collection and scheduling stage), to increase scheduling efficiency and reduce response time. Patients were classified into being normal or in a critical state in minimal time, the researchers integrate Smart Health Care system with the Cloud environment, which makes it possible for the system to ensure patient prioritization according to disease prevalence.

Microsoft IoT Central was released in 2017 and the platform allows every company all over the world to build up its own IoT application without concerning about the platform architecture and technology, Microsoft also announced in 2018 to invest us $ 5 billion on IoT, e.g. Microsoft Azure IoT, through cloud computing, operating system and facilities. Nokia, Siemens and other enterprises are competing in the field. In China, Baidu combined cloud computing, big data and artificial intelligence together and developed its IoT platform, Alibaba's Link platform built Internet of Beings to promote networks at daily life, industry and city construction. Tencent, based on its huge users on QQ and Wechat, built an open platform for wearable devices, smart home, smart Auto, and traditional hardware, to realize a stable and reliable users-devices-devices-devices automatic interconnection and intercommunication. Other enterprises, including China Mobile and China Telecom joined the team as well, OneNet has advantage on its low cost, while NB-IoT of China Telecom is built on 4G network, which covers the largest area and boasts the most stable IoT platform.

2.3   Sensors, Wearable Devices and Smart Home

Scientists and engineers have successfully connected sensors and intelligent devices to monitor the people remotely so that they can obtain some physical checkup results to help build up healthy habit, avoid sudden illness and get instant warning and rescue in danger. Aminian, K. et al. (2011) did several researches on smart sensing equipment and technology and he set a shoe-worn inertial module to detect and prevent falling for the elderly people by inserting wearable sensors in shoes and collecting diverse parameters to assess daily physical activities of the old people, including the status of sitting and standing [6]. In 2013, a project named "Trillion Sensors Universe" was proposed at TSensors Summit in U.S, to promote and improve efficiency over the world through a trillion of sensors. Current sensors can be wearable, portable, fixed, movable, non-contact, in which wearable devices are the most popular. Intelligent wearable devices are smart, handy, convenient and multifunctional they can keep monitoring and intervene when something is wrong with the old. The wearable devices collect the checkup results and upload the data automatically and instantly to the health center and guardian or relatives. The process of uploading, saving, analyzing and feeding back can be easily achieved on the basis of Person Digital Assistant (PDA), a smart phone or pad, with Wi-Fi, Bluetooth, Global Positioning System (GPS) and Global System for Mobile Communications (GSM), no matter 2G, 3G, 4G, or even 5G. Current wearable devices are working well to monitor the old people's heartbeat, breathing, temperature, blood pressure, blood glucose, blood oxygen, etc. There are also floor sensors, kitchen sensors, door sensors, light sensors... you name it! Consumers can buy various intelligent devices, like smart bracelet, smart crutch, smart watch, and smart clothes like hat, hairband, socks and even shoes in the market, which would be a trend in the near future.

In the field of academic research, Kyung Hee University in Korea and Chinese Academy of Sciences published the largest amount of papers in recent years. The former researchers designed wearable devices and smart home for the seniors and make effort to improve life quality of the old, including individual activity sensor, health monitor for single seniors and wireless sensor networks and its usage in sensitive monitoring and tracking applications. They also noticed the importance of ensuring complete security for the old; researchers of the later academy focus on interaction design and IoT environment architecture, they devoted to design health smart devices, the purpose is to improve life quality, they also work on assistant environment design, sensor devices and senior concerned illness and cases research.

Chan M (2009) defined smart home as a housing system, equipped with sensors, electronic stoppers and biomedical monitors, to help monitor the inhabitants living alone and keep them in physical and mental health. He predicted that smart home system would be the mainstream of future medical care [7]. Skubic M (2015) focused his research on sensor devices usage of the old people, he surveyed old people's requirement and preference on household sensor technology and assessed old people at home, especially those who live alone. He proposed a health change detection model. He monitored continuously in the home through sensors embedded in the environment to capture behavior and activity patterns and detected potential signs of changing health. The system alerts and provides a method for detecting health problems at very early time to make early treatment possible [8]. Several countries and enterprises followed on and a lot of smart home products were put into market. Amazon pushed Echo to the public in 2014, together with its voice assistant Alexa, later the company developed and opened API, to join in smart home market. Alexa has been making progress from the day it was created, and can control Microwave or even auto in 2018. Apple company released HomeKit into market in 2015, which is compatible with Apple devices, like iPhone, IPad, Ipod Touch, the accessories can control lights, outlets, thermostats, windows, air conditioners, doorbells, locks, speakers, fans and other household applicants, the number grows and it comes to over 200 now. In 2016, Google introduced Brillo and Nest which were extended of Android to the smart home and built on the work of Nest, later the company launched Google Home, boasts to enjoy music and entertainment throughout the entire house, easily manage everyday tasks and get answers from Google, now Google Assistant is compatible with over 5000 and supports nearly all the main household appliance in the U.S. Up to Sep. 2019, Alexa has become the most popular intelligent voice assistant in Northern American market, and Amazon is leading the industry with supporting over 12,000 smart home products. Windows and Sumsung (SmartThings) also joined the competition these years. Microsoft, cooperated with Harman/Kardon, released Ivoke to market in 2018. Ivoke is integrated with voice assistant Cortana, which can connect Win 10, iOs and Android, and Skype, the hottest instant communication software, to talk freely. Invoke supports facilities from other smart home products, like SmartTHings and Nest. China is the fastest growing smart home market in the world, Hi-tech manufactures like Huawei, Baidu, Xiaomi and other companies launched their smart home products and boom the market in recent years. It is estimated by Global Market Insight that smart home market will grow up to US \$53.45 billion in 2022. Being inserted with modern sensors into smart home, it can do fall prevention, help old people with weak health status and communicate with them and solve some mental problems like depression and loneliness.

Consumers have witnessed the flourish in research towards clinical rehabilitation systems in smart home applications, which are needed to provide instant and timely motion information about patients. Tongqian Peng (2019) proposed a motion detecting approach, on the basis of IoT architecture and fuzzy neural network (FNN), to collect the human movement information efficiently, wearable sensing devices are used In the research and achieved a high accuracy [9]. Most smart home products are based on voice assistant, for the seniors with poor earring, they would not work so well as the youngsters, what's more, a set of smart home is not cheap at present, and it needs a lot of preparation to set them.

Some research was done from the users' perspective. Kharrazi et al. (2012) evaluated stand-alone mobile personal health record (mPHR) applications for iOS, Black-Berry, and Android, which are the top 3 leading cellular phone platforms [10]. They also assessed the content, function, security, and marketing characteristics of each platform separately. They referred that more people are concerning about their health, and mPHR is an emerging health care technology. Microsoft's software "healthy storage library" is another platform that recorded personal health data. Consumers are allowed to track their own health information, and safely share their health information with relevant service and individuals, like clinicians, nursing staff, family members and so on. Wei Peng, Shupei Yuan et al. (2016) adopted the Extended Unified Theory of Acceptance and Use of Technology (UTAUT2) Model, the purpose is to examine the users' intention to use health and fitness apps and determine the design and elements of health apps that facilitate or impede usage. They did research on challenges and opportunities of health apps and make suggestion on development and evaluation to health Apps [11].

2.4 Smart Care System

Smart care system is a loop system connecting the seniors, information collective devices, platform and clinicians, nursing staff and first-aid service. A system was introduced by Lemlouma, T. (2013), who built a framework for automatic dependency evaluation to monitor the changes of the elderly dependency, on a flexible architecture and an extensible model linked to opened data, referring to a wide variety of services, e.g. hardware sensors, software, simple or composed services. The purpose is to provide required services in time [12]. Chien-Nan Lee (2012) proposed a home care service platform for mobile health care with a smart phone as a platform to effectively assist medical staff in carrying out home visits and home care services [13]. The platform aids with tasks such as data download, synchronized operation, and photo or video recording, it also helps to track the patients' health status as well. To meet the requirements of assistance services of disabled and old people, Alberto and his team (2019) designed automatic eAssistance home system that can be widely used and integrated into users' home to monitor the user's activities and to improve the self-sufficiency of dependents [14]. The system is based on Ambient Intelligence (AmI) and good at Activity recognition and Behaviour patterns inference. At present, smart elderly care is mainly based on GIS, GPS, LBS, SMS, MAS, TTS, database and various APPs to set loop systems and establish O2O community elderly care service platforms. The government in China encourages and supports various sets of smart care system to improve the senior' life experience with the help of social service workers and local community. As for the cost, some system are set up by government, for free, some are set by enterprises, the government pays for part of the construction, operation and maintenance, others are paid by enterprises themselves.

2.5 Sojourners

The word "sojourner" was originated from "The Chinese Migrant in Hawaii", a PH.D thesis written by Click, C.E in 1938. In 1952, Paul C.P. Siu, a Chicago PHD student, defined a sojourner as an individual who has lived abroad for a long time without being assimilated by it (Siu 1952: 34) and still being a stranger or marginal man to the nearby neighborhood. The concept changed with time. According to "Evaluation Standard for Senior Sojourners Services" [15] issued in 2015 in China, senior sojourners are those who stayed at places outside of their inhabitant areas or countries for over 15 days and returned home after the tour. World Tourism Organization surveyed and made an analysis that a vacation tour is widely accepted when average GDP is over 5,000 US Dollars per person. At present, sojourners are mainly consists of people who were born before the 1960s, who are going to their 60 s in a few years and retire from work, most of the group are well educated and better paid, they have leisure time, money and interest for sojourn life. Statistics show that most economies are stepping into aging society, especially in Asia and Europe. China is the fastest aging country in the world, with 2410 million people over 60 years old, in 2020, the number would be over 2500 million. It is for sure that the huge number of seniors would boom great smart care market.

Unlike traditional seniors, these people with higher pension are proficient internet and high-tech products users, and they are better-educated, and more energetic and independent in wealth, hobbies and lifestyle. They long for qualify senior life with dignity, self-fulfillment and better experiences. According to AgeClub and Chinese Sojourn Bluebook (2018), a large number of newly retired people in big cities prefer sojourn life to elderly care at home, alone or with families and close friends, to enjoy fresher air, more beautiful view, diverse cultures and more relaxed lifestyle before they are getting too old to travel and stay at satisfying places. Statistics (from Homelink Research) shows in the first half of the year 2018, most aged tourists are those people from 60–75 years old, and over 80% of which are between 60 and 70, most of them are willing to take a long-term tour, 47% chooses a tour lasts 2–3 months, 31% likes 4–5 months. As for sojourn tourist destination, the most prevailing ones are in Europe, with Japan and Australia to follow up. Although they don't have a definite destination or time to travel in general, American seniors like the coast or Mexico for a sojourn, whereas Japanese prefer small places in Philippines, and some Chinese people move with seasons, for example, they go to Hainan or Guangxi provinces for winter, others go abroad to accompany their children or babysit their grandchildren of just for fun. Most of the senior sojourners are experienced tourists and willing to pay for improved service and seniors-oriented AI products. The booming market, which would be a trend in fast developing countries, is updating current tourism industry and appealing to integrated smart sojourn care. In developed countries, after retirement sojourn care emerged long time ago and has set several successful models in European countries, like those in Bo01, Malmo, Sweden; Greenwich, London and Fliedner, Germany, etc. They are costumed to intelligent products, like smart phones, wearable devices, and online communications. They would even live together with a multifunctional AI robot in the future.

Fengman Xu (2014) analyzed the seniors in Taiwai and found old people are concerned more about physical and economy safety, and they long for social involvement, communal participation and self-fulfillment [16] Ying Guo (2015) investigated the old people in community in Wuhan, China, trying to set up an information framework based on local senior requirements [17].

Problems: With similar technology and function, devices of different major brands cannot be interconnected, every product has its own service system of unique a device terminal server, users have to buy various of smart devices and purchase, learn and operate various smart system, which is a complicated and complex task, especially for the old. Each system works under its platform, and is bad at compatibility, what's more, most wearable devices can deal with limited illness, it would be a burden for the dependent seniors to handle different illnesses that are bothering them. What's more, the safety of personal data cannot be guaranteed. Lack of efficient design at top level is another problem, there is no basic systemic framework that is approved by most researchers or manufacturers. Most communities developed platform of their own, there is no compatibility among them, and it costs a lot for the old. There is no mature business module at present, and a general criteria is missing.

Solutions: It is necessary to set up an integrated platform system and unite all the terminal service ports, correspondence and service, on the basis of internet of everything, a IoT platform is needed to provide safe and reliable correspondence service, connecting trillions of information and equipment, upload the data to icloud API, the service port makes use of the uploaded data and orders the electronic devices to fulfil remote control task.

3 Survey

The objective is to understand the principal demands of senior sojourners through analyzing their physical and mental health, economic status, social participation, and expectations for senior sojourn support.

3.1 Content and Objective of the Survey

The questions to be answered are as follows:

A. The willingness and reasons to choose a sojourn life.
B. Besides basic demands, what are they emotionally longing for? e.g. loneliness or isolation problem, social participation and communication needs?
C. How much do they rely on their relationship with children and relatives in elderly care?
D. How well do they know about smart elderly care, what services supported them effectively?
E. Do they have a stable pension, are they economically independent to cover their sojourn expense?
F. What are the most concerned problems of these senior sojourners?

3.2 Methodology

Questionnaires: The author prepared 300 questionnaires designed on the above questions and handed out to international tourists aged from 50–70 years old at international airports by tour guides and leaders, most of whom are former students in our college. The author also asked Mr. Cao Chengde, one of the colleagues who attended the 2nd World Senior Tourism Congress, which was held on May 24–26, 2019, in Yantai, Shandong province, P.R.C., to hand out the questionnaires to researchers and entrepreneurs at the meeting. In the end, 282 questionnaires are collected and 275 of them are completed and valid.

Interviews: The author interviewed three of the acquaintances for detailed senior sojourners information, either by Smart phone or online. One is a 65-year-old friend who is babysitting his grandchildren in Melbourne, Australia, another one is a former colleague who is retired and accompanying her daughter, a postgraduate student in University College London. The last one is a 51-year-old friend who spent 1 month in Kumanon, Japan for a month tour during last winter vocation.

3.3   Results

Basic information of the participants: 73.4% of the participants are female, and 62% of them are aged between 51 and 60, 61% of them prefer to spend a sojourn life with close friends, 43% would like to join sojourn centers with the help of agencies, while 36% choose to spend the time quietly with one's spouse, only 16% is willing to be a sojourner living alone. As for educational background, nearly half of the participants accepted higher education and have a degree, over 1/4 of them finished their high school learning, only 15% of them finished 9-year-education or below. 96% of them have been to an overseas country, and 53% of them have stayed at a place out of their permanent residence for over 1 month. The hottest dream destinations are those with beaches, sunshine for a slow and leisurely life. Answers to questions to be surveyed are as follows: A: we found that 89.3% of the participants are interested in or has been experienced some pattern of sojourn life, no matter going abroad or at home, although the reasons are multiple and various. The most popular reason goes to fresh air and pleasant climate, which takes the highest percentage (93.1%), sightseeing comes after with a percentage of 86.2%, and culture experience (68.2%) follows, 64.7% of them choose to sojourn because of their children need them to help with housework and babysitting, other reasons are business (9.1%), job opportunity (6.3%), further learning (4.6%), disease treatment (7.9%) and lower elderly care cost (3.7%).

B: participants agree that living at a strange place for a long time is not an easy thing, after a few days of enjoyment, people become depressed and blue in some degree, some would feel lonely, eager to talk and share the feeling with someone, some would even feel isolated from the society, most of them think they cannot live without communicating with others, only few of them think it is a valuable period to calm down and do something quietly.

C. Most of the respondents do not rely their children or relatives on elderly care. 86% of them would take care of their own, together with a spouse, some friends or a partner, when they become independent, they would choose a senior care center for the rest of life.

D. Most of the respondents know how to use a smart phone, but only half of them have experienced wearable devices and voice assistants, actually, nearly all of them do not believe in smart elderly care, because they think the devices are complicated to setup and inconvenient to use, the products do not meet their requirement in daily life, what's more, the cost is really high.

E. The economic status are shown in the table below (Table 1):

Table 1. Economic resources of the respondents

Economic resources	Age (years old)		Sex	
	50–60	61–70	Female	Male
Pension	52.3%	48.4%	33.7%	67%
Children's income	9%	17.2%	21.5%	3.7%
Salary	6%	15%	3%	18%

(*continued*)

Table 1. (*continued*)

Economic resources	Age (years old)		Sex	
	50–60	61–70	Female	Male
Government welfare	4.3%	7.5%	7.3%	4.5%
Spouse's salary	6.5%	12.1%	10.5%	3.7%
Real estate rent income	35%	20%	56%	50%
Savings	60%	57%	75%	28%
Investments/shares	31%	47%	58%	56%
Business	3.9%	11%	3%	12%
Others	0.7%	0.9%	0.6%	0.9%

The survey shows most respondents are economically independent, and 97% of them has a monthly income of over $ 1,200 (US dollars), and they would pay for the cost in health and quality life. Nearly all of them has medical care or medical insurance to cover the disease treatment.

F: Major demands and concerns of the senior sojourners are shown in Table 2.

Table 2. Major demands and concerns of respondents

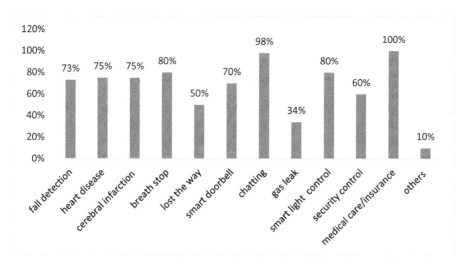

It is clear that most respondents concern about the physical health and safety the most, especially emergency happens, in time support is what they really need when enjoying a sojourn life, and communication with others is a must for nearly all of them, they need to share and have someone to listen. All of them agree with the importance of medical care or insurance to cover their disease treatment.

F. Getting old, most respondents admitted they are suffering from some chronic diseases, like heart disease, high blood pressure, diabetes, early Alzheimer's disease, arthritis and so on. Some carries at least two of the diseases. Being a sojourner, they would worry about health problems and safety concerns, especially in emergency, a smart health and security care is necessary and a low pay is acceptable, which is contradiction to their answers in D.

G. In the near future, there would be a great number of senior sojourners staying at unacquainted environment for a long period of time, with a beautiful vision in mind, which would be a chance and challenge for smart care market. The potential sojourners care more about their health and safety, which means an easygoing, integrated and efficient smart care system with little barriers among different brands and developers would be popular, which is still missing in current market.

4 Proposed Design

To meet the senior sojourners' need in their daily life, an integrated smart care system is proposed by the author.

As we can see from Fig. 1, the proposal is a senior sojourners- oriented smart care system, with Microsoft Azure IoT as its platform. Microsoft has the largest amount of users in the world. The platform is open and compatible with iOS and android, which is supporting nearly all the smart phones in the world and convenient for setting up wearable devices Apps, what's more, Microsoft Ivoke can work well in smart home to meet basic security and communication need. The elder sojourner is connected with all necessary sensors, e.g. intelligent medicine package, KIT-blood pressure meter, either with Apps in smart phone or with Ivoke and Cortana, the voice assistant of Microsoft smart home, the data is collected by Azure platform continuously, which is monitoring the sensors and analyzing the information automatically all the time, when abnormal information appears, the platform would alert and make a decision, to correct the error or warn all the concerned ports, e.g. first aid service, 911, clinics, hospitals, doctors, nurses, or social workers, user's children or guardians... each port is connected automatically as well. The platform sets layers of codes to make it safer. To make the system work smoothly, local government also plays a role in joining the system, for senior sojourners would need the medical care or insurance, to cover first aid, checkup, diagnosis, treatment and nursing service from local doctors, nurses and social workers, online or face-to-face, which is a cost for the local government, although the patients have paid for it. IoT automatically collect, analyze and process information instantly and alert in time, which makes it possible to keep dependent senior sojourners in safe hands.

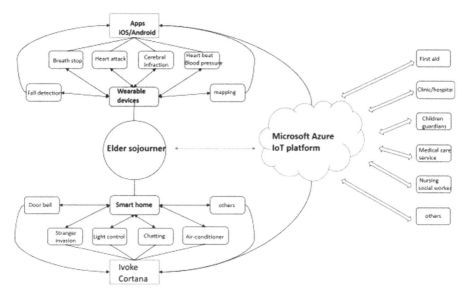

Fig. 1. Smart care system for elder sojourners

With the improvement of interconnection among platform, users of various sites and services, the danger of hackers attack and personal information leaking is definitely increasing. It is becoming a vital barrier to keep elderly users from buying the service. By leading in threat surface, threat assessment at Requirement Analysis stage; review and risk analysis during Design Stage, and secure coding, static analysis, test automation to support Implementation Stage; secure configuration and penetration testing at Integration and Test Stage, adding user Verification and authentication and system encryption. The devices developers and software servers can significantly decrease the net danger, and boom the senior sojourners market, to make it a win-win situation among enterprises, users and even the government.

5   Conclusion

Although it is not an easy job to persuade the government, the IT companies to make the designed system real, it would benefit the elder sojourners and help them enjoy a decent, dependent and quality life, they would pay, although not much for each, but a huge amount of potential users for the market bring magnificent income. An ideal smart care system is to control household appliances and monitor senior movement and health with modern information technology, plus a remote call service. The proposed system would be one of them for it meets the elder sojourners basic needs and it is not complicated.

Acknowledgement. I would like to take this opportunity to thank a number of people who have offered invaluable assistance in the preparation of the paper. My deepest gratitude goes first and foremost to one of my colleagues, Mr. Cao Chengde, who helped me hand out questionnaires when he worked as a French interpreter at the 2nd World Senior Conference in 2019. I would like to express my heartfelt thanks to my friends and former coworker, Ms. Miao Xuemei, Mr. Di Baorong, and Ms. Guo Suzhen, who have well helped me with the interview survey because have been abroad and become experienced senior sojourners. I am also obliged to my former students, Ms. Chen Yuting and Mr. Hou Fangdong, who handed out hundreds of questionnaires at the airport when they are working as tour guides and leaders. Their help is quite important for the completion of the paper. I also greatly appreciate the assistance offered by the authors and scholars mentioned in the references, without whose works, the research would not have been possible.

Lastly, I am deeply indebted to my beloved parents and daughter, who always supported me and offered valuable insights. Their support have accompanied me through the difficult course.

References

1. Wang, J., Zhang, Y., Zhu, Q.: The status quo and hot spot analysis of smart elderly care. J. Inf. Resour. Manag. **1**, 11–20 (2019)
2. Zuo, M.: My Understanding and Suggestion to the Development of Smart Care. China Society News, no. 004, 22 May 2017
3. Avinash, M., Sathwik Rai, M.S., VIjay Kumar, P.: Home for elder care. Int. J. Adv. Res. Comput. Eng. Technol. (IJARCET) **6**(6), 866–869 (2017)
4. Schah, J., Danve, S.R.: IOT based smart e-care system. Int. J. Innov. Res. Sci. Eng. Technol. (IJIRSET) **6**(5), 9865–9872 (2017)
5. Manikandan, R., Patan, R., Gandomi, A.H., Sivanesan, P., Kalyanaraman, H.: Hash polynomial two factor decision tree using IoT for smart health care scheduling. Expert Syst. Appl. (2019). https://doi.org/10.1016/j.eswa.2019.112924
6. Mariani, B., et al.: Foot worn inertial sensors for gait assessment and rehabilitation based on motorized shoes. In: Annual International Conference of the IEEE Engineering in Medicine and Biology Society (EMBC), 30 August–3 September 2011 (2011). https://doi.org/10.1109/iembs.2011.6091440
7. Chan, M., Campo, E., Esteve, D.: Smart homes-current features and future perspectives. Maturitas **64**(2), 90–97 (2009)
8. Skubic, M., Guevars, R.D., Rantz, M.: Autumated health alerts using in-home sensor data for embedded health assessment. IEEE J. Transl. Eng. Health Med. **3**, 1–11 (2015)
9. Peng, T.: A novel motion detecting strategy for rehabilitation in smart home. Comput. Commun. **150**, 687–695 (2019). https://doi.org/10.1016/j.comcom.2019.11.043. Accessed 03 Jan 2020
10. Kharrazi, H., Chisholm, R., Van Nasdale, D., Thompson, B.: Mobile personal health records: an evaluation of features and functionality. Int. J. Med. Inf. **81**, 579–593 (2012). https://doi.org/10.1016/j.ijmedinf.2012.04.0072012
11. Peng, W., Kanthawala, S., Yuan, S., Hussain, S.A.: A qualitative study of user perceptions of mobile health apps. MBC Public Health **16**(1), 1158 (2016). https://doi.org/10.1186/s12889-016-3808-0
12. Lemlouma, T., Laborie, S., Roose, P.: Toward a context-aware and automatic evaluation of elderly dependency in smart homes and cities. In: IEEE Conference 2012 (2012). https://doi.org/10.1109/WoWMoM.2013.6583501

13. Lee, C.-N.: A home care service platform for mobile healthcare. In: International Conference on Machine Learning and Cybernetics (2012). https://doi.org/10.1109/icmlc.2012.6359670
14. Poncela, A., et al.: Smart care home system: a platform for eAssistance. J. Ambient Intell. Humaniz. Comput. **10**(10), 3997–4021 (2019). https://doi.org/10.1007/s12652-018-0979-9
15. Live News. http://tv.cctv.com/2015/12/16/VIDE1450248001514305.shtml
16. Xu, F.: Exploration to internet information service for senior citizens by public libraries in Taiwan. Library World (4), 92–94 (2014). https://doi.org/10.3969/j.issn.1005-6041.2014.04.025
17. Guo, Y., Fu, W., Xia, N.: Investigation and analysis on information demand and path of the aged people in wuhan urban community. China. J. Mod. Inf. **35**(10), 97–103 (2015)

A Prototype of Patient Decision Aid for Treating Obstructive Sleep Apnea

Hsin-Chang Lo[1(✉)], Mei-Chen Yang[2], and Fu-Nien Lin[1]

[1] Department of Product Design, Ming Chuan University, Taoyuan, Taiwan
{lohc,funien}@mail.mcu.edu.tw
[2] Division of Pulmonary Medicine, Department of Internal Medicine,
Taipei Tzu Chi Hospital and School of Medicine, Tzu Chi University,
New Taipei City, Taiwan
mimimai3461@gmail.com

Abstract. According to a cross-country research in 2018, there are approximately 936 million people worldwide who suffer from obstructive sleep apnea (OSA), which is almost ten times the World Health Organization estimate before ten years. People with untreated sleep apnea stop breathing repeatedly during their sleep. This means the brain and their body may not get enough oxygen which may cause the development and progression of cardiovascular conditions. Actually, different people may have different traits and value preferences, so each patient may have different opinions and choices about various clinical decisions facing this disease. In order to help medical staffs and patients with OSA to discuss more closely, the process of share decision making (SDM) based on the evidence is the most important information for the patient. Patient decision aid (PDA) can ensure that patients have the knowledge and tools necessary to make the best health decisions with as much assistance as they want and need from their clinicians. Therefore, this study regards SDM for OSA examination, diagnosis and treatment as a service system. First, explores the interaction between physicians and patients through observations and interviews. Then, we draw stakeholder map and customer's journey map according to the result of the interviews to define the shared decision making gap for clinical diagnosis or disposition to reveal design opportunities. Finally, we used scenario to build the script and propose the visualized prototype of PDA, which could be the useful tool for SDM for OSA. This tool makes it easier for clinicians and patients to combine their own preferences and values before making medical decisions related to sleep apnea. Through the participation of clinical staffs and patients, it is hoped that this innovative service model can achieve the purpose of SDM and support patients to make medical decisions that more closely meet user needs.

Keywords: Patient decision aid · Shared decision making · Obstructive sleep apnea

1 Introduction

Shared decision making (SDM) is a widely recognized approach to cultivate patient-centered care [1, 2]. Clinicians and patients work together to make optimal health care decisions that align with what matters most to patients. SDM focusses on ensuring that

© Springer Nature Switzerland AG 2020
Q. Gao and J. Zhou (Eds.): HCII 2020, LNCS 12208, pp. 128–137, 2020.
https://doi.org/10.1007/978-3-030-50249-2_10

patients have the knowledge and tools necessary to make the best health decisions with as much assistance as they want and need from their clinicians. The characteristics of shared decision making were that [3]:

- at least two participants-physician and patient be involved;
- both parties share information;
- both parties take steps to build a consensus about the preferred treatment;
- an agreement is reached on the treatment to implement.

Patient decision aids (PDAs) are tools to help make SDM practical in the busy world of health care delivery. They are available as brochures, videos, web programs, or decision tables, and they incorporate various goals and teaching strategies. These tools help patients make better decisions by providing standardized information regarding treatment options and clarifying benefits and risks of each choice [4]. In addition, PDAs allow patients to make informed decisions about healthcare choices taking into account their personal values and preferences. This can be for both diagnostic and therapeutic procedures. They make it easier for patients and clinicians to discuss treatment options. A PDA has the following objectives [5, 6]:

- Inform patients of the evidence base to the available options;
- Enable patients to identify what is important to them so that their choices reflect their preferences and values;
- Encourage active participation by the patient in the decision-making process.

Obstructive sleep apnea (OSA) is a common chronic sleep-related breathing disorder characterized by repetitive upper airway collapse during sleep [7]. Some adverse health outcomes associated with untreated OSA include cardiovascular disease, cerebrovascular events, diabetes, and cognitive impairment. In middle-aged adults in the United States, the estimated prevalence of OSA is 10% for mild OSA and 3.8% and 6.5% for moderate to severe OSA. In Taiwan, the average prevalence of OSA is 2.6% in adults (3.4% in adult males and 1.9% in adult females) [7, 8]. It is noteworthy that estimated 80% to 90% of people with OSA remain undiagnosed. Untreated moderate to severe OSA has a potentially huge impact on health, therefore effective treatment is essential. The presence and severity of OSA are usually determined by polysomnography (PSG), a multimodal analysis that measures neurologic (electroencephalogram) and cardio-respiratory parameters during sleep. Treatments for OSA include behavioral modification, weight loss, medication, continuous positive airway pressure, oral appliance therapy, and surgical procedures [7, 8].

Generally, clinical physicians of a sleep center will give relevant information to patients with OSA, ask them the extent of their understanding of treatment plans, and arrange examinations appropriate for them. In the face of choosing various treatment modalities and directions, patients may become hesitant when they consider the effectiveness of treatments in improving the quality of sleep, cost and convenience of treatment, and so on. In a SDM model, physicians provide treatment modalities, patients offer their preferences, both sides share information, and they come to a consensus on the treatment. However, clinically, patients often do not fully understand the treatment modalities that clinicians have provided, making it difficult for patients to actually participate in the SDM process. Therefore, this study regards SDM for OSA examination, diagnosis and treatment as a service system. Through the design thinking method to discuss the core of patient-clinician communication and PDA. Then hoping to propose a PDA prototype that closely meets the needs of clinicians and patients.

2 Methods

This study is based on a double diamond design process to develop shared decision making process for the treatment of obstructive sleep apnea. This model is graphically based on a simple diagram describing the divergent and convergent stages of the design process and each phase starts with a 'D': Discover, Define, Develop and Deliver [9]. The first initial divergent part of the project is the Discovery phase, in which the designer is searching for new trends, new insights or unmet need. The second is Define phase, a kind of filter where the first insights are reviewed, selected and discarded. This stage also covers the initial development of project ideas, in which the designer must engage with the wider context of the identified opportunity. The key activities during the definition phase are define design target, project management. In the Develop phase the project has been taken through a team resolution, it finds ourselves again in a divergent period. Design solutions are developed, iterated and tested by multi-disciplinary teams and under the use of design thinking tools such as brainstorming, sketches, scenarios, renderings. The last D is a converge stage, Deliver phase. The final concept is taken through prototypes, final testing, fabricate and launched [10].

In the Discovery phase of this study, researchers conducted interviews with patients with OSA and sleep center staffs (including thoracic physicians, sleep case managers, etc.) to understand the patient's medical history; physicians' clinical diagnosis and treatment methods. We also focus on the problems and difficulties often encountered in the process of diagnosis and treatment. The outline of the interview is as follows:

Patients

- How do you know whether you suffer from OSA?
- What is the most significant difficulty in communicating with clinicians?
- Do you understand the examinations, diagnosis and treatments that clinicians have proposed?
- Do you think that there are other ways that will more easily help you decide whether to participate in the examinations or accept the treatments?

Clinicians

- How to diagnose and treat OSA?
- What is the most significant difficulty in communicating with patients?
- Presently, what tools do you use to make decisions with patients to jointly arrive at decisions on examinations, diagnosis and treatments?
- What is the most common demand from patients when you execute SDM? How did they express their demand?

In the define phase, research team, clinicians and patients with OSA discuss together and draw stakeholder map and customer's journey map according to the result of the interviews. In the Develop phase, we used scenario to build the script for OSA SDM service. Finally, in the Deliver phase, we using the proposed script to create the prototype of the PDA.

3   Results

3.1   Define Phase

After Interviewing with the a chief of a sleep center, a thoracic physician, a case manager, and three patients with OSA (Fig. 1), it showed the following results.

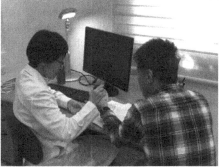

Fig. 1. In-depth interview to the clinicians.

In the patient site

- OSA often occurred during sleep. The people were unaware of it. They have sought treatment only after their snoring have affected their spouses or families.
- People may use the relative questionnaires, e.g. Pittsburgh sleep quality index (PSQI), Epworth sleepiness scale, Berlin questionnaire, STOP-Bang sleep screening questionnaire to conduct preliminary self-assessment of sleep apnea
- People needed to undergo multiple tests under polysomnography monitoring while being diagnosed to find the cause of the sleep problems. Often the lengthy test periods caused patients to resent the tests.

In the clinician site

- OSA is a heterogeneous disease. Potential genetic risk factors include weight and fat distribution, craniofacial morphology, ventilation control, and upper airway control. However, not all patients with these risk factors develop OSA. Additionally, there is individual susceptibility to OSA consequences. Not all patients will be sleepy and not all patients will develop cardiovascular diseases. It potential differential effects of OSA depending on the cardiovascular outcome studied, severity of OSA, and gender.

- As for clinical treatments, mild symptoms may be alleviated by having patients modify their daily routine and do orofacial myofunctional exercise therapy that strengthen the muscles of upper respiratory tract.
- Continuous positive airway pressure is the most commonly used non-invasive treatment, but most patients are unwilling to use it because they are initially unable to sleep while wearing the mask and they are unable to become accustomed to the continuous pressure and the noise of the machine. The noise makes it hard for them to fall asleep. Many patients give up on the treatment, or they do not wear the mask through the night, diminishing the effectiveness of the treatment.
- Surgery can improve symptoms, but it comes with risks. Furthermore, there is no guarantee that soft tissues will not grow back to obstruct breathing again, and there is rehabilitation and side effects to contend with.
- When assessing or treating patients, they hope to have pictures or videos available to help them communicate with patients, but patients don't understand medical videos and they are scared when they see realistic photographs. In addition, they hope to have a platform with which to easily judge whether a patient is suffering from OSA.

3.2   Discover Phase

With the interview results, the stakeholder map divided the parties interested in the current course of OSA examination, diagnosis and treatment into the following categories: thoracic physicians, chest surgeons, case managers, patient with OSA, and family members of patients (Fig. 2). Thoracic physicians and patients with OSA are the direct providers and recipients of the medical service, so they are classified as internal grades. Case managers and patients' families are external grades.

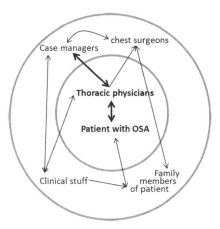

Fig. 2. The stakeholder map of OSA examination, diagnosis and treatment.

The customer's journey map is shown in Fig. 3. It is divided into pre-examination, SDM1, during examination, post-examination, and SDM2. The treatment is divided into medical treatment and surgery, which include 10 stages before, during, and after treatment.

	Pre-Exam	SDM1	Exam	Post-Exam	SDM2	Pre-Internal Treatment	Internal Treatment	Post-Internal Treatment	Pre-Surgical Treatment	Surgical Treatment	Post-Surgical Treatment
FIELDS	Home	OPD	SDC	OPD	OPD	SDC	Home	Home	Surgery clinic	Operating room	Home
CUSTOMER ACTIVITIES	• See the doctor • Self assessment	• Physician examines • Execute SDM	• PSG examination • Epworth Sleep scale	• Physician evaluation • Referral to OPD	• Execute SDM	• CPAP Assessment	• Wear CPAP during sleep	• Continue to use CPAP • Regular follow-up	• Surgery assessment	• Surgery	• Regular follow-up • Regular Daily routine
EXPERIENCE (5 4 3 2 1)	Irritable and tired	dispirited and worried	Get rid of worried and rejecting	Go along with the examinations	Worried and dispirited	Go along with the assessment	At ease and peace	Relaxed and at ease	Restless and anxiety	none	Cheerful and bright
USER PAIN POINTS	• Loud snoring • sleepiness during the day • emotionally unstable	• Is PSG scheduled?	• Several monitors on the body. • Spend the night elsewhere	• Diagnosis confirmed	• Options of Treatment	• Learning to wear the mask	• Getting used to the mask	• Use CPAP before bed. CPAP • Regular follow-ups	• Too much red tape before surgery	• Family waiting surgery is finished	• Post-surgery rehab • improve daily routine
TOUCH POINTS	• Family	• Thoracic physicians	• Sleep medicine physician • Sleep case managers	• Thoracic physicians • Exam instruments	• Sleep medicine physician • Medical records	• Sleep case managers • C PAP	• Sleep case managers • C PAP	• Sleep case managers • Family • C PAP	• Surgeon • Family	• Surgeon • Operating room	• Caretaker

SDM: Shared Decision Making
OPD: Outpatient Department
SDC: Sleep Disorders Centers

PSG: Polysomnography
CPAP: Continuous Positive Airway Pressure

Fig. 3. The customer's journey map of OSA examination, diagnosis and treatment.

3.3 Develop Phase

With the results of the Discovery and Define stages, this research used the scenario to develop the script for OSA SDM service. The first one introduces the causes of OSA and its examinations and diagnosis. The second one covers diagnosis and treatments for OSA, including behavioral changes, oral appliances, positive airway pressure, surgery, as well as their effectiveness and side effects. Please refer to Fig. 4.

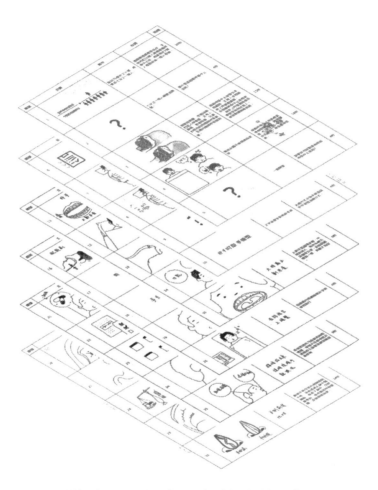

Fig. 4. The script of PDA for OSA SDM service.

3.4 Deliver Phase

After repeated discussions with sleep center staffs and modifications, the research team has devised a PDA prototype as shown in the diagram. The final PDA prototype is shown in Fig. 5.

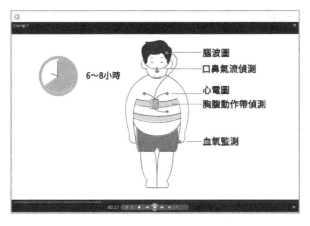

(a)
Through the polysomnography (PSG) test, the apnea-hypopnea index (AHI) can be used to determine whether it is sleep apnea and its severity.

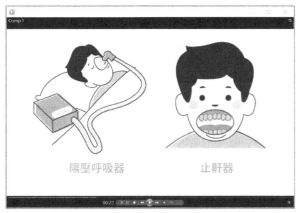

(b)
People can choose continuous positive airway pressure machine (CPAP) or oral appliances for internal treatment.

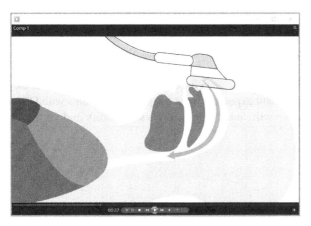

(c)
When the patient using continuous positive airway pressure machine, fresh air is injected under pressure and propped up the collapsed airway.

Fig. 5. Video PDA prototype for OSA SDM.

4   Discussion

In the 1980s, sleep laboratories mostly focused on the diagnosis of sleep disorders but rarely provided ongoing patient care. Modalities for treatment of OSA were few and surgery or positive airway pressure was typically recommended, often with little patient education or follow-up. Healthcare at this time was disease-centric rather than patient-centric, therefore clinicians rarely make treatment decisions based on the patient's opinion or discuss the medical condition with patient [11]. It has been advocated in recent years that in the process of providing medical care empirical medicine should be combined with communication skills in order to raise the quality and effectiveness of medical care. In the SDM process, the patient's preferences, values, and opinions are joined with those of the clinicians to arrive at a consensus for medical treatments. It is an effective method of providing health care. But clinical stuffs at various facilities have pointed out that the most common reason for the failure to execute SDM has been time constraints. They generally consider it very time consuming for them to explain treatment options to patients and to know patient's preferences and values. In the busy medical environment of Taiwan, the main roadblock to achieving patient-centered SDM has been a lack of facilities and tools for physicians and patients to communicate.

This research also found that the expert knowledge of clinicians includes that obtained from training in medical school and from clinical site. Therefore, they can easily use specialized medical terms to describe clinical situations or clinical questions. Even though physicians believe that they have substituted spoken language for medical jargon to explain medical situation, patients who lack medical training still find it hard to fully understand and absorb the options that clinicians have offered because their usual sources of medical knowledge are personal experience, experience of friends, and popular medical magazines. Furthermore, the health literacy, acquire, analyze, and use health-related knowledge of people is usually inadequate, making it very difficult for patients to actually take part in SDM [12].

Video is one of the useful decision support tool, which have been created to complement patient-clinician communications and ensure that patients remain active participants in shared decision making process. It also has the potential to further enhance verbal discussions by providing realistic visual images of treatment options and outcomes [4]. This research has built a visualized PDA proto-type based on the communication between physicians and experts to meet the needs of patients with OSA and clinicians. In the next stage we will conduct clinical tests to modify and verify its effectiveness.

5   Conclusions

OSA contributes to the development and progression of cardiovascular conditions like systemic arterial hypertension, heart failure, metabolic syndrome, cardiac arrhythmia, and coronary artery disease. SDM allows patients and physicians to make joint medical treatment decisions, which are based on evidence in applied medicine and patient's values. Effective PDA can help people with varying degrees of health knowledge to make decisions that are best for their needs. This research used the double diamond design process to clarify the gap of SDM service through the clinical staffs and patients. Then it used the scenario to build a script for OSA SDM services to finish the PDA prototype. In the future, it is hope to introduce this video PDA prototype into the SDM service flows for patient with OSA. Through the joint participation of clinicians and patients, they arrive at a joint medical decision, which also accommodates the preferences of the patients.

Acknowledgements. The authors appreciate the participations and clinical stuffs from sleep center. This work was sponsored under grant MOST 108-2410-H-130-012-MY2 by the Ministry of Science and Technology, Taiwan.

References

1. Barry, M.J., Edgman-Levitan, S.: Shared decision making - the pinnacle of patient-centered care. N. Engl. J. Med. **366**, 780–781 (2012)
2. Hoffmann, T.C., Montori, V.M., del Mar, C.: The connection between evidence-based medicine and shared decision making. JAMA **312**, 1295–1296 (2014)
3. Elwyn, G., Laitner, S., Coulter, A., Walker, E., Watson, P., Thomson, R.: Implementing shared decision making in the NHS. BMJ **341**, 971–975 (2010)
4. Volandes, A.E., et al.: Randomized controlled trial of a video decision support tool for cardiopulmonary resuscitation decision making in advanced cancer. J. Clin. Oncol. **31**(3), 380–386 (2013)
5. Stacey, D., Legare, F., Lewis, K.B.: Patient decision aids to engage adults in treatment or screening decisions. JAMA **318**(7), 657–658 (2017)
6. Jha, S., Duckett, J.: Utility of patient decision aids (PDA) in stress urinary incontinence surgery. Int. Urogynecol. J. **30**(9), 1483–1486 (2019)
7. Chang, H.P., Chen, Y.F., Du, J.K.: Obstructive sleep apnea treatment in adults. Kaohsiung J. Med. Sci. **2019**, 1–6 (2019)
8. Schwartz, M., Acosta, L., Hung, Y.L., Padilla, M., Enciso, R.: Effects of CPAP and mandibular advancement device treatment in obstructive sleep apnea patients: a systematic review and meta-analysis. Sleep Breath. **22**(3), 555–568 (2018)
9. UK Design Council: What is service design? (2005). http://www.designcouncil.org.uk/. Accessed 10 Aug 2019
10. Tschimmel, K.: Design thinking as an effective toolkit for innovation. In: Proceedings of the XXIII ISPIM Conference: Action for Innovation: Innovating from Experience, Barcelona (2012)
11. Hilbert, J., Yaggi, H.K.: Patient-centered care in obstructive sleep apnea: a vision for the future. Sleep Med. Rev. **37**, 138–147 (2018)
12. McCaffery, K.J., et al.: Addressing health literacy in patient decision aids. BMC Med. Inform. Decis. Mak. **13**(Suppl. 2), S10 (2013)

The Design of Electronic Tagging and Tracking Solutions to Improve the Safety and Person-Centered Care for People with Dementia

Anders Kalsgaard Møller[(✉)]

Aalborg University, 9000 Aalborg, Denmark
ankm@learning.aau.dk

Abstract. This paper presents results from a study about the design of new electronic tagging and tracking solutions for people with dementia with the aim of increasing the safety for people with dementia and the caregivers. The results are based on workshops involving caregivers, dementia advisors, nursing home leaders and people in local government positions. In the study challenges with current technology are identified such as low battery capacity, poor reliability and usability and issues with people with dementia removing the device. The participants suggested that the technology could be used to support the caregivers when they were not present, provide safety for people with dementia when going for a walk and prolong the time before they had to leave their own home to live at a care facility. The results suggest that solutions are introduced in the early stage of the disease while the person with dementia is still conscious about the technology and can get familiar with the device. Flexible solutions where the functionality and design can be adjusted to the individual person with dementia could increase the likelihood that the device stays on and thereby increase the safety of the person with dementia.

Keywords: Dementia · GPS · Person-centered care · Co-design

1 Introduction

In line with the demographic trend we see an increasing number of elderly and people being diagnosed with dementia. This results in increased demands and needs for dementia care. One of the challenges encountered in the dementia care is that people with dementia leave their homes with the risk of getting lost. Often people with dementia are unable to take care of themselves and risk suffering harm due to e.g. dehydration or hypothermia that in worst case can lead to fatality [1, 2]. In addition, the wandering behavior represents a considerable workload and concern for caregivers and relatives [3]. One solution to this problem is electronic tracking systems such as GPS that helps to preserve the independence of people with dementia and provide the caregivers with reassurance about the person with dementia's wellbeing. However, many challenges exist with the current GPS systems. Many relatives and professionals find the GPS systems difficult to operate [4] and are reluctant to use the systems due to

© Springer Nature Switzerland AG 2020
Q. Gao and J. Zhou (Eds.): HCII 2020, LNCS 12208, pp. 138–148, 2020.
https://doi.org/10.1007/978-3-030-50249-2_11

technical shortcomings; it may run out of power and a lack of reliability and accuracy in the tracking data [4]. Other challenges apply to the appearance, shape and design of the systems which may cause people with dementia to not be interested in using and carrying the solutions [5, 6]. The formal caregivers are, however, very innovative in how they place the devices and play an important role in making the people with dementia accept the system [5] why we believe that the development of the solutions could benefit from the expertise of the formal caregivers.

In this paper, we take a person-centered approach [7] to study how the use of a tracking solutions can improve the safety of people with dementia and help them to retain their daily activities. While doing so we study the different reasons for removing the tracking device and look at designs strategies that could make it more acceptable for people with dementia to keep it on.

The study is part of a project with the overall goal of improving electronic tracking and tagging solutions for people with dementia. The project involves a collaboration between private companies, research institutions and municipalities where the solutions and strategies for implementation and usage are developed and examined in close collaboration with the users and stakeholders [8]. In this study we use a co-design [24] approach to create new solutions and strategies with caregivers, dementia advisors, nursing home leaders and people in local government positions.

2   Background

Dementia is a neurological disorder with no cure or preventive treatment. It is characterized by cognitive and behavioral symptoms caused by degenerative changes in the central nervous system [9]. The incidence and prevalence of dementia are increasing due to demographic factors [10]. It was estimated that almost 47 million people were living with dementia worldwide in 2015 and that number will grow to over 131 million by 2050 [11].

A common issue in healthcare is that people with dementia wanders away from the care facility without being able to take care of themselves. Different studies point towards a prevalence of approximately 20% shows some type of wandering behavior [12–14]. The term, wandering or wandering behavior covers many types of wandering behaviors, such as: trailing caregivers and other residents, inappropriate walking (going to places they should not), night-time walking, and attempts to leave the house/facility [15, 16]. Often these are related to previous life routines, e.g., going to work each day, going to the bus stop, working under cars, going to the stable and/or the physical need to move. These types of wandering behavior occur for different reasons and is not always obvious why. Cognitive impairment is often a causative factor for wandering and a correlation between the severity of the impairment and the behavior have been shown [1]. Other factors also affect when, and how often, the wandering behavior is triggered, with factors such as stress, boredom and environmental factors (e.g., too busy, too much noise) [1, 17]. The risk of endangering oneself often causes relatives and caregivers to keep people with dementia at home. It is, however, important for people with dementia to be able to retain their current activity level e.g. walking biking and exercising [6].

Assistive technology can be used to support safety, monitoring and healthcare [19]. This can help to reduce distress and burden of caregivers and prolong the time where family caregivers can take care of the person with dementia [21]. Different tracking solutions exist with the purpose of aiding caregivers with ensuring the safety of the person with dementia. The solutions can typical pinpoint the location of the person with dementia, trigger an alarm, when leaving a predefined area, or a combination of both [4, 21].

Studies of electronic tracking solutions and other assistive technologies have included professionals and relatives which have provided insights into the challenges that exist with current solutions [4, 5, 19–21]. A number of studies have also involved people with dementia [6, 22, 24]. According to [20] the systems needs to become intelligent and practical issues such as user acceptance and usability need to be resolved as most current systems are ineffective, difficult to use and have a low acceptance rate. In many cases people with dementia remove the tagging device or forget to put it on [4, 5]. One of the reasons for removing the device is because they don't accept the device due to the size or the design of the device [5]. People with dementia dislike devices attached to their clothes and prefer something small such as a bracelet or wristwatch or necklace [5]. There is, however, a considerable variation in the group of people with dementia and thus also a large difference in preferences, acceptance of diagnosis and level of self-reliance [10]. It is, therefore, important to understand the needs, wants and capabilities of people with dementia to avoid designing inappropriate or useless technologies [21]. Therefore. assistive technologies need to be designed with an in-depth understanding of constraints on interaction caused by the disease [19].

3   Methods

In the project we hosted two workshops where caregivers, dementia advisors, nursing home leaders and people in local government positions were invited. Workshop 1 focused on functionality: In which situations the technology could be used, issues with current solutions and wishes/needs for new solutions. Workshop 2 focused on the design of the solutions with focus on shape, size, color and wearability of the technology.

3.1   Workshop 1

Fifteen people participated in workshop 1. They were divided in three mixed groups (different positions and different municipalities). First the participants were asked to list situations where they needed technical assistance. This could be situations were the current technology failed or where no solutions existed. Afterwards specific wishes and needs to the solution in the specific situation were discussed. The participants first discussed situations and solutions in groups and later in plenum where they agreed on what situations and solutions should be given priority. The different situations were written on a paper and post-it where needs and problems were added to each case. The whole session was also recorded (one recorder at each table) and transcribed for further data-analysis.

3.2   Workshop 2

After workshop 1 the rumor had spread about the project within the different municipalities why more people wanted to join the next workshop. Therefore, twenty-four people attended workshop 2. They were divided in 5 mixed groups. In the beginning of the workshop small plastic components were shown to the participants to indicate the size of the electronic components see Fig. 1. Subsequently, the participants were asked to evaluate and rate 12 different designs of existing products not only for location tags, but also other wearables see Fig. 2. The designs varied in shape, color and material. This was used as an elicitation method and not because we wanted to use the specific ranks. By allowing the participants to compare and discuss the different designs, information about important aspects of the design such as, color, shape and material would be discussed. The participants were also asked to draw a concept drawing of their ideas for the design in each group to give them an opportunity to express their own ideas of a potential design. Like workshop 1 this workshop was held as a mix between ingroup and plenum discussions.

Fig. 1. 3D models were used to indicate what size and shape the technology could have.

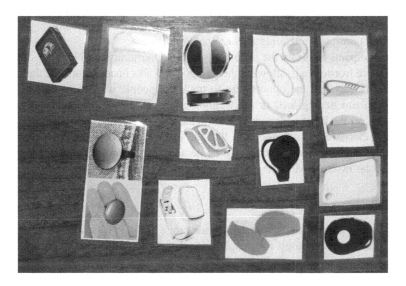

Fig. 2. The 12 different designs of existing products that were used for the elicitating method

3.3 Analysis Approach

The recordings from each workshop were transcribed, thematized and analyzed with inspiration from Yin's five phase approach [18] using the software Nvivo. This is an inductive approach to qualitative data analysis where the research iterates between the five phases Compiling, Disassembling, Reassembling, Interpreting and Concluding. Although no predefined themes were used in the analysis the participants in the workshop were asked to find situations where they needed support from assistive technology and to find challenges with existing technologies. Therefore, these themes naturally emerged in the analysis. In conjunction with the analysis of the transcribed data the concept drawings were also analyzed to shed light on potential solutions and designs.

4 Findings

First the situations where technology was needed is listed followed by the challenges they experienced with the current technology. Next the wishes and needs and some more overarching themes such as early-interventions and ethical considerations are presented.

4.1 Situations Where the Technology is Needed

The participants stated that they needed support from technology in situations where they did not have the opportunity to be present or in situations where something goes wrong or something unexpected happens. The caregivers are very focused on maintaining the same routines to ensure the safety of people with dementia. If something unexpected happens it might set off the residents making them more likely to leave. Things such as: *"new faces, new neighbors, new routines. It may be that you have an infection"* could potentially lead to a person with dementia leaving the nursing home as the caregivers are busy attending to the other residents.

The participants also saw the technology as an opportunity to give the people with dementia more freedom e.g. allowing them to go for walks inside or outside the nursing home area. If they had the opportunity to track the people with dementia in case of emergency (them getting lost) or the technology could aid the person with dementia with staying on the right path it could allow them to roam more freely.

Finally, the participants suggested that the technology could aid the people with dementia and their relatives in their own home and thereby prolonging the time before they had to be institutionalized.

4.2 Challenges

The results from the workshop revealed a wide range of difficulties in the practicality of handling tracking technology for people with dementia. On top of this a number of technical issues were reported about the current technology which lowers the reliability of the technologies and limited the options for using the systems.

Battery. The current GPS solutions needs to be recharged daily to ensure that the devices do not run out of power. Furthermore, this problem is compounded by the lack of battery indicators, so the caregivers never knows if there is enough power left unless it is fully charged. Some even uses 2 GPS devices to be able to have one in the charger while the other one is being used. The caregivers typically use the exact same procedures for changing to avoid errors or forgetting to charge it but nevertheless there is a risk of either forgetting it or it not sitting properly in the charger, each time it is recharged.

Precision and Reliability. The precision and update frequency of the current GPS technologies is very low. The caregivers have experienced deviations of 2 km and update rates of 30 min is not uncommon for some of the systems. Due to the electronic devices being based on GPS, the systems are not able to track people indoor or if they stay beneath a tree. Sometimes the systems are using a functionality called Geofencing where the system are supposed to give an alarm if the person wearing the device is leaving a predefined area – e.g. the nursing home. In these situations, the caregivers have experienced several false alarms and situations where the alarm have not been triggered despite the person leaving the nursing home. Some of these issues could again be the result of the systems inability to track people indoor.

Usability and Human Errors. The caregivers were also concerned that they would make mistakes or forget something related to operating the device due to usability with very limited feedback and information about the system state. This meant that the caregivers were constantly in doubt if they had charged the device correctly, turned it on and activated the right settings.

People Removing the Device. The participants reported that they were always worried if the people with dementia were wearing the tracking device: *"So we never know if they are wearing it. It is false security in some way"*.

The participants mentioned several reasons why this challenge exist. In some cases, the people with dementia would simply remove everything shoes, watches, cloth, while others forget to bring the device with them. When the device is introduced at a late stage of the disease, the person with dementia might remove the device because they do not recognize it and do not understand what the purpose of it is. Others remove it, because they do not wish to be monitored or they lack an understanding of the course of their disease and do not find it necessary. Lastly, some chose to take the device off because it is uncomfortable to wear and is bothering the person wearing it.

4.3   Functionality and System Requirements

The participants suggested a system with different zones where it was possible to set up alarms or notifications upon leaving a zone. It could be upon leaving the house or the area surrounding the nursing home. This solution is similar to the existing geofence options, however, this system should have the option to adjust the security level quickly – e.g. if the person with dementia is ill or for some other reason is more disoriented than normal it should be possible to instantly change the security setting such as adding an alarm. The participants also asked for more intelligent tracking solutions such as having the option to receive more frequent and precise location information in case of emergency – e.g. the person with dementia being gone for too long – leaving without a jacket etc.

The system must be easy to operate for both the busy nursing staff and the housewife at work. One suggestion to this was to be able to simply click things on and off as needed and be able to change and adjust geofence zones through a mobile application. The solution needs to have very high degree of self-service and have as long battery time as possible.

4.4   The Design

Quite a few ways of designing the tracking technology was brought up during workshops. Overall the participants seemed to agree on round-shaped items with no sharp edges that could be easily cleaned and waterproof in case they were accidently put in the washing machine. There seemed to be two general directions in terms of the design ideas for the technology which came from two different user groups: The first group being the ones who want something new, smart and fancy and the other group who would immediately remove an object if they did not recognize it. To accompany the first group the participants suggested creating a new artifact for the people with dementia to be used as a tracker e.g. a watch bracelet, rings or a necklace. Once these things have become habitual the risk of them removing it would be significantly lower.

The other design direction was to create something that attached itself to something else or as an integration option into an existing item. This was also shown with one of the concept drawings see Fig. 3. In this example the participants wanted a rather neutral but round button-shaped item that could be attached to various items. By integrating the technology into existing items, you can avoid that the people with dementia first must get familiar with the item before they want to use it. Many participants stressed that this design direction was more useable than the first one, as they often see the person with dementia still being attached to a certain object, they have worn for years before the disease that a loved one might have given to them.

In one group the participants had the idea of a solution designed as a LED-band. The reasoning behind this idea was that the system could be used in a variety of ways with many different known artifacts and that the band itself should be flexible in size and shape to correspond to the object often worn. At the same time, it should be possible to add or remove technology to the band by simply extending its lenght. This was one example of the participants who wanted to create options for customizing the design and functionality for each individual which were also mentioned several times during the workshop e.g. from one participant stating: *"You have to look at the individual and what they wear, and the it needs to integrate into this – watches, jewelry, glasses and so on"*

It was highlighted that you must look at the individual when designing the solution as all people with dementia have lived different lives, with different routines and a "one size fits all" solution cannot meet the needs required for the technology to be a success.

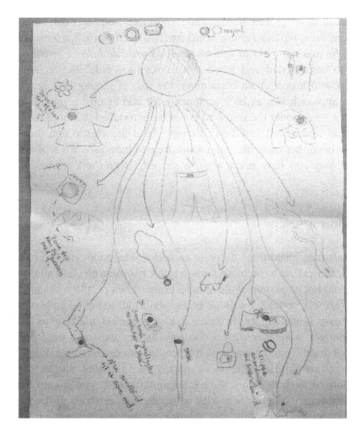

Fig. 3. Concept drawing from the workshop of a round button-shaped item that could be attached to other items

4.5 Early Intervention

The participants believed that technology should be introduced early. The earlier in a process they start using the solution, the greater the level of confidentiality and meaning is created by the person with dementia. In this way, people with dementia can decide for themselves what technology they want and what design they think is appropriate. In this way, the person with dementia would also be used to wear the technology and as the disease progress it will become a habit and reduce the risk of the people with dementia removing the object because they forget what it is for. This is exemplified by this quote: *"Early in the process, they understand what the GPS is, and once they have learned it, they often want to keep it."*

4.6 Ethical Considerations

It was highlighted that the purpose of the system was not to replace care or to continuously track the person with dementia. Instead the solution should be used to ensure that the caregivers can be two steps ahead, one of the participants emphasized that technology could never replace human care: *"technical solutions can be a good help, but it can never, ever, replace human hands and hearts, it can't, but it can help support us so we can be two steps ahead just be ready to provide help"*

It was also discussed if and when it was okay to "hide" the technology inside something else and aspect about consent vs. the risk of getting lost. It was not clear what the best approach was as both arguments for and against came up. However, it was agreed that "the sooner the solutions could be introduced the more the person with dementia would understand and be conscious about the choice and thereby have a chance to give his or her consent. *"the sooner we can introduce this tool the more self-determination they can have about what it should contain and what situations it is needed"*

5 Discussion

The participants mentioned three different scenarios where they needed or could see a potential for technical aid to increase the safety for people with dementia: In situations where they could not be present at the nursing home, when people with dementia leaves the nursing home e.g. to take a walk or as a support tool to help people with dementia stay in their own home longer. In relation to the current tracking technology four different challenges were identified – too low battery capacity, poor precision and reliability, poor usability and issues with the people with dementia removing the device. These challenges are similar to the ones reported from previous studies [4–6, 21].

In the solutions to these issues the participants focused on a system that could be customized to the individual person with dementia both in terms of functionality and design. The caregivers can tailor the solution to the specific person adjusting the solution to meet the needs in preferences, acceptance of diagnosis and level of self-reliance raised in [10] and thereby provide an opportunity for the person to e.g. go for a walk without having to worry about getting lost which increases both the safety and the wellbeing of the person with dementia. This is in line with [7] and his approach to person-centered care, which is based on the individual's preferences and needs, instead of the disease.

The participants emphasized that the solutions were not supposed to be used as a surveillance system and not to replace care but as a mean to support the caregivers in providing care and safety for the people with dementia. Furthermore, the participants were keen on introducing the solutions early while the people with dementia were still in the early stage of the disease before the cognitive impairments become too sever and while the people with dementia can make a conscious choice about wearing a tracker and when it is appropriate for the caregivers to track them.

This would also increase the chance that the people with dementia would accept the system and not remove it on a later stage of the disease. While this paper provides several ideas for how the system can be designed it is still only concepts, which could prove challenging to transfer to a physical design and even so there is still no guarantee that people will not remove the solutions for other reasons. It does, however, provide insights into some of the issues and potential solutions to the problems raised by the caregivers and serves as a starting point for the future development of assistive technology with the purpose of increasing the safety of people with dementia.

While informal caregivers, dementia advisors, nursing home leaders and others have a good understand of people with dementia the study would benefit from incorporating the perspective of the actual users. This is however, outside of the scope of this paper.

6 Conclusion

This study showed different scenarios where electronic tracking solutions could be used to increase the safety of people with dementia. The caregivers are hesitant to use and insecure about current solutions due to different technical challenges such as low battery capacity, poor reliability and usability. Furthermore, people with dementia often remove the device because they do not recognize it or understand the purpose of the system. The participants from the workshop came up with ideas to how these challenges can be overcome by designing flexible solutions where the functionality and design can be adjusted to the individual person with dementia. Hereby supporting person-centered care and a person-centered approach. It is recommended that the solutions are introduced early while the person with dementia is still conscious about the technology and can get familiar with the device.

References

1. Algase, D.L.: Wandering: a dementia-compromised behavior. J. Gerontol. Nurs. **25**(9), 10–16 (1999)
2. McShane, R., Gedling, K., Keene, J., Fairburn, C., Jacoby, R., Hope, T.: Getting lost in dementia: a longitudinal study of a behavioral symptom. Int. Psychogeriatr. **10**(03), 253–260 (1998)
3. Miyamoto, Y., Ito, H., Otsuka, T., Kurita, H.: Caregiver burden in mobile and non-mobile demented patients: a comparative study. Int. J. Geriatr. Psychiatry **17**(8), 765–773 (2002)
4. Wan, L., Müller, C., Wulf, V., Randall, D.W.: Addressing the subtleties in dementia care: pre-study & evaluation of a GPS monitoring system. In: Proceedings of the 32nd Annual ACM Conference on Human Factors in Computing Systems - CHI 2014, pp. 3987–3996. ACM Press (2014)
5. Mahoney, E.L., Mahoney, D.F.: Acceptance of wearable technology by people with Alzheimer's disease: Issues and accommodations. Am. J. Alzheimer's Dis. Dement. **25**(6), 527–531 (2010). https://doi.org/10.1177/1533317510376944
6. Robinson, L., Brittain, K., Lindsay, S., Jackson, D., Olivier, P.: Keeping in touch everyday (KITE) project: developing assistive technologies with people with dementia and their carers to promote independence. Int. Psychogeriatr. **21**(3), 494–502 (2009). https://doi.org/10.1017/S1041610209008448
7. Kitwood, T.: Dementia Reconsidered: The Person Comes First. Open University Press, Buckingham (1997)
8. Møller, A.K., Christensen, T.S.: Designing electronic tracking and tagging solutions for people with dementia: experiences from a public-private project collaboration. In: Dementia Lab 2018 Proceedings (2018). https://doi.org/10.6084/m9.figshare.9936422.v1

9. Rafii, M.S., Aisen, P.S.: Recent developments in Alzheimer's disease therapeutics. BMC Med. **7**, 7 (2009)
10. Winblad, B., et al.: Defeating alzheimer's disease and other dementias: a priority for european science and society. Lancet Neurol. **15**(5), 455–532 (2016)
11. Alzheimer's Disease International: World alzheimer report 2015. The global impact of dementia. An analysis of prevalence, incidence, cost and trends. Alzheimer's Disease International, London (2015)
12. Klein, D., et al.: Wandering behaviour in community-residing persons with dementia. Int. J. Geriat. Psychiatry **14**, 272–279 (1999)
13. McShane, R., Gedling, K., Kenward, B., Kenward, R., Hope, T., Jacoby, R.: The feasibility of electronic tracking devices in dementia: a telephone survey and case series. Int. J. Geriatr. Psychiatry **13**(8), 556–563 (1998)
14. Cooper, J.K., Mungas, D., Weiler, P.G.: Relation of cognitive status and abnormal behaviors in Alzheimer's disease. J. Am. Geriatr. Soc. **38**(8), 867–870 (1990)
15. Hope, T., Tilling, K.M., Gedling, K., Keene, J.M., Cooper, S.D., Fairburn, C.G.: The structure of wandering in dementia. Int. J. Geriatr. Psychiatry **9**(2), 149–155 (1994)
16. Hope, T., Keene, J., McShane, R.H., Fairburn, C.G., Gedling, K., Jacoby, R.: Wandering in dementia: a longitudinal study. Int. Psychogeriatr. **13**(02), 137–147 (2001)
17. Cohen-Mansfield, J., Werner, P.: Environmental influences on agitation: an integrative summary of an observational study. Am. J. Alzheimer's Dis. Dement. **10**(1), 32–39 (1995)
18. Yin, R.K.: Qualitative Research from Start to Finish. Guilford Publications, New York (2015)
19. Evans, J., Brown, M., Coughlan, T., Lawson, G., Craven, M.P.: A systematic review of dementia focused assistive technology. In: Kurosu, M. (ed.) HCI 2015. LNCS, vol. 9170, pp. 406–417. Springer, Cham (2015). https://doi.org/10.1007/978-3-319-20916-6_38
20. Chernbumroong, S., Cang, S., Atkins, A., Yu, H.: Elderly activities recognition and classification for applications in assisted living. Expert Syst. Appl. **40**(5), 1662–1674 (2013)
21. Landau, R., Werner, S., Auslander, G.K., Shoval, N., Heinik, J.: Attitudes of family and professional caregivers towards the use of GPS for tracking patients with dementia: an exploratory study. Br. J. Soc. Work **39**(4), 670–692 (2009). https://doi.org/10.1093/bjsw/bcp037
22. Suijkerbuijk, S., Nap, H.H., Cornelisse, L., IJsselsteijn, W.A., De Kort, Y.A., Minkman, M.: Active involvement of people with dementia: a systematic review of studies developing supportive technologies. J. Alzheimer's Dis. **69**, 1041–1065 (2019)
24. Sanders, E.B.N.: From user-centered to participatory design approaches. In: Design and the Social Sciences, pp. 1–7. Taylor & Francis (2002)

Co-designing Strategies to Provide Telecare Through an Intelligent Assistant for Caregivers of Elderly Individuals

Mateus Monteiro[1(✉)], Luciana Salgado[1], Flávio Seixas[1],
and Rosimere Santana[2]

[1] Instituto de Computação, Universidade Federal Fluminense,
Av. Gal. Milton Tavares de Souza, s/n, Niterói, Brazil
mateusmonteiro@id.uff.br, {luciana,fseixas}@ic.uff.br
[2] Universidade Federal Fluminense, Escola de Enfermagem Aurora de Afonso Costa,
Rua Dr Celestino, 94, Niterói, Brazil
rfsantana@id.uff.br

Abstract. Worldwide, the number of people who are over 60 is growing more than any other age group. In the scenario of this research, a medium-sized city in Brazil, elderlies with Chronic Noncommunicable Diseases can have home care services. However, the healthcare professionals who assist these patients regularly face challenges in the visits, such as persistent fear of violence in certain areas. This research proposes the use of Intelligent Conversational Agents as a tool for supporting Telecare practices and tame these challenges. Our literature review, however, has demonstrated that previous works did not follow a methodology to promote a co-design of these agents in a scenario such as ours. There is also a lack of works that balance technological and social issues with non-technological experts in the design process (conceptualization, dialogues elaboration, intelligent agent goals and evaluation). We, thus, have performed a study following a qualitative methodology with the participation of health professionals. The first step aimed to raise the context, dialogues, and objectives of the agent. The second step, using observational and interviewing in a controlled environment, aimed to determine and evaluate the design goals, usefulness, compatibility with the reality, and find out additional requirements to aid the development of an Intelligent Conversational Agent. Results have led us to propose the agent MarIANA (Maria Intelligent conversAtioNal Agent). Therefore, it will act to prevent the clinical complications of these older adults suffering from Chronic Noncommunicable Diseases pointed as a critical matter in a recent work conducted in the city of the scenario of this research.

Keywords: Telecare · Intelligent Conversational Agents · Elderly

The authors want to thank the Brazilian funding agencies that support this project in different ways: CAPES, CNPq and FAPERJ. They would also like to express their gratitude to the volunteers who participated in the study.

Q. Gao and J. Zhou (Eds.): HCII 2020, LNCS 12208, pp. 149–166, 2020.
https://doi.org/10.1007/978-3-030-50249-2_12

1   Introduction

One of the main challenges facing society is the aging of the population [38]. All over the world the number of people who are over 60 is growing more than any other age group [30]. Brazil, by 2025, will be the sixth country in number of elderlies worldwide [38]. This increase is mainly due to the rise in life expectancy and the decline in birth rates [1,18]. Accompanied by these demographic changes, there is a need to ensure the elderly with positive and healthy aging [29,38].

In our research scenario, a medium-sized city in Brazil, elderlies with some mobility difficulties, or elderlies who need a multidisciplinary health team can have home care service. In a majority of cases, due to socioeconomic aspects, the patients have an informal familiar caregiver, which means a person with an uninterrupted task, which, in general, suffers from physical and psychological burnout that indirectly affects the patient and the caregiver him/herself [17].

However, the homecare is negatively affected, because the healthcare professionals who assist the patients regularly face challenges in carrying out the visits, such as lack of time, work overload, and persistent fear of violence in certain areas [23]. In this sense, this research assumes the use of a Telecare assistance to prevent clinical complications with intelligent agents, where the caregiver may act as a bridge between the professionals and those older adults' health [25], during the interval between the healthcare professionals visits.

According to Denecke, Tschanz, Dorner, and May [15], intelligent agents can provide care in places where people would not have or have limited access. However, few studies are focused on the challenges and benefits of Intelligent Conversational Agents (ICAs) usage for elderlies [26]. Besides that, none of them focuses on the caregiver. Our literature review has also demonstrated that previous works did not follow a methodology to design an ICA in a challenging scenario like ours, that is, high illiteracy rates, poverty as well as high rates of motor disability. There is also a lack of works that balance technological and social and cultural issues with non-technological experts (the health professionals) in the design process (conceptualization, dialogues elaboration, ICA goals, and evaluation).

This research, thus, aims at investigating the design of ICAs as a tool for supporting Telecare practices and tame these challenges. In this sense, a research question emerges: "Which communicative strategies should be adopted in an Intelligent Assistant to support caregivers of elderly patients in a Telecare assistance context?"

We, thus, have performed a study following a qualitative methodology [10, 16,28,40] with the participation of health professionals. The first step aimed to raise the context, dialogues, and objectives of the agent. The second step, using observational and interviewing in a controlled environment, aimed to determine and evaluate the design goals, usefulness, compatibility with the reality, and to find out additional requirements to aid the development of an ICA for our Telecare context.

Results have led us to propose the agent MarIANA (Maria Intelligent communicAtioN Agent). It will act to prevent the clinical complications of these older adults suffering from Chronic Noncommunicable Diseases (NCDs), pointed as a critical matter in a recent work conducted in the city of the scenario of this research. This paper has been divided as follows. In Sect. 2, we present our theoretical foundation. In Sect. 3, we present an overview of some related works. Section 4 presents our methodology and the results from the studies, including MarIANA. Finally, we discuss and conclude our results in Sect. 5.

2   Conversational Agents in Healthcare

According to Jusoh [22], a conversational agent is one of the emerging applications of natural language processing. According to Montenegro and Costa da Righi [26], the definition of conversational agents consists of a computer program or artificial intelligence capable of holding a conversation with humans through natural language processing.

Recently, applications of ICAs include emergent fields such as healthcare or even online business. A significant benefit of deploying an ICA is that it is available 24 h a day, seven days a week, and has a high potential to reduce the cost of hiring human personnel [22]. According to Denecke, Tschanz, Dorner, and May [15], agents can provide care in places where people would not have access. Possibilities of use in the medical field include, for example, a virtual nutritionist for diabetic patients, in which chatbot asks questions and ultimately prepares a diet, or an electronic medication management assistant or even music therapy.

Nonetheless, the authors Tsiourti et al. [34] affirm that real-world applications of conversational agents require in-depth exploration and a more scenario-based approach. Besides, it increases the chances of success in terms of acceptance, perceived usability, and usefulness. The authors King et al. [24] presented the efficiency of a culturally and linguistically adapted virtual agent. Results indicate a meaningful increase in physical activity relative of some of the older adults from the study.

In the work of Amato et al. [2], the authors investigate the effectiveness of a chatbot in a clinical context. In that scenario, the chatbot is used as a medical decision support system, having the goal of providing useful recommendations concerning to several disease prevention pathways. More in detail, the chatbot has been developed to help patients in choosing the most proper disease prevention pathway. The intention is to support the related prevention check-up and the final diagnosis. Preliminary experiments report the possibility of scalability of such system.

In the mental healthcare for elderlies scenario, there is a need to consider that the feeling of loneliness may come up when a patient lacks company or when they do not receive attention, which is common [21]. According to Eschweiler and Wanner [21], in the case of moderate dementia, patients tend to talk again and again about the same past events, which may lead to the adverse reaction of their conversation partners.

In this context, the role of an ICA could consist of dedicated affirmative responses that encourage the patients to continue their story [21]. Other applications for company could comprehend the support for locating objects, offering reminders, and guidance with household activities [34]. However, this implies the consideration of data privacy and data protection issues, both the patients themselves and the individuals possibly mentioned or commented upon in the conversation.

Another application for ICA in healthcare is the early identification of some diseases or the diagnosis of age-related diseases, affirms Eschweiler and Wanner [21]. As an example, Parkinson includes reduced perception and distinction of odors and disturbed sleep. Through the instruction of the caregivers or identification calls to the patient, some questions could be made to identify such issues. Still, according to Eschweiler and Wanner [21, pp. 8], the ICA could be programmed to apply geriatric assessment tools and questions of different aspects, such as Geriatric Depression Scale (GDS); Quality of life in Alzheimer's disease; Mini-Mental State Examination (MMSE); ADL/IADL; the revised memory and behavior problem checklist (RMBPC); among others.

In a work presented by the authors Montenegro, da Costa, and Righi [26], five categories concerning to the challenges of using conversational agents emerged: dialogue generation, integration with other technologies, adaptation and use of conversational agents by the older adults, user experience, and new approaches to methodology and architecture. Still, according to the authors, all papers that sought to solve the challenges of ICA for the older adult [24,27,31,33], focused on the patient scenario.

Among these works are three major fronts: prevention [24], training [27], and assistance with daily activities [33]. In the work of Nikitina, Callaioli, and Baez [27], the authors describe the requirements, models, and designs of inexperienced professional training for reminiscence, which is a reminder of important aspects of the life of older adults. Concerning prevention, ICAs can contribute in choosing the best path for treating the disease, preventing suicide, and even dealing with depression [26].

Regarding the initial and exploratory topic, which is the use of ICA with older adults, many applications, benefits, and challenges are upon ahead. Among the benefits, according to Jusoh [22], ICAs are available 24/7, can provide care in places where people would not have access, reduce the cost of hiring human personnel. About the applications, it is possible to mention, in the clinical context, to support physicians with the appropriate treatment path [2], mental healthcare regarding companionship [21], or even the support of locating objects, reminders, and guidance with daily activities [33,34]. In nursing, the ICA application includes the diagnosis of age-related issues using geriatric assessment tools and questions of different aspects [21]. Other usages cover prevention [24], training of inexperienced healthcare professionals [27], preventing suicide, dealing with depression [26], and many others. As seen, there are many challenges regarding to older adults' ICA application [24,27,31,33]. Real-world applications require in-depth exploration, and, in some cases, a longitudinal study [34]. According to Tsiourti et al. [34], this increases the chance of success in terms of acceptance, perceived usability, and usefulness. Moreover, including the agent in culturally and linguistically adapted developing, indicates a meaningful increase in behavior change of its users [24].

3   Related Works

Many studies have addressed some challenges of ICA for older adults by promoting mental health, such as reminiscence [27], training for cognitive [20,37], companions for the older adults who live in isolation [6,36,39], suicide prevention, how to deal with depression [26], and even palliative care [35]. Literature regarding agents for older adults with NCDs, in turn, is not extensive. Efforts are placed in the self-care promotion in the domain of endocrinology [7], cardiology [3,41], or pneumology [19]. The lack of research of NCDs is, perhaps, related to a concentration of the efforts in first-world countries, such as the United States [4–6,32], Ireland [3], France [37], United Kingdom [19] and Portugal [7,34].

Moreover, similar to agents that focus on improving mental health (see [11]), agents for physical health should not address the communicative strategies as a secondary issue. For example, Tsiourti and colleagues [34] argue that the agent for isolated older adults should not be intrusive, should avoid proactivity when monitoring and be informal when remembering the daily activities. So, anticipating communicative strategies for an ICA to support caregivers of older adults with NCDs is not only related to improve the social abilities of agents but also to avoid risks.

Even in the same domain as Tsiourti and colleagues [34], in the study of Vardoulakis et al. [36], one of the participants commented she was feeling worse after the study because the interactions with the agent has made the participant realize the lack of communication with humans and friends that she desired in her life. In a longitudinal study with elderlies reported in Bott et al. [6], participants emphasized discontent with the repetitive nature of the agent and inappropriate dialogues - "I love you (the agent's dialog) [...] it meant nothing to me, there was no reason why it would love me". These reports highlight the need for prior co-creation and evaluation process with health professionals before the evaluation stage with the older adults. Zhang and colleagues [41] claim that previous interaction with professionals during the development phase allows a more assertive opinion and anticipates possible embedded risks.

Therefore, we can conclude that there is a lack of research about how to develop and ICA focusing on communicative strategies and attributes, especially for older adults with NCDs. Even more, the development of ICAs should consider socioeconomic and cultural factors of older adults. The complexity of variables from our research scenario urges for anticipating risks and avoiding more barriers to the older adults' health.

4   Co-designing Intelligent Conversational Agents in Healthcare

4.1   Goal and Methodology

As already mentioned in the introduction, the goal of these studies was to investigate which communicative strategies should be adopted in an Intelligent Assistant for support caregivers of elderly patients in our scenario. This is the first step of a larger research project to create a framework to inform the design of such agents and to allow the design team to anticipate and deal with known problems in a specific context.

To this purpose, we have designed a qualitative study with two steps to investigate who the health professionals think the users are, the context and scenario details, the clinical expectations and conditions, the objectives to be achieved in Telecare assistance (engage, monitor, for instance). The option for a qualitative methodology derives from the fact that we want to learn in-depth and, in detail, the particularities of a specific scenario.

Given our goal, we had to choose how to characterize and frame our phenomenon of study. So, we chose to anchor our study in Semiotic Engineering (SE) theory [12–14], because it puts together the two themes of interest in our research, the communicability of ICAs and Human-Centered Computing (HCC) [13]. The procedures and analysis presented below have thus been carried out with constant reference to dimensions proposed by SE authors.

In the first step, we performed an exploratory study to discover context issues, dialogues and strategies that could provide prevention of clinical complications to the elderly in the context. The second step, using observational and interviewing in a controlled environment, aimed to determine and evaluate the perception of the agent design goals, usefulness, compatibility with the reality, and to find out additional requirements to aid the development of the ICA.

The recruitment process has selected academic and professional community, with no distinction of gender or age. The participants should be health professionals (nurses, doctors, psychologists, therapists, among others), preferably nurses, based on the level of technical/scientific/practical knowledge.

4.2 Step 1

Through the process of recruitment of health professionals who have experience in the home care setting, two health professionals were selected based on their previous experiences with older adults and knowledge about our research scenario. The first participant (P1) is a nursing student who is in the ninth semester. Her final essay project is related to monitoring postoperative seniors through a messaging application and she also has experience in a local project of Telecare. The second participant (P2) is a nurse, graduated since 2012, specialist in health care for the older adults who is currently a master student. Besides, the participant also has experience in working in several critical home care scenarios, as manager of a Telecare company.

Concerning the data collection, before the workshop, an initial survey was applied to select the participants, based on the level of technical/scientific/practical knowledge regarding the context of the research. This survey consisted basically in demographic information and a Likert scale for the subjects in which the study aims in the workshop. During the workshop, an empirical collection took place through audio, video, and artifacts from the Design Thinking stages.

Design Thinking has three steps (Immersion, Ideation, and Prototyping), in which we intend to:

- Immersion - build a Persona with demographic information (name, age, education, technology skills, bio, frustrations, limitations) and two points from the Empathy Map ("Need to change" and "Works out"), i.e., improvements and solutions, techniques that are not working;
- Ideation - the technique "How Might We" is applied. The participants must raise questions, for example, "How Might We - reduce the clinical complications in the scenario?" and seek answers for the resulting issues, regarding the ICA;
- Conversational flow prototyping - co-create the dialog between the ICA and the Persona from the Immersion step. In general terms, the participants are thinking in creative solutions that could occur with a human-human interaction intermediated by the telephone or any communication source, thinking in solutions that meet the particular needs of the Persona. To do so, the participants should elaborate on the conversation, in a tree structure, with the materials (post its, styrofoam, pins, among others).

Data analysis of the transcribed info followed a non-predictive and interpretive paradigm with the coding approach of collected and transcribed empirical data [8]. The analysis started with an open coding naming sentence by sentence and an axial coding that used the most significant codings to organize, synthesize, integrate, and organize large amounts of data.

The main products of this step were a: Persona containing demographic information (e.g., name, age, among others), frustrations (e.g., lack of technical knowledge, informality, among others), limitations (e.g., social, economic, and cultural aspects), what the participants consider as pain points in the context and should be improved, and what the participants already use as solution for the pain points; "How Might We" answers, that is, possible solutions for the Persona, as well as the respective positive and negative impacts; and a "hands-on" conversational flow prototype of interactions between the agent and the Persona. Besides, with the analysis of the products of step 1 and the transcribed data, preliminary communicative strategies were elaborated.

To conclude, having the results from step 1, we developed on Dialogflow[1] an initial interactive prototype. This version was deployed on a Facebook[2] page and had a programmed dialogue to verify and guide the caregiver of older adults with hypertension, as shown in Fig. 1.

---

[1] https://dialogflow.com/.
[2] https://www.messenger.com/.

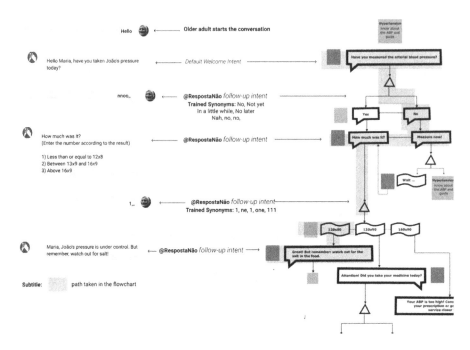

Fig. 1. From the "hands-on" conversational flow prototype to an initial interactive prototype on Dialogflow.

4.3   Step 2

The second step, using observational and interviewing in a controlled environment, aimed to determine and evaluate the perception of the agent design goals, usefulness, compatibility with the reality, and to find out additional requirements to aid the development of the ICA.

There were three participants, and each interview took place at the participant's preferred location. In general, participants presented a good knowledge concerning older adults, self-care, clinical complications, informal/formal caregivers, hypertension, and Telecare. The first participant (P1) is a nurse, a Ph.D. Candidate, and works in a government secretary of health, where our research is being carried out. The second participant (P2) is a professor and researcher in nursing and a doctor in cardiovascular sciences. Finally, the third participant (P3) is a nurse, postgraduate in intensive care, and has a master degree in nursing. Both second and third participants have worked for years on projects to assist the elderly with socioeconomic challenges.

Regarding data collection, before the interviews, pursuing the same goal as in Step 1, demographic information and the level of knowledge of the participants with the topics of our objective were collected. During the interviews, we collected the audio recorded, video recordings of the interaction with the initial prototype, and participants' notes on the "hands-on" conversational flow prototype (printed in paper).

Hence, sessions of observational and interviews determined the perception of other specialists on the design goals, compatibility with the reality, and additional requirements to aid the development of the ICA. The research followed the semi structured steps below:

– Present the research;
– Ask the participant about more details related to the context and Persona;
– Ask the participant to use the initial interactive prototype with the Thinkaloud protocol [9];
– Show the participant the "hands-on" conversational flow (printed in paper) and ask for corrections, annotations or observations of any mistakes;
– Ask the participant about the communicative strategies and attributes.

For the analysis step of the collected data, we combined discourse analysis [8] with semiotic analysis [12,14], while examining records of what participants said, how they behaved in the workshop, kinds of comments they build, and so on. The semiotic analysis was conducted with the SigniFYIng Message tool [13]. In this tool, the following SE-based meaning categories are used to identify and describe: [13, pp.64]:

– (i) Designers' (in our context, the health professionals) beliefs about
    – (a) The logic of the user's context?
    – (b) User's needs;
    – (c) User's preferences;
    – (d) User's profile; and/or
    – (e) User's goals;
– (ii) the Developer's (in our context, the health professionals) intentions and expectations with respect to
    – (a) The Logic of the system's design?
    – (b) The System's mode of use;
    – (c) The System's description; and/or
    – (d) The System's functionality;
– (iii) the Developer's (in our context, the health professionals) provisions and support for alternative modes/purposes of use that are compatible with the system's design? of the system.

The main products of this step were: additional information (profile, context, user preferences, among others) for the Persona; critical paths which the health professionals anticipate in light of the scenario, on the "hands-on" conversational flow (through notes), and the interactive prototype (through interaction). To conclude, with the analysis of the products of step 2 and the transcribed data, additional communicative strategies were elaborated, and previous strategies from step 1 were refined.

4.4 Findings

Step 1. Regarding the first step (resulting artifacts in Fig. 2), it has showed that male elderlies between 70–75 years old are the most common profile that faces high hospitalization rates due to lack of self-care, causing clinical complications (injuries, mutilations, and even in extreme cases, death). This profile generally proves to be dependent on specific activities. Also, they do not properly maintain the treatment until the next service. Due to the neglect of their health, relatives such as their wives, aged about 60–65, end up taking care of their husbands for themselves. However, this can often happen without the relative having the proper technical preparation to be a caregiver.

Regarding the communicative aspects, the interaction human-human of the participants' daily routine allowed the elicitation of communication models within the current Telecare context. Textual interaction enables professionals to receive short responses and with more agility. On the other hand, the use of voice interaction enables the reduction of subjectivity, allows illiterate older adults to interact with the application. One of the participants in the first step affirms that "The older adults [...] in applications such as Facebook or Whatsapp [...] guide themselves through figures and icons [...] and even with low literacy, they manage to send voice notes".

Another result is the social skills of the agent: An incisive posture is noted in the dialogues with messages such as "Measure now"; Simpler dialogues denote the need for dialogues without subjectivity and reformulation of phrases. According to the report of one of the participants - "I saw an older adult who once said to me - Young man, do not go around. Speak exactly what I need to hear"; Repetition is the need to repeat the dialog. According to the participants, the negligence of actions happens intentionally or unintentional, "You can ask him to do it [...], but he may end up not remembering or not doing it at all. The ideal would be for you to get in touch again".

As a result of the last stage from step 1, conversational flow prototyping, the participants developed 17 dialogues interaction between the agent and Persona, including questions as if the caregiver measured the older adult's blood pressure. According to the immersion phase, our Persona's husband does not apply the self-care.

Step 2. Regarding the (i) first category of the SigniFYIng Message, the discourse of the participants about (a) the context was related to dealing with actions promoted by educational institutions and movements of the public power about permanent education on the health of the elderly. Another part of the discourse (i.c) is associated with issues of the elderly and health professionals. It is interesting to notice the depth of the participants' discussion when they stressed the use of digital meters and disconnection with part of the dialogues presented in the prototype (e.g., 120×80). According to the participants, this would create a barrier. This barrier is necessarily related to the caregivers' when they see a different sign in the dialogue other than they are used to in the digital blood pressure monitor (e.g., 12×8), causing a communicational rupture.

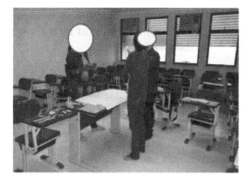
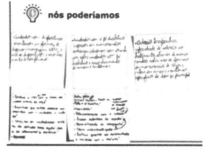
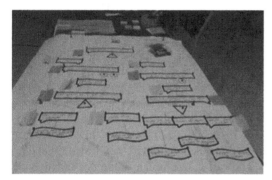

Fig. 2. Resulting artifacts from the Step 1.

Besides that, according to the participants, 13×9 is not considered hypertension, even in a generic context without considering the health history of the older adult. In a scenario in which the older adult presented this pressure and was referred to the emergency room, it would lead to a denial by the professionals, indicating the absence of hypertension and possible disbelief with technology, consequently affecting the care process. Still, on breaks in the dialogues, the participants also stressed the importance of promoting physical exercise and not only changing eating habits.

Regarding the profile of the actors (i.d) in the scenario, the participants stressed the difficulty of changing the habit of the elderly, the need to engage in the care process and with technology, such as using festive dates in the dialogues, and finally, the real possibility of wrong medicalisation by caregivers. Finally, about the item, (i.e.), the emotional stress of the caregivers(s), as already stated above, affects not only the older adult but the wife caregiver who is often also elderly. This statement conducts the goal of technology to something more than just the health of the husband, but a relational agent in an indirect way to the caregiver.

About the (ii) second category of the SigniFYIng Message, the Developer's intentions and expectations discourse was related to the design logic (ii.a), mode of use (ii.b), and functionality (ii.d). The sub-category (ii.a) refers to factors necessary for the interaction to occur correctly. Participants raised questions regarding strategies before and during use. Before use, promotion of interviews and training with caregivers were suggested by the participants.

Furthermore, during the use, for example, clarity in the way information should be entered by the user. Firstly, the use of simple agent dialogue for simple responses from the caregivers is evident, specially when considering that there is the possibility of answers in disconnected phrases. Limiting text input to predefined responses would be an obvious answer to the challenge, using, for example, buttons or checkboxes. However, according to one of the participants, the ideal would be to map tracks and common words. In that sense, it is continuously detecting words or phrases that may cause a warning and helping the health professionals in the decision-making process about the next medical appointment or acting immediately.

This alert to professionals is deeply associated with the "symbiotic" discourse of the participants in the second step. This discourse is a variation compared to the works of literature. Agent strategies are often very much associated with a context, when, in fact, the agent will be placed in a setting with several actors, such as the health professionals. Strategies for both the caregiver and the professionals allow a closer relationship and value the opinion of professionals about the technology, for example encouraging responsible nurses, from time to time, to analyze caregivers with good practices and make contact to congratulate them. According to one of the participants, the call makes much difference in the care of the elderly, because, on certain occasions, the call from the responsible nurse is the only call that the older adult receives over a long period.

Regarding the ways of Use (ii.b), the participants warned about the distance between the participants with long-term care and technology. The participants stressed how caregivers can fail to notice essential parts of the dialogue, needing something that promotes contrast or Use of visual aids. Besides, playful strategies are necessary to get him to use the technology for a longer time, thus avoiding the standardization of the care process. One of the participants suggested the Use of festive dialogues according to the date of the year. However, by the end of the study, the participant himself anticipated a possible barrier, saying that each patient has their religion (or not) and that not everyone celebrates specific dates.

Regarding the resulting functionalities and strategies (ii.d), new strategies point to improvements in the dialogues, promoting retention through the mentioned festive approach and personalized dialogues, promoting more assertive care through the mapping of the so-called target values and keywords. The discussion about the trade-off of the limitation or not of the user input enabled two points: limiting the target ranges when questioning the pressure at first. So, if the user responds with a critical option such as "Higher than 16×9", ask them how much higher. Thus, acknowledge if it is necessary to refer the older adult to the health center. In the case of target words, keep open and allow the agent to be continually listening to the user's speeches, and if they enter a term that may be dangerous to the life or well-being of the elderly, notify the nurse linked to the elderly – finally, the Use of contrast in the parts that need the caregiver's attention.

Also, call to congratulate when the caregiver is getting good results with the care – in this way, further strengthening the institutional bond between the elderly and caregiver with public health. Finally, personalizing the dialogues for the profile of the elderly is essential for the assertive care process, as each patient has his or her depth of context, culture, health, and beliefs.

Regarding the last item of the SignFYing Message, (iii) provisions and support for alternative modes/purposes, the participants' discourse brought the possibility of using the agent with independent older adults – these, lonelier, also a profile with difficulties such as the caregiver profile, previously anticipated. Also, carelessness in these older adults' care can cause a regression in the health condition, generating a further increase in the statistics of clinical complications. Specially because in some cases, they refuse the need of a caregiver, living alone without the help of a third party in self-care of their health.

MarIANA. The resulting agent MarIANA, it is essentially conceptualized to orient a caregiver of an older male adult with hypertension. Also, the agent promotes emotional support to the caregiver through valuing the care with pieces of dialog and by fostering the contact between health professionals and the caregiver. There are mainly two actors in the design space of MarIANA, the informal caregiver and the health professionals of the primary care. The informal caregiver, usually the wife of the patient, is susceptible to some conditions that can directly influence the care of the spouse. These conditions are low education, lack of technical knowledge (of the care procedures), pressure and lack of family support, among many others. On the other hand, professionals in primary care are vulnerable to external conditions of access to care, that is, difficulties in access and excessive activities and responsibilities.

For this reason, the benefits of the intelligent agent divide into promoting for professionals through MarIANA: the possibility of noting caregivers' behavioral changes; receive requests for help from patients or caregivers; view in real-time or the records of the dialogues between agent and caregiver; promote the recognition of good practices; have inputs for the next visits; have general information about care for micro or macro-regions, and receive notifications that alert the patient is in risky situations. For the caregivers, it is: guide on some activities of the care, receiving monitoring by the agent for eventual emergencies; receive emotional support through dialogues and contacts from health professionals.

It is noteworthy that those benefits are derived from communication aspects. The first strategy (S1) is related to the dialog definition, which is determined by the objective (i.e., greeting, health orders, collection, guidance, reminders) of the message. That objective determines the (a) temporality (i.e., instant, daily, weekly), (b) means of transmitting (i.e., textual, videos, visual resources), and the (d) social ability (i.e., non-subjective, imperative, repetition, contextual language). For example, when the message is about health orders, the health professionals in the prototype instantiated an imperative posture - "Measure now!".

The second strategy (S2) is related to personalizing the resulting hypertension dialog individually. In this sense, in order to make the dialog elements individual, some data are required from the caregiver (name, age, region) and from the older adult (name, age, health history, current medicines usage, family beliefs, interests, associated health professional).

The third strategy (S3) it is about clarity in the way the user should enter the information. Certain dialogues require different approaches since the "freedom" that a natural language conversation allows can be a barrier or a path for intervention. See the following example of the interaction between the agent and the caregiver:

- (Agent) Did you measure John's blood pressure today?
- (Caregiver) yes
- (Agent) How much was it? Select (or write) one of the options, Maria.
    - (1) Up to 12×8
    - (2) Between 12×8 and 14×9
    - (3) Higher than 16×9
- (Caregiver) 3
- (Agent) How much higher, Maria?
- (Caregiver) 19

The first time that the agent asks for BP, then predefined BP is used. However, if the third option is selected, then the agent asks, "How much higher?". This happens because a critical condition is relative to each individual. If this number is considered critical for the patient, then the patient is guided to the emergency. Since there is the possibility of "he goes to the hospital [...], and then the health professional himself will underestimate it [...] (the elderly person) leaves home [...] and (will have to) go back". Not only putting the elderly, the caregiver, and the family in an alert situation but can also make the technology as untrustworthy as if it was placed by one of the participants.

The fourth strategy (S4) is related to another way to concede intervention. MarIANA will be capable of identifying words that can characterize a danger. For example, if, through audio or text, the caregiver sends the word "sleepy" then the health professional associated with the family should be warned. Besides, as in the case of the "critical words", when the blood pressure is in dangerous levels, the team is also notified. One of the participants from step 1 said - "[...] maybe notify the team that he (older adult) was instructed to go to the hospital [...] because then at the end of the month they (health professionals) [...] could call to ask if he went to the hospital [...] and it is no longer the problem of the agent, it is the problem of the team that will take the necessary provisions".

The fifth strategy (S5) is related to communication models. So that both the agent can process the information and the health professional make trusting decisions, the dialogues need to allow direct and straightforward interactions, agility in the interaction, detect sings and avoid questions that allow subjective answers.

Other strategies with great potential in care are the (S6) Engagement and (S7) Symbiosis. Regarding (S6), the participants argued the need to keep them engaged with technology and care:

– a. Dialogues of interest - dialogues embedded during the flowchart, to comment on something of interest to the participant. For example festive dialogues, a Merry Christmas message.
– b. Visual Resources - these visual resources depend on the means of transmitting. In the case of MarIANA, the use of emojis, figures, and even GIFs was recommended. Also, presenting contrast through stronger colors in alert messages, colorful or cheerful emojis, such as, for example, the second participant of the second step said, "Something that would show an OK here [...], a thumbs up".
– c. Dynamism - another concept inherited from human-human practice. Protocol dialogues like Mariana's tend to become nauseating. Therefore, the use of (S5.a) or (S6.b) may be essential in this process of patient improvement, changing, for example, different visual resources, colors or even adding a dialog related to the caregiver interest.

Regarding (S7) Symbiosis, the participation of professionals in this context is essential. The cooperative participation between agent and scenario allows caregivers (and adjacent actors) to realize that it is not just a technology; there is a team behind it. This symbiosis occurs through:

– Mapping of executions - how many times the agent needed to ask the caregiver to perform a certain task. For example, if it is needed many times, the agent should, in this case, contact the team. The Mapping of executions can also happen with a non-punitive intention. One example may be that, after a specified time, contact the health team. Then the associated professional get in touch to congratulate that the care is being adequate;
– Mapping of target words and blood pressure values - once the agent maps this data, when it presents any risk, send an alert to the responsible professional or team.

5   Conclusions

The in-depth co-design approach of the ICA, with the participation of specialists, allowed the design of MarIANA. It is noteworthy that the use of agents in this scenario does not propose the replacement of human contact, essential for overcoming loneliness, cognitive, and emotional decline of the older adults [21]. In step 1, participants have cooperated by defining the profile and needs of the Persona, proposing solutions for the scenario, and prototyping a conversational flow for the hypertensive Persona's husband. Additionally, challenging socioeconomic and cultural characteristics reflected directly in the intentions and expectations of the co-designers concerning the agent. In step 2, participants have brought additional information for the design space and additional communicative strategies; evaluated design decisions from step 1, such as the conversational flow; and also anticipated intricacies that were not compatible with the reality and needs of the health professionals.

Therefore, this research brings three main contributions. First, our research presented an initial exploration of a methodology for co-designing an ICA to such a socioeconomic and culturally challenging scenario. That may serve as a detailed approach to future investigation and possibly providing a starting point. Second, communicative aspects of a conversational agent, which we did not have the goal to offer definitive answers but plausible strategies and attributes to guide further development. Finally, our third contribution relates to the computational artifact for our research scenario, which may act as a tool for older adults with NCDs, specifically hypertension, in the scenario. Future work includes another co-design and evaluation cycle of the actual prototype and the inclusion of the caregivers in the design process. Also, more research is needed to reveal the potentials as well as the limitations of using such technology and the resulting behavior changes from such technology.

References

1. de Aguiar Sá Azeredo, Z., Neto Afonso, M.A.: Solitude from the perspective of the elderly. Revista Brasileira de Geriatria e Gerontologia **19**(2), 313–324 (2016)
2. Amato, F., Marrone, S., Moscato, V., Piantadosi, G., Picariello, A., Sansone, C.: Chatbots meet eHealth: automatizing healthcare. In: WAIAH, pp. 40–49 (2017)
3. Barrett, M., et al.: Artificial intelligence supported patient self-care in chronic heart failure: a paradigm shift from reactive to predictive, preventive and personalised care. EPMA J. **10**(4), 445–464 (2019). https://doi.org/10.1007/s13167-019-00188-9
4. Bickmore, T., Gruber, A., Picard, R.: Establishing the computer-patient working alliance in automated health behavior change interventions. Patient Educ. Couns. **59**(1), 21–30 (2005)
5. Bickmore, T.W., et al.: Patient and consumer safety risks when using conversational assistants for medical information: an observational study of Siri, Alexa, and Google assistant. J. Med. Internet Res. **20**(9), e11510 (2018)
6. Bott, N., et al.: A protocol-driven, bedside digital conversational agent to support nurse teams and mitigate risks of hospitalization in older adults: case control pre-post study. J. Med. Internet Res. **21**(10), e13440 (2019)
7. Buinhas, S., et al.: Virtual assistant to improve self-care of older people with type 2 diabetes: first prototype. In: García-Alonso, J., Fonseca, C. (eds.) IWoG 2018. CCIS, vol. 1016, pp. 236–248. Springer, Cham (2019). https://doi.org/10.1007/978-3-030-16028-9_21
8. Charmaz, K.: Constructing Grounded Theory. SAGE, London (2014)
9. Charters, E.: The use of think-aloud methods in qualitative research an introduction to think-aloud methods. Brock Educ. J. Educ. Res. Pract. **12**(2), 68–82 (2003)
10. Creswell, J.W.: Qualitative Inquiry and Research Design. SAGE Publications, Thousand Oaks (2007)

11. Cruz-Sandoval, D., Favela, J.: Incorporating conversational strategies in a social robot to interact with people with dementia. Dement. Geriatr. Cogn. Disord. **47**(3), 140–148 (2019)
12. De Souza, C.S.: The Semiotic Engineering of Human-Computer Interaction. MIT Press, Cambridge (2005)
13. Sieckenius de Souza, C., Fontoura de Gusmão Cerqueira, R., Marques Afonso, L., Rossi de Mello Brandão, R., Soares Jansen Ferreira, J.: Software Developers as Users. Springer, Cham (2016). https://doi.org/10.1007/978-3-319-42831-4
14. De Souza, C.S., Leitão, C.F.: Semiotic engineering methods for scientific research in HCI. Synth. Lect. Hum. Center. Inf. **2**(1), 1–122 (2009)
15. Denecke, K., Tschanz, M., Dorner, T., May, R.: Intelligent conversational agents in healthcare: hype or hope? Stud. Health Tech. Inf. **259**, 77–84 (2019)
16. Denzin, N.K., Lincoln, Y.S.: Collecting and interpreting qualitative materials, vol. 3. SAGE Publications, Thousand Oaks (2008)
17. Diniz, M.A.A., Monteiro, D.Q., Gratão, A.C.M.: Education for informal elderly caregivers (educação em saúde para cuidadores informais de idosos). Soc. Health Soc. Change (Saúde & Transformação) **7**(1), 028–040 (2016)
18. Dohr, A., Modre-Opsrian, R., Drobics, M., Hayn, D., Schreier, G.: The Internet of things for ambient assisted living. In: Seventh International Conference on Information Technology: New Generations (ITNG), Las Vegas, NV, USA, pp. 804–809. IEEE (2010)
19. Easton, K., et al.: A virtual agent to support individuals living with physical and mental comorbidities: co-design and acceptability testing. J. Med. Internet Res. **21**(5), e12996 (2019)
20. El Kamali, M., Angelini, L., Caon, M., Andreoni, G., Khaled, O.A., Mugellini, E.: Towards the nestore e-coach: a tangible and embodied conversational agent for older adults. In: Proceedings of the 2018 ACM International Joint Conference and 2018 International Symposium on Pervasive and Ubiquitous Computing and Wearable Computers, pp. 1656–1663. ACM (2018)
21. Eschweiler, G.W., Wanner, L.: How can intelligent conversational agents help? The needs of geriatric patients and their caregivers. In: Intelligent Conversation Agents in Home and Geriatric Care Applications, Stockholm, Sweden, pp. 1–9. CEUR-WS (2018)
22. Jusoh, S.: Intelligent conversational agent for online sales. In: International Conference on Electronics. Computers and Artificial Intelligence (ECAI), Iasi, Romania, pp. 1–4. IEEE (2018)
23. Kebian, L.V.A., Acioli, S.: The home visit of nurses and community health agents of the family health strategy. Revista Eletrônica de Enfermagem **16**(1), 1–9 (2014)
24. King, A.C., Bickmore, T.W., Campero, M., Pruitt, L.A., Yin, J.L.: Employing virtual advisors in preventive care for underserved communities: results from the compass study. J. Health Commun. **18**(12), 1449–1464 (2013). https://doi.org/10.1080/10810730.2013.798374. pMID: 23941610
25. Ministry of Welfare and Social Assistance of Brazil (Ministério da Previdência e Assistência Social do Brasil): Publicity of the role of caregiver (Publicização do papel do cuidador domiciliar) (1998). Accessed 17 Jan 2020
26. Montenegro, J.L.Z., da Costa, C.A., da Rosa Righi, R.: Survey of conversational agents in health. Expert Syst. Appl. **129**, 56–67 (2019)
27. Nikitina, S., Callaioli, S., Baez, M.: Smart conversational agents for reminiscence. CoRR abs/1804.06550 (2018). http://arxiv.org/abs/1804.06550
28. Olson, J.S., Kellogg, W.A. (eds.): Ways of Knowing in HCI. Springer, New York (2014). https://doi.org/10.1007/978-1-4939-0378-8

29. World Health Organization: Global action plan on the public health response to dementia 2017–2025 (2017)
30. Schneider, R.H., Irigaray, T.Q.: Aging today: chronological, biological, psychological and social aspects. Estudos de Psicologia **25**(4), 585–593 (2008)
31. Shaked, N.A.: Avatars and virtual agents-relationship interfaces for the elderly. Healthcare Technol. Lett. **4**(3), 83–87 (2017)
32. Sidner, C.L., et al.: Creating new technologies for companionable agents to support isolated older adults. ACM Trans. Interac. Intell. Syst. (TiiS) **8**(3), 17 (2018)
33. Tokunaga, S., Horiuchi, H., Tamamizu, K., Saiki, S., Nakamura, M., Yasuda, K.: Deploying service integration agent for personalized smart elderly care. In: 2016 IEEE/ACIS 15th International Conference on Computer and Information Science (ICIS), pp. 1–6, June 2016. https://doi.org/10.1109/ICIS.2016.7550873
34. Tsiourti, C., et al.: A virtual assistive companion for older adults: design implications for a real-world application. In: Bi, Y., Kapoor, S., Bhatia, R. (eds.) IntelliSys 2016. LNNS, vol. 15, pp. 1014–1033. Springer, Cham (2018). https://doi.org/10.1007/978-3-319-56994-9_69
35. Utami, D., Bickmore, T., Nikolopoulou, A., Paasche-Orlow, M.: Talk about death: end of life planning with a virtual agent. IVA 2017. LNCS (LNAI), vol. 10498, pp. 441–450. Springer, Cham (2017). https://doi.org/10.1007/978-3-319-67401-8_55
36. Vardoulakis, L.P., Ring, L., Barry, B., Sidner, C.L., Bickmore, T.: Designing relational agents as long term social companions for older adults. In: Nakano, Y., Neff, M., Paiva, A., Walker, M. (eds.) IVA 2012. LNCS (LNAI), vol. 7502, pp. 289–302. Springer, Heidelberg (2012). https://doi.org/10.1007/978-3-642-33197-8_30
37. Wargnier, P., Carletti, G., Laurent-Corniquet, Y., Benveniste, S., Jouvelot, P., Rigaud, A.S.: Field evaluation with cognitively-impaired older adults of attention management in the embodied conversational agent louise. In: IEEE International Conference on Serious Games and Applications for Health (SeGAH), pp. 1–8. IEEE (2016)
38. World Health Organization (WHO): Global Health and Aging (2011)
39. Yaghoubzadeh, R., Kramer, M., Pitsch, K., Kopp, S.: Virtual agents as daily assistants for elderly or cognitively impaired people. In: Aylett, R., Krenn, B., Pelachaud, C., Shimodaira, H. (eds.) IVA 2013. LNCS (LNAI), vol. 8108, pp. 79–91. Springer, Heidelberg (2013). https://doi.org/10.1007/978-3-642-40415-3_7
40. Yin, R.K.: Case Study Research. SAGE Publications, Thousand Oaks (2008)
41. Zhang, L., Babu, S.V., Jindal, M., Williams, J.E., Gimbel, R.W.: A patient-centered mobile phone app (iHeartU) with a virtual human assistant for self-management of heart failure: protocol for a usability assessment study. JMIR Res. Protoc. **8**(5), e13502 (2019)

Tablet-Based Comprehensive Cognitive Rehabilitation in Daily Life Using Virtual and Augmented Reality Technology

Sayaka Okahashi[1]([✉]), Saori Sawada[2], and Ayae Kinoshita[1]

[1] Kyoto University, Kyoto, Japan
okahashi.sayaka.7c@kyoto-u.ac.jp
[2] Advanced Science, Technology & Management Research Institute of KYOTO,
Kyoto, Japan

Abstract. One major concern for people with dementia is the decline in their cognitive functions such as memory or attention, which can significantly affect their ability to perform instrumental activities of daily living. It is important to observe the patients in an environment similar to the daily life in order to understand their actual problems. Previous studies have shown that an approach using Virtual Reality technology has the advantage of providing realistic scenario repeatedly, cost-effectively and safely for patients. In the series of our studies, we have developed a computer-based Virtual Shopping Test (VST), which introduces shopping tasks in a virtual shopping mall in order to assess comprehensive cognitive ability in routine daily tasks. One of unresolved issues with VST was a lack of clinical usability (e.g. custom-made task level adjustability, device portability). We then revised VST into Virtual Shopping Applications (VSA) for iOS with some additional functions using virtual and augmented reality technology. In this paper, we describe the development of VSA, a tablet-based comprehensive cognitive rehabilitation system in daily life. We discuss the development of the system, as well as feasibility studies in people with dementia.

Keywords: Virtual Reality · Augmented reality · Cognitive rehabilitation · Elderly people · Dementia

1 Introduction

The Japanese population is aging rapidly. The percentage of elderly people with cognitive impairment and physical disability has increased. Cognitive dysfunction related to memory, attention, and calculation due to aging and brain damage lead to many difficulties in everyday life. Such patients have difficulties not only in fundamental activities of daily living (ADL), such as eating and clothing, but also in other practical instrumental activities of daily living (IADL), such as shopping, cooking, use of public transport, etc. It has been reported that the results of conventional assessment methods with a paper and pencil sometimes disagree with the actual cognitive level of patients [1–3]. Therefore, the development of more effective assessment/training methods with new technology is required to assist in cognitive rehabilitation. For such rehabilitation, it is important to observe patients in an environment that is similar to daily life in order to understand their actual problems.

Q. Gao and J. Zhou (Eds.): HCII 2020, LNCS 12208, pp. 167–176, 2020.
https://doi.org/10.1007/978-3-030-50249-2_13

Virtual Reality (VR) technology provides access virtually thus offering benefits when far or while at home or hospital. Augmented Reality (AR) technology allows us to behave in a real environment containing additional artificial information. VR/AR technologies have great possibilities in not only entertainment industry but also for medical care and/or patient rehabilitation. VR techniques have been applied the assessment of cognitive impairment since the 1990s. Previous studies [4–7] reported that VR technology has significant potential for clinical cognitive rehabilitation. However, there were problems when we applied these systems for Japanese patients with brain damage in terms of complicated operation, cultural difference and difficulty of tasks.

In the series of our study [8, 9], we developed the Virtual Shopping Test (VST), which introduces shopping tasks in a virtual shopping mall in order to assess comprehensive cognitive ability in routine daily tasks. The hardware system included a personal computer and a 19-inch touch screen. We found that one of unresolved issues is with this system was a lack of clinical usability (e.g. custom-made task level adjustability, device portability). In this research, we first revised the VST into "Virtual Shopping App_1 (VSA_1)" for iOS tablets to assess everyday problems related to dementia using VR technique. Second, in order to investigate the possibilities in expansion of existing the VST, we revised the VST into "Virtual Shopping App_2 (VSA_2)" for iOS tablets using AR technique. We hypothesized that the system with VSA_2 provides a more self-directed rehabilitation environment for subjects cognitively and physically. We then conducted feasibility studies of VSA_1 or VSA_2 in several patients with dementia. In this paper, we describe two kinds of new tablet-based systems and discuss the applicability of VSA to people with cognitive impairment based on their behavioral data.

2   Related Works

2.1   Traditional Cognitive Assessment Methods

There are some methods of assess cognitive functions clinically. Occupational therapists and speech-language-hearing therapists use neuropsychological tests with pencil and paper in a quiet room for objective assessment of cognitive functions traditionally. They usually use a specific a test battery for each cognitive function. In addition, questionnaires are sometimes used for patients and/or their family or main caregivers to evaluate patients' disability in daily life. There are several popular clinical tests and questionnaires about attention, memory, and executive functions. For example, Symbol Digit Modalities Test [10] is used to assess general attention. Star/Letter Cancellation Task [11, 12] are used to assess spatial attention. the Rey-Osterrieth Complex Figure Test [13] is used to assess visual memory. Rivermead Behavioural Memory Test [14] and Everyday Memory Checklist [15] are used to assess everyday memory. Behavioural Assessment of the Dysexecutive Syndrome (BADS) and Dysexecutive Questionnaire [16, 17] are used to assess executive functions.

2.2   Virtual Reality in Cognitive Assessment

Conventional assessment methods are effective for each cognitive function precisely, however it is reported that results of neuropsychological tests sometimes disagree with the cognitive function level in real life of the patients [1–3]. It is difficult to evaluate the daily cognitive ability of people with cognitive dysfunction by only conventional neuropsychological tests. Therefore, in cognitive rehabilitation, before planning the detailed training program, it is important to understand that we should not only evaluate each cognitive function using these tests, but also clarify the problems for the patients in their real life. VR technology provides one of the most advanced interaction between human and computers. This approach has the advantage of providing realistic scenario repeatedly, cost-effectively and safely for patients [18, 19]. New types of cognitive assessment based on IADL performance in virtual environment have been reported mainly since the 2000s [4–7].

Titov and Knight et al. [5, 6] reported a virtual street for assessment of deficits in prospective memory following chronic traumatic brain injuries. In the series of their study, the virtual street was created by taking a series of 1500 photographs every few meters inside and outside of shops in the downtown shopping precinct of a real city in New Zealand. Subjects could move along the street by pressing buttons on the PC screen and complete ongoing and prospective memory tasks while walking along the virtual street under conditions of high and low distraction. They were required to do ten errands with a checklist and respond to three targets that appeared repeatedly. Patients performed both tasks poorly compared with the controls as well as more affected by distractions. Zhang et al. [7] developed a virtual kitchen for assessment of executive function in meal preparation task. In this task, subjects operate PCs by using a mouse and wearing head-mounted display. They investigated the correlation among VR performance, actual kitchen performance, occupational therapy evaluation, and neuropsychological evaluation of people with brain injury. The VR system showed adequate reliability and validity as a method of assessment.

2.3   Virtual Shopping Test (VST)

In our previous works [8, 9], we have developed a VST, which introduces shopping tasks in a virtual shopping mall in order to assess comprehensive cognitive ability in routine daily tasks. The hardware system included a personal computer and a touch screen (1928L 19" LCD Desktop Touch monitor 5000series, Tyco Electronics, DE, USA). We conducted studies to clarify the significance of VST by comparing VST with other conventional tests, the applicability of VST to brain-damaged patients, and the performance of VST in relation to age differences. We reported the results suggest that VST is able to evaluate the ability of attention and everyday memory in patients with brain damage. The time required of VST performance is increased by age [8]. Sakai et al. examined differences in VST performances among healthy participants of different ages and correlations between VST and general cognitive screening tests. It was indicated that VST may be useful for assessing general cognitive decline; effects of age must be considered for proper interpretation of the VST scores [9].

3   Virtual Shopping Application for iOS

3.1   Virtual Shopping App_1 (VSA_1) Using VR

We have developed VSA_1 by using VR technology. Figure 1 shows experimental environment during the performance. Each user was provided with an Apple iPad tablet computer with VSA_1. In this App, the visual environment was made up of a Japanese shopping mall with 20 shops and a train station. An audio environment of the natural sounds in a shopping mall was also provided. Users can move in the virtual shopping mall freely, enter shops, and buy items by touching a button or a picture on the screen. A log file was recorded automatically. In a task of VSA_1, they were required to memorize specific items to buy, to look for shops in the mall, choose the items in each shop, pay at the cash register, and to perform the entire task smoothly. The scores for evaluation included the number of items bought correctly, the number of times hints were used, the number of movements, and the total time spent to complete the task.

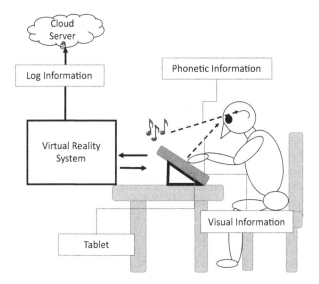

Fig. 1. Experimental environment during VSA_1 performance.

Basic Program and Operation Procedure. This App has two modes, namely BASIC MODE (Fig. 2) and SHOP MODE (Fig. 3). As shown in Fig. 2, in BASIC MODE users could move in virtual shopping mall by touching four kinds of arrow buttons to look for shops or reach a station as a goal. Three hint buttons (e.g. List, Bag, and Map) were provided to allow users to view some hints during the shopping task. They could refer to the hints when they lost their way or did not know what to buy. As shown in Fig. 3, in SHOP MODE users could enter a shop, select one or more shopping items in a showcase and pay at the cash register. After finishing shopping, they would be transferred to BASIC MODE.

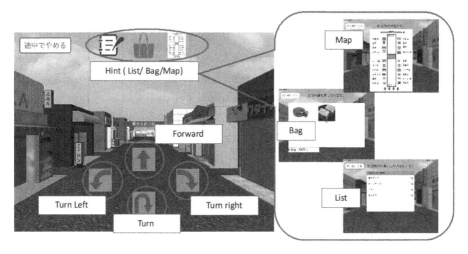

Fig. 2. A screenshot of BASIC MODE in VSA_1.

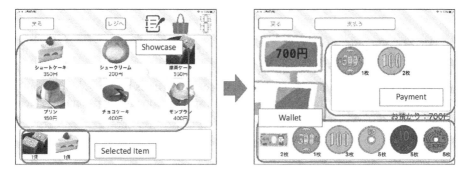

Fig. 3. A screenshot of SHOP MODE in VSA_1.

Data Output. The operation of buttons during the VSA_1 performance was recorded automatically and outputted as a log file after finishing the test. Figure 4 (left) shows a result summary of task performance for users and Fig. 4 (right) shows an example of a flow line display on the map by a log data analysis.

Task Setting. VSA_1 has a practice task and four kinds of tasks with different twenty shop arrangement each other. A therapist customizes the task difficulty level depending on a user's cognitive ability and conducts this App for assessment/training cognitive functions in clinical rehabilitation.

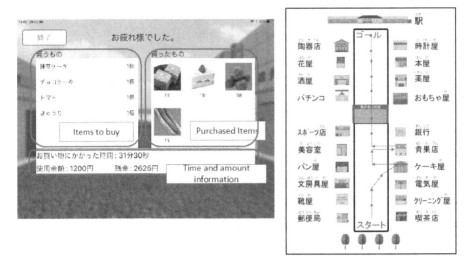

Fig. 4. A screenshot of a result summary (left) and a flow line display on the map based on a log data (right).

3.2   Virtual Shopping App_2 (VSA_2) Using AR

We have developed VSA_2 by using Apple's ARKit 2 on iOS. Figure 5 shows experimental environment during the performance. When users held a 9.7-inch Apple iPad tablet in front of their faces, they could see a specific shop or shops on the screen as shown in Fig. 6. As users changed the direction, the screen changed. They shopped in accordance with the VSA_1 rules.

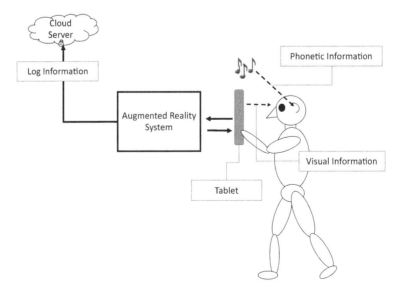

Fig. 5. Experimental environment during VSA_2 performance.

Fig. 6. A screenshot of shop appearance a in BASIC MODE in VSA_2.

Basic Program and Operation Procedure. This App has two modes, namely BASIC MODE (Fig. 6) and SHOP MODE. In BASIC MODE, when users detected floor near their feet with a camera of a tablet, shops appear around the user at real environment. They could see the shops on the screen as shown in Fig. 6. As users changed the direction, the screen changed. When they went toward a specific shop or touched a shop image, they could enter the shop. SHOP MODE in VSA_2 was as same as in VSA_1 basically. In addition, we set two types of shop arrangement as shown in Fig. 7 in case users perform it while sitting in a narrow apace like a test room in a hospital or walking about in a wide space.

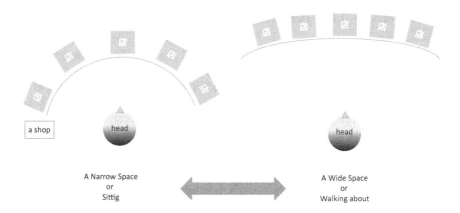

Fig. 7. Two types of shop arrangement in VSA_2.

4 Clinical Feasibility Study

4.1 Study of VSA_1 in Dementia Patients

We conducted two clinical pilot studies using VSA_1/VSA_2 as described below. The protocol of the study was approved by Kyoto University Graduate School and Faculty of Medicine ethics committee.

Methods. We conducted a feasibility study of VSA_1 with three female elderly patients with dementia. Demonstration of a 12.9-inch Apple iPad pro touchscreen was provided to the subjects with an A4-sized shopping mall map by an occupational therapist, and then the subjects performed the 2-item shopping task including payment at the cash register for practice. Next, they shopped in virtual mall freely.

Results and Discussion. The subjects completed the task with some advice about location and how to refer to hints (e.g. a shopping list and inside of a bag) in the specific 2-item shopping task and 2–4 free shopping task. Most participants performed payment intuitively. Some patients could choose a correct target shop and entered it however could not remember what to buy while they retrieved a specific item name aloud until just a minute ago. They referred to the shopping list 1–2 times and inside of a bag 0–2 times during the 2-item shopping performance by following tester's advices. In the free task, they dropped in a baker, a flower shop, and a book store and bought something they like. It took about thirty minutes including instruction for one session.

Three words recall task is used to evaluate immediate recall and delay recall of memory in the most popular general cognitive screening test, Mini-Mental State Examination (MMSE) [20]. In consideration of this point, this result indicated that a 2–3-item shopping task was appropriate for a dementia screening test. We also consider that patients need to get used to operate it by repeated daily use, for utilization of a tablet with this App in clinical rehabilitation.

4.2 Study of VSA_2 in a Dementia Patient

Methods. We conducted a feasibility study of VSA_2 in a male elderly outpatient with dementia, who was in his early eighties. His MMSE score was 26/30 due to disorientation, working memory deficit, and failing recent memory. He goes shopping at the hardware store and supermarket with his wife usually. Demonstration of a 9.7-inch Apple iPad touchscreen was provided to the patient by an occupational therapist, and then he performed the 2-item shopping tasks including payment at the cash register.

Results and Discussion. He understood the task procedure generally and completed it with some advice about location and commodity selection. He looked for shops voluntarily and performed almost correct payment intuitively. However, he needed some help to refer to hints because of his memory problem and made some mistakes during his VSA_2 performance:

- He confused the first trial and the second trial and retrieved a shopping item on the list in the 1st trial during the 2nd trial performance.

- He mistook a cucumber for an eggplant in memorizing at a fruit and vegetable shop.
- He remembered to go to the electricity shop, but it was difficult for him to retrieve the detail on the shopping list (e.g. AAA battery or size C battery).
- He bought his favorite two cakes which were different from that he was asked to buy in advance.

We found that finding a target shop in VSA_2 was easier than in VSA_1, but the patient made mistakes similar to those in VST [8, 9] and VSA_1 caused by attention deficit and failing memory. In order to investigate the applicability of VSA_2, we will need to collect data in patients at various cognitive levels. We will discover the hypothesis that the system provides a more self-directed rehabilitation environment for subjects cognitively and physically in the next step.

5   Conclusion

In this paper, we revised our previous computer-based VST system into two types of Virtual Shopping Applications for iOS with good clinical usability, VSA_1 and VSA_2 using VR/AR respectively, for comprehensive cognitive rehabilitation in a usual shopping scenario. In feasibility studies in people with dementia, they completed the VSA_1 task with some advice about location and how to refer to hints. Most participants performed payment intuitively. We found that finding a target shop in VSA_2 was easier than in VSA_1, but a subject made similar mistakes caused by attention deficit and failing memory. In the future, we will examine the effects of these applications for clinical cognitive rehabilitation and prevention/treatment of dementia in the elderly. We will also investigate their effectiveness in a future remote medical system.

Acknowledgements.   This research was supported by KAKENHI; Grant-in-Aid for Young Scientists (B) (16K16461).

References

1. Alderman, N., Burgess, P.W., Knight, C., Henman, C.: Ecological validity of a simplified version of the multiple errands shopping test. J. Int. Neuropsychol. Soc. **9**(1), 31–44 (2003)
2. Chaytor, N., Schmitter-Edgecombe, M., Burr, R.: Improving the ecological validity of executive functioning assessment. Arch. clin. Neuropsychol. **21**(3), 217–227 (2006)
3. Ord, J.S., Greve, K.W., Bianchini, K.J., Aguerrevere, L.E.: Executive dysfunction in traumatic brain injury: the effects of injury severity and effort on the wisconsin card sorting test. J. Clin. Exp. Neuropsychol. **32**(2), 132–140 (2010)
4. Kang, Y.J., et al.: Development and clinical trial of virtual reality-based cognitive assessment in people with stroke: preliminary study. Cyberpsychol. Behav. **11**(3), 329–339 (2008)
5. Knight, R.G., Titov, N., Crawford, M.: The effects of distraction on prospective remembering following traumatic brain injury assessed in a simulated naturalistic environment. J. Int. Neuropsychol. Soc. **12**(1), 8–16 (2006)

6. Titov, N., Knight, R.G.: A computer-based procedure for assessing functional cognitive skills in patients with neurological injuries: the virtual street. Brain Inj. **19**(5), 315–322 (2005)
7. Zhang, L., Abreu, B.C., Seale, G.S., Masel, B., Christiansen, C.H., Ottenbacher, K.J.: A virtual reality environment for evaluation of a daily living skill in brain injury rehabilitation: reliability and validity. Arch. Phys. Med. Rehabil. **84**(8), 1118–1124 (2003)
8. Okahashi, S., Seki, K., Nagano, A., Luo, Z., Kojima, M., Futaki, T.: A virtual shopping test for realistic assessment of cognitive function. J. NeuroEng. Rehabil. **10**, 59 (2013)
9. Sakai, H., Nagano, A., Seki, K., Okahashi, S., Kojima, M., Luo, Z.: Development of a cognitive function test using virtual reality technology: examination in healthy participants. Aging Neuropsychol. Cogn. **25**, 1–15 (2017)
10. Smith, A.: Symbol Digit Modalities Test Manual. Western Psychological Services, Los Angels (1982)
11. Ishiai, S.: Cognitive Dysfunction. Ishiyaku Publishers Inc, Tokyo (2012). (in Japanese
12. Wilson, B.A., Cockburn, J., Halligan, P.: Behavioural Inattention Test. Thames Valley Test Company, England (1987)
13. Lezak, M.D., Howieson, D.B., Bigler, E.D., Tranel, D.: Neuropsychological Assessment. Oxford University Press, New York (2012)
14. Wilson, B.A., Cockburn, J., Baddeley, A., Hiorns, R.: The development and validation of a test battery for detecting and monitoring everyday memory problems. J. Clin. Exp. Neuropsychol. **11**(6), 855–870 (1989)
15. Kazui, H., Watamori, T.S., Honda, R., Mori, E.: The validation of a Japanese version of the everyday memory checklist. No to Shinkei **55**(4), 317–325 (2003). (in Japanese)
16. Evans, J.J., Chua, S.E., McKenna, P.J., Wilson, B.A.: Assessment of the dysexecutive syndrome in schizophrenia. Psychol. Med. **27**(3), 635–646 (1997)
17. Wilson, B.A., Alderman, N., Burgess, P., Emslie, H., Evans, J.: Behavioural Assessment of the Dysexecutive Syndrome: Test Manual. Thames Valley Test Company, England (1996)
18. Morganti, F., Gaggioli, A., Strambi, L., Rusconi, M.L., Riva, G.: A virtual reality extended neuropsychological assessment for topographical disorientation: a feasibility study. J. Neuroeng. Rehabil. **4**, 26 (2007)
19. Vincelli, F., Molinari, E., Riva, G.: Virtual reality as clinical tool: immersion and three-dimensionality in the relationship between patient and therapist. Stud. Health Technol. Inform. **81**, 551–553 (2001)
20. Folstein, M.F., Folstein, S.E., McHugh, P.R.: "Mini-mental state". a practical method for grading the cognitive state of patients for the clinician. J. Psychiatr. Res. **12**(3), 189–198 (1975)

Technological Care

Health Professionals' Discourses on Technology in Home-Based Services Seen Through a Capability Approach

Erik Thorstensen[1]([✉]) [iD], Torhild Holthe[2] [iD], Liv Halvorsrud[3] [iD],
Dag Karterud[3], and Anne Lund[2] [iD]

[1] OsloMet, Work Research Institute, 0130 Oslo, Norway
erikth@oslomet.no
[2] Faculty of Health Sciences, Department of Occupational Therapy,
Prosthetics and Orthotics, OsloMet, 0130 Oslo, Norway
[3] Faculty of Health Sciences, Department of Nursing and Health Promotion,
OsloMet, 0130 Oslo, Norway

Abstract. This article is a contribution to the reflection upon what forms of assistive technologies societies should provide to users of home-based services. The material is collected from five focus group interviews conducted in Oslo in 2016 as part of a research project into assistive technologies with the purpose to gain knowledge of how such technologies were used in the home-based services. The interviews are analyzed on the basis of Martha Nussbaum's capability approach in order to see what forms of technologies influenced the users' capabilities. Thereafter, the technologies are classified as either public or private technologies in order to see what forms of capabilities the public care for and which technologies that are in the domain of private initiative. Based on the focus groups, it seems that public technologies are targeted at bodily health and integrity, while private technologies on communication and infrastructure, with some notable exceptions. The paper ends with discussions on the seemingly paradoxical situation that publicly supported technologies aim at the private sphere while the privately acquired technologies focus on public activities.

Keywords: Capability approach · Assistive technologies · Ethics · Focus groups · Ageing ethics

1 Introduction

Life is technological as technologies are an integrated part of most peoples' lives in several countries. Technologies promise – or, rather, humans promise technologies – to solve large social and political challenges. One such challenge is how to prepare for a future with an expanding ageing population with ensuing less capacity in the care and health systems. Much attention has been payed to question as to what are the most useful and promising solutions [1, 2]; how to successfully deploy novel technologies [3]; and different perspectives on the ideals of active ageing and ageing at home [4]. However, the underlying values for the selection of useful and promising technologies

© Springer Nature Switzerland AG 2020
Q. Gao and J. Zhou (Eds.): HCII 2020, LNCS 12208, pp. 177–195, 2020.
https://doi.org/10.1007/978-3-030-50249-2_14

and their relations to the ideals of the good life seems still to be an area where a tacit consensus reigns [5]. Dimensions of the good life is central to assessing the value of assistive technologies [6].

It is the ambition of this article to contribute to this discussion by observing what technologies health professional value in practice and their reasons for these valuations. In the setting of creating ideas for and developing assistive technologies for older adults, five focus groups were conducted in order to map and discuss assistive technologies intended to, for or with older adults with mild cognitive impairments, but also technologies more broadly in daily life. Reading all the transcripts, we sensed a differentiation between how the informants described the values and purposes of public assistive technologies and private leisure technologies as well a range of different human values connected to such technologies. One question this impression raised was to investigate possible connections between the different values and public or private technologies – or to see if themes arise through closer readings of such possible interconnections. In this article, we will look into what forms of care for older adults that are mediated through technologies. Care is an ambivalent term and phenomenon [7, 8]. Care might strengthen autonomy, but patient autonomy might conflict with utilitarian concerns – and conflict with the autonomy of the patient even though the caregiver has no such intention at all [9–11]. This opposition is not in any way linked uniquely to older adults, but is rather symptomatic of the way all humans are both social and independent beings [12]. Interaction with others entail that one is allowed to exercise one's free will within constraints set by the surroundings. One might even learn to integrate these constraints as a value system and find them to be meaningful – and thus in accordance with an autonomous act [13]. Thus, we will not make any judgements whether or not the views expressed by the health professionals are respectful of the subjects that they might have in mind or not, but merely investigate their own judgements of how technological solutions in the home affects the persons they encounter in their professional lives.

2   The Capability Approach

Mark Coeckelbergh [14] has suggested that and demonstrated how the capability approach might be useful and illuminating in assessing technologies in and for care of older adults. Amartya Sen and Martha Nussbaum developed the capability approach as an alternative to understanding human development [15]. Nussbaum and Sen promoted a view that emphasized individuals' possibilities to live their lives as they themselves wanted to. They thereby suggest the capability approach to be an account that accentuates both freedom and equality. Freedom to act based on basic capabilities, but also with an eye on how such freedoms are distributed in a society. Now, Sen and Nussbaum have developed the capability approach in different directions [12, 16]. Whereas Sen [17] see capabilities as conditions for realizing freedoms in a general sense, Nussbaum [18] has concretized the capabilities to a list of entitlements that all humans need in order to live dignified lives. These actual or potential capabilities would be termed "functionings" in Sen's version of the capability approach [16].

Using the capability approach in assessing care for older adults is an established approach [19–22] and care technologies [14, 23, 24]. According to Coeckelbergh, the connection of Nussbaum's approach to the valuation of care lies in that the capability approach takes as a point of departure how social arrangements, such as care, affect well-being and agency:

> From this perspective, the promise and goal of using information technology in elderly care can be framed as empowering people to live independently, to enjoy a higher quality of life, and to live their lives in dignity. This puts the emphasis on what people can do with the technology (the goal) rather than on the technology itself and its particular technical details [14].

An analysis of how technologies in care aim at fulfilling such basic entitlements, as suggested by Nussbaum, gives an indication of what the ethical issues or questions might be. Nussbaum's list of central capabilities is,

1. Life: 'Being able to live to the end of a human life of normal length; not dying prematurely, or before one's life is so reduced as to be not worth living.'
2. Bodily health, including nourishment and shelter
3. Bodily integrity: free movement, freedom from sexual assault and violence, having opportunities for sexual satisfaction
4. Being able to use your senses, imagination, and thought; experiencing and producing culture, freedom of expression and freedom of religion
5. Emotions: being able to have attachments to things and people
6. Practical reason: being able to form a conception of the good and engage in critical reflection about the planning of one's life
7. Affiliation:
   a. being able to live with and toward others, imagine the other, and respect the other
   b. having the social bases of self-respect and being able to be treated as a dignified being
8. Other species: being able to live with concern to animals, plants and nature
9. Play: being able to laugh, to play, to enjoy recreational activities
10. Control over one's environment:
    a. political choice and participation,
    b. being able to hold property, being able to work as a human being in mutual recognition (After Coeckelbergh [14], but with modifications based on Nussbaum [18]).

Nussbaum explicitly underlines that this list is open-ended, i.e. that additional items could be added, but also that the specifications should be made to local contexts.

Seen from the point of view of Nussbaum's capability approach, no one should live a life under a minimum of any of the suggested capabilities. The goal of analyzing the private technologies in relation to the public assistive technologies is based on a thought to open up for more reflection on what forms of capabilities (in Nussbaum's sense) that are perceived to be in the public domain, or under public responsibility and which ones are placed in the private domain. The reason for this is that there is still an open discussion concerning what forms of technologies should be prioritized in care for elderly in their own homes – and this debate should include a reflection on values [25].

3   Methods

In the autumn 2016, a total of seven researchers conducted five focus groups consisting of different health care professionals working in or close to the home-based services. All participants signed a letter of consent to take part in the focus group and for the material to be used in research. Each interview had two interviewers. One interview had only two respondents, whereas the remaining four had four, five, six and seven participants. All interviews were recorded digitally, transcribed and read through by the interviewers for approval.

We started the interviews with presentation of ourselves and the purpose of the study. The purpose of the study was presented as 1) how they work with assistive technologies with users with mild memory problems, 2) how they assess needs and meet the users' needs for technology as support in their daily lives, and 3) how they cooperate with others (such as users, next of kin, developers or others) related to assistive technologies. We did not pose any direct questions regarding other technologies, but the respondents themselves mentioned these several times.

We imported the word transcripts into Nvivo 11 and created the nodes according to Nussbaum's list of capabilities and specified the nodes according to the usage in Nussbaum (2007) where for example "Bodily health" is understood as "good health", "reproductive health", "nourishment" and "shelter" in order to see if there were dimensions of the capabilities that predominated over others. We found mentions of different technologies and whether these could be understood to be private and public. This amounts to a type of analysis closely related to thematic analysis committed to a realist epistemology conducted in a deductive manner. Such a manner of deductive qualitative research can be used when addressing issues that are set prior to the investigation itself by some external institution (often a funding body) to address political priorities [26].

First, we chose to see what form of capabilities the health professionals mentioned regarding their experiences in the home based services in general. This means looking at all the coding for different capabilities in the interviews regardless of technology. This approach was chosen because it provided an overview of capabilities first and technologies to support such capabilities second. This approach is the correct direction for investigation of capabilities-preserving measures since it implies taking the health professionals' experiences of care-recipients' capabilities as the primary object of study rather than the technologies.

This approach suggests a combination of a deductive approach with the division of private and public and with the capabilities' list and an inductive approach with no preconfigured list of technologies. Such an combination of a deductive frame with sets of rules (the capabilities) and an attention towards a range of unstructured phenomena that should be accounted for by the deductive frame has been termed abduction, and is often used for generating hypotheses for further investigations [27].

The division of private and public is not in any way set in stone, but is cultural specific and has different meanings in different contexts [28, 29]. However, in the current context no respondents raised the issue that they were unsure of whether some device was privately owned or something acquired through the public aid system.

The content of the division between private and public is in our case consequently based on induction. Private technologies are further *market technologies*, and the market is understood as private as it does not affect the whole community of citizens even though it is accessible to all, which are two possible criteria for distinguishing between the private and the public [30]. Likewise, we did not provide any definition of "technology", but used what the respondents identified as technologies.

Furthermore, we worked inductively in our approach to the difference between assistive technologies and technologies in general. This means that we did not provide any form of definition or other guiding questions as to how to delineate between the two. Our focus has been more generally on the difference between private and public technologies regardless of their intended purpose in order to study the valuation of the different solutions.

Since focus group discussions as a method is more related to eliciting different perspectives and exchanging experiences and build upon these [31], we will not try to summarize what the groups meant, but rather use the material as the outcome of interactive discussions and not differentiate between consensus positions and outlier positions. It is valuable to collect all forms of community health care workers' experiences, and we as researchers and interviewers do not, in the focus groups setting, have any direct tools to validate or invalidate the utterances. This being said, the findings in the focus groups are not characterized by conflict, but by a range of nuances in their opinions over the potentials and values of a variety of technological solutions.

4   Results

In the following, we will explicate what the informants said concerning the different capabilities that were positively or negatively impacted in the daily lives of older adults. We will relate these impacts to technologies where there is support to do this in the material.

4.1   Life

Being able to live to the end of a human life of normal length; not dying prematurely, or before one's life is so reduced as to be not worth living.

In a strict reading of the transcript, which we hold to be a virtue, the issue of quality of life was only discussed in one group.

> R 23: *Maybe one should think about the quality of life for people if it is the robots and such stuff. That they get even more isolated ...*[1]

In this utterance, in the discussion of possible future assistive technologies, R 23 states that loneliness is already a problem and introduction of further advanced technologies is a threat to a life worth living.

---

[1] The originals are in Norwegian and are translated by the authors.

4.2   Bodily Health, Including Nourishment and Shelter

The large majority of utterances here addressed mainly nourishment and shelter and not bodily health narrowly defined.

Bodily Health

Bodily health, and possible changes in health condition, came across as belonging to the domain of professional discretion. Physical visits from care workers and health professional and continued and regular observation of patient behavior and talk could indicate changes in health condition that create the foundation for mastery of technologies.

Technologies that could improve the bodily health of older adults were talked about as medical technologies measuring for example heart rhythm and blood pressure and transmitting these to the health professionals through the internet. Other examples were installations in the bathroom that could facilitate for using the shower and the toilet and through such installations manage maintain personal hygiene and normal bodily functions without aid. Neither of these are classified as assistive technologies in the Norwegian nomenclature, but rather as medical technologies and assistive devices.[2] The application of novel assistive technologies that might improve health was connected to video communication training for older adult. Connected to a video camera or a 3D depth sensor producing images training and fitness in order to strengthen muscles and balance could be distributed more rationally and conducted with high quality. A comment to this position regarded who should decide and observe the extent to which the users should be challenged to perform more and more advanced exercises.

Nourishment

Nourishment was the most discussed capability in the focus groups. It is necessary here to remind that not wanting to eat for any purpose does not mean that one lacks access to food or proper nourishment. It might well be that a refusal to eat (properly) might be the result of a voluntary decision or an indication of some underlying issue. There is furthermore a range of other concerns related to food and eating and an instrumental focus on food as nourishment seems to conflict with other capabilities. Consequently, we mention briefly some of these tensions here. Many persons have the sensation that the meal should also be a social event, and the lack of sociability might influence the decision to eat. Furthermore, several persons attached value to preparing meals, and the lack of ability to do so might affect eating and nourishment. However, if or when such factors influence nourishment, it would seem preferable from every perspective to try to remedy the situation so that a person becomes adequately nourished.

> R22: ... we cooperate with them in ordering food in order for them to present proposals and ideas – and nourishment is very important. Many seldom leave the home. They don't know what is in the stores. So we try to take the users with us when we come to their homes ...

---

[2] Seemingly, the notion of assistive technologies in the literature carries with it a relation to automation or information and communication technology that is absent from the notion of home aids 1. Haux, R., Koch, S., Lovell, N.H., Marschollek, M., Nakashima, N., Wolf, K.H.: Health-Enabling and Ambient Assistive Technologies: Past, Present, Future. Yearb Med Inform Suppl 1, S76-91 (2016).

As, stated by R22, the planning of shopping might also be a way of activation and mental training and going out shopping can be a way of getting out. Another informant told us how cooking might be a field for versatile training.

The process of acquiring food is experienced as burdensome for older adults by several informants, and some see it as a positive development that one can use tablets, computers or phones to order food online – which is now becoming an increasingly frequent way of ordering food. However, others place the purchase of food in stores as an important element for the feeling of coping and as influencing what people actually eat – and this will be addressed under capability 3, free movement.

Some informants told stories of how cognitive decline also affected the ability to be adequately nourished: some forgot that they had eaten or that they had a full refrigerator, others forgot that they had not eaten or not had food. No technological solutions were connected to such discoveries, but some related this to the need for spending more time with the users.

One of the barriers to buying food for persons in the home-based services was how to pay for the groceries. Some told that they could only use cash or shop if the person in question had a client account in a shop. They were not allowed to use debit or credit cards, and in some instances, this was connected to the trouble that some have in remembering pin codes.

All informants who discussed the social aspect of eating recognized this as important, and discussed possible solutions to eating alone: new forms of co-habitation, tours to senior centers, robot companions and video communication. Of these, only the robot eating-companions were valued negatively.

One theme discussed extensively in two of the groups regarding cooking was the stove timer. Stove timers come in several varieties, but the forms discussed were a timer and/or a temperature sensor. There was a general expression that it was a useful aid, but with important shortcomings, which could affect negatively cooking activities for people with cognitive decline or impairment. In terms of safety and security, the most important weakness is that the stove timer does not react when paper, plastic or cloth is placed on the stove. Whereas the main limitation regarding cooking activities is that the sensor on stove guard might turn off the stove if a kettle is placed so that the heat element is not totally covered. Furthermore, the stove timer will always turn off the stove after a pre-set time regardless of what one is cooking – and leave the person with unfinished food. Here, nourishment might be imperiled by safe living conditions.

Adequate Shelter

In addition to discussion regarding fire safety based on stove guards discussed above, the main theme for shelter was locks, keys and entrance into apartments. The informants provided a range of idiosyncratic ad hoc solutions from their practice, such as messages to the residents written on the door "Do not let strangers in", to key exchanges, central key depot, video calling system, calling system in the form of a telephone etc. One informant provided an example of a resident who got locked out, another of a resident that could not hear the doorbell, and a third an example of a person running down all the stairs to open. Being able to exit and enter ones domicile is of course also central for maintaining a social life and keeping unwanted visitors out. The different forms of exchange of keys between professionals in the home-based services was seen upon with some unease, since the residents lacked control over who entered at what time, logistics between different types of home assistance, and a risk for keys being lost – which is stressful for residents and time-consuming for the workers since it entails searching and getting permissions for making new copies. When discussing different forms of electronic locks, one group had positive experiences with automated doors, but introducing codes was viewed with some hesitation in another group since they perceived it to involve some kind of chip and also with possible administrative procedures for recoding.

Some other themes concerning adequate housing departed from reflections around falls. Here, one informant talked about the carpets people had in their homes as a risk factor, another of how a resident stayed in the dark around the clock since he did not have the energy to operate the wall mounted switches and fell, and a third about the fear of fire connected to electronic installations that caused residents to pull all plugs, which of course affects electronic aids and consumer electronics. A central theme was the safety alarm, a body-worn alarm button around the neck or wrist connected to the phone system and that one can push and an alarm reaches the services. As a rule, the safety alarm was discussed as a positive aid, but some talked of over-use and others talked about non-use due to nervousness, anxiety or social factors.

4.3   Bodily Integrity

Being able to move freely from place to place; to be secure against violent assault, including sexual assault and domestic violence; having opportunities for sexual satisfaction and for choice in matters of reproduction.

Freedom of movement was brought up in two different contexts, but with a similar background. The first context was that of GPS locators. GPS locators were presented in four of the groups as a condition for being able to move around in the city and in nature, and one informant said that his/her client experienced the possession and the use of the GPS locators as contributing to a feeling of safety. In a different group, the GPS was perceived positively in itself and for the user, but it could create administrative difficulties and furthermore contribute to an increased inequality since the municipality gave GPS locators to those with next-of-kin who could receive an eventual alarm. This might deteriorate the relative level of service given to those without next-of-kin nearby since they do not qualify for a service that could contribute to freedom of movement at the same time as they are likely to receive less visits and assistance from their family. A third position was that GPS locators are given to people who are too ill to really benefit from the possible freedom the tracker could provide, but is mainly used as a location tool in case a person wanders off rather than as a safety measure against getting lost. One informant made the connection between the ability to move around safely from a GPS and going to the shop, which is the second context. Being able to move freely around relates to having a social life. In addition to the fear of getting lost, one informant mentioned how public transportation is designed such that it is hard to enter if one is dependent on walking aids. Here, personal aids becomes an obstacle to social life since walking aids are constructed and performed in a way that make them difficult to combine with the designs and constructions of public trams and busses. This combination serves to exclude some older adults.

4.4   Senses, Imagination, and Thought

Being able to use your senses, imagination, and thought; experiencing and producing culture, freedom of expression and freedom of religion.

The informants discussed this aspect only in two brief instances in the material. The first context was that of a female blogger aged 92 years who used her blog to tell others about the experiences of being elderly. She was talked about with enthusiasm by one informant and others joined the chorus. The second context was that of audio books on CDs. Here, one informant told about the experience she/he had in trying to obtain a portable CD player for a woman. Because of the new streaming technology, the municipal assistive technology supplier had discontinued such products that the woman knew how to operate and thus risked to be deprived of cultural experiences. However, the supplier managed to find one "laying around in the corner of the storage" so this case ended happily.

4.5   Emotions

Being able to have attachments to things and people outside ourselves.

The most important device mentioned as the source of connection with the outside world and with which the elderly had the strongest attachment was the television. A common frustration in this context is the complexity of the remote controls. The importance of television is so strong that one informant even suggested that patients complaining that television is boring really had lost mastery over the remote control.

Several informants raised the issues of solitude and loneliness in the focus groups. The sensation of being isolated from the outside world seems to deprive many older adults from the possibility to create attachments. One issue raised by many informants was how the elderly sought social contact from people in the home-based services, and the put forward the view that technologies could not compensate for this contact. As examples, the informants mentioned automatic pill dispensers and robot vacuum cleaners. Positive actions against solitude consisted in organizing trips and social eating. However, there are some mentions, which will also be addressed under Affiliation: Live with and towards others, that seems to run counter to the view that technologies cannot help against loneliness. We encountered informants saying that iPads were one way elderly kept in touch with others and stayed informed. Skype and video communication was both experienced and imagined as useful tools in creating bonds between people.

4.6   Practical Reason

Being able to form a conception of the good and to engage in critical reflection about the planning of one's life.

We could not find that this theme was raised in the focus groups.

4.7 Affiliation

Being Able to Live with and Toward Others
Only one of the subcategories, being able to live with and toward others, was identified in the material. As mentioned above, in the few mentions of living with and towards others, skype and video communication plays a central part. One interviewer raises the issue of using such technologies to create a virtual social club for older adults, and the respondents seem to accept that this could be a viable route forward. Skype seems to be gradually replacing the telephone as means of communication. In a few instances, skype seems to be included in tablets provided by the municipality as a part of a calendar function. On the opposite side, breakdown of television and radio – or the loss of capacity to operate them – was also raised as loss of sociality by one informant. She/he also connected such loss of capacity to loss of self-respect, which is the theme in Nussbaum's next capability. Here, we should also signal that the theme of updates, charging, and product malfunctioning was raised by some in connection to such tablets.

Treated as a Dignified Being and having the Social Bases of Self-respect
Here, we combine these two items since the material suggests that these are highly interlinked. Technologies are social products: they are created with a specific group of users in mind. Clearly, several of the technologies used by older adults, both commercial and those issued by the home-based services might possibly affect a person's self-respect. This issue was raised in connection with different cooking activities and the stove timers, remote controls and operating doors and locks. Failure in mastery of daily tasks, such as remembering appointments, knowing what day it is and what time of day, and organizing oneself seems to the informants to affect the self-respect of older adults. Some informants said that such failure could result in persons becoming confused, which they portrayed as negative. One device mentioned by three different informants in two different locations was a calendar with photos that one might use to have such overview. One informant even talked about having this calendar connected to the television. However, when asked, one group was able to tell us how the content entered the calendar while a different group had no knowledge of this process. Such a difference in mastery of technologies provided by the home-based services is not in any way a surprise, but should be kept in mind.

The fine line between activation of persons as a tool for increasing their self-esteem and leaving them in a vulnerable position was raised by one informant. The theme was a reminder system for persons with cognitive impairment or decline. While useful in general, one informant stressed that such a system might give a person increased mastery in everyday life on the condition that she or he understands the concept of a reminder system- If the person does not grasp this concept, such a system might create a false sense of security for the services, the next-of-kin and the person in question. In addition, the reminder system can be a cause for worries and thus making the person even more vulnerable.

4.8 Other Species

Being able to live with concern for and in relation to animals, plants, and the world of nature.

Only in one group, one informant mentioned a new assisted living facility in Hammerfest where they had plants and animals in what the informant referred to as a "garden of senses".

4.9   Play

Being able to laugh, to play, to enjoy recreational activities.
We could not find that this theme was raised in the focus groups.

4.10   Control Over One's Environment

Political
Being able to participate effectively in political choices that govern one's life; having the right of political participation, protections of free speech and association.

Under this theme, we arranged discussions relating to surveillance, a theme often associated with technologies and especially GPS, since surveillance can be seen as an obstacle to free political participation [32]. Now, the discussions regarding surveillance related to GPS tracking only in one dialogue. In the remaining talk, surveillance was related to the presence of personnel from the home-based services and to potential mass measuring of health data in the homes.

Material
Being able to hold property (both land and movable goods), and having property rights on an equal basis with others.

With control over the material environment in the current discussions, I identified to main themes: money and unwarranted entry. In one instance, there was a discussion of how people themselves needed to decide on spending money on technologies not covered by the public or remain without a service the health professionals saw as useful, and the informants believed that the users would need to pay even out of their own pocket in the future. Unrelated to this, was a discussion on how the home-based services could assist persons with paying for their goods and services. Paper money seems to be the easiest monetary infrastructure for the services since informants said that are not allowed to use the users' cards. Pin codes and online banking had advantages as long as the user remained cognitively unimpaired and had continuous use of these, but informants gave examples that these became barriers to coping.

When discussing different versions of locks and door controls, the informants separated between the feeling of control and actual control. Control over exit and entry into one's home is both a subjective state of mind and an objective affair. Subjectively, one's cognitive state influences feelings of vulnerability and might be both an obstacle to and a driver for giving access to unknown persons – regardless of these are part of the home-based services or not. Reversely, also the persons employed in the home-based services had reservations against how easy they gained access to other people's personal space. One informant also raised the issue that not being in a state of constant waiting for health personnel who do not keep their appointments also increases the feeling of control.

5   Discussion

Nussbaum and Sen's capability approach focuses on the conditions for the good life and the distributive concerns of these conditions. From the analysis above, technologies largely affect such conditions both negatively and positively. On a basic and concrete level, one can identify how devices as disparate as iPads and digital door locks might positively affect social encounters, but they also depend on a specific configuration of the services with updates, passwords, pin codes that might also constitute an obstacle to realize other capabilities such as adequate shelter or living with and towards others. A very interesting finding is how technologies seem to play a part in transforming the way we relate to each other, as the examples provided by skype connections seen as valuable and senior blogging as a way of providing new voices into the semi-public blogosphere. Arie Rip and René Kemp [33] make the point that technologies and societal norms co-evolve and that this interaction is a fruitful approach rather than technological determinism, the view that technology will take society in one pre-determined direction. Closer studies of how technologies change the actual social reality of older adults is needed [7, 34] and Coeckelbergh's contribution discussed above does so only hypothetically.

5.1   Technologies and Capabilities

Returning to the initial question behind this article regarding the relationships between the different capabilities and whether these relate to publicly funded technologies through the home-based services or to private technologies, we would suggest that there are some patterns. Bodily health understood as physical health relate uniquely to public technologies. Whereas discussions regarding nourishment pertained both to public and private technologies where the public technologies typically referred to stove guards and the private technologies concerned monetary technologies, kettles or microwaves, i.e. either the means of procuring or preparing nourishments. Now the stove timers can also be understood as a part of adequate shelter since they should protect against fires. Likewise social alarms can be considered as an element of adequate shelter since they reduce the risk of accidents in homes not because the likelihood becomes less, but because the consequences might be less severe. With the exception of proper illumination technologies, private technologies for adequate shelter concern the border or the threshold between public and private spaces, namely keys, locks and doors. The informants relate bodily integrity, understood primarily as freedom of movement, uniquely to public technologies such as the GPS locator.[3] It is further of

---

[3] Even though GPS locators might be privately acquired, the informants discussed GPS locating systems as part of the municipal care system.

interest that the informants related cooking and stove timers to safety as older adults themselves tend to relate cooking to self-respect [6].

For what regards Nussbaum's relational and emotional capabilities, they seem overwhelmingly connected to private technologies with a clear exception for novel video communication technologies implemented in some parts of the home-based services. Television, radio, skype and the blogger are all instances of private technologies providing fun, connections, and creativity for older adults. Whereas they relate public technologies to how these fail to provide dignity or might lead to increased isolation.

When it comes to the capability of relating to nature, animals and plants, given that the focus was the home, it is unsurprising that nature does not play a part. However, as 40% of the Norwegian population hold animals as pets [35], and this number falls below 10% for older adults [36], this area might be explored; especially as pets have positive effects on well-being [37]. Experiments with digital pets have produced varied results, but with a positive tendency [7, 38, 39].

The informants saw some technologies as (experienced as) possible surveillance technologies, but they also told about discrepancies between the way society at large handles money transfers and the situation in the home-based services. There seems to be a gap between the fully digitalized current money exchange and the paper money practice in parts of the home-based services, and furthermore a need for systems less based on passwords and pin codes.

From this argument one conclusion could be that the home-based services should provide a wider selection of technologies (or abstain from some). However, Nussbaum [40] further writes that there are three types of capabilities: basic, internal and combined (or combined) capabilities. The most basic are the capabilities for seeing and hearing, while the internal capabilities are "mature conditions of readiness" [40], and the combined capabilities is the above quoted list. Nussbaum's point is that if people have internal capabilities that can flourish through access to the combined capabilities, then they should have reasonable access to these. de Maagt and Robeyns [21] build upon Nussbaum and argue that lack of potential for internal capabilities, such as is the case for persons with severe cognitive decline, means that access to a range of the combined capabilities will not provide them with an increased quality of life. They state that, "In fact, we may harm these persons since they may be given options with potential harmful outcomes, without having the internal capabilities for responsible choice" [21]. However, the home-based service do not only provide technologies for persons with highly reduced internal capabilities, but also to persons with other sets of needs. Furthermore, the ambition of the health authorities is that assistive technologies shall become an integrated part of all home-based services – regardless of age – by 2020 in Norway [41].

5.2 Private and Public Realms of Technologies

When considering the scope of the publicly provided assistive technologies compared to the private technologies of the users, the contrast between the attention to the body and the home as a containing device among the publicly available technologies versus the focus on communication and infrastructure among the private technologies is striking. This suggests a politics of old age where the private sphere has become the domain for public care and, conversely, that participation in the public sphere is left to private initiative. In a fairness perspective, active participation in society and in democratic processes such as debates and elections presupposes active facilitation by the state to reach groups and individuals who have different preconditions for participation than the majority. Use of digital communication technologies declines with age, and ageing users wish for more training [42]. Furthermore, as discussed above, several of the new food, purchasing and social services presuppose digital competences that users in the home-based services often lack, according to the respondents. Several care providers have experimented with distribution of tablets that seem to work well for facile tasks [43], but they pose challenges for more diversified actions [44] and require staff to help with updates and maintenance [6]. Such insights suggest that active participation presupposes more than a single device and that mastery does not follow with the device.

The role of the state in providing for individuals' needs is a central element in political philosophy. If one applies a perspective from Nozick and his arguments for a minimal state [45], then the public domain becomes reduced to enforcement of contracts and policing. In such a system of thought, the state has no obligation towards providing for public participation and every state action should be kept at a minimum. From a dialectical perspective, needs are seen as dependent on and constituted by the actual social forms to meet these needs. Personal needs, individual needs, human needs always take some form, and we cannot but meet then in some form. These forms are on one level a matter of choice [46].

Seen from a capability perspective, the central notion of equality refers to what Sen has called equality of basic capabilities in reaching what individuals see as good in their lives [47]. Good health and bodily safety are central to what is usually seen as good in peoples' lives. One reason that Sen seems reluctant to define good health and bodily safety as basic capabilities such as Nussbaum does, is that some people voluntarily expose themselves to situations where they trade off health or safety in the search for other goals. Such goals can be helping others or one's own amusement [12]. Both Sen's and Nussbaum's approaches to equality of capabilities have clearer affinities with the dialectical notion of needs fulfilment than with the libertarian approach. The core of the matter is that freedom to realize what one conceives of as good cannot be decided by others for an individual based on the assumed preferences of that individual due to an imagined group identity [48]. An individual cannot be assumed to share the common norms of one's group – and especially so if this assumption affects the individual's access to pursue what is good [49]. Seen from the perspective of negative freedoms, the responsibility of a care providing system becomes that of not barring access to individual realisation of goods by introducing assistive technologies [50]. Seen from the perspective of positive freedom, the responsibility of a care providing system becomes that of facilitating for giving access to individual realisation of goods by introducing assistive technologies.

The justification of aiming at publicly funded assistive technologies limited to the private sphere seems to depend upon an individual's internal capabilities. In situations where an individual lacks this potential, safety and bodily integrity are important. In other cases, to limit the public provision of assistive technologies to shelter, bodily integrity and nourishment might lack justification if they negatively affect other capabilities. The case of the GPS locator seems to be the only instance where the informants addressed lacking internal capabilities of a person as contributing to a possible loss of safety.

In terms of the practice of prioritizing assistive technologies and how care systems should allocate their resources, the view from negative freedom suggests that solutions that obstruct a person from realising one's capabilities should be avoided. Examples of such solutions for some persons in the current material were stove timers, reminder systems and different forms of new locks or other access controls.

What is the right action to pursue? Wareham [51] argues for an ethic of ageing which takes as a point of departure the situation of an ageing person and investigates the ethical issues facing this person as an ageing person. This position leaves open the definition of ageing, and there exists a vocal debate that spans from whether ageing is valuable in itself [52] or a condition to be altered or annihilated through medical research [53]. As indicated in the material, and as supported by Stahl and Coeckelbergh [54], novel technologies change or impact on how we create, uphold and end meaningful relations with our surroundings. Whether or not technological solutions will change dramatically the way societies value old age remains an open question, but this value is connected to social norms [55], and novel evaluations of age groups makes up a part of slow changes in history [56]. However, for the immediate and near future few such deep changes in the perception of ageing seems unlikely. What seems to constitute some of the respondents' valuation of communication devices might be understood as transforming the older adults from being frail and needy and towards being masters of their life-situation. On the contrary, one can see how technologies related to the body and to a physical place seem to be less valued. This dichotomy resonates well with how Oudshoorn [34] understand the transformation of care in assistive technologies where the physical aspect of care is seen as a stage to be overcome and replaced by novel devices. Accordingly, there seems to be instances of an unreflexive normative ideal of ageing as a condition to be altered towards mastery.

Seen from the perspective of positive freedoms, there is a vast range of possible technological solutions that enhance the realisation of different capabilities. From the perspective of citizenship, the main lacunae are in solutions that facilitate for social participation. A different perspective to this question would be to look at the private sphere as intimate, and that the public ought to remain from interfering – or even facilitating for – changes in peoples' private spheres [30].

6   Conclusion

This article contributes to the discussion of how we can theorize and discuss priorities in home-based care. Such prioritization has a moral component. By addressing capabilities as constitutive of a good life, priorities can be separated from each other with reference to their capabilities. In addition, this article presents a case in the discussion over the value-ladenness of technologies. As discussed by Brey [57], when technological products are correlated with specific social impacts, a view on technologies as neutral with respect to values becomes untenable.

There are some limitations to the generalizability of this study. The first consists in that the researchers did not address capabilities directly and these are just searched for at a later stage in the material so there was no way of validating the findings with the users in context. However, when conducting interviews it might be beneficial not to address the theoretical terms directly since these might create a power imbalance between the researcher and the respondents. The second, and maybe most important limitation, is the context of the interviews. We conducted the interviews in Oslo, Norway, a medium size city in European context in a country where the arrangement of assistive technologies is tightly connected to the health services rather than to individual responsibilities or to social work as can be the case in other European countries [58].

How should the considerations in this article influence the way in which we envisage technologies for living at home for a longer time? On the one side, there are technologies and solutions intimately connected to the municipality responsibility for the safety of their citizens. If some of these technologies were to be removed, then such a removal would have to be based in changes in legislation, i.e. that health professionals are absolved from parts of their legal duties towards their care recipients. As becomes clear from these interviews, there are some new connections to the outside world that can be established through technologies, such as video communication, but also to find and establish well-functioning payment services that are less cumbersome and less open for fraud than the current technologies. Being able to hold and remaining in control of one's finances seems to be important in the eyes of the health professionals. Furthermore, older adults should be able to benefit from the company of pets and plants, just as any other person, and they should be able to have fun with their technologies. Recently, Moors asked whether current decisions regarding ageing and technology would favour solutions aiming at self-management and agency as citizens and consumers or solutions aiming at reducing fear or portraying older adults as needy [59]. The current research shows an inclination towards the latter.

On an overarching level, individuals, civil society, industry and service providers need to start a discussion on the different purposes of technologies in the homes that extend beyond ensuring the recipients' basic capabilities. It is through paying attention to the realization of specific values or capabilities through technologies that service providers and industry might change a focus beyond safety and economics [60].

Acknowledgements. The project, 'The Assisted Living Project: Responsible innovations for dignified lives at home for persons with mild cognitive impairment or dementia', is financed by the Research Council of Norway under the SAMANSVAR strand (247620/O70). I wish to thank everyone involved in the Assisted Living project for access to data and collegial discussions, and all the health professionals and residents who have provided us all with time, effort, insights and fun. The material for this article is also used in an article by [61] but there the methodological approach has been purely inductive, the research question regards how the informants view the technologies in relation to their work and the theoretical analysis based on health professionals as street-level bureaucrats.

References

1. Haux, R., Koch, S., Lovell, N.H., Marschollek, M., Nakashima, N., Wolf, K.H.: Health-enabling and ambient assistive technologies: past, present. Future Yearb Med. Inform. Suppl. **1**, S76–S91 (2016)
2. Dawson, A., Bowes, A., Kelly, F., Velzke, K., Ward, R.: Evidence of what works to support and sustain care at home for people with dementia: a literature review with a systematic approach. BMC Geriatr. **15**, 59 (2015)
3. Meiland, F., et al.: Technologies to support community-dwelling persons with dementia: a position paper on issues regarding development, usability, effectiveness and cost-effectiveness, deployment, and ethics. JMIR Rehabil. Assist. Technol. **4**, e1 (2017)
4. Aceros, J.C., Pols, J., Domènech, M.: Where is grandma? Home telecare, good aging and the domestication of later life. Technol. Forecast. Soc. Change **93**, 102–111 (2015)
5. Thorstensen, E.: Stakeholders' views on responsible assessments of assistive technologies through an ethical HTA matrix. Societies **9**, 51 (2019)
6. Thorstensen, E.: Responsible help at home: establishing indicators for a product assessment methodology. In: Bowman, D.M., et al. (eds.) The Politics and Situatedness of Emerging Technologies, pp. 167–182. IOS Press, Berlin (2017)
7. Pols, J., Moser, I.: Cold technologies versus warm care? on affective and social relations with and through care technologies. ALTER – Eur. J. Disabil. Res./Revue Européenne de Recherche sur le Handicap **3**, 159–178 (2009)
8. Roberts, C., Mort, M.: Reshaping what counts as care: older people, work and new technologies. ALTER – Eur. J. Disabil. Res./Revue Européenne de Recherche sur le Handicap **3**, 138–158 (2009)
9. Pellizzoni, L.: Responsibility and environmental governance. Environ. Politics **13**, 541–565 (2004)
10. Dworkin, G.: Paternalism. In: Zalta, E.N. (ed.) The Stanford Encyclopedia of Philosophy. The Scholarly Publishing and Academic Resources Coalition, Washington, D.C. (2016)
11. Woodward, V.M.: Caring, patient autonomy and the stigma of paternalism. J. Adv. Nurs. **28**, 1046–1052 (1998)
12. Svendsen, L.: A Philosophy of Freedom. Reaktion Books, London (2014)
13. Durkheim, E.: The Elementary Forms of Religious Life. Free Press, New York (1995)
14. Coeckelbergh, M.: "How I Learned to Love the Robot": capabilities, information technologies, and elderly care. In: Oosterlaken, I., van den Hoven, J. (eds.) The Capability Approach, Technology and Design, vol. 5, pp. 77–86. Springer, Netherlands (2012). https://doi.org/10.1007/978-94-007-3879-9_5
15. Nussbaum, M., Sen, A. (eds.): The Quality of life. Clarendon Press, New York (1993)
16. Robeyns, I.: The capability approach: a theoretical survey. J. Hum. Dev. **6**, 93–117 (2005)
17. Sen, A.K.: Development as Freedom. Oxford University Press, Oxford (1999)
18. Nussbaum, M.C.: Frontiers of Justice: Disability, Nationality, Species Membership. The Belknap Press of Harvard University Press, Cambridge (2007)
19. Breheny, M., Stephens, C., Henricksen, A., Stevenson, B., Carter, K., Alpass, F.: Measuring living standards of older people using sen's capability approach: development and validation of the LSCAPE-24 (Living Standards Capabilities for Elders) and LSCAPE-6. Ageing Soc. **36**, 307–332 (2016)
20. Stephens, C., Breheny, M., Mansvelt, J.: Healthy ageing from the perspective of older people: a capability approach to resilience. Psychol. Health **30**, 715–731 (2015)
21. de Maagt, S., Robeyns, I.: Can person-centered care deal with atypical persons? Am. J. Bioeth. **13**, 44–46 (2013)

22. Meijering, L., Van Hoven, B., Yousefzadeh, S.: "I think I'm better at it myself": the capability approach and being independent in later life. Res. Ageing Soc. Policy **7**, 229 (2019)
23. Hoven, J.: Human capabilities and technology. In: Oosterlaken, I., Hoven, J. (eds.) The Capability Approach, Technology and Design, vol. 5, pp. 27–36. Springer, Netherlands (2012). https://doi.org/10.1007/978-94-007-3879-9_2
24. Oosterlaken, I.: The capability approach, technology and design: taking stock and looking ahead. In: Oosterlaken, I., Hoven, J. (eds.) The Capability Approach, Technology and Design, vol. 5, pp. 3–26. Springer, Netherlands (2012). https://doi.org/10.1007/978-94-007-3879-9_1
25. Hofmann, B.: Hvordan vurdere etiske aspekter ved moderne helse- og velferdsteknologi? Tidsskrift for omsorgsforskning **5**, 99–116 (2019)
26. Pope, C., Ziebland, S., Mays, N.: Analysing qualitative data. BMJ **320**, 114–116 (2000)
27. Eco, U.: The Limits of Interpretation. Indiana University Press, Bloomington (1990)
28. Habermas, J.: The Structural Transformation of the Public Sphere: An Inquiry into a Category of Bourgeois Society. MIT Press, Cambridge (1989)
29. Casanova, J.: Private and public religions. Soc. Res. **59**, 17–57 (1992)
30. Taylor, C.: Modern Social Imaginaries. Duke University Press, Durham (2004)
31. Hennink, M.M.: Focus Group Discussions. Oxford University Press, Oxford (2014)
32. Solove, D.: A taxonomy of privacy. Univ. Pennsylvania Law Rev. **154**, 477–560 (2006)
33. Rip, A., Kemp, R.: Technological change. In: Rayner, S., Malone, E.L. (eds.) Human Choice and Climate Change, vol. 2. Battelle Press, Columbus (1998)
34. Oudshoorn, N.: Physical and digital proximity: emerging ways of health care in face-to-face and telemonitoring of heart-failure patients. Soc. Health Illn. **31**, 390–405 (2009)
35. Svendsen, L.F.H.: Å forstå dyr: filosofi for hunde- og katteelskere. Kagge, Oslo (2018)
36. Kristiansen, J.E.: Som hund og katt?; kjæledyr i norske husholdninger. Samfunnsspeilet **8**, 18–21 (1994)
37. Gee, N.R., Mueller, M.K.: A Systematic review of research on pet ownership and animal interactions among older adults. Anthrozoös **32**, 183–207 (2019)
38. Robinson, N.L., Cottier, T.V., Kavanagh, D.J.: Psychosocial health interventions by social robots: systematic review of randomized controlled trials. J. Med. Internet Res. **21**, e13203 (2019)
39. Abbott, R., et al.: How do "robopets" impact the health and well-being of residents in care homes? a systematic review of qualitative and quantitative evidence. Int. J. Older People Nurs. **14**, e12239 (2019)
40. Nussbaum, M.C.: Women and Human Development: The Capabilities Approach. Cambridge University Press, Cambridge (2000)
41. Helse-og omsorgsdepartementet: Omsorg 2020. Regjeringens plan for omsorgsfeltet 2015–2020. Helse-og omsorgsdepartementet (2015)
42. Slettemeås, D., Mainsah, H., Berg, L.: Eldres digitale hverdag. En landsdekkende undersøkelse om tilgang, mestring og utfordringer i informasjonssamfunnet. Forbruksforskningsinstituttet SIFO (2018)
43. Delello, J.A., McWhorter, R.R.: Reducing the digital divide: connecting older adults to iPad technology. J. Appl. Gerontol. **36**, 3–28 (2017)
44. Dahle, H.A.: Eldres muligheter til å bruke iPad som styringsverktøy for smarthusteknologi-betydningen av kognisjon, mestringstro og teknologierfaring. Universitetet i Stavanger (2012)
45. Nozick, R.: Anarchy, State, and Utopia. Blackwell, Malden (2012)
46. Fraser, I.: Hegel and Marx: The Concept of Need. Edinburgh University Press, Edinburgh (1998)

47. Sen, A.: Inequality Reexamined. Harvard University Press, New York (1992)
48. Sen, A.: Identity and Violence: The Illusion of Destiny. Penguin Books, London (2007)
49. Thorstensen, E.: Ateismekritikk: om reduksjonisme, religion og samfunn. Akademika forlag, Oslo (2013)
50. Berlin, I.: Two Concepts of Liberty: An Inaugural Lecture Delivered Before the University of Oxford on 31 October 1958. Clarendon Press, Oxford (1958)
51. Wareham, C.S.: What is the ethics of ageing? J. Med. Ethics **44**, 128–132 (2018)
52. Kass, L.R.: Ageless Bodies, Happy Souls, vol. 9–28. The New Atlantis, Washington, D.C. (2003)
53. Bostrom, N.: The fable of the dragon tyrant. J. Med. Ethics **31**, 273–277 (2005)
54. Stahl, B.C., Coeckelbergh, M.: Ethics of healthcare robotics: towards responsible research and innovation. Robot. Auton. Syst. **86**, 152–161 (2016)
55. Beauvoir, S.D.: La vieillesse. Gallimard, Paris (1970)
56. Ariès, P.: Centuries of Childhood: A Social History of Family Life. Vintage Books, New York (1962)
57. Brey, P.: The strategic role of technology in a good society. Technol. Soc. **52**, 39–45 (2018)
58. Knarvik, U., Rotvold, G.-H., Bjørvig, S., Bakkevoll, P.-A.: Kunnskapsoppsummering: Velferdsteknologi. Nasjonalt senter for e-helseforskning (2017)
59. Moors, E.H.M.: Responsible innovation and healthy ageing. In: Von Schomberg, R., Hankins, J. (eds.) International Handbook on Responsible Innovation, pp. 271–284. Edward Elgar Publishing, Cheltenham (2019)
60. Thorstensen, E.: Responsible assessments. frameworks for a value-based governance of assistive technologies. OsloMet, Centre for the Study of Professions, Oslo (2020)
61. Holthe, T., Halvorsrud, L., Thorstensen, E., Karterud, D., Laliberte Rudman, D., Lund, A.: Community health care workers' experiences on enacting policy on technology with citizens with mild cognitive impairment and dementia. J. Multi. Healthc. **13**, 447–458 (2020)

Active Aging AI Community Care Ecosystem Design

Hsiao-Ting Tseng[1] (iD), Hsieh-Hong Huang[2] (iD),
and Chen-Chiung Hsieh[3]([✉])

[1] National United University, Miaoli 36003, Taiwan, R. O. C.
appleapple928@gmail.com
[2] National Taitung University, Taitung 95092, Taiwan, R. O. C.
[3] Tatung University, Taipei 104, Taiwan, R. O. C.
cchsieh@ttu.edu.tw

Abstract. Many countries are facing a severe population ageing problem. The aging environment of the population, the trend of declining birthrate, the decline of family care function and the sense of loneliness in elderlies are impacting the lives of the elderlies. Even though there are many long-term care services at the national level it has been in implementation, there are still many restrictions on the recipients receiving service. Many elderly people in the healthy life stage are not eligible for service. However, based on the concept of "prevention is better than cure", these healthy elders needs to be cared for in order to prevent the heavy resources and manpower generated in the future stage of treatment. The demand for long-term care is not only to meet their physiological needs, but also for their psychological needs. Therefore, this study hopes to use the standardization and information privacy protection for the elderly to care for huge amounts of health care data, and apply machine learning and statistical techniques, and deep learning to find out the hidden information of the elderly care, to find key decision points, and to establish alert and notification mechanism. Through this process, this study hopes to not only care for the physical and mental health of the elderly, but also to take care of the hearts and minds of the elderly and relatives around the elderly, and to establish a blessed smart community care sharing model.

Keywords: Community care · Artificial intelligence · Active aging

1 Introduction

1.1 Research Background and Motivation

Well-known journalist Fishman raised the major issues of population aging and a series of chain effects in his book "Shock of Gray" after visiting many cities and towns in various countries, aging not only affects the physical and mental safety and health of the elderly, but also affects the middle-aged, youth, and young children [1]. Therefore, society has gradually evolved many long-term care tragedies [2]. For example, many middle-aged people should be at the peak of their lives, but because they have elderly people to take care of, they must give up their careers and become the guardian of the

© Springer Nature Switzerland AG 2020
Q. Gao and J. Zhou (Eds.): HCII 2020, LNCS 12208, pp. 196–208, 2020.
https://doi.org/10.1007/978-3-030-50249-2_15

elderly. However, the restricted lifestyle and time schedule have greatly restricted its development, and it will be more difficult to earn a living in the countryside. From an economic perspective, it is quite inefficient, but from an emotional and family perspective, it is priceless. In addition, there are many modern families who, because of their heavy burden of taking care of the elderly [3, 4], and because of the limited allocation of time resources, dare not to have the next generation, or sacrifice the growth education resources of the next generation.

Many countries are facing a severe population ageing problem [5–7]. The aging environment of the population, the trend of declining birthrate, the decline of family care function and the sense of loneliness in elderlies are impacting the lives of the elderlies. Therefore, in the environment of aging population, how to promote our society to achieve the Confucius philosophy "[8]… That makes the aged have the appropriate last years, those in their prime have the appropriate employment, and the young have the appropriate growth and development…" is an important issue of long-term care that we as a member of the aging environment cannot ignore.

Due to the rapid changes in social structure, countries around the world must develop long-term strategic planning and resource reorganization related to the care of the elderly [9]. And the rapidly aging population has always been the Taiwan government's biggest concern. With the rapid growth of the elderly population, the resulting long-term care needs and home care responsibilities will become heavier and heavier. In order to establish a long-term care system that meets the needs of the elderly and the physically and mentally disabled, the Taiwan Executive Yuan adopted the "Long-Term Care Ten Year Plan 2.0" in 2016. At the same time, the Taiwanese government has strongly used various IoT applications in the "Long-Term Care Ten Year Plan 2.0" and hopes to improve the long-term care system with the intervention of in-formation and communication technology [10, 11].

Even though there are many long-term care services at the national level it has been in implementation, there are still many restrictions on the recipients receiving service. Many elderly people in the healthy life stage are not eligible for service. However, standing in the concept of "prevention is better than cure", these healthy elders needs to be cared for in order to prevent the heavy resources and manpower generated in the future stage of treatment. The demand for long-term care is not only to meet their physiological needs, but also for their psychological needs.

In addition, Taiwan is a highly democratic society [12], and care for the elderly living in various regions should not deviate from the fairness and equality of social welfare due to geographical location, resource allocation and sparse population conditions. Moreover, the right to life and health of the basic hu-man rights of the elderly living in rural areas should not be put at a disadvantage. The United Nations introduced "Proclamation on Aging" as early as 1991, revealing the five principles of "independence, participation, care, self-realization, and dignity" that older people should have [13]. The WHO pro-posed an "active ageing" policy framework in 2002, advocating the three aspects of health, participation and safety to improve the quality of life of the elderly [14]. The Ministry of Health and Welfare in Taiwan has established an active aging indicator framework and monitoring system since 2015 [15]. Aiming at important impact factors and key results, develop a data collection and intervention model that spans the health process, across levels, and across fields, and establishes a data warehouse and decision support system. Promote the successful and active aging of individuals and society, reduce cowardice, disability, dementia, care costs and premature death.

1.2 Research Purpose

In a highly democratic society, care for the elderly living in various regions should not deviate from the fairness and equality of social welfare because of geographical location, resource allocation, and sparse population conditions, let alone the basic human rights of rural elderly living at a disadvantage with the right to health. The United Nations introduced the "Proclamation on Aging" as early as 1991, revealing the five principles of "independence, participation, care, self-realization, and dignity" that older people should have. The World Health Organization (WHO) proposed an "active ageing" policy framework in 2002, advocating to improve the quality of life of the elderly from the three aspects of health, participation and safety [16]. The Ministry of Health and Welfare has established an active aging indicator framework and monitoring system since the Taiwan in 2015. In response to important impact factors and key results, it has developed a cross-health history, cross-level, and cross-domain data collection and intervention model, and established a data warehousing and decision support system. Promote the successful and active aging of individuals and society, reduce cowardice, disability, dementia, care costs and premature death.

Thus, this study mainly establishes an active aging AI community care ecosystem as the main task. With the success of this active aging AI community care ecosystem, it can help to deal with the problems faced by aging, effectively prevent and reduce the waste of healthcare resources at early stage. With the current state of aging in advanced countries, AI healthcare robots is a vast market to be developed. Therefore, this study hopes to use the standardization and information privacy protection for the elderly to care for huge amounts of health care data, and apply machine learning and statistical techniques, and deep learning to find out the hidden information of the elderly care, to find key decision points, and to establish alert and notification mechanism. Through this process, this study hopes to not only care for the physical and mental health of the elderly, but also to take care of the mental status of the elderly and relatives around the elderly, and to establish a blessed smart community care sharing model.

Every elder is a treasure with rich experience and it is the love of many family members and friends. How to protect the last mile of the dignity of the elders in the life stage and make them older is our major mission and responsibility. Therefore, based on the severe resource aging and resource issues faced by elder care mentioned above, this research will apply new-generation information technologies such as big data, deep learning, the Internet of Things, artificial intelligence and blockchain technology to bionic technology Robot dog as a carrier (considering the effects of the Valley of Terror theory, this study does not use robots as a carrier to provide services), to build a comprehensive and community-based AI community elder care program for the elders, which is close to the elders'real lives and needs Based on the researcher's mission and responsibility, design a care plan for the elderly on the last mile of life. And in combination with the development of telecommunications technology to minimize the possible inequality between the urban and rural areas and the gap. Finally, through the intervention of technology, the life stories and experiences of the elders can be passed down and become the treasures of the community and society in the present and the future.

2 Artificial Intelligent Applications in Elderly Care

In recent years, the development of telematics has been quite rapid and matured and diversified [17]. For example, Japan is a best example of the use of next-generation telematics technology in elderly care. Artificial Intelligence (AI) is to make computers through a series of deep learning to make machines intelligent, and then used to solve real-life problems [18]. In many countries, robots have gradually been introduced as caregivers in response to manpower shortages. For example, Japan has been developing AI to support the elderly's life since 2015, and has vigorously developed a robot that combines huge amounts of data and AI to help support future long-term service.

In Japan, robots are the main development direction of elderly care. At present, the robots on the market can be divided into three categories, namely: nursing support robots, self-assistance robots, and chat robots [19–21]. This study will provide comprehensive care services through the integrated solution of the nursing support robot and chat robot. But no matter which type, AI robots should have a human temperature, and currently the provision of human emotional connections and spiritual care is quite a missing link. The European Union has also developed some robots for elderly care programs, such as SocialRobot, ENRICHME… [22, 23]. Some researchers even shouted slogans to encourage everyone to seize the opportunity to develop smart elderly care robots [24].

Another study points out that the biggest criticism of such applications is that they may have deeper loneliness or fear of lack of humanity in robots [25]. AI robots should have a human temperature, and the current overall international development trend is currently quite lacking in the provision of human emotional connections and spiritual care. For a robot that is applied in daily life, it is very important to be able to grow with the changes in technology and needs. Because of this, research intends to use an enhanced deep learning method to allow AI robot to enhance themselves at any time. This type of growth way allows us to stay at the forefront of technology and serve humanity.

In 2019, Gartner proposed ten strategic technological trends with the core concept of "human-oriented smart space", which is consistent with the direction of this project. The biggest needs of silver-haired people in China are physiological and safety needs [26], but in the process of accompanying the elderly, they often find that the elderly need more, but it is because of dignity and some factors that cannot truly convey the true needs And this often causes them to feel lonely and worthless, which is often the main reason for the elderly's depression.

3 Active Aging

The World Health Organization (WHO) began promoting the concept of active aging in 2002 [27]. The main appeal of active aging is to enable the elderly to improve the quality of life in old age, and strive to improve the process of health, participation and safety. The vision of active aging requires the joint efforts of multiple parties, not just the health system alone.

In 2003, researchers in Taiwan began to study issues related to active aging, and eventually created an age-friendly city [28]. According to the "Global age-friendly cities: A guide" by WHO [29], there are eight major areas for friendly cities for the elderly: housing, transportation, telecommunications, accessible and safe public space, social participation, community and health services, work with volunteering, respect for the elderly and social integration.

Taiwan began to build the first age-friendly city program in Chiayi in 2010 [30], and counties and cities have subsequently joined the initiative. At the same time, it has also led to the development of the silver economy. The involvement of science and technology in the silver economy does not cost a lot of money, but to re-conceive and design the multi-level intervention of technology, environment, services and systems from an age-friendly manner.

The focus of active aging is on the concept of "prevention". It is hoped that the prevention perspective can be used to affect the improvement of the health of the elderly and prevent the occurrence of disability. At the same time, in 2013, 1,672 community care points were deployed nationwide to promote the health promotion of the elderly [31]. It is hoped that this will make our elders not only live old but also live well.

4 Taiwan's Current Long-Term Care Policy

At this stage, Taiwan's long-term care policy mainly promotes long-term care 2.0, focusing on the realization of local aging and providing multiple care services for the elderly from family, community, and institutions. It is mainly to build community-based care-based communities to promote local elderly's quality of life.

Long-term care 2.0 Establish community-integrated service centers (A), composite service centers (B), and alleys of long-term care station (C) in each township to provide care services with high accessibility, flexibility and convenience. At the same time, we also set up community-based dementia common care centers for dementia, provide related resources to build a safe community environment for dementia, and strengthen the prevention and delay of disability [32].

In addition, the National Health Agency also promotes related elderly friendly health environment and service plans [33], including: transformation of medical services, adjustment of medical care institutions, distribution of community services, and upgrading of counties and cities.

The transformation of medical services is mainly to build a high-quality chronic care network for the elderly; the adjustment of medical care institutions is to promote an elderly friendly care environment that promotes the dignity, participation and health of the elderly; the community service network is to build a community health promotion network that is active in the physical, mental and social functions of the elderly Road; county and city construction and upgrading is to promote an age-friendly city suitable for the active life of the elderly.

5   Active Aging AI Community Care Ecosystem Design Concept and Process

Based on the above-mentioned deficiencies in activating the lives of the elderly. This study considers the elders who have been in bed for a long time and have limited mobility. At present, they have been involved in the mechanism of nursing and caring staff and have been doing so for a long time. Therefore, this study first excludes these two types of elderlies, and only focuses on the health and sub-health elderlies that can take care of themselves. Conceptual care for seniors, prevention is better than cure. Therefore, this study hopes that this is a temperature-based application plan, which not only protects the elderly's physical and safety, but also integrates the characteristics of the community into the elderly's social partners in the old age and personalization. The integration of nursing care applications enables the elderly to actively age from the process of social and self-improvement. Finally, through the integrated application of chatbots, they interact with the elders and retain their life experiences and stories, which not only provides elders with full care, but also uses these valuable life materials as the treasure of humanity's knowledge in the future.

In the past, there were many related researches on population aging using information technology. At the beginning, most of the development process was in the clinical medical and nursing level. For example, Li [34] proposed a bed monitoring system centered on the bed and not prejudicing the privacy of the elderly. Then, government officials have gradually adapted health information technology from the electronic medical records at the clinical end to the concept of "returning health information to patients" [35].

However, the elders are relatively weak in information ability and literacy, and there are obvious problems of unequal information for the above-mentioned health-related data. Therefore, the promotion of elders' health is not only achieved through the introduction of information technology. To assist, we must also think about how to make the large amount of health information they generate can be effectively and properly applied based on professional health care background, not just partial fragmentation, but a perfect solution.

Many current researches only address fragmented current long-term care problems, but the development of information diffusion practices in the subject is quite limited due to the limitations of the elderly's own conditions, such as: Chen [36] summarizes the leisure needs for active aging of middle-aged and elderly And health information needs to build active and aging leisure and health apps, but not all elderly people make good use of mobile phones and apps, and the development of health information assistants also lacks room for growth. In addition, there are also many home care design products for the elderly in the current environment. However, there are still many shortcomings in terms of functionality and meeting the needs of the elderly. In particular, the satisfaction and promotion of the social and self-realization of the elderly are still lacking.

Therefore, this plan designs an AI elder care solution using artificial intelligence technology combined with the new generation of information technology. Through professional and impartial third parties with health care knowledge and portable health care equipment, it provides care for the elderly in the community such as urban areas. Prevention is better than cure. I hope that through the design of this study, we will help rural elders who are far away from medical institutions. They will not sacrifice their own health and the right to equality in survival because of time and space constraints, so that the elderly is active.

In addition, it is hope that through the design of the AI community elderly care, the rural elderly can no longer be lonely, and the young people can leave the country and struggle more safely. Finally, human beings are group animals and should not be lonely or lack a stage to play because of their age and restrictions on their place of residence. Therefore, this study will design a mechanism for rural elders to meet social needs and respect needs. Toward self-realization, let the soul of the elderlies on the last mile of the village be rich.

The robot's mission achievement is very good, but it supports logic. Although it lacks emotion, morality, self, and loyalty, we can give human logic to its logic. Just as in the movie Robot and Frank, Frank and Robot live and interact as normal [37]. Therefore, this research and development technology combines the knowledge of bionics to inject active temperature into the robot dog. Hamlin, Wynn, and Bloom [38] has used experimental methods to understand the distinction between good and bad infants at six and ten months. The study uses different design characters to show babies to show the positive events and animations with matching animations. Negative events prove that babies choose characters who are combined with positive events. It proves that babies have developed simple social ability and judgment ability in the early stage. Zoologists also point out that dogs understand our emotional changes by watching us [39].

Attila [40] points out that dogs understand the meaning of words with the left brain, and the meaning of intonation is distinguished with the right brain. Therefore, considering biological instincts, we will continue to use deep reinforcement learning (RL) to allow robot dogs to learn by observing the environment, and continue to self-grow at any time based on new data., And the data in the collection process for analysis and application in order to obtain maximum efficiency, efficiency and benefits.

Finally, the development of a chatbot model and the analysis results of the voice database to guide the elderly to share life experiences and stories, thereby retaining valuable life trajectory assets and becoming Taiwan's huge database of elderly care with the concept of holistic care. In addition, this research focuses on system integration and data analysis and application, in order to minimize the risk of equipment instability and provide stable, perfect, and future-oriented care for the elderly. The AI community care ecosystem including following three main processes:

1. Design and build the prototype and basic capabilities of an elderly AI community care system and environment. This stage mainly integrates hardware, including smart bracelets, edge computing home butler cores, intuitive reflection cores, brain

control cores, depth cameras, GPS receivers, array microphones, wireless network cards, servos, etc. Connected to each other.

2. Then, through the integrated environment of the previous stage, collect the physiological data of the community elders (heart rate, meal time, drinking water\work and rest\medication time, movement trajectory), image data (faces from different angles\expressions\relationships\contacts pictures), Audio file data (daily discourse, topical discussion, emotional classification, personal characteristics and preference attribute classification) are stored in the AI community care big data center established by this study.

3. By integrating these collected data, it can analyze personal care patterns, not only reminding the elderly to develop regular meals, rest, water and medication, and emotional and health precautions.

In this study, a four-legged robot is used as the carrier, that is, a robot dog. The reason why robot dogs are used instead of robots is based on the following advantages: superior load bearing and cross-terrain capabilities, more mature balance and movement functions, and the possibility of developing into pet shapes in the future to reduce the theory of valley of terror caused by robots. In addition, this study also combines wearable smart bracelets as companion components, mainly based on the following advantages, including: mature products with waterproof and dustproof capabilities, long standby time, years of experience, and diverse functional forms You can choose to transfer data directly with Android or iOS. This research device is composed of the core of the housekeeper, and with edge computing and blockchain technology, it can consume less power and could report at the first time. Furthermore, it can also avoid the worry of missing data or difficult backup. Once some terminals are broken, just replace the hardware and all the data will be stored in the blockchain. Because personal data has been de-personalized using SHA encryption, only you can find the correct backup from the blockchain, thereby reducing user concerns about information security and privacy protection of personal data (Fig. 1).

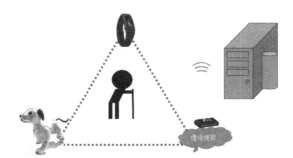

Fig. 1. Active aging AI community care ecosystem design concept

This study mainly designed the following four major work items to complete the AI community care ecosystem:

1. AI elderly care robot dog and AI elderly care big data center planning, design and construction

The robot interpretation of the elderly's behavior by analysis based on Google Atomic Visual Actions (AVA), this data set distinguishes human behavior into three categories (1) posture or movement performance during movement (2) person-to-item interaction behavior (3) person-to-person interaction behavior, and 96,000 individual-type actions are labeled, resulting in 210,000 Action tags. By extending this database and training AI to judge the behavior of the master, the advantage of this database is that it takes only three seconds to complete the interpretation.

2. Identification of the elderly

This method uses fast.ai as a template. The advantage of this method is that it is mature and uses python as the basic syntax to call various function libraries including C. In the first stage, I started training AI to identify the master with a deep learning course. First, I collected photos of the master from various angles to establish a training database and used this database as a template to start training AI. Use Google's massive crawling text to collect many photos of people and things as a non-master feature database (Confusion matrix). At the beginning of the project, the AI was trained using a server computer. Load it into the electronic dog and test its accuracy to identify the owner. This study uses convolutional neural network image recognition as the basis. The visual images seen by AI dogs are first simplified by convolution operations and pooling methods to facilitate subsequent comparison and data transmission. The advantage of the convolution operation is that it retains the nature of 2D pictures but simplifies the amount of data and complexity and uses the GPU's parallel operation capabilities to effectively complete the comparison of pictures and libraries.

3. Detection and application of classification methods for elder behavior and health status development with deep learning technology

We use deep learning technology to teach robotic dogs to classify elder behavior into moods, griefs, sadness, and other categories based on their facial expressions or physiological information. The basic and important skills for identifying facial expressions and emotions in the early stages of bionic interaction with human society. Each node is calculated from the weighted input values of multiple nodes in the previous layer. These weights can be adjusted to perform special image recognition tasks.

In order to train a deep neural network to recognize photos with happy faces, we show them happy pictures as raw data (image pixels) on the input layer. For example: when we know that the final result is hi, the network will recognize the pattern in the picture and adjust the node weights to minimize the errors of the category pictures judged as hi Every picture that shows favor will help optimize picture weight. With enough input information and training, accurately analyze and recognize patterns corresponding to hilarious expressions. Since the early elders have just joined the initial stage of the database establishment, the plan uses deep reinforcement learning. The deep reinforcement learning method can respond to the initial stage of our environment. Currently, the information is less complete. The robot dog acts based on the environment to maximize the expected benefits. In addition, under the environment's feedback stimulus, the expectation of stimulus can be gradually formed gradually, resulting in the habitual problem of obtaining the maximum benefit.

In this study, the human action understanding data set AVA is used as an auxiliary database to establish an elderly behavior understanding database in Taiwan. With the help of the bracelet's real-time tracking of health information, the health status is divided into three levels according to the emergency level.

4. Matchmaking for elder networks based on social network analysis and semantic analysis

Liu [41] reported that elders love social networking sites, more than 90% are LINE users, and nearly 60% also play Facebook. Using the connection between the robot dog and the mobile phone can act as a Bluetooth transmission terminal, presetting the basic voice activation function of several communication software. First save the record by streaming, develop the "Verbatim Tool" to convert speech into text, and gradually improve its conversion accuracy through deep learning. The word processing is turned into a dataset, and the natural language processing tool Google Natural Language API is used to analyze the positive and negative scores of each sentence, combined with the Chinese word segmentation system developed by the Central Research Institute of Taiwan to find out the characteristics of the elderly (keywords of interests or behaviors).

Use the semantic database to calculate topics or common behaviors that elders are interested in (such as singing, drawing, chatting, playing chess, etc.), and list keyword functions and analyze text or voice to collect data, and also analyze the types of attractions often visited by the elderly, the length of stay, the frequency and the time period through the trajectory data, and match up similar potential late-life partners. This function will calculate the score of each item with different score weights, so it may be necessary to establish a suitable formula after obtaining a more credible weight decibel through a questionnaire.

6   Conclusion

This study takes care of the physical and mental health of the elders through artificial intelligence technology. It also uses the judgment of physiological information to provide their concepts of health and wellness. The interaction between humans and dogs promotes the elders to carry out some healthy activities, thereby effectively shortening the elderly's bedtime, improve physical health functions and functions, and make it a good social circle through the matching of social networks.

Finally, this research uses the blockchain structure as the material for the elderly, which not only allows the elderly to live happily and with dignity from the design and planning of this project, but also focuses on "people-oriented" for individualized care.

Kate Swaffer, chairman of the International Dementia Union, mentioned that although a patient with dementia is a patient, we should also allow him/her to participate in or engage in activities of interest, but his/her family or the institution takes the dominance of the demented, not the elderly [42]. The elder has his own life history and interests and can also express his feelings. Good care is based on him to help him develop his preferences. It is everything he decides, not standard arrangements. We should give basic respect to the human rights of the elderly and give him the right and opportunity to choose. Although the decline in function may affect the elderly's decision-making, identification, language, sense of space, direction, etc., if we respect their human rights, we can still Provide different options to match their existing functions, giving him the right and opportunity to choose, not at the discretion of caregivers or institutions.

In this study, it is emphasized listening and respect. Let us understand the elders, accompany the elders, and listen to the elders. Through the practice of artificial intelligence technology and huge amounts of data, we understand and give the elders the real needs. Leaving a huge amount of valuable elderly assets in the field can also enable technology to help everyone more to leave more memories of the elders' voices, words and pictures, so that the miss is no longer far away. Of course, while retaining the data, the elders need not worry about their own information privacy. The block-chain structure designed in this study will properly protect the elders 'data and guard the elders' human rights.

References

1. Fishman, T.: Shock of Gray: The Aging of the World's Population and How it Pits Young Against Old, Child Against Parent, Worker Against Boss, Company Against Rival, and Nation Against Nation. Simon and Schuster, New York City (2010)
2. Agich, G.: Dependence and Autonomy in Old Age: An Ethical Framework for Long-Term Care. Cambridge University Press, Cambridge (2003)
3. Oura, A., Washio, M., Izumi, H., Mori, M.: Burden among caregivers of the frail elderly and its correlation with the introduction of a long-term care insurance system for the elderly in fourth year. Nihon Ronen Igakkai zasshi, Jpn. J. Geriatr. **42**, 411–416 (2005)
4. Brodsky, J., Resnizky, S., Citron, D.: Issues in Family Care of the Elderly: Characteristics of Care, Burden on Family Members and Support Programs. Myers-JDC-Brookdale Institute, Jerusalem (2011)
5. Kalache, A.: Ageing in developing countries. Crit. Pub. Health **2**, 38–43 (1991)
6. Arltová, M., Langhamrová, J.: Migration and ageing of the population of the Czech Republic and the EU countries. Prague Econ. Pap. **19**, 54–73 (2010)
7. Raju, S.S.: Studies on Ageing in India: A Review, Population Ageing in India, p. 180. Cambridge University Press, Cambridge (2014)
8. Tan, C.: Beyond rote-memorisation: confucius' concept of thinking. Educ. Philos. Theory **47**, 428–439 (2015)
9. Vishnevskiy, K., Karasev, O., Meissner, D.: Integrated roadmaps for strategic management and planning. Technol. Forecast. Soc. Chang. **110**, 153–166 (2016)
10. Cheng, P.-F., Chen, H.-Z., Pan, H.-C.: Outcome of Discharge Planning Linked to Long-Term Care Plan 2.0 for Elderly Orthopedic Surgery Patient (2019)
11. Tseng, H.-T., Hwang, H.-G., Hsu, W.-Y., Chou, P.-C., Chang, I.: IoT-based image recognition system for smart home-delivered meal services. Symmetry **9**, 125 (2017)
12. Hsieh, J.F.: Democracy in a Mildly Divided Society, Democratization in Taiwan, pp. 29–42. Routledge, London (2016)

13. Veras, R.P., Oliveira, M.: Aging in Brazil: the building of a healthcare model. Ciencia & saude coletiva **23**, 1929–1936 (2018)
14. De São José, J.M., Timonen, V., Amado, C.A.F., Santos, S.P.: A critique of the active ageing index. J. Aging stud. **40**, 49–56 (2017)
15. Lin, Y.-Y., Huang, C.-S.: Aging in Taiwan: building a society for active aging and aging in place. Gerontologist **56**, 176–183 (2016)
16. Formosa, M.: Active ageing through lifelong learning: the university of the third age. In: Formosa, M. (ed.) The University of the Third Age and Active Ageing. IPA, vol. 23, pp. 3–18. Springer, Cham (2019). https://doi.org/10.1007/978-3-030-21515-6_1
17. Chang, S.-H., Fan, C.-Y.: Identification of the technology life cycle of telematics: a patent-based analytical perspective. Technol. Forecast. Soc. Chang. **105**, 1–10 (2016)
18. Koohsari, M.J., et al.: Cognitive function of elderly persons in Japanese neighborhoods: the role of street layout. Am. J. Alzheimer's Dis. Other Dementias® **34**, 381–389 (2019)
19. Maruyama, K., et al.: Food frequency questionnaire reproducibility for middle-aged and elderly Japanese. Asia Pac. J. Clin. Nutr. **28**, 362 (2019)
20. Osuka, Y., Matsubara, M., Hamasaki, A., Hiramatsu, Y., Ohshima, H., Tanaka, K.: Development of low-volume, high-intensity, aerobic-type interval training for elderly Japanese men: a feasibility study. Eur. Rev. Aging Phys. Act. **14**, 14 (2017)
21. Kobayashi, T., et al.: Dementia screening system based on SNS agency robot. In: 2019 IEEE 9th International Conference on Consumer Electronics, ICCE-Berlin, pp. 306–309. IEEE (2019)
22. Riva, G., Riva, E.: ENRICHME: an interactive social robot capable of moving autonomously in an elderly person's house. Cyberpsychol. Behav. Soc. Netw. **22**, 565–566 (2019)
23. Agrigoroaie, R., Tapus, A.: Contactless physiological data analysis for user quality of life improving by using a humanoid social robot. In: Battiato, S., Gallo, G., Schettini, R., Stanco, F. (eds.) ICIAP 2017. LNCS, vol. 10485, pp. 696–706. Springer, Cham (2017). https://doi.org/10.1007/978-3-319-68548-9_63
24. Sifeng, Z., Min, T., Zehao, Z., Zhao, Y.: Capturing the opportunity in developing intelligent elderly care robots in China challenges, opportunities and development strategy. In: 2016 IEEE Workshop on Advanced Robotics and its Social Impacts, ARSO, pp. 61–66. IEEE (2016)
25. Cylkowska-Nowak, M., Tobis, S., Salatino, C., Tapus, A., Suwalska, A.: The robot in elderly care. In: Psychology and psychiatry, sociology, health care and education-SGEM 2015 (2015)
26. Yanwei, C., Yue, S., Zifeng, C.: Towards smarter cities: Human-oriented urban planning and management based on space-time behavior research. Urban Planning Int. **6**, 31–37 (2014)
27. World Health Organization: The World Health Report 2002: Reducing Risks, Promoting Healthy Life. World Health Organization, Geneva (2002)
28. Kang, M.J.: Regenerating public life for ageing communities through the choreography of place-ballets and the weaving of memory tapestries. In: Chong, K.H., Cho, M. (eds.) Creative Ageing Cities, pp. 91–120. Routledge, London (2018)
29. World Health Organization: Global Age-Friendly Cities: A Guide. World Health Organization, Geneva (2007)
30. Sun, Y., Chao, T.-Y., Woo, J., Au, D.W.: An institutional perspective of "Glocalization" in two Asian tigers: The "Structure − Agent − Strategy" of building an age-friendly city. Habitat Int. **59**, 101–109 (2017)
31. Hsiao, F.-Y., Hsieh, P.-H., Gau, C.-S.: Ten-year trend in prescriptions of z-hypnotics among the elderly: a nationwide, cross-sectional study in Taiwan. J. Clin. Gerontol. Geriatr. **4**, 37–41 (2013)

32. Lee, P.Y.: Case Study of the Long Term Care 2.0 Barriers on the Hospice Share Care Patient's

33. Scharlach, A.E., Lehning, A.J.: Ageing-friendly communities and social inclusion in the United States of America. Ageing Soc. **33**, 110–136 (2013)

34. Li, N., Becerik-Gerber, B., Krishnamachari, B., Soibelman, L.: A BIM centered indoor localization algorithm to support building fire emergency response operations. Autom. Constr. **42**, 78–89 (2014)

35. Shy, B.D., et al.: Increased identification of emergency department 72-hour returns using multihospital health information exchange. Acad. Emerg. Med. **23**, 645–649 (2016)

36. Ku, P.-W., Fox, K.R., Chen, L.-J.: Leisure-time physical activity, sedentary behaviors and subjective well-being in older adults: An eight-year longitudinal research. Soc. Indic. Res. **127**, 1349–1361 (2016)

37. Schreier, M.: Qualitative Content Analysis in Practice. Sage publications, Thousand Oaks (2012)

38. Hamlin, J.K., Wynn, K., Bloom, P.: Social evaluation by preverbal infants. Nature **450**, 557–559 (2007)

39. Greenebaum, J.B.: Training dogs and training humans: Symbolic interaction and dog training. Anthrozoös **23**, 129–141 (2010)

40. Andics, A., Miklósi, Á.: Neural processes of vocal social perception: dog-human comparative fMRI studies. Neurosci. Biobehav. Rev. **85**, 54–64 (2018)

41. Liu, J., Guo, M., Xu, L., Mao, W., Chi, I.: Family relationships, social connections, and depressive symptoms among Chinese older adults in international migrant families. J. Ethnic Cult. Diversity Soc. Work **26**, 167–184 (2017)

42. Low, L.-F., McGrath, M., Swaffer, K., Brodaty, H.: Communicating a diagnosis of dementia: a systematic mixed studies review of attitudes and practices of health practitioners. Dementia **18**, 2856–2905 (2019)

A Study on the Preference of Elderly Diabetic Patients to Blood Glucose Meters

Yixiang Wu[✉]

Yiwu Industrial and Commercial College, No. 2,
Xueyuan Road, Yiwu 322000, Zhejiang, China
1951601836@qq.com

Abstract. Fully exploring the hidden inner feeling of elderly diabetic patients, and satisfying the feeling in the research and development stage of blood glucose meter will improve the design process of blood glucose meters and improve the design quality. Therefore, a study is carried out on the preference of elderly diabetic patients to blood glucose meters. Starting with the study on the psychological feelings of elderly diabetic patients, the user's preference factors are extracted through the Evaluation Grid Method of Miryoku Engineering. First, the blood glucose meter samples on the market are selected, and an in-depth interview is made for more than 8 elderly diabetic patients, to construct the relationship between the semantics of user preference at the upper level (the psychological feeling of users) and the specific preference characteristics at the lower level. Then the KJ method is adopted for integration and sorting, to sort out the evaluation grid diagram of 8 elderly diabetic patients, which can link the correlation between the user's psychological feelings and specific features. In this way, it improves the satisfaction of elderly diabetic patients, and provides a new method for the design of blood glucose meters.

Keywords: Elderly diabetic patients · The elderly · Preference · Design of blood glucose meters

1 Background and Purpose

In recent years, due to the development of medical technology, the average life of the people has increased year by year. According to the statistical data of *Selected Papers on China's Population Aging*, the report introduces the problems and policy suggestions brought about by China's population aging. The report points out that China in the 21st century will be an irreversible aging society. From 2001 to 2020 is a period of rapid aging. China would add an average of 5.96 million elderly people every year. [1] By 2020, the elderly population will reach 248 million and the aging level will reach 17.17%. [1] From 2021 to 2050 is the accelerated aging stage. The number of elderly people in China has begun to accelerate, increasing by 6.2 million on average every year. [1] By 2050, the total elderly population will exceed 400 million. From 2051 to 2100 is a stable stage of severe aging. [1] In 2051, China's elderly population will reach a peak of 437 million, about twice the number of children, entering a plateau of high aging. [1]

© Springer Nature Switzerland AG 2020
Q. Gao and J. Zhou (Eds.): HCII 2020, LNCS 12208, pp. 209–218, 2020.
https://doi.org/10.1007/978-3-030-50249-2_16

With the increase of age, the physical health of the elderly is getting worse and worse, and the rate of chronic diseases is also increasing. According to the statistics of the National Health Bureau, the probability of elderly people over 60 years old suffering from chronic diseases such as coronary heart disease, hypertension and diabetes is 3–7 times higher than that of 15–45 years old, of which 43.2% are elderly people suffering from two diseases and 43.8% are chronic diseases. Diabetes is a chronic lifelong disease, its hyperglycemia can cause acute and chronic complications, and complications are the main causes of disability and death rate of patients. Blood sugar level is an important indicator to reflect the control of the disease, and good blood sugar control is the main measure to prevent diabetic complications, so the compliance of blood sugar monitoring of patients is very important. Attention should be paid to improving patients' awareness and skills of self-monitoring blood sugar.

The American Diabetes Association recommends diabetic patients to test their glucose three or more times a day with a blood glucose meter to avoid possible complications. Due to the reduction of the elderly's living ability and mobility, most activities are at home, and most of them still have to take care of themselves. Therefore, the elderly must have the ability to operate their own living products and monitor their own health. In order to avoid the trouble of blood glucose measurement in hospitals every day, the household blood glucose meter and test paper provide a convenient choice. More and more attention has been paid to the development of commercial home medical equipment products, such as blood sugar machines and sphygmomanometers, so that the elderly can be tested at home without having to go to the hospital frequently. However, there are still many interface design defects in blood glucose meter products at present, which are easy to cause operation errors. It is challenging to design medical equipment for non-professional users, especially for the elderly who suffer from physiological and psychological deterioration and are more likely to make cognitive errors in the perceptual information provided by products than young people. They may have various physical, cognitive or perceptual disorders, and their educational background and understanding of clinical background may differ greatly.

Product designers should provide more perceptual information, especially in the area of artificial intelligence, to help elderly users understand how to use household medical devices, such as blood glucose meters. There are still many designs of the existing commercial household blood glucose machines, which will cause inconvenience in operation for the elderly due to cognitive errors. In view of this, this study wants to know whether the perceptual information provided by the product can help the elderly to use and operate correctly. Through appropriate devices, the product can significantly induce the response of the elderly users, so that the first-time users can complete the operation correctly without too much explanation. The purpose of this study is to explore the usability test of the elderly when using blood glucose machines based on the perceptual information provided by the products, and to investigate and study the blood sampling pens of four blood glucose machines, so as to understand the cognitive ability of the elderly to the operation of the products and further improve the attractive factors in product design.

2   Research Methods

Japanese scholars Junichiro Sanui and Masao Inui [2] refer to the concept of clinical psychology and put forward the word "Miryoku Engineering" [2], which is a design concept based on user needs. Attractive factor, in Japanese, is "Miryokuyouso" or "Miryokuyinsi" [2] English translation is "Attractiveness", "Attractiveness Factor" or "Attractive Factor". It is a factor that makes something have positive attraction. Its concept was put forward by Japanese charm engineering researchers [3] From the point of view of product design, the extraction of attractive factor is what many designers are trying to find in the process of product design. Evaluation Grid Method is an important research method in Miryoku Engineering, which originates from the category of psychology and is helpful to deeply understand the psychological cognition of the subject to something. This method is mainly through personal interviews, through the paired comparison of objects A and B, to clearly discuss the similarity or difference between objects, and then to sort out the individual characteristics of the target objects [4]. To further develop this method, firstly, in the evaluation of the target object, the interviewee must answer his likes or dislikes of the object. The second step is to clarify the meaning or conditions of the interviewee's answers through additional questions, to integrate their answers, to specifically analyze the attractive factors of products to consumer preferences, and to sort out their related construction networks. This research method is called evaluation construction method. [2]

The evaluation construction method provides stimulation according to the scope of the topic by means of in-depth interviews, and the process is carried out hierarchically. The consumer's preference for products is obtained by layering. First, prepare the blood sampling pens of the 4 blood glucose machines used in the interview, then start the interview, ask each subject to experience according to the operation process of the blood sampling pens, and pick out the blood sampling pens he thinks he likes. The appearance and interface of the blood sampling pen will provide information on how to operate the blood sampling pen, enabling elderly users to feel the product visually and tactilely and understand how to use it. The appearance and interface information of the blood sampling pen induce the elderly users to associate with how to operate the product. These appearance and interface information that induce the elderly users to operate correctly are their original concepts to stimulate the subject, thus guiding the subjects to make a clearer analysis of their concepts, then extending the concepts to two items: concrete reasons and abstract feelings, and finally sorting out the attractive factors for the subjects to evaluate the product (Fig. 1).

Fig. 1. 4 blood sampling pens used

3 Steps for Operating Blood Sampling Pen

3.1 Blood Collection Operation Task Instructions

Taking the blood sampling pens of 4 blood glucose machines as a case study, the blood collection operation steps are shown in Fig. 2. Its detailed steps are as follows:

1. Hold the blood sampling pen nib in one hand and the pen holder in the other. Apply a slight upward force and pull open the blood collection nib.
2. After the pen nib is separated from the pen holder, pull it out to both sides.
3. Place the blood collection needle into the needle holder of the blood sampling pen.
4. Rotate to remove the protective cover of blood collection needle and keep the protective cover.
5. Press back and close the pen nib of the blood sampling pen.
6. Rotate the pen nib to select the depth and confirm that the selected depth is aligned with the window so as to obtain the appropriate blood volume. The depth setting is based on the skin condition of the individual.
7. Hold the blood sampling pen with one hand and pull it to the end with the other hand. The blood sampling pen will buckle the release button. Release the handle, and the handle will automatically return to the original position close to the release button.
8. Align the blood sampling pen and stick to the fingertip for blood collection, and then press the release button for blood collection.
9. Pull the blood sampling pen nib, do not touch the blood collection needle, hold the blood sampling pen and directly put the blood collection needle under the protection cover.
10. Press and hold the release button first, and pull the handle of the blood sampling pen back to the end with the other hand to safely withdraw the blood collection needle covered with the protective cover.
11. Discard the used needle in a container that will not hurt others.
12. After the test, replace the pen nib of the blood sampling pen.

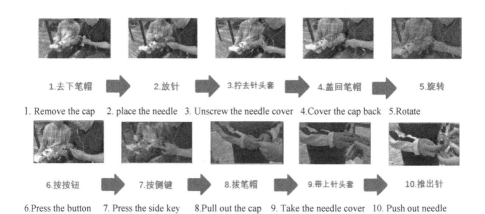

1.去下笔帽 2.放针 3.拧去针头套 4.盖回笔帽 5.旋转

1. Remove the cap   2. place the needle   3. Unscrew the needle cover   4.Cover the cap back   5.Rotate

6.按按钮 7.按侧键 8.按笔帽 9.带上针头套 10.推出针

6.Press the button   7. Press the side key   8.Pull out the cap   9. Take the needle cover   10. Push out needle

Fig. 2. Blood collection steps

3.2 Interviewees

The in-depth experience interview subjects of this study are specific or representative figures, including 8 elderly people, who participated in a 2-h in-depth experience interview. These elderly people are residents of two different communities in Shanghai. Their ages range from 60 to 70 years old, including 4 women and 4 men.

4 Extraction of Attractive Factor

The following are the attractive factors of the selected 3 elderly users after in-depth experience (Figs. 3, 4, 5).

Comfortable	←	Release button	→	The length and area of the button are the same as the area of the first thumb joint contact button
Skidproof Comfortable	←	Finger grip	→	The concave shape conforms to the shape of the muscle in the finger belly
Easy to understand	←	Spring press button	→	The direction in which the push button is tilted indicates the direction in which the push button to push
Clear	←	Pen cap	→	The concave groove is skidproof and indicates that the pen nib can rotate. The digital blood collection depth gauge conforms to the reading habit of people.
Intuitive		Depth indicator		Number represents needle depth
Reasonable	←	Needle withdrawal device	→	Pull off the cap and push the needle withdrawal button to remove the needle
Skidproof Comfortable	←	Spring pen bolt	→	There are many skidproof points on the shape of the thumb fingertip-shaped handle, indicating that the handle needs to be pinched and pulled upward by fingers.
Thoughtful	←	Joint of pen nib and pen holder	→	There is a clear small arrow icon to indicate the exact position where the cap and pen holder are combined.
Clear	←	Transparent plastic pen nib cover	→	The transparent pen cover indicates that the pen cover needs to be removed before the needle is installed.
Powerful	←	Release button	→	The button protrudes higher from the pen holder and has a round protrusion which is compact to press.

Fig. 3. Interview result of elderly user 1

Accurate	←	Nib	→	The pen nib is made of transparent plastic and has a small area, so the blood collection position can be well found during blood collection.
skidproof Obvious	←	Release button	→	There are many concave points on the button to prevent slipping.
Reasonable Elastic	←	Spring press button		When the push button is pushed upwards, the spring force is very large, which can prevent misoperation.
Clear	←	Size	→	The length of the blood sampling pen is short, and the three fingers can just hold it when collecting blood.
Feel at ease Easy	←	Release button	→	The front area of the release button is large, and the rear area is small. The front end of the release button will bulge to a part after loading, so it is easier to press it down.
Smooth Fitted	←	Nib	→	The front end of the pen nib is a flat plane, which can be attached to the fingertip when taking blood.
Elastic	←	Spring pen bolt	→	After being pulled up, the spring handle will automatically rebound with sound effect, and there will be no sound feedback after being pulled down in the loaded state.
Accurate Clear	←	Transparent plastic pen nib cover	→	The specific position of the needle can be seen when the transparent plastic pen nib cover takes blood, thus avoiding the situation that the needle can not be seen to be biased.
Comfortable	←	Appearance	→	The blood sampling pen is thin, which is suitable when holding it.

Fig. 4. Interview result of elderly user 2

Neat Representative	←	Color	→	The overall appearance of white is closely related to the medical field.
Intuitive	←	Release button	→	The release button is located in the middle of the blood sampling pen and is distinguished by gray color different from that of the pen holder.
Small Portable	←	Appearance		The overall appearance of the blood sampling pen is small and convenient to store and carry.
Comprehensive	←	Depth indicator	→	Nine numbers represent nine different blood collection depths, which can be used by most people.
Humanized	←	Needle withdrawal device	→	Pushing the needle withdrawal button can safely withdraw the needle after blood collection.
Clear	←	Release button	→	The release button of transparent material can see a red part inside the blood sampling pen to indicate whether the loading is completed or not.
Reasonable	←	Spring pen bolt	→	The color and texture of the spring bolt is different from that of the pen holder. When two fingers pull upward to hear the sound, release the bolt.
Intuitive Clear	←	Depth indicator	→	The number of the depth indicator is exposed at the nib of the blood sampling pen, and the white arrow on the pen holder indicates the current depth.
Comfortable	←	Spring pen bolt	→	A part of the spring pen bolt is embedded in the pen holder, which makes it easier to pull it up.

Fig. 5. Interview result of elderly user 3

In the study, the author used the KJ method used by Japanese scholar Kawakita [133] for induction and collation. By analyzing and comparing the evaluation structure diagrams of each test subject and combining the approximate descriptions with KJ method, the evaluation structures of all test subjects will be summarized (Fig. 6).

Clear	Clear 6 times, distinct 4 times
Comfortable	Comfortable 6 times, easeful 4 times
Skidproof	Skidproof 7 times
Reasonable	Reasonable 6 times, easy to understand twice , lucid once, suitable once, easy once
Intuitive	Intuitive 8 times, obvious 3 times, concise once
Thoughtful	Thoughtful twice, fitted once, Humanized once, feel at ease once
Accurate	Accurate 3 times, specific twice
Elastic	Powerful twice, elastic twice, compact once
Neat	Smooth once, neat twice, beautiful once, concise once
Portable	Portable twice, convenient once
Comprehensive	Comprehensive twice, high performance once, high efficiency once, multipurpose
Stable	Symmetrical once, steady once, firm once, stable once, tight once
Sensitive	Easy once, fast once, flexible once, sensitive once, advanced once

Fig. 6. Simplified results of KJ method

After all evaluation items are consolidated and simplified by KJ method, an overall evaluation structure diagram of attractive factors of blood sampling pen can be drawn, as shown in the (Figs. 7, 8, 9, 10, 11, 12, 13).

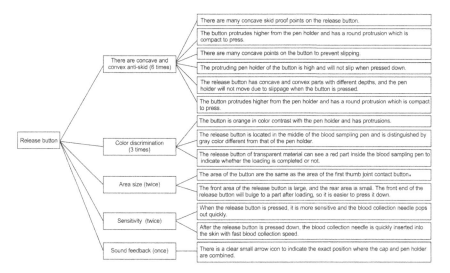

Fig. 7. Attractive factors of blood sampling pen component 1

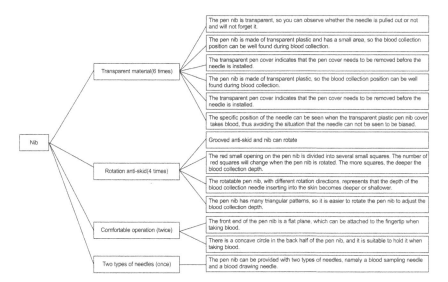

Fig. 8. Attractive Factors of Blood Sampling Pen Component 2

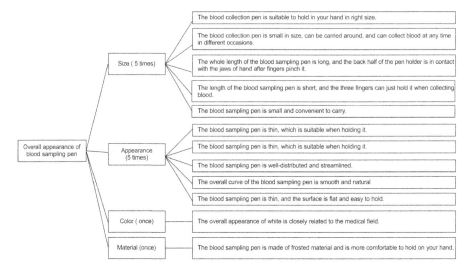

Fig. 9. Attractive factors of blood sampling pen component 3

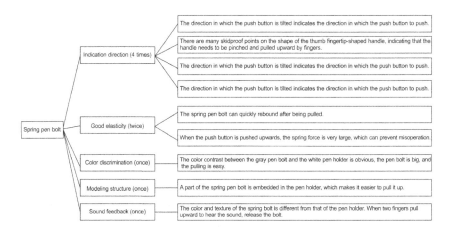

Fig. 10. Attractive factors of blood sampling pen component 4

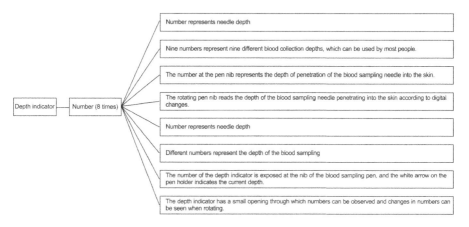

Fig. 11. Attractive factors of blood sampling pen component 5

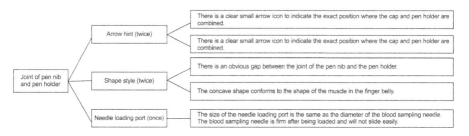

Fig. 12. Attractive factors of blood sampling pen component 6

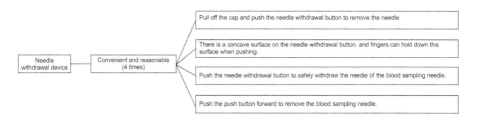

Fig. 13. Attractive factors of blood sampling pen component 7

When operating different blood glucose machines, it is mainly to identify the usage mode of the blood sampling pen. The ranking of all attractive factors of the elderly users after using the blood sampling pen is shown in the figure. It is suggested that the design of future home medical products should provide clearer information according to the ranking of attractive factors, so that the elderly users can intuitively respond to the operation and increase the satisfaction degree of the products (Fig. 14).

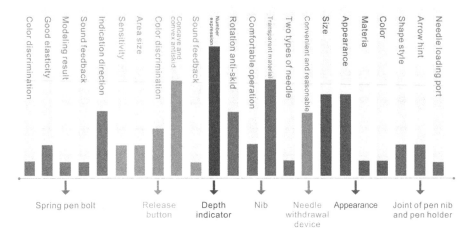

Fig. 14. Sequence of attractive factors of blood sampling pen

References

1. Cao, B.: Selected Papers on China's Population Aging. Hualing Publishing House, Beijing (2010)
2. Sanui, J., Inui, M.: Phenomenological approach to the evaluation of places: a study on the construct system associated with place evaluation. J. Architect. Planning Environ. Eng. **367** (2), 816–817 (1986)
3. Miryoku Engineering Research Institute, Miryoku Engineering, 1 edn. Haiwentang, Tokyo (1992)
4. Kelly, G.A.: The psychology of personal constructs, vol. 1, 2. Norton, New York (1955)

Well-Being, Persuasion, Health Education and Cognitive Support

Choice-Based User Interface Design of a Smart Healthy Food Recommender System for Nudging Eating Behavior of Older Adult Patients with Newly Diagnosed Type II Diabetes

Wen-Yu Chao and Zachary Hass[(⊠)]

Purdue University, West Lafayette, IN 47906, USA
zhass@purdue.edu

Abstract. Information Retrieval (IR) and Recommender System (RS) has its potential to assist patients to make an informed decision on healthy food and influence their food choices which inferring the chance of nudging dietary behavior. However, the potential users of the system, older adult patients, is a unique group of people with heterogeneity of the computer proficiency and the latency of technology acceptance. In this context, the effective User Interface (UI) design of such a personal health decision support system for older adults remains undetermined. To fill in the research gap, a choice-based UI of healthy food recommender system for older adults was proposed based on the literature review of ageing-centered design principles. A further user testing study was conducted to systematically examine the effectiveness of the critical UI design variables, search result layouts and nutrition information formats, in a 2×2 full factorial experiment. Fifteen older adults aged 60 years and older (mean = 66.8) were recruited to participate a scenario-based evaluation of the proposed prototype system, another fifteen college students between the ages of 20–35 (mean = 28.6) were recruited as the control group of the study. The results are collected by both quantitative data of subjective questionnaires and qualitative data of the transcriptions from interview and think aloud notes. This article presented and discussed the results of older adults' perceptions of the system collected by mixed methods in comparison to the student groups.

Keywords: Gerontechnology · UI/UX design · Recommender System

1 Introduction

Evidence indicates that healthy eating is an effective way to slow down the progression of diabetes mellitus [1]. In recent decades, an increasing knowledgebase about the disease has been built and moved into the digital sphere. Online communities provide strong support for dietary behavior change, particularly for the patient newly diagnosed with prediabetes or type II diabetes. However, for newly diagnosed older adults, that digital health-related information may not be easily accessible due to difficulty in adapting to new technology. To reduce this barrier, it is expedient to design a smart system adopting an

Q. Gao and J. Zhou (Eds.): HCII 2020, LNCS 12208, pp. 221–234, 2020.
https://doi.org/10.1007/978-3-030-50249-2_17

appropriate technology to aid in diet change. A potentially useful technology for this problem is a healthy food recommender system. This is essentially a decision support tool aimed at optimizing the nutritional intakes for an individual by providing recipe recommendations tailored to their particular health related dietary needs.

Recommender systems have been found useful in different domains such as e-commerce and scientific literature to solve the problem of information overload, leveraging big data analytics of user behavior, ratings, and user-defined tags [2–4]. In recent years, researchers in the food recommender system domain have focused on developing algorithms that incorporate health aspects into the system [5–9]. However, there is limited research focusing on the user interface design and evaluation of a food recommender system, factors which are likely to have a direct impact on guiding user behavior. What's more, the technology is not currently designed for older adults, users of the system who may stand to gain substantially from the health benefits of diet change, but who may struggle to learn the system due to low computer proficiency and self-efficacy of adopting technology into their daily life.

For the purpose of beginning to fill in the research gap around the design of a healthy food recommender system for older adult users, a prototype app with a choice-based user interface design was created. In this article, two critical user interface design variables were selected to be systematically examined by a 2×2 full factorial experiment; presenting the choice options on a vertical list-view layout or a side-by side layout; presenting the nutrition information in a text-list label (FDA Nutrition Facts Panel style) or in a symbolic, interpretative label (FSA Nutri-scores). The outcome variables were collected by a scenario-based human factors evaluation study. The usability and human workloads of using the system were evaluated by the USE questionnaire and NASA-TLX questionnaire after participants performed a healthy food choice task in a breakfast cereal selection scenario.

The purpose of this research is to gain insight on the optimal user interface design for the proposed healthy food recommender system. Our intent is to fill the research gap surrounding ageing-centered design of a healthy food recommender system by testing potential design guidelines within the paradigm of a user-centric evaluation framework. The paper is organized as follows: we begin with a literature review around the issues of technology and older adults and two key design variables, we then briefly describe the development of a prototype recommender system, proceeding next to describe the methods of our pilot experiment to test the system, and we finish with results from the experiment and concluding remarks.

2 Literature Review

2.1 Technology Acceptance Gap of Dietary Apps for Older Adults

Developing technology for older adults is a unique problem. Compared to younger adults, older adults aged over 55 are less likely to be engaged with food-related technologies [10]. This lower likelihood of older adult consumers adopting mHealth apps can be explained by the Technology Acceptance Model (TAM) proposed by Davis (1985), within which a consumer's attitude towards technology is mainly determined by Perceived Usefulness

(PU) and Perceived Ease of Use (PEOU) [11]. In the perspective of PU, it appears that researchers have overestimated users' enthusiasm for tracking their health using technology [12]. According to the 2013 Pew Study of the Quantified-Self movement, as many as 69% of adults track their own health-related measures such as weight, body circumstances, and food intakes. However, half of these do so by roughly keeping such information in their head, seldom using technology [13, 14].

Older adults may also have a lower PEOU for food tracking apps. Orso et al. (2019) developed a food-tracking app called 'Salus' and invited older adult users to evaluate the usability. Overall they found positive results for perceived ease of use and satisfaction, but the learnability and error prevention of the app were relatively low and they found that older adults were not particularly engaged in using the app [15]. Guo et al. (2013) also reported finding that older adults were reluctant to use the mHealth app until they were forced to do so, for example, as when "prescribed" by a doctor [16].

Despite their reluctance to embrace mHealth apps, older adults are particularly interested in using nutrition information. For example, Sanjari et al. (2017) performed a literature review about customer's attitude and response to front-of-package (FOP) nutrition labels, from 1990 to 2016. They found that when compared to younger adults, older adults' food choices are more influenced by the nutrition labels on packaged food during grocery shopping [17]. There is reason to believe that the older adult perceived usefulness in nutrition information can remain intact even when the information is delivered through a digital platform. Ali et al. (2012) developed a digital nutrition education package on platforms using touch-screen technology (i.e. smartphone and tablets). The app was designed based on appropriate guidelines for older adults. In the context of this digital education package, they found that older adults accepted the usefulness of the content for promoting a healthy lifestyle and the delivery mode as easy to use [18].

Focusing on perceived ease of use, the groundwork has been laid for promoting older adult friendly mHealth apps. Watkins et al. (2014) performed a heuristics evaluation of a small set of commercial dietary apps available in the Apple App store in 2012. They derived 14 heuristics from Nielsen's general usability heuristics [19], older adult-friendly design heuristics by Chisnell et al. [20], iOS-specific heuristics, and the usability issues from user feedback [21].

2.2   Search User Interface Design

An important choice point for the design of a food recommender system is the Search User Interface (SUI). The human user of such an mHealth app interacts with the Information Retrieval (IR) and Recommender System (RS) or the database through the SUI. SUI development has evolved from a query search on a command-line system to a keyword search on a graphical user interface. There has been less recent research in the SUI design area as the Google search engine UI has been established as the keyword search paradigm. The Google search engine UI has been found relatively easy to use and easy to learn for older adults and novice users as compared to other search engine UIs [22]. Despite this, some usability problems for older adults still occur due to confusion with the information architecture, which may be a new idea to some older adults [23].

Given Google's dominance of the search engine market as the most frequently used landing homepage of internet browsers, modern SUI features are defined by and compared against its well-known layout and features including input, control, informational, and personalizability [24]. However, given the fast-paced development of new technologies, it is important that SUIs continue to evolve to accommodate new innovations. A prime example is the faceted search used on mobile devices to adapt to the limitation of smaller screen size [25, 26]. Faceted metadata search allows users to refine the searching results with filters of its metadata, which defined the search space [27, 28]. Faceted systems can be more dynamic and have been found to improve the search experience for exploratory search type tasks compared to keywords searches [29]. It could facilitate the "Berrypicking" browsing model of Bates, which is close to searchers' natural behavior of searching, by effectively collecting metadata of needed information from various resources [30].

2.3   Nutrition Information Format Design

A widely accepted and a cost-effective method to nudge consumer dietary behavior is by providing nutrition information in the context of daily food selection. One of the primary vehicles is the nutrition label on the packaged food provided to support a consumer's decision-making process. In the United States, the government (Food and Drug Administration; FDA) established a packaged food regulation policy through the Nutrition Labeling and Education Act of 1990, introducing the standardized format nutrition label called the Nutrition Facts Panel (NFP). The Nutrition Facts Panel is a Back-of-Package (BOP) nutrition label, displaying information including serving size, number of servings, total energy, and a selection of nutrients such as energy from fat, total fat, saturated fat, trans fat, cholesterol, sodium, carbohydrates, dietary fiber, sugar, protein, vitamin A, vitamin C, Vitamin D, calcium, and iron. In response to the related evidence-based research in academia about the risks regarding trans-fat the FDA made a 2006 amendment to require data on Trans fat. In 2016, a revision was made to require a line on added sugar, bringing the NFP in alignment with the 2015–2020 Dietary Guidelines for Americans regarding limiting added sugar intake to less than 10% of daily calories [31].

In many countries of Europe, a variety of symbolic labels, such as health claims, Guidelines Daily Amounts (GDA), traffic light system, and Nutri-scores, have been developed as the Front-of-Packaged (FOP) labels [32]. The GDA, developed in the UK around 1998, is a list of the absolute amount per serving and the percentage of daily value for five key nutrients: calories, fat, saturated fat, sugar, salt. It's a simplified nutrition facts panel with the general guidelines for healthy adults and children. The traffic light system further adds the color-coding of a traffic light signal to further interpret healthiness with the high-, medium-, and low-level content of those nutrients corresponding to a color. Nutri-scores integrates the weighted sum of the GDA and the color-coding of the traffic light system to interpret the healthiness with a 5-point scale of a letter grading system.

3   Prototype

In order to test a pair of UI design variables, the prototype of a smart food decision support system for an mHealth app was designed and developed by the User-Centered Design (UCD) process. The design project began with a thematic analysis of literature and also included informal interviews with older adults from the local community. From this information a use case was development surrounding dietary planning as a part of informal caregiving for a spouse newly diagnosed with Type II diabetes. The sketch of the design was drawn based on this use scenario, and a cognitive walkthrough was performed by the designer to develop a low-fidelity prototype as shown in Fig. 1. This system integrates the food composition and nutrition database and the recipe recommender system to provide a decision support feature to users.

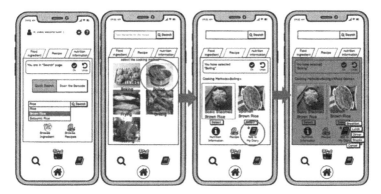

Fig. 1. Fig. 1: Keywords search and browsing the recipe for the ingredient and adding the recipe to the grocery list.

4   Methods

Two critical UI design variables, search result layout and nutrition information format were addressed in the literature review and were examined in a user testing pilot experiment. For the search result layout, the designer proposed a choice-based UI design which facilitated the faceted search by presenting two side-by-side alternatives at a time. For the purpose of comparison, a browsing-based UI with a vertical list-view layout was used as the baseline. For the nutrition information format, the designer adopted FSA Nutri-score labels [33, 34] to compare to the FDA NFP label. A smart healthy food recommender system prototype was developed in the NodeJS environment as a web application to implement the subset of desired functionalities required to test the design variables. A within-subject test was employed across four user interfaces, varying the testing order to protect against confounding with a learning effect.

4.1 Participants

Thirty participants were recruited for this experiment from the greater Lafayette area in Indiana. Participants came from two populations: the first group consists of 15 older adults age 60 years and older, who consider themselves capable of meal planning. These individuals are likely to represent at least a subset of those who would most benefit from diet change required by a chronic health condition diagnosis and use a food recommendation system for this purpose.

The second group was recruited from college and graduate students aged from 20–35 who were attending Purdue University. These individuals are more likely to be early adopters of technology to enhance personal health management in their daily lives. Data from this second group permits us to draw some inference about how ageing impacts the design of the application.

4.2 Procedures

All subjects were asked to fill out a preliminary questionnaire and then follow a scripted use scenario using the web-based application on a computer. A small subset of participants who volunteered to do so, completed the computer-based task on a desktop equipped with an eye tracker located in a lab in the Discovery Learning Resource Center (DLRC) at Purdue University. Remaining participants completed the computer task on a laptop without an eye tracker in a designated meeting room or public area at the recruitment location. For each UI in the computer task, participants filled out a usability questionnaire about their perceived ease of use and perceived ease of learning for the system.

Preliminary Questionnaire. The preliminary questionnaire consisted of basic demographic information, questions adapted from the Computer Proficiency Questionnaire [35], and Health Literacy Questionnaire [36]. Demographics included age and gender. The Computer Proficiency Questionnaire is designed to assess an individual's experience using computers and provides an overall score as well as three sub-domain scores. This information allows us to control for an individual's experience using a computer. The Health Literacy Questionnaire is a nutrition facts label comprehension test for evaluating an individual's knowledge level in health and nutrition and serves as a proxy to control for the participant's experience in making food choices based on nutrition information.

Computer Task. For the study, participants sat at a table with a laptop with the experimenter close at hand for assistance. The experimenter first explained and demoed the standard operation procedures of the system to the participant. The participant was then permitted to freely try out the various features of the system until they indicated they were confident in how to use the system. The subject was informed by the experimenter that their task was to use the web-based application to make a choice of cereal for breakfast for an informal care recipient (e.g. Spouse). The experimental task was to choose a cereal out of six (or six pairs of) alternatives within the context that the participant was planning a meal for their care recipient who was newly diagnosed with type II diabetes. The care recipient strongly wants to have breakfast cereal in their meal plan, and the consulting dietitian has suggested an allowable amount of cereal for breakfast, and recommend using the food recommendation system to assist in meal planning. The participants were encouraged to think aloud when they performed the task to give further insight to the experimenter in how they were interacting with the system.

Each participant encountered four UI alternatives of the recommendation system. These included the combinations of browsing-based user interface or choice-based user interface and text-list nutrition information or symbolized nutrition information. The order of the four versions were randomized to avoid confounding results with a learning effect. After finishing each version of the recommendation system, participants completed the USE questionnaire for measuring the Perceived Usefulness (PU), Perceived Ease Of Use (PEOU), Perceived Ease Of Learning (PEOL), and Satisfaction; and a NASA-TLX subjective workload questionnaire for measuring the mental workload. The experiment concluded with a short interview were participants were asked for their comments and suggestions to improve the system design.

4.3   Measures and Analysis

The self-rated metrics of subjective workload and perceived usability were the quantitative measures collected. The subjective workload was measured by NASA-TLX questionnaire with the weighted total scores as the primary output metric. The perceived usability was measured by four instruments with 7-point Likert scales from the USE questionnaire. The output metric from those four instruments were the total score of PU, the total score of PEOU, the total score of PEOL, and the total score of Satisfaction.

A General Linear Model was used for analysis. The models' main effects were the two design variables estimated as fixed effects. A random effect for subject was used to capture the within subject correlation. All possible interactions between fixed effects were estimated. Significance was set at 5% and all data analyses were performed in Minitab® statistical software. A secondary analysis was performed using the within subject Z-score adjustment to increase the test power given the high degree of variability between subjects [37]. For each test, an individual's outcomes (e.g. workload rating) were standardized using that individual's mean and standard deviation (e.g. from their four workload ratings).

Qualitative data were collected in the form of notes during the experiment as the participants practiced thinking aloud and from the brief interview at the conclusion of the experiment. These data were first transcribed and then printed out on paper so that they could be marked up. The experimenter read each transcript several times, each time marking important themes. After marking all transcripts, these themes were collected from all participants and the differences and similarities were analyzed for basic tendencies.

4.4   Hypotheses

The goal of the experiment was to examine two UI design variables for a relationship with participants perceived usability and subjective workload rating. We tested two key hypotheses:

H1: The search result layout is a significant predictor of the self-rated metrics (weighted total of NASA-TLX, PU, PEOU, PEOL, Satisfaction).
H2: The nutrition information format is a significant predictor of the self-rated metrics (weighted total of NASA-TLX, PU, PEOU, PEOL, Satisfaction).

5   Results

5.1   Quantitative Results

General linear models with a random effect for subject were fit to assess for a relationship between the design variables (search result layout and nutrition information format) and the outcome variables of workload and perceived usability (PU, PEOU, PEOL, Satisfaction). The main results are given in Table 1. For the outcome of subjective workload, the nutrition information format is a statistically significant predictor of the total score from NASA-TLX ($P = 0.000$). The main effect of search result layout was not found to be statistically significant ($P = 0.294$). Nutrition information format was a statistically significant predictor of PEOU scores ($P = 0.008$) and also of PEOL scores ($P = 0.01$). Neither the search result layout main effect ($P = 0.167$ for PEOU and $P = 0.208$ for PEOL) nor the two-way interaction ($P = 0.387$ for PEOU and $P = 0.803$ for PEOL) were statistically significant for both PEOU score and PEOL score. The FSA Nutri-scores nutrition information format had the lowest mean workload score and highest mean PEOU and mean PEOL. For the models with PEOL, PU, and Satisfaction as the outcome variable neither main effect nor the interaction were significant.

Table 1. ANOVA table of GLMs

Analysis of variance of GLM for		NASA-TLX		PU		PEOU		PEOL		Satisfaction	
Source	DF	F-Value	P-Value	F-Value	P-Value	F-Value	P-Value	F-Value	P-Value	F-Value	P-Value
Search result layout (list-view v.s. side-by-side)	1	1.110	0.294	1.870	0.175	1.940	0.167	1.600	0.208	0.700	0.405
Nutrition information format (NFP vs. FSA Nutri-scores)	1	**21.650**	**0.000****	0.030	0.859	**7.430**	**0.008****	**6.970**	**0.01****	2.290	0.134
Subjects	32	**4.900**	**0.000****	**4.230**	**0.000****	**3.680**	**0.000****	**4.050**	**0.000****	**4.590**	**0.000****
Search result layout * nutrition information format	1	2.200	0.141	0.410	0.523	0.750	0.387	0.060	0.803	0.020	0.885
Error	94										
Total	129										

Notably, for each of the general linear models, variability in the outcome was dominated by the between subject variability. For the purpose of reducing this impact and thereby increase the power of the tests we used a within subject z-score adjustment approach. This allowed us to get a better feel for whether or not subjects tended to prefer a particular design variable level even if there was no consensus on how they ought to be rated numerically. We repeated the General Linear Model analysis on the transformed data, results are given in Table 2.

Table 2. ANOVA table of GLMs using z-scores standardization

Analysis of variance of GLMs for	NASA-TLX		PU		PEOU		PEOL		Satisfaction	
Source	DF	F-Value	P-Value	F-Value	P-Value	F-Value	P-Value	F-Value	P-Value	F-Value	P-Value
Search result layout (list-view v.s. side-by-side)	1	0.430	0.516	0.770	0.381	1.490	0.225	0.730	0.396	0.870	0.354
Nutrition information format (NFP v.s. FSA Nutri-scores)	1	**18.850**	**0.000****	1.500	0.224	**10.200**	**0.002****	**4.750**	**0.032***	**4.940**	**0.029***
Subjects	32	0.000	1.000	0.520	0.981	0.640	0.925	0.870	0.671	0.630	0.930
Search result layout * nutrition information format	1	2.030	0.158	**3.980**	**0.049***	**8.870**	**0.004****	1.530	0.220	2.440	0.122
Error	94										
Total	129										

The within subject standardization of the outcome variables had the intended effect of reducing the between-subject variance such that the random effect was no longer statistically significant. The main effect of nutrition information format remained significant for workload (P = 0.000), PEOU (P = 0.002), PEOL (P = 0.032), and was now found to be statistically significant for the outcome of Satisfaction (P = 0.029). The two-way interactions of the design variables was significant in the PEOU model (P = 0.004), and was now statistically significant in the PU model (P = 0.049). The optimal combination of design factors for Perceived Ease of Use were list-view search result layout and FSA Nutri-label nutrition information format.

5.2   Qualitative Results

For the purpose of better explaining the meaning of quantitative results, several sources of qualitative data were collected. These include experimenter notes derived from the participant practice of thinking aloud during the experiment and the short interview about participant impressions of and suggestions for the food recommender system.

The qualitative results support the quantitative results since there was not a consensus on which Search Result Layout was preferred. It appears that an individual's preference of the search results layout may be influenced by their search strategy. For example, three students and two younger older adults (early 60s) who were all familiar with using computers, specifically mentioned that they preferred the vertical list view over the horizontal side-by-side view as it requires fewer steps to do an exhaustive search of all alternatives. On the other hand, one student and three older adults showed a strong preference for the side-by-side view layout as it made pairwise comparisons straightforward. One of the older adults noted that they preferred the list-view layout for the exhaustive search, but also appreciated the horizontal presentation of the alternatives, for the ease of comparison.

The qualitative results regarding nutrition information format also aligned with the quantitative results as most participants preferred the Nutri-scores labels. Four students and two older adults raised some important concerns about the Nutri-score label. First, they pointed out correctly that the label was not specifically designed for the patient with type II diabetes and so might not be appropriate for decision making when caregiving for such a care recipient. Secondly, they pointed out that the absence of information such as serving size and sugar content are absent from the Nutri-score label making it difficult to control daily intake values. Along that same line, two older adult participants mentioned they were unsure in deciding between NFP and Nutri-scores when they were asked about their preference. They both thought they should choose the NFP for its detailed information but they both desired a simple, easy to use label for decision making.

Another theme that arose from the notes is that it takes a little time to learn how to use and to trust the Nutri-score labels. Most of the participants saw the Nutri-scores label for the first time during the experiment and requested some explanation about the context of the label and how to interpret it. Once participants learned that the rating was created by government authorized experts and became familiar with its interpretation, they were willing to use it. Participants did not fully trust the label until they felt that it conformed with their expectations. Only a minority of participants trusted the label implicitly without going through this process.

To our surprise, most participants needed some instruction in how to interpret the Nutri-score rating system. One student and one older adult reported a comprehension issue, noting that the Nutri-score label was in the reverse order, in terms of quality, from what they found intuitive. Nutri-score marks a letter grades on an A to E scale with the traffic light color coding, A being the best and E being the worst. The current design drew the scale such that it starts at "A" on the left-hand side. These two participants were most familiar with thinking of mathematical scales (increasing numerical order) and so experienced difficulty at first in interpreting the label.

Given the exploratory nature of the experiment, several participants gave suggestions for improvement of the design. The majority of participants preferred the vertical list-view of search results, but two older adults suggested a horizontal list-view layout, which follows their natural reading behavior. Given the different searching strategies, the most compelling suggestion came from a student who recommended a faceted search with a dynamic layout design alternative. Search results would first be presented in a list-view layout on the main page from which the user could pick multiple alternatives before advancing to a secondary page. On this secondary page, the selected alternatives would be shown in a side-by-side layout to aid in pairwise comparison decision making.

6 Discussion

In our pilot study, we examined the relationship of search result display and nutrition information format with workload and ease of use outcomes in the context of a food recommender system. We collected quantitative data using subjective questionnaires, which is the most frequently used usability evaluation method in empirical UI design studies for older adults [38]. The variability in our outcome was dominated by between subject variability. We took several steps to try to reduce the impact of this such as allowing participants to check their previous answers as they evaluate subsequent UI designs and encouraging them to consider the first UI they encounter as the baseline UI during the experiment. Additionally, we performed a secondary analysis with transformed outcomes using the within subject Z-standardization approach. In order to supplement the quantitative analyses we collected qualitative data. We consider each of these

We originally expected to find that older adults would consider the choice-based UI to be easier to use. Quantitatively there was not a significant difference between choice-based and list-view browsing-based UIs, but a divide between two UIs was born out in the qualitative data. We can think of at least two reasons that may have led to this contrary finding. First, it may simply be that we have an underpowered study, and given a sufficiently sized and representative sample of older adults we might find the choice-based UI was preferred. While our sample size was certainly small, we think the second reason is more compelling. Our qualitative data made it clear that at least two search strategies were being employed. If an individual was seeking the optimal choice through an exhaustive search of the options, list-based UI was preferred. However, if participants were more focused on picking a quality (but not globally optimal) choice using the satisficing rule, the choice-based UI was a natural preference. Which search strategy is most likely to be used and which UI is most natural to first time users will likely depend, at least in part, on the most common application designs dominating user experience, such as Google's search engine UI.

In terms of quantitative results, we prefer the standardized outcomes over the raw data. We think it is easier for the novel user to make relative comparisons between different UI designs than to make an unbiased judgement on an absolute scale. The question being answered on the standardized scale is more a matter of which UI does the user prefer as opposed to the overall quality of the UI design. Although this is the question we are after in this study, it does reduce generalizability of the findings overall. For example, it may be clear that a design is preferred, but that does not establish that the design is good (i.e. the best of four poor designs).

In the interest of limitations, the fact that we performed unplanned secondary analysis on a small sample size is likely to inflate Type I error of statistical tests. This reduces the strength of the quantitative findings. However, given the agreement from the qualitative data, we have at least convinced ourselves of some potentially interesting improvements that can be made to the UI design of a food recommender system. In particular, it was noted that the Nutri-score label was generally preferred for ease of decision making, but that some additional information from the NFP would still be required to support diet management for the care recipient with a chronic condition. Additionally, the multiple search strategies suggest that a fully faceted search UI beginning with a list of alternatives to select from and ending in the choice-based UI is likely to be more useful than either UI by itself.

Our measures were subjective, but it is possible to have objective data in this same setting. In particular it is possible to measure human task performance or eye tracking data to better assess the impact of these and other UI design decisions [24, 39].

We leave these explorations for future work.

7 Conclusion

In this article, we describe a pilot experiment using a food recommender application prototype developed using the ageing-centered design process. Such an app could be used to support healthy diet change in individuals facing a chronic health condition or disease. As the knowledgebase surrounding diet specific strategies to combat various conditions and diseases, such an app could be tailored to support the individuals care needs. We identified two critical design variables from the literature for this context, search result layout and the nutrition information format. We expected the choice-based UI design would be preferred. The study results suggested that users may be split on the list vs choice-based UI and an optimal design may actually be a combination of the two (list to choose a subset of alternatives which are fed into the choice-based second stage for deeper comparison). We also found a general desire for the simplicity of the interpretive Nutri-score label, but also a noted need to maintain certain elements from the NFP to support proper food intake management. Design is an iterative process and the insights from this step suggest the next step should be towards the faceted search feature development.

References

1. Povey, R.C., Clark-Carter, D.: Diabetes and healthy eating. Diabetes Educ. **33**, 931–959 (2007). https://doi.org/10.1177/0145721707308408
2. Ge, M., Elahi, M., Fernández-Tobías, I., Ricci, F., Massimo, D.: Using tags and latent factors in a food recommender system. In: ACM International Conference Proceeding Series, pp. 105–112. Association for Computing Machinery (2015). https://doi.org/10.1145/2750511.2750528
3. Schäfer, H., et al.: Towards health (aware) recommender systems, vol. 5 (2017). https://doi.org/10.1145/3079452.3079499
4. Calero Valdez, A., Ziefle, M., Verbert, K., Felfernig, A., Holzinger, A.: Recommender systems for health informatics: state-of-the-art and future perspectives. In: Holzinger, A. (ed.) Machine Learning for Health Informatics: State-of-the-Art and Future Challenges, pp. 391–414. Springer, Cham (2016). https://doi.org/10.1007/978-3-319-50478-0_20
5. Freyne, J., Berkovsky, S.: Recommending Food: reasoning on recipes and ingredients. In: De Bra, P., Kobsa, A., Chin, D. (eds.) UMAP 2010. LNCS, vol. 6075, pp. 381–386. Springer, Heidelberg (2010). https://doi.org/10.1007/978-3-642-13470-8_36
6. Freyne, J., Berkovsky, S., Baghaei, N., Kimani, S., Smith, G.: Personalized techniques for lifestyle change. In: Peleg, M., Lavrač, N., Combi, C. (eds.) AIME 2011. LNCS (LNAI), vol. 6747, pp. 139–148. Springer, Heidelberg (2011). https://doi.org/10.1007/978-3-642-22218-4_18

7. Ge, M., Ricci, F., Massimo, D.: Health-aware food recommender system. In: RecSys 2015 - Proceedings of the 9th ACM Conference on Recommender Systems, pp. 333–334 (2015). https://doi.org/10.1145/2792838.2796554

8. Harvey, M., Ludwig, B., Elsweiler, D.: Learning user tastes: a first step to generating healthy meal plans? In: CEUR Workshop Proceedings, pp. 18–23 (2012)

9. Harvey, M., Ludwig, B., Elsweiler, D.: You are what you eat: learning user tastes for rating prediction. In: Kurland, O., Lewenstein, M., Porat, E. (eds.) SPIRE 2013. LNCS, vol. 8214, pp. 153–164. Springer, Cham (2013). https://doi.org/10.1007/978-3-319-02432-5_19

10. Doub, A.E., Levin, A., Heath, C.E., LeVangie, K.: Mobile appetite: consumer attitudes towards and use of mobile technology in the context of eating behaviour. J. Direct Data Digit. Mark. Pract. **17**, 114–129 (2015). https://doi.org/10.1057/dddmp.2015.44

11. Davis, F.D.: A technology acceptance model for empirically testing new end-user information systems : theory and results (1985). http://dspace.mit.edu/handle/1721.1/15192

12. Ancker, J.S., Witteman, H.O., Hafeez, B., Provencher, T., Van De Graaf, M., Wei, E.: "You get reminded you're a sick person": Personal data tracking and patients with multiple chronic conditions. J. Med. Internet Res. **17** (2015). https://doi.org/10.2196/jmir.4209

13. Fox, S., Duggan, M.: Health online 2013: 35% of U.S. adults have gone online to figure out a medical condition; of these, half followed up with a visit to a medical professional. http://pewinternet.org/Reports/2013/Health-online.aspx. Accessed 24 Jan 2020

14. Ramirez, E.: Pew Internet Research: 21% Self-Track with Technology. https://quantifiedself.com/blog/pew-internet-research-the-state-of-self-tracking/. Accessed 24 Jan 2020

15. Orso, V., Spagnolli, A., Viero, F., Gamberini, L.: The design, implementation and evaluation of a mobile app for supporting older adults in the monitoring of food intake. In: Leone, A., Caroppo, A., Rescio, G., Diraco, G., Siciliano, P. (eds.) ForItAAL 2018. LNEE, vol. 544, pp. 147–159. Springer, Cham (2019). https://doi.org/10.1007/978-3-030-05921-7_12

16. Guo, X., Sun, Y., Wang, N., Peng, Z., Yan, Z.: The dark side of elderly acceptance of preventive mobile health services in China. Electron. Mark. **23**, 49–61 (2013). https://doi.org/10.1007/s12525-012-0112-4

17. Sanjari, S.S., Jahn, S., Boztug, Y.: Dual-process theory and consumer response to front-of-package nutrition label formats. Nutr. Rev. **75**, 871–882 (2017). https://doi.org/10.1093/nutrit/nux043

18. Ali, N.M., Shahar, S., Kee, Y.L., Norizan, A.R., Noah, S.A.M.: Design of an interactive digital nutritional education package for elderly people. Inform. Health Soc. Care **37**, 217–229 (2012). https://doi.org/10.3109/17538157.2012.654843

19. Nielsen, J.: 10 usability heuristics for user interface design (1995). https://doi.org/10.1145/191666.191729, http://portal.acm.org/citation.cfm?doid=259963.260333

20. Chisnell, D.E., Redish, J.C., Lee, A.: New heuristics for undeNielsen, Jakob. Heuristic evaluation. In: Nielsen, J., Mack, R.L., (eds.) Usability Inspection Methods. Wiley, New York 1994, rstanding older adults as web users (2006). https://www.ingentaconnect.com/content/stc/tc/2006/00000053/00000001/art00006

21. Watkins, I., Kules, B., Yuan, X., Xie, B.: Heuristic evaluation of healthy eating apps for older adults. J. Consum. Health Internet. **18**, 105–127 (2014). https://doi.org/10.1080/15398285.2014.902267

22. Sayago, S., Blat, J.: A preliminary usability evaluation of strategies for seeking online information with elderly people (2007)

23. Aula, A.: User study on older adults' use of the web and search engines. Univ. Access Inf. Soc. **4**, 67–81 (2005). https://doi.org/10.1007/s10209-004-0097-7

24. Wilson, M.L.: Search user interface design. Synth. Lect. Inf. Concepts Retrieval Serv. **3**, 1–143 (2011). https://doi.org/10.2200/s00371ed1v01y201111icr020

25. Kleinen, A., Scherp, A., Staab, S.: Interactive faceted search and exploration of open social media data on a touchscreen mobile phone. Multimedia Tools Appl. **71**, 39–60 (2014). https://doi.org/10.1007/s11042-013-1366-3

26. Karlson, A.K., Robertson, G., Robbins, D.C., Czerwinski, M., Smith, G.: FaThumb: a facet-based interface for mobile search (2006)

27. Wilson, M.L., André, P., Schraefel, M.C.: Backward highlighting: enhancing faceted search. In: UIST 2008 - Proceedings of the 21st Annual ACM Symposium on User Interface Software and Technology. pp. 235–238 (2008). https://doi.org/10.1145/1449715.1449754

28. Wagner, A., Ladwig, G., Tran, T.: Browsing-oriented semantic faceted search. In: Hameurlain, A., Liddle, Stephen W., Schewe, K.-D., Zhou, X. (eds.) DEXA 2011. LNCS, vol. 6860, pp. 303–319. Springer, Heidelberg (2011). https://doi.org/10.1007/978-3-642-23088-2_22

29. Stoica, E., Hearst, M.A.: Nearly-automated metadata hierarchy creation (2014). https://doi.org/10.3115/1613984.1614014

30. Bates, M.J.: The design of browsing and berrypicking techniques for the online search interface (1989). https://doi.org/10.1108/eb024320

31. Malik, V.S., Willett, W.C., Hu, F.B.: The revised nutrition facts label: a step forward and more room for improvement (2016). https://doi.org/10.1001/jama.2016.8005

32. Hodgkins, C., et al.: Understanding how consumers categorise nutritional labels: a consumer derived typology for front-of-pack nutrition labelling. Appetite, **59**, 806–817 (2012). https://doi.org/10.1016/j.appet.2012.08.014

33. Egnell, M., et al.: Objective understanding of nutri-score front-of-package nutrition label according to individual characteristics of subjects: comparisons with other format labels. PLoS ONE **13**, e0202095 (2018). https://doi.org/10.1371/journal.pone.0202095

34. Szabo de Edelenyi, F., Egnell, M., Galan, P., Druesne-Pecollo, N., Hercberg, S., Julia, C.: Ability of the Nutri-Score front-of-pack nutrition label to discriminate the nutritional quality of foods in the German food market and consistency with nutritional recommendations. Arch. Public Heal. **77** (2019). https://doi.org/10.1186/s13690-019-0357-x

35. Boot, W.R., et al.: Computer proficiency questionnaire: assessing low and high computer proficient seniors. Gerontologist **55**, 404–411 (2015). https://doi.org/10.1093/geront/gnt117

36. Weiss, B.D., et al.: Quick assessment of literacy in primary care: the newest vital sign. Ann. Fam. Med. **3**, 514–522 (2005). https://doi.org/10.1370/afm.405

37. McIntosh, A.R., Grady, C.L., Haxby, J.V., Maisog, J.M., Horwitz, B., Clark, C.M.: Within-subject transformations of PET regional cerebral blood flow data: ANCOVA, ratio, and Z-score adjustments on empirical data. Hum. Brain Mapp. **4**, 93–102 (1996). https://doi.org/10.1002/(sici)1097-0193(1996)4:2%3c93:aid-hbm1%3e3.0.co;2-j

38. Zapata, B.C., Fernández-Alemán, J.L., Idri, A., Toval, A.: Empirical studies on usability of mHealth apps: a systematic literature review. J. Med. Syst. **39**, 1–19 (2015). https://doi.org/10.1007/s10916-014-0182-2

39. Sharit, J., Hern, M.A., Czaja, S.J., HernándezHern, M.A., Czaja, S.J.: Investigating the roles of knowledge and cognitive abilities in older adult information seeking on the web. ACM Trans. Comput. Interact. **15** (2008). https://doi.org/10.1145/1352782.1352785

"Older and Younger People": Towards a Cross-Generational Online Peer Support About Cancer. The Example of Glioblastoma on French Digital Platforms

Juliette Charbonneaux[(⊠)] and Karine Berthelot-Guiet[(⊠)]

CELSA Sorbonne Université-GRIPIC-Siric CURAMUS APHP.6, Paris, France
{juliette.charbonneaux,
karine.berthelot-guiet}@sorbonne-universite.fr

Abstract. The present paper, based on science communications, deals with interferences and reconfiguration at work between generations due to digital devices dedicated to discussion about one particular type of brain cancer: Glioblastoma. Glioblastoma is a rare brain cancer more than often diagnosed at a late stage, with a very poor prognosis and huge and disabling neurological impairments at the time of identification of the disease. Thereby, when a web patient chat room happens to deal with glioblastoma, the discussion happens most of the time between close relatives. This paper analyzes these digital testimonies to explore how they enable, build, and give access to a "parent expertise" instead of patient expertise, and this through intergenerational solidarity. This specific corpus of web discourse is analyzed, which a semio-communicational analysis mixed with thematic content analysis, discourse analysis, a pragmatic, narrative, and socio-semiotic analysis. This analysis first shows how the architexts of the forums promote the emergence of a figure of intergenerational, then focuses on the variations of the two major types of exchanges carried out, between generations, within these digital frameworks: a relationship to illness experienced as extraordinary upheaval, and to the accompaniment of the disease in the very ordinary of everyday life.

Keywords: Communication · Cancer · Forum · Glioblastoma · Intergenerational solidarity · Parent

1 Introduction

"[Status confusion]. For months, I have been her mother. It is as if I had lost my daughter (a greater grief than that? It had never occurred to me.)" [1].

Roland Barthes wrote these very words about his late mother in his *Mourning*. This example of Barthes' famous rhetoric of fragmented discourse [2] gives in a simple, explicit and condensed way the stakes of the present paper, dealing with interferences and reconfiguration at work between generations due to digital devices dedicated to discussion about one particular type of brain cancer, that is glioblastoma.

© Springer Nature Switzerland AG 2020
Q. Gao and J. Zhou (Eds.): HCII 2020, LNCS 12208, pp. 235–249, 2020.
https://doi.org/10.1007/978-3-030-50249-2_18

This research is part of an Integrated research site on Cancer, called Siric Curamus (Cancer United Research Associating Medicine, University & Society) linked to Pitié Salpêtrière Hospital and Sorbonne Université. The eight French Siric research centers have a common mission, which is to foster integrated multidisciplinary research programs "to optimize and accelerate the production of new knowledge and promote its diffusion and application to cancer treatments."

Curamus Siric Center currently works on three integrated programs about rare cancers in neuro-oncology, immuno-hematology, cancers with microsatellite instability concept; these programs are linked to a Human and Social Sciences transversal program that aims to provide multidisciplinary approaches about technical expertise, patient preferences, ethical and equity issues regarding access to care and solidarity. In this respect, ideas such as "health democracy" or "patient expert" are examined.

The concept of "health democracy" is institutionalized in France since the 2002 law on "patients' rights and health system quality." This law defines the participation of users in the health system functioning and puts the stress on the idea of "approval of the associations of patients and the training of users' representatives." 2016 law on "modernization of our healthcare system" strengthen health democracy and increases the role of users within the healthcare system, especially in national and regional authorities; at the same times this law specificities users rights such as cost information, health data [https://www.ars.sante.fr/quest-ce-que-la-democratie-sanitaire].

The concept of "patient expert" arises in this context. National institutions strongly highlight "patient expert." However, the notion is problematic [3]. A "patient expert" is defined as "a patient who gained over time a solid knowledge about his pathology, thanks to patient therapeutic education. He does not take the place of the caregiver, but he can enable dialog between medical teams and patients, facilitate the expression of other patients and improve their understanding of the discourse of medical teams" [Haute Autorité de Santé].

The idea "patient expert" is an essential field for the Human and Social sciences team in Siric CURAMUS. Its analysis is based on philosophy, sociology, anthropology, and communication. This is very important since some of the cancers implied in the medical programs are rare and with bad prognostic, and this implies to think about complex limits regarding cure, care, and human aspects. This paper, based on science communications, deals with one of these limits. Glioblastoma is, indeed, a rare brain cancer more than often diagnosed at a late stage, with a very poor prognosis and huge and disabling neurological impairments at the time of identification of the disease. Thereby, when a web patient chat room happens to deal with glioblastoma, the discussion happens most of the time between close relatives. Due to brain impairment, the patient direct expression is scarce.

We intend to work on these testimonies of close relatives to explore how they enable, build, and give access to a "parent expertise" instead of patient expertise. We will analyze this "parent expertise" through intergenerational solidarity. For this purpose, we initially gathered a vast corpus of web discourses which embraces general discourses about glioblastoma and patients chat rooms and finally focuses on discourses dealing with "generational" topics.

We, at first, entered "glioblastome" (French for *Glioblastoma*) in Google, which is the most frequently used web search engine both in France and worldwide (except for

China). In a second step, we entered the group of terms "glioblastoma forum." This choice is not free of bias, but it enables us a first overview, precise enough, of the main circulation of discourses about this rare brain cancer, which has limited attention from the mass media and, therefore, is little-publicized. In both cases, we gathered the elements given in the first four pages of results to build two corpora. We conducted this research and gathering in April 2019. The first responses to our "gliosblastome" request put forward the following websites, in order of appearance: Wikipedia, Passeport Santé (a web information publisher dedicated to health and medical issues targeting the general public), Orphanet (a web portal and information providing server in open access for all and dedicated to rare disease, disorders, and orphan medicinal products), Ligue contre le cancer (a state-approved non-profit organization dedicated since 1918 to the fight against cancer), Roche (the Swiss pharmaceuticals laboratory that produces the drug Avastin, one of the key chemicals in chemotherapy against glioblastoma), La Revue Médicale Suisse (a weekly specialized publication of French-language expression for the continuing training of practitioners), Imagineformargo.org (the website of the Imagine for Margo – Children without Cancer association and foundation, established respectively in 2011 and 2017. They aim to raise awareness and funds to accelerate research against childhood cancers) and Le Quotidien du Médecin (a French journal dealing with medical information for health professionals, whether they are practitioners or policymakers).

This overview gives the first picture of glioblastoma as a rare, rapidly growing cancer, with fatal outcome, as evoked through palliative are. Its primary treatment is surgery and chemotherapy. Mention is made of a new treatment, a therapeutic vaccine. La Ligue contre le Cancer mostly redirects to patient forums and when Imagineformargo.org tells the story of a young patient. A very complex picture comes out of this first macro-exploration and reveals an under-known and under-explained and described brain cancer, given as mostly rapidly fatal.

The digital public space of glioblastoma, as sketched by our Google search, builds, for those who know only its name, a piece of information from different sources. The first one is Wikipedia, which is easily predictable since Wikipedia usually appears first in Google responses. In this respect, the glioblastoma knows classical digital processing. We also find media bodies related to the health professions (Passeport Santé, Orphanet, La Revue Médicale Suisse, and Le Quotidien du Médecin), two associations (la Ligue contre le cancer and Imaginformargo), one pharmaceutical company (Roche). Public authorities, hospitals, doctors, and patients do not appear in these results. They do not appear as primary key players of the digital public space of glioblastoma and therefore are not part of the first corpus.

The second corpus comes from the Google search "glioblastome forum" and counts six out of twenty-eight results explicitly linked to a testimony ("témoignage de XXX glioblastome grade" – *testimony from XXX, grade 4 glioblastoma*). That is why we retained the six following forums: Allodocteurs (a website linked to a bunch of French television programs about health and medicine, broadcasted by France 5, national channel part of France TV group), Santé médecine Journal des femmes (this is a health website link to Journal des femmes, a pure player, first French women's online magazine created in 2003 – https://sante-medecine.journaldesfemmes.fr/forum/affich-1655002-glioblastome, https://sante-medecine.journaldesfemmes.fr/forum/affich-1401164-glioblastome-grade-iv), Forum-doctissimo (Doctissimo is a francophone website dedicated to health and well-being. In its field, the site is one of the most important in terms of audience- http://forum.doctissimo.fr/sante/cancers/glioblastome-avis-sujet_177892_1.htm, http://forum.doctissimo.fr/sante/cancers/atteint-glioblastome-voulezvousenparler-sujet_171031_1.htm, http://forum.doctissimo.fr/sante/cancers/glioblastome-maman-sujet_165141_1.htm, http://forum.doctissimo.fr/sante/cancers/glioblastome-besoin-soutien-sujet_170658_1.htm, http://forum.doctissimo.fr/sante/cancers/glioblastome-besoin-temoignages-sujet_156853_1.htm), Guérir du cancer (a website initiated by a French oncologist to promote what he calls metabolic treatment), Forumcancer.ch (this Swiss website is moderated by the Ligue Info cancer which is the information and advisory service of the Swiss Cancer League - https://www.forumcancer.ch/forum3_fr/viewtopic.php?f=6&t=1119), Forum ligue-cancer.net linked to La Ligue contre le cancer as introduced above (https://www.ligue-cancer.net/forum/45530_glioblastome?page=1, https://www.ligue-cancer.net/forum/40821_remission-ou-guerison-dun-glioblastome).

We made one last final selection and extracted from these six forums of patients about glioblastoma all the exchanges referring to generations in any way. A first "floating reading" of these digital exchanges [4] confirmed the importance of the issue of generations. This appears through the evocation of children's support for their parents, sibling mutual self-help, the concern, and the revolt of parents for their children.

These online exchanges, collected in a systematic way, gather thirty-six enunciators/authors of one single post or multiple ones when they take part in an online conversation.

This specific corpus was analyzed, which a semio-communicational analysis mixed with thematic content analysis, discourse analysis, a pragmatic, narrative, and sociosemiotic analysis. Our theoretical position regarding the methodology is one of a socio-semio-communicational approach [5, 6]. This kind of analysis takes place in some of the French Information and Communication Sciences contemporary approaches [7, 8]. We chose, in French Communication Sciences, to rely on researches focused on the conceptualization, description, or analysis of social and media discourses in a comprehensive purpose to understand how discursive items circulate between different social and media spaces building their media and public exposure.

This point of view is neither psychological, sociological, nor semiotic; these researchers intend to build intermediate positions. Thus, the methodology is recrafted to match every new corpus. It implies what we call "creative methodology" in research. We intend to find each time the best set and organization of qualitative methods to question our specific research topic, accurately.

The corpora we obtained as explained above were gathered in Spring 2019 and we applied the semio-qualitive method as presented in the preceding paragraph. In this respect, we will take into account the specificities of the social link on social media sites, and we chose to rely on the theory of recognition [9]. This theory, developed by Axel Honneth [10], pays particular attention to relationships involving social links through which subjects develop experiences of caring, mutual attachment, normative obligations, and solid relationships with themselves and others. These intersubjective dynamics are all forms of social bond from which an individual can experience himself as an autonomous subject developing confidence, respect, and self-esteem.

Our purpose is to identify how the mediation of digital writing encourages intergenerational relations and promotes the recognition of the parent as a potential expert of the disease. In this perspective, we will first show how the architexts of the forums promote the emergence of a figure of intergenerational. The concept of architextual software is a kind of writing, as explained by Jeanneret and Souchier: "when you write in one [software], somebody has yet written upstream of you the forms in which you can compose a text. From the moment we created the term, architexts have constantly been proliferating amazingly so to demonstrate their extraordinary power. Architexts shape the forms (word processors, presenters), the exchange of correspondence (mail, chat), information retrieval (search engines), the intertextual relations (RSS readers), and so on. To summarize, we can say that architexts are software objects that go on industrializing the capacity of written forms to shape practices, as explained above, leading in those conditions on a renewed economy of writing" [8].

We will then analyze the variations of the two major types of exchanges carried out, between generations, within these digital frameworks: first, a relationship to illness experienced as extraordinary upheaval, then the relationship to the accompaniment of the disease in the very ordinary of everyday life. We develop the hypothesis that, in this particular type of very aggressive brain cancer, rises a specific figure of "parent expertise", linked to patient expertise and carers expertise. Our question is to approach how the parent expert is part of negotiation of generational places.

2 Digital Conditions of Possibility for Intergenerational Dialogue

All the exchanges we analyze were written by a writer directly related to the patient. They all highlight the intergenerational dimension and show the digital forums as "techniques of self" [11] that is to say "practices whereby individuals, by their own means or with the help of others, act on their own bodies, souls." The point is the co-building identity using both the writing the self and the supports given by relationships (communities of belonging, family, friends), at the same time, intellectual and physical.

These exchanges produce complex self-writing, including the writer, the sick parent, and the rest of the family. These exchanges are individual at first and become after the collective say of families, the collective say of the digital forum, and beyond a collective statement from the community of families whose members have this cancer. They take up and transform, discursive norms by producing and weaving, in the same text, individual biographies of patients and/or exemplary writers and collective biographies that reverse/neutralize common generational relationships. In the latter, intra-family and inter-family histories offer product standards and promote the emergence of the cross-sectional figure of the "parent."

2.1   Individual Biographies: Digital *Exempla*

The first intervention of a newcomer in the forum is, in most cases, a biography of the patient, his illness, and the parent writer whose "biographical competence" [12] is thus set out. The contributions set biography as the accepted and implemented narrative standard. The subject, as a global enunciator, is "the parent." The patient, because of the cognitive impairment due to this cancer, is an "object of discourse" or "secondary actor" [13].

The biographies produced are brief forms, with a strong presence of discursive shifters [14]: many personal pronouns and their equivalents, dates, precise time intervals, locations build a pregnant deictic system. Most often, the "parent" comes back to systems for designating parents attached to childhood (mon papa-ma maman: *my daddy-my mommy*). Although very brief, these forms strike by the degree of detail they condense and their explicit, direct approach to the disease and its symptoms.

The patient, the writer, and their community are strongly present in a condensed narrative that includes all the characteristics of a narrative and a specific form of narrative schema and actancial model [15]. The initial situation is rarely mentioned, the story focuses on the disruptive event (the diagnosis, its announcement), events (treatment, information search, remission, tumor return, death) and resolution (the experience of the disease and a form of expertise to be transmitted). Globally, these exchanges are quite different from the central media representations of cancer patients. Nevertheless, the same motifs of the soldier, the vanquished, the hero can be found as expressed in the idea of a fight, will, and courage [16]. They appear as non-standard cancer stories compared to standard media treatment since they do not follow the usual narrative conventions, as described in previous researches about cancer media treatment. The biographies written by the parents" are so detailed that they lead to very incarnate anonymity.

These individual biographies are close to the particular form of *Exemplum*; they include the micro-narrations, the "narrative detours" that act as discourse shifters and produce a singularized and singular narrative that is linked to a collective value through the creation of a kind of common repertory for participants [17]. The device of the digital forum redoubles, by the model of the listing, the series specific to the exemplum. These exchanges thus produce an induced or explicit exemplarity. The work linked to the writing of a "life story" has a specific direction, a narrative logic. It creates a before and an after. This given direction makes sense [18]. The individual, serialized in a micro-form, becomes collective and allows to go towards exemplarity for others and society. It is a "monument" prepared by the writer/parent to his or her sick parent: "the Monument […] is an act, an action, an activity that brings recognition." [1]

2.2   Collective Biographies and et Neutralization of Generations

These exchanges produce a triple family biography through the prism of the glioblastoma, the biography of the patient, of the writer's parent, and the other parents. This triple family biography co-exists with other biographies and opening up a threefold narrative perspective: that of the illness of one's parent in "his" family, embedded in those of others to form a collective biography, some kind of exemplary stories expanding into as many intrafamily and interfamily stories.

The intra-family narrative, due to the specificity of this aggressive brain cancer, tells about violent, rapid, and irreversible changes and recompositions to which the stories try to oppose, by the emphasis on age and normal family relationships [19]. The family and the parent with cancer know the same micro-narrative treatment, so it is idealized, and the figure of the combatant is extended to the spouse, the writer, and the whole family. They show courage, they surround with love, give support, strength, and understanding, reassure, give confidence, say their love and sometimes become, through a break or a celebration, an average family again. The biography also has a value of exemplarity. It erects a Family Monument that can enter the circle of other stories to create interfamily stories These interfamily stories are facilitated by the formal series of individual biographies as well as by the digital devices of the forums which propose/impose forms of speech typical of the imaginaries and codes of the sociodigital networks (pseudonym, familiar tone and scheme of the commentary).

The tone of the exchanges (generalized tutoring, low language formalism, use of emojis, and use of nicknames) produces a kind of generational erasure: one is the "parent," whatever the generation. This tone smoothes the ages and weaves itself into "caritatism" as defined by Roland Barthes [20] as "pet name or affectionate appella-tion" [21], through the small family names of childhood and community names, pseudonyms, digital discourse shifters enthusiasts, "anonymous ligator" [22]. When one moves to a deeper relationship, often marked by strong polylogism, masks fall to return to identity of the civil status: "Kiss kiss, Françoise (aka Minoï)."

Interfamily stories also unfold in the regime of extended comment, which is pregnant into socio-digital interactions. The device is commented for the connections it allows, the connection with other "files," which are recommended or indicated: "Hi Datine, I'm muscling into your file. How's your Mommy?" [http://forum.doctissimo.fr/ sante/cancers/atteint-glioblastome-voulezvousenparler-sujet_171031_1.htm].   General comments focus on the purpose of these exchanges and their effects: "Here, you started talking to other people about what's burdening you." The digital device is invested as a quasi-physical place. Finally, we find many comments of solidarity, mutual aid, and advice giving broad guidelines for individual and collective conduct facing the disease; they especially appear in polylogic exchanges where the writers follow each other and exchange over time. It allows the communication partners to invest their self-representation in a continuum of action [22]. The digital forums thus act fully as "techniques of self" by allowing to "distinguish the memorable from the insignificant" [23]. This will create stability and allow the intra and interfamily "Monument."

In the course of the exchanges, a collective "we" emerges that comes to position itself alongside the family "we" and the "I" of the writer parent. These exchanges show several figures of the "We-I" [18, 24]: that of the I-parent/we-family; of the I-parent/we-parents; I-parent/we-patients, up to the I as part of a "we" on the digital forum/we parents and we as the forum community, etc. From the exemplary person to the expert, from the patient to the "parent," from "parent" to "parent," then "parents," the case of digital conversational forums about glioblastoma exacerbates the forms and postures due to the relentless aspect of the disease and makes visible what is subject to exchange when it comes to this rare brain cancer.

3   Core Exchange: An Extra-Ordinary Relationship to Illness and Medicine

The individual and collective biographies also produce narratives of cancer. This narrative activity is here analyzed in terms of its normative power. Olivier Voirol explains how media narratives provide social esteem, values and shape symbolic recognition [9]. In this perspective, the following part of the paper is dedicated to the analysis of this question: how do the narratives of the "extra-ordinary" (the announcement, the treatments) produce an evaluation of the care path and, therefore, a questioning of the medical authority?

3.1   The Pattern of Announcement: The Tipping Point

The diagnosis announcement represents a particular pattern in the parent's narratives. The announcement of the disease marks a temporal break in the story of the family and can, therefore, be seen as an event that tears the habits, the daily routines, the projects and the memories [25].

The announcement pattern takes place at the very beginning of the parent's narratives since it justifies their on-line speeches. The story only gets its meaning from the initial diagnosis, which is marked by the mention of the date.

On the swiss forum forumcancer.ch, one can, for instance, read the following testimony: "Hi everyone, my name is Jonathan, I am 25 years old. On October 14, 2014, my father's life, mine and my mother's switched completely. My father was at his mother's, surrounded by his sisters and had just called in to tell us that he was about to arrive." (all quotes from the forums are translated from French) [https://www. forumcancer.ch/forum3_fr/viewtopic.php?t=1529].

In his book called "Semiotic of the event", the French researcher Bernard Lamizet underlines the significance of dating and temporal scansion in the narrative of an event. According to him, dating acts as a kind of time horizon that makes the social time readable and intelligible [26]. While reconfiguring the temporal horizon of the family, the announcement also transforms the places and roles of the family members in the narratives. From this event, some become patients, and some others become parents, even if they may question these new functions. This is the case of Din 92 mg who tells the story of her mother's cancer on the french forum Doctissimo "health/cancer/ glioblastoma": "Mummy took it with a lot of courage… but I immediately noticed that she had not really understood… indeed, she used to tell me that getting cancer at her age (64) was not such a big deal, that she had only 7 or 8 years left anyway (…) … Must a daughter announce that to her mother?! I wanted to talk with my father but he did not want to hear about it… until it was written down on the biopsy results."

Even if fora appear as privileged media to tell about the diagnosis announcement, one can see there how it stays a medical acts in the eyes of parents [27].

3.2   Discourses Around Discursives Absences

Antoine Spire et Rollon Poinsot mention the "conspiracy of silence" that might be felt by the patients at the moment of the announcement and how it can generate suffer for them and their parents. In the case of glioblastoma, the conspiracy and the suffering are first to be found after the announcement, when the medical care and the support of the patient begin [27]. The parents express a feeling of incomprehension, at different stages of cancer and towards different people. The incomprehension is related to the rarity of the disease and, therefore, the rarity of institutions or media discourses able to explain it. Kika writes: "On Tuesday, we found out that my daddy has two inches frontal glioblastoma, the doctor used the term "rare". By reading some articles on line, I realize that it is not that rare… it's frontal, is this the rarity of it?" [https://www.ligue-cancer.net/forum/40821_remission-ou-guerison-dun-glioblastome].

Kika's interrogation also reveals the other cause of suffering expressed by the parents: the opacity of the medical speech. "I searched answers on every possible forum I could find, because the doctors did not want to tell me exactly how it was going to end while I wanted to know (translated from French)", tells for example Lou. [https://sante-medecine.journaldesfemmes.fr/forum/affich-1401164-glioblastome-grade-iv].

We can notice that the *fora* are mobilized by the parents as a source of information and, at the same time, as a space of expression, to question and criticize the medical authority. Silence and opacity are not the only claims. Parents also express their regret regarding the lack of concerns shown by the doctors, especially when they keep using numbers in their explanations. Alexandra, the mother of a young woman called Cyrielle, writes the following sentences: "Doctors give us numbers; despairing statistics. (…) The doctor told me that I had to be prepared for the time when Cyrielle is going to «sink» because, according to the statistics, "the vital prognostic is close to zero".   [http://forum.doctissimo.fr/sante/cancers/atteint-glioblastome-voulezvousenparler-sujet_171031_1.htm].

"The family has nothing to say about it either. The sick man is taken away by the institution that takes charge not of the individual, but of his illness, an isolated object transformed or eliminated by technicians devoted to the defense of health the way others are attached to the defense of law and order or tidiness", wrote Michel de Certeau in the part of his book *The Practice of Everyday Life* called "The Unnamable: dying" [28]. We can see here, through the questioning, how parents are using on-line *fora* to get to say something about the disease and to give back to the patient his/her individuality and singularity.

3.3   Invention and Collective Production of Experiential Knowledge

While facing this kind of uncertainty, the patient's parents develop speeches that express a kind of reconquest of power on the information. They show their deep knowledge of the disease through accurate descriptions of cancer and of its treatments. Rose writes about her daughter's case: "My daughter has a stage IV multiocular glioblastoma, that was diagnosed in 2018. She had surgery twice and the neurologists who did the surgery in Bordeaux were satisfied and had achieved their goals, so they said. She just finished the concomitant phase of her treatment (radiation therapy for

7 weeks and chemo pills for 49 days). She is now resting for 3–4 weeks and has to get back to the stage of the monotherapy chemo treatment. For that, she is going to have an MRI in Bordeaux on February 7 and her new treatment protocol will be adjusted afterward". [https://www.ligue-cancer.net/forum/40821_remission-ou-guerison-dun-gli oblastome].

The support experience legitimates the parent's expertise. The parent will then develop another kind of knowledge by actively searching for pieces of advice or therapeutical complements. This research activity is another specific pattern of the supporting narratives. "We are all fighting the same enemy, I keep on searching, looking for therapeutical advances, for testimonies that give hope", writes Anarafa. [https://sante-medecine.journaldesfemmes.fr/forum/affich-1401164-glioblastome-grade-iv].

In this online context, parents make discoveries that may concern a new protocol, a medicine, or a well-know specialist. Here is, for example, Laura Stehlin's narrative: "I managed to get an appointment with a glio-specialist: M. Olivier Chinot in a hospital in Marseille (France). In the frame of a clinical study, he had tested a new treatment. (…) It does not extend the life duration but improves its quality by "blocking" the progress of cancer during a certain among of time. It would give us some rest as long as my father stays in this good state." [https://sante-medecine.journaldesfemmes.fr/forum/affich-1401164-glioblastome-grade-iv].

These "quest-stories" transform the parent's figure: it was a passive spectator; it becomes an actor in the fight against cancer. The parent also becomes an actor by sharing his or her requests with others, on the fora. To help her step-daughter, Cocotinette asks all the members of the «glioblastoma forum» of the french Cancer League : "I just found articles about doctor David Fortin in Canada who has been researching for several years and can make his patients live longer in good conditions. Has someone heard about him? Thank you for your answers." [https://www.ligue-cancer.net/forum/45530_glioblastome?page=1].

When the "Cancer Plan" was launched in France in March 2003, it was presented by the government in these terms: "Several hundred thousand of patients (…) would like to be real actors in the battle against the disease. This battle is not a technical one; it can not be limited to the medical staff: it is a shared battle, and it is a human battle" [13].

In this perspective, the glioblastoma case appears quite exceptional since the patients can not get involved in the collective fight against the disease.

Therefore, regarding the doctors-patients-parents relationship, the glioblastoma fight has to be considered as a parallel battle. However, online, at the level of the conversations between parents, it appears as a shared one. It is shared between and by different generations, who exchange about extra-ordinary and about ordinary as well.

4   Core Exchange: A New Relationship to the Ordinary

The analysis reveals another level of interlocking with the insertion, in these narratives of the unexpected and the extraordinary, of statements that tell the daily life during the illness. The discussion of the medical authority and the parallel fight it generates is thus articulated to parents' investment in a more neglected and open field that enables, as a result, a form of parallel expertise: that of daily care and the emotions it involves.

4.1   Reinventing Hyperdaily Through Hypercontextualization

Parent-to-parent discussions on the forums make visible and readable a disease that also plunges families into a meticulous daily routine that which at the same time is who is close to and stands out from the classical media discourses on cancer. We find the same decontextualization of the illness and the patient since there are, in these messages, very few evocations and precisions about the working conditions or the socioeconomic aspects. However, a great deal of emphasis is placed on the "care" of the sick and the disease within the family.

In fact, biographies and messages in general are hyper-shifted. Beyond a meticulous use of first and second person pronouns and family nicknames or caritatisms, the daily life of the disease is recorded and specified to the extreme, to the day, to the place, to the date. The gestures are described, the exchanges recorded and the emotions laid down in this micro book of hours of the patient, his illness and the family that marks out and chants afterwards a chaotic period, which thus finds order and qualification of its various stages. These emphasis on the body and the daily life [22] result from the multiple self-writing that intertwines these micro-events to enable all families and generations who live under the rule of the glioblastoma small regains of control on biographies that seem to escape them.

4.2   Living with: Towards a Transgenerational "Emotional Community"?

The hyperdaily life told by the parents also consists of "on-line affective feelings", seen as an ability to feel or to make live emotions [28]. According to Fanny George and Virginie Julliard, the use of signs that carry an emotional value plays a role in the construction of subjective [29]. In the case of glioblastoma, parents become subjects and actors of the disease through the expression of emotions about it.

The first kind of emotion is linked to a feeling of deep unfairness regarding the specificities of this cancer. "This is a painful and unfair disease", writes, for instance, Idyl on the "Journal des femmes" ("Women diary") forum. The suffer is expressed towards one-self and others as well. The parent's narrative shows an empathy that goes far beyond the generation's borders. "We are scared for her, scared to see her suffer, but also scared for our son and our grand-son", explains Cocotinette about her step-daughter's illness [https://www.ligue-cancer.net/forum/45530_glioblastome?page=1]. Bic writes the following about her mother: "It is always hard to see her condition gradually worsen, and I ask myself what her fun can be while staying in bed all day, eating horrible mixed food... I am negative." [http://forum.doctissimo.fr/sante/cancers/glioblastome-maman-sujet_165141_1.htm].

These last words also show a parent's reflexivity regarding their feelings. This reflexivity leads to the expression of the second kind of emotions, a positive kind, which is based on two major feelings: courage and hope. "My father is still alive after 5 years now and keep hope, try always to keep hope, there are exceptions. Good luck to those who are in this situation", writes Cin [https://www.ligue-cancer.net/forum/40821_remission-ou-guerison-dun-glioblastome].

The expression of negative feelings, therefore, does not provide from the parallel expression of a positive one. On the contrary, they are encouraged by another kind of reflexivity: the one parent's mention about the role of the one-line fora in the way they deal with the disease. Therefore, "on-line feelings and emotions" can also be seen as feelings that are expressed towards on-line devices.

For example, Doko 2 writes the following paragraph: "At the beginning, I refused to look at fora or even to meet associations that provide support to sick people, but I must say that it is important to have external help – despite family support –, I feel it more and more. Is may sound silly, but it feels good to be able to express oneself in writing to say one's piece". [http://forum.doctissimo.fr/sante/cancers/glioblastome-avis-sujet_177892_1.htm]. This kind of feeling also makes the parents become subjects/actors in/of the disease because some of them, when they realize the meaning of the on-line support, will then want to pass it on to others and to tell it. "I will republish your post so that you get more answers and encouragement, one should not stay alone with this great pain", says Pri08al [http://forum.doctissimo.fr/sante/cancers/glioblastome-besoin-soutien-sujet_170658_1.htm].

Virginie Julliard and Fanny Georges consider that a shared way of expressing emotion can suggest the existence of an "emotional community" (Georges, Julliard XX). In our case, the repeated and converging expression of the three kinds of feelings we mentioned participate in the production of an emotional parent's community in a transgenerational way. The similarity of the emotional experiences indeed neutralizes the gaps between generations.

4.3   Living Already Without: Regarding "Death in the Future"

The specificities of glioblastoma lead to the addition of another temporal aspect in the narratives of the everyday-life: a future marked by the seal of death.

"Considered on the one hand as a failure or a provisional halt in the medical struggle, and on the other, removed from common experience and thus arriving at the limit of scientific power, and beyond familiar practices, death is an elsewhere", wrote Michel de Certeau [28]. In this case, death represents an elsewhere of the family life, but, like a horizon, it is also fully integrated into the "shared experience" of the disease. "The limit" is, therefore, also a constitutive pattern in the building of the "emotional community": parents share a particular perception of time, which is reconfigured under a deadly perspective.

The "ordinary" as it is told expresses "death in the future" [30] through several anticipation patterns. The first one appears as the last race to the death, such as the one written by Kristall 13: "When we look at the vital prognosis of this disease, we get terrified. And still, mummy is still here. She lives by herself, goes grocery shopping, does the cleaning, and she is here, alive, with us. This is the most beautiful thing." [http://forum.doctissimo.fr/sante/cancers/atteint-glioblastome-voulezvousenparler-sujet_171031_1.htm].

The search for a time extension is also contained in the incentive to enjoy the present, despite the certain future. "The piece of advice I could give you is to enjoy as much as possible the presence of your sister, to get all prepared and to get her children ready when the time comes, it is also important for them to understand that the disease may sometimes be stronger than anything else", entrust Lou to Thyli [https://sante-medecine.journaldesfemmes.fr/forum/affich-1401164-glioblastome-grade-iv].

The children, as we can see, plays a particular role in the "future death" narratives. Whereas the mourning anticipation neutralizes the meaning of generations, the presence of a child reassigns and reaffirms the places and functions in the family line. It mostly happens when the helpers just had a baby and anticipate a future without his/her grandparent. Bic writes on Doctissimo: "this bloody glioblastoma hits one person out of 100 000 and it had to be my mum, I know that I sound selfish by saying that, but I wish so bad that she could see my baby grow." Through the mention of this new presence - which connotes future, continuity, and renewal of generations - the anticipated absence becomes all the more significant.

Michel de Certeau also wrote these words about dying: "The dying are outcasts because they are deviants in an institution organized by and for the conservation of life. An "anticipated mourning," a phenomenon of institutional rejection, puts them away in advance in "the dead man's room"; it surrounds them with silence or, worse yet, with lies that protect the living against the voice that would break out of this enclosure to cry: "I am going to die". This cry would produce an embarrassingly graceless dying. The lie ("Of course not; you're going to get better") is a way of assuring that communication will not occur" [28]. In this perspective, the exchanges and narratives built through and in the on-line *fora* form a kind of "deviation" relative to the medical institution. It is an active deviation since it does not offer the dying the silence but, on the contrary, a discursive space that maintains them, for a while, at the threshold of "the dead man's room". This deviation is also active from a parent's point of view since they make themselves actors of everyday life through cancer by presenting themselves as to its authors. In doing so, they create their own authority space.

5 Conclusion

At the end of this incursion in the very special universe built by generational on-line exchanges about glioblastoma, we note the extreme richness of their communicational and identity constructs. These exchanges, through their serialization, do not only focus on individual cases but create community and reach to the universal. They also draw a plural figure of profane expertise: the figure of the "expert-parent" on-line, on these *fora*, appears as richer and more complex than the one that the institutions (associations, medical reference web-sites...) tend to raise and promote. Through the extraordinary dimension of this disease, the default "expert-parent" becomes an expert of his/her ordinary life, becomes the "one who knows," the one who cares and supports not only the patient but also the family and other families as well. Online *fora* seem to be spaces where their experiences are expressed and therefore formalized [16], which is usually what associations do. To that extent, we can ask if these biographies, Monument of "exemplary lives", are known by the medical staff and if they can play a role in the relationship between patients, parents, and health-care professionals.

Our hypothesis about the rise, in this particular type of very aggressive brain cancer, of a specific figure of "parent expertise", linked to patient expertise and carers expertise finds here a first stage of confirmation. So does the question regarding the negotiation of generational places in this context. This research will have to be carried out further to understand all the implications that we have not been able to address here. First within the digital space and digital patients' forums, we could question the content of the exchanges according to the degree and kind of authority of the websites hosting them. We could also try to specify the figure of parent expert according to age, gender and rank in generations. In a second phase, we could explore, as much as possible, the socio-economic implications on the produced discourses and the mere ability to speak out.

References

1. Barthes, R.: Mourning Diary. Hill and Wang, New York (2010)
2. Barthes, R.: A Lover's Discourse: Fragments. Penguin Books, London (1990)
3. Gross, O., Gagnayre, R.: Hypothèse d'un modèle théorique du patient-expert et de l'expertise du patient: processus d'élaboration, Hors-Série «les Actes». Revue Recherches Qualitatives **15**, 147–165 (2013)
4. Bardin, L.: L'analyse de contenu. PUF, Paris (2013)
5. Berthelot-Guiet, K.: Analyser les discours publicitaires. Armand Colin, Paris (2015)
6. Berthelot-Guiet, K.: Older people are the future of consumption: great expectations and small starts for brands and new media. In: Zhou, J., Salvendy, G. (eds.) HCII 2019. LNCS, vol. 11593, pp. 33–45. Springer, Cham (2019). https://doi.org/10.1007/978-3-030-22015-0_3
7. Jeanneret, Y., Ollivier, O.: Les Sciences de l'Information et de la Communication. Hermes, 38. CNRS Editions, Paris (2004)
8. Jeanneret, Y.: The relation between mediation and use in the research of information and communication in france. RECIIS – Elect. J. Commun. Inf. Innov. Health **3**(3), 25–34 (2009)
9. Voirol, O.: Le pouvoir normatif du narratif, Réseaux, 23 (2005)
10. Honneth, A.: The Struggle for Recognition: The Moral Grammar of Social Conflicts. MIT Press, Cambridge (1996)
11. Foucault, M.: Technologies of the Self: A Seminar With Michel Foucault. MIT Press, Cambridge (1998)
12. Wrona, A.: Small Lives, Exemplary Lives: Personal Accounts and News. The Example of "Portraits of Grief" in the New York Times after 9/11. Réseaux, 132, pp. 93–110 (2005)
13. Azzedine, L.: Le cancer et ses récits : quelles places des malades et des maladies. Les enjeux de l'information et de la communication (2007)
14. Jakobson, R.: Shifters, Verbal Categories and the Russian Verb. Harvard University, Cambridge (1957)
15. Greimas, A., Courtes, J.: Semiotics and Language: an Analytical Dictionary. Indiana University Press, Bloomington (1982)
16. Azzedine, L., Blanchard, G., Poncin, C.: Le cancer dans la presse écrite d'information générale. Questions de communication **11**, 111–127 (2007)
17. Abiven, K.: L'exemplum: un modèle opératoire dans la lettre familière ?. Exercices de rhétorique 6 (2016)
18. Wrona, A.: Face au portrait. De Sainte-Beuve à Facebook. Hermann, Paris (2012)
19. Caradec, V., Glevarec, H.: Age et usages des médias. Réseaux, 119, pp. 9–23
20. Barthes, R.: How to Live Together. Columbia University Press, New York (2012)

21. Gundersen, K.: Noum. In: Stene-Johansen, K., Refsum, C., Schimanski, J. (eds.) Living Together: Roland Barthes, the Individual and the Community, Transcript Culture and Theory, vol. 179 (2018)
22. Georges, F.: Représentation de soi et identité numérique. Une approche sémiotique et quantitative de l'emprise culturelle du web 2.0, Réseaux, 154 (2009)
23. Coutant, A.: Des techniques de soi ambivalentes. Hermès, La revue **59**, 53–58 (2011)
24. Elias, N.: The Society of Individuals. Basil Blackwell, Cambridge (1991)
25. Arquembourg, J.: Le Temps des événements médiatiques. De Boeck Supérieur, Louvain-la-Neuve (2003)
26. Lamizet, B.: Sémiotique de l'événement. Hermès Lavoisier, Paris (2006)
27. Spire, A., Poinsot, R.: L'annonce en cancérologie. Questions de communication (2007)
28. De Certeau, M.: The Practice of Everyday Life. University of California Press, Berkeley (1984)
29. Georges, F., Julliard, V.: Produire le mort. Pratiques d'écriture et travail émotionnel des deuilleurs et des deuilleuses sur Facebook, Réseaux, 210 (2018)
30. Barthes, R.: Camera lucida. Hill and Wang, New York (1980)

Are Digital Twins Becoming Our Personal (Predictive) Advisors?

'Our Digital Mirror of Who We Were, Who We Are and Who We Will Become'

Christel De Maeyer[1,2(✉)] and Panos Markopoulos[2(✉)]

[1] Department Graphical and Digital Media,
Artevelde University of Applied Science, Ghent, Belgium
christel.demaeyer@arteveldehs.be
[2] Department of Industrial Design, Eindhoven University of Technology,
Eindhoven, The Netherlands
p.markopoulos@tue.nl

Abstract. In this paper we look at the notion of a Digital Twin and what it could entail for an aging population. A Digital Twin refers to a digital replica of potential and actual physical assets (physical twin), processes, people, places, systems and devices that can be used for various purposes. Today's evolution of smart devices, mobile application used in different domains, could be ways of nurturing a Digital Twin. Moreover, these smart device and mobile applications are often equipped with NUI's (Natural User Interfaces), which make them more affordable for an aging population in terms of usability. In this paper we focus on the affordance and appropriation of these assistive digital technologies. We first do a literature review on related work on 'Aging in Place' in combination with 'Digital Twin' theory. Furthermore, we conducted in-depth qualitative interviews with boomers (1946–1964) 60+ and 70+, mixed gender and mixed education, but predominately higher educated boomers living in Belgium. In addition we conducted in-depth interviews with stakeholders active in a medical environment.

Keywords: Digital Twins · Quantified Self · Personal informatics · Data selves · Aging population

1 Introduction

With the evolution of quantified-self tools, smart devices and mobile applications, we are now entering a new era which can be described as that of 'Modern Wellbeing'. Modern wellbeing pertains to the extensive adoption of new technologies that track different facets of our lives and activities over time, resulting in varied impacts on our bodies, minds, our environment and our communities [40]. The abundance of data that such technologies generate can serve a variety of purposes and fusing such data can provide new and often unexpected insights.

© Springer Nature Switzerland AG 2020
Q. Gao and J. Zhou (Eds.): HCII 2020, LNCS 12208, pp. 250–268, 2020.
https://doi.org/10.1007/978-3-030-50249-2_19

By combining a variety of all the data that we gather as humans in a digital world, the possibility emerges of creating a 'Digital Twin'. A Digital Twin refers to a digital replica of potential and actual physical assets (physical twin), processes, people, places, systems and devices that can be used for various purposes [12, 19]. A Digital Twin could hold information on different biomarkers, cognitive information, lifestyle and environmental data would give the ability to look at an individual's well-being in a different way. Such a synthesized artefact opens up the possibility for predictive analyses and early detection of anomalies that occur during the lifecycle of humans.

When creating the Digital Twin, we can map a medical layer and lifestyle layer of individuals. In some ways, we already have such information on a micro and on a macro level. On a micro level, lots of our medical information today is already digitized (MRI's, radiographies, results of breast cancer examination and so forth). Such information is used to learn and understand the data collected during examinations, to show them to patients and to explain their condition. Such data can also be given to third parties for providing personalized solutions and services, e.g., it can be shared with a manufacturer in case a tailor-made prosthesis needs to be made for example. But Digital Twins can also be more commonplace and mundane than this example might suggest. More familiar and popularized is self-tracking with mobile applications and wearable devices, which is quite pronounced in relation to the whole Quantified Self phenomenon. Even on a macro level, we can conceive Facebook as a coarse grain Digital Twin, capturing parts on what we do, who we are. Considering systems supporting a Digital Twin applies also for several other applications that are available in the social media space and used extensively [44].

Digital Twins can be used to serve a variety of purposes resulting in valuable societal benefits but could lead to negative consequences as well. In the health domain the potential application of Digital Twins for predicting health conditions could result in substantial cost savings for the healthcare system and improving the effectiveness of health interventions. For patients this could lead to improved quality of life, e.g., by keeping patients longer in their own environment, avoiding premature hospitalization, especially since smart devices and mobile applications getting more and more financially affordable.

The smart home today looks very different from the smart homes from years ago. With the introduction of Internet of Things (IoT) these 'smart devices' or 'smart objects or things' can be equipped with Natural User Interfaces (NUI), which makes them more accessible and easier to use. Interacting with these 'smart things' can combine voice, gesture, motion or touch; these new ways of interacting with smart objects come very natural to humans to use. It also broadens the discussion of the embodiment and the social relation humans develop with these new digital technologies [27].

Discussing the opportunities this technological trend offers is one thing, but equally imported are the possible negative aspects, the socio-political impact it has on the individual and society as a whole. One of the consequences of Digital Twin concepts is that it could lead to surveillance resulting in social sorting of a population, changing policies based on the social sorting and the data that is gathered by individuals, resulting in inequality in certain populations [28, 30, 32]. On an individual or patient level, it can create empowerment for the patient but at the same time disempower them. Self-tracking asks for self-discipline, self-examination and as we will see further, individuals have to have the means and the knowledge to engage in managing one's health through assistive digital technologies [25, 48]. In this paper, we would focus our research on the affordance [15] of these technologies and how these technologies are appropriated. We aim to get insight into how older adults make sense of the new technologies in their everyday life [27] and to answer the following research questions:

1. To which extent do technologies such as wearable device and mobile applications, leading towards a 'Digital Twin' concept within preventive and predictive health-care give human enhancement towards personal healthcare?
2. How do elderly users handle or think about the data they (might) gather?
3. How do they give meaning to their gathered data?
4. How will different stakeholders within the healthcare and care giving organizations be organized around the concept of a Digital Twin.

The research methods we will use are first a literature review on related work and in depth-interviews with 8 individuals, more specifically boomers (1946–1964), 60+ and 70+, mixed gender and mixed education, but predominately higher educated boomers living in Belgium. In addition, we interview 3 stakeholders in the care cycle of elderly people, a general practitioner, CEO of a caregiver's platform and an MRI radiologist.

2 Related Work

2.1 From Data Selves to Digital Twins

In 2007 Gary Wolf and Kevin Kelly founded the Quantified Self Movement, with the stated aim to explore what these new self-tracking tools could mean on a human level. Today self-tracking has become mainstream and is entering in different areas of our lives. Self-tracking is very promising for preventive healthcare solutions and healthcare in general. Furthermore, with the rise of 'smart objects' or 'smart things' internet of things in general, we can evolve to a connected self. In these environments, humans are gathering and measuring a mass of data for themselves but also for others. These technologies could enhance human lives as we surround ourselves with the new knowledge about our bodies but also in a broader sense, as the way we live, our lifestyle and our surroundings are mapped and digitally modelled.

Such data might allow us to have more detailed self-knowledge and allow for optimization of a variety aspects of our human existence and experiences. We can have at easy reach information about our health status, our physical activity, our mental well-being, our environments we live in, in fact we have the opportunity to create a better self of ourselves with the help of these assistive digital technologies. Today scholars discuss the emergence of humans akin to 'walking sensory platforms' [47] or 'data selves' [31], referring to networked humans, the 'networked self', it extends the discussion of self-tracking humans. As humans today are engaging with digital technologies in different ways on a variety of platforms, mobile applications and lately with 'smart objects' and 'smart things'. The discussion extends on the level of embodiment and the social relation humans have with these digital technologies, on a micro and macro level. These scenarios are leading towards the idea or the notion of a 'Digital

Twin' of ourselves. The concept of a Digital Twin refers to a digital replica of potential and actual physical assets (physical twin), processes, people, places, systems and devices that can be used for various purposes. The data is a live, it is 'lively data' [29], we could look at this as human-data assemblages, which goes beyond quantifying ourselves. Human-data-assemblages according to Lupton, are created through the interaction and encounters humans have during their life cycle with software, digital platforms, devices and other humans in time and space. In the next topic we will look what a possible Digital Twin could mean for seniors and aging in place. Further in our research methods we use a cultural probe (Fig. 2) to illustrate a possible example of a Digital Twin concept.

2.2 Aging in Place

In the 'city of people' project a 'Hello Jenny' living lab research project was launched in Ghent. Twelve seniors received a 'smart speaker' and a sensor to monitor how frequently the front door goes open and closed to check how many visitors seniors have during the day. When it is detected that the door hasn't been opened a lot, Hello Jenny, the smart speaker gets a signal. The speaker will ask if the senior wants to have a visit to have a little conversation or to do a walk, to play some cards or other socializing events or activity. The senior can then push a button 'yes or no'. A buddy gets a message through messenger in the pilot project, the buddy types when is a good moment to come over for a visit, the sentences are converted to speech and the senior gets the message through the smart speaker. The senior can then again push yes or no, and the visit is confirmed [22] (Fig. 1).

Fig. 1. Hello Jenny, prototype © Michiel Devijver [22]

As aging in place [51] today is an important evolution in our society today [52] mainly because elderly want to stay at their home longer and postpone the transfer to a care home, but also because care homes want to postpone the entrance of elderly people to cut costs [18]. The ecosystem of care services is changing and is preparing for the elderly aging in place. To fulfill the promise of aging in place, it is important that elderly people can rely on the community they live in and the necessary resources to live independently. Resources for aging in place have been researched in recent years by scholars on different levels. A large body of research has been done on smart homes [20, 36], but also for the daily domestic tasks, new digital technologies arise [5], doing groceries today can be organized online and delivery at home is already a widespread practice. Furthermore quantified-self tools are also entering the aging population, the emergence of 'quantified aging' [33].

Several living labs and experiments done in quadruple helix models, stimulate that process in investigating how technologies possibly could facilitate aging in place [22, 23, 26 48]. In addition, research is showing that the adoption of new digital technologies within the older population is growing, especially with the baby boomers [41]. Given enough time, these assistive digital technologies will become more popular as user-interfaces will get more user-friendly and more intuitive like we already see in the Natural User Interface of today. Humans can be expected to interact with newer digital technologies by voice, gesture, motion and touch. Furthermore, as all these 'smart devices' and 'smart things' are connected to each other, overviews can be aggregated into dashboards or in Digital Twins. The usage of assistive digital technologies can give overviews on a daily, weekly or monthly basis or when needed. Data logs can help the caregivers who work and service the elderly population in getting deeper insights of the day to day activities of the elderly. Below we return to the notion of the Digital Twin and look at the different aspects on how a Digital Twin could be built, what the possible motivation could be for feeding the digital twin with data and how this could affect the future caregiver and healthcare eco systems in general. We also consider whether one or more Digital Twins should be supported.

2.3   Digital Twins, a Connected Self

This is not a Black Mirror episode but let's look at the Digital Twin as a connected self, a sidekick of yourself. As humans move around, do different activities, travel, are active in different work settings and live different lifestyles, one can imagine Digital Twins to have different categories in the Digital Twin that are in relation with each other. For example, a medical layer, a lifestyle layer, a home and a workplace layer. A Digital Twin could potentially simulate health risks on a longer term, help athletes to get more insights in their training schedules, risk management at work, get more insights on performance and productivity and all this on a micro but also on macro scale, on society as a whole [44]. One would get also more insight in the aging process and how to facilitate this process towards 'dignified' aging. Or creating or working towards 'a better you'. One of the interviewees mentioned: 'it would be great to have a view on an ideal Digital Twin of oneself and get advice on how you would be able to get there', considering the abilities of the individual. As we will see in our findings, security will be very important if we evolve towards a Digital Twin. Briggs worked on the notion of a Biometric Daemon, authentication system through an electronic pet. The electronic pet not only provides possible secure ways to authentication, but at the same time can develop a relationship with its owner. The more the biometric daemon is nurtured by means of the behavior (conversation, familiar behavior, idiosyncratic movements) of the owner who is identified with the Biometric Daemon, the more they will bond with each other and develop an intimate relationship. Briggs also suggest that the Biometric Daemon will be unhappy when it is separated from its owner and eventually will die if separated to long from its owner. 'Daemons have a number of interesting properties. They are animal in form but share an identity with their owner – and exhibit an intimacy based upon seamless communication of a shared emotional state. Any separation between daemon and owner will result in the death of the daemon' [4]. The Biometric Damon is a dynamic object, capable of adapting. This means that overtime the Biometric Daemon can adapt based on the owners behavior, it becomes a digital companion, a sidekick of yourself with the capability to become a personal coach, a companion in a secure way, because of its biometric features of identification and authentication, a Digital Twin could be born.

The notion that a Digital Twin could be materialized as a social robot, like the example of a biometric daemon we discuss here, brings us also to research that has been done on how older adults perceive social robots as companions. Most of this research has been done in controlled environments like care centers [6, 24, 35]. These studies show a positive outcome in general, however it is still early days in the field of social robots.

If we think further about these robotic technologies and the empathy they give to older adults in this case is maybe also worrying. While these technologies know what our preferences are after a while, what we like to eat, what physical activity we like, what our daily habits and routines are, do they also know what they mean? Can we actually have a dialogue that goes further than the coded dialogues, even when AI is deployed? If one relates this back to the quantified self, the feedback we get from those technologies are very blunt and don't show any empathy at all. They just report facts and figures [43]. They will never ask the question 'why you haven't run for a week' or even considering context around 'the why you haven't run for a week'.

Turkle, speaks of 'pretended empathy' as robots don't really have a past or lived a life, it is all programmed and coded, they don't have real empathy nor feelings. "What is the value of interaction that does not contain shared life experiences and contributes nothing to a shared story of human-meaning-and indeed may devalue it" [50]? Social robots will challenge us and should make one think about the commitment we can give to the older adults or those who need care in general. One should look at these technologies as enablers and facilitators to create a balance between human commitment and the help of social robots and/or quantified self-tools, in making 'aging in place' still human, enabled, facilitated by technology and humans. Let's explore further the notion of a Digital Twin, what motivates individuals to nurture a Digital Twin.

2.4 Motivation for Feeding a Digital Twin

A Digital Twin needs to be fed or nurtured with data, such as medical data, archived in a hospital, data gathered by approved medical devices, data from lifestyle wearable devices or data from domestic smart devices, individuals have in their home. In the Biometric Daemon example, researchers speak about imprinting and nurturing. Imprinting 'when it becomes exposed to the identify information of an individual but simultaneously bonds to that individual'. Nurturing is a process where the daemon learns about the individual by conversation, touch and behavior of the owner [4].

The motivation to do this could be found in the reasons for which humans are tracking themselves with wearable devices and other tools that are available today. Within the quantified self-domain, lots of research has been done on the motivations and the reasons why humans are tracking themselves, as well as the negative aspects [9, 10, 12, 45]. The main reasons that individuals track themselves are curiosity, leisure and health. In addition, research shows that there is a lot of drop out with self-trackers, among the main reasons are failure of technologies, individuals track themselves when things are going well, the data is always the same and the effort and time it requires to reflect on the results. If we look further into motivation for health reasons, Gimpel et al. [17] provides a framework of five motivational factors that motivate humans to track themselves.

- *Factor 1: Self-entertainment*: motivation because of the pleasure it brings to the self-tracker, this motivation lies into the aspect that the user has fun and enjoyment in using these digital devices.
- *Factor 2: Self-association*: the prospect of being associated within a community, 'community citizenship'. This is less about one's self, but more 'how one relates to a community or understanding her or his individualization within a certain environment, self-individualizing aspects within the community. The idea that a self-tracker needs a counterpart to understand him or herself mainly by comparison'.
- *Factor 3: Self-design*: motivation by the possibilities of self-optimization. Self-trackers are interested in controlling and optimizing their life, whether they track mood, physical activity or other tracking aspects of their daily life.
- *Factor 4: Self-discipline*: motivation due to self-gratification. The self-tracker is more motivated by the prospect of achieving certain goals, getting rewarded, or not being penalized and avoiding negative consequences.
- *Factor 5: Self-healing*: motivation by the possibilities of self-healing. The self-tracker doesn't have a lot of trust in the current health system, carrying some sort of rebellion attitude towards healthcare systems. They want to have a certain independence from traditional healthcare systems. Further research will give more insight why elderly might be motivated to feed their Digital Twin with data.

2.5 Digital Twin and the Environment

As mentioned before, a large body of research has been done on smart homes for aging in place and on Ambient Assistive Living (AAL). However today, IoT (Internet of Things) technologies are entering homes bringing closer the prospect of a smart home, also making it relatively affordable financially and acceptable in terms of usability and user-experience.

Smart homes can be monitored in a detailed way. The smart home can be managed locally but also remotely; it has the potential to detect 'red flags', having an alarming function and service providers can be integrated in the whole process, in viewing and controlling their patients from a far. As mentioned before these IoT based systems can be supported by natural user interfaces and the underlying technology can be transparent to end users [11].

The IoT environment is connecting 'humans to things', as mentioned before in the human data assemblage [31], 'things to things', smart devices talk to each other and there could be an interoperability between them. IoT is also connecting 'humans to humans' [22]. One could state that IoT is fulfilling the needs of AAL (Ambient Assisted Living), namely:

- Monitoring health status of a human in the smart home environment to provide peace of mind for the owner but possibly also for the family, trusted friends and caregivers.
- The ability to live independently and therefore stay longer in place.
- Giving a sense of security/safety and the ability to maintain the social network of the elderly, giving the possibility to engage with their community remotely but also in real life [11, 21, 48].
- Exploring different scenarios with the gathered data, to change or alter data to make simulations, to predict the future in a way with 'the what if…' or 'if this then this…' scenarios so to speak. In the next chapter we can examine how this could work.

2.6   Digital Twins Integrated in a Healthcare System

Mr. P is 61 years old is in good health and trains regularly and likes to run a marathon at least once a year. His health, sports and physical activity are monitored by his sports doctor on a regular basis. Based on his heart rate (cardiovascular screening), acidification of muscles (musculoskeletal screening) and performance screening, Mr. P gets a forecast of what his performance will be and what kind of sensitivities may arise in his next marathon season. Mr. P relies on the input and output of data to adjust his lifestyle and behavior towards a successful marathon season without injuries.

Mr. D, is a general practitioner, is a type 1 diabetes patient and sports person. He switched towards a glucose system (patch) that gives real time data on his glucose level. Mr. D now has much more insights on his glucose, more accurate. Furthermore, he gets insights on trends of his glucose status. Mr. D now feels more insecure than before. Because he has real insights on his status, his life experience has become different, he has more peace of mind, but at the same time also feels insecure. Mr. D uses these patches for already two or three years as an early adaptor.

Miss C. is 75 years old and has recently suffered a stroke. Today she is surrounded by care givers helping her in her domestic tasks and her revalidation process. This is all scheduled very precisely. Miss C. has a strong community around her, the neighbors, friends and medical care, since one of her family members is a specialist in a hospital. Miss C. sees potential in the Digital Twin concept. She thinks that it could have given her and her surroundings more insight in her bio-medical data, which could have helped her maybe prevent the stroke. In addition, she thinks that she could enjoy more control if the Digital Twin would be easy to use and help her to organize her life, especially with caregivers visiting her today.

These are scenarios derived from real situations that came up during interviews using the thematic analysis method [3] in the first scenario (P1 from the stakeholders participants) bikes on regular basis with his friend and observed him when his friend made the switch from a traditional glucose measuring system towards the new patch system, where his friend now gets real-time data in. The second and the third scenario, were testimonials from the participants P1 and P6, which we will discuss further in our research results. When thinking about Digital Twins, one tends to think immediately about the medical impact it could have. To get more insights on the self through a lens of a 'virtual self'. As the Digital Twin is a data-driven approach, the power not only lies in the one-person, personalized medicine, but also in the scale of data or big data and give a 'high resolution' view on what is the 'normal or healthy state' today in a given population.

We've been looking in this paper at digital assistive technologies that could give the ability, considering the enablement and constraints or advantages and disadvantages for an aging population to stay longer in place. The notion of Digital Twin looks more at how we can predictively look at an individual and a society as a whole to explore human enhancements or human life extension [7] combining data information on biomedical data information but also lifestyle and behavior data information.

> '...whereas the means used to achieve life extension – food, physical activity – clearly fall into the field of natural remedies, the broader process of scientific acquisition of data and of (social) design of which they are part may turn the process into a form of engineering, and therefore, arguably, of human enhancement. In fact, if the same group of people would obtain the same life extension effect, but this time because they have the financial means to access some complex biotechnological interventions, intuition would probably lead us to classify this as enhancement' [7], p7.

With the Digital Twin comes new responsibility pertaining to maintaining data integrity, ensuring appropriate access and use of the information it encodes. Achieving these goals raises several questions such as: Where will the Digital Twin reside? Who will have access to it? What are legitimate uses of this information? What are suitable mechanisms for providing consent? Who is accountable for decisions made based on the Digital Twin? Such discussions will inevitably accompany the emergence of the Digital Twin. As mentioned before there are ethical questions to be resolved, among the lines of data privacy, transparency, patient autonomy (human agency and oversight). Governance is needed in the whole discussion to make it transparent, considering accountability as well, to be able to become a trustworthy human oriented technology [2, 8, 46, 49].

3   Research Methods

Our research methods consist in a literature review on 'Aging in Place' [51, 52] combined with 'Digital Twin' theory in healthcare. In addition, we conducted in-depth interviews with eight boomers (1946–1964), 60+ and 70+, and three stakeholders in the care cycle of elderly people, a general practitioner, the CEO of a caregiver platform and an MRI radiologist.

During the in-depth qualitative interviews' cultural props [34] in the form of images were used as a conversation starter to explain what a Digital Twin is, without influencing the interviewees too much. The interviews were in verbatim style transcribed, and then analyzed through thematic networks to analyze the patterns [34].

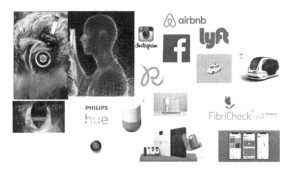

Fig. 2. Digital Twin notion

4   Research Results

In-depth qualitative interviews were conducted with a purposive sample, recruited from the Dutch speaking part of Belgium (5 participants) and from the Netherlands (3 participants). The subjects were all 60+ in a healthy condition. However, two of them have had some severe incidents in the past. One of the subjects had a minor stroke in 2018 and another subject could avoid a stroke because of early detection of a blood clot behind the eye. Another subject survived breast cancer. Subjects enjoyed a higher education in general, worked or are still working in a cultural setting and in higher education. In addition, we conducted a stakeholder sample, recruited in Belgium, which contained three stakeholders, one radiologist, specialized in Magnetic Resonance Imaging (MRI) and active in a hospital, one general practitioner and one CEO of a caregiver platform. We used images to start the conversation and to explain the concept of a Digital Twin as none of the interviewees were knowledgeable in the domain of Digital Twin concepts, especially the boomers. Even though some of them gather quite some data for several purposes, they were not really aware of the emergence of the Digital Twin concept in a medical or preventive healthcare environment. We transcribed the interviews in a verbatim style and then used the thematic analysis and thematic network methods [3, 33] to analyze the patterns that occurred in the interviews.

Two sets of questions were conducted, one set for the boomers and one set for the professionals active in healthcare. With the questions we explore how boomers would perceive a Digital Twin and what it could mean for them and what would motivate them to feed a Digital Twin. Furthermore, we also had questions about the preparation for the end-of-life care, considering the presence of the Digital Twin embedded in the life cycle of boomers.

4.1   The Boomers (1946–1964) 60+ and 70+

The Boomers and Motivation for Feeding a Digital Twin
In the in-dept interviews, all of the subjects agreed on the usefulness of feeding a Digital Twin with their medical data and other data if it would help them to get more

insights, to adjust lifestyles if needed. Such as eating and physical activity were the most important ones. One subject is already working together with his sports doctor to optimize his results in the marathons and other smaller running events he is running. Together they analyze the possibility for injuries, what his performance could be during a marathon and the diets he needs to follow. One subject was more motivated to do this out of curiosity and at the same time to see how the children possibly could be affected. If their health conditions would be genetically transferred or if it would be more behavior related.

The motivation aspects are in line with the framework of Gimpel [17], more specifically on the factors of 'Self-design' and 'Self-discipline', as subjects are willing to control and optimize their lives if it helps them and achieve certain goals to get rewarded in a sense of positive influence on their quality of life and not to get penalized or get negative consequences from certain behaviors. Within this perspective is also a self-gratification factor.

A sub question we asked was, if there should be a need to cheat in the data, for example on your diet, drinking or smoking habits. However, none of the subjects were interested to cheat on the Digital Twin, they all agreed it would have no sense to do so. One subject (P2) says *'no, the Digital Twin is my 'higher conscious' as it were. So, if I say that I drink only one glass of wine and I had two glasses, the twin would say you had two glasses'*.

Forecasting Diagnoses and Life Expectations
None of the subjects were interested in their life expectations in terms of when they are going to die. One subject (P5) said *'if I have a severe bicycle accident I could die too, this is all very relative'*. One subject (P6) would find it creepy to know about his life expectations through DNA samples for example. Another subject (P2) would find it interesting if there would be a diagnosis of cancer for example, in this case it would be interesting to know whether it is possible to survive it or how many months you still have with a certain cancer diagnosis, this is something that is possible today, but maybe more accurate in the future, considering the possibility of a holistic view through a Digital Twin.

Getting forecasts on certain diagnosis would have an added value for the subjects. All of them would find that very helpful to adjust behavior if necessary and to know what they need to watch in order to keep a good health. For example, to know cholesterol levels or sugar levels would be helpful. Which they already do when they have a yearly check-up, but then it would be more frequently. On the other hand, one subject (P6) mentioned that too much information could lead to inducing behavior, leading towards a restricted life somehow, not a naturel and spontaneous life anymore. Feeling controlled by personal surveillance.

Ethics and Privacy Implications with a Digital Twin
With this question we wanted to explore how the subjects felt about collecting their data as an individual, but furthermore if one looks at a bigger scale on society level or even a certain population, how it could enable social sorting, or even discriminate and exclude a certain population [1, 28].

Most of the subjects are worried about their data privacy on an individual level. If the medical data would stay secured within a hospital or general practitioner, they would not worry but if this would not be the case, it would be a big worry. One subject said (P5) *'not personally, I have a good job, if I retire I will need downsize a bit, so I'm privileged in a sense. I would not really be worried as long as people stick to the rules'.* Another subject (P2) *'I would not take a Digital Twin if the law on privacy is not in place'.* Yet, another one said (P1), *I'm am who I am, so no I'm not worried.* Then another one was thinking more ahead (P3) *'I think today it is a general worry how we evolve as a society. You are going to be punished on your behavior and on what you say, it is already happening in some cultures and I see it in ours as well'.*

With Whom Would We Share the Digital Twin and Who Owns It?

This question is getting more deeper on how humans in general could or would prepare for the end-of-life. Whom they would trust to hand things over when they are not conscious or not able anymore to decide for themselves. Forms of dementia that might emerge or other critical situation where the subjects cannot decide themselves anymore. Is there a role for the Digital Twin, or who would have access to Digital Twin besides the medical staff?

Most of the subjects see themselves having ownership of the data they produce through the Digital Twin. For some it might be a layered relationship and ownership, where the user gives consent to certain aspects of the Digital Twin. All of them would share the information or give consent to the medical staff where they are in treatment in order to get professional feedback. They would not necessarily share their information with their family when they are in a healthy state but appoint them as trustees in the case they cannot decide anymore for themselves. One of the subjects said (P5) *'I don't know if I would trust a Digital Twin that far to make decisions, it is best to have still humans involved in the process and have the ability to discuss things'.*

The Concept of the Digital Twin or the Materialization of a Digital Twin

Most of the subjects see the Digital Twin as database combined with an algorithm. There are some variations, subjects see it also as an object, that could be installed at home, some kind of a robot, a social companion maybe that helps you. Others see it as a dashboard on their computer where they have an overview. In some ways it is already available in hospitals in Belgium when you had examinations, but you need to ask for access at the moment.

Another subject finds it difficult to conceptualize it. The subject said (P4) *'I find it difficult to grasp this. I don't think I would like a database telling me or nudge me to do things. If I can use a metaphor, for me life is a conversation not a database'.* In general, the subjects don't see the need of having multiple twins, two subjects (P3), (P6) argued that it could be useful if used as a test environment, referring to the control and test groups that were or are being used in research methods today.

Could a Digital Twin help in 'Aging in Place'?

There was a general positive agreement that the evolution of today's assistive digital technologies would most probably work for the subjects to stay longer at home. However, this agreement was conditional upon it being user friendly and privacy respecting. One subject argued (P2) *'Information would be extremely important, how to use it what it holds. I need to be fully informed. I know exactly what is for and how it is used. What I get out of it. So, I don't want to have surprises. And not that there are some hidden elements, like the hospital can automatically download your data. Or the government can say, people over 80 in a certain region should live there or so and so. That should be absolutely to be avoided'.*

Another discussion that came up was: (P6) *'What does it mean 'aging in place?' Maybe we need to go to new ways of living, co-living, what is home? Maybe a new environment, where the soup man comes by to deliver soup, like we had in the old days, or the milkman and the bakery'*, a more personal approach.

What Happens with the Digital Twin When You Die?
Today when people die, the access to their medical file is closed and will come to an end, and the relationship with caregivers and medical staff will be ended. However, the medical data stored in hospitals is archived for 30 years according to Belgian law. In this research all subjects would prefer that their Digital Twin dies with them. Either a symbolic burning or a lock down. Some would donate their data for medical purposes on an anonymous basis. In all cases medical data would be archived as the law foresees it today.

The Extra Comments on This Questionnaire
A few subjects made extra comments. Most of them found it an interesting debate really worthwhile investigating this. The concerns they had was on the usability of the Digital Twin concept. How it would unfold and how they could access it. For all of them this was a new way of thinking. One of the subjects said (P4): *'this is not about data systems but about social systems.' It is a question of democracy. The question is what is the nature of our society. And the question is what we are going to do about it. These are political debates. Furthermore, the question is what do we do about these oligarchies that run and ruining our lives and rule the world'.*

4.2   The Stakeholders

As mentioned before the stakeholders are participants working in a medical environment. Participants are active as CEO of caregiving platform, as a radiologist, specialized in Magnetic Resonance Imaging (MRI) and active in a hospital and a general practitioner.

Motivation to Feed a Digital Twin from a Medical Staff Perspective
According to the stakeholders, the motivation of patients in feeding a Digital Twin were diverse. According to (P1) in order to get patients on board, simplicity would be a key element. For (P1) simplicity lies in the ease of use of devices or software in general. Software or mobile applications should not need a manual, devices have a simple on or off button and so forth, they are simple. In Fogg's behavior model [13] there are six simplicity components, one of them is brain cycles, this complies to what (P1) is referring to, do users have to think deeply or hard to use assistive digital technologies. (P1) also is convinced that caregivers can have an import role as trustees of the aging population to make them familiar with assistive digital technologies. Most caregivers enjoy the trust of the individuals they visit they are taking care of on a

regular basis. For (P2), the motivation lies the potential a Digital Twin could have as a digital personal coach, which functions as an awareness creator, a digital advisor which also could refer individuals to human coaches, such as dietitian or sleep coaches and so forth. (P2) also pointed out that the lifestyle of humans is important to evaluate the whole process of patients. Combined with the medical data one would get a more holistic view on the individual. (P3) argued that the ability to stay longer at home would be a big motivator for individuals, also to avoid illness, but that is difficult to do. (P3) also mentioned that some individuals would not be able to cope with the thought of getting all that information on themselves and that patients already today say no, they don't want to know all the details on what possibly could happen to them.

The findings of patients not being able to cope with all the knowledge digital data might give, is something that also rises in the second question we discussed. What would a medical staff see as a worry with all the digital data that could come available for the patient through a Digital Twin. Patients would share the data with the caregivers, but whether they are resilient enough to grasp and deal with the information is another question. This is depending on the personality of the patient.

How Could the Ecosystem Work with a Digital Twin?

All the stakeholder participants were convinced that there is a need to have open and uniform standards of all the systems that are in use or will come in use in the future. This is not an easy task, and this is a responsibility of the government (P1, P2), that hospitals have open standards towards the caregivers and general practitioners, to create interoperability of the systems. Patients have access and can or have to give consent to look at their data if it is someone outside the medical environment. The medical data that comes in, is always discussed with the general practitioner. The general practitioner gives advice, for example, to start a trial for a week to measure their heartrate with a digital application for example, to see when there are critical moments. This was conceived as very helpful. (P2) mentioned again the functionality of a digital personal coach before going to a human coach, the complementarity between the two could be very helpful.

Is There a Need for a Cheating Function with the Digital Twin?

In contrast with the boomers, all three of the stakeholder participants were convinced that it is human to cheat. Humans are always presenting themselves better than they are. (P1) said: *'If I go to my general practitioner to have a check-up and to have a blood sample, the three days before I will eat differently, drink less, be aware of my behavior, while I shouldn't do that. I should behave as I normally do, but I don't'.* (P2) said: *'I don't believe in objective evaluations by patients'. Take smoking for example, smoking you cannot monitor unless you do it manually and if they are addicted it is even a bigger problem'.* (P3) argued that the patient always has the right to say no or to stop for a while in giving data or to monitor themselves.

Who is the Owner of the Digital Twin?

Just as with the boomers, they all agreed that the patient is the owner of his or her Digital Twin. *'It is a sine qua non'* says (P2).

What Happens When You Die with the Digital Twin?
(P3) Today the data is anonymized, and it is archived for 30 years when patients die, this is defined by the Belgian law. (P2) *'It would be interesting to have access to the data of a population to see how a certain city or even country is doing health wise. This might be a role for the WHO (World Health Organization)'* But the patient always gives consent what happens with the data. He or she decides, he or she is in control.

How Do We Conceptualize a Digital Twin?
Depending on the personality, maybe people can choose? (P1) says: *'In my experience it would be a database where we work with algorithms. Although I'm always apprehensive, it is only an algorithm, what is it going to invest and what will it exactly do?* (P2): *'It could be a little robot. Maybe other people prefer something else, maybe there are options. The question is also how the data is entered, who can see the data and where does it stop?'* (P2) sees it possible that a social sorting could be possible. But in Belgian healthcare this would not be possible, he argues. But of course, it can be done. Practice shows that a lower class excels in messing with their health, social sorting would underline that phenomenon. (P3): *I think the data would be in the cloud, something like that. The medical data is separated from the other data such as lifestyle data and so forth in terms of accessibility. I think China has probably the most Digital Twins, 'I saw this documentary, the surveillance that is going on, this is absolutely to be avoided. These applications exist and applied'*, (P3) continues *'I'm always worried about this surveillance, the abuse or misuse of these applications'*.

Should It Be a Bottom-Up or Top-Down Initiative?
(P1) thinks it might be bottom-up initiative in forms of living labs, although a lot of living labs die and face the 'valley of death'. Somehow one should be able to get over that point and try to create a fit-to-market. If it would happen in a top-down scenario, (P1) thinks in that case, there would be a lot of resistance from the potential users to get a Digital Twin.

Both (P2) and (P3) are convinced that security is a top priority. In that sense both also argued it should not reside within a government, *'you never know what regime one will get in the future'*. Although both find that regulation is something that should come from the top through privacy commissions or an 'order of ethics in medicine'.

To conclude, data leaks and security are the biggest concerns in a digital twin concept from a medical point of view but also from the boomer's perspective.

5   Conclusions, Limitations and Future Research

In this paper we presented a theoretical overview on 'Aging in Place' combined with 'Digital Twin' theory. To understand the notion of the Digital Twin we also build on the notion of a 'Biometric Daemon' [4], this is the notion of an electronic pet researched for authentication and identity recognition, we see possible similarities in this concept for the notion of a Digital Twin. Further in our research we conducted in-depth interviews with eight boomers (1946–1964), 60+ and 70+, and three stakeholders in the care cycle of elderly people to get more insights on following research questions: *"To which extent do technologies such as wearable device and mobile applications, leading towards a 'Digital Twin' concept within preventive and predictive healthcare give human enhancement towards personal healthcare?"* The added value or human enhancement for participants lies in the medical and lifestyle overview participants might get from a Digital Twin. Participants would use it to adjust their behavior when needed, in that sense participants are also convinced it could help them to stay longer at home and have the ability to 'Aging in Place". For the stakeholders the latter has a lot of added value as well. They could perform short trials based on the information they get from the patients Digital Twin leading towards personal medicine. On the flip side, participants worry about the privacy and security of the data, although the security side was more a worry on the stakeholder side, but privacy of data is a concern for all, it has to comply with the rules of 'Privacy by Design [8] and AI Trustworthy guidelines [2]. The discussion that big data could be used for social sorting and stimulating inequality was something participants perceived as a threat in our democracy and is part of the political debate. The next research question we explored in our research was *"how do elderly users handle or think about the data they (might) gather?"* Our findings show that in general participants would be motivated to nurture a Digital Twin if it would help them to make decisions about certain health issues they might have or health issues that could occur in the future. However most of the participants were not interested in forecasting life expectations through a data-driven approach. Furthermore, some participants argued that today, forecasting on certain diseases or possible injuries is already possible today and possibly more accurate in the future. In addition, participants also stressed on the affordability of assistive digital technologies in terms of usability and user-experience. The ease of use and rules of simplicity should apply [14, 37, 38] no complex brain cycles, no manuals to learn, on and off buttons should be as easy to push the button, see 'Hello Jenny' [22]. Related to the previous research question we also want to go deeper on *"how the elderly would give meaning to their data"*. The participants who already track themselves for several reasons (prepare for marathons or recovering from health issues), mainly track their physical activity, nutrition aspects or other biomarkers such as blood pressure, glucose, are discussing their data with a general practitioner as to understand the data they gather. However the medical stakeholders argued that patients are not always eager to know about their health or the risks they have when they continue their lifestyle and not making any changes. In addition, they also argued that patients are not always honest about their lifestyle they lead either. This was a big contrast, as on the participant's side they didn't see any reason to cheat with the Digital Twin. Our last research question was specifically towards the medical stakeholders: *"How will different stakeholders within the healthcare and caregiving organizations be organized around the concept of a Digital Twin?"* It is clear that the stakeholders active in a medical environment are concerned about the security of the digital data that is gathered through a Digital Twin. On an individual level, data from the patient but also as a whole, the big data phenomenon from today. What it can entail in terms of social sorting and the possibility to evolve to an exclusive society instead of an inclusive society, creating inequality as a norm [39]. Stakeholders argued this is already happening today, but when everything becomes data-driven, the stakes are even higher. For now, digital technologies don't have empathy, there is no context within the data-driven world today [42]. This is a point of attention; therefore, these assistive digital technologies have to be complementary and have a facilitating function for the medical professionals.

On the other hand, the stakeholders see a lot of positive elements to stimulate awareness and behavior change possibilities when necessary with patients. Furthermore, they see value in starting little trials to help patients whether they need adjustments of medication, going towards more personalized medicine. As a last comment they had, in order to get a full potential out of a Digital Twin, there need to be standards in the systems that are in place today in the hospitals and caregiving organizations, they need to be interoperable in order to look at correlations and to create more context around a certain individual and his or her Digital Twin.

The limitations of this research lies in the fact that the notion of a Digital Twin is an abstract concept for the participants, especially for the boomers. As researchers we paid less focus on the constraints of the notion of a Digital Twin, this is subject for further research.

Future research should give more insight on how we can conceptualize a Digital Twin, will it be an object or just AI software or both. Furthermore, we could explore the design requirements taking in account also the constraints that these assistive digital technologies could induce and considering the affordance for an aging population. In addition, exploring design research on adaptive technologies and adaptive objects.

References

1. Adams, S.: Digital 'solutions' to unhealthy lifestyle 'problems': the construction of social and personal risks in the development of eCoaches. Health Risk Soc. **17**(7–8), 530–546 (2016)
2. AI HLEG: Ethics Guidelines For Trustworthy AI, Brussels (2019). https://ec.europa.eu/digital-single-market/en/news/ethics-guidelines-trustworthy-ai
3. Braun, V.: Using thematic analysis in psychology. Qual. Res. Psychol. **3**(2), 77–101 (2006)
4. Briggs, P.: Biometric daemons: authentication via electronic pets. In: Proceedings of the 1st Conference on Usability, Psychology, and Security (UPSEC 2008), San Francisco (2008)
5. Broadbent, E.: Acceptance of healthcare robots for the older population: review and future directions. Int. J. Soc. Robot. **1**(4), 319 (2009). https://doi.org/10.1007/s12369-009-0030-6
6. Broekens, J.: Assistive social robots in elderly care: a review. Gerontechnology **8**, 94–103 (2009)
7. Bruynseels, K.: Digital twins in health care: ethical implications of an emerging engineering paradigm. Front. Genet. **9**, 31 (2018)
8. Cavoukian, A.: Privacy by design, seven foundational principles (2009). https://www.ryerson.ca/pbdce/certification/seven-foundational-principles-of-privacy-by-design/
9. Choe, E.: Understanding quantified-selfers' practices in collecting and exploring personal data. In: CHI 2014. ACM, Toronto (2014)
10. De Maeyer, C.: Exploring quantified self attitudes. In: Biomedical Engineering Systems and Technologies (BIOSTEC 2018), pp. 253–260 (2018)
11. Dohr, A.: The Internet of Things for ambient assisted living. In: Seventh International Conference on Information Technology: New Generations. IEEE (2010)
12. El Saddik, A.: Digital Twins: the convergence of multimedia technologies. IEEE Multimedia Comput. Soc. **25**, 87–92 (2018)

13. Epstein: Beyond abandonment to next steps: understanding and designing for life after personal informatics tool use. In: CHI 2016, 07–12 May 2016, San Jose, CA, USA. ACM, San Jose (2016)
14. Fogg, B.J.: A behavior model for persuasive design. In: Proceedings of the 4th International Conference on Persuasive Technology (Persuasive 2009) (2009)
15. Gibson, J.: The Ecological Approach to Visual Perception, 1st edn. Routledge, Abingdon (1986)
16. Giddens, A.: Agency, structure. In: Giddens, A. (ed.) Central Problems in Social Theory. Contemporary Social Theory. Palgrave, London (1979)
17. Gimpel, H.: Quantifying the quantified self: a study on the motivations of patients to track their own health. In: Thirty Fourth International Conference on Information Systems, Milan (2013)
18. Graybill, E.M.: Can aging in place be cost effective? A systematic review. PLoS One **9**, e102705 (2014)
19. Grieves, M.: Digital Twin: Manufacturing Excellence through Virtual Factory Replication, USA (2014)
20. Himmel, S., Ziefle, M.: Smart home medical technologies: users' requirements for conditional acceptance. i-com **15**(1), 39–50 (2016)
21. Hsu, Y.L.: Design and implementation of a smart home system using multisensor data fusion technology. Sensors (Basel) **17**, 1631 (2017)
22. iMec: Hello Jenny (2019). https://www.imec-int.com/nl/imec-magazine/imec-magazine-april-2019/how-can-you-help-lonely-seniors-not-with-a-talking-flowerpot-but-by-having-people-actually-go-and-visit-them-courtesy-of-technology
23. iMec, et al.: Proact2020 (2016–2019). http://proact2020.eu/
24. Kanamori, M.M.: Evaluation of animal-assisted therapy for the elderly with senile dementia in a day care program. Am. J. Alzheimer's Dis. Other Dementias **16**(4), 234–239 (2001)
25. Karvonen, S., et al.: Who needs the sociology of health and illness? A new agenda for responsive and interdisciplinary sociology of health and medicine. Front. Sociol. **3**, 4 (2018)
26. Longueville, L.: AIPA (2014–2016). https://www.flanderscare.be/project/zorgproeftuin-aipa-ageing-place-aalst
27. Loos, E.: Generational Use of New Media. Ashgate, Farnham (2012)
28. Lupton, D.: Self-tracking Modes: Reflexive Self-Monitoring and Data Practices. Imminent Citizenships: Personhood and Identity Politics in the Informatic Age (2014)
29. Lupton, D.: Living Digital Data Research Program (2016). https://simplysociology.wordpress.com/2016/02/28/living-digital-data-research-program/
30. Lupton, D.: The Quantified Self. Polity Press, Cambridge (2016)
31. Lupton, D.: Data Selves. Polity Press, Cambridge (2019)
32. Lyon, D.: Surveillance, power and everyday life. In: David, L. (ed.) The Oxford Handbook of Information and Communication Technologies, Oxford (2009)
33. Marshall, B.: How Old Am I? Digital Culture and Quantified Ageing. DCS (Digital Culture and Society), vol. 2, issue 1 (2017)
34. Martin, B.: Universal Methods of Design. Rockport Publishers (2012)
35. Moyle, W., Cooke, M., Beattie, E., et al.: Exploring the effect of companion robots on emotional expression in older adults with dementia: a pilot randomized controlled trial. J. Gerontol. Nurs. **39**(5), 46–53 (2013). https://doi.org/10.3928/00989134-20130313-03
36. Mynatt, E.D.: Increasing the opportunities for aging in place. In: Proceedings on the 2000 Conference on Universal Usability (CUU 2000), pp. 65–71. ACM, New York (2000)
37. Norman, D.: Things That Make Us Smarter. Diversion Books, New York (1993)
38. Norman, D.: Living with Complexity. MIT Press, Cambridge, London (2010)
39. O'Neil, C.: Weapons of Math Destruction. Penguin Books, New York (2016)

40. Owyang, J.: Modern Wellbeing (2019). http://www.web-strategist.com/blog/category/modern-wellbeing/
41. Pew Research, Vogels E.: us-generations-technology-use (2019). https://www.pewresearch.org/fact-tank/2019/09/09/us-generations-technology-use/ft_19-09-03_digitaldividegenerations_1/
42. PWC: BodyLogic (2018). https://www.youtube.com/watch?v=dzy9G18Bn_8
43. Ruckenstein, M., Pantzar, M.: Beyond the quantified self: thematic exploration of a dataistic paradigm. New Media Soc. **19**(3), 401–418 (2017). https://doi.org/10.1177/1461444815609081
44. Saracco, R.: can-we-have-a-digital-twin/. IEEE.org (2017). https://cmte.ieee.org/futuredirections/2017/09/27/can-we-have-a-digital-twin/
45. Schwanda, V.: Side effects and 'gateway' tools: advocating a broader look at evaluating persuasive systems. In: CHI 2011. ACM, Vancouver (2011)
46. Sloane, M., Moss, E.: AI's social sciences deficit. Nat. Mach. Intell. **1**, 330–331 (2019). https://doi.org/10.1038/s42256-019-0084-6
47. Smith, J.G.D.: Surveillance, data and embodiment: on the work of being watched. Body Soc. **22**(2), 108–139 (2016)
48. Stojkoska, B.R.: Internet of Things framework for home care systems. Wirel. Commun. Mob. Comput. **2017**, 1–10 (2017)
49. Sharon, T.: Self-tracking for health and the quantified self: re-articulating autonomy, solidarity, and authenticity in an age of personalized healthcare. Philos. Technol. **30**(1), 93–121 (2017). https://doi.org/10.1007/s13347-016-0215-5
50. Turkle, S.: Reclaiming conversation. Penguin Press, New York (2015)
51. Wiles, J.L., et al.: The meaning of "aging in place" to older people. The Gerontologist **52**(3), 357–366 (2012)
52. World Health Organisation: World report on ageing and health 2015. World Health Organisation (2015)

Persuasive Design Strategy of Online Health Education for Elderly Adults Based on TAM Model

Yongyan Guo[✉]

School of Art Design and Media,
East China University of Science and Technology, Shanghai, China
g_gale@163.com

Abstract. With China's entering into an aging society, health education on aging has been attached great importance. Health education refers to planned, organized and systematic social education activities. The core of health education is to help people to establish health awareness, promote people to change unhealthy behavior and life style, develop good behavior and life style, so as to reduce or eliminate the risk factors affecting health. However, there are some problems in the current health education of aging. The elderly lack of health awareness and learning ability. The community lacks high-quality health education personnel and teaching materials. The emergence of online health education media helps to overcome some existing problems and improve the accuracy and systematization of health education for the elderly. In order to improve the acceptance effect of online health education technology, this paper combined the technology acceptance model (TAM) and persuasive strategy design (PSD) model to study the elderly's acceptance of online health education APP, as well as the influencing factors of the elderly's technology acceptance attitude.

Keywords: Aging · Online health education · Technology acceptance model · Persuasive design strategy

1 Introduction

China's aging population is deepening. It is estimated that in 2025, the population over 60 years old will exceed 300 million, and China will become a super aged country. It can be seen that the population aging problem of China is imminent [1]. In order to reduce the medical pressure brought by aging population, Healthy Aging and Active Aging are put on the agenda. Du Xiaoping [2] explored the implementation effect and method of community health management in the context of population aging. It was found that the implementation of health education management for the elderly can improve their unhealthy living habits and control the occurrence of chronic diseases.

Therefore, the health awareness and health literacy of the elderly should be improved through mobile health education technology. The research aim of this paper is to combine TAM and PSD, to study the comprehensive technology acceptance model of online health education for the elderly. The influencing factors and the path relationship among the elements are also explained.

© Springer Nature Switzerland AG 2020
Q. Gao and J. Zhou (Eds.): HCII 2020, LNCS 12208, pp. 269–281, 2020.
https://doi.org/10.1007/978-3-030-50249-2_20

2   Related Work

2.1   Research on Health Education Technology

The main methods of traditional health education include oral health education, education cards and manuals, health lectures, telephone follow-up and so on, which have low sustainability and compliance. With the development of mobile Internet technology, instant messaging programs based on smart phones are more widely used, and mobile medical service has been used in health education by foreign scholars [3].

Most of the existing research focuses on health education based on Wechat platform. The research content is mainly about the effectiveness of health education with Wechat [4]. Cui Huaqian [5] combined with the relevant theory of PRECEDE-PROCEED model, compared the excellent health management experience at China and abroad. The personalized service mode for the health management of urban community residents is explored combined with the modern Internet of things information technology.

2.2   Technology Acceptance Theory for the Elderly

The commonly used Technology Acceptance model (TAM) is a model proposed by Davis [6] to study the user's acceptance of information system. This model is widely used to study the decisive factors of the user's acceptance of new technologies. Technology acceptance model includes perceived usefulness, perceived ease of use, attitude toward using, and behavioral intention to use (Davis [6], Davis et al. [7]) (Fig. 1).

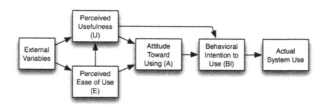

Fig. 1. Technology Acceptance Model (TAM)

Braun [8] used the TAM to study the barriers of 124 people over 60 years old to use social network services. The results showed that social pressure and perceived ease of use did not significantly affect the behavior intention of the elderly to use social network services, while self-enabling factors indirectly affected the behavior intention through perceived usefulness and of use. Yong et al. [9] used TAM and PBT to study the influencing factors of the elderly people's acceptance of social media. The results show that perceived usefulness and perceived ease of use have significant influence, while perceived ready availability of service has indirect influence through perceived usefulness. Chakraborty [10] explore the privacy problems of the elderly when using social network services from the information sharing behavior through the research on the use of Facebook by the elderly. The initial adoption of information technology does not guarantee that users will continue to use the technology. However, the traditional TAM provides a universal model to explain or predict the use of information technology, but due to the wide range of types of information technology, the model should be expanded in different usage situations.

2.3   Persuasive Design Model

Persuasive design is a design method to promote users to use information technology. Oinas-Kukkonen and Harjumaa [11] proposed PSD model, which is mainly used for persuasive information system development and evaluation. This model focuses on the detailed analysis of persuasive situations, events and strategies. 28 persuasive design strategies are provided and four dimensions are divided: primary task support, dialogue support, system credibility support and social support.

Table 1. PSD model

PSD	
Primary task support:	Reduction, Tunnelling, Tailoring, Personalization, Self-monitoring, Simulation, Rehearsal
Dialogue support:	Praise, Rewards, Reminders, Suggestion, Similarity, Liking, Social role
System credibility support:	Trustworthiness, Expertise, Surface credibility, Real-world feel, Authority, Third-party Endorsements, Verifiability
Social support:	Social learning, Social comparison, Normative Influence, Social facilitation, Cooperation, Competition, Recognition

Based on the model, many researchers have studied the effect and internal relationship of different persuasive strategies on user behavior. Sitwat Langrial [12] suggests that when developing persuasive system, customized information for different user groups should be provided, human-computer interaction should be promoted by integrating software functions (such as social prompts, feedback and virtual rewards), and users' behavior should be encouraged by enhancing social support. A structural model is studied to explain the effect of perceived persuasiveness on behavior change support system (Filip Drozd, Tuomas Lehto and Harri Oinas-Kukkonen [13]). This model verifies that dialogue support has a positive impact on perceived persuasiveness and perceived credibility, while perceived persuasiveness and non-abruptness have a positive impact on willingness to use.

However, in the context of persuading elderly users to use Health Education APP, we need to know which persuasive dimensions have a positive impact on perceived usefulness, perceived ease of use, accept attitude and behavior intention of elderly users, so as to use reasonable persuasive strategies in the future design. Therefore, the main purpose of this paper is to combine the PSD model and TAM to study the persuasive factors that affect the elderly users' health education technology acceptance behavior, as well as the relationship between the factors in the TAM model.

3 Research Methods

3.1 Conceptual Model and Research Hypothesis

Persuasive Factors. After literature review and content analysis of Health Education APP, Delphi method is used and six main persuasive factors are discussed by five experts: Perceived ease of use (PEOU), Perceived Credibility (PC), Perceived Social Support (PSS), Perceived Persuasiveness (PP), Sense of Achievement (SOA) and Perceived Entertainment (PE). The hypotheses for forming persuasive factors are as follows:

H1: PEOU has a positive effect on PC
H2: PEOU has a positive effect on PSS
H3: PC has positive effect on PP
H4: PC has positive effect on PE
H5: PEOU has a positive impact on SOA
H6: PEOU has a positive effect on PP
H7: PEOU has a positive effect on PE
H8: PSS has a positive impact on SOA
H9: PSS has a positive effect on PP
H10: PSS has a positive effect on PE
H11: SOA has a positive impact on PC

Factors of TAM. Because the measurement content of Perceived Main Task Support and Perceived Ease of Use is similar, the firs factor is kept in this paper. With the three factors of TAM model, Perception Usefulness (PU), Attitude (at) and Behavior Intention (BI), the following assumptions are formed.

H12: SOA has a positive impact on PU
H13: PP has a positive effect on PU
H14: PE has a positive effect on PP
H15: Pu has a positive effect on BI
H16: Pu has a positive effect on at
H17: PP has a positive impact on BI
H18: PP has a positive effect on at
H19: PE has a positive effect on at
H20: at has a positive effect on BI

The structure model is shown in Fig. 2.

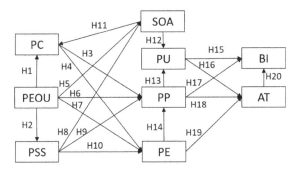

Fig. 2. Construct model

3.2   Measurement Index

The questionnaire consists of three parts: introduction, personal information measurement and variable measurement. The introduction is the notes for filling in the questionnaire. The personal information measurement is the basic information of the respondents, involving age, gender, education background, etc. In the scale questions, Likert five level scale is used to score, in which 1 = non conformity, 2 = relatively non conformity, 3 = general, 4 = relatively conformity, 5 = conformity. All variables were measured by more than three measures, which were adapted from the existing literature to ensure the validity of the scale.

The measurement indexes include: Perceived ease of use (PEOU), Perceived usefulness (PU), Perceived Credibility (PC), Perceived Social Support (PSS), Perceived Persuasiveness (PP), Sense of Achievement (SOA), Perceived Entertainment (PE), Attitude (AT) and Behavioral intention (BI). According to the mature scale in the existing literature, the measurement indicators of the structure model are formed, and the detailed items of each structure are listed in Table 2.

Table 2. Questionnaire content (HEA-Health Education APP)

Variable	Serial number	Item	Source
Perceived Ease of Use (PEOU)	PEOU1	I think HEA is clear and easy to understand	Davis et al. [14]
	PEOU2	I find HEA doesn't need much mental work	
	PEOU3	I found HEA easy to use	
Perceived Usefulness (PU)	PU1	Using HEA will improve my effectiveness in managing my personal health	Davis et al. [14]
	PU2	Using HEA will improve my efficiency in learning health knowledge	
	PU3	HEA will improve my health knowledge	

(continued)

Table 2. (*continued*)

Variable	Serial number	Item	Source
Perceived Credibility (PC)	PC1 PC2 PC3	In my opinion, HEA is reliable/credible In my opinion, the content of HEA is professional HEA is reliable in protecting users' privacy	Lehto, T., et al. [15]
Perceived Social Support (PSS)	PSS1 PSS2 PSS3	My family thinks I should use HEA My doctor thinks I should use HEA My peers will think (suggest, encourage) that I should use HEA	Venkatesh, V., et al. [16]
Perceived Persuasiveness (PP)	PP1 PP2 PP3	HEA has an impact on my health concept HEA asked me to rethink my healthy lifestyle I think HEA helps to increase my healthy behavior	T. Lehto, et al. [17], Y.K. Bartlett [18]
Sense of Achievement (SOA)	SOA1 SOA2 SOA3	When I learned new health knowledge, I was very excited When I learn new health knowledge, I feel a sense of achievement I think it's worth the time and effort to use HEA	L. Meng [19]
Perceived Entertainment (PE)	PE1 PE2 PE3	It's fun to use HEA It is pleasant to use HEA Using HEA can satisfy my curiosity	Venkatesh, et al. [16]
Attitude (AT)	AT1 AT2 AT3	I think it's a good idea to use HEA I think it's good for me to use HEA I have a positive view on the use of HEA	Fishbein and Ajzen [20]
Behavioral Intention (BI)	BI1 BI2 BI3	I plan to use HEA in the future In my daily life, I will always try to use HEA I plan to use HEA often	Venkatesh, et al. [16]

3.3   Data Analysis

Data Collection and Sample Information. According to the purpose of the survey, online questionnaire and paper questionnaire were used. Because the aim of this study is to understand the technical acceptance of Health Education APP in the context of aging, we mainly invited the people beyond 50 years old who have experience in using Health Education APP. Finally, total of 380 questionnaires were distributed on the Wenjuanxing internet platform and offline, and 333 valid questionnaires were obtained, with a recovery rate of 87.6%. The sample size meets the statistical needs of the next empirical study. The basic information statistics of the total sample size of the effective questionnaire is shown in Table 3.

Table 3. Basic information statistics

Gender	Frequency	Proportion
Male	166	49.85%
Female	167	50.15%
Total	333	100%
Age	Frequency	Proportion
50–59 years old˙	111	33.33%
60–69 years old	170	51.05%
Over 70 years old	52	15.62%
Education level	Frequency	Proportion
Below junior middle school	173	51.95%
High school	136	40.84%
Undergraduate	17	5.11%
Master's degree or above	7	2.1%
Monthly income	Frequency	Proportion
Under 2000 yuan	38	11.41%
2001–5000 yuan	253	75.98%
5001–10000 yuan	23	6.91%
Over 10001 yuan	19	5.71%

Reliability Test and Validity Test of Questionnaire. In this paper, software SPSS 20 is used to analyzed the reliability and validity of the sample data. By analyzing the KMO value of the nine core variables, the validity was analyzed to determine the correctness of the questionnaire. Generally, the higher the validity coefficient is, the better the sample can be measured. KMO value of this sample is shown in Table 4. The KMO value is 0.978, more than 0.9, Sig. coefficient is less than 0.05, indicating that the sample data has a high validity.

Table 4. Validity value (KMO and Bartlett's test)

Kaiser-Meyer-Olkin measure of sampling adequacy		.978
Bartlett's test of sphericity	Approx. Chi-Square	6735.385
	df	351
	Sig.	.000

The Cronbach alpha value of the core variable means the credibility and stability of the questionnaire. Cronbach's α $(0 < \alpha < 1)$ is used to measure the reliability of the scale. Generally, the larger the α coefficient is, the higher the reliability of the questionnaire is. When the α coefficient is greater than 0.6, the reliability of the scale is better. The core variable Cronbach's α of this sample is shown in Table 5. The analysis shows that the combined reliability of each factor of the sample data is greater than 0.70, which indicates that the questionnaire has a good reliability.

Table 5. Reliability and composite reliability (CR).

Variable	Cronbach's Alpha	Item
Perceived Ease of Use (PEOU)	0.737	3
Perceived Usefulness (PU)	0.742	3
Perceived Credibility (PC)	0.753	3
Perceived Social Support (PSS)	0.754	3
Perceived Persuasiveness (PP)	0.753	3
Sense of Achievement (SOA)	0.752	3
Perceived Entertainment (PE)	0.759	3
Attitude (AT)	0.739	3
Behavioral Intention (BI)	0.768	3

According to the correlation coefficient matrix (Table 6), the AVE values of all variables are higher than 0.5, indicating that the questionnaire has good convergence validity. In addition, the square root value of the mean variance extraction value (AVE) is higher than the correlation coefficient between the variables, indicating that the validity of the questionnaire is good.

Table 6. Correlation coefficient matrix and square root of AVE

	PEOU	PSS	SOA	PC	PE	PP	PU	AT	BI
PEOU	**.844**								
PSS	.722	**.859**							
SOA	.720	.716	**.831**						
PC	.749	.740	.733	**.873**					
PE	.738	.734	.688	.747	**.874**				
PP	.753	.747	.706	.763	.758	**.876**			
PU	.716	.710	.693	.726	.715	.733	**.804**		
AT	.724	.719	.679	.733	.722	.734	.698	**.842**	
BI	.776	.770	.737	.787	.778	.797	.757	.763	**.943**

In conclusion, the reliability and validity of each variable in this study meet the requirements of further hypothesis testing.

Analysis and Modification of Path Model. In this study, software Amos 24 was used to analyze the path model of questionnaire data. First, the fitting degree is analyzed, and the fitting indexes are shown in Table 7. The results show that all the indexes are within the acceptable range, so the theoretical model established in this paper has a good fit.

Table 7. Path model fitting index analysis

Index	P	X^2/df	GFI	RMR	RMSEA	AGFI	NFI	CFI	IFI
Standard	>0.05	1–3	>0.9	<0.05	<0.1	>0.9	>0.9	>0.9	>0.9
Measure	0.200	1.331	0.990	0.005	0.032	0.961	0.997	0.999	0.999
Result	Yes	Yes	Yes	Yes	Yes	Yes	Yes	Yes	Yes

Import the data in Amos model. In Table 8, the path coefficient of two hypotheses is not significant because the path significance coefficient P > 0.05, and the CR value of one path (PP <— PSS) is negative (−1.596). Therefore, this path is delated firstly to make model correction.

Table 8. Regression weights: (group number 1 - default model)

			Estimate	S.E.	C.R.	P	Label
PSS	<—	PEOU	.855	.029	29.153	***	par_19
SOA	<—	PSS	.415	.047	8.875	***	par_2
SOA	<—	PEOU	.499	.047	10.588	***	par_7
PC	<—	SOA	.296	.051	5.775	***	par_8
PC	<—	PEOU	.635	.050	12.655	***	par_24
PE	<—	PSS	.303	.044	6.897	***	par_3
PE	<—	PC	.296	.047	6.244	***	par_22
PE	<—	PEOU	.352	.047	7.411	***	par_23
PP	<—	PC	.576	.162	3.548	***	par_1
PP	<—	PEOU	.793	.261	3.037	.002	par_6
PP	<—	PE	.226	.038	6.015	***	par_21
PP	<—	PSS	−.713	.447	−1.596	.110	par_25
PU	<—	SOA	.082	.064	1.281	.200	par_16
PU	<—	PP	.872	.067	12.950	***	par_20
AT	<—	PE	.704	.080	8.792	***	par_5
AT	<—	PP	.142	.060	2.358	.018	par_10
AT	<—	PU	.136	.060	2.275	.023	par_17
BI	<—	PP	.500	.060	8.395	***	par_4
BI	<—	AT	.142	.052	2.726	.006	par_9
BI	<—	PU	.413	.059	6.983	***	par_18

Recalculate the modified model and obtain the hypothesis results by observing the significance coefficient of the path (Table 9). The results show that four hypotheses are 0.01 < P < 0.05, and 15 hypotheses are very significant (P < 0.001).

Table 9. Modified regression weight

Hypothesis	Route			Estimate	S.E.	C.R.	P	Result
H1	**PC**	<—	PEOU	.631	.050	12.610	***	Support
H2	**PSS**	<—	PEOU	.855	.029	29.083	***	Support
H3	**PP**	<—	PC	.323	.040	8.000	***	Support
H4	**PE**	<—	PC	.296	.047	6.241	***	Support
H5	**SOA**	<—	PEOU	.499	.047	10.606	***	Support
H6	**PP**	<—	PEOU	.398	.043	9.318	***	Support
H7	**PE**	<—	PEOU	.352	.047	7.434	***	Support
H8	**SOA**	<—	PSS	.415	.047	8.897	***	Support
H10	**PE**	<—	PSS	.303	.044	6.895	***	Support
H11	**PC**	<—	SOA	.301	.051	5.901	***	Support
H12	**PU**	<—	SOA	.142	.049	2.921	.003	Support**
H13	**PU**	<—	PP	.815	.053	15.274	***	Support
H14	**PP**	<—	PE	.238	.038	6.180	***	Support
H15	**BI**	<—	PU	.403	.058	6.925	***	Support
H16	**AT**	<—	PU	.136	.060	2.276	.023	Support*
H17	**BI**	<—	PP	.513	.059	8.619	***	Support
H18	**AT**	<—	PP	.142	.060	2.365	.018	Support*
H19	**AT**	<—	PE	.704	.081	8.740	***	Support
H20	**BI**	<—	AT	.141	.052	2.687	.007	Support**

Note: if $P < 0.05$, the significance level is acceptable (*); if $P < 0.01$, the significance level is good (**); if $P < 0.001$, the significance level is very high (**)

After path deletion, the PSD-TAM model and path coefficient are obtained (Fig. 3).

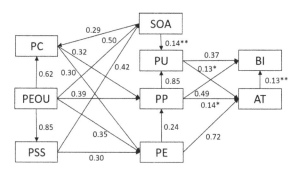

Fig. 3. PSD-TAM model and standard path coefficient (Note: path p value without asterisk is very significant***)

4   Discussion

The aim of this study is to explore the influencing factors and behavioral intentions of elderly users when using online health education technology, and to combine persuasive design model and Technology Acceptance Model (TAM) for research. There are seven persuasive elements in the model: Perceived Ease of Use (PEOU), Perceived Usefulness (PU), Perceived Credibility (PC), Perceived Social Support (PSS), Perceived Persuasiveness (PP), Sense of Achievement (SOA) and Perceived Entertainment (PE). The experimental results provide a new perspective for constructing PSD-TAM models. PU, PP and PE are the key factors influencing user acceptance attitude (AT). PU and PP are the key factors that influence Behavioral Intention (BI). From the perspective of significance, PU has a very significant impact on AT and BI, while PP has a significant impact on AT and BI, which indicates that persuasive factors have a positive impact on elderly usage of Health Education APP, but its impact is less than PU. According to the analysis results, in order to improve the elderly users' acceptance Attitude and behavior Intention of Health Education APP, we need to design better product Perceived Usefulness (PU) and Perceived Persuasiveness (PP).

In this study, Persuasive Design Technology Acceptance Model (PSD-TAM) was developed to predict the technology acceptance attitude and behavior intention of Chinese elderly people using Health Education APP. PP has a significant direct effect on PU. SOA has a significant effect on PU. PEOU, PC and PSS have significant direct effects on SOA and PE, respectively. PEOU and PC have a significant direct impact on PP. These conclusions are consistent with the research of other scholars. Therefore, persuasive factors should be added to promote the use of health education APP for the elderly. However, PSS has no significant direct effect on PP. PSS has a significant direct impact on PE, and then indirectly on PP. In order to improve the effect of Perceived Persuasiveness (PP), entertainment elements should be introduced in the design of Health Education APP for elderly users. For example, through the gamification user experience design, the user's sense of pleasure should be improved, so as to enhance the user's acceptance attitude and behavior intention.

There are some limits in this paper. Firstly, the small-scale user survey was taken at present, and a larger scale survey should be carried out in the future to verify the reliability of this model. Secondly, the persuasive factors that affect the elderly users' intention and behavior of using health education App need to be further studied. In the future, we will study the adoption method of persuasive strategies for different elderly users.

5   Conclusions

Based on the TAM model, the aim of this study is to find out the key factors and the internal mechanism that affect the elderly's technology acceptance attitude and behavior intention of using Health Education APP. The results showed that the Perceived Usefulness (PU) and Perceived Persuasiveness (PP) of products had a significant positive impact on user's Acceptance Attitude (AT) and Behavior Intention (BI). The results of this study provide some significant theoretical contributions to the literature of persuasive design and TAM research. The PSD-TAM model explains the influencing factors and influencing mechanism of technology acceptance of Health Education APP for elderly users. This study will help designers and developers to better understand the behavior characteristics of elderly people. These findings provide valuable information for the online system and health care stakeholders to promote the Health Education APP that the elderly is more willing to accept and use.

Acknowledgements. This study is supported by the Youth Fund for Humanities and Social Sciences Research of the Ministry of Education, No. 17YJCZH055.

References

1. Zhiyan Consulting Network: China's population aging Market Research and Development Trend Research Report 2019–2025. http://www.chyxx.com/industry/201805/641672.html
2. Du, X.: Research on community health management model in the context of population aging. World Clin. Med. **11**(5), 59–62 (2017)
3. Wang, P., Zhao, Q., et al.: Application progress of mobile medicine in health education of patients with coronary heart disease. China Nurs. Manag. **18**(7), 953–958 (2018)
4. Luo, J., Fu, J., et al.: The impact of health education based on Wechat platform on the health literacy and healthy lifestyle of residents in three municipal districts of Sichuan Province. China Health Educ. **35**(3), 231–234 (2019)
5. Cui, H.: Construction of community health management model based on PRECEDE-PROCEED Model – Based on the survey of health management willingness of community residents in Guangzhou. Southern Medical University, Guangzhou (2017)
6. Davis, F.D.: Perceived usefulness, perceived ease of use, and user acceptance of information technology. MIS Q. **13**(3), 319–340 (1989)
7. Davis, F.D., et al.: User acceptance of computer technology: a comparison of two theoretical models. Manag. Sci. **35**, 982–1003 (1989)
8. Braun, M.T.: Obstacles to social networking website use among older adults. Comput. Hum. Behav. **29**, 673–680 (2013)
9. Ji, Y.G.: Older adults in an aging society and social computing: a research agenda. Int. J. Hum.-Comput. Interact. **26**(11–12), 1122–1146 (2010)
10. Chakraborty, R.: Privacy preserving actions of older adults on social media: exploring the behavior of opting out of information sharing. Decis. Support Syst. **55**(4), 948–956 (2013)
11. Oinas-Kukkonen, H., Harjumaa, M.: A systematic framework for designing and evaluating persuasive systems. In: Oinas-Kukkonen, H., Hasle, P., Harjumaa, M., Segerståhl, K., Øhrstrøm, P. (eds.) PERSUASIVE 2008. LNCS, vol. 5033, pp. 164–176. Springer, Heidelberg (2008). https://doi.org/10.1007/978-3-540-68504-3_15
12. Langrial, S.: Native mobile applications for personal well-being: a persuasive systems design evaluation. In: PACIS 2012 Proceedings, p. 93 (2012). http://aisel.aisnet.org/pacis2012/93
13. Drozd, F., Lehto, T., Oinas-Kukkonen, H.: Exploring perceived persuasiveness of a behavior change support system: a structural model. In: Bang, M., Ragnemalm, E.L. (eds.) PERSUASIVE 2012. LNCS, vol. 7284, pp. 157–168. Springer, Heidelberg (2012). https://doi.org/10.1007/978-3-642-31037-9_14
14. Davis, F.D., Bagozzi, R.P., Warshaw, P.R.: User acceptance of computer technology: a comparison of two theoretical models. Manag. Sci. **35**(8), 982–1003 (1989)

15. Lehto, T., Oinas-Kukkonen, H.: Explaining and predicting perceived effectiveness and use continuance intention of a behaviour change support system for weight loss. Behav. Inf. Technol. **34**, 176–189 (2015)
16. Venkatesh, V., Morris, M.G., Davis, G.B., Davis, F.D.: User acceptance of information technology: toward a unified view. MIS Q. **27**, 425–478 (2003)
17. Lehto, T., Oinas-Kukkonen, H., Drozd, F.: Factors affecting perceived persuasiveness of a behavior change support system. In: Proceedings of the Thirty Third International Conference on Information Systems, Orlando, FL, USA, pp. 16–19 (2012)
18. Bartlett, Y.K., Webb, T.L., Hawley, M.S.: Using persuasive technology to increase physical activity in people with chronic obstructive pulmonary disease by encouraging regular walking: a mixed-methods study exploring opinions and preferences. J. Med. Internet Res. **19**, e124 (2017)
19. Meng, L.: The Relationship Between the Sense of Achievement, Achievement Motivation and Socioeconomic Status; Soochow University, Taipei, Taiwan (2012)
20. Fishbein, M., Ajzen, I.: Belief, Attitude, Intention and Behavior: An Introduction to Theory and Research. Addison-Wesley, Reading (1975)

Supporting Information Recall for Elderly People in Hyper Aged Societies

Tatsuya Ishigaki$^{(\boxtimes)}$, Jingyi You, Hiroki Takimoto, and Manabu Okumura

Tokyo Institute of Technology, 4259 Nagatsuta-cho, Midori-ku,
Yokohama, Kanagawa 226-8503, Japan
{ishigaki,youjy,takimoto}@lr.pi.titech.ac.jp, oku@pi.titech.ac.jp
http://lr-www.pi.titech.ac.jp

Abstract. As people become elderly, they often suffer from memory loss. This can present itself in a conversation where the participants cannot recall, for example, the name of a place they visited or a person they met. In this work, we present a support system for people in such situations that 1) recognizes utterances that trigger situations where information recall is required and then 2) retrieves the necessary information from data sources such as news articles. Our system is composed of two modules: a recognizer for utterances that trigger information recall and a search engine to retrieve necessary information. We describe the task of detecting utterances that trigger information recall and present a novel corpus. Then, we present the details of the search engine. The performances of baseline models for detecting utterances that trigger information recall suggest that these models achieve excellent performances in terms of recall but there is still have room for improvement in terms of precision. Moreover, the performance of the overall proposed system suggests that the retrieval task is somewhat difficult and merits further investigation.

Keywords: Information recall · Utterance classification · Non-task-oriented dialogue · Dialogue corpus

1 Introduction

When people become elderly, they encounter various kinds of problems. One of the most significant is memory loss [3], which often presents itself in situations where individuals cannot recall specific information such as the name of a place they visited or a gift they gave for a friend's birthday. For example, Fig. 1 shows a situation where the conversation is interrupted because the older man cannot remember the specific name of a place he used to visit. Memory loss can cause serious problems in communication, especially between seniors. As an aid to help deal with memory loss, Chen and Okumura [2] proposed an idea for a support system for information recall of past events. In this paper, we present how we built this system and evaluate its performance.

Our system helps users recall information by three steps: 1) the system recognizes utterances that trigger the need for information recall, 2) it then searches

© Springer Nature Switzerland AG 2020
Q. Gao and J. Zhou (Eds.): HCII 2020, LNCS 12208, pp. 282–291, 2020.
https://doi.org/10.1007/978-3-030-50249-2_21

the knowledge base for useful information in order to recall necessary experiences or events, and then 3) the retrieved information is represented as an utterance by a bot. We can use, for example, newspaper articles, user-supplied lifelogs, or posts from social network services as the knowledge bases. For this study, we use a corpus of newspaper articles as the knowledge base.

The support system described in this paper is composed of two modules: an utterance recognizer that is capable of recognizing information recall triggers and an article searcher. The former monitors the conversation and decides whether an utterance triggers the need of information recall. The task can be considered a binary utterance classification task. We implement the classifier through two approaches, one based on rules and the other on machine learning, and compare their performances. Once the recognizer recognizes the need for an information recall, the utterance that triggered the information recall is passed on to the article searcher. The searcher then retrieves useful articles from the corpus.

Our main contributions are as follows:

1. We manually created a dataset containing 99 conversations between two participants: an interviewer and a senior interviewee. This dataset is particularly useful for analyzing the characteristics of utterances that trigger information recall. According to our analysis, sentences that tend to trigger information recall usually include questions about the interviewee's own experience or attributes, or the current attributes of individuals or entities other than the interviewee.
2. Through experiments on this dataset, we found that both simple rule-based recognizers and machine learning-based recognizers show excellent performances in terms of recall, but there is still room for improvement in terms of precision.
3. We also tested our system using human participants and collected their feedback. The results indicated that a simple keyword matching-based search engine struggles to retrieve useful news articles for information recall. This demonstrates that the retrieval task is somewhat difficult and merits further investigation.

2   System Overview

The overview of our system is shown in Fig. 2. We assume that two human participants have a conversation on Slack[1], a text-based chat system. Our system is connected to Slack as a bot. The bot posts an utterance when users require support with information recall. The system achieves this by two modules: the `recognizer` and the `article searcher`. Every time the user posts an utterance, the utterance is passed on to the recognizer. If the recognizer classifies the utterance as an information recall trigger, our system assumes that the user is in a situation that requires information recall. The utterance is next passed

---

[1] https://slack.com.

Fig. 1. Example of a situation where information recall is needed and how our system supports the user.

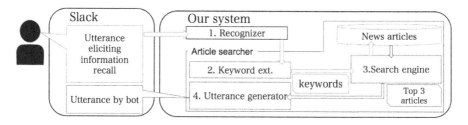

Fig. 2. System architecture of our support system for information recall

on to the article searcher, which is composed of three sub-modules: a keyword extractor, a search engine and an utterance generator. The searcher eventually generates an utterance by the bot through these three sub-modules. Note that the utterances by the bot are only visible to those users who need the support. We describe the recognizer and article searcher in more detail in the following subsections.

2.1 Recognizer

The recognizer monitors the conversation and identifies the utterances that trigger informational recall. The task of automatically detecting such utterances has not been addressed in the field of natural language processing, so it is not necessarily obvious how a system can detect them. To analyze this task, we created a dataset that contains utterances that trigger information recall. This dataset also enables us to quantitatively evaluate models for the detection task. The details of the dataset creation, utterance analysis, and evaluation of three baseline models for this task are provided next.

Dataset. We recruited 13 participants who were not experts in linguistics or natural language processing and divided them into two groups: three interviewers and ten interviewees. The interviewers were aged in their 30s to 40s and the interviewees in their 40s to 70s. We extracted interviewer-interviewee pairs and asked them to have a natural conversation on Slack. Interviewers were asked to give utterances that trigger information recall and interviewees responded to them. Then, the interviewers were asked to annotate the utterances that triggered information recall.

The resultant corpus contains 99 conversations. There are a total of 2,129 utterances, and each utterance can consist of multiple sentences. We collected 1,081 utterances provided by interviewers, of which 549 (52.5%) utterances were marked as triggers.

Analysis of Utterances that Triggered Information Recall. In this subsection, we describe our manual analysis of the conversations. The objective of this analysis was to clarify the characteristics of the trigger utterances. We analyzed 110 utterances extracted from ten randomly selected conversations. The insights from our analysis are as follows:

1. Most of the trigger utterances include at least one question.
2. The tense and the question focus in an utterance are important cues for distinguishing whether the utterances including questions trigger information recall or not.
3. We found only a few utterances that triggered information recall without any question.

Examples of the first insight are shown in examples 1) to 4) in Table 1. For the second insight, we found that a question often triggers information recall when the question is about the interviewee him/herself and is phrased in the past tense (see example 1) in Table 1). Furthermore, when a question is about people or entities other than the interviewee, it often triggers information recall regardless of whether the past tense is used (see example 2) and 3)). An example of the third insight is shown in example 6), but such cases are very rare. We refer readers to the paper by Ishigaki et al. [7] for a more detailed analysis of the utterances in this dataset.

Methods for Detecting Utterances that Trigger Information Recall. We compared three baseline models: POSITIVE, RULE, and SVM. POSITIVE classifies all utterances as positive, i.e., all utterances trigger information recall. RULE determines whether the utterances are questions or not by using the rule exemplified in Tamura et al. [15]. SVM uses a support vector machine (SVM)-based classifier. We utilized the linear kernel SVM implemented in Liblinear [4] with the N-gram, word embeddings and a binary feature representing utterances include (or do not include) at least one interrogative. We used pretrained GloVe vectors [12] for the embedding feature. Interrogatives are identified by the same method as RULE.

Table 1. Examples of utterances.

Trigger ∩ Question	1) (What kind of movies did you mainly watch when you were young Which genres?)
	2) (What are your parents' interests?)
	3) (Your father used be a university professor. What did he teach?)
	4) (What is the birthday of your favorite actor?)
not Trigger ∩ Question	5) (Do you usually cook by yourself?)
Trigger ∩ Not Question	6) (I guess your children would have enjoyed their stay at your parents' house in the summer vacation?)
not Trigger ∩ Not Question	7) (I often cook too)

2.2 Article Searcher

Once an utterance is recognized as an information recall trigger by the recognizer, it is passed on to the article searcher. The article searcher then retrieves useful news articles. The bot presents the retrieved articles as an utterance that is only visible to the user who needs support.

The article searcher can be divided into three sub-modules: a keyword extractor, a keyword-based article searcher, and an utterance generator. The keyword extractor extracts content words from the utterance. It uses a Japanese morphological analyzer (Janome[2]) to determine nouns, verbs, adjectives and adverbs. These morphologies are extracted as keywords and then passed on to the keyword matching-based search engine. The search engine is implemented by using a Python library (Whoosh[3]). The engine conducts an OR search for retrieving related news articles from the Mainichi Shimbun corpus[4], which contains news articles published from 1994 to 2004. The list of the top three related articles obtained by Whoosh is passed on to the utterance generator. Finally, the generator combines the three top-ranked articles into one utterance. The following three contents are included in each utterance (see Fig. 3 for an example of a bot utterance):

1. article titles
2. first sentences of articles
3. dates of issue

---

[2] https://github.com/mocobeta/janome.
[3] https://bitbucket.org/mchaput/whoosh.
[4] https://ndk.co.jp/newspaper-mainichi/.

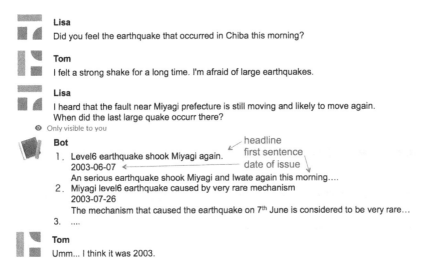

Fig. 3. Translated example of conversations in our system. Two humans and a bot participate in the conversation. The fourth utterance is by the bot

3 Evaluation

We report the results of our experiments to evaluate the performances of the recognizer and article searcher in this section.

3.1 Recognizer

Table 2 shows the precision, recall, and F-value scores obtained by the three models we compared. The hyperparameter C in SVM was tuned by 5-fold cross-validation, and we report the average scores for SVM. All compared models achieved high scores in terms of recall (1.0, 0.93 and 0.96). POSITIVE scored the lowest in terms of precision (0.53). SVM and RULE scored better in terms of both precision (0.68 and 0.67) and F-value (both 0.79). Although SVM had a slightly higher precision than RULE, RULE had a higher recall (0.93 vs. 0.96). These results suggest that RULE has the advantage in a situation where recall is more important, while SVM has the advantage in terms of precision.

We found that SVM classified most of the utterances containing at least one question sentences as positive i.e. as utterances that trigger information recall. One possible reason for this is the imbalance of positive and negative labels in the dataset. Since 74% of the utterances containing at least one question are annotated as positive in the training set, utterances containing at least one question are often wrongly classified as positive. For example, the fifth example in Table 1 was wrongly classified as positive although it does not trigger information recall. This type of error lowered the precision scores. Thus, the models still have room for improvement in terms of classifying the utterances containing questions correctly.

Table 2. The results of quantitative evaluation of the recognizer

	Precision	Recall	F-value
POSITIVE	0.53	**1.00**	**0.68**
SVM	**0.68**	0.93	**0.79**
RULE	0.67	**0.96**	**0.79**

3.2 Article Searcher

For evaluating our search engine, we asked four human participants to use our system. They were asked to have a conversation with us approximately 30 min on Slack. We attempted to give them utterances that triggered information recall and they responded to our utterances. The utterances by the bot were posted if the recognizer recognized a situation where information recall was required. We used the RULE-based recognizer in this experiment to take advantage of its higher recall. After the conversation, we asked participants to annotate the utterances using a two-step procedure: 1) annotate the utterances by us that actually triggered a situation where they needed information recall, and then 2) annotate the utterances by the bot as to whether they were useful or not. If the bot did not provide an utterance, the annotation would be negative (i.e. not useful).

Participants annotated 78 utterances in total. 30 out of which were annotated as ones that actually triggered a situation where information recall was required. We used these 30 for our evaluation. The remaining 48 utterances did not trigger the need for information recall, for two reasons: 1) 26 of the 48 were simply greetings or acknowledgements and 2) 22 were our attempts to trigger information recall but the human participants already knew the necessary information to respond.

Table 3 shows the proportion of the utterances by the bot that human participants judged as useful. Twelve out of the 30 utterances were judged as useful and 18 as not useful. This suggests that searching for news articles that are useful for information recall is a somewhat difficult task. Two of the 12 utterances by the bot that were judged useful actually provided wrong information, but human participants did not realize this and treated the information as if it was correct.

These results suggest that the search engine could be improved by two extensions: using context information and using a semantic vector-based search engine. For the first, context information from previous utterances might be useful. For example, the utterance "What is the name of the big earthquake that happened that year?" triggers information recall, but the expression "that year" references specific information mentioned in a previous utterance. Thus, it is difficult for our current system to retrieve the proper news article because of the lack of information. For the second, expressions of spoken language are used in text-based chats and they are often informal. In contrast, written language is used in news articles. For this reason, a simple keyword matching-based search engine often fails. To solve this problem, semantic vector-based [13] search engines would likely prove useful.

Table 3. Useful / not useful utterances by the bot, and the reasons.

Useful	12 utterances
- Bot provided correct information	10 utterances
- Bot provided wrong information	2 utterances
Not useful	18 utterances
- Bot did not provide related articles	15 utterances
- Bot did not give any utterances	3 utterances

3.3   User Feedback

Finally, we asked the participants to freely describe their impressions on the use of the system or comment on the future extension of our system. All four participants stated that the prototype system was useful when the bot provided the necessary news articles. One participant mentioned that even if the bot's utterances were not useful for information recall, he could discuss a wider range of topics thanks to the information provided by the bot, and thus could continue the conversation for longer than if he had not been using our system. This feedback is useful because it means our system not only helps with memory loss but also makes human communications smoother and more diverse.

4   Related Work

The task of detecting utterances that trigger information recall can be viewed as a type of utterance classification. Various utterance classification tasks have been proposed, such as dialogue act classification [14] and utterance intent classification [9]. These tasks use a set of pre-defined tags, but none of the tags represent a situation where information recall is necessary. The most similar tasks to ours are classification tasks that target questions. Tamura et al. [15] proposed a classifier that selects the most salient sentence from a multi-sentence question to improve the performance of question-answering systems. Ishigaki et al. [8] summarized questions posted on community question-answering sites by means of binary classification. Olney et al. [11] classified question sentences by students into pre-defined types to improve the performance of an automatic tutoring system. Although these works have formulated tasks as binary classification tasks similar to ours, no existing tasks have been designed to detect utterances that trigger information recall.

The task of retrieving news articles to support information recall can be viewed as a type of information retrieval [10]. The target documents of existing information retrieval systems are diverse, ranging from web documents [10] to lifelogs [1]. In many previous settings, a query for a search engine is a set of words. In contrast, in our research, we consider the utterance as a query and apply keyword extraction to obtain a set of words. It is necessary to develop sophisticated keyword extraction methods that can deal with the history of a conversation. It might be useful to integrate a method that converts spoken language into a written one with our search engine or to use a feature vector-based engine [13].

Our proposed corpus contains annotated text-based dialogues by two participants. Various types of dialogue corpora have previously been released. Our corpus is classified as non-task-oriented [6], but there are also corpora of task-oriented dialogues [5]. Furthermore, our corpus consists of text-based conversations by two human participants whereas other corpora have been created from spoken dialogues [5], multi-party chats [16], and dialogues between a human and a system [6]. The conversation participants in our corpus are aged in their 30s to 70s whereas the construction methods for other dialogue corpora do not consider the ages of participants.

5   Future Work

In this paper, we have described a support system for information recall of elderly people in hyper aged societies. We newly proposed a dataset to analyze utterances that trigger information recall and automatically evaluate the recognizers for such utterances. Experimental results showed that while the performance of the recognizer in terms of recall is high, there is room for improvement in terms of precision. For a future direction on this task, exploiting the information extracted from the dialogue history should prove useful. The performance of the article searcher suggests that the retrieval task is somewhat difficult and merits further investigation. Our plans include extending our search engine by using context information or semantic vectors instead of using a simple keyword matching. We also want to broaden the target text of the search engine to data linked to individuals, such as lifelogs and social media posts.

Acknowledgments. This research was conducted as part of the joint research project "Information Recall Support for Elderly People in Hyper Aged Societies" between the Tokyo Institute of Technology and National Taiwan University.

References

1. Chang, C.C., Fu, M.H., Huang, H.H., Chen, H.H.: An interactive approach to integrating external textual knowledge for multimodal lifelog retrieval. In: Proceedings of the ACM Workshop on Lifelog Search Challenge, pp. 41–44. ACM (2019)
2. Chen, H.H., Okumura, M.: Information recall support for elderly people in hyper aged societies. In: Proceedings of the The Web Conference, pp. 431–432 (2018)
3. Craik, F.I., Byrd, M., Swanson, J.M.: Patterns of memory loss in three elderly samples. Psychol. Aging **2**(1), 79 (1987)
4. Fan, R.E., Chang, K.W., Hsieh, C.J., Wang, X.R., Lin, C.J.: LIBLINEAR: a library for large linear classification. J. Mach. Learn. Res. **9**, 1871–1874 (2008)
5. Hakkani-Tur, D., et al.: Multi-domain joint semantic frame parsing using bi-directional RNN-LSTM. In: Proceedings of Interspeech (2016)

6. Higashinaka, R., Funakoshi, K., Inaba, M., Tsunomori, Y., Takahashi, T., Kaji, N.: Overview of dialogue breakdown detection challenge 3, vol. 6 (2017)
7. Ishigaki, T., Okumura, M.: Detecting utterances eliciting information recall. In: Proceedings of the 12th Edition of its Language Resources and Evaluation Conference (LREC2020) (2020, under review)
8. Ishigaki, T., Takamura, H., Okumura, M.: Summarizing lengthy questions. In: Proceedings of The 8th International Joint Conference on Natural Language Processing (IJCNLP2017), vol. 1, pp. 792–800 (2017)
9. Kato, T., Nagai, A., Noda, N., Sumitomo, R., Wu, J., Yamamoto, S.: Utterance intent classification of a spoken dialogue system with efficiently untied recursive autoencoders. In: Proceedings of the 18th Annual SIGdial Meeting on Discourse and Dialogue (SIGDIAL2017), pp. 60–64 (2017)
10. McCallum, A., Nigam, K., Rennie, J., Seymore, K.: A machine learning approach to building domain-specific search engines. In: Sixteenth International Joint Conference on Artificial Intelligence (IJCAI99), vol. 99, pp. 662–667 (1999)
11. Olney, A., Louwerse, M., Matthews, E., Marineau, J., Hite-Mitchell, H., Graesser, A.: Utterance classification in autotutor. In: Proceedings of the HLT-NAACL 03 Workshop on Building Educational Applications Using Natural Language Processing, pp. 1–8 (2003)
12. Pennington, J., Socher, R., Manning, C.D.: Glove: Global vectors for word representation. In: The 2014 Conference of Empirical Methods in Natural Language Processing (EMNLP2014), pp. 1532–1543 (2014)
13. Platzer, C., Dustdar, S.: A vector space search engine for web services. In: Third European Conference on Web Services (ECOWS 2005), pp. 9–16 (2005)
14. Raheja, V., Tetreault, J.: Dialogue act classification with context-aware self-attention. In: Proceedings of the 2019 Conference of the North American Chapter of the Association for Computational Linguistics: Human Language Technologies (NAACL2019), pp. 3727–3733. Association for Computational Linguistics, Minneapolis (2019)
15. Tamura, A., Takamura, H., Okumura, M.: Classification of multiple-sentence questions. In: Dale, R., Wong, K.-F., Su, J., Kwong, O.Y. (eds.) IJCNLP 2005. LNCS (LNAI), vol. 3651, pp. 426–437. Springer, Heidelberg (2005). https://doi.org/10.1007/11562214_38
16. Uthus, D.C., Aha, D.W.: The ubuntu chat corpus for multiparticipant chat analysis. In: Proceedings of 2013 AAAI Spring Symposium Series (2013)

Older Adults' Motivation for Physical Activity Using Gamified Technology: An Eight-Week Experimental Study

Dennis L. Kappen[1]([⊠]), Pejman Mirza-Babaei[2],
and Lennart E. Nacke[3,4]

[1] Humber Institute of Technology and Advanced Learning,
Toronto, ON, Canada
dennis.kappen@humber.ca
[2] Faculty of Business and Information Technology,
Ontario Tech Unversity, Oshawa, ON, Canada
pejman.m@acm.org
[3] Drama and Speech Communication, University of Waterloo,
Waterloo, ON, Canada
Lennart.Nacke@acm.org
[4] Stratford School of Interaction and Business, University of Waterloo,
Waterloo, ON, Canada

Abstract. While gamification strategy has been used in many areas such as marketing, education, health and wellness, only a few projects have investigated the relevance of longer study durations. There are limited number of long-term studies in the usage of gamification elements to facilitate motivation and engagement of users in a physical activity (PA) setting, especially for the older adult demographic. We conducted a synchronous, three-condition (gamified, non-gamified and control), eight-week, experimental study which randomized 30 participants in the 50+ age group. Results from quantitative analysis indicated that the addition of motivational affordances increased engagement of participants. Perceived competence, perceived autonomy was significant for the gamified group against the non gamified (traditional PA monitor – pedometer) and control group. Results from the quantitative analysis rejects the null hypothesis that there was no change between the groups as measured by motivation, enjoyment and engagement. Furthermore, the results also support our hypotheses that enjoyment and engagement was less in groups with pedometers (non-gamified PA monitors) than in the group with gamification elements. Results highlight the possibility of adaptive engagement where gamification elements can be customized to participants for the 50+ age group to foster engagement tailored to suit their current health conditions and prevalent barriers to participate in PA.

Keywords: Motivational affordances · Gamification · Intrinsic motivation · Extrinsic motivation · Physical activity · Older adults · Perceived competence · Perceived autonomy · Adaptive engagement

Q. Gao and J. Zhou (Eds.): HCII 2020, LNCS 12208, pp. 292–309, 2020.
https://doi.org/10.1007/978-3-030-50249-2_22

1 Introduction

As the general population in Western countries shifts towards an aging demographic, older adults are trying to lead healthy lifestyles [1] while maintaining physical and mental wellness. Maintaining an active lifestyle by engaging in activity equivalent to walking more than three miles per day, in addition to independently carrying out normal daily activities contributes to physical wellness [2]. Additionally, technology assisted physical activities contribute to overcoming cognitive decline thereby facilitating mental wellness [3–5]. Information technology has evolved over time to enable the creation of fitness apps [6] and wearable technologies to help adults participate in physical activity (PA) with health benefits [7, 8]. However, cognitive and physical challenges faced by older adults poses barriers and limitations for them to participate in PA [9, 10]. These barriers and limitations can be mitigated through the use of persuasive technologies that encourage physical activity [11]. Research has indicated the advantages of games [12], gamification [13] and persuasive technology [14, 15] to motivate older adults for PA. Therefore, it is important to investigate the reasons for lack of engagement and motivation with PA, and the potential increase in PA motivation through the use of motivational affordances. Motivational affordances *are game elements which help foster intrinsic and extrinsic motives* [6, 16] *especially in mundane activities like PA.* This idea follows from gamification, which is the application of strategies from game design (e.g., actions, challenges, and achievements) to non-game activities to help make people's actions more engaging [17]. Persuasive technologies like gamification have been instrumental in effecting behaviour change in users in diverse fields ranging from education, marketing, crowdsourcing, management information systems to health and wellness domains, to mention a few.

To investigate the influence of gamification elements on older adults' motivation and engagement in PA, we designed a synchronous, three condition, long-term study over an eight-week duration in which participants were randomized into three groups (gamified, non-gamified and control) (cf. Sect. 3.2). Quantitative analysis indicated significant differences between the groups with higher engagement for gamified and non-gamified groups. These results suggest the relevance of gamification elements as behaviour change elements to motivate and engage older adults in PA.

2 Theory and Background

2.1 Gamification

Persuasive technologies using gamification as a strategy have been used to foster motivation indicated emergent themes such as feedback and monitoring, reward and threat, and goals and planning [13]. While many definitions of gamification exist, its role as a behaviour change agent is more inspiring.

Effective gamification is influencing human behaviour through engaging experiences, using game design principles in non-game applications and services [18]. Gamified app-based interventions to improve diet, physical activity and exercise indicated significant health improvements in comparison to stand-alone apps [19].

Tailoring these apps based on the personality traits of users could increase their efficacy [20]. While incorporating challenges and accountability facilitated usage of persuasive strategies within a gamified design, challenges with privacy (sharing personal information) and reduced self-confidence hindered effective deployment of these gamified apps [21]. A systematic review of empirical studies on gamification in the health and wellbeing domains indicated a positive impact towards health behaviours [22]. While this study indicated that targeted health and well-being domains were: physical health (exercise and fitness), healthcare utilization (dispensing, medication usage and monitoring glucose levels, patient empowerment), and mental health (stress and anxiety reduction, it also indicated that several studies reviewed reported mixed or neutral effects of gamification. Gamified web interventions for rheumatoid arthritis patients indicated increased empowerment, app usage and PA than the control group [23]. Systematic reviews on gamication literature have called for comparing gamified interventions with non-gamified interventions [24–26]. This inspired the comparison of the differences between gamified and non-gamified PA interventions [27].

Many commercial systems have combined gamification with PA [6] as a behaviour change strategy to help individuals achieve health and fitness goals. As part of this, fitness trackers motivate workout activities by providing feedback [26]. Gamification or gameful design as a form of persuasive technology offers many hedonic (pleasure, enjoyment, comfort, absence of distress) and eudaimonic (growth, meaning, authenticity, excellence) [28, 29] pathways to implement persuasive strategies to motivate older adults to initiate, maintain, and adhere to healthy behaviour.

2.2   Gamification and Older Adults' Physical Activity

While research on the general intrinsic and extrinsic motivation of older adults [30] affirmed interest levels towards engaging in PA, more research on player personality characteristics from gamer personality is needed to understand attitudes and motivation of players (users) [31]. Existing research explores age-related needs of older adults [32], barriers and motivations towards PA, and activity levels [30, 33].

Persuasive technologies in the form of exergames (games involving physical exercise), web-based interventions and fitness applications involving gameplay, provide a diverse spectrum of available technologies to initiate and maintain PA among older adults. Seniors preferred games that simulated true-to-life scenarios, provided cognitive training and digital games that helped to improve their reflexes [34]. Systematic reviews on exergames and older adults' PA indicated clustering of studies into rehabilitation, training and wellness themes with focus on theories such as self-determination theory and social cognitive theory [35, 36]. Playing video games also contributes to improving health outcomes in areas of psychological therapy and physical therapy and improving balance among older adults [37, 38]. However, designers must consider age-related functional limitations such as declining vision, hearing, hand-to-eye coordination and cognition issues of older adults [39]. Furthermore, in-person and electronically mediated interventions through persuasive games [40] and inter-personal communications [41] were shown to be effective for influencing and motivating health behaviour change [42]. Additionally, home-based health monitoring practices [43], as researched in Mediframe [44] and in-home rehabilitation technologies [45] discuss challenges in the implementation of these technologies due to age-related infirmities and diseases. Gamification applications like Superbetter (www.superbetter.com) focused on negotiating life's challenges such as depression, anxiety, pain, finding a job, improving a skill and strengthening a relationship to mention a few, into a gamelike experiential play supported by motivational affordances. Habitica (www.habitica.com) and coach.me (www.coach.me) are also examples of gameful technology that provide the impetus to role playing life in the form of setting up goals, with in-game rewards, punishments and social facilitation.

Many older adults are growing accustomed to evolving technologies and omnipresent video games [23, 46, 47]. New input technologies for these games are becoming more intuitive for an aging demographic of gamers (e.g., movement interfaces such as the Microsoft Kinect [48], the Nintendo Wii controllers [49], large screens present on mobile tablet computers and smartphones). Adaptive engagement, defined as tailoring of older adults' engagement through customization and personalization of motivational affordances is important to address age-related changes, current health conditions and barriers to do PA [27, 50–52].

Research has explored the design of motion-based games with the goal of facilitating occupational therapy and rehabilitation among older adults. Recent examples include motion-based games for stroke rehabilitation where the patient recovered significant motor abilities over a six-week period [53], therapy for older adults with Parkinson's disease [54], and balance training to reduce the risk of falls among older adults [55, 56]. Motivating older adults in PA with focused gameplay over long periods was seen as an advantage of exergaming [57].

Different approaches have been taken with regard to the promotion of exercise and PA. Non-commercial games like UbiFit Garden provided feedback in the form of flowers based on daily physical activities [11] and Flowie provided feedback on increased number of daily steps taken by the participants [58], targeted the older adult population, and aimed to encourage PA through persuasive technology intervention [59]. While this helps to promote PA, mobile apps can also promote activity using smartphones, focusing on individually tailored feedback and advice [60]. While playful persuasive solutions [61], embodied gaming [62] and augmented gaming [63] can facilitate fun and socially engaging activities, key intrinsic and extrinsic reasons for sustaining motivation in these activities have not been identified. While prior research investigated older adults and PA motivation, little research has been conducted in the intersection of older adults, motivation and gamified PA technology. Therefore, we conducted a synchronous three condition experimental study which included a control group, to investigate the motivational affordances specific to older adults PA technology.

3   Experimental Study

This study was conducted to investigate motivational affordances in PA technology over a longer period. This was undertaken to understand older adults' preferences and challenges with motivational affordances in a controlled study [50, 51].

3.1   Research Design

In comparison to existing PA technology available commercially the rationale for selecting Spirit50.com as a technology intervention for this study was because it was a gamified fitness activity intervention website for use by older adults. Spirit50 was specifically designed for adults over 50 years of age and incorporated the following gamification elements: goal definition (quest), daily challenges (sub-goals), goal progression meter, points and badges (stars) as motivational affordances (gamification) [27, 51]. Using pedometers was considered to be the non-gamified PA intervention.

Prior research indicated that a minimum effective exercise program for habit formation was six weeks [64–66]. Therefore, a randomized experimental study investigating PA over an eight-week duration was designed. This study was a synchronous, three-condition, eight-week study with a total of thirty participants. Participants above 50 years of age were randomized to one of three conditions:

1. Physically active and use a gamified physical activity app (Spirit50.com)
2. Physically active and use a pedometer
3. Physically active (control group)

All three groups had participants who were physically active. The inclusion of a control group was done to make effective comparisons the two groups receiving the intervention.

3.2   Research Question and Hypotheses

The primary question driving this research was:

Can gamification elements be used to foster the intrinsic and extrinsic motivations for physical activity and daily exercise routines among older adults?

Hypotheses. The hypotheses are rooted in established and validated studies which have investigated the following: the benefits of web based interventions to promote PA by sedentary older adults [67]; improved engagement of older adults with dementia when using artificially intelligent assistive technology [68]; improved motivational benefits of using a telehealth intervention using Nintendo Wii Fit Balance Boards [69]; and changes in attitude towards individual health [70].

Brawley et al. reported that self-monitoring was the behaviour modification strategy that led to maximum participation in PA [3]. Theory-based behaviour change methods for motivating adults' in participating in PA, providing self-monitoring and socialising modifiers can be done using gamification strategies [13, 71–73]. The question is to investigate whether such strategies can be used to foster intrinsic and extrinsic motivation for older adults PA.

These studies provide evidence to support the usage of technology artifacts for PA challenges faced by older adults. Our methodical approach was to leverage this evidence to investigate the effectiveness of gamified technology artifacts as influencers of health behaviour change for improving PA in older adults'. Because of this, my hypotheses are:

H0: If older adults use traditional or classic physical activity applications interventions, there is **no difference** as measured by **enjoyment and engagement** compared to when they use gamified physical activity applications to influence change in health behaviour.

H1: If older adults use traditional or classic physical activity applications interventions, they are **less engaged** as measured by **enjoyment and engagement** than when they use gamified physical activity applications to influence change in health behaviour.

H2: If older adults use traditional or classic physical activity applications interventions, they are **less motivated** than when they use gamified physical activity applications to influence change in health behaviour.

3.3   Measures for Dependent Variables

A prior systematic review on the enjoyment of digital games attributed the experience of enjoyment as key to engagement in digital videogames [74, 75]. Boyle et al. (2021) and Mekler et al. (2014) conceptualised the subjective experience of engagement as a moment-to-moment feelings of enjoyment that players experience while gaming [74, 75]. Game enjoyment has been equated with the experience of flow as in the state of immersion or an experiential state of play when interacting with the gaming system [74–80]. The most frequently used measures of enjoyment was the IMI [75]. Doing an activity for its inherent satisfaction (intrinsic motivation) [81, 82], as opposed to an external outcome translates to paratelic engagement [83–85]. Researchers have also used the IMI as a measure of engagement [74, 85]. Therefore, the Intrinsic Motivation Inventory (IMI), an instrument that stemmed from the constructs of the Self-Determination Theory (SDT) [81] was selected as a measure of enjoyment and engagement.

From a motivation to participate in PA, the Psychological Need Satisfaction in Exercise (PNSE) scale has been used by researchers to measure perceived autonomy, perceived autonomy and perceived relatedness [86–88]. Preliminary eligibility to participate in the study was established through the PAR-Q [89] document. Baseline assessment of current PA condition of each participant was assessed using the International Physical Activity Questionnaire (IPAQ) [90]. Participants from the three conditions filled in a questionnaire once a week, for eight-weeks, which combined the scales measuring the following dependent variables:

1. Measuring the *enjoyment* and *engagement* of the participants over the eight-week period using the IMI Scale [91, 92].
2. Measuring the *motivation* aspect of the participants over the eight-week period using the PNSE scale [87].
3. User Experience: Measuring *exertion* using the Rating of Perceived Exertion scale (RPE) [93] after each participant session.

4 Analysis

4.1 Participants

At the onset, there were three groups of participants, 10 participants in each group, and eight weeks of sessions leading to 240 instances of data collection points.

4.2 Data

Quantitative Analysis. SPSS was used to analyze the data for normality and subsequent significance testing. Data from the PNSE and IMI scales were tested for normality within each group using the Kolmogorov-Smirnov (K-S) and the Shapiro-Wilk tests.

For the PNSE scale, the dimensions of perceived competence, perceived autonomy and perceived relatedness, $D(80)$, $p < 0.05$, were significantly non-normal. The Shapiro-Wilk statistic yields exact significance and is more accurate than the K-S test [94]. All dimensions in the three groups, $D(80)$, $p < 0.05$, were significantly non-normal.

5 Results

5.1 Findings from Quantitative Analysis

The PNSE scale [87] measures perceived need satisfaction and is based on the view that psychological needs are a motivating force in achieving certain goals [95]. This scale was used to measure participants' motivation for PA and exercise routines on a weekly basis. The IMI was used to evaluate the participants' subjective experiences, and engagement related to the specific intervention associated with each group. The Rate of Perceived Exertion (RPE) scored participants feeling of exertion, weekly, on a scale of 0 (no exertion at all) to 10 (highest exertion).

Answers from participants for these two scales, collected over an eight-week period were compared between the three groups (Group 1 = gamified, Group 2 = non-gamified, Group 3 = control). This study had 10 participants in each group with a total of 80 responses in each group.

5.2 Overall Tests for Repeated Measures Within Groups

Friedman's ANOVA was used to test for differences within groups in a repeated measures design where each participant within a group did the exercise routines on a weekly basis and reported their experiences using the PNSE and the IMI scales.

Friedman's ANOVA (PNSE)
For the **PNSE scale**, the analyses are shown in Table 1.

Table 1. Output from Friedman's ANOVA (PNSE)

Ranks (Friedman's ANOVA)		
Please input your group number		Mean rank
1	Perceived competence	1.96
	Perceived autonomy	2.45
	Perceived relatedness	1.59
2	Perceived competence	2.07
	Perceived autonomy	2.56
	Perceived relatedness	1.38
3	Perceived competence	1.67
	Perceived autonomy	2.79
	Perceived relatedness	1.54

The three dimensions of the PNSE scale: perceived competence, perceived autonomy and perceived relatedness indicated significance ($p < 0.05$) depending on which type of intervention.

There was a statistically significant difference in Group 1 ($\chi2(2) = 44.5, p < 0.05$), Group 2 ($\chi2(2) = 66.6, p < 0.05$) and Group 3 ($\chi2(2) = 80.3, p < 0.05$). This indicated that the interventions helped to significantly change the dependent variables over the course of eight-weeks. Follow-up tests were carried out and are explained in Sect. 5.4.

Friedman's ANOVA (IMI)

For the **IMI scale**, the data analyses are shown in Table 2.

Table 2. Output from Friedman's ANOVA (IMI)

Ranks (Friedman's ANOVA)		
Please input your group number		Mean rank
1	Interest/enjoyment	4.99
	Perceived competence	5.19
	Effort/importance	2.66
	Pressure/tension	1.87
	Perceived choice	4.33
	Value/usefulness	5.79
	Relatedness	3.17
2	Interest/enjoyment	4.82
	Perceived competence	4.58
	Effort/importance	2.18
	Pressure/tension	2.32
	Perceived choice	5.34
	Value/usefulness	6.30
	Relatedness	2.46

(continued)

Table 2. (*continued*)

Ranks (Friedman's ANOVA)	
Please input your group number	Mean rank
3 Interest/enjoyment	4.46
Perceived competence	4.71
Effort/importance	2.40
Pressure/tension	1.61
Perceived choice	5.72
Value/usefulness	5.84
Relatedness	3.26

The dimensions of the IMI scale indicated significance ($p < 0.05$) depending on which type of intervention. There was a statistically significant difference in Group 1 ($\chi2(2) = 222.0$, $p < 0.05$), Group 2 ($\chi2(2) = 286.4$, $p < 0.05$) and Group 3 ($\chi2 (2) = 274.6$, $p < 0.05$). This further indicated that the interventions helped to significantly change the dependent variables over the course of eight-weeks. Follow-up tests were carried out and are explained in Sect. 5.4.

5.3 Overall Tests Between Groups

Data were ordinal, non-normal and were binned into the three groups using the grouping variable and tested using the Kruskal-Wallis test for differences.

Based on the Kruskal-Wallis test for the PNSE scale, motivation was significantly affected by the interventions for the dimensions related to perceived competence $[H(2) = 28.77$, $p < 0.5]$, perceived autonomy $[H(2) = 8.76$, $p < 0.5]$, and perceived relatedness $[H(2) = 17.60$, $p < 0.5]$.

Jonckheere-Terpstra test also revealed a significant trend between the groups in the perceived competence ($J = 6491$, $z = -5.33$, $r = -.34$) and the perceived relatedness dimension ($J = 8064$, $z = -2.63$, $r = -.17$). Since the groups were coded as $1 =$ gamified, $2 =$ non-gamified and $3 =$ control, and the negative value of the z statistic indicated a trend of descending medians as the coding variable got bigger, which indicated a rising trend toward the gamified group.

Based on the Kruskal-Wallis test for the IMI scale, significance was indicated in specific dimensions (all effects are reported at $p < 0.5$). Engagement was significantly affected by the interventions: interest/engagement ($H(2) = 12.45$), perceived competence ($H(2) = 39.65$), effort/importance ($H(2) = 6.21$), pressure/tension ($H(2) = 12.56$), perceived choice (H(2) = 12.5), value/usefulness (H(2) = 6.43), relatedness (H(2) = 10.42).

Jonckheere-Terpstra's test for the IMI scale revealed a significant trend in the data: since the groups were coded as $1 =$ gamified, $2 =$ non-gamified and $3 =$ control, and the negative value of the z statistic indicated a trend of descending medians as the coding variable got bigger, which indicated a rising trend toward the gamified group. Significant trend in the data was seen in the following dimensions: Interest/Enjoyment: $J = 7602$, $z = -3.42$, $r = -.22$; Perceived Competence: $J = 5824$, $z = -6.46$, $r = -.41$; Effort/Importance: $J = 8272$, $z = -2.28$, $r = -.14$; Perceived Choice: $J = 11616$, $z = 3.45$, $r = .22$; Value/Usefulness: $J = 8116$, $z = -2.60$, $r = -.16$

Kruskal-Wallis Test (RPE). The comparison for RPE showed significant exertion between the groups $H(2) = 24.3$, $p < .05$. The Jonckheere-Terpstra's test revealed a significant trend in the data: $J = 12277$, $z = 4.618$, $r = .30$. The positive z statistic indicates a rising trend of medians as the coding variable increased, indicating that the participants in the gamified group (Group 1) felt lower exertion compared to the participants from the control group (Group 3).

5.4 Follow-Up Tests

Mann-Whitney test were used to follow up the findings by comparing Group 1(gamified) and 2 (non-gamified), Group 1 and 3 (control), and Group 2 and 3. Bonferroni correction was applied and all effects are reported at 0.0167 (p < 0.05/3) level of significance.

Mann-Whitney Test (PNSE). Exercise need satisfaction was compared between groups and the results are indicated below:

Gamified (Group 1) – Non-gamified (Group 2): Comparing the mean ranks between the groups, Group 1 (gamified) indicated higher perceived competence and perceived relatedness in comparison to Group 2.
Tests indicated that perceived competence ($U = 2341$, $r = -0.23$) and perceived relatedness ($U = 2125$, $r = -0.29$) were significant at this level and ranked higher in Group 1.
Gamified (Group 1) – Control (Group 3): Comparing the mean ranks between the groups, Group 1 (gamified) indicated higher perceived competence and perceived relatedness in comparison to Group 3.
Tests indicated that perceived competence ($U = 1629$, $r = -0.42$) and perceived relatedness ($U = 2125$, $r = -0.26$) were significant at this level and ranked higher in Group 1.
Non-Gamified (Group 2) – Control (Group 3): When comparing the mean ranks between the groups, Group 2 (non-gamified) indicated higher perceived competence in comparison to Group 3. However, while Group 3 indicated significance in the perceived autonomy dimension ($p < 0.0167$). Tests indicated that perceived autonomy ($U = 2712$, $r = -0.13$) were significant at this level and ranked higher in Group 3.

Mann Whitney Test (IMI). Experience and engagement in the intervention routines were compared between groups as a follow-up test. Results are indicated as follows:

Gamified (Group 1) – Non-Gamified (Group 2): While the mean ranks of perceived competence and perceived relatedness were higher in Group 1 (gamified), the rankings in perceived choice were higher in Group 2 (non-gamified) than in Group 1.

All effects reported at p < 0.0167, perceived competence ($U = 2312$, $r = -0.24$), perceived choice ($U = 2489$, $r = -0.19$) and relatedness ($U = 2345$, $r = -0.23$) were significantly different between the groups.

Gamified (Group 1) – Control (Group 3): While interest/enjoyment, perceived competence, effort/importance dimensions ranked higher for the non-gamified group, perceived choice was ranked higher in the control group. All effects reported at $p < 0.0167$, interest/enjoyment ($U = 2201$, $r = -0.27$), perceived competence ($U = 1481$, $r = -0.46$), effort/importance ($U = 2448$, $r = -0.20$), perceived choice ($U = 5440$, $r = -0.27$) dimensions indicated a significant difference between groups.

Non-Gamified (Group 2) – Control (Group 3): All effects reported at $p < 0.0167$, interest/enjoyment ($U = 2482$, $r = -0.19$), perceived competence ($U = 2030$, $r = -0.31$), and pressure/tension ($U = 2139$, $r = -0.29$) dimensions showed significant differences between the two groups. The above three dimensions also ranked higher in the non-gamified group compared to the control group.

6 Discussion

We conducted a synchronous, eight-week study with three groups: gamified, non-gamified and a control group to investigate whether gamification elements or motivational affordances could foster older adults PA.

To understand older adults' enjoyment and experiential aspects of using technology for PA, it was critical to examine the relevance of technology in the context of PA motivation, setting up goals, feeling of accomplishments, fears and barriers, and rewards, and tracking. By investigating the influence of gamification elements in PA technology, this paper extends prior work of using web-based interventions to promote PA by sedentary older adults (55+) [67], supporting improved behavioural changes and effective changes in PA of older adults (50+) [96] due to computer-tailored interventions and justifying the need for improved web-based interventions for older adults (50+) for better sustainability [97].

The quantitative analyses indicated that adding gamification elements such as goal-based fitness quest scaffolded short-term goals focussed on working towards long-term goals and increased older adults' engagement in PA. Adding the choice of difficulty levels and differentiated exercise intensity levels in (Group 1) fostered perceived autonomy, and perceived competence, two of the three major constructs of the SDT [81]. These results supported prior game based PA intervention studies where rules, challenges, competition, rewards and feedback mechanisms served as motivational strategies for PA [98, 99]. Perceived autonomy was significant in the non-gamified group (pedometers) with increased walk distance and duration than the participants in the control group. These findings extend the results of prior studies on PA and older adults using gaming technologies [48, 100]. Addition of motivational affordances (gamification elements) in Group 1 provided older adults with the choice of keeping track of their progression, achievements and providing them with an improved sense of control of their exercise selections and establishing a validation of their PA efforts on a weekly basis. These results also extend the results of prior studies on improving PA in older adults through mail-based interventions [101, 102] in the context of gamified PA interventions. Furthermore, this shows us that technology facilitation of PA can be achieved through the usage of motivational affordances through the gamification construct and quantification of PA.

These results reject the null hypothesis (H0) and supports the hypothesis that gamified PA applications would increase participant engagement and motivation in PA activity (H1, H2). This further shows that gamification elements or motivational affordances can help with improving engagement because these provide opportunity for improving one's skill sets (competence), choice of challenges, intensity levels and type of exercises (autonomy). Furthermore, addition of these elements serves as a basis for customization and personalization of PA technology. This allows for tailoring fitness apps for older adults PA mindful of their physical limitations, barriers to exercise and current health conditions. Therefore, this paper extends the concept of *adaptive engagement* [27, 50] where tailoring of the user's experiences can be designed to foster unique enjoyment through customized PA technology.

7 Conclusion and Limitations

While motivational affordances or gamifications elements have been used in many areas, research studies are often limited to pre-test and post-test intervention designs which were carried out over a short timeframe. However, effectiveness of the inclusion of gamification elements into PA technology for older adults can be determined only over a long-term engagement with such technology. To bridge this gap, we conducted a synchronous, three condition, eight-week study which included three groups: gamified, non-gamified and a control group. Participants (50+ years old) were randomized into the three groups and answered the IMI [91, 92], PNSE scale [86–88] and long form questionnaires. Results indicated that engagement was higher in the gamified and the non-gamified group compared to the control group. Furthermore, engagement was higher in the gamified group compared to the non-gamified group implying that gamifications elements can contribute to the enjoyment of PA over a longer period of time. Therefore, gamification elements or motivational affordances can help to foster competence and autonomy among older adults mindful of their physical limitations, barriers to exercise and current health conditions. While gamified technology for PA can help with motivation, engagement and enjoyment, participants in the gamified group may be biased due to novel features in the gamified PA application. Maintaining enrolment in the eight-week program or fatigue was also a major concern during the experimental study. Three participants from the control group decided to drop out from the study which required enrolment of new participants to this condition. Additionally, personalities and temperament of older adults also change with age-related impairments and current health conditions. Finally, older adults' perception of the games and gamification in the context of their understanding of gamification can be different in comparison to younger adults already adept with such PA technology. Therefore, onboarding of older adults with the stages and complexities of gamification technology could help alleviate their fears of technology acceptance.

Acknowledgements.   This paper is adapted from the first author's PhD dissertation, Adaptive Engagement of Older Adult's Physical Activity through Gamification and is an extended version of a prior publication [27, 50]. The authors would like to thank the Faculty of Applied Sciences and Technology, Applied Research and Innovation Department at Humber College of Applied Technology and Advanced Learning, and the Humber Employees Scholarship fund for their financial support of this research.

References

1. Barwais, F.A., Cuddihy, T.F., Tomson, L.M.: Physical activity, sedentary behavior and total wellness changes among sedentary adults: a 4-week randomized controlled trial. Health Qual. Life Out. **11**, 183 (2013)
2. Hu, F.B., Neuhouser, M.L., Perez-Escamilla, R., Martinez-Gonzalez, M.A., Willett, W.C.: U.S. dietary guidelines. Ann. Intern. Med. **165**, 604–605 (2016)
3. Brawley, R.L., Rejeski, W.J., King, A.C.: Promoting physical activity for older adults: the challenges for changing behavior. Am. J. Prev. Med. **25**, 172–183 (2003)
4. Bianchi-Berthouze, N., Kim, W.W., Patel, D.: Does body movement engage you more in digital game play? and why? In: Paiva, A.C.R., Prada, R., Picard, R.W. (eds.) ACII 2007. LNCS, vol. 4738, pp. 102–113. Springer, Heidelberg (2007). https://doi.org/10.1007/978-3-540-74889-2_10
5. Kooiman, B.J., Sheehan, D.P., Wesolek, M., Girginov, V.: Technology assisted reciprocal physical activity (TARP activities). Cogent Soc. Sci. **2**, 1209966 (2016)
6. Lister, C., West, J.H., Cannon, B., Sax, T., Brodegard, D.: Just a Fad? Gamification in health and fitness apps. JMIR Serious Games **2**, 1–12 (2014)
7. Shin, G., Jarrahi, M.H.: Studying the role of wearable health-tracking devices in raising users' self-awareness and motivating physical activities. In: WISH 2014 - Workshop on Interactive Systems in Healthcare, pp. 1–5 (2014)
8. Blobel, B., Pharow, P., Sousa, F., McCallum, S.: Gamification and serious games for personalized health. In: 9th International Conference on Wearable Micro and Nano Technologies for Personalized Health, pHealth 2012, pp. 85–96 (2012)
9. Bethancourt, H.J., Rosenberg, D.E., Beatty, T., Arterburn, D.E.: Barriers to and facilitators of physical activity program use among older adults. Clin. Med. Res. **12**, 10–20 (2014)
10. Czaja, S.J., Lee, C.C.: Information technology and older adults. In: Sears, A., Jacko, J.A. (eds.) Human-Computer Interaction Handbook: Fundamentals, Evolving Technologies and Emerging Applications, pp. 777–792. CRC Press, Boca Raton (2007)
11. Consolvo, S., Everitt, K., Smith, I., Landay, J.A.: Design requirements for technologies that encourage physical activity. In: Proceedings of SIGCHI Conference on Human Factors Computing System - CHI 2006, p. 457 (2006)
12. Payne, H.E., Moxley, V.B., MacDonald, E.: Health behavior theory in physical activity game apps: a content analysis. JMIR Serious Games **3**, e4 (2015)
13. Edwards, E.A., et al.: Gamification for health promotion: systematic review of behaviour change techniques in smartphone apps. BMJ Open **6**, e012447 (2016)
14. Yoganathan, D.: Designing Fitness Apps Using Persuasive Technology: A Text Mining Approach (2015)
15. Loos, E., Kaufman, D.: Positive impact of exergaming on older adults' mental and social well-being: in search of evidence. In: Zhou, J., Salvendy, G. (eds.) ITAP 2018. LNCS, vol. 10927, pp. 101–112. Springer, Cham (2018). https://doi.org/10.1007/978-3-319-92037-5_9

16. Hamari, J., Koivisto, J., Sarsa, H.: Does gamification work? - A literature review of empirical studies on gamification. In: Proceedings of Annual Hawaii International Conference on System Sciences, pp. 3025–3034 (2014)
17. Deterding, S., Dixon, D., Khaled, R., Nacke, L.E.: From game design elements to gamefulness: defining " gamification." In: MindTrek 2011, Tampere, Finland, 28–30 September 2011, pp. 9–15 (2011)
18. Kappen, D.L., Nacke, L.E.: The kaleidoscope of effective gamification: deconstructing gamification in business applications. In: Proceedings of the First International Conference on Gameful Design, Research, and Applications – Gamification 2013, pp. 119–122 (2013)
19. Schoeppe, S., et al.: Efficacy of interventions that use apps to improve diet, physical activity and sedentary behaviour: a systematic review. Int. J. Behav. Nutr. Phys. Act. **13**, 127 (2016)
20. Orji, R., Nacke, L.E., DiMarco, C.: Towards personality-driven persuasive health games and gamified systems. In: Proceedings of SIGCHI Conference on Human Factors Computing System (2017)
21. Orji, R.: Why are persuasive strategies effective? Exploring the strengths and weaknesses of socially-oriented persuasive strategies. In: de Vries, P.W., Oinas-Kukkonen, H., Siemons, L., Beerlage-de Jong, N., van Gemert-Pijnen, L. (eds.) PERSUASIVE 2017. LNCS, vol. 10171, pp. 253–266. Springer, Cham (2017). https://doi.org/10.1007/978-3-319-55134-0_20
22. Johnson, D., Deterding, S., Kuhn, K.-A., Staneva, A., Stoyanov, S., Hides, L.: Gamification for health and wellbeing: a systematic review of the literature. Internet Interv. **6**, 89–106 (2016)
23. Allam, A., Kostova, Z., Nakamoto, K., Schulz, P.J.: The effect of social support features and gamification on a web-based intervention for rheumatoid arthritis patients: randomized controlled trial. J. Med. Internet Res. **17**, e14 (2015)
24. Cota, T.T., Ishitani, L.: Motivation and benefits of digital games for the elderly: a systematic literature review. Rev. Bras. Comput. Appl. **7**, 2–16 (2015)
25. Bleakley, C.M., et al.: Gaming for health: a systematic review of the physical and cognitive effects of interactive computer games in older adults. J. Appl. Gerontol. **34**, NP166–NP189 (2015)
26. Pereira, P., Duarte, E., Rebelo, F., Noriega, P.: A review of gamification for health-related contexts. In: Marcus, A. (ed.) DUXU 2014. LNCS, vol. 8518, pp. 742–753. Springer, Cham (2014). https://doi.org/10.1007/978-3-319-07626-3_70
27. Kappen, D.L.: Adaptive Engagement of Older Adults' Fitness through Gamification (2017). http://hdl.handle.net/10155/881
28. Huta, V., Waterman, A.S.: Eudaimonia and its distinction from hedonia: developing a classification and terminology for understanding conceptual and operational definitions. J. Happiness Stud. **15**, 1425–1456 (2014). https://doi.org/10.1007/s10902-013-9485-0
29. Tondello, G.F., Wehbe, R.R., Diamond, L., Busch, M., Marczewski, A., Nacke, L.E.: The gamification user types hexad scale. In: Proceedings of the 2016 Annual Symposium on Computer-Human Interaction in Play (2016)
30. Dacey, M., Baltzell, A., Zaichkowsky, L.: Older adults' intrinsic and extrinsic motivation toward physical activity. Am. J. Health Behav. **32**, 570–582 (2008)
31. Bartle, R.: Hearts, Clubs, Diamonds, Spades: Players who suit MUDS. http://mud.co.uk/richard/hcds.htm
32. Gerling, K.M., Livingston, I., Nacke, L.E., Mandryk, R.: Full-body motion-based game interaction for older adults. In: Proceedings of 2012 ACM Annual Conference on Human Factors Computing System – CHI 2012, pp. 1873–1882 (2012)
33. Schutzer, K.A., Graves, B.S.: Barriers and motivations to exercise in older adults. Prev. Med. (Baltim) **39**, 1056–1061 (2004)

34. Nap, H.H., De Kort, Y.A.W., IJsselsteijn, W.A.: Senior gamers: preferences, motivations and needs. Gerontechnology **8**, 247–262 (2009)
35. Kappen, D.L., Mirza-Babaei, P., Nacke, L.E.: Older adults' physical activity and exergames: a systematic review. Int. J. Hum. Comput. Interact. **00**, 1–28 (2018)
36. Kooiman, B., Sheehan, D.: Exergaming theories: a literature review. Int. J. Game Based Learn. **5**, 1–14 (2015)
37. Primack, B.A., et al.: Role of video games in improving health-related outcomes: a systematic review. Am. J. Prev. Med. **42**, 630–638 (2012)
38. Zhang, F., Kaufman, D.: Physical and cognitive impacts of digital games on older adults: a meta-analytic review. J. Appl. Gerontol. **35**, 1189–1210 (2015)
39. Loos, E.: Exergaming: meaningful play for older adults? In: Zhou, J., Salvendy, G. (eds.) ITAP 2017. LNCS, Part II, vol. 10298, pp. 254–265. Springer, Cham (2017). https://doi.org/10.1007/978-3-319-58536-9_21
40. Rovniak, L.S., et al.: Engineering online and in-person social networks to sustain physical activity: application of a conceptual model. BMC Public Health **13**, 753 (2013)
41. Riche, Y., Mackay, W.: PeerCare: supporting awareness of rhythms and routines for better aging in place. Comput. Support Coop. Work **19**, 73–104 (2009). https://doi.org/10.1007/s10606-009-9105-z
42. Orji, R., Mandryk, R.L., Vassileva, J., Gerling, K.M.: Tailoring persuasive health games to gamer type. In: Proceedings of SIGCHI Conference on Human Factors in Computing Systems – CHI 2013, pp. 2467–2476. ACM Press, New York (2013)
43. Grönvall, E., Verdezoto, N.: Beyond self-monitoring: understanding non-functional aspects of home-based healthcare technology. In: Proceedings of UbiComp 2013, pp. 587–596 (2013)
44. Daalgard, L.G., Grönvall, E., Verdezoto, N.: MediFrame: a tablet application to plan, inform, remind and sustain older adults medication intake. In: In IEEE International Conference on Healthcare Informatics, pp. 36–45 (2013)
45. Axelrod, L., Fitzpatrick, G., Burridge, J., Mawson, S., Smith, P., Rodden, T., Ricketts, I.: The reality of homes fit for heroes: design challenges for rehabilitation technology at home. J. Assist. Technol. **3**, 35–43 (2009)
46. Jung, Y., Li, K.J., Janissa, N.S., Gladys, W.L.C., Lee, K.M.: Games for a better life: effects of playing wii games on the well-being of seniors in a long-term care facility. In: Proceedings of Sixth Australasian Conference on Interactive Entertainment – IE 2009, pp. 1–6 (2009)
47. Anguera, J.A., Gazzaley, A.: Video games, cognitive exercises, and the enhancement of cognitive abilities. Curr. Opin. Behav. Sci. **4**, 160–165 (2015)
48. Brox, E., Konstantinidis, S.T., Evertsen, G.: User-centered design of serious games for older adults following 3 years of experience with exergames for seniors: a study design. JMIR Serious Games **5**, e2 (2017)
49. Jung, Y., Li, K.J., Janissa, N.S., Gladys, W.L.C., Lee, K.M.: Games for a better life: effects of playing Wii games on the well-being of seniors in a long-term care facility. In: Proceedings of the Sixth Australasian Conference on Interactive Entertainment – IE 2009, pp. 1–6. ACM Press, New York (2009)
50. Kappen, D.L., Mirza-Babaei, P., Nacke, L.E.: Gamification of older adults' physical activity: an eight-week study. In: Proceedings of the 51st Annual Hawaii International Conference on System Sciences, pp. 1–12 (2018)

51. Kappen, D.L., Mirza-Babaei, P., Nacke, L.E.: Motivational affordances for older adults' physical activity technology: an expert evaluation. In: Zhou, J., Salvendy, G. (eds.) HCII 2019. LNCS, vol. 11592, pp. 388–406. Springer, Cham (2019). https://doi.org/10.1007/978-3-030-22012-9_28

52. Kappen, D.L.: Adaptive engagement of older adults' fitness through gamification. In: Proceedings of CHIPLAY 2015 (2015)

53. Alankus, G., Lazar, A., May, M., Kelleher, C.: Towards customizable games for stroke rehabilitation. In: Proceedings of 28th International Conference on Human Factors Computing System – CHI 2010, p. 2113 (2010)

54. Smeddinck, J., Siegel, S., Herrlich, M.: Adaptive difficulty in exergames for parkinson's disease patients. In: Proceedings of Graphics Interface Conference 2013, pp. 141–148 (2013)

55. Smith, S.T., Sherrington, C., Studenski, S., Schoene, D., Lord, S.R.: A novel Dance Dance Revolution (DDR) system for in-home training of stepping ability: Basic parameters of system use by older adults. Br. J. Sports Med. **51**, 441–444 (2009)

56. Laufer, Y., Dar, G., Kodesh, E.: Does a Wii-based exercise program enhance balance control of independently functioning older adults? A systematic review. Clin. Interv. Aging. **9**, 1803–1813 (2014)

57. Brox, E., Åsheim-olsen, H., Vognild, L.: Experiences from long-term exergaming with elderly. In: Proceedings of AcademicMindTrek 2014, pp. 216–220 (2014)

58. Albaina, I.M., Visser, T., van der Mast, C.A.P.G., Vastenburg, M.H.: Flowie: a persuasive virtual coach to motivate elderly individuals to walk. In: Proceedings of the 3D International ICST Conference on Pervasive Computing Technologies for Healthcare, pp. 1–7. ICST (2009)

59. Fan, C., Forlizzi, J., Dey, A.: Considerations for technology that support physical activity by older adults. In: Proceedings of ASSETS 2012, pp. 33–40. ACM Press, New York (2012)

60. Geurts, L., et al.: Digital games for physical therapy: fulfilling the need for calibration and adaptation. In: Proceedings of the Fifth International Conference on Tangible, Embedded, and Embodied Interaction, pp. 117–124 (2011)

61. Romero, N., Sturm, J., Bekker, T., de Valk, L., Kruitwagen, S.: Playful persuasion to support older adults' social and physical activities. Interact. Comput. **22**, 485–495 (2010)

62. Aarhus, R., Grönvall, E., Larsen, S.B., Wollsen, S.: Turning training into play: embodied gaming, seniors, physical training and motivation. Gerontechnology **10**, 110–120 (2011)

63. Al Mahmud, A., Mubin, O., Shahid, S., Martens, J.-B.: Designing social games for children and older adults: Two related case studies. Entertain. Comput. **1**, 147–156 (2010)

64. Kaushal, N., Rhodes, R.E.: Exercise habit formation in new gym members: a longitudinal study. J. Behav. Med. **38**, 652–663 (2015)

65. Martinson, B.C., et al.: Maintaining physical activity among older adults: 24-month outcomes of the Keep Active Minnesota randomized controlled trial. Prev. Med. (Baltim) **51**, 37–44 (2010)

66. van der Bij, A., Laurant, M.G.H., Wensing, M.: Effectiveness of physical activity a review. Am. J. Prev. Med. **22**, 120–133 (2002)

67. Irvine, A.B., Gelatt, V.A., Seeley, J.R., Macfarlane, P., Gau, J.M.: Web-based intervention to promote physical activity by sedentary older adults: randomized controlled trial. J. Med. Internet Res. **15**, e19 (2013)

68. Leuty, V., Boger, J., Young, L., Hoey, J., Mihailidis, A.: Engaging older adults with dementia in creative occupations using artificially intelligent assistive technology. Assist. Technol. **25**, 72–79 (2013)

69. Imam, B., et al.: A Telehealth intervention using nintendo Wii fit balance boards and iPads to improve walking in older adults with lower limb amputation (Wii.n.Walk): study protocol for a randomized controlled trial. JMIR Res. Protoc. **3**, e80 (2014)

70. Brauner, P., Calero Valdez, A., Schroeder, U., Ziefle, M.: Increase physical fitness and create health awareness through exergames and gamification. In: Holzinger, A., Ziefle, M., Hitz, M., Debevc, M. (eds.) SouthCHI 2013. LNCS, vol. 7946, pp. 349–362. Springer, Heidelberg (2013). https://doi.org/10.1007/978-3-642-39062-3_22

71. Romero, N., Sturm, J., Bekker, T., de Valk, L., Kruitwagen, S.: Playful persuasion to support older adults' social and physical activities…Do not use. Interact. Comput. **22**, 485–495 (4392)

72. Hamari, J., Koivisto, J.: Social motivations to use gamification: an empirical study of gamifying exercise. In: 21st European Conference on Information Systems, ECIS 2013. Association for Information Systems (2013)

73. Cadmus-Bertram, L.A., Marcus, B.H., Patterson, R.E., Parker, B.A., Morey, B.L.: Randomized trial of a fitbit-based physical activity intervention for women. Am. J. Prev. Med. **49**, 414–418 (2015)

74. Boyle, E.A., Connolly, T.M., Hainey, T., Boyle, J.M.: Engagement in digital entertainment games: a systematic review. Comput. Hum. Behav. **28**, 771–780 (2012)

75. Mekler, E.D., Bopp, J.A., Tuch, A.N., Opwis, K.: A systematic review of quantitative studies on the enjoyment of digital entertainment games. In: Proceedings of the 32nd Annual ACM Conference on Human Factors in Computing Systems – CHI 2014, pp. 927–936. ACM Press, New York (2014)

76. Douglas, Y., Hargadon, A.: The pleasure principle: immersion, engagement, flow. In: Hypertext 2000, pp. 153–160 (2000)

77. De Kort, Y.A.W., Ijsselsteijn, W.A.: People, places, and play: player experience in a socio-spatial context. ACM Comput. Entertain. **6**, 1–11 (2008)

78. McLaughlin, A., Gandy, M., Allaire, J., Whitlock, L.: Putting fun into video games for older adults. Ergon. Des. Q. Hum. Factors Appl. **20**, 13–22 (2012)

79. Jennett, C., et al.: Measuring and defining the experience of immersion in games. Int. J. Hum Comput Stud. **66**, 641–661 (2008)

80. Nacke, L., Drachen, A., Göbel, S.: Methods for evaluating gameplay experience in a serious gaming context. J. Comput. Sci. Sport. **9**, 1–12 (2000)

81. Ryan, R.M., Deci, E.L.: Intrinsic and extrinsic motivations: classic definitions and new directions. Contemp. Educ. Psychol. **25**, 54–67 (2000)

82. Deci, E.L., Eghrari, H., Patrick, B.C., Leone, D.R.: Facilitating internalization: the self determination theory perspective. J. Pers. **62**, 119–142 (1994)

83. Apter, M.J.: The structural phenomenology of play. In: Kerr, J.H., Apter, M.J. (eds.) Adult Play: A Reversal Theory Approach, pp. 13–30. The Netherlands, Amsterdam (1991)

84. Suits, B.: The Grasshopper—Games, life and utopia. University of Toronto Press, Toronto (1972)

85. Lieberoth, A.: Shallow gamification testing psychological effects of framing an activity as a game. Games Cult. **10**, 229–248 (2015)

86. Teixeira, P.J., Carraça, E.V., Markland, D., Silva, M.N., Ryan, R.M.: Exercise, physical activity, and self-determination theory: a systematic review. Int. J. Behav. Nutr. Phys. Act. **9**, 78 (2012)

87. Wilson, P.M., Rogers, W.T., Rodgers, W.M., Wild, T.C.: The psychological need satisfaction in exercise scale. J. Sport Exercise Psychol. **28**, 231–251 (2006)

88. Direito, A., Jiang, Y., Whittaker, R., Maddison, R.: Smartphone apps to improve fitness and increase physical activity among young people: protocol of the Apps for IMproving FITness (AIMFIT) randomized controlled trial. BMC Public Health **15**, 635 (2015)

89. Physical Activity Readiness Questionnaire - PAR-Q. (2002)
90. IPAQ-Group: Guidelines for Data Processing and Analysis of the International Physical Activity Questionnaire (IPAQ) – Short and Long Forms. Ipaq, pp. 1–15 (2005)
91. Description, S.: Intrinsic Motivation Inventory (IMI) (1994)
92. Lavigne, G.L., et al.: On the dynamic relationships between contextual (or general) and situational (or state) motivation toward exercise and physical activity: a longitudinal test of the top-down and bottom-up hypotheses. Int. J. Sport Exerc. Psychol. **7**, 147–168 (2009)
93. Borg, G.A.V.: Psychophysical bases of perceived exertion. Med. Sci. Sports Exerc. **14**, 377–381 (1982)
94. Field, A.: Discovering Statistics Using IBM SPSS Statistics. SAGE Publications Ltd., London (2013)
95. Ryan, R.M., Frederick, C.M., Lepes, D., Rubio, N., Sheldon, K.M.: Intrinsic motivation and exercise adherence. Int. J. Sport Psychol. **28**, 335–354 (1997)
96. Peels, D.A., et al.: Development of web-based computer-tailored advice to promote physical activity among people older than 50 years. J. Med. Internet Res. **14**, 15–27 (2012)
97. van Stralen, M.M., de Vries, H., Bolman, C., Mudde, A.N., Lechner, L.: Exploring the efficacy and moderators of two computer-tailored physical activity interventions for older adults: a randomized controlled trial. Ann. Behav. Med. **39**, 139–150 (2010)
98. Kappen, D.L., Nacke, L.E., Gerling, K.M., Tsotsos, L.E.: Design strategies for gamified physical activity applications for older adults. In: IEEE 49th Proceedings of the Annual Hawaii International Conference on System Sciences, pp. 1309–1318. IEEE Computer Society (2016)
99. Tabak, M., Dekker-van Weering, M., van Dijk, H., Vollenbroek-Hutten, M.: Promoting daily physical activity by means of mobile gaming: a review of the state of the art. Games Health J. **4**, 460–469 (2015)
100. Far, I.K., et al.: The interplay of physical and social wellbeing in older adults: investigating the relationship between physical training and social interactions with virtual social environments. PeerJ Comput. Sci. **1**, 1–25 (2015)
101. Martinson, B.C., Crain, A.L., Sherwood, N.E., Hayes, M., Pronk, N.P., O'Connor, P.J.: Maintaining physical activity among older adults: Six-month outcomes of the Keep Active Minnesota randomized controlled trial. Prev. Med. (Baltim). **46**, 111–119 (2008)
102. Peels, D.A., et al.: Long-term efficacy of a printed or a Web-based tailored physical activity intervention among older adults. Int. J. Behav. Nutr. Phys. Act. **10**, 104 (2013)

Implementing a Digital Wellness Application into Use – Challenges and Solutions Among Aged People

Tuomas Kari[1,2(✉)], Anna Sell[1,3], Markus Makkonen[1,2], Stina Wallin[4],
Pirkko Walden[1,3], Christer Carlsson[1,3], Lauri Frank[2],
and Joanna Carlsson[5]

[1] Institute for Advanced Management Systems Research, Turku, Finland
[2] Faculty of Information Technology,
University of Jyvaskyla, Jyvaskyla, Finland
{tuomas.t.kari,markus.v.makkonen,lauri.frank}@jyu.fi
[3] Faculty of Social Sciences, Business and Economics,
Åbo Akademi University, Turku, Finland
{anna.sell,pirkko.walden,christer.carlsson}@abo.fi
[4] Faculty of Education and Welfare Studies,
Åbo Akademi University, Vaasa, Finland
stina.wallin@abo.fi
[5] Faculty of Science and Engineering, University of Turku, Turku, Finland
joanna.p.carlsson@utu.fi

Abstract. The ageing population is a growing priority area for policy makers and healthcare providers worldwide. Life expectancy is improving, but at the same time, insufficient physical activity threatens older age. Thus, an important question arises: how to improve the probability of people living a healthy and active life in older age. One potential solution to support physical activity and healthy aging is digital wellness technologies. However, digital wellness technologies are still typically designed for younger populations, yet a growing need and potential also among aged people is prevalent. Aged people are a user group with distinct needs and challenges. The main purpose of this study was to identify challenges and suggest solutions for implementing digital wellness applications into use among aged people. The focus was on the implementation phase. This study was based on a research program where groups of aged people implement into use a digital wellness application that is meant for tracking, following, and supporting physical activity and exercise. In total, 14 main challenges in implementing digital wellness applications into use among aged people were identified. These challenges are categorised into 1) technology-based challenges, 2) physical activity-based challenges, and 3) participant-related challenges. In addition, possible solutions for each challenge are suggested. The findings of this study provide both researchers and practitioners with insights on aspects that would be beneficial to be taken into account in designing digital wellness applications and building digital wellness interventions for aged people.

Keywords: Wellness technology · Implementation · Physical activity · Exercise · Digital Wellness Services · Aged people · Older adults · Young elderly · Later life · Smartphone applications · Digital practices

© Springer Nature Switzerland AG 2020
Q. Gao and J. Zhou (Eds.): HCII 2020, LNCS 12208, pp. 310–328, 2020.
https://doi.org/10.1007/978-3-030-50249-2_23

1 Introduction

The ageing population is a growing priority area for policy makers and healthcare providers worldwide. Life expectancy is improving not just at birth but also at older ages. Globally, a person aged 65 could expect to live an additional 17 years in 2015–2020 and an additional 19 years by 2045–2050 [1]. The increasing life expectancy includes an important question: how to improve the probability of people living a healthy and active life in older age?

This is an imperative question as insufficient physical activity is a global problem across all age groups [2]. Insufficient physical activity is one of the leading risk factors for non-communicable diseases and death worldwide, whereas physical activity has significant health benefits across all age groups and contributes to the prevention of non-communicable diseases [2]. Researchers in various fields have begun serious effort to find solutions to battle the problems associated with a sedentary lifestyle, which are becoming increasingly common in our society. One of the research streams concerning this has focused on investigating wellness technologies and their use, as well as on how different wellness technologies could be used to promote physical activity.

There is a great variety of different digital wellness technologies, such as devices, applications, and services aimed for different target groups with diverse physical activity levels. Such technologies have become increasingly popular and are used by varying types of users and for various purposes [3]. However, digital wellness technologies as well as information technology in general are still typically designed for younger populations, yet a growing need and potential among aged people is prevalent [e.g., 4]. Indeed, this seems to be the case as persons aged 65 years or older represent around 18 to 22% of the population in most EU countries and around 20% in EU-28. Moreover, the share of the population aged 65 years or older is increasing in every EU member state, EFTA country, and candidate country [5]. On a global scale, the number of people aged over 65 years is projected to double to 1.5 billion by the year 2050 [1]. Similarly, as there is a rising need for digital wellness technologies designed for aged people, there is a rising need to study digital wellness practices of the aged people [e.g., 6, 7].

Digital wellness technologies can support physical activity in numerous ways. For example, such technologies can be used to increase physical activity levels – albeit with modest evidence [e.g., 8–10], they can be used for goal-setting [e.g., 11, 12], they can provide instructions and coaching [e.g., 13–15] as well as social support [e.g., 16], and they can make physical activities more entertaining through exergames [e.g., 17, 18] – see also [19, 20]. Studies also suggest that feedback from wellness technologies can increase their user's awareness of personal physical activity and motivate towards it [e.g., 21–24]. However, although tracking wellness-related activities can result in an improved awareness of daily activity, it is not always sufficient for sustained use of wellness technologies [25], which in turn can affect maintaining wellness routines [26]. Furthermore, discontinued use of wellness technology is often followed by a reduction in activity levels [27]. Hence, providing convincing reasons and guidance for using such technologies would probably increase their use adherence, and subsequently, adherence to wellness and physical activity related routines. One potential way to do this is through physical activity programs and interventions [16].

Wellness technologies in general can be implemented into use by the users themselves or via the support of a physical activity program or an intervention. In either case, when looking for suitable solutions and testing different alternatives to meet the existing needs, the implementation phase is crucial for technology adoption: does the technology bring sufficient added value or not [28]? Related to technology adoption, the implementation phase is where the user makes the decision on whether to continue using the technology (continued adoption) or to reject the technology (discontinuance). Indeed, [29] confirm that an initial positive response to wellness technology use does not guarantee continued use among older adults. Therefore, it is essential to study the implementation phase when examining the adoption of wellness technology.

The main purpose of this study is to identify challenges and to suggest solutions for implementing digital wellness applications into use among aged people. The main research questions are: 1) What are the central challenges in implementing digital wellness applications into use among aged people? and 2) What kind of solutions can be used to meet these challenges? The focus of the study is on the implementation phase. This study draws from a research program where groups of aged people implement into use a digital wellness application meant for tracking, following, and supporting their physical activity and exercise. The findings of this study provide both researchers and practitioners with insights on aspects that would be beneficial to be taken into account in designing digital wellness applications and building digital wellness interventions for aged people. Ultimately, the aim is to contribute to physical activity routines that will lead to increased long-term physical wellness among older populations.

2 Background

World Health Organization provides research-based guidelines and recommendations for physical activity [2]. These guidelines state, among others, that adults aged 65 years or older should do at least 150 min of moderate-intensity physical activity or at least 75 min of vigorous-intensity physical activity throughout the week, or an equivalent combination of moderate- and vigorous-intensity activity. For additional health benefits, they should increase moderate-intensity physical activity to 300 min per week, or equivalent. Additional physical activity to enhance balance and muscle-strength as well as to prevent falls should also be conducted [2]. All these are important to ward off age-related illness and frailty [30]. Moreover, studies [e.g., 31, 32] show that systematic physical activity contributes to a better quality of life during senior years. As mentioned, insufficient physical activity is a global problem among all age groups [2]. This is the case also in Finland [33]. However, when asked, 77% of the people in the 55–75 age group in Finland would like to be physically more active [33].

2.1   Digital Wellness Services for Young Elderly (DigitalWells) Program

This study originates from the *Digital Wellness Services for Young Elderly (DigitalWells)* research and development program [34], which is carried out in the years 2019 to 2021 in Finland. DigitalWells aims to recruit first 1000, then 2500, and finally 10000 participants during the three years of the program from the 60+ age group with the purpose of helping them to build and to adopt sustainable wellness and physical activity routines in their daily lives. The program's focus is on people aged 60+, because of 1) the possibility to build a strong impact on better health for the ageing population, 2) which will potentially have significant effects on the escalating costs for elderly care, and 3) contribute to better quality of life and more healthy years for the elderly. Further, while the definition of elderly or older person is somewhat arbitrary, "it is many times associated with the age at which one can begin to receive pension benefits. At the moment, there is no United Nations standard numerical criterion, but the UN agreed cutoff is 60+ years to refer to the older population" [55].

In the beginning, the main focus of the DigitalWells program is on promoting and supporting physical activity and exercise. The ultimate goal is to increase the probability for better health during the senior years and to contribute to better quality of life, which could also subsequently lead to reduced costs of senior health care. DigitalWells cooperates with the Finnish unions and associations of retired people. With the help of these nationwide unions and associations, field groups for the interested local associations are formed. Each group consist of approximately 25 to 50 voluntary participants and is assigned a field researcher who guides the group and provides support in different phases. To help to achieve the adoption of daily wellness routines and to support physical activity and exercise, a digital wellness mobile application is offered to and used by all the participants. For a more comprehensive description of the program, refer to [35], however, several refinements have taken place since the initial phase in 2019.

The first field phase of the DigitalWells program with the first wave of field groups from different parts of Finland started in June 2019. At that time, the participants in the groups implemented the DigitalWells mobile application into use. These groups acted as pilot groups, and the experiences and feedback from the interaction between them and the field researchers were used to refine the program and the mobile application as well as its deployment process before the next wave of field groups started in November 2019. During the program, new waves of field groups are started on a regular basis. The present study focuses on the implementation phase of the application in the first wave of field groups and participants who started in June 2019.

The DigitalWells Mobile Application. The DigitalWells mobile application is an application within an application. It operates on the Wellmo [36] application platform, where the DigitalWells application features constitute their own entity. The application and its use are free for the participants. However, the participants are required to have a smartphone of their own. The application works on iOS and Android platforms. Thus, most smartphones are capable of running it. The DigitalWells application is aimed to support the forming of wellness routines in everyday life and it is designed specifically for aged people. The first central features in the DigitalWells application are related to tracking physical activity and exercise. A key feature is the ability to transfer the collected personal wellness data to My Kanta Personal Health Record (Kanta PHR), which is a Finnish national repository for personal wellness records [37]. The Wellmo application platform also supports importing exercise data and other wellness data from certain external services, for example, Polar, Fitbit, iHealth, and Google Fit. The DigitalWells application is under constant development. New versions are planned to be released twice a year and minor updates more often. Features such as the ability to plan exercise programs, digital coaching features [13–15], gamification features [38, 39], and the ability to directly connect to an exercise tracker device are planned to be introduced in the future.

The version that was implemented into use among the first field groups in June 2019 was numbered the 1.0 version. This version included, for example, features for tracking and following one's physical activity and exercise, simple weekly and monthly reports about the conducted physical activity and exercise, and the possibility to import data from certain external wellness services supported by Wellmo. Data transfer to Kanta PHR was not yet active. In the released newer versions of the DigitalWells application the procedure of taking the application into use has remained quite similar.

2.2 Implementation Phase

The implementation phase is a stage of the innovation-decision process presented in the innovation diffusion theory (IDT) by Rogers [28, 40]. Implementation has been a widely included component in different theories and models regarding information technology [c.f. e.g., 41, 42]. The innovation-decision process reflects the decision-making process linked to the adoption of an innovation. It is defined as "the process through which an individual passes from first knowledge of an innovation to forming an attitude toward the innovation, to a decision to adopt or reject, to implementation and use of the new idea, and to confirmation of this decision" [28, p. 475].

There are five phases included in the innovation-decision process: 1) knowledge, 2) persuasion, 3) decision, 4) implementation, and 5) confirmation. The first phase, where the process begins, is the knowledge phase. During it, the individual becomes aware of the innovation. The process continues with the persuasion phase, during which the individual seeks information regarding the innovation and forms an attitude towards it. Next is the decision phase, during which the individual makes a preliminary decision to either adopt or reject the innovation, that is, either to take the innovation into use or not. This decision is affected by the individual's attitude towards the innovation and perceived characteristics of the innovation. After the decision phase, the implementation phase takes place. The implementation phase is where the individual implements the innovation into use (i.e., becomes a user) and determines its usefulness. Following the decision and the implementation phase, in the confirmation phase, the user makes the final confirmation decision on whether to continue or discontinue the use of the innovation. Should the user's positive perceptions of using the innovation be strengthened during the implementation phase, the use is likely to continue. Respectively, should the user perceive contradictions with his or her preliminary decision to adopt, the decision can turn into rejection and the use discontinue. If the perceptions affecting the preliminary decision to reject are positively strengthened, it is also possible that the preliminary rejection decision can change and later adoption occur.

Generally, the different choices and functions related to the innovation-decision process can extend to a longer period of time [28]. Rogers [28] also introduces prior conditions related to the individual (i.e., decision maker) that affect the process. These include innovativeness, previous practice, felt needs, and norms of the social system. Furthermore, there are perceived characteristics of an innovation which influence the individual's evaluation of the innovation: Relative advantage, that is, "the degree to which an innovation is perceived as better than the idea it supersedes"; Complexity, that is, "the degree to which an innovation is perceived as difficult to understand and use"; Compatibility, that is, "the degree to which an innovation is perceived as being consistent with the existing values, past experiences, and need of potential adopters"; Trialability, that is, "the degree to which an innovation may be experimented with on a limited basis"; and Observability, that is, "the degree to which the results of an innovation are visible to others" [28, pp. 15–16]. Innovations that are perceived to have greater relative advantage, compatibility, trialability, and observability as well as to have less complexity will more likely be adopted.

It is evident that the implementation phase can have a significant influence on the final adoption decision. This also applies to digital wellness technologies. Kari et al. [43], for example, found that the experiences during the implementation phase of a digital wellness technology have an influencing role on the final adoption decision. Moreover, several studies [e.g., 44] suggest the commonness of users' disengagement with digital wellness technologies during the first months of use, that is, during the implementation phase. This applies also among older adults; an initial positive response to wellness technology use does not guarantee use maintenance [29]. Thus, different aspects connected to the implementation phase and the challenges related to it are an important matter to study.

3   Methodology

This study has a qualitative approach. The general goal of qualitative research is to understand real life and find new knowledge [45]. It aims to understand people, their actions, as well as the social and cultural context in which their actions occur. One of the central benefits of qualitative research is enabling the researcher to see and understand the underlying contexts in which actions happen and decisions are made [45].

The focus of the study is on the first field phase of the DigitalWells program that began in June 2019. At that time, the first wave of eight field groups with a total of 142 participants implemented the DigitalWells mobile application into use. These groups acted as pilot groups before the next wave of field groups was launched in November 2019. Each group had one field researcher who organised field meetings, guided the group in the program, assisted in taking the application into use, and provided support through the implementation phase. The implementation phase lasted for five months, consisting of a one-month introduction period in which the program was introduced and the application was installed and taken into use, followed by a four-month use period, during which the participants used the application in their daily lives but were able to get support by request.

The data for this study consisted of field notes made during and after the field meetings, textual communication (e.g., emails) between the field researchers during the implementation phase, and notes on the communication between the field researchers and the participants during the implementation phase. In addition, the participants also filled forms where they could describe their experiences from the implementation phase regarding the application and its use. Finally, all field researchers made a personal list based on their own experiences about the central challenges and solutions concerning the implementation phase. All these different data sources were combined into one data set before the analysis and then analysed by using thematic analysis.

Thematic analysis is a method for "identifying, analysing and reporting patterns (themes) within data" [46, p. 79]. It is the most widely used method of analysis in qualitative research [47]. It supports interpreting the research topic from various aspects and organising and describing the data set in rich detail [46]. To support the analysis, guidelines presented by [46] and [48] were applied. As suggested, these were applied flexibly to fit the research setting and the collected data. The analysis began by reading and rereading the data set to get familiar with it, concurrently marking all interesting features in it. Next, common tendencies were recognised. Based on the recognised tendencies, recurring themes were identified and analysed in more detail. A spreadsheet program was used as a tool to aid in this. As [46] suggest, the analysis process was recursive, meaning that the analysis moved back and forth between the different phases. Finally, a report was produced. After thematic analysis, the findings were further refined with the field researchers.

3.1 Participants in the Field Groups

In the first phase, the implementation of the application into use was conducted among eight field groups. In total, these groups comprised of 142 participants. Of them, 36.9% were male and 63.1% were female. The age of the participants ranged from 62 to 89 years, the average being 70.3 years (standard deviation 4.3 years). Descriptive statistics concerning gender, age, education, marital status, and perceived physical activity level of the 142 participants in the eight field groups are reported in Table 1.

Table 1. Descriptive statistics of the participants in the field groups (N = 142).

	n	%
Gender		
Male	52	36.9
Female	89	63.1
Other	0	0.0
N/A	1	–

(*continued*)

Table 1. (*continued*)

	n	%
Age		
60–64 years	6	4.4
65–69 years	51	37.5
70–74 years	55	40.4
75– years	24	17.6
N/A	6	–
Highest education		
Primary education	5	3.6
Vocational education	44	31.6
Upper secondary school	0	0.0
Further vocational education	35	25.2
University of applied sciences degree	12	8.6
University degree	39	28.1
Other	4	2.9
N/A	3	–
Marital status		
Married	97	68.3
Common-law marriage	5	3.5
Registered partnership	0	0.0
Unmarried	1	0.7
Divorced	20	14.1
Widowed	17	12.0
Other	2	1.4
N/A	–	–
Perceived physical activity level		
Very high	1	0.7
High	28	19.9
Moderate	97	68.8
Low	6	4.3
Very low	9	6.4
Sedentary	0	0.0
N/A	1	–

In addition to general demographics, we investigated the participants' physical activity levels and the personal innovativeness in the domain of information technology (PIIT) [49]. This was done to check and ensure that the field groups were not comprised of just certain types of people, for example, those considering themselves to be physically already very active or those being very interested in new information technologies. Seifert et al. [7] found that older adults with a high interest towards new technology or who exercise frequently have a higher likelihood of using mobile devices for physical activity tracking. As can be seen from Table 1, the perceived physical activity level of the participants was mostly moderate, as it was stated by almost 69% of the participants. In addition, there were about twice the number of more active (very high and high, 20.6%) than less active (low and very low, 10.7%) people. As a methodological consideration, it should be noted that this was a subjective perception and can vary from objective measurements due to the general limitations of assessing physical activity by self-report [e.g., 50]. Yet, it suggests that reaching those "most in need" in terms of physical inactivity can be challenging.

PIIT is defined as "the willingness of an individual to try out any new information technology" [49] and reflects individual's earliness or lateness in adopting information technology innovations [49]. User's personal innovativeness is understood to be connected to a higher likelihood to test and adopt new technologies, including wearable healthcare devices [51]. We measured PIIT by using the 7-point scale of four items proposed by [49]. The scale was found to have a Cronbach's alpha of 0.81, suggesting good internal consistency. The mean of the four items among participants varied from 1.25 to 7.00 and averaged at 4.75 (standard deviation 1.44), meaning that there was considerable variance in the interest of the participants towards new information technology. On average, the participants were slightly more interested than uninterested toward trying out new information technology.

4 Findings

Based on the analysis, 14 main challenges in implementing the application into use were identified. These challenges could be categorised into 1) technology-based challenges, 2) physical activity-based challenges, and 3) participant-related challenges. However, it is to be noted that some challenges overlap between different categories, and the presented categorisation is not entirely unambiguous.

Each presented challenge is also accompanied with suggested solutions. These solutions are based on the analysis and our own experiences on utilising the solutions. However, all suggested solutions were not (yet) employed in the field, but rather are insights we have learned along the way.

4.1 Technology-Based Challenges

Five main technology-based challenges were identified: 1) app-in-app issues, 2) variety of different phone models, 3) technical issues in using the application, 4) need to register and login to use the app, and 5) issues with external data sources.

Challenge 1: App-in-App Issues. This challenge originates from using an application within an application and an application platform that is not self-developed. Therefore, although it is possible to control the features of the own application, there could be little control over the application platform. There can be, for example, software bugs, notification screens, compatibility issues with certain phone models, or similar issues, which one has no control on, and which may come as a surprise. This challenge also applies to other applications, commercial and non-commercial, that are not self-developed.

Suggested solution: If using an application within an application, it is imperative to have a good communication relationship with the application platform provider: First, in order to be able to find out as much as possible about the application platform features and to prepare for issues beforehand; Second, in order to quickly receive answers from the application platform provider when something unexpected occurs. Naturally, it is also recommended to conduct extensive testing before launching the application.

Challenge 2: Variety of Different Phone Models. This challenge relates to the great variety of different phone models that are used in the field. It is unfeasible to pre-test the application with all the different models. Thus, unexpected issues can occur either while installing the application or when using it. This can also present a challenge to the field researchers in terms of how to solve these issues. This is notable especially with Android phones, as they are often implemented with modified operating systems, but even more so with the so called "senior phones" that are designed to be simpler to use, to show bigger fonts, and so forth. Hence, issues related to those can occur, for example, with screen scaling.

Suggested solution: Instruct the field researchers to be prepared for such issues, both mentally and practically. Enquire beforehand from the application provider or the application platform provider if there are any known issues with "senior phones" (or any phones for that matter). If possible, acquire different phones and test the application with them before going into the field. These challenges are mostly solvable but can require some heuristic approach. Instructing the field researchers to document and communicate the encountered issues to the research group is a good practice.

Challenge 3: Technical Issues in Using the Application. There is always the possibility that some technical issues occur while using the application, the reason for which can often be difficult to pinpoint at first. Besides causing possible issues with functionality, this can cause disturbance or frustration especially among people who possess relatively low technology skills. They may think they did something wrong even if it was the application malfunctioning, which acts as the cause for their frustration.

Suggested solution: Communicate with the participants. Ask for patience if an issue is encountered. Inspect the issue and if so, let them know that it was the application that was malfunctioning and it is not the user's fault (and that the issue will be fixed). Provide support on need-basis, preferably via instant messenger, such as WhatsApp (fast to respond and possible to ask detailing questions). Finally, fix the issue.

Challenge 4: Need to Register and Login to Use the Application. There is often a need to first register an account in order to be able to use an application, and also often a need to login when using the application for the first time. Registering accounts and logging in might not be familiar procedures in general for aged people. Whilst the registration is mostly unproblematic, issues can occur with logging in. Participants may not remember their password, or they may mix the application login password with their phone or email passwords despite having created the account for the application – sometimes just before trying to log in. A password's visibility replaced by stars (e.g., *********) when typing it, for example during creating an account and logging in, can also cause issues.

Suggested solution: Provide support through the account registration and the first time use of the application when there is the need to login and set up the application. It is encouraged to give this support in field meetings if possible. Also, present clear instructions for which credentials to use when logging in to the application. There should be a forgotten password recovery option on the login screen.

Challenge 5: Issues with External Data Sources. This challenge relates to importing data to the application from external services if such feature is supported. From some services the (physical activity and exercise) data is imported without any problems and in a compatible way, but from some other services there can be issues or errors related to how the imported data is handled and how it is displayed in the application. This can lead to false markings or erratic reporting of physical activity.

Suggested solution: Test beforehand data import from available external data sources in order to establish which external services work correctly with the application. Recommend using only those and no others. If possible, disable data import from external services that are not fully compliant with the application. Depending on the research goals, the use of external data sources can also be discouraged.

4.2   Physical Activity-Based Challenges

Three main physical activity-based challenges were identified: 1) physical activities not available in the application's listing, 2) physical activity can be perceived challenging among aged people, and 3) communicating the received physical activity benefit from using the application.

Challenge 1: Physical Activities not Available in the Application's Listing. Most applications and services that can be used to store data on physical activities and exercise provide a list of activities from which the user can choose the appropriate ones. Typically, these lists are rather extensive. However, there are types of exercises that are modified or specifically designed for aged people. Thus, they are not necessarily very common and are often missing from the applications' list of activities. Yet, these activities can be very dear to certain users. Not being able to select such an activity can cause frustration or annoyance as users are not able to mark their exercises with correct terms.

Suggested solution: Collect feedback and wishes from the field on such activities that are often conducted but missing from the application's list of activities. Make additions based on the requests and let the participants know that their feedback and wishes are welcomed and appreciated. Before new activities are added to the list, a potential solution is to guide the participants to mark the missing activities as a listed activity that resembles the conducted activity the most, which aids in the estimation of the physical exertion.

Challenge 2: Physical Activity can be Perceived Challenging Among Aged People. This challenge can be related to a variety of things, such as low self-efficacy towards physical activity or exercise, which can be an issue especially among aged people and act as a barrier to being physically active. In many cases, this challenge can be traced to a participant not having routines or good practices for physical activity.

Not actually being able to conduct any physical activity or exercise due to health or similar problems barely existed in the field groups.

Suggested solution: Collect good practices for physical activity from the field and present them to all participants. Such practices are likely to be perceived more reachable when they come from a peer group of same aged people in the same city/town with more or less the same possibilities and services. As an example, we first collected and then presented the following five good practices from and to the field groups: 1) have a specified schedule, 2) have a varying selection of activities, 3) exercise in the morning or day time, 4) exercise with a friend or in an organised group, and 5) if it feels unappealing to get going, think about the positive feeling that exercising offers.

Challenge 3: Communicating the Received Physical Activity Benefit from Using the Application. This challenge relates to some participants questioning the benefit from using the application, for example, for their physical activity levels. This is apparent especially if a participant perceives to be already conducting "enough" physical activity or misses the benefit of tracking one's own activities in general instead of just doing something when feeling like it. Some might also perceive that using the application "takes extra time". There is a risk for drop-out if the application use is not perceived useful enough during the implementation phase.

Suggested solution: Highlight the features that support tracking and following one's own physical activity and exercise on a longer-term, for example, informative weekly/monthly/yearly reports and the ability to follow own progress. Reason that following one's own physical activity can increase understanding, motivation, and adherence towards it. Also highlight the (possible) upcoming new features that offer more benefits. In some instances, it is also valuable to mention about the altruistic reasons for use, such as contributing to research and greater good.

4.3   Participant-Related Challenges

Six main participant-related challenges were identified: 1) variation in technology skills among the participants, 2) variation in physical activity literacy among the participants, 3) participants being unable to describe the problem or its details, 4) some participants not having an email account, 5) some participants not having email access in their phones, and 6) not everyone can be present in the field meetings at the same time.

Challenge 1: Variation in Technology Skills Among the Participants. This challenge relates to a high variation in the technology skills among aged people. Whereas some participants are fluent with technology, some others have very low technology skills in general or low skills related to smartphone use. For example, some might have never installed any applications from application stores or do not know the functions of their own phones. However, they might still be using applications installed by someone else, typically by their children. A challenge lies also in taking the application into use in the field: how to present the information in a way that it is easy enough for all to understand but not too tiresome for some.

Suggested solution: Avoid presenting too much new information or too many new concepts at a given time. Consider what is a suitable amount of new information or instructions considering the target group. Often the rule "keep it simple" is valuable. Prepare to provide support during the field meetings, especially in the beginning when installing the application and learning how to use it. It might also be good to encourage peer support: let the more advanced users assist those who need more support. Moreover, the field researchers should naturally be very skilled with the application.

Challenge 2: Variation in Physical Activity Literacy Among the Participants. There are generally challenges among people in understanding basic physical activity related concepts, or they might be unaware of the many benefits of physical activity. The participants may also have misbeliefs about physical activity and exercise related things. For example, some participants may present bizarre statements or questions related to physical activity, which by nature contradict common scientifically agreed consensus. This, in turn, can cause confusion or bafflement among the peers.

Suggested solution: As for the first challenge, avoid presenting too much new information or too many new concepts at a given time. Keep it simple, taking into account that some have very limited understanding and knowledge on physical activity related things. If misconceptions or misbeliefs about physical activity related things are presented (in public or in person), it is best to politely correct them then and there and, if needed, provide rationalisations and proper solutions. Moreover, the field researchers should naturally be knowledgeable of the key concepts of physical activity.

Challenge 3: Participants Being Unable to Describe the Problem or its Details. At times, a participant faces an issue or a problem with the application or its use but is unable to describe it in adequate detail for the researcher or the support person to comprehend what actually is the problem or the issue. These kinds of situations are more common with people who have low technology skills. In such cases, it can be difficult to provide a solution for the problem at hand unless being able to get more information.

Suggested solution: Provide support through communication mediums that allow real-time communication and the sharing of screen captures straight from the phone, such as WhatsApp. This enables asking more detailing questions, responding faster, and potentially solving the problems more efficiently. If the problem arises or is presented during a field meeting, then it is valuable to provide instant hands-on support, as it is possible to "see it yourself" and interact with the problem or issue.

Challenge 4: Some Participants not Having an Email Account. Although not common, some (aged) people do not have an email account. If an email address is needed to use the application, the participant will need to create an account or one needs to be created for the participant.

Suggested solution: If an email address is only needed for registering and taking the application into use, instead of demanding the participant to create an account, it might be easier to use an artificial or dedicated email address. Develop a method for creating artificial email addresses for those not having an email account. The registration mails sent to these artificial addresses can be automatically redirected to another mailbox. Moreover, do not rely on email as the only means for communication and informing participants. Instead, prepare to distribute information also through other means. For example, certain instant communication applications seem to have good reachability.

Challenge 5: Some Participants not Having Email Access in their Phones. Not having an email access in their phones is much more common than not having an email account at all. If the mobile application requires an invitation (email or code) to set up an account and to start using it, do not solely rely on email invitations. If the application invitations are sent by email, some participants might not be able to access it if installing the application away from a computer, for example, in a field meeting.

Suggested solution: If possible, allow creating an account from inside the application without the need to access one's email simultaneously. If using invitations, instead of using only email invitations, consider also invitation codes which can be inserted within the application. This removes the need to have direct email access to set up the account.

Challenge 6: Not Everyone can be Present in the Field Meetings at the Same Time. In cases where the application is supposed to be taken into use during a field meeting, it is good to acknowledge that not every participant is able to attend the meetings at the same time. Still, the benefit in taking the application into use in field meetings is that a field researcher can provide hands-on support for those in need of it. Nevertheless, there might be cases where some participants need to install the application on their own without the immediate support of the field researcher.

Suggested solution: Step-by-step instructions with informative images can be sent to the participants in order for them to take the application into use by themselves without personal assistance. Extra meetings can also be arranged, though this is not always feasible. Peer support can also be encouraged; if the participant has familiar persons in the group or there are group coordinators who have already installed the application themselves, they can possibly provide support for installing and taking the application into use. Remote support can also be provided to these participants if a common and suitable time for conducting the installation can be arranged.

5   Conclusions

The main purpose of this study was to identify challenges and suggest solutions for implementing digital wellness applications into use among aged people. The focus was on the implementation phase. More specifically, this study was based on a research program where groups of aged people implement into use a digital wellness application that is meant for tracking, following, and supporting physical activity and exercise. The main research questions (RQ) studied in this paper were: 1) What are the central challenges in implementing digital wellness applications into use among aged people? and 2) What kind of solutions can be used to meet these challenges?

As an answer to RQ 1, in total, 14 main challenges in implementing digital wellness applications into use among aged people were identified. These challenges could be categorised into 1) technology-based challenges, 2) physical activity-based challenges, and 3) participant-related challenges, although with some overlap among the categories. In addition to identifying the challenges, and as an answer to RQ 2, we also suggested possible solutions for each challenge. The challenges and the suggested solutions are summarised in Table 2.

T. Kari et al.

Table 2. Main challenges and solutions.

Technology-based challenges
1. App-in-app issues
Solution: communication with the application platform provider; testing
2. Variety of different phone models
Solution: groundwork; communication with the application (platform) provider; testing
3. Technical issues in using the application
Solution: communication with the participants; reassurance; support
4. Need to register and login to use the app
Solution: support; instructions; forgotten password recovery option
5. Issues with external data sources
Solution: testing; recommend only fully compatible ones; disable incompatible ones
Physical activity-based challenges
1. Physical activities not available in the application's listing
Solution: collect feedback; make additions; provide an option
2. Physical activity can be perceived challenging among aged people
Solution: collect and offer good practices
3. Communicating the received physical activity benefit from using the application
Solution: highlight features and benefits for longer-term tracking; provide reasoning
Participant-related challenges
1. Variation in technology skills among the participants
Solution: level of information; keep it simple; peer support
2. Variation in physical activity literacy among the participants
Solution: level of information; keep it simple; correct and provide reasoning
3. Participants being unable to describe the problem or its details
Solution: support with suitable communication mediums; hands-on support
4. Some participants not having an email account
Solution: artificial email address; other means of communication besides email
5. Some participants not having email access in their phones
Solution: do not require direct email access; allow other means
6. Not everyone can be present in the field meetings at the same time
Solution: step-by-step instructions; peer-support; remote support

Although the application used in our program is an application within an application, most of the challenges and solutions are also applicable to situations in which standalone applications are used. Although necessary, some of the suggested solutions are work-arounds to overcome the present barriers, and not always ideal for the user. For example, using artificial email addresses for registration is likely to be perplexing for a user who has never used email. In such cases, the field researcher has to intervene in the process in ways which the participant might not completely understand. This can possibly undermine the user's agency.

In this paper, we have suggested solutions to challenges that are frequently encountered in the implementation of digital wellness technologies among aged people. It is, however, equally important that the special characteristics of the target population and their typical challenges would be considered already in the design phase of digital wellness solutions and interventions. The findings of this study provide both researchers and practitioners with insights on aspects that would be beneficial to take into account when designing digital wellness applications and building digital wellness interventions and programs for aged people. At the same time, this study highlights the importance and the growing need to research digital wellness practices among aged people. We call for more research efforts on the topic and dare to say – *grey is the new black.*

6   Limitations and Future Research

There are two main limitations in the study. First, the identified challenges and solutions are based on our own program. Thus, other challenges may also occur and not all suggested solutions are possible or feasible to be employed in every use case. However, we believe that the identified challenges are likely to be faced by others also, and the suggested solutions are aimed to be useful in most instances. Second, we did not yet employ and test every suggested solution ourselves, but they rather are insights we have learned. Thus, we cannot be entirely sure about their effectiveness. However, we believe in the efficacy of these solutions and plan to utilise them in the future.

As the program continues, we will include larger numbers of aged participants. We are continuously building on our own expertise with this specific group of consumers, and thereby we are able to improve the design of the implementation process. This is not possible unless we are engaged in a continuous iterative process of implementation, evaluation, and improvement, building on both our own data collection and analysis as well as on other relevant research.

A typical weakness of many studies on technology implementation and adoption is their short duration; many studies span only a few weeks or months. It is one of our central goals to gather longitudinal data, which has been deemed important by many [e.g., 52–54]. When writing this (January 2020), the first groups of participants have been involved in the project for eight months. We intend to follow the participants through the implementation phase and the confirmation phase as in Rogers' [28] innovation-decision process. The participants can at any point, based on their own will and choice, discontinue their use of the studied wellness technologies, or completely depart from the project. Among others, we intend to investigate the reasons for discontinuance. Further, we are planning to design interventions utilising gamification mechanisms and mixed reality applications in order to investigate their possible impact on adherence to wellness technology use as well as to physical activity and exercise habits.

Acknowledgments. We are thankful to The Social Insurance Institution of Finland for funding the DigitalWells program and research project.

References

1. United Nations: World population ageing 2019 (2019). https://www.un.org/en/development/desa/population/publications/pdf/ageing/WorldPopulationAgeing2019-Highlights.pdf. Accessed 5 Jan 2020
2. World Health Organization: Physical activity (2018). https://www.who.int/news-room/fact-sheets/detail/physical-activity. Accessed 4 Jan 2020
3. Kettunen, E., Kari, T., Moilanen, P., Vehmas, H., Frank, L.: Ideal types of sport and wellness technology users. In: Proceedings of the 11th Mediterranean Conference on Information Systems, Genoa, Italy. AIS (2017). 12 pages
4. Carlsson, C., Walden, P.: Digital coaching to build sustainable wellness routines for young elderly. In: Proceedings of the 30th Bled eConference "Digital Transformation – From Connecting Things to Transforming Our Lives", Bled, Slovenia, pp. 57–70. University of Maribor (2017)
5. Eurostat: Population structure and ageing (2019). https://ec.europa.eu/eurostat/statistics-explained/index.php/Population_structure_and_ageing#Past_and_future_population_ageing_trends_in_the_EU. Accessed 5 Jan 2020
6. Allmér, H.: Servicescape for digital wellness services for young elderly. Åbo Akademi University Press, Turku, Finland (2018)
7. Seifert, A., Schlomann, A., Rietz, C., Schelling, H.R.: The use of mobile devices for physical activity tracking in older adults' everyday life. Digit. Health 3, 1–12 (2017)
8. de Vries, H.J., Kooiman, T.J., van Ittersum, M.W., van Brussel, M., de Groot, M.: Do activity monitors increase physical activity in adults with overweight or obesity? A systematic review and meta-analysis. Obesity 24(10), 2078–2091 (2016)
9. Larsen, R.T., Christensen, J., Juhl, C.B., Andersen, H.B., Langberg, H.: Physical activity monitors to enhance amount of physical activity in older adults – a systematic review and meta-analysis. Eur. Rev. Aging Phys. Act. 16(1), 7 (2019)
10. Romeo, A., et al.: Can smartphone apps increase physical activity? Systematic review and meta-analysis. J. Med. Internet Res. 21(3), e12053 (2019)
11. Gordon, M., Althoff, T., Leskovec, J.: Goal-setting and achievement in activity tracking apps: a case study of MyFitnessPal. In: Proceedings of the World Wide Web Conference, New York, NY, pp. 571–582. ACM (2019)
12. Kirwan, M., Duncan, M., Vandelanotte, C.: Smartphone apps for physical activity: a systematic review. J. Sci. Med. Sport 16, e47 (2013)
13. Kari, T., Rinne, P.: Influence of digital coaching on physical activity: motivation and behaviour of physically inactive individuals. In: Proceedings of the 31st Bled eConference "Digital Transformation – Meeting the Challenges", Bled, Slovenia, pp. 127–145. University of Maribor Press (2018)
14. Kettunen, E., Kari, T.: Can sport and wellness technology be my personal trainer? Teenagers and digital coaching. In: Proceedings of the 31st Bled eConference "Digital Transformation – Meeting the Challenges", Bled, Slovenia, pp. 463–476. University of Maribor Press (2018)
15. Sell, A., Walden, P., Carlsson, C., Helmefalk, M., Marcusson, L.: Digital coaching to support university students' physical activity. In: Proceedings of the 32nd Bled eConference "Humanizing Technology for a Sustainable Society", Bled, Slovenia, pp. 599–618. University of Maribor Press (2019)
16. Sullivan, A.N., Lachman, M.E.: Behavior change with fitness technology in sedentary adults: a review of the evidence for increasing physical activity. Front. Publ. Health 4, 289 (2017)

17. Kari, T.: Exergaming usage: hedonic and utilitarian aspects. Jyväskylä studies in computing, (260) (2017). Jyväskylä, Finland
18. Loos, E., Zonneveld, A.: Silver gaming: serious fun for seniors? In: Zhou, J., Salvendy, G. (eds.) ITAP 2016. LNCS, vol. 9755, pp. 330–341. Springer, Cham (2016). https://doi.org/ 10.1007/978-3-319-39949-2_32
19. Kari, T.: Can exergaming promote physical fitness and physical activity? A systematic review of systematic reviews. Int. J. Gaming Comput. Med. Simul. **6**(4), 59–77 (2014)
20. Loos, E.: Exergaming: meaningful play for older adults? In: Zhou, J., Salvendy, G. (eds.) ITAP 2017. LNCS, vol. 10298, pp. 254–265. Springer, Cham (2017). https://doi.org/10. 1007/978-3-319-58536-9_21
21. Faghri, P.D., Omokaro, C., Parker, C., Nichols, E., Gustavesen, S., Blozie, E.: E-technology and pedometer walking program to increase physical activity at work. J. Prim. Prev. **29**(1), 73–91 (2008)
22. Kang, M., Marshall, S.J., Barreira, T.V., Lee, J.O.: Effect of pedometer-based physical activity interventions: a meta-analysis. Res. Q. Exercise Sport **80**(3), 648–655 (2009)
23. Kari, T., Kettunen, E., Moilanen, P., Frank, L.: Wellness technology use in everyday life: a diary study. In: Proceedings of the 30th Bled eConference "Digital Transformation – From Connecting Things to Transforming Our Lives", Bled, Slovenia, pp. 279–294. University of Maribor (2017)
24. Wang, J.B., et al.: Mobile and wearable device features that matter in promoting physical activity. J. Mob. Technol. Med. **5**(2), 2–11 (2016)
25. Miyamoto, S.W., Henderson, S., Young, H.M., Pande, A., Han, J.J.: Tracking health data is not enough: a qualitative exploration of the role of healthcare partnerships and mhealth technology to promote physical activity and to sustain behavior change. JMIR mHealth uHealth **4**(1), e5 (2016)
26. Warraich, M.U.: Wellness routines with wearable activity trackers: a systematic review. In: Proceedings of the 10th Mediterranean Conference on Information Systems, Paphos, Cyprus. AIS (2016). 13 pages
27. Attig, C., Franke, T.: Abandonment of personal quantification: a review and empirical study investigating reasons for wearable activity tracking attrition. Comput. Hum. Behav. **102**, 223–237 (2020)
28. Rogers, E.M.: Diffusion of Innovations, 5th edn. Free Press, New York (2003)
29. Kononova, A., et al.: The use of wearable activity trackers among older adults: focus group study of tracker perceptions, motivators, and barriers in the maintenance stage of behavior change. JMIR mHealth uHealth **7**(4), e9832 (2019)
30. Hoogendijk, E.O., Afilalo, J., Ensrud, K.E., Kowal, P., Onder, G., Fried, L.P.: Frailty: implications for clinical practice and public health. Lancet **394**(10206), 1365–1375 (2019)
31. Jonasson, L.: Aerobic fitness and healthy brain aging: cognition, brain structure, and dopamine. Umeå University, Sweden (2017)
32. Wallén, M.B., Ståhle, A., Hagströmer, M., Franzén, E., Roaldsen, K.S.: Motionsvanor och erfarenheter av motion hos äldre vuxna. Karolinska Institutet, Stockholm, Sweden (2014)
33. The Finnish Institute for Health and Welfare: Aikuisten terveys-, hyvinvointi-ja palvelu-tutkimus ATH: n perustulokset 2010-2017 (2017). http://www.thl.fi/ath. Accessed 12 Jan 2020
34. IAMSR: Digital Wells (2020). https://www.iamsr.fi/digitalwells.html. Accessed 19 Jan 2020
35. Carlsson, C., Walden, P.: Digital support to guide physical activity – augmented daily routines for young elderly. In: Proceedings of the 32nd Bled eConference "Humanizing Technology for a Sustainable Society", Bled, Slovenia, pp. 783–802. University of Maribor Press (2019).

36. Wellmo: Mobile health platform (2019). https://www.wellmo.com/platform/. Accessed 4 Jan 2020

37. Social Insurance Institution of Finland: Kanta personal health record (2019). https://www.kanta.fi/en/wellbeing-data. Accessed 4 Jan 2020

38. Kari, T., Piippo, J., Frank, L., Makkonen, M., Moilanen, P.: To gamify or not to gamify? Gamification in exercise applications and its role in impacting exercise motivation. In: Proceedings of the 29th Bled eConference "Digital Economy", Bled, Slovenia, pp. 393–405. University of Maribor (2016)

39. Koivisto, J., Hamari, J.: The rise of motivational information systems: a review of gamification research. Int. J. Inf. Manage. **45**, 191–210 (2019)

40. Rogers, E.M.: The Diffusion of Innovations. Free Press, New York (1962)

41. Ely, D.P.: Conditions that facilitate the implementation of educational technology innovations. Educ. Technol. **39**, 23–27 (1999)

42. Ensminger, D.C., Surry, D.W., Porter, B.E., Wright, D.: Factors contributing to the successful implementation of technology innovations. Educ. Technol. Soc. **7**(3), 61–72 (2004)

43. Kari, T., Koivunen, S., Frank, L., Makkonen, M., Moilanen, P.: Critical experiences during the implementation of a self-tracking technology. In: Proceedings of the 20th Pacific Asia Conference on Information Systems, Chiayi, Taiwan. AIS (2016). 16 pages

44. Lazar, A., Koehler, C., Tanenbaum, J., Nguyen, D. H.: Why we use and abandon smart devices. In: Proceedings of the 2015 ACM International Joint Conference on Pervasive and Ubiquitous Computing, New York, NY, pp. 635–646. ACM (2015)

45. Myers, M.D.: Qualitative Research in Business and Management, 2nd edn. SAGE, Los Angeles (2013)

46. Braun, V., Clarke, V.: Using thematic analysis in psychology. Qual. Res. Psychol. **3**(2), 77–101 (2006)

47. Guest, G., MacQueen, K.M., Namey, E.E.: Applied Thematic Analysis. SAGE, Los Angeles (2012)

48. Patton, M.Q.: Qualitative Research & Evaluation Methods, 3rd edn. SAGE, Thousand Oaks (2002)

49. Agarwal, R., Prasad, J.: A conceptual and operational definition of personal innovativeness in the domain of information technology. Inf. Syst. Res. **9**(2), 204–215 (1998)

50. Sallis, J.F., Saelens, B.E.: Assessment of physical activity by self-report: status, limitations, and future directions. Res. Q. Exercise Sport **71**(sup2), 1–14 (2000)

51. Park, E., Kim, K.J., Kwon, S.J.: Understanding the emergence of wearable devices as next-generation tools for health communication. Inf. Technol. People **29**(4), 717–732 (2016)

52. Schaie, K.W., Hofer, S.M.: Longitudinal studies in aging research. In: Birren, J.E., Schaie, K.W. (eds.) Handbook of the Psychology of Aging, vol. 5, pp. 53–77. Academic Press, San Diego (2001)

53. Larsen, L.H., Schou, L., Lund, H.H., Langberg, H.: The physical effect of exergames in healthy elderly—a systematic review. Games Health J. **2**(4), 205–212 (2013)

54. Loos, E., Kaufman, D.: Positive impact of exergaming on older adults' mental and social well-being: in search of evidence. In: Zhou, J., Salvendy, G. (eds.) ITAP 2018. LNCS, vol. 10927, pp. 101–112. Springer, Cham (2018). https://doi.org/10.1007/978-3-319-92037-5_9

55. World Health Organization: Proposed working definition of an older person in Africa for the MDS Project (2002). https://www.who.int/healthinfo/survey/ageingdefnolder/en/. Accessed 24 Jan 2020

A Study on the Effect of Gamification on Alleviation Anxiety Levels of the Elderly in China

Fumie Muroi[✉], Xinyi Tao[✉], and Ting Han[✉]

School of Design, Shanghai Jiao Tong University,
No. 800 Dongchuan Road, Shanghai 200240, China
MFumie@163.com, {taoxinyi,hanting}@sjtu.edu.cn

Abstract. As the problem of aging becomes increasingly serious, anxiety symptom has seriously affected the mental health of the elderly as a ubiquitous phenomenon in the elderly of China. Recently, a lot of researches show that gamification plays a positive role in relieving negative moods. This paper sorts out the gamification design strategies for the elderly to relieve anxieties and develops a collage game for the elderly according to this strategy: background, text and picture materials are used to make different subject patterns of collage and create own collage works. This game is used to verify the influence of gamification intervention means on the anxieties of the elderly as an intervention of control experiment. In this experiment, 42 participants were divided into two groups. The experiment group used gamification intervention, while the control group did not; STAI scale and galvanic skin were used to measure the change in the anxiety level of participants. According to the results, collage game for the elderly can relieve the anxiety state of the elderly, and most of the participants were free from usage pressure and relieved their anxieties during the game. Gamification seems to be a promising way to relieve the anxieties of the elderly. In the future work, it is necessary to make long-term experiments with a large sample size, so as to verify the influence of gamification intervention means on the reduction of anxieties, explore the influence of demography factor on the reduction of anxieties and sort out more targeted gamification intervention means.

Keywords: Gamification · Elderly · Anxiety

1 Introduction

In recent years, aging has gradually become an important social issue, and the realization of active aging has become an important problem to be solved around the world. Literature shows that, according to the national survey of the National Bureau of statistics, by the end of 2018, China's elderly population (aged 60 and over) has reached 249 million, accounting for 17.9% of the total population; the elderly population aged 65 and over 167 million, accounting for 11.9% of the total population [1]. The sudden peak of aging is more likely to cause various psychological problems of the elderly, such as anxiety and depression. According to the World Health Organization (WHO), more than 20% of adults aged 60 and over suffer from mental or neurological disorders (excluding headache), while anxiety affects 3.8% of the elderly population,

© Springer Nature Switzerland AG 2020
Q. Gao and J. Zhou (Eds.): HCII 2020, LNCS 12208, pp. 329–342, 2020.
https://doi.org/10.1007/978-3-030-50249-2_24

and material use problems affect about 1% of the population [2]. The trend of serious psychological problems will become an obstacle in the family life and social life of the elderly, and also a challenge for the international community to achieve the goal of active aging.

Gamification is defined as the application of game elements to non-game environment, which can attract users' attention and improve users' enthusiasm. In recent years, gamification related research has been applied in many fields. A large number of studies have shown that play and gamification play a positive role in calming emotions and reducing stress, especially for children. For example, Elke et al. [3] introduced 'mindlight', a neurofeedback video game to prevent anxiety disorders in children, and recruited 136 subjects to conduct a randomized controlled experiment. The results showed that children's anxiety was significantly reduced after the experiment. Knox et al. [4] recruited 24 children and adolescents who received anxiety treatment to carry out a control experiment to verify whether biofeedback based play can help reduce the anxiety and depression of children and adolescents. The research proved that biofeedback assisted relaxation training in the form of video games can effectively reduce the anxiety of children and adolescents. Barbara et al. [5] described a 2D jump 'n' run game 'mindspace' developed for 7–12-year-old children with anxiety disorder. The game combines cognitive behavior technology and aims to let children understand their own anxiety problems, complete tasks to obtain incentives, and specifically relax these children's patients. In addition, there are also a lot of researches that should apply gamification to stress management. For example, Corinna et al. [6] designed a stress management system with the idea of gamification, which can be used to avatar, agent, complete routine tasks, experience value, virtual currency, badge and other gamification elements to help users manage stress. Alluhaidan and Plachkinova [7] designed a program to reduce the pressure of patients with congestive heart failure (CHF), which integrates meditation breathing. When patients breathe, they can see the interactive images of the lungs. So that the patients can understand their physical condition, improve their participation and reduce anxiety. Mercer [8] designed a game using elements such as natural scenes and animals. Users need to find the specified small animals in the forest within a certain period of time. Through the experiment of questionnaire and blood pressure measurement, the effect of the game on reducing pressure was verified.

In the past, most of the research on game or gamification for the elderly focused on physiological training or cognitive ability. Yu-Hsiang Lin et al. [9] developed a serious game for training the cognitive and physiological functions of the elderly by using sensors and microcontrollers. The elderly can sit in a chair and use modular sensing tools to play rhythm games. They can train the cognitive functions of the elderly through physical activities and serious games, such as reaction speed, short-term memory and working memory. Wlkeogh j et al. [10] used Nintendo Wii video sports fitness game to intervene the elderly in the nursing home for eight weeks. The analysis results showed that the biceps flexion and extension endurance, physical activity level and life quality of the intervention group were significantly improved. Participants also expressed their sense of achievement from the game and believed that the game provided them with a way to social In addition, research on the willingness and motivation of the elderly to play games can help designers design games for the elderly more specifically. Ingmar Wagner and Michael Minge [11] invited 18 pairs of elderly people to play a dice game. They compared their subjective enjoyment and use motivation by providing different social conditions for the elderly. Through repeated scale measurement, it is found that social game elements enhance the elderly's positive mood and willingness to maintain the game, and social contact is an important element of interaction between the elderly and technology.

From the review research on game and gamification, it can be found that there are few researches focusing on the mental health and emotions of the elderly, while game and gamification have shown their advantages in the field of emotions, which seems to be a promising means of intervention in mental health of the elderly. This study aims at alleviating the anxiety of the elderly, and proves the influence of the game design on alleviating the anxiety of the elderly through the control experiment. We hope to design an effective, accepted and widely used game based intervention method to alleviate the anxiety of the elderly.

2 Materials and Methods

2.1 Game Design

In the early research on gamification, the widely accepted point of view is that the game elements are applied to non-game systems to improve user experience and participation. Among them, game design principles, methods, game framework, game mechanism and specific interface design are all game elements [12]. Some research believe that gaming experience depends on game design elements, which should be able to interact to stimulate players' emotional input [13]. Therefore, before the game design, the physical, psychological conditions and preferences of the elderly should be consider to find the design elements that can alleviate the anxiety of the elderly.

After entering middle age, all physiological functions will be decline gradually, but after entering old age, this change will be more obvious. The specific physiological characteristics of the elderly are as follows:

- vision: decreased vision; decreased color perception; decreased spatial perception; decreased dark adaptation and light adaptation.
- touch: with the growth of age, the skin, muscle and nervous system will also lost all hint of youth, so it will cause the tactile response of the elderly to be slow, and the use of touch-screen electronic products will be more difficult than that of the young.
- responsiveness: poor tolerance of stimulation; slower responsiveness.
- memory: learning ability is weakened; short-term memory, near event memory.

Health problems and changes in social roles [14] may cause psychological changes in the elderly. Due to aging and even diseases, the ability of self-care of the elderly has declined. Nowadays, with the rapid development of science and technology, people's life style changes rapidly, and the life of the elderly is more vulnerable to impact. Therefore, the psychological status of the elderly also has several characteristics different from that of the young:

- emotional dependence needs: feeling uneasy and lost; increasing dependence on family members, and possibly on some entertainment activities.
- social support needs: strong expression desire; more pursuit of content in entertainment activities; desire to reflect their own value.
- nostalgia: nostalgia is a kind of complex that most old people have. Nostalgia can remind the aged people of what they did when they were young, and produce a sense of self-identity or good feeling for their past experience. Nostalgia therapy has also been widely used in the intervention of anxiety and depression in the elderly [15, 16], and achieved good results.
- conservative: unwilling to take risks; value accuracy and avoid mistakes.

In addition, different kinds of games will have different effects on emotional relief, and different types of games also correspond to different types of people. Game elements related to emotional relief include:

- attention diversion: when playing games, people need to focus on the current game tasks or the world outlook of the game, which can temporarily separate people from the real world, avoid things that cause anxiety and bad emotions, and play a role in alleviating anxiety.
- weakening stimulating elements: slow rhythm; weakening winning and losing judgment; cooperation mechanism; soft music, etc.
- relaxing elements: some studies have shown that elements related to nature, pictures, etc. can relieve people's pressure to a certain extent [17]; in addition, some studies have proved that nostalgia can alleviate the anxiety of the elderly, and some nostalgic pictures or playing methods can be appropriately used to evoke their old memories.

Based on the physical and psychological characteristics of the elderly and the game elements to ease anxiety, the game design principles suitable for the elderly are extracted (Fig. 1) for application in future design. The principle consists of three dimensions: game planning, interactive design and visual design.

According to the above design principles, flash is used to develop a puzzle game to alleviate the anxiety of the elderly. The game provides picture materials, background materials and text materials. Players can choose the materials they want and drag them to the drawing board area. Through basic operations such as zooming in, zooming out and rotating, they can freely assemble and assemble a picture.

In order to enhance the fun of the game, a wealth of picture materials are provided. Since this experiment is aimed at the elderly in China, the preferences of the elderly in China will be taken into account in terms of material and language. The game material can be divided into three categories: common material, background material and text material. Common materials correspond to different themes, which may be animals, plants, figures, patterns and other illustrations. Background material includes scenery, color block and other materials. Some Chinese poems are used as text materials, which can be matched with other picture materials. For avoid causing tension and anxiety, the slow-paced playing method is adopted, and there is no clear judgment on the winning and losing, and there is no time limit. The elderly can play the game leisurely and relaxed (Fig. 2).

Dimension	Strategy	Description
Game	Low stimulation	Aged people have low tolerance to stimulation, so the playing method with strong stimulation is not suitable for aged people
	Low rhythm	Since aged people react slowly, the games with fast rhythm are hard to play and easy to cause sense of nervousness
	Highlighting accuracy	The setup of the playing method should highlight accuracy, weaken speed, which makes aged people complete the tasks in a relatively casual way.
	Weakening judgement of winning and loss	The desire for winning a game will increase psychological pressure, so the game without strict judgement of winning and loss is more suitable for relaxing and killing tim.
	Encouragement	Reduce the negative information, positive stimulation is conducive to increasing the confidence of aged people who can generate the feeling of happiness.
	Simple functional structure	The too complicated playing method is not set up and only the basic functions are maintained.
	Coordination mechanism	It is conducive to strengthening communication, increasing social relations and alleviating the sense of loneliness and anxiety for aged people.
	Share mechanism	Encourage the aged people to share their achievements with others, which satisfies their desire to express and enhance social connections.
	Cultural connotation	The game containing cultural content is much more welcomed by the aged people and it is also able to enrich the spiritual world of the aged people.
	Knowledge popularization	The integration of knowledge popularization, such as the information related to health care will make them master information through games and reduce their anxiety caused by unknown.
	Relaxing elements	Nature, nostalgia and other elements can alleviate the anxiety of aged people.
Interactive Design	Simple operation	The structure is clear in terms of interface design, the basic clicking functions, dragging forms should be used in operation and the complicated operations should be reduced.
	Specific prompt information	The specific explanation should be used as much as possible in the charts, buttons, note information and so on, which avoids misunderstanding.
	Size of design element	In terms of interface design, the functional components, proportion of words size should be highlighted, which helps to reduce visual recognition difficulty of aged people.
	Soft color matching, clear contrast	It should have high contrast ratio for convenient recognition, at the same time, the colors with high brightness, high saturation and dazzling elements should be avoided.
Visual Design	Warm tones	Aged people are easier to recognize warm tones while their ability to recognize cold tones as blue, green and so on has been degenerated, so more warm tones should be used.
	Integrated visual effects	The ability of the aged people's eyes to adapt to the light is weakened and it is very hard for them adapt to the sudden light shifts, so the sudden brightness shift should be avoided.
	Strong sense of button-clicking feedback	When the visual image for the functional buttons that can be clicked is designed, the stronger sense of clicking should be highlighted and there is specific prompt information indicating such area can be clicked.
	Combined with the elements aged people like	The visual styles, such as nature, patterns and so on that aged people like can be integrated, which is conductive to reducing the anxiety of the aged people.

Fig. 1. The design strategy for the elderly

Fig. 2. The homepage

There are three modes in the game: Chinese style, nature and family portrait, with different kinds of materials built in. In addition to the core playing method, the game also has some additional functions. In the process of puzzle, users can save the progress at any time. After completing the puzzle, they can also share the work to the social platform, which is helpful to strengthen the social communication, satisfy the expression desire, reflect the self-worth of the elderly, and has a positive effect on improving their self-identity and reducing their anxiety (Figs. 3 and 4).

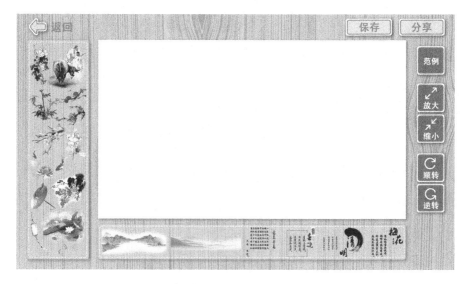

Fig. 3. Chinese style mode

Fig. 4. Example of Chinese style

2.2 Participants

42 elderly participants were recruited in this experiment, including 18 males and 24 females, aged 60–78 years, with an average age of 67.79 years. The participants were included in the following conditions: clear consciousness, smooth communication; normal vision, no eye disease; independent action, no serious disease affecting action.

2.3 Procedure

First, the participants who met the criteria were randomly divided into experimental group and control group. There were 23 participants in the experimental group, including 10 males and 13 females, aged 60–76 years, with an average age of 67.52 years. There were 19 participants in the control group, including 8 males and 11 females, aged 62–78 years, with an average age of 68.11 years. They all signed the consent before the experiment and filled in the pre-STAI. The control group did not use game intervention to keep the participants calm for seven minutes. The experiment group was intervened by playing the puzzle game. In the process, the researchers conducted process guidance, but only when the participants had difficulty in playing. The time limit of the game was seven minutes. Participants in each experimental group need to complete the same task flow:

1. Start the game.
2. View the introduction pictures and enter the game homepage.
3. Click the entrance of game mode, enter the puzzle game operation page, view the styles of material, exit and go back to the homepage.
4. View the styles of three modes for puzzle game respectively, choose one style for the game.

5. Click the mode entrance, enter the operation page of the puzzle game.
6. Choose the picture material, drag it to the area of painting board, click the function button for operation, adjust the material.
7. Drag other materials, adjust and combine them in the area of painting board.
8. Click to save after completing the puzzle game.
9. Click sharing button to share the painting to the social media software (the step is up to the option of the participants).
10. Go back to the homepage of the game, click the entrance of my painting album, enter painting album.
11. View the paintings browsed and saved.
12. End the game.

Before starting the task, the researcher will help the subjects to wear the skin electric sensor and record the skin electric signal. After that, the subjects need to fill in the STAI again and accept the interview. All participants will be asked about two aspects: (1) recent living conditions and the causes of anxiety; (2) experience of playing video games. In addition, the subjects in the experimental group were asked about their feelings and difficulties in playing the puzzle game.

2.4 Measurement Indexes

The independent variable of the experiment is intervention means based on games and the dependent variable is the anxiety level of the tested. Among them, the relevant assessment for the anxiety level of the tested is mainly divided into two aspects. The first one is to rely on the subjective assessment questionnaire STAI to assess the anxiety level of the participants. The second one is to test the physiological index-skin electricity SC/GSR of the tested as the objective index. With the combination of the subjective and objective indexes, it will be able to assess the anxiety level of the participants more comprehensively.

- Subjective indexes

STAI is used to measure the anxiety level of the participants. The scale is the self-assessment type and divided into two sub-scales, including 40 description items in total: S-AI includes 20 items. S-AI describes the temporary unhappy mood experience, such as worry, tension, fear, nervousness and so on which are accompanied with hyper function of autonomic nervous system, so it can be used to measure the temporary anxiety level of the tested and it is also able to induce the experience of situation anxiety. T-AI includes 21–40 items. T-AI describes the anxiety tendency which is relatively stable and becomes different in different individuals. T-AI can be used to identify the frequent anxiety level of the tested within the specific time duration, moreover, it is also able to assess the effectiveness of psychological consultation and treatment.

- Objective indexes

In the experiment, the skin electricity of the tested is measured. In terms of skin electricity, it refers to a kind of emotional physiological index being able to reflect the emotional changes of the participants, so it is used as the mutual evidence with anxiety inventory. The hardware equipment for measuring the physiological index include: one unit of Psytech-10 multichannel physiological instrument, PC, skin electric sensor, BioTrace+acquisition and observation of piezoelectricity signal used in software.

3   Results

3.1   Baseline Data Analysis

The S-AI sub-score and T-AI sub-score of the participants in the experimental group are compared with that in the control group before the experiment for carrying out T test of independent samples. The STAI total score and T-AI total score in the two groups are not significantly different before the experiment ($P > 0.05$). STAI total score in the experimental group is compared with the control group before experiment for carrying out T test of independent samples. The result shows that there is no significant difference between STAI total scores in the two groups before experiment ($P > 0.05$) (Table 1).[1]

Table 1. Comparison of STAI scores between experimental group and control group before experiment

| | Group ($\bar{x} \pm$ s) | | t | p |
	Experiment group (n = 23)	Control group (n = 19)		
S-AI	40.09 ± 5.51	39.95 ± 6.51	0.075	0.940
T-AI	41.78 ± 4.72	41.21 ± 5.93	0.348	0.729
STAI total	81.87 ± 10.18	81.16 ± 12.39	0.204	0.839

Therefore, it shows that there is no significant difference between the initial anxiety levels in the experimental and control groups before experiment. Moreover, the baseline data of S-AI sub-score, T-AI sub-score are in line with that of the STAI total score. They can be further used to carry out comparison analysis with the score changes of anxiety scales after experiment (Table 2).[2]

Table 2. Comparison of SC/GSR data between experimental group and control group before experiment

| | Group ($\bar{x} \pm$ s) | | t | p |
	Experiment group (n = 23)	Control group (n = 19)		
SC/GSR	1.25 ± 0.72	1.24 ± 0.71	0.045	0.964

---

[1] Data comparison * $P < 0.05$, * * $P < 0.01$.
[2] Data comparison * $P < 0.05$, * * $P < 0.01$.

The skin electricity SC/GSR score in the experimental group is compared with that in the control group before experiment for carrying out T test of independent samples. There is no significant difference between the initial skin electricity SC/GSR values of the tested ones in the two groups before experiment (P > 0.05). Therefore, it shows that there is no significant difference between the initial skin electricity levels in the experimental and control groups before experiment. Moreover, the baseline data of SC/GSR is in line with each other. The comparison analysis of the changes of skin electricity SC/GSR data after experiment can be carried out, which is of great significance.

3.2   The Change of Anxiety Level in the Control Group

In the control group, S-AI sub-score, T-AI sub-score before experiment are compared with those after experiment for carrying out T test. The results show that there is no significant difference between S-AI sub-score, T-AI sub-score before and after experiment (P > 0.05). In the control group, the STAI total score before experiment is compared with after experiment for carrying out matching T test. The results show that there is no significant difference between STAI total score before and after experiment (P > 0.05). It is obvious that there are no significant differences for S-AI sub-value, T-AI sub-value and STAI total score in the control group before and after the experiment and there are no obvious changes for these values after the experiment. When the intervention means based on games is not carried out, there is no obvious change for the anxiety level of the aged people measured by STAI (Tables 3 and 4).[34]

Table 3. Comparison of STAI scores before and after the experiment in the control group

	Control group before and after the experiment ($\bar{x} \pm s$)		t	p
	Before the experiment (n = 19)	After the experiment (n = 19)		
S-AI	39.95 ± 6.51	40.05 ± 6.49	−0.294	0.772
T-AI	41.21 ± 5.93	41.16 ± 5.91	0.165	0.871
STAI	81.16 ± 12.39	81.21 ± 12.28	−0.092	0.928

The initial skin electricity SC/GSR value of the 19 tested ones in the control group before the experiment is compared with that after the experiment for carrying out matching T test. There are no significant differences for skin electricity SC/GSR values before and after the experiment (P > 0.05). It is obvious that there are no significant differences for skin electricity SC/GSR values before and after the experiment in the control group and there are no obvious changes for the values before and after the experiment. When the intervention means based on games is not carried out, there is no obvious change for the anxiety level of the aged people showed by physiological index skin electricity signal, which is consistent with the previous measurement results measured by STAI.

---

[3] Data comparison * P < 0.05, * * P < 0.01.

[4] Data comparison * P < 0.05, * * P < 0.01.

Table 4. Comparison of SC/GSR data between control group and control group before experiment

	Control group before and after the experiment ($\bar{x} \pm$ s)		t	p
	Before the experiment (n = 19)	After the experiment (n = 19)		
SC/GSR	1.24 ± 0.71	1.23 ± 0.70	0.335	0.742

3.3   The Change of Anxiety Level in the Experiment Group

In the experimental group, the S-AI sub-score experiment is compared with that after the experiment for carrying out matching T test. There are significant differences for S-AI sub-score before and after the experiment (P < 0.01). After the experiment, the S-AI sub-score is reduced obviously. The T-AI sub-value in the experimental group before experiment is compared with that after the experiment for carrying out matching T test. There are differences for T-AI sub-value before and after the experiment (0.01 < P < 0.05). After the experiment, the T-AI sub-score is reduced, but the extent is not obvious. The STAI total score in the experimental group before experiment is compared with that after the experiment for carrying out matching T test. There are obvious differences for STAI total score before and after the experiment (P < 0.01). After the experiment, the STAI total score is reduced obviously (Table 5).[5]

Table 5. Comparison of STAI scores of experimental group before and after the experiment

	Experiment group before and after the experiment ($\bar{x} \pm$ s)		t	p
	Before the experiment (n = 23)	After the experiment (n = 23)		
S-AI	40.09 ± 5.51	38.04 ± 3.78	3.792	0.001**
T-AI	41.78 ± 4.72	41.09 ± 4.51	2.113	0.046*
STAI	81.87 ± 10.18	79.13 ± 7.98	4.188	0.000**

In the experiment group, after the tested ones finish the puzzle game designed for aged people as the intervention means based on games, the anxiety level of aged people measured by STAI decreases, which indicates that such puzzle game can alleviate the anxiety level of the tested ones, but what is noteworthy is that the S-AI-immediate anxiety level of the tested ones is obviously alleviated while its alleviating effect on the T-AI-anxiety feelings in recent period is not so obvious (Table 6).[6]

---

[5] Data comparison * P < 0.05, * * P < 0.01.

[6] Data comparison * P < 0.05, * * P < 0.01.

Table 6. Comparison of SC/GSR data of the experimental group before and after the experiment

	Experiment group before and after the experiment ($\bar{x} \pm$ s)		t	p
	Before the experiment (n = 23)	After the experiment (n = 23)		
SC/GSR	1.25 ± 0.72	1.04 ± 0.58	4.652	0.000**

The skin electricity SC/GSR in the experimental group before experiment is compared with that after the experiment for carrying out matching T test. There are significant differences for skin electricity SC/GSR before and after the experiment (P < 0.01). After the experiment, the skin electricity SC/GSR is reduced obviously.

In the experiment group, after the tested ones finish the puzzle game designed for aged people as the intervention means based on games, the anxiety level of aged people measured by physiological index skin electricity signal decreases, which is in line with the measurement results of STAI. The results indicate that the experimental intervention stuff-puzzle game for the aged people can alleviate the anxiety of the tested ones.

4 Discussion and Conclusion

It is found out in the research that intervention means based on games can reduce the anxiety of the aged people to some extent. The matching T test is carried out for STAI total score, S-AI sub-value, T-AI sub-value, skin electricity SC/GSR value before and after the experiment in the experimental group, then it is found out that those in the experimental group show reduction of anxiety level in both aspects of STAI and physiological index-skin electricity signal. Moreover, those in the experimental group are compared with those in the control group receiving no intervention means based on games and showing no difference in anxiety level. The result reveals that the aged people in the experimental group receiving intervention means based on games in the subject have lower anxiety level with relatively positive effectiveness.

The intervention stuff in the experiment for the aged people is the video game made in accordance with design strategies based on games for reducing the anxiety of aged people proposed in the previous content. The game is featured with low stimulation, slow rhythm, weak winning and losing judgment, few restrictions, simple functional structure and so on. It is expected that the aged people can play games with relaxing mood, no pressure, no learning difficulties. It is known in the interview after experiment that most of the aged people engaged in the experiment have the habit to play video devices and have higher level of acceptance for video games. The tested ones also show the acceptance attitude for the game and just a small part of the tested ones show that they feel pressure in operation. Some of the participants ones propose suggestions for improvement of the game, such as increasing music used to calm emotions, increasing coordination mechanism which is more specific. All the suggestions will be iterated in the future research.

Additionally, the limitations of the research include the limited number of participants ones, so there is certain restriction for the analysis results, which just represents the reduction of anxiety for the participants ones in the experiment. What is noteworthy is that the S-AI of the tested ones drops obviously and the T-AI of the tested ones drops not obviously in accordance with the changes of the relevant values in the STAI before and after the experiment in the experimental group. It is revealed that the intervention means and ways based on games can obviously alleviate the situation anxiety of the tested ones while their alleviating effect for T-AI anxiety is not obvious, it is possibly caused by the short-term experiment period in the research and only one time of intervention is carried out. Further subsequent research must be carried out for more in-depth exploration. In the future, the long-term and continuous intervention based on games with certain frequency should be carried out to observe whether its effect on reducing T-AI anxiety will be more obvious or not. In the subsequent research, the performance of the participants ones with large sample volume can be mined deeply and the effect of the demographic factors on the means based on games used to alleviate the anxiety level of aged people can be explored. It also further explores the category of aged people that intervention means based on games is suitable for, which helps to carry out further intervention for the anxiety of aged people in accordance with their traits. Moreover, more experimental research can be carried out in accordance with the design strategies based on games extracted in the paper for alleviating the anxiety of aged people, then the variables can be controlled to explore the differences of different design factors based on games for alleviating the anxiety of aged people, which lays a good foundation for subsequent application and designing of intervention means based on games.

To sum up, it is preliminarily shown by the research that intervention means based on games has certain effect on alleviating the anxiety level of aged people. The puzzle game made in accordance with the design strategies of the research can alleviate the anxiety level of the tested ones to some extent. Hopefully, it is possibly the non-drug method used to intervene the anxiety of the elderly.

Acknowledgement. The research is supported by National Social Science Fund (Grant No. 18BRK009).

References

1. He, X., Song, M., et al.: Basic and translational aging research in China: present and future. Protein Cell **10**(7), 476–484 (2019)
2. World Health Organization, mental health and the elderly. https://www.who.int/zh/news-room/fact-sheets/detail/mental-health-of-older-adults. Accessed 12 Dec 2017
3. Schoneveld, E.A., Malmberg, M., Lichtwarck-Aschoff, A., et al.: A neurofeedback video game (MindLight) to prevent anxiety in children: a randomized controlled trial. Comput. Hum. Behav. **63**, 321–333 (2016)
4. Knox, M., Lentini, J., Cummings, T.S., et al.: Game-based biofeedback for paediatric anxiety and depression. Mental Health Family Med. **8**(3), 195–203 (2011). http://www.springer.com/lncs. Accessed 21 Nov 2016

5. Göbl, B., et al.: MindSpace: treating anxiety disorders in children with a CBT Game. In: International Conference on Games & Learning Alliance, pp. 266–275 (2016)
6. Christmann, C.A., Hoffmann, A., Zolynski, G., Bleser, G.: Stress-mentor: linking gamification and behavior change theory in a stress management application. In: Stephanidis, C. (ed.) HCI 2018. CCIS, vol. 851, pp. 387–393. Springer, Cham (2018). https://doi.org/10.1007/978-3-319-92279-9_52
7. Alluhaidan, A., Plachkinova, M.: Designing a game to reduce stress for congestive heart-failure (CHF) patients. In: Hawaii International Conference on System Sciences, pp. 3359–3368 (2016)
8. Mercer, N.: Stress Relieving Video Games: Creating a Game for the Purpose of Stress Relief and Analyzing Its Effectiveness (2015)
9. Lin, Y., Mao, H., Tsai, Y., Chou, J.: Developing a serious game for the elderly to do physical and cognitive hybrid activities. In: 2018 IEEE 6th International Conference on Serious Games and Applications for Health (SeGAH), Vienna, pp. 1–8 (2018)
10. Keogh, J.W., Power, N., Wooller, L., Lucas, P., Whatman, C.J.: Physical and psychosocial function in residential aged-care elders: effect of Nintendo Wii Sports games. Aging Phys. Act. **22**, 235–244 (2014)
11. Wagner, I., Minge, M.: The gods play dice together: the influence of social elements of gamification on seniors' user experience. In: HCI International 2015 - Posters' Extended Abstracts Communications in Computer and Information Science, vol. 57, pp. 334–339 (2015)
12. Deterding, S., Sicart, M., Nacke, L., et al.: Gamification: using game design elements in non-gaming contexts. In: Proceedings of the International Conference on Human Factors in Computing Systems, pp. 2425–2428 (2011)
13. Mullins, J.K., Sabherwal, R.: Gamification: a cognitive-emotional view. J. Bus. Res. **106**, 304–314 (2020)
14. Dooley, E., Kunik, M.E.: Depression and Anxiety Across the Age Spectrum, Depression and Anxiety in Patients with Chronic Respiratory Diseases, Ch. Chapter 2, pp. 11–31 (2017)
15. Jones, E.D.: Reminiscence therapy for older women with depression. J. Gerontol. Nurs. **29** (7), 26–33 (2003)
16. Chiang, K.J., Chu, H., Chang, H.J., et al.: The effects of reminiscence therapy on psychological well-being, depression, and loneliness among the institutionalized aged. Int. J. Geriatr. Psychiatry **25**(4), 380–388 (2010)
17. Kort, Y.A.W.D., Ijsselsteijn, W.A.: People, places, and play: player experience in a socio-spatial context. Comput. Entertain. **6**(2), 1–11 (2008)

ICF-Based Analysis of Barriers and Facilitators for Smartphone Usage in an App-Supported Training Program for Health and Well-Being of Older Users

Anke Osterhoff[1]([✉]), Liane Günther[2], Christian Thiel[1],
Christian Grüneberg[1], and Sascha Sommer[1]

[1] Department für angewandte Gesundheitswissenschaften,
Hochschule für Gesundheit, Gesundheitscampus 6-8, 44801 Bochum, Germany
anke.osterhoff@hs-gesundheit.de
[2] Institut für Medizinische Soziologie, Centre for Health and Society,
Medizinische Fakultät, Heinrich-Heine-Universität Düsseldorf,
Moorenstr. 5, 40225 Düsseldorf, Germany

Abstract. In an integrated cognitive and physical training program for older users (63 and older), smartphones and a new, specially designed app were used to provide digital training elements and to promote social participation. Due to heterogeneous levels of experience with such technologies in this age group, we analyze the barriers and facilitators that influence usage and acceptance. Results of qualitative research confirm varying levels of experience and varying attitudes among the target group, often associated with age-related individual differences. We also found that individual age-related user needs and requirements could usually be satisfied with user-centered support and with enough time for the users to become acquainted with the application. Barriers and facilitators for the use of device and app where analyzed according to the framework of the International Classification of Functioning, Disability and Health of the World Health Organization. Overall, we confirmed that app-supported training programs can be useful tools for health promotion. When developing such app-based programs, it should be borne in mind that older participants may require specific individualized support. This can be time-consuming but is also relatively easy to provide when crucial barriers and facilitators are considered early during development of similar concepts. Peer-based support like "tandems", where an assigned experienced participant provides supports to a less experienced user, or involvement of younger "digital native" relatives like grandchildren may further reduce resources required for support.

Keywords: Health · Well-being · ICF · Older users · Aging · Accessibility · Combined cognitive and physical activity · Social participation · Smartphone support

© Springer Nature Switzerland AG 2020
Q. Gao and J. Zhou (Eds.): HCII 2020, LNCS 12208, pp. 343–353, 2020.
https://doi.org/10.1007/978-3-030-50249-2_25

1 Objective

1.1 Introduction

The research and development project "Agile Quarter" ("Quartier agil"), funded by the German Federal Ministry of Education and Research, designed and evaluated an app-supported program for cognitive and physical training of community-dwelling older persons (age 63 and older) living independently. Besides health and well-being, the main goals of the training program are social participation and autonomy of older people in their own neighborhood [1]. We provided smartphones and a supporting training app for all participants. The supporting app provides timely information about relevant social activities and services in the neighborhood in order to strengthen social contacts among participants of the program. The app also serves as a platform for self-led training with specific tasks for cognition and physical activity.

We conducted analyses of user needs, as well as of barriers and facilitators for older persons with regard to smartphone-based elements of the training concept, based on the International Classification of Functioning, Disability and Health (ICF) [2]. Identifying the individual needs for accessibility is fundamental for the development of health-enhancing smartphone apps for older users. At the same time, according to the principle of *design for all* [3, 4], the highest possible degree of inclusion for vulnerable or technologically inexperienced user groups also generates better ease of use for users without specific extra needs, who also profit from improved usability. Thus, identification of barriers and facilitators for health-enhancing smartphone use can be advantageous for user groups of all ages.

1.2 Cognitive and Physical Training for Older Persons

Aging is associated with a loss of both cognitive and physical performance. This can have negative effects on the ability to lead an active and autonomous lifestyle and also to participate in social activities. A major factor in preventing the loss of cognitive and physical function is training, thus stabilizing existing abilities and possibly adding new ones. A multitude of training programs for cognitive and physical function exists, albeit training the two functional areas only separately. "Agile Quarter" is instead a combined training program, focusing on the interplay of cognitive and physical performance as well as their influence on social participation and well-being.

Although combining cognitive and physical training in dual-task exercises seems to be a promising means of maintaining an active lifestyle [5], only few such multimodal training programs for older people have been published to date [6–8]. "Agile Quartier" was designed to fill this gap, adding another innovation: training cognitive and physical resources specifically relevant to daily living in the neighborhood is supported via smartphones and a specially designed training app. Smartphones were used as a tool for promoting social participation, disseminating training instructions, and recording physical activity.

1.3   The Role of Social Participation in Aging

Social participation is a key component of quality of life. There appears to be a link between participation and cognitive and physical function in aging. Both of these functional areas are closely interconnected, especially in old age [9]. Age-related physical and behavioral changes can affect function and performance, which in turn can negatively impact social participation, overall quality of life, and basic activities such as walking [10, 11].

A fulfilling social life is closely linked to basic physical functions such as mobility (i.e. moving around, the ability to visit friends and events) and cognitive abilities (i.e. processing of information, communication etc.). The goal of "Agile Quarter" is training of all these interconnected factors in one common program to prevent functional loss and support social participation and, if possible, to improve existing abilities. For example, improved physical ability might make it easier for an older person to be able to walk around the neighborhood independently. Improved cognitive ability, in turn, might facilitate better concentration needed for sustaining meaningful conversations with friends. Improving both physical and cognitive function simultaneously might enable an older person to participate socially where it was not possible before due to age-related loss of function.

1.4   Smartphone and App Usage Among Older Persons

Due to demographic change and the associated increase in older people, new media such as smartphones need to be explored as potential resources for alleviating the possible accompanying societal challenges. Communication and information technology could positively affect both physical and psychological health, well-being, and social participation in older users, enabling them to remain independent longer and with higher quality of life [12].

We hypothesized that older people, who often still are not as familiar with these technologies, could benefit from new media such as smartphone apps and that cognitive and physical training for this target group can be improved by employing new media. This was assumed to be partly due to the increased cognitive and physical training frequency (flexible training times afforded by the app) and the added cognitive stimulation via smartphone per se. The "Agile Quarter"-app afforded flexible self-led training times and provided participants with supplementary physical and cognitive training materials.

In addition to this, smartphones and apps are potent tools for enriching social participation, enabling older users to keep contact with friends and family and to make new social connections as well. This is particularly relevant because of the increasing risk of loneliness associated with age [13].

We also assumed that due to varying degrees of technological experience and individual age-related cognitive and physical changes, older users would present with specific needs and challenges with regard to smartphone usage. The present study illustrates the way in which individual needs and differences associated with age interact with the usage of smartphones and apps during health-enhancing cognitive and physical training. Improving awareness of both cognitive and physical demands enables future researchers, trainers, tutors etc. to specifically adapt training programs and training materials or apps for this growing target group.

2 Methods

2.1 Procedure

The cognitive and physical training itself consisted of weekly 90-min group meetings over the course of a six-month training cycles in 2017 to 2018. We conducted two separate six-month training cycles. During the weekly group meetings, participants were offered a range of individual and group activities, such as strength, coordination, and balance exercises, linguistic, attention, memory, and concentration training. The group sessions often combined cognitive and physical training, for example it provided simultaneous training of lexical fluency and balance, when participants were asked to name as many words from a certain lexical category as possible while also going through an obstacle course with different floor conditions and other obstructions. The first and second authors acted as training instructors, focusing on cognitive-linguistic and physical activity, respectively. Both also served as technical support and smart-phone instructors.

In addition to this, we offered further training sessions at different locations throughout the neighborhood, e.g. walks in the local park, games at a café, and scavenger hunts all over the neighborhood. The smartphone app served as another additional training tool, regularly reminding participants to work on specific tasks and offering a range of freely selectable games and exercises that complemented the in-person exercises.

2.2 Participants

Participants were recruited from the urban neighborhood of Altenbochum, part of Bochum, Germany. Bochum is a city in the Ruhr district, Germany's most populous urban area, which is especially affected by demographic change due to its industrial past and associated impact on population structure (e.g. migration). As "Agile Quarter" was only in its development phase, the neighborhood of Altenbochum was selected due to its central location, favorable local resources (i.e. clubs, organizations, and sports facilities) and demographic structure (i.e. more older inhabitants than Bochum average). Participants were recruited via flyers, advertisements in local newspapers, information events, and via referral through other participants.

Inclusion criteria were age (63 and older), absence of major cognitive or physical health impairments, independent residence in the selected neighborhood, and written declaration of consent after written and verbal information. Exclusion criteria included physical health impairments that contradict physical activity, as recommended by the American College of Sports Medicine [14], cognitive impairments that exceed mild cognitive impairment (ICD-10 code F06.7), and existence of a nursing care level.

In total, 39 participants entered the training program, 19 took part in the first six-month training cycle (mean age = 72 ± 7, female = 16, male = 3), and 20 in the second training cycle (mean age = 73 ± 6, female = 17, male = 3).

2.3   ICF-Based Analysis

In a qualitative study, we conducted semi-structured interviews before and after two training cycles (six months each). Information about prior technical experience, digital competency, and about smartphone ownership/usage after participating in the program were also gathered via paper and pencil survey, since many participants reported not owning a smartphone before starting the program. A second source of information about barriers and facilitators were the regular in-person training sessions, where the two training instructors observed the participants and acted as immediate technical support.

The International Classification of Functioning, Disability and Health (ICF) is a standard classification framework by the World Health Organization used to describe and measure health and disability [2]. It was applied to analyze the qualitative findings according to the core dimensions described therein: body functions, activities and (social) participation [15]. We distinguished between smartphone usage barriers and facilitators that arose from the participants and their characteristics (i.e. personal factors) versus the barriers and facilitators that arose from the smartphone, the app, and the training concept itself (i.e. environmental factors).

3   Results

Out of 19 participants in the first cycle, 16 completed the six-month training (drop-outs = 3), while the second cycle was completed by 17 of its original 20 participants (drop-outs = 3). All drop-outs were due to personal reasons, no adverse events related to our training program occurred.

We analyzed our interview data and field notes with regard to technology acceptance, usage, and occurring technical difficulties or malfunctions during the respective six-month training cycles, paying particular attention to the health- and age-related characteristics of our target group.

Following the ICF-based distinction between environmental factors and personal factors, one main finding is that availability of personal support as well as sufficient time for the participants to become acquainted with the device and app are the most relevant environmental factors. Individual cognitive and physical impairments are among the crucial user-dependent personal barriers that have to be taken into account as special user needs. Table 1 and 2 give an overview of the main findings.

Table 1. Summary of key facilitators in smartphone and app usage.

Lessons learned: *Facilitators* for smartphone usage by older users

User-dependent personal factors	Smartphone-dependent environmental factors	Training-dependent environmental factors
Positive attitude, curiosity	Adequate, participative choice of device/data plan	Small groups, tandems
Cognitive and physical ability	Individual configuration & choice of apps	Extra smartphone training by an expert tutor
Cognitive and physical training, activation	Operability of apps, internet, etc.	Regular, personal support
Technical experience, media competency	Affordable devices/data plans	Generous time slots
Motivation, fun	Unlimited operability of features	Repetition & written manuals
Self-efficacy expectation	Low threshold for usability of menus/apps	Development of individual solutions
Group dynamics, encouraging social contact	Providing adequate technical support (e.g. stylus pens, headphones)	Feedback

3.1   Facilitators: Personal Factors

Intact sensory, physical, and cognitive functions in general are obvious key facilitators for smartphone usage in older users. The same holds true for environmental and personal factors, which, in favorable constellation (i.e. adequate devices, faultless functioning, and technology acceptance) can promote the older smartphone users' success.

The cognitive-linguistic part of the six-month training cycle led to positive training effects, which might have had a positive influence on the ability to use the provided smartphone. Conversely, cognitive activation and learning processes might have also had detrimental effects on cognitive resources necessary for successful smartphone usage [16–18]. Overall, heightened cognitive and physical activity should contribute to easier learning and use of new technology, but training instructors need to be cognizant of the potential risk of overwhelming older persons.

Furthermore, the training program's central goal was to increase social participation and well-being. Social networking via smartphone, which was strongly encouraged by the training instructors, might have been a facilitator in itself. Both the participants' individual social contacts and the overall group dynamic encouraged participants to take part in the online and offline group activities and thus influenced technology acceptance and smartphone use positively. The possibility of enhancing one's social life via smartphone added considerably to the users' willingness to engage with the technology.

Overall satisfaction with the training program "Agile Quarter" also influenced smartphone usage, e.g. via increased attendance at group meetings and training sessions, giving the opportunity for regular instruction and interaction with technology [19].

Individual goals and preferences also influenced technology acceptance on a personal level. Positive individual attitudes and strategies with regard to new input (e.g. other group members, training methods, and smartphones) had a possible supporting effect in the case of open-minded participants with relatively higher self-efficacy expectation [20].

3.2   Facilitators: Environmental Factors

The selected smartphone (LG Nexus 5X) was accepted by all participants as a training tool after some adjustments (e.g. larger font size, regulating ringtone volume, changing screen lock settings), repeated use, and provision of a stylus pen for those users who needed it [21]. Some participants also appreciated the possibility to manage individual customizations freely, including unlimited use of the provided amount of data for downloading apps, surfing the web, calling, texting, sharing pictures, videos etc. Our sample also reported enjoying the device due to its "normalcy." Special phones for older users sometimes are perceived as stigmatizing and users are wary of the possibility of not always being offered the full range of functionality.

Not all participants used the device equally for self-led training and social participation. Some could be encouraged by additional personal support or by eliminating individual obstacles such as changing the smartphone settings or undoing changes the participants had made inadvertently, for example entering flight mode or downloading costly apps. This high level of customizability also made flexible troubleshooting a necessity. Participants required great personal availability of the training instructors. Written manuals for basic functions were helpful to a certain point, but most users preferred reaching out to the training instructors immediately and personally so as not to delay their problems. Regular training sessions and additional meetings in the neighborhood also always included time slots for troubleshooting, which played a key role in ensuring successful smartphone usage and later adoption of new technology. Older users in our sample showed a great need for personal and timely support [22, 23]. Delayed problem solving led to frustration. Situations in which participants were able to learn solution strategies for themselves where optimal, e.g. teaching what to do when the smartphone screen remains black (i.e. check the battery light, charge the device, press power button). Participants tended to worry about broken screens and faulty phones and were pleased to learn solution strategies and experience self-efficacy in troubleshooting independently [20, 24]. Participants often needed to be reassured that they could not do permanent damage with or to the smartphone we provided for them. Trust and absence of fear were important facilitators for technology usage in our case.

Table 2. Summary of key barriers in smartphone and app usage.

Lessons learned: *Barriers* for smartphone usage by older users

User-dependent personal factors	Smartphone-dependent environmental factors	Training-dependent environmental factors
Negative attitude, skepticism	Inadequate choice of device/data plan (e.g. small screen, data restrictions)	Group size
Cognitive and physical impairments (e.g. perception, fine motor skills)	Technical disruptions (e.g. bugs, unforeseen updates)	Delays (e.g. not immediately fixable bugs, support not reachable)
Socioeconomic barriers	Complex menus	Smartphone training by lay tutors
Lack of motivation	Impeded usability (e.g. deactivated downloads)	Focus on training and "work" (new media should be fun)
Fear of contact/breaking things	Hidden cost traps (e.g. subscriptions, microtransactions)	Inflexible solution strategies
Prior negative experiences with new media	Selection of unappealing apps/services	Financial burdens (training fees)

3.3   Barriers: Personal Factors

Following the ICF, there are three subcategories of personal factors that played a part in the participants' usage and acceptance of the smartphone and app. Firstly, we consider the level of body function, which comprises individual sensory or neural processing deficits, which might hamper the usage of complex technology. Some participants were limited perceptually (i.e. auditory, visual, haptic impairments) or with regard to cognitive ability (e.g. attention, memory, cognitive flexibility), all of which can be hampered due to age.

Secondly, the ICF-level of body structure affected participants through diminished neural and physical structures, which also included cognitive and physical loss of function (e.g. difficulty maneuvering a touch screen due to damaged joints and decreased fine motor skills).

Thirdly, personal factors such as individual attitudes towards new media and group dynamic processes also sometimes obstructed successful usage of smartphones and apps. Additionally, personality variables like self-confidence, openness, conscious behavior reflection, and personal goals and motivations played an essential role in mastering new technology and adapting to its functions.

3.4   Barriers: Environmental Factors

Usage barriers due to environmental factors include, among others, the smartphone itself. Although most participants accepted the device after some training, troubleshooting, and personalization, it proved to be a barrier as well. Participants often perceived it as too small, with buttons that were hard to maneuver, and complex navigation through its menus. Touchscreens were unfamiliar to many participants as well and posed another large barrier that required extensive training. Because we worked with a smartphone that was not especially geared towards older users, it was customizable and working to its full extent, sometimes leading to unexpected events such as updates, activation of airplane mode, unintended changing of font size, background image, screen brightness etc. Some participants also struggled with third-party content and although playing around with the smartphone and downloading apps that participants might find fun or useful was encouraged some issues arose due to this. Occasionally, participants downloaded unintended or non-functional apps and files, sometimes even activating micro-transactions in games or subscribing to services that affected the available data and credit. Our sample found these errors highly distressing, because they were not aware of potential cost traps and thus sometimes felt confirmed in their skepticism of downloadable content and new media in general.

Further usage barriers are its fundamental services and systems, such as internet reception, operating system, and the training app we developed. Since the "Agile Quarter" training app was developed during the training cycles, we sometimes experienced server problems and unforeseen problems with the app itself, which also posed a considerable barrier to user acceptance. Unreliable technology frustrated the older users and led to dissatisfaction.

Especially during the second training cycle, it also became evident that the data plan we provided for the participants offered too many units for calling and texting, which our sample hardly used, but too little data volume, which often ran out before the end of the billing period and thus also constituted a usage barrier.

Further key environmental usage barriers are a lack of time to instruct participants, solve problems, and monitor individual progress. The group of participants also hindered user success at times, for example when many participants had questions or were confused, noise levels rose and attention was affected. Although the training instructors were experienced with the target group of older users and were "digital natives" themselves, they were laymen in terms of smartphone instruction and had to rely on their own everyday knowledge of new technology. This might also have been a usage barrier caused by the logistics of the training setup.

4   Discussion

Being aware of what makes a new device or a new app usable and attractive, and what barriers can arise for a specific target group is essential for user-centered design. This is especially true for older persons and in health-related contexts with a high proportion of vulnerable users. By applying the ICF framework to qualitative data from the research and development project "Agile Quarter," various personal and environmental factors were identified that can be understood as facilitators or as barriers for older users participating in app-supported training programs for health and well-being. The facilitators and barriers specified in this qualitative study can thus serve as orientation for the future design of smartphone-based training programs for older users in health-related contexts.

Future app-supported training programs must strike a balance between barriers and facilitators, for example when smartphones are provided, it is essential to balance the pros and cons of possible customization. We found it helpful for the participants to be able to experience all facets of this new technology, without being limited by certain settings or special phones for older users. Many participants decided to invest in a smartphone for themselves after the training cycle had ended and are glad to have learned something new and to have found access to this modern technology. User adoption was dependent on instruction and resources, though, which was only manageable in the context of this project because personal support was prioritized.

Another resource that could improve adoption of new technology by older users is group training, especially tandems with more experienced peers. "Agile Quarter" aimed to take advantage of its heterogeneous group constellations by pairing more experienced older users and inexperienced peers. Helping and instructing others solidifies the experienced users' knowledge while also teaching digital competency to group members who still had much to learn [25, 26]. Another possibility is the involvement of younger relatives such as grandchildren who are familiar with the technology as "digital natives," who often might be more readily accessible than professional tutors or instructors.

Acknowledgments. The German Federal Ministry of Education and Research (BMBF SILQUA-FH 03FH0085SA5) supported this research. This study was approved by the ethics committee of the German Physiotherapy Association (Deutscher Verband für Physiotherapie) (2016-06).

References

1. Thiel, C., et al.: Implementierung und erste Effekte Smartphone-unterstützter körperlich-kognitiver Aktivitäten im Wohnquartier zur Förderung der sozialen Teilhabe älterer Menschen. Bewegungstherapie und Gesundheitssport **35**, 235–245 (2019)
2. DIMDI – Deutsches Institut für Medizinische Dokumentation und Information: Internationale Klassifikation der Funktionsfähigkeit, Behinderung und Gesundheit. World Health Organization, Geneva
3. EIDD Design for all Europe Homepage. http://dfaeurope.eu/what-is-dfa/dfa-documents/the-eidd-stockholm-declaration-2004/10. Accessed 24 Jan 2020
4. Persson, H., Åhman, H., Yngling, A., Gulliksen, J.: Universal design, inclusive design, accessible design, design for all: different concepts – one goal? On the concept of accessibility – historical, methodological and philosophical aspects. Univ. Access Inf. Soc. **14**(4), 505–526 (2015)
5. Schoene, D., Valenzula, T., Lord, S., de Bruin, E.: The effect of interactive cognitive-motor training in reducing fall risk in older people: a systematic review. BMC Geriatrics **14**(107), 1–22 (2014)

6. Barnes, D., et al.: The mental activity and eXercise (MAX) trial. JAMA Intern. Med. **173**(9), 797–804 (2013)
7. Hopman-Rock, M., Westhoff, M.: Development and evaluation of "aging well and healthily": a health-education and exercise program for community-living older adults. J. Aging Phys. Act. **10**, 364–381 (2002)
8. Oswald, W., Gunzelmann, T., Ackermann, A.: Effects of a multimodal activation program (SimA-P) in residents of nursing homes. Eur. Rev. Aging Phys. Act. **4**(9), 91–102 (2007)
9. Huxhold, O., Schafer, S., Lindenberger, U.: Age-associated interactions of sensorimotor and cognitive functions. Zeitschrift für Gerontologie und Geriatrie **42**, 93–98 (2009)
10. Verbrugge, L., Jette, A.: The disablement process. Soc. Sci. Med. **38**, 1–14 (1994)
11. Reid, K., Fielding, R.: Skeletal muscle power: a critical determinant of physical functioning in older adults. Exerc. Sports Sci. Rev. **40**(1), 4–12 (2012)
12. Siegel, C., Dorner, T.: Information technologies for active and assisted living – influences to the quality of life in an ageing society. Int. J. Med. Informatics **100**, 32–45 (2017)
13. Tesch-Römer, C., Wiest, M., Wurm, S., Huxhold, O.: Loneliness trends in the second half of life: results from the German ageing survey (DEAS). Zeitschrift für Gerontologie und Geriatrie **46**(3), 237–241 (2013)
14. ACSM: ACSM's Guidelines for Exercise Testing and Prescription, 9th edn. Lippincott Williams & Wilkins, Philadelphia (2014)
15. Osterhoff, A., Günther, L., Thiel, C., Grüneberg, C., Sommer, S.: ICF-basierte Analyse der Barrieren und Förderfaktoren für die Smartphonenutzung im Rahmen eines App-gestützten kognitiv-körperlichen Trainingsprogrammes für Nutzer*innen ab 65 Jahren. Nutzerorientierte Gesundheitstechnologie. Hogrefe, Bern (2019)
16. Dunning, T.: The internet exercises the mind. Act. Adapt. Aging **28**(3), 71–72 (2004)
17. Shapira, N., Barak, A., Gal, I.: Promoting older adults' well-being through internet training and use. Aging Mental Health **11**(5), 477–484 (2007)
18. Beitzel, B.: How not to forget your next appointment: use technology to combat the effects of aging. J. Commun. Inf. **8**(1) (2012). http://ci-journal.net/index.php/ciej/article/view/888
19. Van Deursen, A., Helsper, E.: A nuanced understanding of internet use and non-use among the elderly. Eur. J. Commun. **30**(2), 171–187 (2015)
20. Schmidt, L.: Technikhandhabung im höheren Alter – Zur Rolle von kognitiver Leistungsfähigkeit, Technikeinstellung und Technikerfahrung. Springer, Wiesbaden (2017). https://doi.org/10.1007/978-3-658-16161-3
21. Díaz-Bossini, J., Moreno, L.: Accessibility to mobile interfaces for older people. In: 5th International Conference on Software Development and Technologies for Enhancing Accessibility and Fighting Info-Exclusion, DSAI (2013)
22. Damodaran, L., Olphert, W., Sandhu, J.: Falling off the bandwagon? Exploring the challenges to sustained digital engagement by older people. Gerontology **60**(2), 163–173 (2014)
23. Schelling, H., Seifert, A.: Internet-Nutzung im Alter: Gründe der (Nicht-)Nutzung von Informations- und Kommunikationstechnologien (IKT) durch Menschen ab 65 Jahren in der Schweiz. http://www.zora.uzh.ch/id/eprint/33811/. Accessed 24 Jan 2020
24. Tsai, H., Shillair, R., Cotton, S., Winstead, V., Yost, E.: Getting grandma online: are tablets the answer for increasing digital inclusion for older adults in the U.S.? Educ. Gerontol. **41**(10), 695–709 (2015)
25. Buboltz-Lutz, E., Gösken, E., Kricheldorff, C., Schramek, R.: Geragogik – Bildung und Lernen im Prozess des Alterns – Das Lehrbuch. Kohlhammer, Stuttgart (2010)
26. Kim, Y.: Reviewing and critiquing computer learning and usage among older adults. Educ. Gerontol. **34**(8), 709–735 (2008)

The Use of New Information and Communication Technology for Health Information Among Older Icelanders

Ágústa Pálsdóttir[✉]

Information Science, University of Iceland,
Oddi v/Sæmundargötu, 101, Reykjavík, Iceland
agustap@hi.is

Abstract. The paper examines the adoption and use of information and communications technologies (ICTs) for health information among Icelanders' aged 56 years and older. A survey explored how Icelanders' who are 56 years or older have taken new health ICT into use, and how they perceive their possibilities to do so. Following research questions were asked: 1) How do older adults use recently available ICT to access information about their health history and about healthy lifestyle? 2) How do they evaluate their capabilities to start using new ICT? 3) How do they perceive their possibilities to receive help at using ICT? A random sample was used, and after weighing the data by gender, age, place of residence and education it corresponds with the distribution in the population. The results demonstrate that the participants were motivated towards getting health information, also in digital form. The majority of them had, however, not yet adopted new ICT for health information into use but used older technology, such as blood pressure monitors to track and record their health information. About half of them, however, considered it difficult to take new ICT into use and the majority claimed that it was not easy for them to get help at using technology when they needed it. The main finding of the study is that it is not sufficient to make new ICT systems available in order to provide older adults with information about their health history and healthy behaviour. For them to be ready to accept new technology and take it into use, they need training and technical support.

Keywords: Health ICT · eHealth literacy · Older adults · Technology acceptance

1 Introduction

People's potential for life-long learning and informed decisions making about their health is a crucial issue. In the past years there have been great advancements in the way that information can be communicated and accessed. Health information is increasingly being disseminated digitally and people are constantly required to adjust to and learn about recent advances in their information environment. Given the growing amount of information that can be gathered from digital sources it is essential to recognize how people accept new technology and make use of it to gather information

© Springer Nature Switzerland AG 2020
Q. Gao and J. Zhou (Eds.): HCII 2020, LNCS 12208, pp. 354–364, 2020.
https://doi.org/10.1007/978-3-030-50249-2_26

about their health history and healthy lifestyle. The paper will examine the adoption and use of information and communications technologies (ICTs) for health information among Icelanders' aged 56 years and older.

Advances in digital technology and the growing amount of digital health information has brought new possibilities for people to manage their own health, practice better self-care and improve their health behaviour. Norman and Skinner [1] have introduced the concept of eHealth literacy and defined it as "the ability to seek, find, understand, and appraise health information from electronic sources and apply the knowledge gained to addressing or solving a health problem". Thus, to be able to benefit from digital health information demands that people possess the informational and technological competence which is required to take advantage of the digital information environment [2].

Older adults have been found to adopt new technology at a slower rate than those who are younger [3–5]. The argumentation is sometimes that technological solutions are targeted more towards those who are younger, leaving the older generation behind. Various factors have been identified which can cause challenges and have an impact on older peoples use of information technology. This includes, for example, weak physical condition and health problems [3], problems with the visual and auditory presentation of information [6–8], and changes in the motor ability which people can experience as they grow older [6, 9]. In addition, factors such as lack of confident in their abilities to use ICT and the need for help from others to start to use new technology [3] have been found to influence their use of ICT. Rosales and Fernández-Ardèvol [7] have found indications that older adults choice of information channels is based on their "values, style, habits and long-term perspective" (p. 63), which are among the reasons that limit their use of smartphones and leads them instead to gather information by means that are well known to them.

Several studies have pointed out that a lack of confidence in an information source can also be a hindrance. In particular, digital health information may be regarded as less reliable than information from other sources or channels [10–13]. Previous results have for example revealed that, although Icelandic senior citizens sought health information on the internet more frequently in 2012 than they did in 2007, they had at the same time also become more critical of the information and considered it both less useful and less reliable [14]. Furthermore, there are indications that people prefer to get support from health professionals to identify reliable health information [15]. It is therefore vital to guide them as to where they can access quality digital health information, that they can trust. Otherwise, they will be cut off from using it to make rational decisions about their health-related behaviour.

Nevertheless, there has been a substantial growth in older adults use of digital sources. This includes the use of the internet from home, as well as the use of mobile technology such as smartphones [4]. Mendiola, Kalnicki and Lindenauer [16] have suggested that the use of health apps in smartphones will create increasing opportunities for people to practice health care management. Their findings indicate that it is important that health apps are simple and intuitive to use, with an easy input of health data, and that they possess features that save time over current methods. This corresponds to previous evidence, that if older people find the technology easy to use, they are more inclined to do so [17]. Thus, the usability of the ICT matters. Likewise, it is of significance how older people perceive the benefit of the information that can be reached by ICT. There are indications that their attitude towards the adoption of smartwatches for health information is influenced by how they perceive the value of it [18]. If they believe that digital information has a high value for them, for example by receiving information that is tailored to their own needs, they are more encouraged to use digital solutions [19]. Thus, the relevance of digital information is important, and if older people consider it to be high, they are more motivated and prone to make more effort at seeking it [20].

In Iceland access to the internet is widespread. In 2014, a total of 95% of the population was reported to connect to the internet at least ones a week [4]. Thus, the conditions for obtaining digital health information can be considered excellent in that regard. It must, however, to be kept in mind that access to the internet does not necessarily translate into the use of digital health information [21].

Nevertheless, steps have been taken to improve access to health information. A new legal framework was set in 2009 to ensure people access to their health history through their health records, however many of the files are not yet in a digital form [22]. The latest initiative is the development of the ICT system 'Heilsuvera' which is supposed to provide people with a better and more direct access to information about their own health. The system allows people, for example, to book appointments with their doctors, to view drug prescriptions, and to communicate with doctors or other health professionals to get various health information tailored to their own needs. Some parts of people's health history are already being recorded into the system on a daily basis, while other types of access are still under development. This includes for example health records made during doctors' appointments, which are not accessible yet through the system. In addition to this, the system provides access to various reliable information about healthy lifestyle [23].

Aim and Research Questions

The aim of the study is to explore how Icelanders' who are 56 years or older have taken new health ICT into use, and how they perceive their possibilities to do so. The study will seek answers to the following research questions: 1) How do older adults use recently available ICT to access information about their health history and about healthy lifestyle? 2) How do they evaluate their capabilities to start using new ICT? 3) How do they perceive their possibilities to receive help at using ICT? The purpose of addressing this is to understand better how older adults can benefit from development in ICT and enhance their abilities to adopting healthier lifestyle through health information. An improved awareness of the issue may help to identify their needs for support at using health ICT and increase the efficiency of providing them with digital health information.

2   Methods

2.1   Data Collection

Data were gathered in from November 2018 to January 2019 from two samples using an internet and a telephone survey. The total sample for the survey consisted of 1.800

hundred people, 18 years and older. For the telephone survey, a sample of 300 people aged 60 years and older from the whole country, randomly selected from the National Register of Persons in Iceland, was used. For the internet survey a random sample of 1.500 people at the age of 18 to 59 years, from the Social Science Research Institute at the University of Iceland net panel, was used. The net panel consists of people aged 18 years or older from the whole country. The choice of participants in the net panel follows strict methodological rules to avoid convenience sampling. The net panel is updated regularly to ensure that it corresponds with the distribution in the population, regarding sex, age and residence. Both datasets were merged, allowing answers from all individuals belonging to each set of data. The total response rate was 39%.

The current paper focuses on participants who have reached the age of 56 years and older. The data were weighed by gender, age, place of residence and education so that it corresponds with the distribution in the population. Table 1 shows the number of participants before and after the data has been weighed.

Table 1. Number and rate of participants within the sample

Participants 56 years and older	Before weighing the data no (%)	After weighing the data no (%)
	173 (24.8%)	221 (31.7%)

2.2   Measurements and Analysis

The measurements consisted of four sets of questions:

1. Motivation to healthy lifestyle was examined by two questions. The first question asked how interested the participants were in information about health and lifestyle and the second, how often they discussed the topic with others. A five-point response scale was used (Very interested/often – Very low interest/Never).
2. One question examined how important it was for the participants to have full access to their health history through electronic health records. A five-point response scale was used (Very important – Very low important).
3. Use of health information and communication technology (ICT) was examined by four questions: 1) The use of the health ICT system "Heilsuvera" to communicate with doctors or to get information about their health, for example to book appointments, view drug prescriptions, or send messages to their doctor; 2) The use of "Heilsuvera" to seek information about healthy lifestyle, such as nutrition or exercise; 3) The use of smartphones or smartwatches to monitor or record health information; 4) The use of a blood pressure monitor to record their health information. A five-point response scale was used (Very often – Never).
4. Possibilities of taking new health ICT in use was examined by two questions in the form of statements. The first asked if they found it difficult to begin to use new technology; and the second, how easy it was for them to get help at using technology when they were in need for it. A five-point response scale was used (Strongly agree – Strongly disagree).

The analysis of the data is descriptive. All analysis is based on weighed data.

3 Results

The chapter starts by presenting results about the participants motivation towards receiving health and lifestyle information and the importance of having access to health records. This will be followed by results about the use of the information and communication system Heilsuvera, the use of smartphones/smartwatches, and blood pressure monitors. Finally, results about the participants experience of taking new information and communication technology in use and their possibilities of getting help at it will be introduced.

Figure 1 presents results about the participants motivation towards receiving health and lifestyle information.

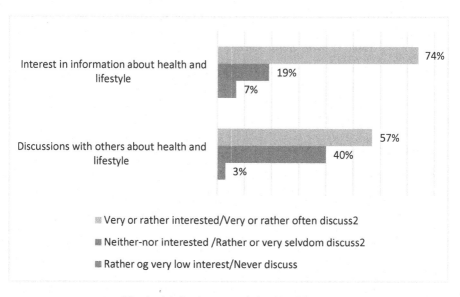

Fig. 1. Motivation towards healthy lifestyle

Figure 1 shows that the participants are in general motivated towards healthy lifestyle. The great majority of the claimed to be either very or rather interested in information about the topic and over half of them discuss it very or rather often with others. The rates of those who have rather or very low interest in the matter and claim that they never have discussions about it with others is low.

The participants were asked how important it was for them to have full access to their health history through electronic health records. A total of 71% of them considered this to be either very or rather important, 14% replied that it was neither important nor unimportant, while 15% found it to be either rather or very unimportant.

Furthermore, they were asked about how often or seldom they had used the Icelandic health information and communication system "Heilsuvera" to communicate with their doctors or to get information about their health, for examples to book appointments, view drug prescriptions, or to send messages to their doctor. In addition, they were asked about their use of the system to seek information about healthy lifestyle, such as about nutrition or exercise. Figure 2 shows the results.

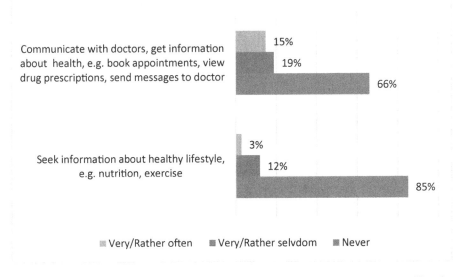

Fig. 2. Use of 'Heilsuvera' to communicate and to seek information about healthy lifestyle

The results in Fig. 2 show that a total of 34% of the participants had used 'Heilsuvera' to communicate with their doctors or to get information about their health. However, only 15% had used it either very or rather often, while 19% claimed that they had used it very or rather seldom. The majority of the participants had never used 'Heilsuvera' to communicate with their doctors or to get information about their health. Furthermore, when asked if they had sought information about heathy lifestyle, the results show an even lower use of 'Heilsuvera'. Only a total of 15% of the participants had sought information there, while the great majority of them replied that they had never done so.

They were furthermore asked about their use of equipment, such as smartphones, smartwatches, and blood pressure monitors, to record their health information. The results are presented in Fig. 3.

As can be seen in Fig. 3, the majority of the participants have never used smartphones or smartwatches to monitor or record their health information. Only 24% of them had done so. The results, however, were reversed when they were asked about their use of a blood pressure monitor to record health information. The majority of the participants had used them, with only 25% claiming that they had never done so.

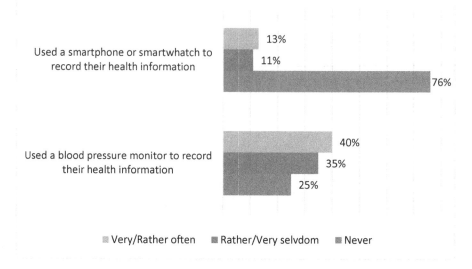

Fig. 3. Use of smartphones/smartwatches and blood pressure monitors

Results about the respondents' experience of taking new health information and communication technology, as well as how easy they found it to get help at using technology when they were in need for, are presented in Fig. 4.

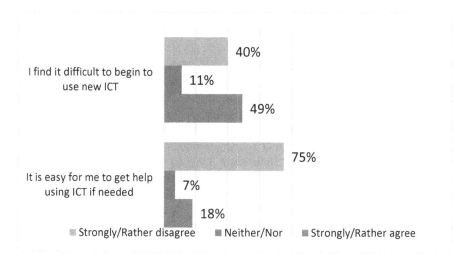

Fig. 4. Difficulties at taking new ICT in use – Access to help

When asked if they found it difficult to take new information and communication technology into use, the results in Fig. 4 revealed that about half of the participants agreed with it, while 40% of them were in a disagreement with it. In addition, the majority of them did not consider it easy to get help at using technology when they were in need for it (Fig. 4).

4 Discussion

Innovations in information technology have brought about major changes in healthcare. New possibilities of disseminating and accessing digital health information have emerged that give people the chance to better monitor their health, and to more actively manage their healthy behaviour. The current study explored how people at the age of 56 years, living in Iceland, have adopted new ICT for health information.

The participants in the study were both interested in information about healthy lifestyle and they discussed the topic of healthy living with others. Furthermore, over 70% of them also expressed the opinion that it is important to have full access to their own health history through electronic health records. Thus, the results clearly demonstrate that this is a group that is motivated towards getting health information, also in digital form.

About half of them, however, considered it difficult to take new ICT into use. In addition, the majority claimed that it was not easy for them to get help at using technology when they needed it. These are factors that can have a bearing on whether or not people are ready to make the effort of starting to use new technology. Previous studies have for example reported that the ease of using new technology, the confidence that people possess at being able to handle new technology and being able to get help at taking it into use, is of importance for older adults [2, 3, 16, 17].

The results about the adoption of new ICT for health information show that the majority of participants had not yet taken it into use. They were, on the other hand, using older technology, such as blood pressure monitors to track and record their health information. This corresponds with the previous finding that older adults prefer to choose information channels based on the practices that they have created over time, as well as their values and long-term perspectives [7]. Hence, well established means to gather information, which older people are familiar with and have grown accustomed to use, may have more value for them than new technology.

For people to be able to make informed health decisions it is essential that they have access to quality information about their health history and healthy lifestile. Health ICT can open up possibilities for them to retrieve more information about their health history, as well as offering new ways to communicate with health professionals. Providing access to information, however, is of little value if it is not done in a way that meets the needs of the intended users.

The results about the low use of the system 'Heilsuvera' are perhaps not surprising considering the short time that the system has been in use. It may always be expected that it takes time and effort, first of all to introduce and get people acquainted with new technology, and secondly to get them engaged with using it. Nevertheless, the system can be seen as an opportunity for improvement in access to high quality health information, as well as for people to communicate with doctors or other health professionals and receive various tailored information about their health. The value of the information itself is essential. The possibility to receive health information that are tailored to peoples own needs has been found to be a motivator that encourages older people to make an effort at using digital solutions [19, 20]. Hence, given time for people to become knowledgeable about the possibilities that 'Heilsuvera' offers, and provided that they will also be offered support at taking it into use, it can be concluded that the system makes promising possibilities for the future.

The overall study is limited by a total response rate of 39%. Although his may be considered satisfactory in a survey it raises the question whether or not those who answered the survey are giving a biased picture of those who did not respond. In order to compensate for this bias the data were weighed by gender, age, place of residence and education, so that it corresponds with the distribution in the population. Thus, the findings may provide valuable information about the adoption, acceptance, and use of new ICT among older Icelanders.

5 Conclusions and Limitation

In order to recognize how older adults accept new technology and make use of it to gather health information, the study sought answers to three research questions. Firstly, how do older adults use recently available ICT to access information about their health history and about healthy lifestyle? Secondly, how do they evaluate their capabilities to start using new ICT? And, thirdly, how they perceive their possibilities to receive help at using ICT? The results revealed that the majority of the participants had not yet adopted new ICT for health information. Furthermore, they do not perceive their possibilities for doing so to be good. About half of them considered it difficult to take new ICT into use and the majority did not find it easy to get help at using technology when they needed it. Thus, the conclusion of the study is that it is not sufficient to make new ICT systems available in order to provide older people with information about their health. For older adults to be ready to accept new technology and take it into use, they must be offered training at using it and technical support as needed.

The results from the study help to shed a light on older adult's potentials to benefit from the development in ICT, and to identify their needs for support at using health ICT. There is, however, a great deal more to learn about the topic. In particular, the study is limited by the use of quantitative research methods and further research using more varied methods is needed. Especially, there is a need for qualitative studies, that can explore more deeply why older people do not use new technology and what kind of support they need and prefer to receive. This is particularly important because ICT develops rapidly, which is a progress that can be expected to continue in the coming years.

Acknowledgments. The research project was supported by the University of Iceland Research Fund.

References

1. Norman, C., Skinner, H.: EHealth literacy: essential skills for consumer health in a networked world. J. Med. Internet Res. **8**(2), e9 (2006). https://doi.org/10.2196/jmir.8.2.e9
2. Bol, N., van Weert, J.C., Loos, E.F., Romano Bergstrom, J.C., Bolle, S., Smets, E.M.: How are online health messages processed? Using eye tracking to predict recall of information in younger and older adults. J. Health Commun. **21**(4), 387–396 (2016). https://doi.org/10.1080/10810730.2015.1080327
3. Anderson, M., Perrin, A.: Tech adoption climbs among older adults: roughly two-thirds of those ages 65 and older go online and a record share now own smartphones: although many seniors remain relatively divorced from digital lifel. Pew Research Centre (2017). https://www.pewinternet.org/2017/05/17/tech-adoption-climbs-among-older-adults/
4. Statistics Iceland: Computer and internet usage in Iceland and other European countries 2013. Statistical Series: Tourism, Transport and IT **99**(1) (2014). https://hagstofa.is/lisalib/getfile.aspx?ItemID=14251
5. Vorrink, S.N.W., Antonietti, A.M.G.E.F., Kort, H.S.M., Troosters, T., Zanen, P., Lammers, J-W.J.: Technology use by older adults in the Netherlands and its associations with demographics and health outcomes. Assist. Technol. **29**(4), 188–196 (2017). https://doi.org/10.1080/10400435.2016.1219885
6. Loos, E.F., Romano Bergstrom, J.: Older adults. In: Romano Bergstrom, J., Schall, A. J. (eds.) Eye Tracking in User Experience Design, pp. 313–329. Elsevier, Amsterdam (2014)
7. Rosales, A., Fernández-Ardèvol, M.: Smartphone usage diversity among older people. In: Sayago, S. (ed.) Perspectives on Human-Computer Interaction Research with Older People. HIS, pp. 51–66. Springer, Cham (2019). https://doi.org/10.1007/978-3-030-06076-3_4
8. World Health Organization: Global Age Friendly Cities: A Guide. WHO, Geneva (2007). http://www.who.int/ageing/publications/Global_age_friendly_cities_Guide_English.pdf
9. Hoogendam, Y.Y., et al.: Older age relates to worsening of fine motor skills: a population-based study of middle-aged and elderly persons. Front. Aging Neurosci. **6**, 259 (2014). http://www.ncbi.nlm.nih.gov/pmc/articles/PMC4174769/
10. Bradford, W.H., et al.: Trust and sources of health information the impact of the internet and its implications for health care providers: findings from the first health information national trends survey. JAMA Intern. Med. **165**(22), 2618–2624 (2005)
11. Eriksson-Backa, K.: Finnish 'silver surfers' and online health information. In: Eriksson-Backa, K., Luoma, A., Krook, E. (eds.) WIS 2012. CCIS, vol. 313, pp. 138–149. Springer, Heidelberg (2012). https://doi.org/10.1007/978-3-642-32850-3_13
12. Pálsdóttir, Á.: Icelanders' and trust in the internet as a source of health and lifestyle information. Inf. Res. **16**(1), paper 470 (2011). http://InformationR.net/ir/16-1/paper470.html
13. Soederberg Miller, L.M., Bell, R.A.: Online health information seeking: the influence of ag, information trustworthiness, and search challenges. J. Aging Health **24**(3), 525–541 (2012)
14. Pálsdóttir, Á.: Senior citizens, media and information literacy and health information. In: Kurbanoğlu, S., Boustany, J., Špiranec, S., Grassian, E., Mizrachi, D., Roy, L. (eds.) ECIL 2015. CCIS, vol. 552, pp. 233–240. Springer, Cham (2015). https://doi.org/10.1007/978-3-319-28197-1_24
15. Lee, K., Hoti, K., Hughes, J.D., Emmerton, L.: Dr Google is here to stay but health care professionals are still valued: an analysis of health care consumers' internet navigation support preferences. J. Med. Internet Res. **9**(6), e210 (2017). https://doi.org/10.2196/jmir.7489

16. Mendiola, M.F., Kalnicki, M., Lindenauer, S.: Valuable features in mobile health apps for patients and consumers: content analysis of apps and user ratings. JMIR Mhealth Uhealth **3**(2), e40 (2015). https://www.ncbi.nlm.nih.gov/pmc/articles/PMC4446515/

17. Tsai, H.S., Taiwan, H., Shillair, R., Cotton, S.R., Winstead, V., Yost, E.: Getting grandma online: are tablets the answer for increasing digital inclusion for older adults in the U.S.? Educ. Gerontol. Educ. Gerontol. **41**, 695–709 (2015)

18. Todd, M.M., et al.: Perception of older adults toward smartwatch technology for assessing pain and related patient-reported outcomes: pilot study. JMIR Mhealth Uhealth **7**(3), e10044 (2019). https://doi.org/10.2196/10044

19. Jimison, H., et al.: Barriers and drivers of health information technology use for the elderly, chronically Ill, and underserved. Evidence Report/Technology Assessment No. 175. AHRQ Publication No. 09-E004. Agency for Healthcare Research and Quality, Rockville, MD (2008)

20. Loos, E.: Senior citizens: digital imigrants in their own country? Observatorio **6**(1), 1–23 (2012)

21. Ono, H., Zavodny, M.: Digital inequality: a five country comparison using microdata. Soc. Sci. Res. **36**(3), 1135–1155 (2007)

22. Health Records Act nr. 55 April 27 2009. https://www.government.is/media/velferdarraduneyti-media/media/acrobat-enskar_sidur/Health-Records-Act-No-55-2009-as-amended-2016.pdf

23. Directory of Health: Heilsuvera: mínar heilbrigðisupplýsingar (2016). https://www.landlaeknir.is/gaedi-og-eftirlit/heilbrigdisthjonusta/rafraen-sjukraskra/heilsuvera-minar-heilbrigdisupplysingar/

Chronic Health Problems of Older Workers and Their Occupational Safety: A Meta-Analysis

Lu Peng$^{(\boxtimes)}$ ⓘ, Rita W. L. Yu, Alan H. S. Chan, and Hin Piu Yim

Department of Systems Engineering and Engineering Management,
City University of Hong Kong, Kowloon, Hong Kong
lupeng2-c@my.cityu.edu.hk

Abstract. Ageing is accompanied by a general decline in physical health and a rise in chronic health problems. The increasing rate of workforce ageing and prolonged work life are likely to result in more workers working at older ages with potential diseases and disabilities. This study aims to examine the relationships between a series of chronic health problems and occupational safety risks of older workers using the meta-analysis technique. Literature search was conducted through Google Scholar. Literature published in the last 30 years (from 1989 to 2019) was collected. Eighteen journal articles were included. Sixty records were extracted from these studies. The overall effect size indicated that the odds ratio of occurrence of occupational accidents for older workers with chronic health problems is 1.455 times as high as those without any health problems included. The aggregated effect sizes of 12 categories of health problems showed that older workers with hearing impairment, visual impairment, musculoskeletal disorder, obesity, urogenital problems, chronic bronchitis/emphysema, substance abuse, or not specified health problems suffer significantly higher occupational safety risks than those without such health problems. However, the aggregated odds ratios for cancers, cardiovascular problems, diabetes, and neurotic disorders showed insignificant associations of these diseases with the adverse safety outcomes of older workers. In addition, type of health problem, gender, and cutoff age moderated the focused relationships. Policies related to ageing workforce, e.g., prolonging work life, should consider chronic health problems concerning older workers protection from occupational safety risks.

Keywords: Chronic health problem · Occupational safety · Older worker

1 Introduction

In the 21st century, people have longer life span than before. The ageing workforce has become a popular issue around the world, as more people keep working and retire at an older age comparing to the past. In Australia, the participation rate of workers aged 55 or over increased from 22% in 1985 to 35% in 2015 (Gahan et al. 2016). According to the Census and Statistics Department of Hong Kong (2017), the share of workers aged 55 or over was projected to increase from 20.2% in 2016 to 26.8% in 2066.

© Springer Nature Switzerland AG 2020
Q. Gao and J. Zhou (Eds.): HCII 2020, LNCS 12208, pp. 365–380, 2020.
https://doi.org/10.1007/978-3-030-50249-2_27

Ageing is accompanied by a general decline in physical health and a rise in chronic health problems. Prince et al. (2015) indicated that approximately 23% of the total global burden of diseases is caused by cardiovascular, respiratory, and musculoskeletal disorders for people aged 60 years and older. The Labour Force Survey of the Health and Safety Executive in the UK (2008) reported that females aged 45 to 59 years and males aged 55 to 64 years have the highest estimated prevalence rate of illness.

Researchers had reported that ageing is related to elevated occupational safety risks. The odds ratio of suffering fatal/severe occupational accidents for older workers is twice as high as those of younger workers (Peng and Chan 2019). Evidences had shown that increasing occurrence of chronic health problems suffered by older workers closely associated with their elevated occupational safety risks. For example, Lam (2008) and Zwerling (1996) found that workers who have poor visual capability had an increased risk of occupational injury. Jadhav et al. (2015) indicated that health problems are significant risk factors leading to injuries in agricultural industry. With the trend of global ageing, employers will have to rely on older workers to remain competitive in the global marketplace (Loeppke et al. 2013). However, the increasing rate of workforce ageing and prolonged work life are likely to result in more workers working at older ages with potential diseases and disabilities. Even many older workers with health problems may exit the labor market, there are still many workers choose to stay in their jobs (Silverstein 2008). This will lead to elevation of occupational safety risks.

An investigation on the influences of specific health diseases on occupational safety risks of older workers can help in identifying the critical health problems and improving safety management. The aim of this study is to examine the relationship between a series of chronic health problems and the occupational safety outcomes for older workers using the meta-analysis technique. In addition to the overall effects of chronic health problems on occupational safety of older workers, the effects of specific problems, such as influences of hearing and vision impairments on the safety of older workers, would also be examined. Three potential moderators, including occupation, gender and cutoff age, were presumed to have influences on the focused relationship. Chronic health problems lead to changes in the physical ability of workers. Fraade-Blanar et al. (2017) reported that job demand of different occupations and physical ability of older workers and mismatch between these two factors were related to the likelihood of occupational injury. Thus, it is reasonable to expect that different occupations with different job demands would influence the relationship between chronic health problems and occupational safety. Gender was another possible moderator. Côté (2011) stated that females have different movement strategies and muscle coordination comparing to males. Female workers are more likely to have neck-shoulder problems at work than males. The differences in the risk of suffering specific health problems may influence the focused relationship. Cutoff age refers to the cutoff point of defining older workers. Different studies may define older workers with different cutoff age. The impacts of chronic health problems on the physical ability of workers may be moderated by age, and thus the risks of suffering occupational accidents would vary with the age of workers. Therefore, the influence of cutoff age on the focused relationship should be likewise examined.

2 Method

2.1 Literature Collection

Collection of literature was conducted through a searching in Google Scholar. The keywords used for search were the combinations of (health problems) AND (occupational OR workplace OR agricultural) AND (injury OR accident OR safety OR fatality) AND (older OR age OR ageing). Thereafter, the keyword "health problems", was replaced by "disease", "hearing", "vision", "obesity", "mental", "psychosocial factors", "depression", "anxiety", "cardiovascular" "heart disease", "musculoskeletal", "arthritis", "disability", "respiratory", "diabetes" or "cancer" for further searches as some literature focus on specific types of health problem. Only the literature published within 30 years (from 1989 to 2019) were retained. In addition, some inclusion criteria were set for further filtering. First, studies should be published in English. Second, the samples of workers should be active in the labour market. Third, the study should provide enough information for calculating effect size on the relationship between health problems and occupation safety for older workers. Finally, the targeted relationship should be of individual level rather than organization- or team-level. A total of 721 articles were collected from the initial search, and 102 studies were kept after reading the abstracts. In the end, 18 studies were retained after reading the whole context and applying all the inclusion criteria.

2.2 Coding for Studies

The common information and potential moderators were coded for each included study. They were author information, year of publication, country, sample size, data collection method, type of health problem, gender, occupation, and cutoff age defining older workers. Effect sizes were calculated and converted into odds ratio. If more than one health problems were found in one study, the effect sizes of each problem would be calculated separately. A total of 60 records were extracted from the 18 studies.

To have a better analysis of the studies, the health problems examined in the studies were classified into different categories on the basis of the health categories advised by UK Clinical Research Collaboration (2018). Twelve categories were summarized, including cancer, cardiovascular, hearing impairment, musculoskeletal disorder, obesity, substance abuse, urogenital, vision impairment, chronic bronchitis or emphysema, diabetes, neurotic disorder, and not specified. Substance abuse is a mental illness and brain disorder. It is categorized in substance use disorder in the Diagnostic and Statistical Manual of Mental Disorders by the American Psychiatric Association (National Institute on Drug Abuse 2018). The term, 'not specified', refers to the health problems that were not specified in the articles but only mentioned as general health problems, such as 'chronic physical health conditions' used by Baidwan et al. (2018). The coding method is shown in Table 1. The details of the coded records are demonstrated in Appendix 1.

Table 1. Coding information for some variables

Variable	Category	Coding method
Gender	Both, male	N/A
Type of health problem	Cancer, cardiovascular problem, hearing impairment, musculoskeletal disorder, obesity, substance abuse, urogenital problem, vision impairment, chronic bronchitis or emphysema, diabetes, neurotic disorder, not specified	– Cancer: cancer, skin cancer and other cancers – Cardiovascular problem: heart attack, stroke, high blood pressure, hypertension, cardiovascular disease and heart disease – Chronic bronchitis or emphysema: chronic bronchitis or emphysema – Diabetes: diabetes – Hearing impairment: hearing impairment – Musculoskeletal disorder: arthritis, musculoskeletal disorders, rheumatism, mobility problems, carpal tunnel, back problems, osteoporosis and osteoarthritis – Neurotic disorder: neurotic disorder – Obesity: obesity and obese – Substance abuse: substance abuse, alcohol Abuse and alcohol dependence – Urogenital problem: prostate problems, incontinence and urinary tract disorders – Vision impairment: vision impairment – Not specified: chronic physical health conditions, presence of disease, disabilities, persistent disabilities and disabled from work
Occupation	Cross-occupation, construction, farming, mining, non-farming	N/A
Cutoff age	40, 45, 50, 51, 55, 60, 66	N/A

2.3 Characteristics of the Included Studies

The sample size of the included studies ranged from 113 to 604,134. The study with largest sample size was conducted by Shi et al. (2015a, b). The data were collected from National Health Interview Survey (NHIS) during 1997–2011 in the United States. Among the 60 records, 43 of them were of 'both' and 17 'male' in terms of gender. Regarding the countries of the included studies, two were in Canada, one in France, one in India and 14 in the United States.

2.4 Meta-Analysis

Comprehensive Meta-Analysis (Version 3.0) was used to perform statistical analyses in this study. Random effects model was adopted to estimate the effect sizes given the variations in participant, type of health problem and region across studies. To evaluate the heterogeneity, Q and I-squared statistics were referred. For estimation and adjustment of publication bias, funnel plots and trim-and-fill method were adopted as suggested by Borenstein et al. (2011). The robustness of the results was evaluated with Rosenthal's Fail-Safe N, which indicates the number of missing studies needed to nullify the overall effect (Borenstein et al. 2011). Lastly, Meta-regression was applied to detect the possible sources of heterogeneity across records.

3 Results

3.1 Aggregated Effect Sizes Based on Random Effect Model

When the risk of occupational injury of older workers with certain health problem were compared to those without the problem, the overall odds ratio of the summarized effect size of 60 records was 1.479 (95% CI: 1.350–1.620, $p < 0.01$). When grouped by health problems, the effect sizes in form of odds ratio for subgroups were also calculated. The aggregated results are shown in Table 2. Figure 1 illustrates the forest plot of the 60 records. In this study, the Fail-safe N is 3,623, which is unrealistically large to nullify the overall effect size ($p < 0.001$). That is, the robustness of the results was confirmed.

Table 2. Aggregated effect sizes of subgroups in form of odds ratio

Subgroup	Effect size in odds ratio	Number of records	95% CI	p-value
Chronic bronchitis or emphysema	2.360	1	1.534–3.630	<0.001
Not specified	1.946	7	1.634–2.317	<0.001
Musculoskeletal disorder	1.683	13	1.394–2.032	<0.001
Substance abuse	1.621	4	1.243–2.114	<0.001
Urogenital problem	1.470	3	1.104–1.958	0.008
Hearing impairment	1.467	8	1.172–1.837	<0.001
Obesity	1.452	4	1.202–1.752	<0.001
Vision impairment	1.359	7	1.058–1.747	0.016
Cancer	1.165	4	0.739–1.838	0.511
Diabetes	1.110	1	0.685–1.798	0.671
Neurotic disorder	1.080	1	0.679–1.718	0.745
Cardiovascular problem	0.991	7	0.819–1.199	0.925
Overall	1.479	60	1.350–1.620	<0.001

3.2   Heterogeneity Test and Public Bias Adjustment

The varied effect size across records can be caused by the real heterogeneity or within-study error (Borenstein et al. 2011). Heterogeneity test is to verify if the variation of effect size is resulted from the real heterogeneity. Both Q and I-squared statistics are heterogeneity indicators, but the former is sensitive to the number of studies and the latter is independent from the scale. Higgins et al. (2003) recommended that I-squared statistic higher than 50% and 75% indicated a moderate and high level of hetero-geneity, respectively. Regarding the total 60 records, its I-squared statistic was 69.98%, indicating a moderate level of heterogeneity.

Trim-and- Fill is a method developed for estimating the effect of the missing studies on the overall outcome of a meta-analysis (Duval and Tweedie 2000). An unbiased estimation of effect will be provided by this method in theory (Borenstein et al. 2011). When the Trim-and-Fill method was performed for the overall records, two data points were added in the left of the mean. The aggregated odd ratio for overall results changed from 1.479 to 1.455 (see Fig. 2). According to the adjusted results, older workers with chronic health problems have a significantly higher chance to suffer occupational safety risks than those without chronic health problems.

3.3   Moderator Analyses with Meta-Regression

The heterogeneity test indicated the existence of real heterogeneity across the included records. Therefore, the single covariate meta-regression was conducted to investigate the power of the potential moderators in explaining the variance of effect size. In addition to the aforementioned three moderators, type of health problem was likewise examined given the variation of aggregated effect sizes for grouped results. Gender, occupation, and type of health problem were categorical variables, while cutoff age was a continuous variable.

The results of meta-regression with random-effect model and maximum likelihood method are shown in Table 3. R^2 refers to the percentage of variance explained by the moderator. The category coefficient for categorical variables refers to the marginal effect (log odds ratio) of the focused category comparing to the reference category. Table 3 shows that occupation was not a significant moderator. However, gender, cutoff age, and type of health problem were all significant moderators that influence the variance of effect size across records. The variance was mainly explained by the difference in type of health problem (59%), following by the cutoff age (23%), and gender (18%).

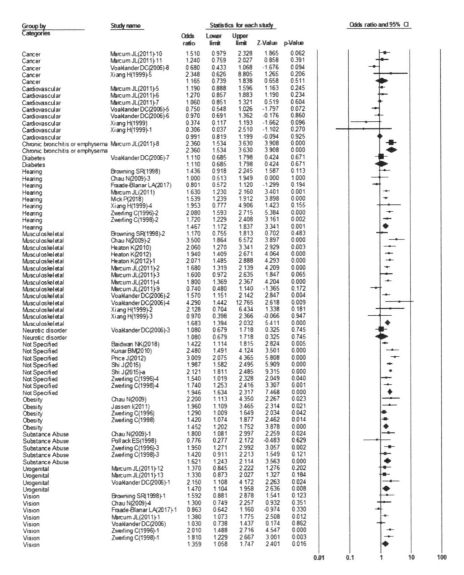

Fig. 1. Forest plot of 60 records grouped by health problems with a mixed-effect model. *Note:* The center of square represents the odds ratio of each record while the area of square is proportional to the given weights of the record. The width of horizontal line represents the confidence interval of effect size for each record. The mid-point of diamond represents the aggregated odds ratio for each subgroup, and its width refers to the corresponding confidence interval.

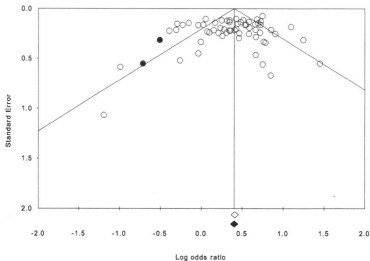

Fig. 2. Funnel plot of all records for publication bias adjustment. Note: The open circles are the original data while the solid circles are the inputted values for filling. The observed point estimate is represented by the open diamond at 0.391 (log odds ratio), corresponding to an odds ratio of 1.479. The adjusted point estimate is represented by the full diamond at 0.375 (log odds ratio), corresponding to an odds ratio of 1.455 (95% CI: 1.326–1.595).

Table 3. Results of moderator analyses with meta-regression.

Covariate	Coefficient	Z-value	2-sided p-value	Test to model	R^2
Gender (reference to both)					
Intercept	0.4449	9.15	<0.001	/	18%
Male	−0.259	−2.41	0.0158	Q = 5.83, df = 1, p = 0.0158	
Health problem (reference to cardiovascular problem)					
Intercept	−0.0133	−0.13	0.8985	/	59%
Cancer	0.1377	0.71	0.4787	Q = 35.57, df = 11, p = 0.0002	
Chronic bronchitis or emphysema	0.8719	2.9	0.0037		
Diabetes	0.1176	0.37	0.7135		
Hearing impairment	0.4054	2.92	0.0035		
Musculoskeletal disorder	0.5301	4.04	0.0001		
Neurotic disorder	0.0902	0.29	0.7734		
Not specified	0.679	4.95	<0.001		
Obesity	0.4286	2.53	0.0114		
Substance abuse	0.4804	2.5	0.0125		

(*continued*)

Table 3. *(continued)*

Covariate	Coefficient	Z-value	2-sided *p*-value	Test to model	R^2
Urogenital problem	0.4166	2	0.0457		
Vision impairment	0.3145	2.21	0.0271		
Occupation (reference to farming)					
Intercept	0.3009	5.12	<0.001	/	18%
Construction	−0.5549	−0.95	0.3433	Q = 8.28, df = 4,	
Cross-occupation	0.1787	1.67	0.0959	p = 0.0819	
Mining	0.6074	1.66	0.0973		
Non-farming	0.2156	1.9	0.0569		
Cutoff age					
Intercept	1.4222	3.98	0.0001	/	23%
Cutoff age	−0.0196	−2.9	0.0037	Q = 8.43, df = 1, p = 0.0037	

4   Discussion

This meta-analysis had studied the relationship between chronic health problems and occupational safety for older workers. The direction and magnitude of the difference of older workers with and without health problem in occurrence of occupational injury had been found out. Substantial variance exists in the effect sizes across records. The potential moderators which can explain the variation of effect size were then examined.

4.1   Overall Relationship Between Chronic Health Problems and Occupational Safety for Older Workers

The overall effect size showed that chronic health problem positively associated with occupation accidents among older workers. It means that older workers with health problem have a higher risk to suffer injuries in their workplace than those without any problem. This finding was consistent with Jadhav et al. (2015) and Palmer et al. (2008). Jadhav et al. (2015) found that workers with health problems have higher probabilities of injury than those without problems. Palmer et al. (2008) indicated that certain types of health problem can lead to increased risks of occupational accidents for general workers. No existing research had examined the influence of chronic health problems on the occupational safety for older workers, while this group of subjects has the highest possibility of suffering chronic health problems.

Demographic changes have brought challenges to employers and management in the society, especially those who strive to resolve labour shortages. One solution to labour shortage is to encourage older workers to stay in the workforce (Bohle et al. 2010). For instance, Hong Kong has prolonged mandatory retirement age for specific occupations, e.g. security personnel. However, such policies should be taken cautiously as the prolonged working lives may lead to increased unhealthy workers involved in the workplace and may result in elevated occupational safety risks of older workers.

4.2   Moderating Factors Explain the Variations of Effect Size

Moderator analyses showed that type of health problem, gender and cutoff of age are critical moderating factors which can explain the variance of effect size. Older workers with hearing impairment, visual impairment, musculoskeletal disorder, obesity, substance abuse, urogenital problem, chronic bronchitis/emphysema, or not specified health problems suffered significantly higher occupational safety risks than those without such health problems. Of these types of health problem, the effect size of chronic bronchitis/emphysema was the greatest. On the contrast, the aggregated odds ratios for cancer, cardiovascular problem, diabetes, and neurotic disorder showed insignificant effects of these diseases on safety outcomes of older workers.

In addition, the effect size for females was greater than males. That implies older female workers were more vulnerable in occupational safety risks when suffering chronic health problems than their male counterparts. Moreover, the aggravating effect of chronic health problems was more salient for younger-old workers than for the older-old workers as the correlation between cutoff age and effect size is negative. The possible explanation is that healthy younger-old workers may have much lower safety risks than their unhealthy counterparts, whereas the difference in occupational safety risks between the healthy and unhealthy older-old workers was smaller than the former.

5   Conclusion

This study found that older workers with chronic health problems suffer more adverse occupational safety outcomes as compared to those without health problems. The relationship between the chronic health problem and occupational safety risk for older workers was influenced by type of health problem, gender, and cutoff age. The findings of this study provide insights for human resource managers and policy makers when addressing the issue of labour shortage by prolonging working life.

Appendix 1

Details of Records Included in the Meta-Analysis

Study name	Health problem	Category of problem	Odds ratio	Lower limit	Upper limit	Sample size	Data collection method	Gender	Country	Occupation	Cutoff age
Baidwan et al. (2018)	Chronic physical health conditions	Not specified	1.422	1.114	1.815	7212	Using data from the U.S. Health and Retirement Study from 2004 to 2014	Both	US	Cross-occupation	50
Browning et al. (1998)	Hearing	Hearing	1.436	0.918	2.245	998	By telephone survey	Both	US	Farming	55
Browning et al. (1998)-1	Vision	Vision	1.592	0.881	2.878	998	By telephone survey	Both	US	Farming	55

(continued)

Study name	Health problem	Category of problem	Odds ratio	Lower limit	Upper limit	Sample size	Data collection method	Gender	Country	Occupation	Cutoff age
Browning et al. (1998)-2	Arthritis	Musculoskeletal	1.170	0.755	1.813	998	By telephone survey	Both	US	Farming	55
Chau et al. (2009)	Obesity	Obesity	2.200	1.113	4.350	2888	By postal questionnaire	Both	France	Cross-occupation	45
Chau et al. (2009)-1	Alcohol abuse	Substance abuse	1.800	1.081	2.997	2888	By postal questionnaire	Both	France	Cross-occupation	45
Chau et al. (2009)-2	Musculoskeletal disorders	Musculoskeletal	3.500	1.864	6.572	2888	By postal questionnaire	Both	France	Cross-occupation	45
Chau et al. (2009)-3	Hearing	Hearing	1.000	0.513	1.949	2888	By postal questionnaire	Both	France	Cross-occupation	45
Chau et al. (2009)-4	Visual	Vision	1.300	0.749	2.257	2888	By postal questionnaire	Both	France	Cross-occupation	45
Fraade-Blanar et al. (2017)	Hearing	Hearing	0.801	0.572	1.120	5586	Using data from Health and Retirement Study from 2010 to 2014	Both	US	Cross-occupation	50
Fraade-Blanar et al. (2017)-1	Vision	Vision	0.863	0.642	1.160	5586	Using data from Health and Retirement Study from 2010 to 2014	Both	US	Cross-occupation	50
Heaton et al. (2010)	Arthritis	Musculoskeletal	2.060	1.270	3.341	1423	Using mailed and telephonic surveys	Both	US	Farming	50
Heaton et al. (2012)	Arthritis/ rheumatism	Musculoskeletal	1.940	1.409	2.671	1419	Using telephoned or mailed surveys	Both	US	Farming	50
Heaton et al. (2012)-1	Mobility problems	Musculoskeletal	2.071	1.485	2.888	1419	Using telephoned or mailed surveys	Both	US	Farming	50
Janssen et al. (2011)	Obese	Obesity	1.960	1.109	3.465	7678	By home or telephone interview	Both	Canada	Cross-occupation	40
Kunar et al. (2010)	Presence of disease	Not specified	2.480	1..491	4.124	2376	By face-to-face interview and questionnaire	Male	India	Mining	45
Marcum et al. (2011)	Hearing	Hearing	1.630	1.230	2.160	1394	By telephone and mail surveys	Both	US	Farming	50
Marcum et al. (2011)-1	Vision	Vision	1.380	1.073	1.775	1394	By telephone and mail surveys	Both	US	Farming	50
Marcum et al. (2011)-2	Arthritis	Musculoskeletal	1.680	1.319	2.139	1394	By telephone and mail surveys	Both	US	Farming	50
Marcum et al. (2011)-3	Carpal tunnel	Musculoskeletal	1.600	0.972	2.635	1394	By telephone and mail surveys	Both	US	Farming	50
Marcum et al. (2011)-4	Back problems	Musculoskeletal	1.800	1.369	2.367	1394	By telephone and mail surveys	Both	US	Farming	50
Marcum et al. (2011)-5	Heart attack	Cardiovascular	1.190	0.888	1.596	1394	By telephone and mail surveys	Both	US	Farming	50

(continued)

(continued)

Study name	Health problem	Category of problem	Odds ratio	Lower limit	Upper limit	Sample size	Data collection method	Gender	Country	Occupation	Cutoff age
Marcum et al. (2011)-6	Stroke	Cardiovascular	1.270	0.857	1.883	1394	By telephone and mail surveys	Both	US	Farming	50
Marcum et al. (2011)-7	High blood pressure	Cardiovascular	1.060	0.851	1.321	1394	By telephone and mail surveys	Both	US	Farming	50
Marcum et al. (2011)-8	Chronic bronchitis or emphysema	Chronic bronchitis or emphysema	2.360	1.534	3.630	1394	By telephone and mail surveys	Both	US	Farming	50
Marcum et al. (2011)-9	Osteoporosis	Musculoskeletal	0.740	0.48	1.140	1394	By telephone and mail surveys	Both	US	Farming	50
Marcum et al. (2011)-10	Skin cancer	Cancer	1.510	0.979	2.328	1394	By telephone and mail surveys	Both	US	Farming	50
Marcum et al. (2011)-11	Other cancers	Cancer	1.240	0.759	2.027	1394	By telephone and mail surveys	Both	US	Farming	50
Marcum et al. (2011)-12	Incontinence	Urogenital	1.370	0.845	2.222	1394	By telephone and mail surveys	Both	US	Farming	50
Marcum et al. (2011)-13	Prostate problems	Urogenital	1.330	0.873	2.027	1394	By telephone and mail surveys	Male	US	Farming	50
Mick et al. (2018)	Hearing	Hearing	1.539	1.239	1.912	107352	Using data from the 1999 to 2012 Medical Expenditure Panel Surveys–Household Component (MEPS-HC)	Both	US	Cross-occupation	50
Pollack et al. (1998)	Substance abuse	Substance abuse	0.776	0.277	2.172	7895	Using the workers' compensation records from 1990 to 1991	Both	US	Construction	45
Price et al. (2012)	Disabilities	Not specified	3.009	2.075	4.365	183676	Using 2006 to 2010 National Health Interview Survey (NHIS) data	Both	US	Cross-occupation	55
Shi et al. (2015)-a	Disabilities	Not specified	1.987	1.582	2.495	604134	Using 1997 to 2011 NHIS data	Both	US	Cross-occupation	55
Shi et al. (2015)-b	Persistent disabilities	Not specified	2.121	1.811	2.485	51254	Using data from Medical Expenditure Panels Survey 2004 to 2011	Both	US	Cross-occupation	45
Voaklander et al. (2006)	Vision	Vision	1.030	0.738	1.437	1692	Using data from Canadian Institute of Health Information (CIHI)	Male	Canada	Farming	66
Voaklander et al. (2006)-1	Incontinence/urinary tract disorders	Urogenital	2.150	1.108	4.172	1692	Using data from CIHI	Male	Canada	Farming	66

(continued)

(continued)

Study name	Health problem	Category of problem	Odds ratio	Lower limit	Upper limit	Sample size	Data collection method	Gender	Country	Occupation	Cutoff age
Voaklander et al. (2006)-2	Osteoarthritis	Musculoskeletal	1.570	1.151	2.142	1692	Using data from CIHI	Male	Canada	Farming	66
Voaklander et al. (2006)-3	Neurotic disorder	Neurotic disorder	1.080	0.679	1.718	1692	Using data from CIHI	Male	Canada	Farming	66
Voaklander et al. (2006)-4	Osteoporosis	Musculoskeletal	4.290	1.442	12.77	1692	Using data from CIHI	Male	Canada	Farming	66
Voaklander et al. (2006)-5	Hypertension	Cardiovascular	0.750	0.548	1.026	1692	Using data from CIHI	Male	Canada	Farming	66
Voaklander et al. (2006)-6	Cardiovascular disease	Cardiovascular	0.970	0.691	1.362	1692	Using data from CIHI	Male	Canada	Farming	66
Voaklander et al. (2006)-7	Diabetes	Diabetes	1.110	0.685	1.798	1692	Using data from CIHI	Male	Canada	Farming	66
Voaklander et al. (2006)-8	Cancer	Cancer	0.680	0.433	1.068	1692	Using data from CIHI	Male	Canada	Farming	66
Xiang et al. (1999)	High blood pressure	Cardiovascular	0.374	0.117	1.193	113	By telephone survey from 1993 to 1995	Male	US	Farming	60
Xiang et al. (1999)-1	Heart disease	Cardiovascular	0.306	0.037	2.510	113	By telephone survey from 1993 to 1995	Male	US	Farming	60
Xiang et al. (1999)-2	Back pain	Musculoskeletal	2.128	0.704	6.434	113	By telephone survey from 1993 to 1995	Male	US	Farming	60
Xiang et al. (1999)-3	Arthritis	Musculoskeletal	0.970	0.398	2.366	113	By telephone survey from 1993 to 1995	Male	US	Farming	60
Xiang et al. (1999)-4	Hearing	Hearing	1.953	0.777	4.906	113	By telephone survey from 1993 to 1995	Male	US	Farming	60
Xiang et al. (1999)-5	Cancer	Cancer	2.348	0.626	8.805	113	By telephone survey from 1993 to 1995	Male	US	Farming	60
Zwerling et al. (1996)	Obesity	Obesity	1.290	1.009	1.649	6854	Using data from the Health and Retirement Study from 1992 to 1993	Both	US	Non-farming	51
Zwerling et al. (1996)-1	Vision	Vision	2.010	1.488	2.716	6854	Using data from the Health and Retirement Study from 1992 to 1993	Both	US	Non-farming	51
Zwerling et al. (1996)-2	Hearing	Hearing	2.080	1.593	2.715	6854	Using data from the Health and Retirement Study from 1992 to 1993	Both	US	Non-farming	51

(continued)

(continued)

Study name	Health problem	Category of problem	Odds ratio	Lower limit	Upper limit	Sample size	Data collection method	Gender	Country	Occupation	Cutoff age
Zwerling et al. (1996)-3	Alcohol dependence	Substance abuse	1.950	1.271	2.992	6854	Using data from the Health and Retirement Study from 1992 to 1993	Both	US	Non-farming	51
Zwerling et al. (1996)-4	Disabled from work	Not specified	1.540	1.019	2.328	6854	Using data from the Health and Retirement Study from 1992 to 1993	Both	US	Non-farming	51
Zwerling et al. (1998)	Obesity	Obesity	1.420	1.074	1.877	5600	Using data from the Health and Retirement Study from 1992 to 1994	Both	US	Non-farming	51
Zwerling et al. (1998)-1	Vision	Vision	1.810	1.229	2.667	5600	Using data from the Health and Retirement Study from 1992 to 1994	Both	US	Non-farming	51
Zwerling et al. (1998)-2	Hearing	Hearing	1.720	1.229	2.408	5600	Using data from the Health and Retirement Study from 1992 to 1994	Both	US	Non-farming	51
Zwerling et al. (1998)-3	Alcohol dependence	Substance Abuse	1.420	0.911	2.213	5600	Using data from the Health and Retirement Study from 1992 to 1994	Both	US	Non-farming	51
Zwerling et al. (1998)-4	Disabled from work	Not specified	1.740	1.253	2.416	5600	Using data from the Health and Retirement Study from 1992 to 1994	Both	US	Non-farming	51

References

Baidwan, N.K., Gerberich, S.G., Kim, H., Ryan, A.D., Church, T.R., Capistrant, B.: A longitudinal study of work-related injuries: comparisons of health and work-related consequences between injured and uninjured aging United States adults. Inj. Epidemiol. **5** (1), 35 (2018). https://doi.org/10.1186/s40621-018-0166-7

Bohle, P., Pitts, C., Quinlan, M.: Time to call it quits? The safety and health of older workers. Int. J. Health Serv. **40**(1), 23–41 (2010)

Browning, S.R., Truszczynska, H., Reed, D., McKnight, R.H.: Agricultural injuries among older Kentucky farmers: the farm family health and hazard surveillance study. Am. J. Ind. Med. **33** (4), 341–353 (1998)

Borenstein, M., Hedges, L.V., Higgins, J.P., Rothstein, H.R.: Introduction to Meta-Analysis. Wiley, Hoboken (2011)

Census and Statistics Department of Hong Kong. Hong Kong Labour Force Projections for 2017 to 2066 (2017). https://www.censtatd.gov.hk/hkstat/sub/sp200.jsp?productCode=FA100042. Accessed 27 Jan 2020

Chau, N., Bhattacherjee, A., Kunar, B.M., Lorhandicap Group: Relationship between job, lifestyle, age and occupational injuries. Occup. Med. **59**(2), 114–119 (2009)

Côté, J.N.: A critical review on physical factors and functional characteristics that may explain a sex/gender difference in work-related neck/shoulder disorders. Ergonomics **55**(2), 173–182 (2011). https://doi.org/10.1080/00140139.2011.586061

Duval, S., Tweedie, R.: Trim and fill: a simple funnel-plot-based method of testing and adjusting for publication bias in meta-analysis. Biometrics **56**(2), 455–463 (2000)

Fraade-Blanar, L.A., Sears, J.M., Chan, K.C., Thompson, H.J., Crane, P.K., Ebel, B.E.: Relating older workers' injuries to the mismatch between physical ability and job demands. J. Occup. Environ. Med. **59**(2), 212–221 (2017). https://doi.org/10.1097/JOM.0000000000000941

Gahan, P., Harbridge, R., Healy, J., Williams, R.: The ageing workforce: policy dilemmas and choices. Aust. J. Public Adm. **76**(4), 511–523 (2016). https://doi.org/10.1111/1467-8500.12232

Health and Safety Executive, UK: Self-reported Work-Related Illness and Workplace Injuries in 2006/07. Results from the Labour Force Survey (2008). https://www.hse.gov.uk/statistics/overall/hssh0607.pdf. Accessed 27 Jan 2020

Heaton, K., Azuero, A., Phillips, J.A., Pickens, H., Reed, D.: The effects of arthritis, mobility, and farm task on injury among older farmers. Nurs. Res. Rev. **2**, 9 (2012)

Heaton, K., Azuero, A., Reed, D.: Obstructive sleep apnea indicators and injury in older farmers. J. Agromed. **15**(2), 148–156 (2010)

Higgins, J.P., Thompson, S.G., Deeks, J.J., Altman, D.G.: Measuring inconsistency in meta-analyses. Bmj **327**(7414), 557–560 (2003)

Jadhav, R., Achutan, C., Haynatzki, G., Rajaram, S., Rautiainen, R.: Risk factors for agricultural injury: a systematic review and meta-analysis. J. Agromedicine **20**(4), 434–449 (2015)

Janssen, I., Bacon, E., Pickett, W.: Obesity and its relationship with occupational injury in the Canadian workforce. J. Obes. **2011**, 1–6 (2011)

Kunar, B.M., Bhattacherjee, A., Chau, N.: A matched case-control study of occupational injury in underground coalmine workers. J. South Afr. Inst. Min. Metall. **110**(1), 1–9 (2010)

Lam, L.T.: Uncorrected or untreated vision problems and occupational injuries among the adolescent and adult population in Australia. Inj. Prev. **14**(6), 396–400 (2008)

Loeppke, R.R., et al.: Advancing workplace health protection and promotion for an aging workforce. J. Occup. Environ. Med. **55**(5), 500–506 (2013)

Marcum, J.L., Browning, S.R., Reed, D.B., Charnigo, R.J.: Farmwork-related injury among farmers 50 years of age and older in Kentucky and South Carolina: a cohort study, 2002-2005. J. Agric. Saf. Health **17**(3), 259–273 (2011)

Mick, P., Foley, D., Lin, F., Pichora-Fuller, M.K.: Hearing difficulty is associated with injuries requiring medical care. Ear Hear. **39**(4), 631–644 (2018)

National Institute on Drug Abuse (2018). Media Guide. https://www.drugabuse.gov/publications/media-guide. Accessed 27 Jan 2020

Palmer, K.T., D'Angelo, S., Harris, E.C., Linaker, C., Coggon, D.: The role of mental health problems and common psychotropic drug treatments in accidental injury at work: a case–control study. Occup. Environ. Med. **71**(5), 308–312 (2014)

Palmer, K.T., Harris, E.C., Coggon, D.: Chronic health problems and risk of accidental injury in the workplace: a systematic literature review. Occup. Environ. Med. **65**(11), 757–764 (2008)

Peng, L., Chan, A.H.: A meta-analysis of the relationship between ageing and occupational safety and health. Saf. Sci. **112**, 162–172 (2019)

Pollack, E.S., Franklin, G.M., Fulton-Kehoe, D., Chowdhury, R.: Risk of job-related injury among construction laborers with a diagnosis of substance abuse. J. Occup. Environ. Med. **40**(6), 573–577 (1998)

Price, J., et al.: Nonoccupational and occupational injuries to US workers with disabilities. Am. J. Public Health **102**(9), e38–e46 (2012)

Prince, M.J., et al.: The burden of disease in older people and implications for health policy and practice. Lancet **385**(9967), 549–562 (2015)

Shi, J., et al.: Characteristics of nonfatal occupational injuries among US workers with and without disabilities. Am. J. Ind. Med. **58**(2), 168–177 (2015a)

Shi, J., Wheeler, K.K., Lu, B., Bishai, D.M., Stallones, L., Xiang, H.: Medical expenditures associated with nonfatal occupational injuries among US workers reporting persistent disabilities. Disabil. Health J. **8**(3), 397–406 (2015b)

Silverstein, M.: Meeting the challenges of an aging workforce. Am. J. Ind. Med. **51**(4), 269–280 (2008)

UK Clinical Research Collaboration: Health Research Classification System (2018). http://hrcsonline.net/wp-content/uploads/2018/01/HRCS_Main_Handbook_v2_Feb2018.pdf. Accessed 27 Jan 2020

Voaklander, D.C., et al.: Pain, medication, and injury in older farmers. Am. J. Ind. Med. **49**(5), 374–382 (2006)

Xiang, H., Stallones, L., Chiu, Y.: Nonfatal agricultural injuries among Colorado older male farmers. J. Aging Health **11**(1), 65–78 (1999)

Zwerling, C., Sprince, N.L., Davis, C.S., Whitten, P.S., Wallace, R.R., Heeringa, S.G.: Occupational injuries among older workers with disabilities: a prospective cohort study of the Health and Retirement Survey, 1992 to 1994. Am. J. Public Health **88**(11), 1691–1695 (1998)

Zwerling, C., Sprince, N.L., Wallace, R.B., Davis, C.S., Whitten, P.S., Heeringa, S.G.: Risk factors for occupational injuries among older workers: an analysis of the health and retirement study. Am. J. Public Health **86**(9), 1306–1309 (1996)

The Impact of User Diversity on the Acceptance of mHealth for Aftercare - Identifying the User Types 'Assistance Seekers' and 'Privacy Supporters'

Eva-Maria Schomakers$^{(\boxtimes)}$ ⓘ, Luisa Vervier ⓘ, and Martina Ziefle ⓘ

Human-Computer Interaction Center, RWTH Aachen University,
Campus-Boulevard 57, 52074 Aachen, Germany
{schomakers,vervier,ziefle}@comm.rwth-aachen.de
http://www.comm.rwth-aachen.de/

Abstract. All around the world, aging societies put pressure on healthcare systems. Information and Communication Technologies (ICT) can offer support for infirm, chronically ill, and older adults in prevention, therapy, and the aftercare of surgery. For that purpose, mHealth apps enhance the quality of patients' lives after surgery thereby offering relieve to the healthcare system. The multi-method approach applied in this study addresses the concerns and wishes that come with the introduction of new technologies. In a qualitative prestudy (n = 17), wishes and requirements that are associated with the use of mHealth apps in aftercare were identified. Key elements turned out to be privacy - especially who has access to the data like emergency calls -, desired type of support, and the kind of assistance in interacting with mHealth apps. In the subsequent quantitative main study (n = 180) these key elements were operationalized in a Choice Based Conjoint (CBC) experiment, additionally focusing on user factors. The results show that the most important aspect is data access, followed by the kind of offered assistance, and finally the features. Moreover, using a Latent Class Analysis, two user groups were detected: Privacy Supporters and Assistance Seekers. Both groups differed in the perceived importance of privacy compared to the kind of assistance offered when introducing the technology. Our results provide practical recommendations for the future roll-out of mHealth apps in aftercare with a special focus on user diversity.

Keywords: mHealth apps · Acceptance · Conjoint · User diversity

1 Introduction

The ongoing demographic change puts healthcare systems under pressure. The aging society causes increasing incident rates of chronic, degenerative, and age-related diseases. At the same time, a growing shortage of physicians leads to the

ⓒ Springer Nature Switzerland AG 2020
Q. Gao and J. Zhou (Eds.): HCII 2020, LNCS 12208, pp. 381–400, 2020.
https://doi.org/10.1007/978-3-030-50249-2_28

insufficient availability of medical care possibly making it next to impossible to provide everyone with adequate medical care in the future. Especially those suffering from chronic diseases requiring special treatment will be affected [10,12]. However, while the number of diseased people is increasing, a digital change is transforming the health care sector. One very promising improvement supporting the health care system by using technical information and communication technologies (ICT) are mobile health applications (short: mHealth apps) [1]. Because mHealth apps are easily accessible by Smartphone – of which almost everyone owns one these days – they can support and improve a patient's care with features like medical reminders, the monitoring of vital parameters, or emergency call functions. Hence, the patients' quality of life and care in the aftercare of surgery can be improved whilst relieving healthcare systems [20,39].

However, the introduction of new digital technologies also introduces concerns, especially regarding privacy since personal and medical information is collected, analyzed, and stored [41]. Additionally, particularly older adults may seek assistance in the interaction with digital technologies. Therefore, it is of great importance to understand the individual motives and barriers associated with a new technical application in medical aftercare treatment. Factors that enhance the willingness to use and increase the acceptance of mHealth apps in aftercare need to be studied. This allows the healthcare system and all stakeholders who are involved in the successful roll-out of mHealth apps in aftercare to consider apps especially tailored for target.

With our study we contribute to the empirical state of research and offer practical recommendations for mHealth apps in aftercare by trying to understand privacy acceptance and the factors that influence the willingness to use digital assistance for aftercare.

1.1   mHealth for Aftercare

mHealth apps increasingly attract the interest from the healthcare system and potential users. The great potential that this technical achievement carries is multifaceted. Since the majority of people nowadays owns or has access to a Smartphone or other mobile device, access to apps – like mHealth apps – is easily obtained. The great advantages of such a technology are its constant availability from any place at any time, its easily transportable size, its equipment with sensors that allow features like, e.g., the measuring of vital parameters, and its possibility to address all kinds of user groups [11]. This enables the private use of mHealth apps for fitness or wellness purposes, but also its medical use. Through the latter, the state of health can be monitored remotely allowing early detection of diseases, supporting the health status, and prolonging life expectancy [12]. mHealth apps could thus contribute to relieving the overburdened healthcare systems [20]. mHealth apps are therefore a welcome technical achievement that can contribute to revolutionizing the healthcare system [21,27] by enabling users to carry out part of their healthcare without the help of medical professionals. Enabling patients to take care of themselves more easily, reduces costs and allows the more targeted use of resources [11,16]. Especially people living in rural regions with a shortage of doctors and poor mobility benefit from the resulting remote care.

However, the use of mHealth apps can only contribute to the health care system if they are of high quality and if both physicians and patients show a high level of willingness to use, and acceptance of, the technology. Since ill people and those in need of rehabilitation show a great desire to recover at home, it is of great importance to improve the scientific state of research on this topic and formulate practice-relevant recommendations for the possible roll-out hereof. All user groups should thereby be taken into account. Even though studies on the acceptance of mHealth apps, like remote monitoring in various fields of practice – e.g., breast and orthopedic surgery [6,32] – already exist, a lot is still left uncovered. Especially the diseases that cost the most lives on a global scale – e.g., types of cardio-vascular disease – need to be studied to improve their treatment and decrease their death rate. It is therefore necessary to understand the motives and barriers which trigger people's willingness to use and finally accept such a technical application.

1.2   Influences on the User Acceptance of mHealth for Aftercare

For the successful roll-out and sustainable use of a technology, its acceptance by potential users is required. From a temporal point of view, the adoption process of a technology starts with the knowledge and awareness by the potential users [28]. After a persuasion phase, a decision to adopt or reject is made. The here described *Diffusion of Innovation Theory* by [28] shows that different factors influence this process. Especially in the persuasion phase, the perceived characteristics of the innovation are important.

Several technology acceptance models summarize the important factors that influence the behavioral intention to use a technology from a user-centered perspective (e.g., the *Technology Acceptance Model* (TAM, [9]), the *Unified Theory of Acceptance and Use of Technology* (UTAUT [34]) and their extensions). With these models, the decision to adopt or reject a technology can hence be explained based on, e.g., the perceived characteristics of the technology (e.g., usefulness, ease of use), the situation (e.g., voluntariness of use, facilitating conditions), and user diversity (e.g., experience, age).

However, research has shown that these models do not properly fit in all contexts of technology use, especially regarding the medical context [15]. For one thing, factors that are important in this specific context are missing from the models. For example, privacy concerns are not considered despite the fact that they are an important barrier for the adoption of digital technologies, both in general [4] and in the medical and mHealth context [13,19,26]. For digital health technologies, it was shown that the most important privacy aspect for potential users was who has access to the data [24,31]. As an important barrier, privacy requirements should thus be considered for mHealth apps for aftercare. Moreover, acceptance and privacy depend on the context and type of the technology [14,23]. The features an mHealth app provides might therefore influence its acceptance and how this is affected by other factors.

Additionally, user diversity needs to be considered [36]. Factors like age, gender, and technical affinity can influence the perception and acceptance of technologies [35,40]. Particularly, older adults – a main target group for mHealth apps for aftercare – represent a special user group regarding the acceptance and use of digital technologies. The perception of technologies is not only influenced by people's upbringing and experience with technologies during their life [29], age also changes perceptual, cognitive and psychomotor skills. These – potentially in combination with illnesses and chronic conditions – can result in difficulties in interacting with technical devices [7]. Ease of use is a decisive barrier for the adoption of digital health technologies, not only for older adults [26,30]. Therefore, technical support and assistance in getting to know and learning to interact with digital technologies are important requirements for mHealth apps.

At the same time, several user groups with different evaluations of acceptance and varying decision patterns may exist [5,25]. For example, [25] found two distinct user groups that differed in their trade-off patterns between the benefits and barriers of Ambient Assisted Living technologies. Whereas privacy was the most important factor for both groups, their preferences regarding the exact wishes for privacy and other factors largely differed, showing very distinct decision patterns. [5] also found different user types in the acceptance of fitness trackers. For the largest user group, their decision for a fitness tracker was mostly based on the privacy design; for another group on the perceived utility; whilst for a third user group the motivational design was most important. These previous studies show that users are diverse regarding their preferences and decision patterns. Similar diversity may exist for the requirements for mHealth apps for aftercare.

1.3 Empirical Approach and Logic of Procedure

This paper addresses the question on which different aspects are relevant to understand the acceptance of mHealth apps in aftercare from the users' perspective. To receive more robust results on this topic, a multi-method approach was chosen. In Fig. 1 an overview of our two-step study is depicted.

In the first step, qualitative data was collected through focus groups. Two focus groups of two different age groups were run. Very general questions were used to guide the group discussions to collect the intended diverse opinions and point of view of the participants:

- *Which features would you like to have when using an mHealth app in aftercare?*
- *Which benefits come to your mind when thinking about using an mHealth app?*
- *What kind of barriers can you think of?*

With the identified requirements, perceived benefits, and barriers, a quantitative study was developed to evaluate and quantify these factors. The use of a Choice Based Conjoint (CBC) experiment allowed the evaluation of preferences

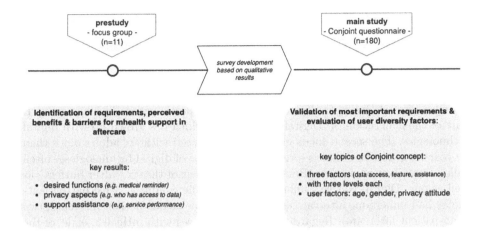

Fig. 1. Overview of the research process showing the qualitative and quantitative measures used to address our research questions.

for different concept alternatives. In that way, the preferences among different levels of three attributes – features of an mHealth app, types of data access, and assistance options for introducing the app – were determined. The choice of these three attributes was based on the results of the prestudy.

The research questions derived from our chosen Conjoint study were:

– *Which factor contributes the most to the decision to use an mHealth app in aftercare?*
– *Are there differences in the response behavior between (groups of) participants?*

The following section is structured according to our study process. First, the procedure and results of the prestudy are presented. Second, the development of the main study will be introduced by explaining the CBC approach in general and in particular related to our study.

2   The Prestudy

Two focus groups were conducted to identify the requirements, perceived benefits, and perceived barriers of potential users for mHealth for aftercare. The advantage of focus groups compared to interviews is the possibility to observe a discussion between participants regarding new topics for which they have been invited as potential users, not as experts. The focus groups were conducted as a part of a master's thesis at the RWTH University in winter of 2018/2019. The participants attended voluntarily and were not compensated. In the following, sample, procedure, and results are shortly outlined.

2.1   The Sample

The participants were acquired from a local medical rehabilitation center and from the social circles of the authors with the aim to include participants of varying gender, with varying technical experience and skills, as well as varying experiences with aftercare and mHealth apps. In the first focus group, five younger adults between the age of 20 to 29 years participated. This age group is part of the generation of 'Digital Natives' [22] which has grown up with digital technologies. The second focus group was conducted with six adults older than 50 years, a generation that is – regarding their use of digital technologies – often called the 'Silver Surfers' or 'Best Agers' [3,8]. Four of the six 'Silver Surfers', as well as one 'Digital Native' suffered from a chronic condition. Five participants (45%) had undergone aftercare of some sort (three as out-patient aftercare, two as in-patient aftercare). Regarding their experiences with mHealth, eight of the eleven (73%) participants had used mHealth apps before, mostly fitness apps. Non of the participants had used an mHealth app for aftercare before.

2.2   The Procedure

First, the participants were informed about data protection and the voluntary nature of the focus groups. After an introduction to mHealth apps in general and for aftercare, the participants discussed their own experiences with, as well as requirements for, such an mHealth app and the pro and contra arguments for the use of it. During the entire focus group, a scenario provided the setting for the discussion. The scenario asked the participants to put themselves in the situation of a patient coming home after a cardio-vascular operation with the option to use an mHealth app free of charge. Cardiovascular illnesses were chosen as they represent the number one cause for death globally [38].

In a practical part, all participants defined their own mHealth app with the features and options they desire. Additionally, each participant evaluated the importance of each characteristic using red (very important), yellow (rather important), and green (rather irrelevant) dots (see Fig. 2). After individually working on their personal preferences for mHealth apps, the participants shared their ideas and requirements with the group and discussed the relevance of the characteristics. The focus groups ended with a short wrap up.

After the focus groups, the participants filled out a short paper-and-pencil questionnaire with questions about demographics, their experiences with mHealth apps and aftercare, as well as their technical affinity. The focus groups were audio-taped and a verbatim transcript was written. A conventional content analysis was conducted to identify important requirements for mHealth apps for aftercare.

2.3   The Main Results

The analysis focused on the requirements for mHealth apps for aftercare. As important aspects, the desired features, privacy requirements, and (technical)

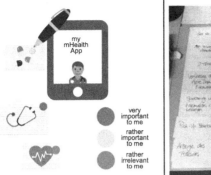 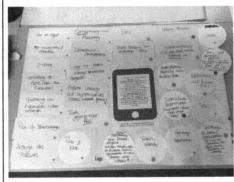

Fig. 2. Sketch of the task to define a personal mHealth app for aftercare (left) and the results of one of the participants (right).

assistance were identified besides other requirements. Perceived benefits and barriers were also analyzed. On overview of the main topics is presented in Fig. 3.

Perceived Benefits and Barriers: The motivation to use an mHealth app for aftercare stemmed from improved rehabilitation and fast help in emergency situations, a higher quality of life, time efficiency, cost savings in the healthcare system, feelings of medical security, the support of research, and monetary bonuses. The particular motivation to provide personal data to other stakeholders is based on the benefit for research, monetary profit, and improved help and recovery. Barriers against the use revolved around stigmatization, feelings of surveillance and privacy concerns, missing trust, and missing technical self-efficacy.

Desired Features: Users wish for the following features in an mHealth app: remote monitoring (e.g., of blood sugar, blood pressure, sleep, weight), medical reminders (e.g., for physical activity, drinking water, medication), information (e.g., about symptoms, allergies, personal medical data), recommendations and advice (e.g., about diet), as well as alarm services to call trusted persons, physicians, or the ambulance.

Privacy Aspects: Privacy requirements were very important to the participants. These included the control over data flow, particularly the consent to it (via legal contracts e.g., a declaration of consent, zipper clause, or a kind of a living will), as well as data security (e.g., encryption, verification of those who have data access) and the varying sensitivity of data types (participants distinguished sensitive from non-sensitive data in how much it needs protection). It was most important for the participants regarding their privacy to have control over who has access to the data (personal physician, care institutions, heath insurance, science, or trusted person).

Assistance: Additionally, the type of assistance for learning to interact with the mHealth apps was discussed as important requirement. The participants discussed who should be responsible (e.g., rehabilitation center/hospital, developer,

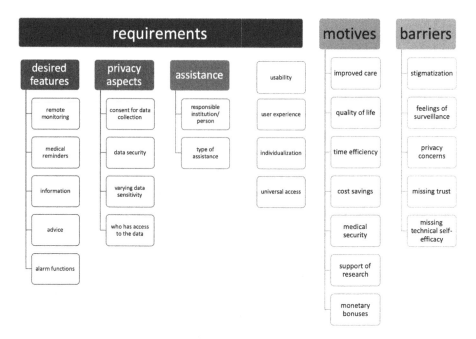

Fig. 3. The main requirements, benefits, and barriers identified in the prestudy.

physician, health insurance) and what type of assistance should be offered (e.g., personal consultation, online tutorial, courses, in-app support).

Additional requirements regarded the usability and user experience of the app, individualization options, and universal access to the app.

3   Method of the Conjoint Study

The results of the prestudy were used to develop a Conjoint study. The goal of the Conjoint study was to gain an understanding of which requirements are most important for potential users of an mHealth app and to analyze the user diversity of these requirements.

3.1   The Choice Based Conjoint Study

In contrast to traditional questionnaires, Choice Based Conjoint studies allow experimental variation of multi-factorial scenarios. The method was originally developed in market research, but has recently been successfully applied in social science for the modeling of technology acceptance [2]. Participants are asked to choose between concrete scenarios in which the characteristics of selected factors are varied. Each participant is presented with several decision scenarios that are randomly generated from the possible combinations. In this way, the influencing factors are not evaluated individually, as they are in a questionnaire, but in combination with, and in a trade-off between, each other. These decisions between the multi-factorial scenarios correspond to the actual decisions that users make about real technologies. Thus, the results are very meaningful and realistic.

Additional, the method provides the option to cluster participants based on their preferences. With this option, the 'Latent Class Analysis', users with similar preferences are identified and grouped in several user groups. Contrary to testing the influence of user diversity factors (e.g., age, gender) or differences between predefined user groups, the data-driven cluster analysis approach of the Latent Class Analysis allows the identification of user groups that differ based on their decision patterns in the Conjoint study. It thus reveals user diversity that may not be influenced by typical factors like age or gender. By combining a traditional questionnaire with a Conjoint study, additional information on, and attitudes of, the participants and the user groups are assessed and can be used to describe the identified user groups.

For CBC studies, a prestudy needs to identify the most important factors since only three to five factors can be included in a CBC. For the operationalization of each *factor*, three to five *factor levels* are set. As requirements for mHealth apps for aftercare, three important factor were identified on the basis of the related work and the prestudy: features of the mHealth app, privacy requirements, and technical assistance. In particular, it was important to the participants who has access to the data of the mHealth app (privacy) and what type of assistance for interacting with the technology is offered (assistance). Therefore, these three factors were included into the CBC study and for each factor three levels were determined. These are depicted in Table 1. The operationalization of the levels reflected realistic characteristics of an mHealth app for aftercare and were based on the answers of the participants in the prestudy. For each level, an icon was designed to help the participants to quickly recognize the levels within the Conjoint tasks.

In each choice task, the participants choose their favorite option out of three different scenarios. Each scenario consisted of a randomly chosen level of each factor. Figure 4 depicts an example of a choice task. Every participant completed ten choice tasks. The efficiency of the design of the CBC study was tested and confirmed as being adequate.

3.2   The Questionnaire

The Conjoint study was embedded into a questionnaire which assessed additional user data. The questionnaire started with an introduction to the topic, the voluntariness of answering the questions, and the consent to data provision. The first questions regarded demographics (age, gender, education), followed by health status and experience with aftercare. Participants were also asked about their use of popular digital technologies (e.g., smartphones) and of mHealth apps. Additionally, perceived privacy risks regarding the use of mHealth apps were assessed (using items by [18]) and the participants' digital health literacy was evaluated (using the

Table 1. Factors and factor levels of the Conjoint experiment.

factor	data access	feature	assistance
levels	medical personnel	remote monitoring of vital parameters	personal consultation
	trusted person	medical reminders	preventative course
	health insurance	emergency call	online video

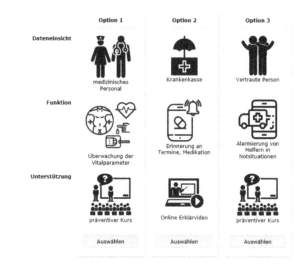

Fig. 4. Example of one Conjoint task consisting of three scenarios varying in the three factors: participants choose the preferred option.

scale by [33]). The digital health literacy scale contains the subdimensions operational skills, navigation skills, information searching, evaluating reliability, determining relevance, adding content, and protecting privacy.

After the Conjoint study, the participants evaluated their intention to use an mHealth app for aftercare (using three items adapted from [34]) and their general attitude towards such an app (using a semantic differential with ten adjective pairs). All items were measured on six point Likert scales. The reliability of the scales was confirmed using Cronbach's Alpha ($\alpha > .7$).

3.3 The Sample

N = 180 participants completed the questionnaire. The participants were recruited within the social network of the authors and through online discussion forums. The age of the participants varied between 15 and 75 ($M = 33.96, SD = 13.4$). 60.6% were women. The level of education of the participants was mixed. Table 2 in Sect. 4 provides an overview of the demographic characteristics of the sample.

Most participants perceive their health status to be rather good (32.8%) or good (41.7%). 13.9% evaluate it as rather bad to very bad. 24.4% have experienced professional aftercare. Regarding their experiences with technologies, 98.9% of participants use a smartphone. 70.6% of the sample use or have used digital health apps. On average, the participants do not agree, nor reject, to perceive privacy risks for mHealth for aftercare ($M = 3.36, SD = 1.19$ on a scale from 1 (very low) to 6 (very high)). Their mean digital health literacy is high ($M = 4.52, SD = .63$).

4 Results

The results of the Conjoint analysis show, on the one hand, how important each factor is for the choice of the optimal mHealth app (relative importance scores), and one the other hand, the relative preference for the levels of each factor (part worth utilities). These values are relative and can only be evaluated in comparison to the other included factors, or factor levels of one factor, respectively. A negative part worth utility does thus not indicate rejection, but that this level is less preferred than the levels with higher part worth utilities.

The software Sawtooth Software was used for the development, acquisition, and analysis of the Conjoint study and the questionnaire. Additionally, analysis of variances and Chi Square Tests were used for the further analysis of the user groups identified in the Latent Class Analysis.

4.1 Average Decision Pattern

Who has access to the data is the most important factor for the decision to use an mHealth app for aftercare with an importance score of 56.6% ($SD = 16.9$) (see Fig. 5). With a large difference, the type of assistance is the second most important factor ($27.5\%, SD = 15.3$). Which features the app provides is the least important of the three included factors ($15.9\%, SD = 8.6$).

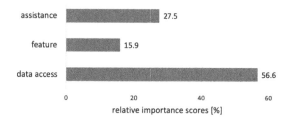

Fig. 5. Relative importance scores of the three factors (n = 180).

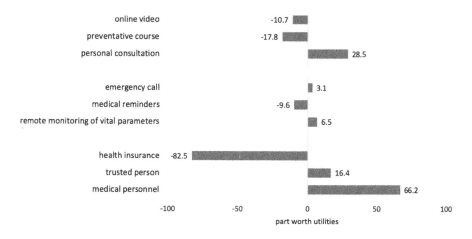

Fig. 6. Part worth utilities of the factor levels (n = 180).

In the part worth utilities (cf. Fig. 6), the importance evaluation is reflected again: For the most important factor, the data access, the participants distinguish largely between the three factor levels. The health insurance is the least preferred party for data access ($-82.5\%, SD = 42.2$). Most preferred is medical personnel ($66.2\%, SD = 39.7$) and trusted persons score in between the other two ($16.4\%, SD = 47.4$).

As kind of assistance for getting to know and interacting with an mHealth app for aftercare, a personal consultation is most preferred ($28.5\%, SD = 32.2$). Least accepted is a preventative course ($-17.8\%, SD = 30.6$), closely followed by the online video option ($-10.7\%, SD = 42$).

Remote monitoring of vital parameters is the most preferred feature ($6.5\%, SD = 21.9$) and the emergency call function is almost as desired ($3.1\%, SD = 21.1$). The medical reminder function is less preferred ($-9.6\%, SD = 23.5$).

4.2   General Evaluation of mHealth Apps for Aftercare

In Fig. 7, the mean evaluation of ten adjective pairs is depicted, showing a generally positive attitude towards mHealth apps for aftercare. They are especially perceived as being useful and practical. Nevertheless, the participants still expect them to isolate them from people and to not be fun or trustworthy. The overall positive attitude corresponds to a rather high use intention with $M = 4.4, SD = 1.04$.

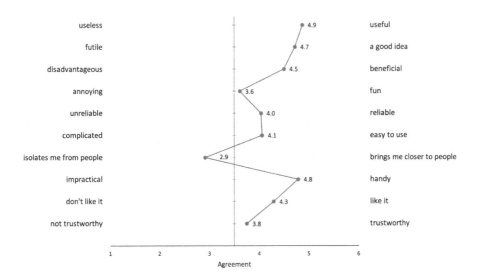

Fig. 7. General evaluation of mHealth apps for aftercare on a semantic differential (n = 180).

4.3   Privacy Supporters and Assistance Seekers

In the Conjoint results, large standard deviations indicate a high variation within the sample. To explain this variance by identifying user segments with differing decision patterns, a Latent Class Analysis was conducted. A two-group segmentation showed the best fit with the data (using the following indices: percent certainty, Akaike information criterion (CAIC), and chi square). The two user groups consisted of 36.4% (n = 61) and 63.6% (n = 119) of the sample showing adequate group sizes for further analysis. In the following, these two user groups are described regarding their decision patterns in the CBC experiments and then further analyzed regarding attitudes and user diversity factors.

Differing Decision Patterns. The juxtaposed relative importance scores for the three factors in Fig. 8 show the main distinction between the two user groups that lend them their names: The *Privacy Supporters* place even more importance on who has access to the data collected by an mHealth app for aftercare (73.3) than the mean sample and the second user group (47.0). In contrast, the type of assistance is less important to the *Privacy Supporters* (13.1). Only little difference can be identified regarding the importance of the provided feature (*Privacy Supporters: 13.6%, Assistance Seekers: 9.0%*). In contrast, for the *Assistance Seekers* the type of assistance and who has access to the data are almost equally important (assistance: 43.9%, data access : 47%).

Differences are also visible in the evaluation of the factor levels (see Fig. 9). Regarding the type of assistance, *Assistance Seekers* strongly prefer a personal consultation (78.1). In comparison, he online video is strongly rejected (−53.7), whereas this is the second best option for the *Privacy Supporters* (8.3).

Different decision patterns regarding who should have access to the data are also prevalent. Whereas the *Privacy Supporters* strongly prefer the medical personnel (105.7) and regard trusted persons as a relatively mediocre option (8.6), the *Assistance Seekers* prefer trusted persons (63.3) and the medical personnel not so much (14.5).

The distinction between the type of feature also varies between the two user groups. The *Privacy Supporters* prefer remote monitoring the most (18.3) and medical reminders the least (−22.4). In contrast, the *Assistance Seekers* prefer emergency call functions the most (12.4) and remote monitoring the least (−14.6).

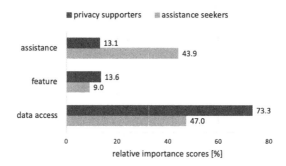

Fig. 8. Relative importance scores of the three factors juxtaposed by the two user types (n = 180).

Characteristics of the Two User Groups. Table 2 shows the differences in age, gender, and education level between the two user groups. Analysis of variance show that the *Assistance Seekers* are significantly older ($M = 37.2, SD = 14.6$) than the *Privacy Supporters* ($M = 32.3, SD = 12.5$) with $F(1, 178) = 5.42, p < .05$. 67.2% of the *Assistance Seekers* are women as are 57.1% of the *Privacy Supporters*. There is no significant gender difference. The education level between the groups does also not differ significantly.

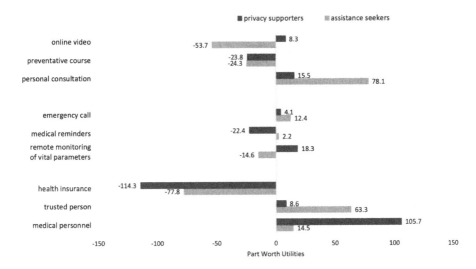

Fig. 9. Part worth utilities (rescaled for comparability) of the factor levels juxtaposed by the two user types (n = 180).

Table 2. Demographic characteristics of the sample and the two user types (N = 180).

		The sample (100%)	Assistance seekers (36.4%)	Privacy supporters (63.6%)
Age	mean (SD)	33.96 (13.4)	37.16 (14.6)	32.32 (12.5)
[years]	15−29	58.3%	47.5%	63.9%
	30−49	23.3%	27.9%	21.0%
	>50	18.3%	24.6%	15.1%
Gender	Women	60.6%	67.2%	57.1%
	Men	39.4%	32.8%	42.9%
College	No	80%	76%	81.5%
education	Yes	20%	23%	18.5%

Furthermore, the groups can be described by their varying attitudes and skills. The *Privacy Supporters* show a significantly lower score of perceived privacy risk for mHealth apps ($M = 3.23, SD = 1.2$) than the *Assistance Seekers* ($M = 3.61, SD = 1.13$) with $F(1, 178) = 5.8, p < .05$. Also, the *Privacy Supporters* score significantly higher in operational skills, a subdimension of digital health literacy ($M_{PrivacySupporters} = 5.6, SD = 0.66, M_{AssistanceSeekers} = 5.32, SD = 0.85$), ($F(1, 178) = 5.82, p < .05$). Operational skills describe basic abilities to use a keyboard, mouse, and website features [33]. The two groups do not differ regarding their intention to use an mHealth app for aftercare, both in the given scenario and in the general evaluation through the semantic differential.

5   Discussion

Particularly in a future with shortages in healthcare resources, digital health technologies show a high potential to improve the quality of healthcare. Especially the use of mHealth apps on Smartphones and other mobile devices – which are nowadays available to almost everybody – is a very promising option to reach patients, e.g., to improve support in aftercare. For a successful roll-out of such technologies, the patients' acceptance is a decisive prerequisite. Therefore, this study investigated the acceptance of mHealth apps for aftercare. The special focus lay on understanding which requirements are most important for mHealth acceptance and how these are influenced by user diversity.

In a qualitative prestudy, the following three factors were introduced as decisive requirements: a) the features and hence type of support offered by the mHealth app for aftercare, b) privacy requirements, for which who has access to the data was most important, and c) the kind of received assistance in getting to know, and learning to interact with, the mHealth app.

In a next step, these three factors were examined using a Choice Based Conjoint approach to not only study the individual influence of each factor on user acceptance, but also the trade-offs between the factors by using a multifactorial design. The Conjoint study confirmed previous empirical work in that the privacy requirement regarding who has access to data is the most important factor for the decision to use digital health technologies [25, 31]. This result once again highlights the importance of privacy and the need to better understand and deal with privacy requirements in the context of mobile and digital health technologies.

The participants in this study did not differentiate much between the three offered features – medical reminders, remote monitoring, or emergency functions. The relatively low importance scores might thus indicate that the type of offered feature is not really important for the acceptance of mHealth apps for aftercare. Another explanation for this result could be that the type of feature is not irrelevant, but that the three used options are equally accepted, so that the choice between them does not influence the decision for an mHealth app. In order to understand which features are preferred and accepted, future work should examine the importance of features more closely by comparing other features that may show a larger distinction.

With a large gap between its importance and the importance of who has access to the data, the type of assistance in getting to know the mHealth app was the second most important factor. However, the high variance within the data indicated that the mean results hide a strong diversity of decisions patterns. For that reason, a Latent Class Analysis was conducted from which two user groups with differing decisions patterns could be identified.

For the first user group, the *Privacy Supporters*, who has access to the data was the only important factor for the choice of an mHealth app for aftercare. Surprisingly, at the same time the *Privacy Supporters* perceived less privacy risks for mHealth than the second user group – which should logically be associated with a lower importance of privacy within the Conjoint. This combination of results thus indicates that the other two factors are even less important to the *Privacy Supporters*. More research is needed to find which factors are important to this user group.

For the second user group, the *Assistance Seekers*, privacy is also very important, but the type of assistance is almost as important. This user group is significantly older and shows lower scores in a subdimension of digital health literacy. They least accept getting to know an mHealth app for aftercare through an online video only and instead prefer a personal consultation. This shows how important user diversity is: the *Assistance Seekers* need more assistance for the mHealth app and prefer personal consultations. Future research is needed to study the importance of assistance – a factor that has not yet drawn much research attention. For a successful roll-out of mHealth technologies, assistance and particularly the option for personal consultations should be provided especially for older target groups and patients who feel insecure in interaction with mobile technologies. Therefore, mHealth apps can support patients but should not substitute face-to-face care.

All in all, a generally positive attitude and high intention to use mHealth for aftercare was observed. This shows that mHealth apps for aftercare can be successful when the diverse patients' requirements – e.g., for data access and assistance – are met. In light of the high user diversity, these may best be met by offering patients different options within a running system, e.g., a choice for who has access to data and how to get assistance for interacting with the technology.

That said, this study is not without shortcomings. The multi-method approach combined the advantage of qualitative research to identify important user requirements with the ability of Conjoint studies to quantify and experimentally modulate the importance and trade-offs between the important factors. But, in Conjoint studies only few factors can be included meaning that the results are only valid for this combination of factors and factor levels. Therefore, all results are restricted to the three included factors and cannot directly be compared to other studies.

Additional caution has to be taken considering the samples. The Conjoint sample included people of all age groups but was quite young on average. Many mHealth apps, especially for aftercare, are used by people of all age groups but show a particularly high potential for older adults. The results showed that older users have different requirements than younger adults. Future research should target older adults to analyze their requirements in more detail since this age group might still be quite diverse.

A last comment addresses the cultural setting of the study. Technology acceptance and privacy attitudes are known to differ between different cultures and in different countries [17,37]. The present results are thus only valid in the German setting of the study. People of other cultures and countries may show different requirements for mHealth for aftercare.

Acknowledgments. The authors thank all participants for sharing their personal opinions. Thanks also to Carolina Tesarczyk for research support. This research has been funded by the German Ministry of Education and Research (BMBF) under project MyneData (KIS1DSD045).

References

1. Aitken, M., Clancy, B., Nass, D.: The growing value of digital health: evidence and impact on human health and the healthcare system. IQVIA Institute for Human Data Science, p. p1 (2017)
2. Arning, K.: Conjoint Measurement. Wiley, Hoboken (2017)
3. Auer-Srnka, K.J., Meier-Pesti, K., Grießmair, M.: Ältere menschen als zielgruppe der werbung: Eine explorative studie zu wahrnehmung und selbstbild der best ager sowie stereotypen vorstellungen vom alt-sein in jüngeren altersgruppen. der markt **47**(3), 100–117 (2008)
4. Bélanger, F., Crossler, R.: Privacy in the digital age: a review of information privacy research in information systems. MIS Q. **35**(4), 1–36 (2011)
5. Burbach, L., Lidynia, C., Brauner, P., Ziefle, M.: Data protectors, benefit maximizers, or facts enthusiasts: identifying user profiles for life-logging technologies. Comput. Hum. Behav. **99**, 9–21 (2019)
6. Cajita, M.I., Hodgson, N.A., Budhathoki, C., Han, H.R.: Intention to use mhealth in older adults with heart failure. J. Cardiovasc. Nurs. **32**(6), E1 (2017)
7. Chen, K., Chan, A.H.S.: Review a review of technology acceptance by older adults. Gerontechnology **10**(1), 1–12 (2011)
8. Choudrie, J., Vyas, A.: Silver surfers adopting and using facebook? A quantitative study of hertfordshire, UK applied to organizational and social change. Technol. Forecast. Soc. Change **89**, 293–305 (2014)
9. Davis, F.D.: Perceived usefulness, perceived ease of use, and user acceptance of information technology. MIS Q. **13**(3), 319–340 (1989)
10. De Bock, F., Shajanian Zarneh, Y., Matusall, S.: The preventive health care act and the future forum public health in Germany: freia de bock. Eur. J. Public Health **29**(Suppl. 4), ckz185–708 (2019)
11. Deng, Z., Hong, Z., Ren, C., Zhang, W., Xiang, F.: What predicts patients- adoption intention toward mhealth services in China: empirical study. JMIR mHealth uHealth **6**(8), e172 (2018)
12. European Commission: Green paper on mobile health ("mhealth") (2014). https://ec.europa.eu/digital-single-market/en/news/green-paper-mobile-health-mhealth
13. Gao, Y., Li, H., Luo, Y.: An empirical study of wearable technology acceptance in healthcare. Ind. Manag. Data Syst. **115**(9), 1704–1723 (2015)
14. Himmel, S., Ziefle, M.: Smart home medical technologies: users' requirements for conditional acceptance. I-Com. J. Interact. Media **15**(1), 39–50 (2016)
15. Holden, R.J., Karsh, B.T.: The technology acceptance model: its past and its future in health care. J. Biomed. Inform. **43**(1), 159–172 (2010)
16. Kaium, M.A., Bao, Y., Alam, M.Z., Hasan, N., Hoque, M.R.: Understanding the insight of factors affecting mhealth adoption. Int. J. Res. Bus. Soc. Sci. (2147–4478) **8**(6), 181–200 (2019)
17. Krasnova, H., Veltri, N.F.: Privacy calculus on social networking sites: explorative evidence from Germany and USA. In: Proceedings of the Annual Hawaii International Conference on System Sciences, pp. 1–10 (2010)

18. Li, H., Wu, J., Gao, Y., Shi, Y.: Examining individuals' adoption of healthcare wearable devices: an empirical study from privacy calculus perspective. Int. J. Med. Inform. **88**(555), 8–17 (2016)
19. Lidynia, C., Brauner, P., Ziefle, M.: A step in the right direction - understanding privacy concerns and perceived sensitivity of fitness trackers. Adv. Intell. Syst. Comput. **608**, 42–53 (2018)
20. Lin, T.T., Bautista, J.R.: Understanding the relationships between mhealth apps' characteristics, trialability, and mhealth literacy. J. Health Commun. **22**(4), 346–354 (2017)
21. Mascolo, C., Musolesi, M., Rentfrow, P.J.: Mobile sensing for mass-scale behavioural intervention. In: NSF Workshop on Pervasive Computing at Scale (PeCS), pp. 27–28 (2011)
22. Millward, P.: The 'grey digital divide': perception, exclusion and barriers of access to the Internet for older people. First Monday **8**(7), (2003)
23. Nissenbaum, H.: Privacy in Context: Technology Policy and the Integrity of Social Life, p. 304. Standford University Press, Standford, California (2010)
24. Offermann-van Heek, J., Schomakers, E.M., Ziefle, M.: Bare necessities? How the need for care modulates the acceptance of Ambient Assisted Living technologies. Int. J. Med. Inform. **127**, 147–156 (2019)
25. Offermann-van Heek, J., Ziefle, M.: Nothing else matters! Trade-offs between perceived benefits and barriers of AAL technology usage. Front. Public Health **7**, 134 (2019)
26. Peek, S.T.M., Wouters, E.J.M., van Hoof, J., Luijkx, K.G., Boeije, H.R., Vrijhoef, H.J.M.: Factors influencing acceptance of technology for aging in place: a systematic review. Int. J. Med. Inform. **83**(4), 235–248 (2014)
27. Rachuri, K.K., Musolesi, M., Mascolo, C., Rentfrow, P.J., Longworth, C., Aucinas, A.: EmotionSense: a mobile phones based adaptive platform for experimental social psychology research. In: Proceedings of the 12th ACM International Conference on Ubiquitous Computing, pp. 281–290. ACM (2010)
28. Rogers, E.M.: Diffusion of Innovations, p. 576. Simon and Schuster, New York (2003)
29. Sackmann, R., Winkler, O.: Technology generations revisited: the internet generation. Gerontechnology **11**(4), 493–503 (2013)
30. Schomakers, E.-M., Offermann-van Heek, J., Ziefle, M.: Attitudes towards aging and the acceptance of ICT for aging in place. In: Zhou, J., Salvendy, G. (eds.) ITAP 2018. LNCS, vol. 10926, pp. 149–169. Springer, Cham (2018). https://doi.org/10.1007/978-3-319-92034-4_12
31. Schomakers, E.m., Ziefle, M.: Privacy perceptions in ambient assisted living. In: Proceedings of the 5th International Conference on Information and Communication Technologies for Ageing Well and e-Health (ICT4AWE 2019) (2019)
32. Semple, J.L., Sharpe, S., Murnaghan, M.L., John, T., Metcalfe, K.A.: Using a mobile app for monitoring post-operative quality of recovery of patients at home: a feasibility study. JMIR mHealth uHealth **3**(1), e18 (2015)
33. van der Vaart, R., Drossaert, C.: Development of the digital health literacy instrument: measuring a broad spectrum of health 1.0 and health 2.0 skills. J. Med. Internet Res. **19**(1), e27 (2017)
34. Venkatesh, V., Morris, M.G., Davis, G.B., Davis, F.D.: User acceptance of information technology: toward a unified view. MIS Q. **27**(3), 425–478 (2003)
35. Wilkowska, W.: Acceptance of eHealth technology in home environments. Advanced Studies on User Diversity in Ambient Assisted Living. Dissertation, RWTH University (2015)

36. Wilkowska, W., Ziefle, M.: User diversity as a challenge for the integration of medical technology into future smart home environments. In: Ziefle, M., Röcker, C. (eds.) Human-Centered Design of E-Health Technologies: Concepts, Methods and Applications, pp. 95–126. Medical Information Science Reference, Hershey (2011)

37. Wilkowska, W., Ziefle, M., Alagöz, F.: How user diversity and country of origin impact the readiness to adopt E-health technologies: an intercultural comparison. In: Work, vol. 41, pp. 2072–2080 (2012)

38. World Health Organization: World Health statistics 2019. Technical report, World Health Organization (2019)

39. Yardley, L., Choudhury, T., Patrick, K., Michie, S.: Current issues and future directions for research into digital behavior change interventions. Am. J. Prev. Med. **51**(5), 814–815 (2016)

40. Zaunbrecher, B.S., Kowalewski, S., Ziefle, M.: The willingness to adopt technologies: a cross-sectional study on the influence of technical self-efficacy on acceptance. In: Kurosu, M. (ed.) HCI 2014. LNCS, vol. 8512, pp. 764–775. Springer, Cham (2014). https://doi.org/10.1007/978-3-319-07227-2_73

41. Zeissig, E.M., Lidynia, C., Vervier, L., Gadeib, A., Ziefle, M.: Online privacy perceptions of older adults. In: Human Computer Interaction International (HCI) 2017 (2017)

Create Video Games to Promote Well-Being of Elderly People – A Practice-Driven Guideline

Marco Soldati[1]([✉])[iD], Carmen Zahn[2], Doruk Bildibay[1][iD], Tabea Iseli[1][iD], David Leisner[2][iD], Mario Niederhauser[2][iD], and Markus Recher[1][iD]

[1] Institute for Data Science (I4DS), FHNW University of Applied Sciences and Arts of Northwestern Switzerland, Windisch, Switzerland
{marco.soldati,doruk.bildibay,tabea.iseli,markus.recher}@fhnw.ch
[2] Institute for Research and Development of Collaborative Processes, FHNW University of Applied Sciences and Arts of Northwestern Switzerland, Olten, Switzerland
{carmen.zahn,david.leisner,mario.niederhauser}@fhnw.ch
http://www.fhnw.ch/myosotis

Abstract. This paper presents a selection of game design concepts to promote social interaction between older people and players from other generations. Hardware-related interaction channels, game mechanics and game content can be used to trigger positive communication between several players. The proposed concepts are based on the experience of 32 game prototypes developed with and for the oldest seniors living in several Swiss nursing and retirement homes. The games are directed at the relatives to make their visits a pleasant and positively perceived experience, with the aim of increasing well-being of all involved.

Keywords: Involving the elderly in HCI methodology · Game design for the elderly · Technology for the elderly's leisure and entertainment · Intergenerational gaming · Social interaction · Increased well-being

1 Introduction

Computer games are fun and can help to improve well-being of elderly people and their relatives [14]. This is the main motivation of Myosotis. Myosotis is the botanical term for a group of flowers colloquially called forget-me-not. And Myosotis is an umbrella term for several research, development, outreach and application projects in which we create, test and play multiplayer video games for and with elderly people. The games should motivate relatives to visit older people more often, so that the elderly are not forgotten.

The common design rationale of Myosotis is to use games to promote positive social interactions between players of different generations. The games build on the strengths of the elderly and do not pursue medical or therapeutic goals. The sole objective of the games is to entertain and make a visit a pleasant and positively perceived experience, where the visitor can find a new and exciting access to the memories and biography of the aged person [3].

© Springer Nature Switzerland AG 2020
Q. Gao and J. Zhou (Eds.): HCII 2020, LNCS 12208, pp. 401–418, 2020.
https://doi.org/10.1007/978-3-030-50249-2_29

Since 2015 we have implemented over 30 game prototypes. Some of them have been developed as part of a research project, most have been implemented by computer science students in more than 20 case studies. All games have been tested in dozens of applied game sessions in eleven nursing homes in Switzerland. More than 100 people have participated in this process, including researchers, students, therapists, caregivers, relatives, volunteers, children, and most importantly, residents of nursing homes.

All game prototypes are designed for two or more players sitting in the same room around or in front of a tablet computer. We are currently focusing on adults playing with seniors living in a retirement or nursing home. The elderly are usually over 75 years old and face different age-related handicaps. We do not differentiate between mental or physical problems, as in our experience, personal preferences and motivation have a greater influence on which game works best in a given situation. There is certainly not one game that suits everyone.

However, the design of such games is not quite as simple and the design principles to be taken into account are manifold. For this publication we focus on the following two questions:

(1) How can video games promote social interaction and how does this relate to well-being of players?
(2) Which game design concepts for multiplayer video games are most suited to promote social interaction?

The response to the first question is based on the self-determination theory [4,5] which defines relatedness as one of the basic universal needs necessary for personal well-being. In Myosotis, we use computer games to reinforce this relatedness by actively triggering communication between multiple players. Hereby we distinguish between non-verbal and verbal communication. Non-verbal communication includes physical contact or emotional expressions such as laughter. Verbal communication is divided into game-related and biographical talk. The latter is particularly interesting because it can trigger longer ongoing conversations. When the players start talking about their lives, Myosotis has reached its goal.

To answer our second question on which game design concepts work best to promote social interaction, we reviewed reports, interviews and test protocols of the Myosotis games already implemented and complemented them with our practical experience. As a result, we compiled a list of game design concepts that have proven to be particularly successful in triggering communication between two players.

Section 2 provides the theoretical background of the self-determination theory. Section 3 gives an overview of the Myosotis project to explain the data source for our findings. A summary of the proposed game design concepts can be found in Table 2, and the details are given in Sect. 4. The publication concludes with Sect. 5, which summarizes the work, highlights the limitations, and provides an outlook on further research topics.

2   Theoretical Background

The design rationale of Myosotis is to use video games to improve well-being of elderly people in retirement homes. It is based on the self-determination theory, which provides the psychological foundation to promote well-being [17].

According to self-determination theory [4,5] three universal psychological needs are relevant for positive motivation, effective functioning and psychological health [5, p. 182]. These basic universal needs are competence, autonomy and relatedness. The self-determination theory assumes that intrinsic motivation to participate in any activity depends on the satisfaction of these basic needs. In turn, activities that satisfy these needs increase energy and can be vitalizing [5].

Empirical results have confirmed that the satisfaction of these basic needs predicts well-being regardless of individual or cultural backgrounds [5]. In other words: If people feel competent, autonomous and related to others, they are intrinsically motivated to perform better and feel comfortable and happy in the long run. If these needs are neglected, people feel less good or even unhappy in the long run.

In Myosotis, we assume that video games can satisfy these basic needs. In this way, they become an intrinsically motivating activity and ultimately can contribute to an increase in well-being. [7] has conducted a controlled study of older people who play video games and found two important results. Playing games was associated with an increase in self-reported well-being and a significant improvement in reaction time.

We claim that playing together with loved ones can satisfy the need for relatedness. This is certainly true during the time of playing and shortly after, but presumably also in the longer term. The need for relatedness encompasses the social dimension of the self-determination theory. A long history of psychological research has shown that positive social interactions are not only beneficial for well-being, but even essential for humans of all ages. Social interaction, social relationships with others and belonging to social groups have been shown to be both protective against depression and curative for an existing depression [2]. Empirical research in media psychology shows that computer-based activities increase psychological well-being and reduce depressive feelings (e.g. [22]). [13] found that "digital games hold the potential to enhance senior's leisure time and social connectedness".

In Myosotis, we look at how video games and specific game mechanics can support positive social interactions. To assess this, we have recently launched a still ongoing study on verbal and non-verbal behavioural indicators of the observed players using video analysis. Verbal interaction is divided into (a) game-related communication, (b) help giving and (c) biography-related communication. As non-verbal indicators we distinguish between (d) laughing together, (e) eye contact and (f) body contact. Well-being is thereby not only understood as the absence of bad feelings, but it is characterized by positive feelings and positive body sensations.

3   The Myosotis Project

The Myosotis project was initiated in 2015 by a very practical issue. While play-ing computer games with her 90-year-old mother-in-law, games expert Bettina Wegenast discovered that many games did not work. They were too complex, too noisy or simply not designed for adults. She contacted our research group at the FHNW and, together with bachelor students, we started to develop first game prototypes in close cooperation with three Swiss retirement homes. In the following years, several other partners joined the project and two research grants were approved. To date, we have developed 32 game prototypes. Each game prototype addresses a different research question, as shown in Fig. 3 in the Appendix. The project is not yet completed and more games will be developed in 2020.

All Myosotis games are tested in regular game sessions with elderly people. In addition, we frequently organise workshops to gather experience and feedback from other stakeholders such as younger children, relatives, caregivers, therapists and students, to name a few.

Table 1 summarises these activities and the corresponding working hours from October 2015 to December 2019. The data is estimated on the basis of internal reports, log files, bachelor theses and diaries. To date, we can draw on the experience of over 11,000 working hours for development, research and doc-umentation. Of these, more than 500 h were in direct contact with the elderly. The seniors, in turn, spent more than 800 h in play with the developers.

Table 1. Estimated work hours for Myosotis games and workshops. The last two columns indicate the person hours elderly people and developers spent together. Further details are provided in Fig. 3 in the Appendix

Project type	#of games	Work hours (dev)	Play hours (dev in home)	Play hours (elderly)
Student games	18	6,940 h	185 h	293 h
Research games	8	3,500 h	90 h	75 h
Experiments	6	485 h	23 h	28 h
Game sessions	–	100 h	210 h	420 h
Workshops	–	100 h	22 h	18 h
Total	32	11,125 h	530 h	834 h

We believe that this broad experience puts us in an ideal position to iterate and evaluate the game design concepts for promoting social interaction. The fact that all projects followed a common, widely accepted research and development methodology supports the credibility of our results.

3.1   Methodology

The pro-active and early involvement of older people in the design process is crucial to the success of Myosotis and is a key driver for the implemented methodology: a user centred design (UCD) approach complemented by participatory design (PD) methods (also see [12]).

There are several variants of UCD, but, in general, the process is divided into four phases [10,16,26]. In phase 1, the context of use is analysed by collecting information about the user group, e.g. through field observations and interviews. In phase 2, requirements are derived from the collected information. These are then implemented in phase 3, in the form of primary design solutions such as prototypes. In the following phase 4, the solutions are tested and discussed with the user group. The resulting findings lead to a further run through the phases until the product meets the user requirements. This iterative approach is one of the three basic principles of the UCD process [8]. The other two are the early involvement of users and the empirical testing of concrete design solutions.

Participatory Design (PD) involves the users directly in the design process, in the sense that they design the product together with the designers [23]. According to [1], direct involvement in the design process aims at increasing the quality of the resulting product. [29] postulates that only through such participation designers can gain a deeper understanding of users' needs. There are various methods of participatory design, such as workshops or cooperative prototyping. The degree of user involvement depends on the field of application and can range from passive observation to active co-decision.

To explain how UCD and PD are used in Myosotis, we now describe the game FoodPlanet, which was developed in 2018 and 2019.

3.2   UCD and PD in FoodPlanet

In FoodPlanet, two players jointly prepare either a Cheese-Fondue or a Hamburger (Fig. 1). The game offers three modes to play. In the creative mode, players freely choose the ingredients for the selected dish. In the cooperative mode, the players prepare the meal as quickly as possible by cooperatively collecting a list of ingredients. In the competitive mode, each player prepares their own meal. The faster player wins the competition. FoodPlanet was tested with over 20 residents from four retirement homes.

In UCD phase 1, the team visited several retirement homes and actively played commercial games with the residents. Through observation and informal discussions, the team established a solid understanding of the needs and challenges of the players. In phase 2, these experiences were consolidated in a short list of requirements.

Phase 3 started with ideation workshops, followed by the implementation of a first prototype. After 6 weeks, this prototype was shown to the elderly and then improved in small iterations. This phase was highly driven by participatory design techniques. Initially, we focused on collecting generic feedback and comments from stakeholders in informal discussions. Then, we presented alternatives of selected features and asked for personal preferences.

Fig. 1. Creative Hamburger and competitive Fondue preparation

A good practice in this phase is to identify and prioritise those functions that can be implemented at low cost. When participants feel that their comments are being taken seriously, they will eventually become more involved in the design process.

In UCD phase 4, we conducted a psychological field study in a retirement home. We primarily investigated the influence of the three game modes "creative", "cooperative" and "competitive" on the social interaction between the players. A total of 10 residents took part in this exploratory study. Each resident played each game mode with a therapist. The game sessions lasted 20 min per mode and were recorded on video to perform an analysis of the social interactions. Although the study has not yet been published, some initial findings are mentioned in the following result sections.

4   Results

To answer our second research question, this paper gives a concrete guideline on how to use different game design concepts to promote social interaction. For this end, we have systematically reviewed reports and protocols of the UCD and PD process from several Myosotis projects and discussed them with stakeholders.

The extracted concepts have been divided into three categories: (1) hardware, (2) game mechanics and (3) game content. Hardware is the physical interface between the game and the real world. It is used to trigger non-verbal communication such as physical contact or movement in space. The game mechanics can motivate players to talk about game-specific topics, e.g. by creating a conflicting situation that requires coordination. Finally, game content can initiate thematic communication, whereby biographical topics are of particular interest. To support the latter, we have integrated personal media such as photos, video or audio into some of the games.

Table 2 provides an overview of these concepts and lists our results and suggestions. The subsequent sections iterate further details on each topic and refer to publications by other research teams. We also indicate the number of

Myosotis games used to validate a particular concept. Where appropriate, we expand the descriptions with exemplary Myosotis games.

4.1   (1) Hardware Channels to Promote Interaction

A tablet computer provides multiple input and output channels for interaction. In Myosotis, we used four of them to achieve our goals: multitouch screen, microphone/speaker, orientation and position sensors and camera.

(1a) Multitouch Screen. A multitouch screen is the most direct and intuitive input channel for the elderly. It makes less demands on hand-eye coordination and the spatial movements of the user [28] than other technologies such as a mouse or game controller. Even complex touch gestures like dragging or pinching can be learned quickly [11].

A shared touch screen area triggers game-related communication when used by multiple players simultaneously [21]. Whether the area is used for interaction or just for display it will provoke a conflict that requires coordination. A split screen can also work, but the interaction between players would have to be enforced by the game's mechanic and not the hardware. In Myosotis, 17 of the games use a shared screen area, while only three use a split screen. The rest are either turn-based multiplayer or single player games.

When designing games for older people, only direct touch input should be used. All experiments with indirect touch control (e.g. when a virtual joystick controls a character) were abandoned during the UCD process. They were just not user friendly.

(1b) Microphone and Speaker. Voice or sound controlled games with audio feedback can work for people with severe visual impairments but still good hearing abilities. In Myosotis, we have recently begun to gain initial experience with two sound driven games [15]. In "Los Emol" ("Listen!"), one player uses headphones to listen to sounds while the other person controls the screen. The game is characterised by a high mutual interdependency. Only by talking to each other, they can solve the audio puzzle (Fig. 2a). To our knowledge, no research has been done in this field so far and we see some potential for further work.

(1c) Orientation and Position Sensors. The orientation and position sensors of a tablet (i.e. the gyroscope, accelerometer and magnetometer) allow the measurement of the tilt of a tablet. [25] discuss games where tilt input is more natural than the other options. However, tilt interaction with large tablets can also cause fatigue because the device must be held in the air.

For Myosotis, we have implemented five collaborative tilt controlled games. Two players hold the tablet with four hands so that each thumb touches a corner of the screen. Together, and in close coordination, players must catch moving objects or solve a puzzle. This leads to game-related communication: "Do you want to take the purple or the brown dot?".

Table 2. Summary of game design concepts and suggestions to promote social interaction through video games

Category	Concept	Techniques and suggestions
(1) Hardware	(1a) Multitouch screen	Sharing a screen area leads to conflicting situations, which require interpersonal communication.
	(1b) Microphone and speaker	Helpful for people with visual impairments. Audio output can add an extra channel on top of visual output.
	(1c) Orientation and position sensor	Tilting a tablet which is held by two players creates an enjoyable multiplayer experience.
	(1d) Camera	Many people refuse or dislike to be taken pictures of. To those who agree, however, camera driven games are entertaining and fun.
(2) Mechanics	(2a) Toy or game	Toys are better suited for people with mental impairments as well as to introduce new technology to non-gamers. Games are better for other people. To promote social interaction, both are equally well suited.
	(2b) Single player games	Single player games are fun to be played together, side by side. Best suited are animated toys and puzzle games.
	(2c) Cooperative play	Cooperative play triggers more game-related communication than competitive play Asynchronous games, where players play a different role or task, are a very promising cooperative variant for elderly.
	(2d) Bi- and multilateral competition	Direct competition should be avoided. Indirect, non-simultaneous competition between a group of personally known players, however, is very motivating.
(3) Story content	(3a) Storytelling	Stories should be short; animated books work best.
	(3b) Emotionally charged game elements	Game elements a user can emotionally engage with lead to discussions and, therefore, to interactions between the players.
	(3c) Personalised media	If photos, videos, audio tracks and texts from the personal environment of a player are embedded in a game, they will trigger communication. The media can be used as a visual design element, as a reward or as part of the core mechanic.

(1d) Camera. We use the camera in two ways for collaborative play: the front camera for live portraits and the rear camera for augmented reality. In both cases our experiences are ambiguous.

For live portraits, we did not implement any games, but rely on existing apps like FaceApp, YouCam Makeup or Chomp, which modify a live image of the player's face in the game. Using the camera in this way is highly individual. Some people enjoy to see and play with their portrait, but many turn away as soon as they see themselves. Interestingly, we have had some of the most enjoyable and memorable two-player gaming sessions with camera-controlled games. It is not clear, however, whether this is because of the games or because the players were simply more extroverted and humorous.

The use of Augmented Reality (AR) on a tablet device is not suitable for elderly. In AR games, a live image taken by the rear camera is supplemented by digital objects. We have tested several AR games and even implemented one by ourselves, but with little success. The players were confused by the digital objects and were overstrained by the coordinative tasks required to control the game. Observing the screen, moving around in a room and simultaneously solving a task is too demanding and leads to frustrating experiences. Therefore we did not investigate further in this direction.

4.2   (2) Game Mechanics to Promote Interaction

Many game mechanics can be customized to promote social interaction, and it would go beyond the scope of this document to list all of them. Instead, we focus on the involved player interaction patterns and, first, on the discussion whether a toy or game is better suited to foster positive social interaction.

(2a) Toy or Game. The distinction between game and toy is controversial [30]. In general, a toy is an object with which you can play as freely and as long as you want. A game specifies goals, rules, restrictions and a final state. [20] condenses a comprehensive discussion on this topic in the statement: "A game is a problem-solving activity, approached with a playful attitude". [18, Chap. 9] says "With a toy, it may be difficult to say exactly when the play begins and ends. But with a game, the activity is richly formalized. The game has a beginning, a middle, and a quantifiable outcome at the end. The game takes place in a precisely defined physical and temporal space of play."

For Myosotis, we have implemented 12 toys and 20 games. The toys seem to be preferred by people with mental disabilities—as long as they are easy to use, entertaining and surprising. Toys do not promote vocal communication per se, but rather through their content.

We often use toys to break the ice when starting a game session with elderly. With a toy, there is no evaluation of a players' actions, there is no right or wrong. Therefore, they are ideal for familiarising oneself with the devices and avoiding exposure of individual impairments. Nevertheless, toys can quickly lose their appeal due to the lack of a challenge or goal. Many players seek a challenge and a purpose. We often meet players, an a majority seems to be male players, who leave the game session because they do not see the purpose.

A toy can be interrupted and resumed at any time. This is more difficult to achieve in a game, but in our experience it is crucial to provide this functionality because the players need the freedom to start a conversation at any time. This implies that time-dependent games are rather unsuitable for the purpose of social interaction. If time-pressure is used, games should be short and goals should be reachable quickly.

(2b) Single Player Games. [6] lists seven common player interaction patterns. Four of them were used in our games: Single player vs. game (six games), cooperative or collaborative play (19 games), bilateral competition (player vs. player, four games) and multilateral competition (all vs. all, five games).

Many single player games can be played together, side by side. One person takes the role of the active player, the other is the advisor. Single-player games do not force interaction per se, but the game environment, the fact that two players participate, makes them a "multiplayer" experience. Puzzle games and animated toys are particularly suitable for this.

(2c) Cooperative Play. In cooperative games, two or more players play together to beat the game [6] or to play with a toy. The development of such local co-op games and in particular toys is a key concept of Myosotis. Indeed, 11 of the 12 implemented toys are cooperative. We believe that multiplayer toys are ideal to establish communication as they leave enough time to start a discussion at any time.

The aforementioned FoodPlanet study supports our assumptions. The creative mode is comparable to a multiplayer toy. Players can freely cook their food and take as much time as they want. First results from the study show that in the creative mode 56% of the overall playtime is related to social interaction as opposed to 47% in the competitive mode and 43% in the collaborative mode under time pressure.

Asynchronous Play. An interesting variant of cooperative games are asynchronous multiplayer games in which the players have different roles. In "Puzzlitekt", two players have to reveal an image covered by a grid of tiles (Fig. 2b). The first player is an architect and constructs Tetris-like pieces. The second player is a painter and searches for free spots to place the pieces on the grid, in order to remove the tiles and find the underlying picture.

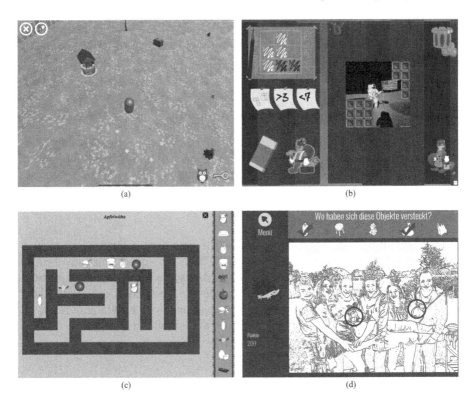

Fig. 2. Screenshots of selected Myosotis games: (a) "Los Emol" ("Listen!") is an asynchronous audio game; player one sees the screen; player two only hears the audio (b) "Puzzlitekt" is an asynchronous puzzle game; left is the playground of the architect; right the one of the painter. (c) In "Was git's z'Ässe?" ("What's for dinner?"), two players collect the ingredients of a meal. (d) In "HiddenObjects", small graphical objects are hidden in an personal image.

(2d) Bi- and Multilateral Competition. [13, 19] have found that older adults cite diversion and social interaction as the main motivating factors for playing games. Challenge is somewhere in the middle and arousal, competition and fantasy are at the bottom. While this is largely consistent with our observations, we found that competition should be discussed in more detail.

Like [28], we also observed that the players enjoyed the indirect competition against other teams. In the FoodPlanet study, we found that beating the high scores of the retirement home was motivation enough to keep trying. A therapist later reported several discussions about who held the record, in the days following the play session.

We noticed that indirect competition only seems to work if the other competitors on the highscore list are known to the player. In games with a global highscore, players never showed interest in beating it or even looking at it.

It is important to avoid a direct one-to-one competition between generations. Elderly people are more likely to become aware of their age-related weaknesses. They also repeatedly expressed their discomfort when younger players let them win: "Don't let me win! I am not a child".

4.3   (3) Game Content to Promote Interaction.

When it comes to biographical communication, the content, topic or story of a game is a key factor. Three core concepts that are helpful for social interaction were identified in our games: storytelling, emotionally charged game elements and personalised media. The concepts are ordered by the increasing degree of individualisation they offer to a game designer.

(3a) Storytelling. In storytelling games, the communication topics are usually influenced by the story itself. Due to the high amount of work involved in developing such games and the limited replayability, we have only experimented with commercial story games. We have made the best experience with short animated books. Longer stories do not seem to appeal to elderly anymore. At all game afternoons since 2015, we only met one woman who was eager to continue a story game from the last session.

(3b) Emotionally Charged Game Elements. Reminiscence work is a form of therapy based on life experiences, memories and stories from the past [27]. Instead of asking questions, people are presented with objects, photos, songs or poems that are connected to their memories. As game designers, we use this method by adding emotionally charged elements to the games. There is no consensus on common topics for such elements, but literature shows different categories that seem to work for many people: holidays, "firsts" like the first car or toy, work and home, sports, animals and food [24].

In Myosotis, we experimented with four games that use cooking ingredients as a topic. In our maze game "Was git's z'Ässe?" ("What's for dinner?"), two players collect ingredients for typical Swiss meals (Fig. 2c). Besides "Food-Planet", our other food game, this is one of the most played Myosotis games. And it works: "I never put raisins in my Muesli, my husband didn't like them", a woman said one day and then continued talking about her husband, her wedding and her family. The game was put aside and her story was put in the foreground.

(3c) Personalised Media. To a large extent, the reminiscence work is based on biographical material, such as personal pictures and objects. Driven by this knowledge, we have developed 13 games that include personal media such as photos, video, audio and personal text snippets. In the games, the media can be used in three different ways: as game mechanics, as rewards and as a visual design element.

Media as Game Mechanic. The use of media as game mechanic places the media at the game's core. A personalised Memory or jigsaw puzzle are simple examples for such game mechanics. But digital jigsaws are not optimal for multiple players and Memory depends on short-term memory, which is not a strength of aged people. In Myosotis, we have implemented five games that use more sophisticated forms of such mechanics.

The most notable Myosotis game is "Hidden Objects". A personal image is algorithmically modified, and small objects are automatically hidden in the image. The players have to recognise the objects (Fig. 2d).

Media as Reward. Media can serve as a reward for a completed level or as a collectible within a game. One of Myosotis' early observations was associated with a famous Swiss dice board game called "Eile mit Weile" ("Haste with time"). Two students created a digital version of the game and added additional fields showing personal photos. As the game proved to be too complex for most players, they spontaneously changed the rules. Instead of trying to get all meeples to the goal area, the new motivation to play was to uncover as many pictures as possible.

Media as Visual Design Element. As a visual design element, personal media can be placed in a game world or used, for example, to personalise an avatar. This area has not yet been investigated by Myosotis, but will be further examined in one of the next Myosotis games.

5   Conclusions and Further Research Topics

In this publication we provide answers to the following questions:

(1) How can video games promote social interaction and how does this relate to well-being of players?
(2) Which game design concepts for multiplayer video games are most suited to promote social interaction?

Question (1) is answered by self-determination theory, which defines relatedness to important others as one of the basic universal needs necessary for personal well-being. Video games can reinforce this relatedness, by using various game design concepts to promote interaction between players from different generations. These games lead to positively perceived, shared experiences and ideally motivate relatives to visit their elderly loved ones more often. Ultimately, this improves the well-being of everyone.

The answer to question (2) is given by the result section of this paper, namely the list of game concepts which are suitable to promote social interaction between multiple players. From over 30 games developed for the Myosotis project, we have extracted the concepts that trigger communication, whether verbal or non-verbal. The concepts are divided into three categories. Hardware related interaction patterns, a selection of game mechanics and the content or story of a game. In particular, the content of a game can establish conversations with a longer duration.

We have also shown that the types of games preferred by different players are highly individual. The players have to agree on a game they like and which is accessible to everyone. Ideally, games for elderly can be played in multiple ways and support both toy-like, creative modes as well as game-like, goal-oriented modes. In either case, it is important to be able to interrupt and resume the game without any disadvantages. Once the players have agreed on a game, playing together is a fun and entertaining social activity, not only for the active players but also for spectators.

This list of game design concepts is by far not exhaustive. Myosotis focuses on the development of touch-based, local multiplayer video games and has not considered other technologies or interaction patterns such as game consoles or playing over a network.

Also, we did not address visual aspects of video games for elderly people. While usability for older people is treated quite well in literature [9], there seems to be a lack of knowledge in the domain of art style and aesthetics. However, we expect that aesthetics and certain usability related facets have a significant impact on social interaction. This is an important field that needs more investigation.

And finally, another important question remains unanswered. How can we compare the effects of the proposed design principles on social interaction and how can we assess the subsequent well-being? In a next step we plan to extend our study to better understand how personalised media in games stimulate communication and what impact this has on social well-being compared to non-personalised games. This will include the development of a method to assess well-being of elderly people.

Acknowledgement. This work was supported by the Strategic Initiative "Myosotis-Garden" funded by the University of Applied Sciences and Arts of Northwestern Switzerland (FHNW). Our special thanks go to all involved students, caregivers, therapists, supporters and the many residents in elderly homes, who provided feedback, insights, ideas and countless hours of fun and enjoyment. They dedicated their precious time to our little flower called forget-me-not or Myosotis, because no one should ever be forgotten.

7   Appendix 1: List of Developed Games

Game	Year	Project	Description	Toy/Game	Media as Game Mechanic	Media as Reward	Media as Design Element	Single Player vs Game	Player vs Player	Cooperative Play	Competition	Asynchronous Coop	Turn-based	Split Screen	Shared Area	Direct Touch	Indirect Touch	Tilt	# Person Visits (Dev)	# Person Visits (Elderly)	# Person Hours (Dev)	# Person Hours (Elderly)	# Work Hours (Dev)
Eile mit Weile	2016	Bachelor	Personalizable "Eile mit Weile"-Game, in which personal pictures, sounds and texts appear during the course of the game.	Game		x					x		x			x			9	4	14	6	360
Hide and Seek	2017	Experiment	Icons are manually hidden and then searched in a personal image.	Game	x								x			x			0	0	0	0	80
KitchenTable	2015	Bachelor	A table with crockery and cutlery, which can be arranged as desired.	Toy					x							x			6	3	9	4.5	20
MyosotisVillage	2017	Bachelor	Game portal. Games are hidden in houses in a village. The houses can be reached by car via roads.	Toy		x				x						x			9	13	15	16	720
ColourBubbles	2017	Bachelor	Mix two colours such that new target colors are created.	Game					x						x	x			2	2	1	1	120
Mystix	2018	Experiment	The players light up a dark surface with fireflies to uncover personal images.	Game		x					x				x	x			1	2	1	2	200
Piano	2016	Experiment	Two sided piano	Toy						x				x	x	x			4	4	2	2	40
Putzspiel	2017	Experiment	Clean a dusty personal picture by wiping away the dirt.	Toy						x					x	x					10	12	120
MusicPong	2016	Bachelor	Two players create musical notes and instruments. Sounds are played when they meet.	Toy						x					x	x			6	8.5	4	7	180
Sternenspiel	2016	Bachelor	Collect stars and interact with planets to produce different sound and graphics effects.	Toy						x					x	x			6	8.5	4	7	180
Verzogene Welt	2017	Bachelor	A personal image is projected onto a virtual rubber skin, which then can be distorted.	Toy	x					x				x		x			7	20	7	20	360
TonSpur	2018	Experiment	Experimental game for sound and graphics effects.	Toy						x	x				x	x			14	13	10	12	40
Familienspaziergang	2016	Bachelor	In this digital board game two players search for object and receive personal pictures as a reward.	Game		x					x		x			x				13	14	13	360
Was gits z'Ässe?	2016	Bachelor	In a maze two players jointly collect ingredients for a meal.	Toy						x		x			x	x			12	24	18	36	1000
HiddenObjects	2018	Bachelor	A photo gets transformed to a black and white line drawing. Graphical objects are then placed in the drawing and have to be found.	Game		x				x				x	x	x			6	6	8.5	8.5	720
MoviePuzzle	2018	Bachelor	Several film snippets must be put in the correct order.	Game	x			x								x			6	9	6	9	360
MovingSouvenirs	2018	Bachelor	Two to four players collect given objects. The player who has found 10 objects wins.	Game							x				x	x			9	19	11	24	360
Wimmelbild-Designer	2018	Bachelor	Cutout pictures of famous people can be placed in an arbitrary scene	Toy	x					x						x			4	14	4	14	180
PuzzliTekt	2019	Bachelor	Asynchronous Puzzle-Game for two players, simultanious or turn based.	Game		x				x					x	x			16	28	34	57	360

Fig. 3. List of games developed for Myosotis (1/2)

Game	Year	Project	Description	Toy/Game	Media as Game Mechanic	Media as Reward	Media as Design Element	Single Player vs Game	Player vs Player	Cooperative Play	Competition	Asynchronous Coop	Turn-based	Split Screen	Shared Area	Direct Touch	Indirect Touch	Tilt	# Person Visits (Dev)	# Person Visits (Elderly)	# Person Hours (Dev)	# Person Hours (Elderly)	Work Hours (Dev)
MyosotisMuseum	2018	Bachelor	Studies about orientation of elderly people in virtual rooms	Toy	x	x		x								x			17	17	14	15	720
CouchPotato	2019	Bachelor	Augmented Reality game in which the player has to grow plants.	Game													x		9	10	9	10	360
ShapeMatch	2019	Bachelor	Recognize touches of multiple players.	Game											x	x			6	22	6.7	24	220
SoundGame	2019	Bachelor	Use a xylophon as input device for a sound game.	Game					x							x			9	25	7.3	21	360
Colordy	2019	Research	By tilting the tablet two players roll a sphere over a coloured checker board,	Game														x			3	3	240
Los Emol	2019	Research	Two players have to find hidden animals by following their noises.	Game						x		x			x	x					3	6	240
Marbelenture	2019	Research	Maze controlled by tilt.	Game						x								x			0	0	240
Dandelion	2019	Research	Two players controll a dandelion flower on its descent by tilting and avoiding harmful objects.	Game						x					x			x			3	3	240
Navigest	2019	Research	Research game to test different navigation types.	Toy						x					x	x	x				10	12	360
FoodPlanet	2018	Research	Two players have to cook a fondue by catching flying ingredients and throwing them in the pot.	Game					x	x					x	x					61	39	1000
The Reunion	2019	Research	Game collection which consists of the five slightly adapted game concepts: Colordy, LosEmol, Marbelenture, Dandelion and Navigest.	Game				x								x		x			10	12	1000
Moving Souvenirs II	2019	Research	Re-implemenetation of Moving Souvenirs	Game							x				x	x			0	0	0	0	180
Hüpfball	2019	Experiment	A puzzle in which a bouncing ball is used to uncover and cover plates underneath. Revealed plates show part of a personal picture.	Game		x				x					x			x					5
Games: 32				12 / 20	5	8	0	5	4	19	5	2	3	3	17	28	2	6	158	252	298	396	10925

Fig. 4. List of games developed for Myosotis (2/2)

References

1. Bødker, S., Ehn, P., Sjogren, D., Sundblad, Y.: Co-operative design-perspectives on 20 years with 'the Scandinavian IT Design Model'. In: Proceedings of NordiCHI 2000, Stockholm, October 2000
2. Cruwys, T., Dingle, G.A., Haslam, C., Haslam, S.A., Jetten, J., Morton, T.A.: Social group memberships protect against future depression, alleviate depression symptoms and prevent depression relapse. Soc. Sci. Med. **98**, 179–186 (2013). https://doi.org/10.1016/j.socscimed.2013.09.013
3. De La Hera, T., Loos, E., Simons, M., Blom, J.: Benefits and factors influencing the design of intergenerational digital games: a systematic literature review. Societies **7**(3), 18 (2017). https://doi.org/10.3390/soc7030018
4. Deci, E.L., Ryan, R.M.: Intrinsic Motivation and Self-Determination in Human Behavior. Springer, Boston (1985). https://doi.org/10.1007/978-1-4899-2271-7
5. Deci, E.L., Ryan, R.M.: Self-determination theory: a macrotheory of human motivation, development, and health. Can. Psychol./Psychologie canadienne **49**(3), 182–185 (2008). https://doi.org/10.1037/a0012801
6. Fullerton, T.: Game Design Workshop, vol. 14, 4th edn. AK Peters/CRC Press, Boca Raton (2018). https://doi.org/10.1201/b22309
7. Goldstein, J., Cajko, L., Oosterbroek, M., Michielsen, M., Van Houten, O., Salverda, F.: Video games and the elderly. Soc. Behav. Pers. (1997). https://doi.org/10.2224/sbp.1997.25.4.345
8. Gould, J.D., Lewis, C.: Designing for usability: key principles and what designers think. Commun. ACM (1985). https://doi.org/10.1145/3166.3170
9. Ijsselsteijn, W., Nap, H.H., de Kort, Y., Poels, K.: Digital game design for elderly users. In: Proceedings of the 2007 Conference on Future Play - Future Play 2007, p. 17. ACM Press, New York (2007). https://doi.org/10.1145/1328202.1328206
10. International Organization for Standardization: ISO 9241–210: Ergonomics of human-system interaction - Human-centred design for interactive systems (2010). https://doi.org/10.1039/c0dt90114h
11. Kobayashi, M., Hiyama, A., Miura, T., Asakawa, C., Hirose, M., Ifukube, T.: Elderly user evaluation of mobile touchscreen interactions. In: Campos, P., Graham, N., Jorge, J., Nunes, N., Palanque, P., Winckler, M. (eds.) INTERACT 2011. LNCS, vol. 6946, pp. 83–99. Springer, Heidelberg (2011). https://doi.org/10.1007/978-3-642-23774-4_9
12. Loos, E., de la Hera, T., Simons, M., Gevers, D.: Setting up and conducting the co-design of an intergenerational digital game: a state-of-the-art literature review. In: Zhou, J., Salvendy, G. (eds.) HCII 2019. LNCS, vol. 11592, pp. 56–69. Springer, Cham (2019). https://doi.org/10.1007/978-3-030-22012-9_5
13. Nap, H., Kort, Y.D., IJsselsteijn, W.: Senior gamers: preferences, motivations and needs. Gerontechnology **8**(4), 247–262 (2009). https://doi.org/10.4017/gt.2009.08.04.003.00
14. Osmanovic, S., Pecchioni, L.: Beyond Entertainment. Games Cult. **11**(1–2), 130–149 (2016). https://doi.org/10.1177/1555412015602819
15. Resch, T., Hädrich, M.: Virtual acoustic spaces unity spatializer with custom head tracker. In: Audio for Virtual, Augmented and Mixed Realities: Proceedings of ICSA 2019; 5th International Conference on Spatial Audio; Ilmenau, Germany, pp. 107–113 (2019). https://doi.org/10.22032/dbt.39936
16. Richter, M., Flückiger, M.D.: Usability und UX kompakt. I. Springer, Heidelberg (2016). https://doi.org/10.1007/978-3-662-49828-6

17. Ryan, R.M., Rigby, C.S., Przybylski, A.: The motivational pull of video games: a self-determination theory approach. Motiv. Emot. **30**(4), 347–363 (2006). https://doi.org/10.1007/s11031-006-9051-8

18. Salen, K., Zimmerman, E.: Rules of Play: Game Design Fundamentals. MIT Press, Cambridge (2003)

19. Salmon, J.P., Dolan, S.M., Drake, R.S., Wilson, G.C., Klein, R.M., Eskes, G.A.: A survey of video game preferences in adults: building better games for older adults. Entertainment Comput. (2017). https://doi.org/10.1016/j.entcom.2017.04.006

20. Schell, J.: The Art of Game Design: A Book of Lenses. Elsevier/Morgan Kaufmann, Amsterdam, Boston (2008)

21. Schild, J., Masuch, M.: Game design for ad-hoc multi-touch gameplay on large tabletop displays. In: Proceedings of the International Academic Conference on the Future of Game Design and Technology - Futureplay 2010, p. 90. ACM Press (2010). https://doi.org/10.1145/1920778.1920791

22. Shapira, N., Barak, A., Gal, I.: Promoting older adults' well-being through Internet training and use. Aging Ment. Health **11**(5), 477–484 (2007). https://doi.org/10.1080/13607860601086546

23. Spinuzzi, C.: The methodology of participatory design. Tech. Commun. **52**, 163–174 (2005)

24. Stinson, C.K.: Structured group reminiscence: an intervention for older adults. J. Continuing Educ. Nurs. **40**(11), 521–528 (2009). https://doi.org/10.3928/00220124-20091023-10

25. Teather, R.J., MacKenzie, I.S.: Position vs. velocity control for tilt-based interaction. In: Proceedings - Graphics Interface, pp. 51–58. Canadian Information Processing Society (2014)

26. Usability.gov: User-Centered Design Basics — Usability.gov (2019). https://www.usability.gov/what-and-why/user-centered-design.html

27. VandenBos, G.R.: APA Dictionary of Psychology, 1st edn. American Psychological Association, Washington DC. (2007)

28. Vasconcelos, A., Silva, P.A., Caseiro, J., Nunes, F., Teixeira, L.F.: Designing tablet-based games for seniors. In: Proceedings of the 4th International Conference on Fun and Games - FnG 2012, pp. 1–10. ACM Press, New York (2012). https://doi.org/10.1145/2367616.2367617

29. Yamauchi, Y.: Power of peripheral designers: how users learn to design. In: Proceedings of the 4th International Conference on Design Science Research in Information Systems and Technology, DESRIST 2009 (2009). https://doi.org/10.1145/1555619.1555637

30. Liu, Y.: Game vs. Toy — IST 446: Game Design and Development (2014). https://sites.psu.edu/ist446/2014/01/17/game-vs-toy/

Stealth-Adaptive Exergame Design Framework for Elderly and Rehabilitative Users

Ramin Tadayon[✉], Wataru Sakoda, and Yuichi Kurita

Hiroshima University,
1-4-1 Kagamiyama, Higashihiroshima, Hiroshima 739-0046, Japan
rtadayon@hiroshima-u.ac.jp

Abstract. Adaptive exergames have been developed to encourage regular exercise and support rehabilitative motion for improved health outcomes in today's ageing population. However, existing approaches often fail to provide evidence for a direct link between physical performance and gameplay outcomes, which makes it difficult to accurately adapt gameplay mechanics. The Stealth-Adaptive Exergame Design (SAED) Framework addresses this limitation by mapping the design of exergame mechanics to performance characteristics and utilizing real-time learning in a seamless (stealth) manner to adapt the system to the individual. Two cases of implementation of the SAED framework from prior work are presented, one modeling the rehabilitative exercise program of a specific individual and physical trainer in a self-defense arm-swing motion and the other utilizing the two-leg standing squat motion to reduce risk of locomotive degeneration in the Japanese elderly population. Design characteristics of the two cases, including the mapping between spatial and temporal characteristics of the motion and corresponding game objectives, are presented along with models for real-time stealth adaptation. Applications of the framework toward a variety of exercise domains are discussed with limitations on usable game scenarios and designs.

Keywords: Exergames · IT for the ageing population · Person-centric design

1 Introduction

As the world's population continues to age, nearly every country has experienced a steady growth in the proportion of its population aged 65 or higher [1]. This is particularly the case in countries such as Japan, wherein the elderly are projected to account for over a third of the population [2]. Consequently, global demand for physical therapy and healthcare to combat the physical disabilities caused by musculoskeletal degeneration and other detrimental health effects of aging has seen a sharp increase, with demand rapidly outweighing availability of therapists and physicians in many cases [3].

A promising solution in recent research has been the usage of exercise-based serious games, or exergames, as a tool for self-driven exercise to benefit elderly physical health and healthy lifespans. A wide variety of exergames have been developed for this purpose, with many recent approaches including adaptation strategies to match the

Q. Gao and J. Zhou (Eds.): HCII 2020, LNCS 12208, pp. 419–434, 2020.
https://doi.org/10.1007/978-3-030-50249-2_30

difficulty of gameplay with performance and physical limitations of the player. These exergames are designed to provide an engaging and meaningful method to motivate regular exercise, and utilize physical motions directly related to those prescribed within rehabilitation programs and therapy in order to relate gameplay to physical health. However, the designs of many such exergame systems share a glaring issue: while it is often shown in resultant data that users of these exergames improve in physical function, due to the lack of a direct link or mapping between the properties and outcomes of the exercise task and the corresponding properties and outcomes of game objectives, it can be very challenging to conclude that the evidence for these improvements in health outcomes are based within gameplay, and therefore the effectiveness of these solutions in practice cannot be effectively determined.

To address this issue, it is proposed that the design of these exergames can utilize a mapping strategy wherein the physical and temporal properties of the motor task, as well as the individual goals, successes and errors within these domains, are linked directly to corresponding gameplay objectives and outcomes, in such a way that evidence for successful and erroneous performance within gameplay serves also as evidence for performance in a motion task. Furthermore, adaptation of the gameplay objectives should utilize a learning backend that learns to link an individual's performance at the exercise task to officially recognized clinical metrics for health and physical function.

These are the key principles in the design of a novel framework for exergame development, the Stealth-Adaptive Exergame Design (SAED) Framework, presented in this work. Related work on exergames for elderly and rehabilitative users and the principles for adaptation and exergame design that serve as the basis for the proposed framework are presented in Sect. 2. Section 3 provides an overview of the SAED Framework and details of the evidence-centered mapping and adaptation strategies described above. In Sect. 4, two cases are presented wherein the SAED framework is utilized in the design of exergames to support rehabilitation, along with details of their respective strategies for individually focused stealth adaptation. Conclusions and directions for future work including implementations of the framework across a variety of domains of exergaming are provided in Sect. 5.

2   Related Work

2.1   Exergames for Elderly and Rehabilitation

The potential for exergames, or exercise-based videogames, to promote the healthy lifespan, rehabilitative recovery, mobility, and physical fitness among the elderly is well-documented in research. Zheng et al. demonstrated the ability of these games to improve multiple health outcomes including strength, balance and other physical characteristics among the elderly population [4]. Liao et al. have further indicated that exergames can assist elderly subjects in recovering from effects of frailty [5]. The primary motivation for utilizing exergames over conventional exercise is also well-noted in research, and is verified by Huang et al. [6]: exergames can create a positive effect on an individual's enthusiasm and perception toward exercise, and may thus assist in improving compliance with regular physical activity requirements over time.

Based on these motivations, and the need for individually adaptive rehabilitative exercise, exergames have been developed and evaluated extensively within this population and have seen a variety of approaches toward adaptation and adjustment to match skill level. As a notable recent example, Garcia et al. developed an asynchronous solitaire exergame wherein gameplay elements requiring cognition were separated from those requiring physical exercise in order to reduce cognitive load in consideration of the preferences of the population [7]. Earlier approaches [8] recognized the need for these exergames to respect the physical and cognitive capabilities of their target population, giving rise to adaptive systems. In some cases, adaptation was facilitated through intervention by a physiotherapist [9]; however, automating the adaptation process becomes increasingly desirable in modern work as the demand for physical therapist time and resources begins to exceed availability.

Adaptive exergames often adopt a default approach to design wherein a predefined game concept or game task is fitted to a motion task and then distributed to a series of users, treating "the elderly" as a group rather than considering interpersonal and intrapersonal variation in design. The Person-Centered Multimedia Computing [10] paradigm argues that even among populations who share common attributes, such as the geriatric population, individuals can be vastly varied from the perspective of technology and human-computer interfaces, especially in the case of physical motion capabilities and limitations. In this regard, adaptation mechanisms such as that of Paliyawan et al. [11] which utilize AI to learn about the player, gradually improving the precision of their adaptation to match their knowledge of that player's attributes, are preferable to more static implementations. The recently-proposed fuzzy logic model by Zhang et al. [12] for assessing adaptation of various exergaming environments using individual characteristics also demonstrates the effectiveness of AI-based dynamic adaptation.

Individual variation also leads to differences in preferred game types, with individuals often preferring games with subject matter they are more familiar with, particularly when these players are elderly users [13]. The choice of subject and mechanics within exergame design should account for these factors in addition to considering the motions themselves. Finding the right game abstraction for an exercise is no trivial task; the chosen game scenario should be the most natural abstraction possible for the motion task. This concept was suggested early in the development of exergame research by Sinclair et al. [14] in their separation of effectiveness and attractiveness of exergames, but was not explored in detail. This places several fundamental constraints on the exergame implementation, which many existing exergame approaches often fail to adequately account for.

Furthermore, the requirements of the trainers, therapists and standard assessments need to be considered and integrated into the AI's assessment of performance in these systems, so that they can be more easily integrated into existing training and exercise programs. Earlier studies relating exercise to physical health in the elderly utilized evidence in physical performance characteristics to support claims about health outcomes [15]. Modern exergame studies utilize validated, trainer-approved evidence of health outcomes to assess the effectiveness of their implementations, but these are often done outside of gameplay, since these instruments of assessment are not mapped into the game's design [16].

2.2 Evidence-Centered Adaptation

When game mechanics are designed merely to accommodate physical activity, rather than to embody it precisely, it is difficult to validate the effectiveness of exergame AI at evaluating and adapting to individual skill level [17, 18]. For example, often it is the case that performance in one of the three primary categories of motion assessment (posture, progression, or pacing) [19] is significantly different than the others, and only the elements of gameplay mapped to that category require adjustment. Recently derived requirements from the elderly population for the design of exergames reflect these concerns, prompting the need for a more flexible adaptation strategy [20].

Studies of adaptation in exergames for the elderly have favored more individually driven and motion-centric design of gameplay. Velazquez et al. [21], for instance, used an action research study to derive several recommendations for the implementation of adaptation within exergames supporting the elderly. Among these is the need to accurately and seamlessly classify motion capabilities of the player concurrently within gameplay. For this classification to relate directly to game performance, it follows that gameplay outcomes should serve as verifiable outcomes for performance results at the motion task. Without this relationship, the claim that adaptation of exergame elements and game mechanics leads to suitable motor learning, and thus improved health outcomes, cannot be easily verified.

Hence, the design of exergames should center itself around the characteristics which serve as evidence for exercise performance, and the physical and temporal characteristics of these mechanics can be mapped directly to the corresponding characteristics of physical performance such that in order to improve their proficiency, users can rely directly on game mechanics, rather than focusing on their own body movements, to guide them [22, 23]. This principle of the application of Evidence-Centered Design [24] toward "stealth" assessment forms the foundation for the "stealth assessment" concept in educational serious games proposed by Shute et al. [25] and is applied in this framework toward adaptive exergames for the elderly.

3 The Stealth-Adaptive Exergame Design (SAED) Framework

3.1 Overview

The Stealth-Adaptive Exergame Design (SAED) Framework, as shown in Fig. 1, is a novel framework for exergame selection and AI design which utilizes Evidence-Centered Design and Stealth Assessment principles [26] to facilitate individually focused machine learning and assessment of motion task performance. In this framework, a specific individual, trainer requirements (when applicable), and motion task properties are utilized as filters to select the best-matching game concept on a case-by-case basis.

Once the exergame implementation is selected, an evidence mapping approach similar to [26] is adopted to map the spatial and temporal attributes of a motor task repetition to a repeating gameplay element, including a relationship between positive and negative task performance and in-game outcomes. Finally, an instrument for performance assessment is chosen from expert standards and a model for AI-based learning is chosen based on the relationships between the chosen assessment instrument and the exercise task properties. This model is used to adapt the game to the player's performance by directly modifying game objectives at a chosen interval and tolerance range for error, resulting in seamless *stealth* adaptation.

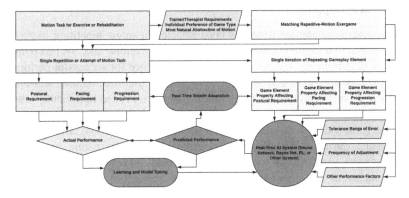

Fig. 1. Overview of the stealth-adaptive exergame design framework.

3.2   Exergame Selection

The first task posed by the SAED framework is the selection of an appropriate exergame by beginning with the motion task. This motion task is provided by a therapist, trainer or physician, and is often tuned to the needs, capabilities and limitations of an individual; however, some common properties exist among rehabilitative or health-improving exercises. Generally, these exercises can be decomposed into three characteristics [19]: *posture*, which represents the requirements of the subject's body configuration while performing the exercise, *pacing*, which represents the rhythm and rate of motion requirements, and *progression*, which represents the degree or precision of motion required to successfully complete the exercise. Furthermore, the exercises themselves are typically repetitive and rhythmic in nature, with each attempt comprising one *repetition* of the task and multiple repetitions forming a *set*.

As discussed in Sect. 2.1, not all game concepts are effective as choices of abstraction for these exercises. When considering the above requirement, the chosen exergame implementation must utilize an interactive game element which is comprised of a uniformly repeating task (for example, a racing track being comprised of a series of turns or curves), with continuously adjustable parameters, and clear, immediate evidence for performance [27]. The game task must also match the motion task in complexity by sharing similar spatial characteristics (posture, progression) and temporal characteristics (pacing) for adaptation to be effective.

In alignment with the requirements of person-centered design, and in respect of the interpersonal and intrapersonal variation within the population, the chosen game objective must match any additional requirements or constraints placed by the trainer or therapist involved in assigning the motion task (such as the use or lack of exercise equipment, and duration of a single session), should respect preferences of the individual toward certain game contexts or subject matter, and should choose a game task which serves as the most natural abstraction for the motion task under assignment. It would be difficult, for example, to associate the game task of flipping a coin to a knee flexion/extension task as input, as coins are typically flipped using the hand.

3.3 Evidence Mapping

Once an exergame implementation has been selected, a single repetition of the game task corresponds to a single attempt or repetition of the exercise task. At this point, it is necessary to determine the factors which serve as evidence for successful performance of this game task and relate one such factor to each of the three requirement domains for performance of the motor task. This task is greatly alleviated in difficulty when the game context is a natural abstraction of the motion task as previously stated. For posture, the game's design should consider what consequences could arise from poor or proper posture during completion of the game task. In the racing track example mentioned earlier, poor posture when driving a vehicle can result in a loss of control at critical moments, as one illustrative example.

Once factors for evidence of game performance are mapped with related factors of exercise performance, a dependency relationship is created wherein the degree of success or failure in each of these mechanics of gameplay is also directly related to the degree of success or failure in performance of a particular attribute. This mapping allows the player to focus entirely on learning how to play the game as effectively as possible, since doing so requires improvement in performance at the motor task. The distinction between these three characteristics of exercise task performance also allows performance in each attribute to be distinguished from the others during gameplay, allowing an individual to learn which areas require improvement more effectively. This matches the type of guidance provided in rehabilitation or exercise with trainers, who utilize their observation and expert knowledge of the individual to give targeted advice for improvement. If the individual's posture is correct, but the pacing is slow, a trainer can point out this distinction so that the individual knows to maintain posture while modifying pacing. Evidence mapping allows an exergame to intuitively embed this guidance into gameplay outcomes, allowing for more effective self-assessment with an external focus [22].

3.4 Stealth Adaptation Using AI

Finally, requirements for the degree of error allowed in each parameter or motion (also referred to as "tolerance range of error"), frequency of adaptation, and other factors such as physiological or affective data, are combined with the real-time performance measures of gameplay as features into the AI component, which can then learn to accurately relate them to motion performance for a specific individual over time using either standard performance measures or trainer-specific measures. This results in real-time adaptation that is argued to more closely reflect the individually variant nature of individuals within the elderly population, as well as the exercise programs and rehabilitative programs most relevant to each.

To achieve this type of adaptation, it is first necessary to select an appropriate metric for performance assessment. Generally, experts such as therapists, trainers, physicians or medical associations provide the instruments of assessment that relate performance at a particular task to predicted health outcomes or functional ability. A range of standard metrics exist for motor function assessment in rehabilitation, for example, such as the Wolf Motor Function Test [28], Barthel Index [29], Fugl-Meyer Assessment [30], and others. However, it is often the case that customized or trainer-specific instruments of assessment are adopted for a particular exercise program. It may also be the case that the relationship between the task performance characteristics and health outcome assessments is not entirely known, in which case it is also possible to learn and characterize automatically using AI. The selected performance assessment metric is used as a calibration or pre-assessment tool to characterize the "actual performance" of the subject in practice (this, of course, can also be provided directly by a trainer or therapist who performs the assessment with the individual externally). This is then used as training data for the AI model to "learn" about the subject by identifying the errors in its prediction of the subject's performance.

Once the metric of assessment is in place, the appropriate learning model can then be selected. The model should account not only for the assessment method and the relationship between that method and the performance parameters of the task, but also for the range of error tolerance for performance of the task, as well as the frequency of adaptation or learning and any other factors present in the implementation, such as the processing power of the exergame platform. When implemented, the model learns about the subject by using the assessment instrument and motion characteristics to predict performance, determining where performance is above or below expectation, and then referring to the mapping to determine what gameplay parameters need to be adjusted to reduce or increase difficulty, and to what degree they should be adjusted based on the severity of error.

4   SAED Case Examples

To illustrate the utilization of the SAED framework, two cases of its implementation are presented in this work. Following the procedure outlined in the framework, each implementation begins by identifying a motion task for improvement of health outcomes, followed by the selection of an exergame implementation accounting for both the task and other influencing factors of the individual, trainer or population. The decomposition of each task into their postural, progression and pacing components is performed, and then evidence mapping with corresponding game mechanics is determined. Finally, instruments for assessment in each case are used to select a learning model for real-time stealth adaptation, and the characteristics of this adaptation are discussed.

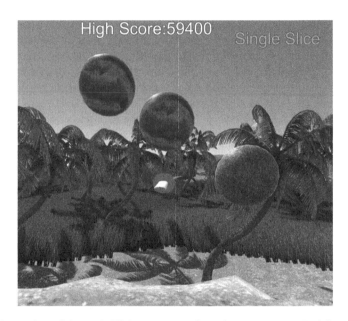

Fig. 2. Screenshot of the Fruit Slicing exergame from the Autonomous Training Assistant.

4.1   The Autonomous Training Assistant: Fruit Slicing Exergame

The first case of SAED implementation is a fruit slicing exergame from [31], shown in Fig. 2. In this case, the role of the exergame was to autonomously monitor, assess and improve function of the paretic arm in a hemiparetic individual whose trainer's reha-bilitative exercise program involved the use of martial arts stick techniques. The assigned motion task by the trainer was an arc swing motion of the stick. The exergame environment for this program, entitled the *Autonomous Training Assistant*, included a customized training stick device (the *Intelligent Stick*) equipped with motion sensing and haptic feedback capabilities, a Kinect depth camera for subject body and joint tracking and the exergame interface played on a television screen at the subject's home (without presence of the trainer). The subject was assigned to swing this device in a horizontal arc at a specific pace while holding it with both hands, in such a way that the functioning arm guided the paretic arm during motion.

The design process for the exergame is detailed in Fig. 3. The trainer's recom-mendation that the subject swing at targets with a sword or stick-like object in gameplay, along with the individual's interest in fruit slicing games such as the commercially-available Fruit Ninja by Halfbrick Studios [32] resulted in the selection of a game task wherein the subject must slice fruit objects along a horizontal path as they fall from the sky. These fruit objects fall together repeatedly in groups; a single repetition of the swing motion thus results in a single swing of the sword at a group of fruit, the objective being to slice as many of the fruit in a single swing as possible.

Postural characteristics of the motion required that both arms should remain on the stick when swinging. This was directly mapped to the requirement that the subject hold the virtual sword with both hands to swing it properly. If the paretic arm loses contact with the stick, the control of the sword is lost and it cannot be swung. The difficulty of this parameter related to the percentage of time during a swing that two-handed contact was maintained.

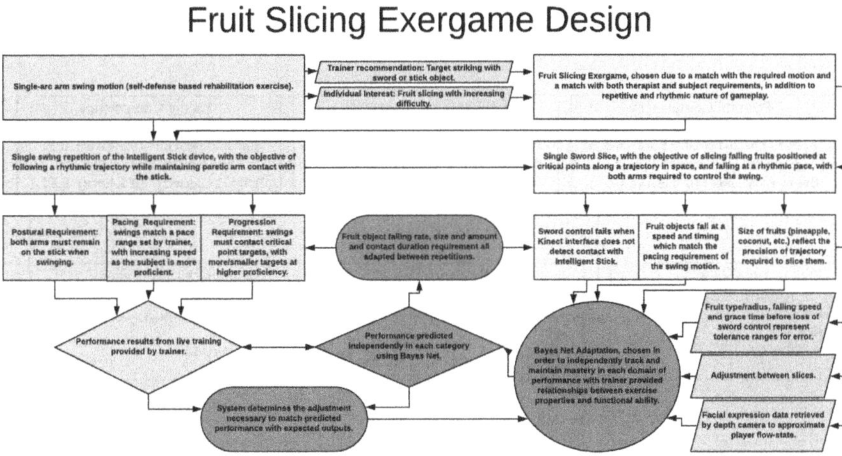

Fruit Slicing Exergame Design

Fig. 3. SAED framework applied in the design of the Fruit Slicing exergame.

Pacing requirements included that the subject must match a specific pace of motion determined by the trainer and adjusted on a regular basis. Since the objective is to slice all of the falling fruit objects, their speed of motion directly corresponds to this pacing requirement. The more rapidly the fruit fall, the less tolerance for error when attempting to slice them, and the faster the motion required to slice all of the fruit in one group.

To maintain optimum progression, the trainer recommended that the subject contact critical points along an arc trajectory when swinging the stick. In the exergame implementation, the fruit objects were selected as the mechanic which represents the critical point concept. In other words, the timing of the fruit's descent is configured in such a way that the subject must contact each object at various points along a horizontal arc trajectory to slice them. Furthermore, the size of the fruit or type of fruit represent the difficulty or tolerance for error in progression, with smaller fruit requiring more precise trajectories.

Having performed the evidence mapping required to directly relate game performance to task performance, the instrument for assessment was then chosen. In this case, the trainer did not utilize a single, combined "mastery" score or assessment but instead assessed each category independently by observation during in-person training sessions with the subject. Thus, the trainer recorded a "correct" template for execution of the motion, and the critical points of this template along with its pacing and postural details were used as the basis for evaluating the subject's task performance. As the three categories needed to be assessed independently, and the relationship between exercise parameters and successful health outcomes was already known and provided by the trainer, a Bayes Net implementation, as illustrated in Fig. 4, was used to learn about the individual and adapt the game difficulty parameters. When the error in a particular category was above a certain trainer-provided-and-adjusted threshold, the gameplay mechanics mapped to that category were automatically adjusted in real-time. The system learned by being supplied information about actual performance in relation to its predictions by regularly provided training session data from the subject and trainer.

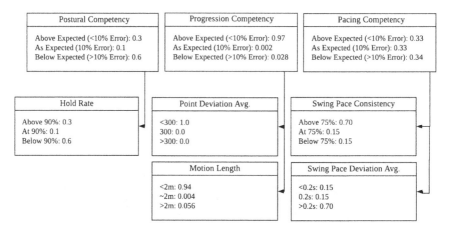

Fig. 4. Bayes Net diagram guiding real-time stealth adaptation of the Fruit Slicing exergame.

The system begins by assuming equal probability that the subject is below, above, and at expectation for performance in each category. For example, it assumes in the case of posture that the subject is equally likely to hold the stick device with both hands for 90%, greater than 90%, and less than 90% of the swing's duration, until data on each swing attempt is used to update the model. As these probabilistic predictions are maintained independently for the three categories, the system makes a decision between each swing attempt (or slice) to adjust difficulty separately for the game mechanics relating to each category. If postural performance is above expectation but pacing and progression are less than predicted, the subsequent slice attempt will require a longer period of time holding the stick with both hands, while using larger fruit that fall more slowly to allow for greater deviations in the motion's pace and trajectory. Facial expression data was used to estimate the subject's emotional response to gameplay, for the system to self-evaluate based on how long the subject maintained the state of optimal engagement, or flow state [31].

4.2   Ski Exergame

The second case of SAED implementation is a ski squat exergame [33] as shown in Fig. 5. This implementation was designed for elderly users to maintain healthy locomotion, mobility, and consequently, improved healthy lifespan by regularly performing the two-leg standing squat in an interactive virtual environment. In this case, the Japanese Orthopaedic Association (JOA) was selected as the expert source for assessment of health outcomes, as they have published extensive work on the characteristics and prevention of Locomotive Syndrome [34]. The exergame environment consists of a RealSense depth camera for tracking motion, and a virtual reality interface for presentation of the ski exergame. In future work, this implementation will be converted to a non-VR format in consideration of the safety of elderly subjects when playing.

Fig. 5. Screenshot of the Ski Squat exergame.

The SAED design process for the ski squat exergame is shown in Fig. 6. The squat motion was selected due to its popularity in Japan as a daily exercise to improve lower extremity strength and balance and to prevent locomotive degeneration. Furthermore, popularity of skiing in Japan and the natural fit of the Ski squat motion, a standard exercise to improve skiing performance, provided the means to select a skiing game which utilizes squats as an obstacle avoidance strategy. In this case, the player is asked to ski through a straight course wherein no turns are required (or they are performed automatically without player intervention). A series of gates appear which can only be cleared by squatting down below a certain height, where each gate along the course requires a single squat motion. The requirements for the postural, progression and pacing aspects of the motion were derived in consultation with an expert health/sports science researcher.

Postural requirements included that the subject maintain stability during the squat (that is, the knees remain firm with as little shakiness as possible) and that the subject's center of mass (CoM) moves in a consistent and smooth motion. Within the exergame implementation, these are naturally fit to the requirement that the subject maintain an average horizontal knee deviation and CoM deviation less than a certain (adjustable) threshold to maintain control during the ski task. The spacing between gates represents this requirement within gameplay.

Pacing of the squat task was simply represented as the number of squats expected over a fixed time interval (such as 30 s or one minute). This time interval was used to determine the length of the ski course, and the number of gates generated in the course represented the number of expected squats to perform. The higher the number of gates over the same length of course, and the shorter the spacing between these gates, the more rapidly the subject is expected to squat to clear all of them.

Progression in this case related to the degree of bending performed during the squat task. A more difficult squat requires the subject to move lower (up to a limit for safe squat completion, beyond which the exercise is considered harmful). This relates directly to the height of each gate obstacle, the lower the gate, the lower the subject is required to squat to clear it when passing through. While an error in progression would normally be considered as a collision with a gate, this collision is not represented realistically in gameplay, as it would be disruptive to the steady pacing requirement of the game. Instead, the subject simply receives points for gates that are successfully cleared, and no points when colliding with a gate obstacle, which the subject simply passes through.

Ski Squat Exergame Design

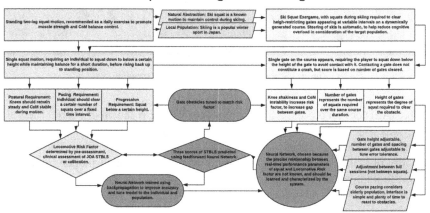

Fig. 6. SAED framework applied in the design of the Ski Squat exergame.

The JOA has derived a standard assessment strategy for determining locomotive risk in elderly subjects, entitled the short test battery for locomotive syndrome (STBLS) [35]. It consists of three assessments: one in which the subject stands up from a seated position at various heights and receives a score based on the lowest height from which he or she could stand without losing balance (sit-stand test), another in which the subject takes two strides as far as possible without falling, and measures the length of the two strides normalized by his or her height (two-stride test), and a third assessment in which the subject answers 25 questions about pain or difficulty with mobility over a time period (25-question assessment). These three tests result in three scores for a subject, which are then combined into a single locomotive risk score (0, 1 or 2) using clinical decision boundaries derived by the JOA and presented in [35]. However, the exact relationship between the above attributes of squat performance and performance in the STBLS is unknown, and needs to be characterized over time by the learning model.

As such, a neural network was deemed appropriate in this case, as it could learn the association between squat input parameters and STBLS scores through training and backpropagation. The structure of this network is shown in Fig. 7. It is initially configured through a set of training data to perform moderately accurate estimations for individuals within the target population (pre-training). The structure of the network is then tuned in real-time according to the error generated between the network's output and the actual STBLS performance of the subject in a pre-assessment. The difficulty of the game is adjusted on a course-by-course basis using the risk value generated by this network as a combination of its outputs.

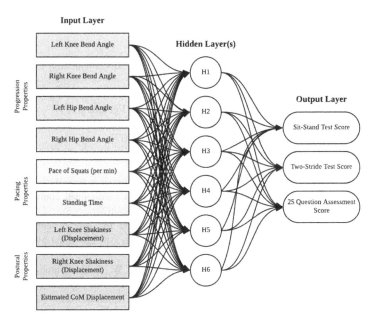

Fig. 7. Diagram of feedforward Neural Network for stealth adaptation in the Ski Squat exergame.

5 Conclusions and Future Work

Initial prototypes of the above case examples in [18] and [33] indicated high accuracy of adaptive capabilities as expressed by real exercise performance and subjective feedback. Quite importantly, these results serve as validation of the effectiveness of adaptation in each case as it relates to physical performance. The Autonomous Training Assistant was adopted for long-term use by the subject and trainer as well, further validating the approach. This serves as a proof of concept that the SAED framework can facilitative effective and verifiable adaptive exergame design centered in evidence and standards of performance and health outcome assessment. Future work should further validate the generalizability of the SAED approach by include game outcome evaluations across a variety of cases and validation through comparison with health outcome measures. One particularly useful effort would be the creation of an exergame concept matching table which provides the most naturally fitting exergame implementation strategies and context across the gamut of rehabilitative motions, individual capabilities and interests.

Acknowledgment. This paper is based partially on results obtained from a project of Development of Core Technologies for Next-Generation AI and Robotics, commissioned by the New Energy and Industrial Technology Development Organization (NEDO), Japan, and partially on results obtained from a project supported by the National Science Foundation under Grant No. 1069125.

References

1. United Nations, Department of Economic and Social Affairs, Population Division: World population ageing, 2019 highlights (2020)
2. Muramatsu, N., Akiyama, H.: Japan: super-aging society preparing for the future. Gerontologist **51**, 425–432 (2011). https://doi.org/10.1093/geront/gnr067
3. Khan, H.T.A.: Population ageing in a globalized world: risks and dilemmas? J. Eval. Clin. Pract. **25**, 754–760 (2019). https://doi.org/10.1111/jep.13071
4. Zheng, L., et al.: Effect of exergames on physical outcomes in frail elderly: a systematic review. Aging Clin. Exp. Res., 1–14 (2019)
5. Liao, Y.-Y., Chen, I.-H., Wang, R.-Y.: Effects of Kinect-based exergaming on frailty status and physical performance in prefrail and frail elderly: a randomized controlled trial. Sci Rep. **9**, 1–9 (2019). https://doi.org/10.1038/s41598-019-45767-y
6. Huang, H.-C., et al.: A randomized controlled trial on the role of enthusiasm about exergames: players' perceptions of exercise. Games Health J. **8**, 220–226 (2018). https://doi.org/10.1089/g4h.2018.0057
7. Garcia, J.A., Sundara, N., Tabor, G., Gay, V.C., Leong, T.W.: Solitaire fitness: design of an asynchronous exergame for the elderly to enhance cognitive and physical ability. In: 2019 IEEE 7th International Conference on Serious Games and Applications for Health (SeGAH), pp. 1–6. IEEE (2019)
8. Gerling, K.M., Schild, J., Masuch, M.: Exergame design for elderly users: the case study of SilverBalance. In: Proceedings of the 7th International Conference on Advances in Computer Entertainment Technology, pp. 66–69. ACM (2010)
9. Rusu, L., Mocanu, I., Jecan, S., Sitar, D.: Monitoring adaptive exergame for seniors. J. Inf. Syst. Oper. Manag., 336 (2016)
10. Panchanathan, S., Chakraborty, S., McDaniel, T., Tadayon, R.: Person-centered multimedia computing: a new paradigm inspired by assistive and rehabilitative applications. IEEE Multimedia **23**, 12–19 (2016). https://doi.org/10.1109/MMUL.2016.51
11. Paliyawan, P., Kusano, T., Nakagawa, Y., Harada, T., Thawonmas, R.: Adaptive motion gaming AI for health promotion. In: 2017 AAAI Spring Symposium Series (2017)
12. Zhang, H., Miao, C., Yu, H.: Fuzzy logic based assessment on the adaptive level of rehabilitation exergames for the elderly. In: 2017 IEEE Global Conference on Signal and Information Processing (GlobalSIP), pp. 423–427 (2017). https://doi.org/10.1109/GlobalSIP.2017.8308677
13. Zhang, H., Miao, C., Wu, Q., Tao, X., Shen, Z.: The effect of familiarity on older adults' engagement in exergames. In: Zhou, J., Salvendy, G. (eds.) HCII 2019. LNCS, vol. 11593, pp. 277–288. Springer, Cham (2019). https://doi.org/10.1007/978-3-030-22015-0_22

14. Sinclair, J., Hingston, P., Masek, M.: Considerations for the design of exergames. In: Proceedings of the 5th International Conference on Computer Graphics and Interactive Techniques in Australia and Southeast Asia - GRAPHITE 2007, Perth, Australia, p. 289. ACM Press (2007). https://doi.org/10.1145/1321261.1321313
15. Daley, M.J., Spinks, W.L.: Exercise, mobility and aging. Sports Med. **29**, 1–12 (2000). https://doi.org/10.2165/00007256-200029010-00001
16. Cacciata, M., et al.: Effect of exergaming on health-related quality of life in older adults: a systematic review. Int. J. Nurs. Stud. **93**, 30–40 (2019). https://doi.org/10.1016/j.ijnurstu.2019.01.010
17. Paulino, T., Muñoz, J., Bermudez, S., Cameirão, M.S.: Design of an integrative system for configurable exergames targeting the senior population. In: Ahram, T., Karwowski, W., Taiar, R. (eds.) IHSED 2018. AISC, vol. 876, pp. 287–292. Springer, Cham (2019). https://doi.org/10.1007/978-3-030-02053-8_44
18. Tadayon, R.: A person-centric design framework for at-home motor learning in serious games (2017)
19. Tadayon, R., et al.: Interactive motor learning with the autonomous training assistant: a case study. In: Kurosu, M. (ed.) HCI 2015. LNCS, vol. 9170, pp. 495–506. Springer, Cham (2015). https://doi.org/10.1007/978-3-319-20916-6_46
20. Muñoz, J.E., Gonçalves, A., Rúbio Gouveia, É., Cameirão, M.S., Bermúdez i Badia, S.: Lessons learned from gamifying functional fitness training through human-centered design methods in older adults. Games Health J. **8**, 387–406 (2019). https://doi.org/10.1089/g4h.2018.0028
21. Velazquez, A., Martínez-García, A.I., Favela, J., Ochoa, S.F.: Adaptive exergames to support active aging: an action research study. Pervasive Mob. Comput. **34**, 60–78 (2017). https://doi.org/10.1016/j.pmcj.2016.09.002
22. Wulf, G., Höß, M., Prinz, W.: Instructions for motor learning: differential effects of internal versus external focus of attention. J. Mot. Behav. **30**, 169–179 (1998). https://doi.org/10.1080/00222899809601334
23. Wulf, G., Shea, C., Lewthwaite, R.: Motor skill learning and performance: a review of influential factors. Med. Educ. **44**, 75–84 (2010). https://doi.org/10.1111/j.1365-2923.2009.03421.x
24. Mislevy, R.J., Almond, R.G., Lukas, J.F.: A brief introduction to evidence-centered design. ETS Res. Rep. Ser. **2003**, i–29 (2003)
25. Shute, V.J.: Stealth assessment in computer-based games to support learning. Comput. Games Instr. **55**, 503–524 (2011)
26. Shute, V.J., Wang, L., Greiff, S., Zhao, W., Moore, G.: Measuring problem solving skills via stealth assessment in an engaging video game. Comput. Hum. Behav. **63**, 106–117 (2016)
27. Richards, C., Graham, T.C.N.: Developing compelling repetitive-motion exergames by balancing player agency with the constraints of exercise. In: Proceedings of the 2016 ACM Conference on Designing Interactive Systems, Brisbane, QLD, Australia, pp. 911–923. Association for Computing Machinery (2016). https://doi.org/10.1145/2901790.2901824
28. Wolf, S.L., Catlin, P.A., Ellis, M., Archer, A.L., Morgan, B., Piacentino, A.: Assessing wolf motor function test as outcome measure for research in patients after stroke. Stroke **32**, 1635–1639 (2001). https://doi.org/10.1161/01.STR.32.7.1635
29. Mahoney, F.I.: Functional evaluation: the barthel index. Md. State Med. J. **14**, 61–65 (1965)
30. Fugl-Meyer, A.R., Jääskö, L., Leyman, I., Olsson, S., Steglind, S.: The post-stroke hemiplegic patient. 1. A method for evaluation of physical performance. Scand. J. Rehabil. Med. **7**, 13–31 (1974)

31. Tadayon, R., Amresh, A., McDaniel, T., Panchanathan, S.: Real-time stealth intervention for motor learning using player flow-state. In: 2018 IEEE 6th International Conference on Serious Games and Applications for Health (SeGAH), pp. 1–8 (2018). https://doi.org/10.1109/SeGAH.2018.8401360
32. Fruit Ninja: Halfbrick Studios. https://fruitninja.com/
33. Tadayon, R., Vega Ramirez, A., Das, S., Kishishita, Y., Yamamoto, M., Kurita, Y.: Automatic Exercise Assistance For The Elderly Using Real-Time Adaptation To Performance And Affect. In: Antona, M., Stephanidis, C. (eds.) HCII 2019. LNCS, vol. 11573, pp. 556–574. Springer, Cham (2019). https://doi.org/10.1007/978-3-030-23563-5_44
34. Nakamura, K.: A "super-aged" society and the "locomotive syndrome". J. Orthop. Sci. **13**, 1–2 (2008). https://doi.org/10.1007/s00776-007-1202-6
35. Ishibashi, H.: Locomotive syndrome in Japan. Osteoporos. Sarcopenia **4**, 86–94 (2018)

Aging in Place

Hermes: A Digital Assistant for Coordinating Invisible Work in Family Elderly Caregiving Scenarios

Andrea Benavides, Francisco J. Gutierrez$^{(\boxtimes)}$, and Sergio F. Ochoa

Department of Computer Science, University of Chile,
Beauchef 851, West Building, 3rd Floor, Santiago, Chile
{abenavid, frgutier, sochoa}@dcc.uchile.cl

Abstract. Family elderly caregiving is one of the preferred approaches for sustaining aging in place. While elderly people usually advocate for such an aging paradigm, supporting it represents an important challenge for family members, particularly in terms of coordination, resource allocation, and articulation of caregiving tasks. This paper presents Hermes, a digital assistant designed to help family caregiving stakeholders deal with the underlying challenges of such a process. Although the system is still at the prototype stage, its usability and perceived usefulness were evaluated with a sample of the target population. The obtained results are highly promising, showing that this challenge can effectively be addressed using technology, as well as generating a potential positive impact on informal family caregivers and older adults.

Keywords: Aging in place · Informal caregiving · Chatbot · Domestic technology

1 Introduction

Aging in place, i.e., encouraging people to live in their homes for as long as possible, is nowadays the preferred option of living for older adults and public services. However, this requires that the elderly become self-sufficient in a large number of daily activities, either independently or with the support of formal or informal caregivers. In most societies, informal care provision is supported partially or fully by members of the older adult's family network, who usually struggle addressing their own professional and personal lives, as well as those of their own families. These informal caregivers contribute with time or resources to help mitigate the needs of their older adults.

In order to support an effective aging in place schema, a collective effort sustained by the involvement of a considerable part of the family network is required. Therefore, informal elderly caregiving is a process that becomes unpredictable in terms of response time, given that assistance and active involvement both depend on the cooperative, voluntary, and articulated action of family members [3]. In that respect, the informal care experience at home needs to address several factors, such as effectively managing the expertise of caregivers, dealing with feelings of social isolation among older adults, and caregiver burden [9].

© Springer Nature Switzerland AG 2020
Q. Gao and J. Zhou (Eds.): HCII 2020, LNCS 12208, pp. 437–450, 2020.
https://doi.org/10.1007/978-3-030-50249-2_31

Given the distributed and interdependent role of family members when fulfilling caregiving tasks, a major challenge that emerges is articulating the distributed collective effort within the network. In particular, this means understanding how to coordinate the actions of family members and allocate resources to improve the efficiency and effectiveness of the process. Building upon the discourse proposed by Star and Strauss on the ecology of visible and invisible work [10], there are confronting visions regarding the informal care provision to their older adults in family networks. In that respect, informal caregivers usually feel overwhelmed and burdened by fulfilling their tasks, which seem to be invisible to other members in the family network [4]. However, the coordination, resource allocation, and articulation of these tasks are all crucial endeavors to sustain the effectiveness of the family elderly caregiving process.

Previous research works have shown that technology-mediated collaboration can help address invisible work in family elderly caregiving scenarios. However, most initiatives have been focused on supporting the needs of the elderly or their caregivers but have not addressed the caregiving process as a holistic system that involves at least these two types of participants. Trying to address such a process in a holistic way, this article proposes a digital assistant named Hermes that helps coordinate the invisible work conducted in family elderly caregiving scenarios. This assistant is autonomous, but it uses as input the information of the caregiving activities that is added by the users (mainly family members) through a mobile application.

Next section presents and discusses the related work. Section 3 presents the architecture of the proposed system and introduces its main components. Sections 4 and 5 describe the system front-end and back-end respectively. Section 6 explains the usability and usefulness evaluations performed to the system and the obtained results. Finally, Sect. 7 presents the conclusions and provides perspectives on future work.

2 Related Work

In HCI literature, the social nuances of caregiving work have not been deeply considered [1]. In particular, the work of family caregivers is typically invisible [2, 4] and lacks formal support [9].

Family caregiving is considered an unstructured (or unframed) process, given that it does not have a predefined workflow that can be specified at the process design time. Instead, only the participants and the potential interactions among them can be specified and supported with technology. In this scenario, the coordination activities are triggered on-demand by the participants, considering their own work context and needs. Therefore, counting on a centralized component, able to successfully coordinate the caregiving activities, is low feasible in practice given the heterogeneity and dynamism of the work context of the participants. In that case, coordination should be promoted through the use of awareness and persuasion mechanisms implemented by distributed as well as centralized components.

Currently, the cooperative foundations of care provision and assistance to older adults is sustained through the involvement of a considerable part of the family network. In that respect, due to the distributed and interdependent role of family members when fulfilling caregiving tasks, a major challenge that emerges is articulating the distributed collective effort within the network [7]. In other words, any socio-technical system aiming to support this application domain needs to sustain the coordination of family members and the allocation of resources to improve the efficiency of the process. According to Star and Strauss [10], family elderly caregiving corresponds to a particular example of invisible work, where duties—and consequent burden—are mainly assumed by one of the adult children in the family the work [6].

Ensuring the assumption of family caregiving roles requires articulating the collective distributed effort of family members. However, this can turn out to be demanding due to the complex and dynamic arrangement of the family network with regard to this process. Indeed, promoting articulation work is more an expectation rather than an established practice in family contexts, where improvisation and individualism are often sources of tension and conflict [4].

According to Schmidt and Simone [7], the articulation of the distributed activities that are part of a cooperative work requires appropriate mechanisms of communication and coordination among the involved participants. Likewise, classical approaches of CSCW design suggest that using common information spaces, such as shared views or board systems [7, 8] could contribute to make visible these aspects of the caregiving process.

Therefore, one plausible alternative to assist older adults into embracing caregiving technology is to design meaningful experiences that do not limit physical exchanges [5]. In addition, respecting the existing routines and expectations of the different involved stakeholders is required, not only for facilitating the technology adoption and promoting effective and meaningful exchanges, but also to try aligning the implicit and explicit asymmetries existing across generations [4].

3   Structural Design of the System

In order to help family members coordinate their caregiving actions and be aware of the activities conducted by others, this section presents Hermes, an autonomous digital assistant that helps reduce the load and tension generated by the assignment and coordination of caregiving duties. This assistant acts as an intermediary that provides awareness to the participants and tries to persuade people to coordinate their activities and help address the needs of older adults.

The system considers the following four user profiles, which were identified based on the roles structure proposed in [4]:

- *Older adult:* This is an elderly person who is the target of the caregiving actions. The participation of the older adult as a user is not mandatory. However, if he/she does, this user can interact with the digital assistant in several ways as well as receiving feedback and notifications.
- *Assistant (or caregiver):* These are people that perform direct activities in favor of the elderly as part of the caregiving process. Typically, they are the children of the older adult that need to coordinate their activities with other caregivers. These users have access to all services provided by the system.

- *Helper:* Users playing this role perform occasional activities in favor of the older adults; for instance, when a caregiver or the older adult asks them for help. Helpers interact with the digital assistant through WhatsApp text messages. A caregiver can propose to assign a specific activity to a helper through the regular task assignment process. Examples of helpers are neighbors and friends of the elderly being cared for, as well as relatives that are not part of the close caregiving network.
- *Health professional:* These users correspond to physicians, nurses, or other medical personnel that are involved in monitoring the health condition of the older adults being cared for, and eventually treat them. If they agree, these users can be contacted by the assistants, in case of need; e.g., about health checkpoints of the older adults being monitored by them.

Figure 1 shows the participation of these user roles and illustrates the structure of the system including its main components. The system considers a front-end application that allows users to interact with the services, and a back-end that provides those services. Typically, the older adults and caregivers use, as front-end, a mobile application specifically designed to interact with the task manager and the chatbot, both providing most of the services offered by the system. The users playing the role of helper and health professional use WhatsApp to interact with other roles and also to receive notifications, invitations, and awareness information sent by the chatbot. The decision of using WhatsApp by these roles was made to ease their participation; i.e., to lower the entry barriers to participate in this caregiving ecosystem. Thus, they do not need to install any extra application in their mobile phones, except WhatsApp.

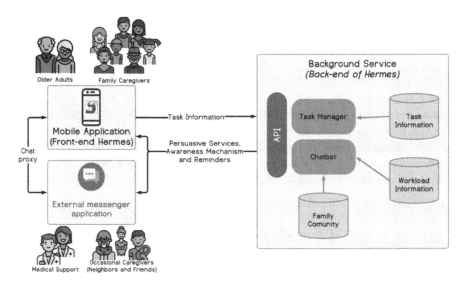

Fig. 1. Structure of the Hermes system.

The main end-users are the family caregivers, who usually add and update tasks into the system (e.g., to make a medical appointment, or buy groceries for the elderlies). They are also the target of the most interactions triggered by the chatbot, e.g., to coordinate tasks or try to get a commitment on those that are pending. The older adults can also use the application, mainly to be aware of the status of the caregiving tasks. As shown in Fig. 1, these users interact with the system through the mobile application that represents the front-end of Hermes. This application allows to create chat groups, without the presence of the virtual assistant.

As mentioned before, the main functionality provided by the back-end involves the task manager and a chatbot. The former manages three types of tasks (or activities) that are scheduled and updated by the users or the chatbot. The latter is mainly in charge to provide awareness about these tasks and reminders to the users in charge of performing them. Next sections explain in more detail the front-end and back-end of the system.

4   Mobile Application

This application manages tasks, contacts, and conversations (chats). The services related to tasks are one of three types: recording medical appointments, where a caregiver has to accompany the older adult to some place; recording a general task that caregivers can perform whenever they need; and recording reminders that help caregivers address periodical activities in favor of the older adults.

Once a task is created, the system runs an "assignment cycle" splitting the caregivers in three priority groups. It then asks each group whether a family member can take the task, until someone does. Then, the task creator is notified about the assignment. On the day of the scheduled event, the virtual assistant sends a task reminder to the user in charge. Once the task is completed, the system will ask for feedback, record it for future events, and post a notification to the Notice panel.

The users can chat with the virtual assistant to ask about the state and history of different tasks, as well as browse the history records as a way to be informed without asking another person. This application also has the feature of adding medical support as another contact, e.g., to perform quick questions or notify emergency situations. In order to do that, the health professional just has to add Hermes (for a specific older adult) as a contact in their personal WhatsApp account. Next sections present a summary of the user interfaces provided by the mobile application to manage tasks and contacts.

4.1   Task Management Front-End

The mobile application has few users interfaces in order to make the user interaction simple and easy. After launching the application, and once the user is logged in, the system shows a main menu with a list of dialogs (or chat rooms) available for that user (Fig. 2 center). This interface contains a message panel, the dialog with the virtual assistant Hermes, and a list of private and group chat rooms.

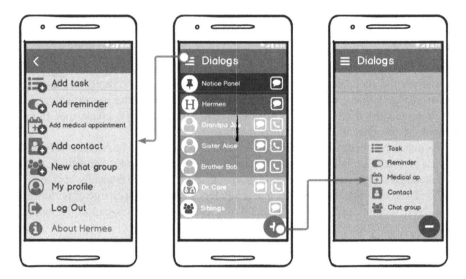

Fig. 2. Sample of the user interfaces of Hermes.

Clicking on the 'message panel', the users can read messages about the coordination process and result of the tasks. The Hermes's chat is the only service that can be utilized by the user to interact with the virtual assistant (i.e., the chatbot). Private chats are 1-to-1 dialogs with other members of the caregiving group and they are sorted by user types starting with older adults, assistants, helpers, and professionals who support the group.

In this first interface the users can make phone calls, if enabled, or directly log into the chatroom. Users can go to the Menu view (Fig. 2 left) or tap a shortcut (Fig. 2 right) for adding elements. These options allow the users to add new contacts, chat groups, or tasks. By tapping onto either of 'Add task', 'Add reminder' or 'Add medical appointment' options, the virtual assistant launches an interactive dialog with the user about creating the selected task type. The 'Add chat group' option shows a list with other family assistants, where the user has the option to create new many-to-many dialogs.

4.2   Contact Management Front-End

Adding a new contact prompts users to the interfaces shown in Fig. 3, where they need to choose the role to be played by the new user. These roles can be older adult (who will receive care), assistant (main responsible for the caregiving activities), helper (who occasionally perform activities in favor of the older adults), or medical support (health professionals). If the new user is an older adult or a helper, such a user needs to fill a data form with their name, phone number, and email. An assistant, helper, or professional contact needs to have an older adult to care for and will receive an email invitation to participate in the caregiving group. The helpers and health professional need to add a contact to their WhatsApp application to accept the invitation. Conversely, an assistant contact has to install the mobile application of Hermes and register him/herself with a family code sent in a personalized invitation.

Fig. 3. User interfaces of Hermes to add contacts.

From the main menu (Fig. 2a), the user can reach "My profile" and "Log Out". In the first option, users can manage their profile data and preferences, quit the caregiving group, deactivate location sharing, or set their absences, i.e., the days when they cannot take any task, except if it is urgent. Figure 4 summarizes the navigation map of the mobile application.

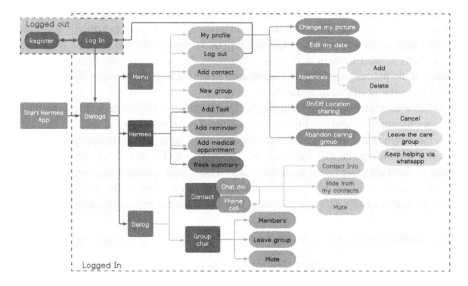

Fig. 4. Navigation schema of Hermes.

5 Back-End

As mentioned before, the main components of the back-end are the task manager and the chatbot. Next we explain each of them.

5.1 Task Manager

The task lifecycle involves four activities: creation, assignment, reminding, and reporting of results. Once finished the cycle, the information is stored and used by the assistant to make decisions in the future.

The system supports three types of tasks (or activities): medical appointments, delivery of a reminder, and general tasks. The first ones require that a caregiver go with the elderly to the medical appointment. The delivery of reminders is related to activities that have short-time periods to be performed or are recurrent. Finally, the general tasks allow addressing the rest of the activities involved in the caregiving process and that require some coordination of the participants in the caregiving network.

Once the information about the activity and its periodicity are recorded, the creator can suggest a participant to perform such an activity. Otherwise, the creator finds a responsible for such a task. The system creates three groups considering users playing the roles of assistants and helpers, as well as taking into account the activities assigned in the past, their absence agenda, and proximity to the place where to perform the activity (if any). As shown in Fig. 5, the groups are ranged from those with less assigned activities (higher priority) to those with more assignments (lower priority).

In this case, the system sends a notification to all users of the first group, asking for a responsible for the task. The process ends if a user accepts the invitation and the virtual assistant informs the assignment to the task creator. If a user explicitly indicates that is not able to address the request, then he is removed from the list for future notifications related to such a request. Otherwise, the users are added to the second group and the process is performed again until getting a responsible to perform the task or complete the notification to the three groups.

When a user accepts to perform a task, the assistant asks if he/she wants to record a reminder for such an activity. Figure 6 shows the steps that the virtual assistant follows to set these reminders. Finally, if the activity is a medical appointment or a general task, after a while the virtual assistant will ask the user committed with the task, what the results of such an assignment were; e.g., it can be completed, pending, or failed. The answer of the user is recorded, and he/she can inform the rest of the group about this result through an automatic message that will be available in the message panel.

5.2 Chatbot

The chatbot provides three major services: (1) to assist family members in the process of adding a caregiving task that requires the support of a family member; (2) to ask family members for help to address particular needs of older adults; and (3) to deliver reminders to the people committed with caregiving tasks and provide awareness about the status of these tasks, e.g., if they are pending, assigned, or addressed.

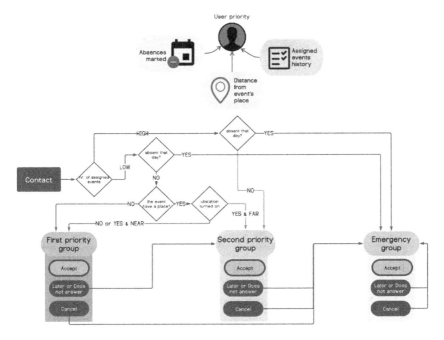

Fig. 5. Algorithm to prioritize groups for assigning an event.

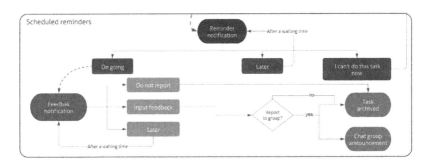

Fig. 6. Reminders and feedback flow.

This chatbot runs in the background of a mobile application and assists their users (usually, the family caregivers, and eventually the older adults) in the three major activities explained before. Figure 7 summarizes the behavior of the chatbot.

First of all, when a family member adds a new caregiving task using the mobile application (e.g., to carry the older adult to the physician), the chatbot helps that user classify and characterize the task. Then, the chatbot identifies a set of candidate members within the family network for completing such an assignment, considering the type of activity to be performed, the usual availability of each person, and the caregiving activities already performed by such a person in favor of the older adult.

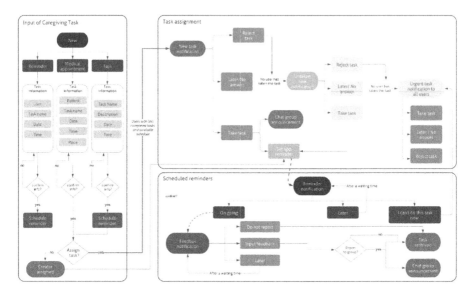

Fig. 7. Caregiving support process performed by the chatbot.

Taking into account these variables, the chatbot finds a voluntary family member that agrees to perform the task. Depending on the results of this process, the chatbot changes its strategy to find new voluntary people if required. Finally, it provides on-time automatic reminders to the involved people trying to ensure the assignment be successfully addressed. The chatbot also provides awareness about the caregiving tasks that are pending, assigned, and successfully/unsuccessfully closed.

6   System Evaluation

As described in the previous section, the chatbot flow depicted in Fig. 7 was developed as a background service of Hermes. The goal of such a service is to coordinate and articulate the activities performed by the family caregivers in a family. Given the complexity of the tightly-coupled cooperative scenario addressed by the system, the design and evaluation of the mobile application followed an iterative and incremental process. This section presents the evaluation of the last version of the prototype, which involved a sample of end-users in a simulated setting.

6.1   Evaluation Setting

Eleven families participated in this process, each composed by an assistant and an older adult or a helper. All families were taking care of an older adult and had an important past experience in this activity. Some of these families have older adults suffering from mental illness as Alzheimer and dementia, while others have an external person as formal caregiver. The participants indicated the role they play in the caregiving process. Next table summarizes the characteristics of the participants (Table 1).

Table 1. Characterization of end-users

	Age range	Female	Male
Older adult	71–80	3	0
Assistant	51–60	8	6
Helper	20–30	3	2

As recognized by Gutierrez et al. [4], the roles assumed by the family members tend to fit their ages and relationship with the older adult. Typically, the older adults are care recipients, middle aged adults (usually child) play the role of assistant, and young adults (usually grandchildren) act as helpers.

In this evaluation process we used the Wizard-of-Oz (WoO) method to present the Hermes system to the users, representing all interfaces needed to reflect the navigation, functions, and processes as a mid-fidelity paper prototypes. We interpreted the chat dialogs between virtual assistant and the user as verbal conversations.

Before the WoO session starts, the users were informed about the objectives and goals of the system as well as about the characterization of three roles supported by the system. During the session, the users assumed the role they interpret in their current caregiving scenario and we asked them to follow the Thinking Aloud method as a way to gather user comments. In the evaluation session, users were asked to make different tasks aimed to let them learn about the system functionalities and to determine whether they were useful. The tasks involved comprised: creating and interacting with contacts, creating and assigning caregiving duties, creating reminders and notifications, and asking for feedback about the status of a task.

Once the session was completed, the participants were asked to fill out an exit questionnaire comprising 20 items graded in a 5-point Likert scale. The first ten items were focused on determining the usability of the system, and the other ten evaluated its perceived usefulness. Next we indicated the obtained results.

6.2   System Usability Evaluation

Table 2 shows the items used to evaluate the usability of the system and their results grouped by role (older adult, assistant and helper), indicating their mean (M) and standard deviation (SD). The instrument that we used for conducting the evaluation was the System Usability Scale (SUS).

Assistants and helpers rated the system with high scores, showing the application is usable for them (>68 pts.). However, it is still not easy-to-use for older adults. The elderly people participating in this evaluation did not use mobile applications to interact with others, and therefore they felt the need of requiring more training for using the system comfortably.

For assistants, the reactions over the things they need to know before using the system vary. It can be caused by their level of exposure or use of mobile technology. In the case of helpers, scores were good. However, these users were uncertain about the capability of their older adults and assistants to quickly learn to use the system.

Table 2. Results of the usability evaluation

Item	Older adult		Assistant		Helper	
	M	SD	M	SD	M	SD
I think that I would like to use this system frequently	4.0	1.0	4.6	0.5	2.8	1.8
I found the system unnecessarily complex	2.0	0.0	1.4	0.5	1.0	0.0
I thought the system was easy to use	3.3	0.6	4.6	0.5	4.8	0.4
I think that I would need the support of a technical person to be able to use this system	3.3	1.2	1.8	1.3	1.2	0.4
I found the various functions in this system were well integrated	3.0	1.0	4.7	0.5	5.0	0.0
I thought there was too much inconsistency in this system	1.7	0.6	1.1	0.3	1.0	0.0
I would imagine that most people would learn to use this system very quickly	3.0	1.0	4.8	0.4	3.6	1.1
I found the system very cumbersome to use	2.3	1.5	1.2	0.4	1.4	0.9
I felt very confident using the system	3.3	0.6	4.5	0.5	4.8	0.4
I needed to learn a lot of things before I could get going with this system	3.3	1.2	1.7	1.4	1.2	0.4
SUS Score	**60.0**	**19.8**	**89.8**	**7.4**	**88.0**	**6.4**

Assistants and helpers have a similar perception of the system usability, perceiving the system as comfortable, easy-to-use and learn, where the functionalities were properly integrated. However, the willingness for using the application is different. Particularly, assistants would use it since they felt the system helped them manage their caregiving agenda and coordinate with other family members. However the helpers, who felt less responsible for the caregiving process, would be 'annoyed' by using the assistant.

6.3   System Usefulness Evaluation

Table 3 shows the items used to evaluate the perceived usefulness of the system and its functionalities. It includes the evaluation results, the average and standard deviation, grouped by role. Concerning the system information handling, support to the lifecycle, and assignment activities, all participants assigned a high score to these services, and recommend to other family members the use of Hermes to coordinate the caregiving activities.

Table 3. Results of the perceived usefulness evaluation

Item	Older adult		Assistant		Helper	
	M	SD	M	SD	M	SD
I consider that the system provides accurate and prompt information concerning the older adult	4.0	0.0	4.6	0.6	4.4	0.6
I think that the coordination of caregiving activities is cumbersome	2.0	0.0	1.8	1.2	2.8	1.3
I feel that the system provides a great assistance in managing caregiving tasks	4.5	0.7	4.2	1.2	4.6	0.6
It is not comfortable enough for me the way in which assigned events are notified	2.0	0.0	1.2	0.6	2.0	0.7
I would ask my family to use the system to coordinate the caregiving duties in favor of our older adult	5.0	0.0	4.8	0.6	4.6	0.6
I think that the older adult in my family will not be able to effectively interact with the system	2.0	1.4	3.7	1.2	3.0	0.7
I would rely on this application to schedule the caregiving tasks in my family	4.5	0.7	4.5	1.2	4.4	0.5
I consider that my family will not respond to the delegation and assignation of caregiving tasks	2.0	0.0	1.8	1.0	3.0	1.4
I think that using this application I would have more time for myself	3.0	0.0	4.2	1.0	4.0	1.0
It is not comfortable enough for me to interact with the virtual assistant	2.0	0.0	1.3	0.6	1.4	0.5

Participating users had mixed feelings about the feasibility of using this application in practice. Particularly, the older adults and assistants would use it since they perceive a benefit on it. However, the helpers are not that sure since they are usually not strongly committed with the caregiving process of the older adults in their families.

Moreover, assistants and helpers think the system would be not easy-to-use for the older adults, mainly due to their usual cognitive impairments and reluctance to use digital technologies. However, the participating older adults wondered where they could have a dedicated interface to interact with friends and family, as they showed themselves to be active and curious about digital devices.

Finally, the obtained results show that most family members were keen on the idea of interacting with the virtual assistant, praising the system as a valuable asset on providing help to manage more smoothly the caregiving process.

7   Conclusions and Future Work

In this paper we presented Hermes, a digital assistant designed to help family caregiving stakeholders deal with the underlying challenges of such a process. As main design principles, Hermes addresses the intrinsic challenges derived from the cooperative practices and articulation work of family caregiving work. We show that this challenge can effectively be addressed using technology, as well as generating a potential positive impact on informal family caregivers and older adults.

In the next step of our research we will conduct a longitudinal in-home deployment study with a representative sample of family networks, aiming to better understand the involvement of family members when caring for their older adults with the assistance of Hermes.

Acknowledgments. This research work has been partially supported by Fondecyt (Chile) under grant #1191516.

References

1. Chen, Y., Ngo, V., Park, S.Y.: Caring for caregivers: designing for integrality. In: Proceedings of the ACM Conference on Computer-Supported Cooperative Work (CSCW 2013), pp. 91–102. ACM Press (2013). https://doi.org/10.1145/2441776.2441789
2. Chen, Y., Cheng, K., Tang, C., Siek, K.A., Bardram, J.E.: The invisible work of health providers. Interactions **21**(5), 74–77 (2014). https://doi.org/10.1145/2645645
3. Gutierrez, F.J., Ochoa, S.F.: Mom, I do have a family!: attitudes, agreements, and expectations on the interaction with Chilean older adults. In: Proceedings of the ACM Conference on Computer-Supported Cooperative Work and Social Computing (CSCW 2016), pp. 1400–1409. ACM Press (2016). https://doi.org/10.1145/2818048.2820000
4. Gutierrez, F.J. and Ochoa, S.F.: It takes at least two to tango: understanding the cooperative nature of elderly caregiving in Latin America. In: Proceedings of the ACM Conference on Computer-Supported Cooperative Work and Social Computing (CSCW 2017), pp. 1618–1630. ACM Press (2017). https://doi.org/10.1145/2998181.2998314
5. Gutierrez, F.J., Ochoa, S.F., Vassileva, J.: Mediating intergenerational family communication with computer-supported domestic technology. In: Gutwin, C., Ochoa, Sergio F., Vassileva, J., Inoue, T. (eds.) CRIWG 2017. LNCS, vol. 10391, pp. 132–147. Springer, Cham (2017). https://doi.org/10.1007/978-3-319-63874-4_11
6. Papastavrou, E., Kalokerinou, A., Papacostas, S.S., Tsangari, H., Sourtzi, P.: Caring for a relative with dementia: family caregiver burden. J. Adv. Nurs. **58**(5), 446–457 (2007). https://doi.org/10.1111/j.1365-2648.2007.04250.x
7. Schmidt, K., Simone, C.: Coordination mechanisms: towards a conceptual foundation of CSCW systems design. Comput. Support. Coop. Work **5**(2), 155–200 (1996). https://doi.org/10.1007/BF00133655
8. Schmidt, K.: Riding a tiger, or computer supported cooperative work. In: Bannon, L., Robinson, M., Schmidt, K. (eds.) Proceedings of the Second European Conference on Computer-Supported Cooperative Work ECSCW 1991, pp. 31–44. Springer, Dordrecht. https://doi.org/10.1007/978-1-84800-068-1_2
9. Schorch, M., Wan L., Randall, D.W., Wulf, V.: Designing for those who are overlooked: insider perspectives on care practices and cooperative work of elderly informal caregivers. In: Proceedings of the ACM Conference on Computer-Supported Cooperative Work and Social Computing (CSCW 2016), pp. 787–799. ACM Press (2016). https://doi.org/10.1145/2818048.2819999
10. Star, S.L., Strauss, A.: Layers of silence, arenas of voice: the ecology of visible and invisible work. Comput. Support. Coop. Work **8**(12), 9–30 (1999). https://doi.org/10.1023/A:1008651105359

Home as a Platform: Levels of Automation for Connected Home Services

Shabnam FakhrHosseini[✉], Chaiwoo Lee, and Joseph F. Coughlin

Massachusetts Institute of Technology,
77 Massachusetts Avenue, Cambridge, MA 02139, USA
{shabnaml, chaiwoo, coughlin}@mit.com

Abstract. Tomorrow's home will not only be a place to live, but will be a platform of services and experiences provided by an interconnected ecosystem of technologies. This platform requires a framework that describes and simplifies the types of homes and services which address consumers' needs and provides current and future directions for researchers and practitioners. Although there have been some efforts to understand homes' types and levels of automation, there is not a commonly established framework. In this paper, we propose a framework outlining types of homes and various levels of home automation: Electric homes, Customized homes, Proactive homes, Support homes, and Companion homes. This framework is built upon previous automation models and is supported by our expert interview panel. The first two levels describe current states and the next three levels discuss future directions and possibilities. Each level varies in terms of the complexity and intelligence of in-home technologies, their interaction and integration with one another as well as with the user, ability to process information based on the stages from information processing theory, and aspects of companionship that a home can provide to its residents. The proposed framework is the first step in achieving a standardized understanding of home automation across stakeholders.

Keywords: Smart home · Automation · Taxonomy

1 Introduction

The world population is aging. Based on [1], by 2050, there will be around 2 billion older adults; a high percentage of them may have conditions that require support and care. Among older adults, aging in place is the preferred lifestyle [2, 3] where they stay in their own homes and communities rather than making a move to an institutional setting. With such growth and demand from those that spend most of their time in their homes alone [4, 5], there is now a greater desire for homes that enable a diversity of activities and to accommodate various capabilities and needs.

New and emerging technologies are well positioned to assist in providing the desired care and support in homes; to enable connection from the home to the outside community; to make jobs convenient and accessible within and around the home; and to maximize residents' independence, as well as to support their caregivers. However, the state of home technologies and services is fragmented with no standard structure for stakeholders to easily access and utilize.

© Springer Nature Switzerland AG 2020
Q. Gao and J. Zhou (Eds.): HCII 2020, LNCS 12208, pp. 451–462, 2020.
https://doi.org/10.1007/978-3-030-50249-2_32

In other domains, such as surface transportation and aviation, standards and taxonomies are in place to define the various levels of automation, as well as the related degrees of human vs. system involvement in a given task. For example, SAE International has defined levels of vehicle automation, from no automation to full automation, to describe and categorize varied levels of human vs. system involvement in the driving task, as well as to classify existing in-vehicle technologies [6]. This framework is widely accepted among industry, academia as well as the public sector and utilized to guide designing, testing and regulating self-driving technologies.

In the areas of smart and connected homes [7–11] and automation [12, 13], there have been efforts to define levels of automation and to create a taxonomy. However, there is not a clear framework on types of homes and levels of automation that stakeholders across different roles and objectives agree on [14]. Moreover, previous efforts have not provided a cohesive model of homes that allows designers and researchers to identify a home's automation level with a user-centered perspective. In other words, most of the existing models focus on in-home technologies as opposed to the home as a platform and user interaction with it. This paper aims at bringing attention to the absence of a framework for levels of automation in homes. The proposed framework is an expansion of the current models in the area of automation to address this question: How can we classify homes and their levels of automation from user-centered perspective? To this end, an in-depth literature review revealed several necessary elements for this framework. Literature from the fields of robotic automation was reviewed to develop a coherent understanding of human-automation interaction. The elements from the previous research on automation were synthesized into a framework that can serve as a tool for designers in identifying the appropriate automation level of a home and to facilitate communications between stakeholders and to enable easier access by consumers. We believe that having a standard definition of home technologies and services, along with a structure to describe the varied levels of automation, can open the horizon to guide future developments and discussions.

2   Defining the Smart Home

Smart homes have been defined mostly as residences augmented with technologies that are built to enhance residents' lifestyle through promoting independence and human-friendly control, comfort, and security while reducing living and care costs [11, 15–17], and responding to the household needs [7, 18].

Recently, Li et al. [19] discussed three generations of smart home technologies:

1. Wireless technology and proxy server home automation approach: This is the first generation of smart home technologies. These technologies were designed to monitor activities in the home and operate electrical devices through Bluetooth, ZigBee, etc.
2. Artificial intelligence controlled electrical devices: The second generation of smart home technologies evolved to the idea of Smart Home Environments (SHE). Unless the first generation that devices were operated based on predefined programs, artificial intelligence, multi-agent systems, and automation run SHE.

3. Robots: The integration of robotics with artificial intelligence differentiates the third generation of smart home technologies from the second generation. These robots can recognize and respond to people's needs through different interaction modalities. Their benefit over the second generation's devices is that they can create a relationship with humans.

3   What Should Be Automated?

The home is a complex domain where multiple activities and tasks take place in various places with different characteristics. The ability to live independently requires the performance of a range of activities. Previous studies on aging in place, ambient assisted living, and helping older adults live independently focused on some activities that are core aspects of everyone's daily life. Based on [20] these activities are categorized as follows:

1. Activities of Daily Living (ADLs): basic tasks that people normally do without any assistance. These activities are eating, bathing, dressing, toileting, transferring, and walking.
2. Instrumental Activities of Daily Living (IADLs): require more complex thinking skills and are essential for people to function in their communities independently. Cooking, driving, using telephone or computer, shopping, keeping track of finance, managing medication, doing laundry, and housekeeping are considered as IADLs.

ADLs and IADLs have been used in many studies. For example, [21] studied detecting ADLs using wearable and non-wearable sensors through different machine learning algorithms. This study was an attempt to create an ambient assisted living environment for older adults to age in place. These efforts are valuable in demonstrating technological capabilities and potential applications. However, based on the varieties of tasks that people accomplish in their homes,, automation should be considered in its context and in regards to holistic user needs, rather than automating every single task within the home. Therefore, instead of moving towards automating all in-home tasks and eliminating the roles of users, technology should be designed in a way to optimize users' experience based on their needs.

4   Understanding Levels of Automation

Automation has been made more affordable recently through the advancement of technology and implementation of IoT and ICT (information and communications technology). Parasuraman et al. [13] defined automation as "the full or partial replacement of a function previously carried out by the human operator" and tried to answer this question: given the technical capabilities, which system functions should be automated and to what extent? In response, they outlined a model of human interaction with automation which was the extension of previous model on levels of automation [22, 23]. In the previous models, a continuum of levels was defined from the lowest level of fully manual performance to the highest level of full automation.

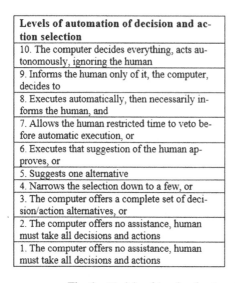
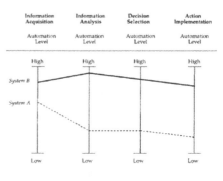

Levels of automation of decision and action selection
10. The computer decides everything, acts autonomously, ignoring the human
9. Informs the human only of it, the computer, decides to
8. Executes automatically, then necessarily informs the human, and
7. Allows the human restricted time to veto before automatic execution, or
6. Executes that suggestion of the human approves, or
5. Suggests one alternative
4. Narrows the selection down to a few, or
3. The computer offers a complete set of decision/action alternatives, or
2. The computer offers no assistance, human must take all decisions and actions
1. The computer offers no assistance, human must take all decisions and actions

Fig. 1. Models of levels of automation (left) [22, 23] vs. (right) [13].

Therefore, the concept of "levels of automation" addresses this continuum from manual to full automation that have been divided into ten [13], eight, and four levels [24] in previous studies. The model suggested by [13] describes four stages of human information processing: 1. information acquisition, 2. information analysis, 3. decision and action selection, 4. action implementation, In this model, input functions (information acquisition and information analysis) that come before decision making process were considered in the continuum. While in the previous models only automation of decision and action selection, or output functions of a system, were explained. They explained: "the automation can differ in type and complexity, from simply organizing the information sources, to integrating them in some summary fashion, to suggesting decision options that best match the incoming information, or even to carry out the necessary action." Based on their view, each of the functions (i.e., stages of information processing) can be automated with various degrees and a system can involve automation of all four functions at different levels. Figure. 1 also shows a 10-point scale of levels of automation, with higher levels representing increased automation of computer over human action [22, 23].

The model described in [13] also suggests that each stage in the model of human information processing has its equivalent in system functions that can be automated. Similar efforts have been seen in other studies [24, 25]. For example, the framework of robot autonomy described by [25] autonomy as "the extent to which a robot can sense its environment, plan based on that environment, and act upon that environment with the intent of reaching some task-specific goal without external control." In this definition, sense, plan, and act refer to the functions from human information processing theory. Table 1 shows the four functions, equivalent automation dimension in a system and a brief explanation.

Table 1. This table shows mapping the four stages of information processing with automation dimensions from [13]

Functions	Automation dimensions	Explanations
Information processing	*Acquisition Automation*	Sensing and registration of input data (raw data)
Information Analysis	*Analysis Automation*	Deriving a list of options through analysis, trend prediction, interpretation, prediction and integration
Decision and action selection	*Decision Automation*	Selection from among decision alternatives and recommend courses of action
Action implementation	*Action Automation*	Execution or authority to act on the chosen option

To avoid treating the model as a static formula and as an iterative method to identify potential design issues, [13] considered primary and secondary evaluative criteria in deciding what type and level of automation should be given to a system. Primary evaluative criteria evaluates consequences for human operator performance (mental workload, situation awareness, complacency, and skill degradation) after automation has been implemented. Secondary evaluative criteria, covers automation reliability and costs of decision/action outcomes. Automation reliability is an important factor in user trust and consequently human use of automated systems. In addition, costs of decisions and associated actions that humans and automated systems take in most systems vary.

5 Method

The proposed framework in this paper is built on the taxonomies and models describing levels of automation [12, 13]. However, this suggested framework includes some key changes and additions to the way which automation should be conceptualized for homes. First, we highlight the importance of home as a whole rather than focusing on tasks and in-home technologies. This factor is important in this framework because with the interoperability and interconnectedness of the emerging systems in the homes, considering tasks and devices alone and apart from the ecosystem of the home is neither helpful nor in line with the current directions. Second, some of the determinant factors to define the levels are variables that are meaningful to this topic. In other words, applying all the key factors from the previous model was not practical. Third, home is a complex and dynamic environment where the number and types of users are unlimited. Although this taxonomy was an effort to simplify the concept for the bigger picture and outlining future directions, automation in each level may change depending on the resident(s), task, and interaction over time.

Besides the in-depth literature review and borrowing concepts and models from the previous studies, this model was discussed and validated in a meeting with experts from different backgrounds. In this meeting, seven experts from different companies involved in the MIT AgeLab's C3 Connected Home Logistics Consortium were presented the framework and the logic behind it. The goal of this consortium is to understand home as a platform with the focus on three main concepts: care, convenience, and connectivity. After the presentation, the framework was discussed in detail. Questions and concerns were explored and the framework, and possible next steps were discussed to validate the framework with more data.

6 Toward a Framework for Levels of Home Automation and Home Taxonomy

The suggested taxonomy is an effort to provide a platform for researchers to discuss the current status of home automation and smart homes, as well as clarifying some perspective of possible future directions and goals. Moreover, this taxonomy is intended to help standardize terminology, instead of using a variety of similar languages such as smart homes, intelligent homes, home networks, home automation, connected living and so on. While stakeholders today are using different vocabularies for similar features and functions in their products, our proposed taxonomy aims to facilitate communication among researchers, designers, and developers which consequently can improve consumers' understanding of the products.

In addition, as is happening in the area of transportation, the taxonomy provides a platform for policymakers. For example, we expect that in near future, sensors and in-home devices that can track people's activities, vital signs, and any abnormal changes. The benefit will be that all these abnormalities, whether minor or major, will be detected and treated in early stages. A related concern, however, can be stated around the potential for related information to be shared with different parties, and also around safeguarding against potential threats to privacy. As policymakers approach regulating how data may be collected, processed, and shared, the proposed framework can help guide the understanding around technical capabilities and interconnectedness of various technologies.

The suggested taxonomy (see Fig. 2) is an effort to address the above concerns. Five levels have been identified and defined in this taxonomy: Electric homes, Customized homes, Proactive homes, Support homes, and Companion homes. Each level is identified based on types of in-home devices, their capabilities in understanding users in terms of receiving information, processing data, decision making, action, human involvement, and user controls.

6.1 Electric Homes

Electric homes describe the majority of homes around the world. These homes are not a platform yet since there is not a central system that can connect and coordinate the tasks and the needs. Results of the discussion with the experts during the meeting showed that everyone agrees on the definition and determinant criteria for this level. Electric homes are described by the following characteristics:

- All the in-home technologies run with pre-determined functions (excluding universal controllers such as smartphone and computer). The pre-determined functions are the default or options that can be selected by users to achieve certain goals.

The available options and functions are the same for all users. In other words, there is no technology with the ability to learn from users and adapt to their needs in electric homes.

- Considering the information processing theory for the levels of automation of devices in electric homes, all the devices can only receive information at the highest level (sense, interpret, decide, and act), and act upon that (stimulus-action response). Stages like interpreting data, making predictions and decisions, and higher-level data processing are missing in this category.
- In-home technologies are not connected with each other. These in-home devices exist in a vacuum. Each performs its function by itself, and all require a high level of human involvement.
- Electric homes do not understand resident needs and/or act upon that. There is no awareness of users, their habits, status, and activities.

6.2   Customized Homes

Customized homes have been adopted vastly during the last decade. Recent smart technologies in many of the homes nowadays, changed user behavior, routine, and the way they interact with in-home technologies. New features like voice recognition systems, or remote controls through apps helped residents to save time and costs. The validated determinant criteria after our discussion with the experts showed that in a customized home:

- There is at least one technology in the home (excluding the universal controllers such as smartphone and computer) that runs with programmable instructions. This technology should be able to learn from the users and adapt to their needs. Users can customize the device to address their needs but still there is a high level of user involvement.
- Considering the information processing theory for the levels of automation of devices in electric homes, devices can autonomously receive information, make decisions and act. However, devices are limited in terms of memory, the types of jobs they can accomplish, and the complexity of data processing and decision making.
- Technologies may be connected with one another, but connection is not a requirement.
- Customized homes have a limited understanding of user needs.

6.3   Proactive Homes

Based on [13], adaptive automation is referring to a flexible level of automation across any of the four stages of automation function dimensions. The level (low to high) and types of automation (acquisition automation, analysis automation, decision automation, action automation) could be designed to vary depending on situational demands during operational use. This context-dependent automation is a concept that was borrowed and applied to the 3rd to 5th level of our taxonomy. Basically, with the capabilities of an adoptive automation system and interoperability and interconnection of in-home devices, the home will be considered as a platform with the below criteria:

- All of the in-home technologies run with a central AI. The central AI receives and processes all the information, makes decisions, and acts if necessary (the same level of information processing as humans). This central AI may be a social robot, a router, a software on a mobile device, or in the cloud, but most of the in-home technologies in the home has to talk to each other through it.
- The intelligence and complexity of each in-home technology does not matter as long as all of them are connected to and being run through the central AI. The central AI manages the in-home activities and requires only a moderate amount of user involvement for managing in home tasks.
- In-home technologies are connected with each other through the central AI.
- Proactive homes understand the residents' needs and/or can act upon them. Homes are aware of users, their habits, status, and activities.
- Proactive homes are connected to other residences and their surrounding communities to increase efficiency of services.

6.4   Support Homes

With the application of context-dependent automation described in level 3, support homes may be even further in the future where technology with the capability of dealing with more complex data like emotions and affect can exceed human intelligence. In these homes:

- All the in-home technologies run with a central AI. The central AI receives and processes all the information, makes decisions, and acts if necessary. The central AI has a higher-level capability of information processing than humans. For example, it can receive and analyze types and ranges of data that human sensory system is limited to receive those. This central AI may be a social robot, a router, a software on a mobile device, or in the cloud, but most of the in-home technologies in the home has to talk to through the central AI.
- The intelligence of each in-home technology does not matter as long as all of them are connected and being run through the central AI. The central AI manages the in-home activities and the level of user involvement in managing in-home tasks is low.
- In-home technologies are connected with each other through the central AI.
- In-home technologies are connected to users and their needs. Homes are aware of users, their habits, status, and activities. They understand users, their emotions, and needs better than themselves. They can make better decisions, provide better options, and act upon them.
- Support homes are connected to other residences and their surrounding communities to increase efficiency of services.

What discriminates level 3 and 4 is the central AI's ability to understand human needs and to adapt. Although homes in both levels have a clear image of users, their routines and behaviors, level 4 is associated with superior abilities in decision making and prediction abilities particularly in complex situations such as residents' emotional needs and affective states.

6.5   Companion Homes

Companion homes have all the capabilities of proactive or support homes but also include the following characteristics:

- In companion homes, there is one or more physical entity that can manage all physical tasks and chores. The physical entity could be built into the in-home technologies or a separate entity like a social robot. This physical entity provides companionship to the residents that go beyond basic functionalities. This companionship encompasses social and emotional aspects.
- The central AI can be built into the physical entity or separately but they should be connected with each other.

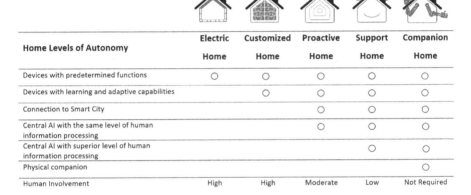

Home Levels of Autonomy	Electric Home	Customized Home	Proactive Home	Support Home	Companion Home
Devices with predetermined functions	○	○	○	○	○
Devices with learning and adaptive capabilities		○	○	○	○
Connection to Smart City			○	○	○
Central AI with the same level of human information processing			○	○	○
Central AI with superior level of human information processing				○	○
Physical companion					○
Human Involvement	High	High	Moderate	Low	Not Required

Fig. 2. A summary of the home taxonomy and levels of automation

Results of our conversations with the experts showed some concerns around the level of human involvement in many of the tasks in homes belong to level 3, 4, and 5 which need to be explored by users in the next steps.

7   Discussion and Conclusion

Home is a complex environment. It is private and shared at the same time. There has been a huge amount of efforts during the last century to make homes more convenient for the residents through different ways. Among all the efforts, in-home technologies have played an important role in changing the layout of the homes, its dynamic, and residents' lifestyle.

With the emergence of IoT and ICT, home automation and smart home technologies have been investigated widely [26]. Assistive technologies, health management systems, safety tools and sensors, communication devices, and energy systems are some examples of the efforts to increase safety, security, and convenience and overall improve residents' lifestyle [30].

Although there has been research in understanding user needs and describing models that can describe smart home technologies, there is no clear framework on types of homes and levels of automation that various stakeholders agree on. In this paper, we proposed a taxonomy outlining various levels of homes automation. This taxonomy describes five types of homes and levels of home automation: Electric homes, Customized homes, Proactive homes, Support homes, and Companion homes. The first two levels describe the current homes and the next three levels discuss the future directions and possibilities.

The highest level in this taxonomy opens discussions and research topics on the area of home as a companion which is capable of satisfying user needs in many dimensions: emotionally, socially, and physically. Each level varies in terms of the complexity and intelligence of in-home technologies, their interaction and integration with one another as well as with the user, home's ability in processing information based on the stages from information processing theory, and aspects of companionship that a home can provide to residents. These determinative factors of levels were selected based on their impact on user mental model. For example, one study examined how different smart home abstractions, priming, and user expectations affect end users' mental models of a hypothetical system [27]. They found that different degrees of system personification (unmediated and agent-mediated) and capabilities (data and devices) influence user interaction with the smart home. They showed that when participants were presented with the unmediated devices abstraction, participants did not assume any connections among the devices.

Results of the MIT AgeLab C3 Connected Home Logistics Consortium expert meeting helped us to understand the application of this framework from different aspects and opened new questions. For example, how much different technologies such as safety and security systems, health systems, assistive devices, social robots, energy systems, housework assistants, and entertainment systems with different capabilities of automation and interoperability in different levels influence user interaction with them and the home and what are the consequences in terms of user trust, preference, frustration, changes in their lifestyle?

As Parasuraman et al. [13] said, "automation design is not an exact science. However, neither does it belong in the realm of the creative arts, with successful design dependent upon the vision and brilliance of individual creative designers." Having a framework that can provide guidance about all facets of a concept is necessary. Although frameworks simplify the concepts and presents an abstract view of a complex idea, they help researchers to situate plans around ideas that are well-grounded in the literature.

The proposed framework is the first step in achieving a standardized understanding of home automation across stakeholders. This framework has been developed with a user-centered perspective and is intended to be used as a reference for designers and researchers in the area of developing smart homes and in-home technologies and products. The taxonomy can also be utilized as a foundation for understanding relationships between people's activities and technological solutions. Future studies need to address how we can improve our current homes (Electric and Customized homes) as they evolve into a more convenient, connected and caring platform. What aspects of users' mental models should we consider to help design the central AI system for highly automated homes? What factors should be addressed when we talk about specific users, e.g. older adults, kids, people with disabilities, etc.?

Although the effort for this taxonomy was to simplify the discussion platform, mechanisms behind user acceptance and adoption of the homes and in-home devices are multi-layered which require a deeper understanding of the users. Next research steps can include rounds of thorough reviews with experts in related fields to define evaluative criteria based human preference and performance, a scan of technologies that are available and in development, and a trends analysis to validate and revise the determinative factors across the levels.

Acknowledgments. Support for this study was provided by the MIT AgeLab C3 Connected Home Logistics Consortium.

References

1. United Nations Department of Economic & Social Affairs: 2017 annual report on World Population Ageing (2017)
2. Benefield, L.E., Holtzclaw, B.J.: Aging in place: merging desire with reality. Nurs. Clin. **49** (2), 123–131 (2014)
3. Marek, K.D.; Rantz, M.J.: Aging in place: a new model for long-term care. Nurs. Adm. Q. **24**(3), 1–11 (2000)
4. Iecovich, E.: Aging in place: from theory to practice. Anthropol. Note-books **20**(1), 21–33 (2014)
5. Roberts, A., Ogunwole, S., Blakeslee, L., Rabe, M.: The Population 65 Years and Older in the United States: 2016. American Community Survey Reports (2018)
6. SAE International: Taxonomy and Definitions for Terms Related to Driving Automation Systems for On-Road Motor Vehicles (2018)
7. GhaffarianHoseini, A., Dahlan, N.D., Berardi, U., GhaffarianHoseini, A., Makaremi, N.: The essence of future smart houses: From embedding ICT to adapting to sustainability principles. Renew. Sustain. Energy Rev. **24**, 593–607 (2013)
8. Mast, M.: User-centered design of a dynamic-autonomy remote interaction concept for manipulation-capable robots to assist elderly people in the home. J. Hum. Rob. Interact. **1**(1), 96–118 (2012)
9. Pilich, B.: Engineering Smart Houses, Lyngby, Informatics and Mathematical Modelling, Technical University of Denmark (2004)
10. Popescu, D., Popescu, S., Bacali, L., Dragomir, M.: Home "Smartness"-helping people with special needs live independently. In: International Conference of Management Knowledge and Learning and Technology Innovation and Industrial Management, Romania (2015)
11. Stefanov, D.H., Bien, Z., Bang, W.C.: The smart house for older persons and persons with physical disabilities: structure, technology arrangements, and perspectives. IEEE Trans. Neural Syst. Rehabil. Eng. **12**(2), 228–250 (2004)
12. Endsley, M.R., Kaber, D.B.: Level of automation effects on performance, situation awareness and workload in a dynamic control task. Ergonomics **42**(3), 462–492 (1999). https://doi.org/10.1080/001401399185595
13. Parasuraman, R., Sheridan, T.B., Wickens, C.D.: A model for types and levels of human interaction with automation. IEEE Trans. Syst. Man Cybern. Part A: Syst. Hum. **30**(3), 286–297 (2000)

14. FakhrHosseini, M., Lee, C., Coughlin, Joseph F.: Smarter homes for older adults: building a framework around types and levels of autonomy. In: Zhou, J., Salvendy, G. (eds.) HCII 2019. LNCS, vol. 11593, pp. 305–313. Springer, Cham (2019). https://doi.org/10.1007/978-3-030-22015-0_24

15. Coutaz, J., Crowley, J.L.: A first-person experience with end-user development for smart homes. IEEE Pervasive Comput. 15(2), 26–39 (2016)

16. Demiris, G.: Smart homes and ambient assisted living in an aging society. Methods Inf. Med. 47(01), 56–57 (2008)

17. Amiribesheli, M., Benmansour, A., Bouchachia, A.: A review of smart homes in healthcare. J. Ambient Intell. Hum. Comput. 6(4), 495–517 (2015). https://doi.org/10.1007/s12652-015-0270-2

18. Wilson, C., Hargreaves, T., Hauxwell-Baldwin, R.: Benefits and risks of smart home technologies. Energy Policy 103, 72–83 (2017)

19. Li, R.Y.M., Li, H., Mak, C., Tang, T.: Sustainable smart home and home automation: Big data analytics approach. Int. J. Smart Home 10(8), 177–187 (2016)

20. Törnquist, K., Sonn, U.: Towards an ADL taxonomy for occupational therapists. Scand. J. Occup. Ther. 1(2), 69–76 (1994)

21. Debes, C., Merentitis, A., Sukhanov, S., Niessen, M., Frangiadakis, N., Bauer, A.: Monitoring activities of daily living in smart homes: understanding human behavior. IEEE Signal Process. Mag. 33(2), 81–94 (2016)

22. Sheridan, T.B., Verplank, W.L.: Human and computer control of undersea teleoperators. Massachusetts Institute of Technology of Cambridge Man-Machine Systems Lab (1978)

23. Riley, V.: A general model of mixed-initiative human-machine systems. In: Proceedings of the Human Factors Society Annual Meeting, Los Angeles, vol. 33, no. 2, pp. 124–128. SAGE Publications (1989)

24. Proud, R.W., Hart, J.J., Mrozinski, R.B.: Methods for determining the level of autonomy to design into a human spaceflight vehicle: a function specific approach. National Aeronautics and Space Administration Houston Tx Lyndon B Johnson Space Center (2003)

25. Beer, J.M., Fisk, A.D., Rogers, W.A.: Toward a framework for levels of robot autonomy in human-robot interaction. J. Hum. Rob. Interact. 3(2), 74–99 (2014)

26. Sharif, M.H., Despot, I., Uyaver, S.: A proof of concept for home automation system with implementation of the internet of things standards. Periodicals Eng. Nat. Sci. 6(1), 95–106 (2018)

27. Clark, M., Newman, M.W., Dutta, P.: Devices and data and agents, oh my: How smart home abstractions prime end-user mental models. Proc. ACM Interact. Mob. Wearable Ubiquit. Technol. 1(3), 44 (2017)

The Influence of Privacy on the Acceptance of Technologies for Assisted Living

Christina Jaschinski[1]([✉]) [iD], Somaya Ben Allouch[2] [iD], Oscar Peters[1],
and Jan van Dijk[3] [iD]

[1] Saxion University of Applied Sciences, Enschede, The Netherlands
c.jaschinski@saxion.nl
[2] Amsterdam University of Applied Sciences, Amsterdam, The Netherlands
[3] University of Twente, Enschede, The Netherlands

Abstract. With population aging and the expected shortage of formal and informal caregivers, emerging technologies for assistive living are on the rise. Focusing on the perspective of the prospective users of these technologies, this study investigates the perceived drivers and barriers that influence AAL adoption. An online survey among 1296 Dutch older adults was conducted. Although loss of privacy was identified as major barrier towards AAL adoption in previous research, the current study provides statistical evidence that these concerns are secondary to the expected benefits of safe and independent living. These findings suggests that older adults consider aging safely in their trusted home environment as a valid trade-off for some loss of privacy. Despite these results, we urge developers to be mindful of privacy aspects when developing AAL applications, as privacy concerns still had a significant negative influence on the attitude towards using AAL.

Keywords: Assisted living · Privacy · Older adults · Technology adoption · Theory of planned behavior (TPB)

1 Introduction

Ensuring good health and wellbeing at all ages is one of the 17 sustainable development goals that were adopted by UN Member states in 2015 [1]. In line with this goal, the European Union has adopted an 'active aging' policy strategy [2]. Emerging assistive technologies, such as smart home technology, mobile and wearable technology, and assistive robotics, are regarded as essential tools to support independent living and healthy aging up to an old age. These technologies are also described as Ambient Assisted Living (AAL) technologies. AAL technologies aim to create supportive environments that help older adult to stay active, monitor their health, preserve their capacities, feel safe, and stay connected with the community. However, their pervasive nature and ubiquitous presence in older adults' personal environments, have serious implications for the older adults' privacy [3].

Indeed, previous studies have consistently shown that concerns about privacy are a major barrier towards AAL adoption [4–7]. Older adults felt uneasy about being permanently monitored and worried about the misuse of their personal information. Third

© Springer Nature Switzerland AG 2020
Q. Gao and J. Zhou (Eds.): HCII 2020, LNCS 12208, pp. 463–473, 2020.
https://doi.org/10.1007/978-3-030-50249-2_33

parties, including family members, might use monitoring data to patronize them and interfere with their personal life. Older adults were also worried that AAL technologies would intrude upon their personal space and interfere with their normal routine [8–10]. On the other hand, some studies have argued that older adults willingly accept some loss of their privacy in exchange for the expected benefits of AAL, such as independent living and an increased sense of safety [11–13].

The current study seeks to provide more insight into this matter by investigating the factors that determine the adoption of AAL technologies among Dutch older adults. More specific, we investigate the importance of potential adoption barriers, such as loss of privacy, compared to potential drivers of AAL adoption. The discussed results are part of a larger AAL adoption survey which was conducted in the Netherlands. For the purpose of this paper, we specifically focus on the insights regarding the attitude towards AAL technology and the underlying behavioral beliefs, with a specific focus on privacy beliefs.

2 Theoretical Background

2.1 User Acceptance

User acceptance is an important pre-condition for the successful implementation of AAL technologies. Several systematic reviews point to user acceptance as one of the big hurdles for the deployment of AAL technologies in real-life settings [5, 7, 14]. Without a profound understanding of user acceptance, there will be a gap between expert opinions and actual user needs [15]. Consequently, AAL designs are likely to be informed by ageist stereotypes and oversimplified or inadequate user profiles [16–18].

The adoption of a new technology is a complex phenomenon and personal, social, contextual and technological influencing factors need to be considered. Drawing on previous literature, we understand technology adoption as a process over time that consists of several stages from the initial awareness of a new technology to the continuous use [19–22]. The current study focusses on early user acceptance, i.e. the factors that influence the initial attitude towards using AAL technologies.

2.2 Privacy

Privacy is one of the top-of-mind concerns when it comes to AAL technologies. While developers discuss privacy predominately in terms of secure data analyses, transfer and storage, the user's perception of privacy goes beyond adequate data management. Leino-Kilpi et al. [26] distinguish four dimensions of privacy: (1) physical, referring to personal space and territoriality; (2) psychological, referring to the need for self-identity and autonomy; (3) social, referring to control over social interactions, and (4) informational, referring to data protection and data integrity. Looking at the nature and objectives of AAL, these solutions influence user's perception of privacy on all four dimensions.

Physical Privacy. Physical privacy refers to the perception of personal space and territoriality. Many AAL applications are designed to operate in the home environment.

The home is traditionally associated with a feeling of happiness and a sense of comfort, familiarity and belonging. It is regarded as a place of self-expression, self-identity and personal control [23]. The ubiquitousness and pervasiveness of AAL technologies can be perceived as invasive to this personal space, thereby threating one's perception of comfort, security and control. Sensors are often placed in sensitive locations such as bedroom, bathroom or toilet. Wearable AAL technologies permeate the user's personal space as they are directly connected to the user's body. This poses additional challenges in terms of physical interaction, intrusion, comfort and aesthetics [24, 25].

Psychological Privacy. Psychological privacy is described as being in control of cognitive and affective processes related to forming personal values. This dimension is also described as the need for personal autonomy and self-identity [26]. Using assistive devices often evokes negative associations of frailty and dependency and can threaten older adults' self-identity as an autonomous person [8, 27]. Previous work showed that older adults are also concerned that family members might utilize monitoring data to interfere with their personal life, habits and decision making [9, 11, 28].

Social Privacy. Social privacy refers to one's control over social interactions in terms of participants, frequency, length and content [26]. As social isolation is a growing concern for older adults, several AAL technologies aim to stimulate and encourage social interactions. This might also include monitoring social interactions and notifying caregivers in case of lacking social activities. Previous research showed that older adults might be skeptical towards these features as they perceive engaging in social interaction to be a personal choice [11].

Informational Privacy. Informational privacy refers the control and confidentiality of personal information and is a frequently discussed topic in the AAL context. AAL technologies collect, store and transmit an abundance of sensitive personal and health-related information, including vital measurement, medication adherence, sleeping patters and toileting behavior. This information is often shared with family members and healthcare professionals. The combination of various interconnected sensors and devices further challenges the implementation of secure data analysis and storage [14]. Indeed, previous studies have consistently shown that older adults worry about data security and misuse of their personal information [9, 10, 29]. There are also individual differences in the willingness to share this personal data with family members and healthcare professionals [6, 10].

Prospective Benefits as a Trade-Off for Privacy. Although privacy appears to be an important barrier towards AAL adoption, there are several researchers that argue that older adults will accept this loss of privacy as a trade-off for the associated benefits of AAL [11, 13, 30]. Townsend et al. [13] conclude that the desire for autonomy and aging in one's own home environment is valued higher than privacy. A similar conclusion was drawn by Wild et al. [12] who found that participants' privacy concerns were secondary to expectations about advanced safety, health and independence. However, these findings are not routed in statistical evidence.

2.3   Modeling the Underlying Beliefs of AAL Adoption

To develop a better theoretical understanding of the underlying beliefs that influence early user acceptance and make statically grounded inferences about their relative importance, we developed a conceptual model of AAL adoption. For the purpose of this paper, we focus on the attitude part of the model together with the underlying behavioral beliefs including loss of privacy.

The theory of planned behavior was used as the theoretical starting point for the AAL adoption model. The theory of planned behavior (TPB) [31] stems from the field of psychology, and offers an integrated and overarching theory of human behavior. TPB has been successfully applied in technology acceptance research [32, 33] and also in the context of assistive devices [34].

Attitude towards behavior is a core construct in the theory of planned behavior, as it is one the immediate ascendants of the intention to perform future behavior [31]. In the context of the current study it is defined as '*the degree to which using AAL technology is positively or negatively valued*'. Attitude towards behavior is determined by several behavioral beliefs that are defined as '*the expected outcomes of using AAL technology*'. We followed Taylor and Todd's approach to decompose the underlying belief structure into multi-dimensional belief constructs. This approach provides a better and more detailed understanding of the underlying belief antecedents and therefore, a better guidance for design and implementation efforts of AAL [35]. The relevant behavioral beliefs for AAL adoption were elicited from previous studies in field of AAL adoption [e.g., 5, 11, 12] and in-depth insights from our own qualitative studies [9, 28]. Besides loss of privacy, loss of human touch (i.e., the fear of technology substituting human care) was hypothesized as a negative belief antecedent of attitude. Safe and independent living and relief of family burden are proposed to be positive belief antecedents (see Fig. 1).

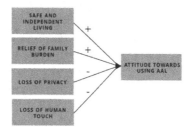

Fig. 1. Extract from the conceptual model of AAL adoption: attitude and the underlying behavioral beliefs

3   Method

3.1   Sample

To test the conceptual model of AAL adoption, we conducted an online survey among Dutch older adults between 55–85 years. The online survey was administered by a

Dutch ISO-certified research agency specialized in online fieldwork. Their panel consists of 110.000 members with diverse demographic background to ensure representativeness of the Dutch population. Participants were invited via e-mail to participate in exchange for credits. For the sampling, we used pre-defined age quota to achieve a sample that was representative for the Dutch older adult population [36]. After screening the data of some cases were removed due to straight lining, exceptionally short response times, incomplete response pattern or insufficient understanding of the AAL concept.

The final sample consisted of $n = 1296$ participants of which 49% were male and 51% were female. The age distribution was aligned with the Dutch population with 43% in the 55–64 years age group, 38% in the 65–74 age group, and 19% in the 75–85 age group. Overall subjective health and quality of life were measured with a single item on a 5-point scale ranging from 1 = poor to 5 = excellent. Subjective health averaged around the midpoint ($M = 2.95$, $SD = .97$) while quality of life had a slight tendency towards the positive end of the scale ($M = 3.21$, $SD = .91$). The majority of the sample (95%) had no direct user experience with AAL applications.

3.2 Survey Materials

Prior to completing the survey, participants viewed a short video animation explaining the concept of AAL (https://youtu.be/TZfy5KW9kOY). The video animation evolved around the persona Ben, an older adult, and his daughter Sophie. The scenario contained several examples of AAL technologie including smart home technology for activity monitoring and fall detection; a reminder system for medication and appointments, and an assistive social robot. Following the video, participants were presented with visuals from actual AAL products that are ready-to-market or already available on the Dutch market: the Sensara activity monitoring system [37]; theDayclocks reminder system [38]; and care robot Zora [39]. The visuals were accompanied by a short description of the key features of each product. To check the participants understanding of the animated video and the visuals, a control question was included after both stimuli. Participants who indicated insufficient understanding were excluded from further analyses. After viewing the video and photos, participants were directed to the AAL adoption survey.

3.3 Measurements and Data Analyses

Measurements were partially based on existing scales, and partially new scales were developed using the topics from AAL literature and our own qualitative pilot work.

A 5-point Likert scale was used as a response scale, ranging from 1 = strongly disagree to 5 = strongly agree. Due to the novelty of the concept of AAL we also included a 'don't know' option. A 5-point semantic differential scale was used as a response scale for the attitude items. Several pre-tests were conducted to improve the psychometric properties of the scales including cognitive interviews with 3 older adults. Finally, a pilot study with $n = 320$ older adults was used as a calibration sample to test the initial measurement model and refine the final survey instrument. The final attitude scale consisted of 6 items ($\alpha = .93$). Safe and independent living was measured with 7 items (α = .88). Relief of family burden was measured with 4 items (α = .85). The loss of privacy scale consisted of 6 items (α = .93) and loss of human touch was measured with 4 items (α = .87) (see Table 1).

Table 1. Measurements

Variable name	No of items	Example item
Attitude towards using AAL	6	I (like/dislike) the idea of using AAL technology
Safe and independent living	7	If I use AAL technology, I will feel safer in my home
Relief of family burden	4	My use of AAL technology will give my family members peace of mind
Loss of privacy	6	Using AAL technology will feel like an invasion into my personal space
Loss of human touch	4	If I use AAL technology, I will get less personal attention

4   Results

4.1   AAL Adoption Model

Before we focus the attitude part of the model, the fit of the greater AAL adoption model is discussed.

Structural equation modelling (SEM) was used to test the proposed adoption model. Prior to testing the structural model the measurement model was specified using maximum likelihood estimation (ML) with FIML for the missing data because the data were approximately normally distributed. All indicators showed good standardized factor loadings (>.50) and loaded significantly on the respective latent variable (p < .001). Some indicators were iteratively removed due to low squared multiple correlation values (<.40). The final measurement model showed adequate model fit (normed chi-square (2.98), RMSEA (.039), SRMR (.05), CFI (.93), and TLI (.92)). In a second step the structural model was tested. The proposed model showed adequate model fit for the observed data (normed chi-square (3.06), RMSEA (.040), SRMR (.06), CFI (.93) and TLI (.92)) and explained 69% of the variance in intention to use.

4.2   Descriptives

The overall attitude towards using AAL technologies was positive among Dutch older adults (M = 3.73, SD = .78). Looking at the underlying behavioral beliefs, participants had strong beliefs that AAL technologies could benefit their safety and independence (M = 3.92, SD = .52). Participant also expected that AAL could relieve the physical and emotional burden of their family members (M = 3.67, SD = .65). Negative beliefs regarding loss of privacy (M = 3.14, SD = .87) and loss of human touch (M = 3.13, SD = .83) were somewhat less prevalent and scored just above the midpoint of the scale (see Fig. 2).

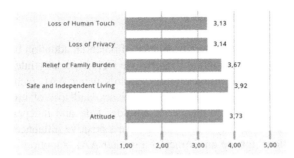

Fig. 2. Mean composite scores of the overall attitude towards using AAL and the behavioral belief constructs

4.3   The Relative Importance of the Behavioral Beliefs

All hypothesized paths between attitude towards using AAL and the underlying behavioral beliefs showed significant standardized path coefficients at a p < .001 level. Together these variables explained 71% of the variance in attitude (R^2 = .71) (see Fig. 3).

Loss of privacy had a negative influence on the attitude towards using AAL technology (β = −.19), but was less important than concerns about the loss of human touch (β = −.25) touch and expectations about safe and independent living. Safe and independent living had a positive influence on attitude towards using AAL technology and was found to be the most important influencer (β = .51). Finally, relief of family burden had some positive influence on attitude (β = .12), but was the least important influencer.

This means that older adults' initial attitude towards using AAL technology is mainly driven by the expectation to feel safer and to be able to age independently, and somewhat less by concerns about privacy and the loss of human touch.

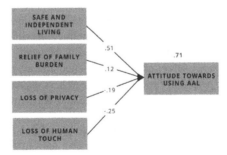

Fig. 3. Extract from the validated model of AAL adoption: attitude and the underlying behavioral beliefs

5 Conclusion and Discussion

This study investigated the relative importance of potential adoption barriers compared to potential drivers of AAL adoption. Hereby, we were especially interested in the role of privacy in informing the initial attitude towards using AAL technologies. In our conceptual model of AAL adoption, loss of privacy and loss of human touch were proposed to have a negative influence on attitude. Safe and independent living and relief of family burden were hypothesized to have a positive influence on attitude. The hypothesized relationships are an extract of a greater AAL adoption model which was validated through an online survey with a representative sample of Dutch older adults ($n = 1296$).

In accordance with our expectations, attitude was affected by older adults' beliefs about loss of privacy, loss of human touch, safe and independent living and relief of family burden. While privacy concerns had a significant influence on the initial attitude towards using AAL technology, these concerns were less important than previous AAL literature implied [4–7]. Our results showed that older adults' initial attitude is mainly driven by expectations about independent aging and increased safety and somewhat less by concerns about privacy and the loss of human touch. Hence, we found statistical evidence for the claim of Townsend et al. [13], who suggest that older adults are willing to accept some loss of privacy as a trade-off for aging independently at home. Townsend et al. [13] argue that the loss of autonomy associated with nursing homes is perceived as more severe than the loss of privacy associated with sensor technology. Wild et al. [12] also found that older adults' privacy concerns were secondary to the perceived benefits of AAL in terms of health, safety and independence. Still, given the prevalence of the privacy discussions in AAL literature, it is still somewhat surprising that privacy was not a stronger driver of attitude among our participants.

An explanation for these findings could be attributed to participants' limited user experience with AAL technologies. The majority of the sample (95%) had never used an AAL application. Hence, answers were based on the material provided in the survey or previous knowledge participants had about AAL technologies. Privacy beliefs might become more prevalent once the technology is in use and users have gained some user experience. Lorenzen Huber et al. [40] and Boise et al. [10] found that privacy concerns can increase over time after active exposure and interaction with the technology. Future research should therefore investigate the trade-off between privacy concerns and expectations about increased safety and independence among participants which have used AAL over a longer period of time. Other researchers attribute lower informational privacy concerns to a limited technical knowledge and consequential lower awareness of security risks [11, 41].

With this in mind, and given the fact that privacy concerns still had a significant negative influence on attitude towards using AAL, we still urge developers to be sensitive to the user's physical, psychological, social and informational privacy and keep privacy protection as a focal point in the development process. Advanced data protection techniques and security protocols have to be implemented to protect the user's personal information. Hardware has to blend seamlessly with the surroundings to minimize interference with the user's sense of home. Older adults should control the decision making regarding sensor types, location and data recipients. Reciprocal [40] or self-monitoring [42] approaches can counter feelings of inferiority and paternalism and stimulate agency.

The results of this study should be considered in the light of some limitations. First, the current study focused on early user acceptance. Consequently, the majority of participants had never used AAL technologies, and opinions were restricted to the participants' expectations towards these applications. While insights on early user acceptance are still very valuable for the design and development of AAL [13, 43], we have already noted that privacy perceptions might change over time. Future research should therefore deploy longitudinal designs that investigate later stages of acceptance. Second, our sample was bias towards older adults with internet connection and basic technology skills as data were collected via an online survey instrument. However, according to Statistics Netherlands [44], most Dutch older adults are active internet users. Hence, we still consider our sample as largely representative for the Dutch older adult population. Third, previous research suggested that privacy concerns are influenced by cultural values [45]. Hence, future research should validate the current findings in a different cultural context.

Awaiting future research to address these issues, the current study provides statistically grounded insights about the acceptability of AAL technologies and specifically the meaning and influence of privacy in forming an initial attitude towards AAL use. Our work therefore contributes to a more user-driven discourse in AAL research and development.

References

1. United Nations: Health - United Nations Sustainable Development. https://www.un.org/sustainabledevelopment/health/
2. Foster, L., Walker, A.: Active and successful aging: a European policy perspective. Gerontologist **55**, 83–90 (2015)
3. Novitzky, P., et al.: A review of contemporary work on the ethics of ambient assisted living technologies for people with dementia. Sci. Eng. Ethics **21**(3), 707–765 (2014). https://doi.org/10.1007/s11948-014-9552-x
4. Yusif, S., Soar, J., Hafeez-Baig, A.: Older people, assistive technologies, and the barriers to adoption: a systematic review. Int. J. Med. Inform. **94**, 112–116 (2016)
5. Peek, S.T.M., Wouters, E.J.M., van Hoof, J., Luijkx, K.G., Boeije, H.R., Vrijhoef, H.J.M.: Factors influencing acceptance of technology for aging in place: a systematic review. Int. J. Med. Inform. **83**, 235–248 (2014)
6. Wilkowska, W., Ziefle, M.: Privacy and data security in E-health: requirements from the user's perspective. Health Inform. J. **18**, 191–201 (2012)
7. Fischer, S.H., David, D., Crotty, B.H., Dierks, M., Safran, C.: Acceptance and use of health information technology by community-dwelling elders. Int. J. Med. Inform. **83**, 624–635 (2014)
8. Beringer, R., Sixsmith, A., Campo, M., Brown, J., McCloskey, R.: The "acceptance" of ambient assisted living: developing an alternate methodology to this limited research lens. In: Abdulrazak, B., Giroux, S., Bouchard, B., Pigot, H., Mokhtari, M. (eds.) ICOST 2011. LNCS, vol. 6719, pp. 161–167. Springer, Heidelberg (2011). https://doi.org/10.1007/978-3-642-21535-3_21

9. Jaschinski, C., Allouch, S.B.: An extended view on benefits and barriers of ambient assisted living solutions. Int. J. Adv. Life Sci. **7**, 40–53 (2015)

10. Boise, L., Wild, K., Mattek, N., Ruhl, M., Dodge, H.H., Kaye, J.: Willingness of older adults to share data and privacy concerns after exposure to unobtrusive home monitoring. Gerontechnology **11**, 428–435 (2013)

11. Steele, R., Lo, A., Secombe, C., Wong, Y.K.: Elderly persons' perception and acceptance of using wireless sensor networks to assist healthcare. Int. J. Med. Inform. **78**, 788–801 (2009)

12. Wild, K., Boise, L., Lundell, J., Foucek, A.: Unobtrusive in-home monitoring of cognitive and physical health: reactions and perceptions of older adults. J. Appl. Gerontol. **27**, 181–200 (2008)

13. Townsend, D., Knoefel, F., Goubran, R.: Privacy versus autonomy: a tradeoff model for smart home monitoring technologies. In: Proceedings of the Annual International Conference of the IEEE Engineering in Medicine and Biology Society, EMBS. pp. 4749–4752 (2011)

14. Rashidi, P., Mihailidis, A.: A survey on ambient-assisted living tools for older adults. IEEE J. Biomed. Heal. Inform. **17**, 579–590 (2013)

15. Piau, A., Campo, E., Rumeau, P., Vellas, B.: Aging society and gerontechnology: a solution for an independent living? J. Nutr. Health Aging **18**, 97–112 (2014). https://doi.org/10.1007/s12603-013-0356-5

16. Östlund, B.: Design paradigmes and misunderstood technology: the case of older users. Sociology **41**, 25–39 (2005)

17. Peine, A., Rollwagen, I., Neven, L.: The rise of the "innosumer"-rethinking older technology users. Technol. Forecast. Soc. Change **82**, 199–214 (2014)

18. Eisma, R., Dickinson, A., Goodman, J., Syme, A., Tiwari, L., Newell, A.F.: Early user involvement in the development of information technology-related products for older people. Univ. Access Inf. Soc. **3**, 131–140 (2004). https://doi.org/10.1007/s10209-004-0092-z

19. Karahanna, E., Straub, D.W., Chervany, N.L.: Adoption across technology information time: a cross-sectional comparison of pre-adoption and post-adoption beliefs. MIS Q. **23**, 183–213 (1999)

20. Karapanos, E., Zimmerman, J., Forlizzi, J., Martens, J.: User experience over time: an initial framework. In: Proceedings of the 27th SIGCHI Conference on Human Factors in Computing Systems, pp. 729–738 (2009)

21. Rogers, E.M.: Diffusion of Innovations. Free Press, New York (2003)

22. de Graaf, M.M.A., Ben Allouch, S., van Dijk, J.A.G.M.: Long-term evaluation of a social robot in real homes. Interact. Stud. **17**, 461–490 (2016)

23. Sixsmith, J.: The meaning of home: an exploratory study of environmental experience. J. Environ. Psychol. **6**, 281–298 (1986)

24. Dunne, L.E., Smyth, B.: Psychophysical elements of wearability. In: Conference on Human Factors in Computing Systems – Proceedings, pp. 299–302. Association for Computing Machinery (2007)

25. Dunne, L.E., et al.: The social comfort of wearable technology and gestural interaction. In: 2014 36th Annual International Conference of the IEEE Engineering in Medicine and Biology Society, EMBC 2014, pp. 4159–4162. Institute of Electrical and Electronics Engineers Inc. (2014)

26. Leino-Kilpi, H., et al.: Privacy: a review of the literature. Int. J. Nurs. Stud. **38**, 663–671 (2001)

27. Bright, A.K., Coventry, L.: Assistive technology for older adults: psychological and socio-emotional design requirements. In: ACM International Conference Proceeding Series, pp. 1–4. ACM Press, New York (2013)

28. Jaschinski, C., Ben Allouch, S.: Listening to the ones who care: exploring the perceptions of informal caregivers towards ambient assisted living applications. J. Ambient Intell. Humanized Comput. **10**(2), 761–778 (2018). https://doi.org/10.1007/s12652-018-0856-6
29. Courtney, K.L.: Privacy and senior willingness to adopt smart home information technology in residential care facilities. Methods Inf. Med. **47**, 76–81 (2008)
30. Van Hoof, J., Kort, H.S.M., Rutten, P.G.S., Duijnstee, M.S.H.: Ageing-in-place with the use of ambient intelligence technology: perspectives of older users. Int. J. Med. Inform. **80**, 310–331 (2011)
31. Ajzen, I.: The theory of planned behavior. Organ. Behav. Hum. Decis. Process. **50**, 179–211 (1991)
32. de Graaf, M.M.A., Ben Allouch, S., van Dijk, J.A.G.M.: Why would I use this in my home? A model of domestic social robot acceptance. Hum.-Comput. Interact. **00**, 1–59 (2017)
33. Pavloe, P.A., Fygenson, M.: Understanding and predicting electronic commerce adoption: an extension of the theory of planned behavior. MIS Q. **30**, 115–143 (2006)
34. Roelands, M., Oost, P.V., Depoorter, A., Buysse, A.: A social-cognitive model to predict the use of assistive devices for mobility and self-care in elderly people. Gerontologist **42**, 39–50 (2002)
35. Taylor, S., Todd, P.A.: Understanding information technology usage: a test of competing models. Inf. Syst. Res. **6**, 144–176 (1995)
36. Statistics Netherlands: StatLine - Bevolking; geslacht, leeftijd en burgerlijke staat, 1 januari. https://opendata.cbs.nl/statline/#/CBS/nl/dataset/7461bev/table?dl=B875
37. Sensara: Sensara|Beter weten, beter zorgen. https://sensara.eu
38. DayClocks International B.V.: DayClocks - Dé tablet voor oriëntatie, planning en verbinding. https://www.dayclocks.nl/
39. Zora Robotics NV: Zorabots - vision and mission. https://zorarobotics.be/
40. Lorenzen Huber, L., et al.: How in-home technologies mediate caregiving relationships in later life. Int. J. Hum. Comput. Interact. **29**, 441–455 (2012)
41. Zeng, E., Mare, S., Roesner, F.: End user security & privacy concerns with smart homes. In: Proceedings of the 13th Symposium on Usable Privacy and Security (SOUPS), Santa Clara, CA, USA, pp. 65–80 (2017)
42. Fitzpatrick, G., Huldtgren, A., Malmborg, L., Harley, D., Ijsselsteijn, W.: Design for agency, adaptivity and reciprocity: reimagining AAL and telecare agendas. In: Wulf, V., Schmidt, K., Randall, D. (eds.) Designing Socially Embedded Technologies in the Real-World. CSCW, pp. 305–338. Springer, London (2015). https://doi.org/10.1007/978-1-4471-6720-4_13
43. Dijk, J.A.G.M., Ben Allouch, S., Graaf, M.M.A., Jaschinski, C.: Toward a process model for selection of theories of technology acceptance. In: 2018 Annual Conference of the International Communication Association, Praag, Czech republic (2018)
44. Statistics Netherlands: CBS StatLine - Internet; toegang, gebruik en faciliteiten. https://opendata.cbs.nl/statline/#/CBS/nl/dataset/83429NED/table?dl=43EC
45. Miltgen, C.L., Peyrat-Guillard, D.: Cultural and generational influences on privacy concerns: a qualitative study in seven European countries. Eur. J. Inf. Syst. **23**, 103–125 (2014)

Home as Experience: The Challenge and Opportunity of Care Home Design

Ying Jiang[1,2(✉)] and Hua Dong[3]

[1] East China University of Science and Technology, Shanghai 200237, China
[2] The Hong Kong Polytechnic University, Hong Kong 999077, China
my.jiang@connect.polyu.hk
[3] Loughborough University, Loughborough LE11 3TU, UK
h.dong@lboro.ac.uk

Abstract. When older people move into care homes from their own homes, they usually face a confusing situation: they live in a care home, but they do not have a homey feeling. In order to help older residents integrate into the institutional environment, this paper proposes the idea of 'home as experience'. The study inquiries how design can play a role in transforming a care home into a home, thus influencing residents to regain their sense of belonging. Firstly, the complex meaning of home is discussed through interdisciplinary literature review, and is used to develop the conceptual framework with four dimensions (cultural, physical, social and spiritual). Secondly, critical issues in care homes are revealed. We visited five care homes in the Putuo District of Shanghai, and identified four problematic aspects based on the conceptual framework. Thirdly, according to Dewey's experience theory, the method of transforming a care home into a home is put forward, including: to identify cultural symbols; to use physical spaces; to build social relations; to discover value believes. Their composition and cooperation construct a process of experiencing being-at-home. This study does not only identify the challenge of care home design by understanding the concept of home, but also provides design opportunities through applying the experience theory.

Keywords: Care home design · The meaning of home · Experience

1 Introduction

With the increase of age and the decrease of self-care capability, many elderly people have to leave their own home and move into care home spending their remaining years. They usually face confusion in this new environment: they are in care home, but they do not have a homey feeling. In order to help residents integrate into the care home environment, this paper proposes the idea of 'home as experience'. The study endeavours to inquiry how design can play a role in transforming 'care home' into 'home', and to help residents to regain their sense of belonging.

Some researchers claim that care home and home are incompatible with each other. For example, Eva Lundgren highlights their differences: boring-comfortable; dangerous-safe; artificial-natural; authoritative-autonomous [1:112]. On the one hand, although some family members continue to be involved in their lives, including frequent visits,

Q. Gao and J. Zhou (Eds.): HCII 2020, LNCS 12208, pp. 474–485, 2020.
https://doi.org/10.1007/978-3-030-50249-2_34

personal care, social and emotional support [2], the role of the family is beginning to blur [3]. On the other hand, the environmental transformation from longer-term living home to new care home requires residents to make extensive changes in their lifestyle. The relocation leads to Person-Environment inconsistencies between older adults' physical, cognitive and emotional competence and new environmental demands [4:380]. Residents often confront with boredom, anxiety, loneliness, obedience, and adherence to rules [1]. These changes will diminish people's wellbeing and life quality.

This study aims to explore how care homes can become home. Firstly, the complex meaning of home was discussed through interdisciplinary literature review and was restructured into the conceptual framework with four dimensions (cultural, physical, social and spiritual). Secondly, the critical issues were identified regarding why residents struggled in care home. Five care homes in the Putuo District of Shanghai were visited, and four problematic aspects were revealed based on the conceptual framework. Thirdly, according to Dewey's experience theory, the method of transforming care home into home was put forward, including to identify cultural symbols; to use physical spaces; to build social relations; and to discover value believes.

2 The Meaning of Home

The meaning of home is diverse and complex. It infuses with multi-disciplinary explanations. Furthermore, the explanation is full of personalized significance, as different people have various understandings in different contexts and times. This study analyzed the meanings of home as a potential design reference.

2.1 Literature Review

Historical and Cultural Aspects. One of the earliest references to home is Hestia in ancient Greek mythology, goddess of the hearth and chief goddess of domestic activity (Merriam-Webster's Collegiate Dictionary). In modern English, home is used to mean 'a place of origin returned to' associated with womb and tomb [5:30]. Many very early explanations of home signify birthplace, one's own place and country [6:21]. At the early seventeenth century, the meaning of home switched to the house [5:37]. An example of home referring to ancestral houses is that: "The stately homes of England! How beautiful they stand" (Felicia Dorothea Hemans, 1793–1835). Since the eighteenth century, home as a family life began to appear in romantic literature [6:23]. Domestic usage of home is exemplified by "There is nothing like staying at home for real comfort" (Jane Austen, 1775–1817). The quotation of home in the twentieth century show more symbolic and idealized meanings. For example, the meaning constructed by the concept of comfort [7].

In the context of Chinese culture, home is made up of two parts: the upper part '宀' means 'house' and the lower part '豕' means 'pig', together the character means raising pigs in a roofed house, indicating the settlement form of dwelling, the living style of raising animals and household economy. It also conveys other meanings: living space; family community composed of consanguinity and the relationship in-laws; a productive economic unit; family discipline and ethics.

Philosophical and Religious Aspects. In the field of philosophy, the study of the home is represented by Heidegger's interest in the dwelling. Dwelling is considered a locus of human living in the world, and it is described as a process of turning a place into a home [8]. Furthermore, Bachelard [9] considers home to be the foundation of the philosophy of space, a corner of our world. Under the influence of these philosophers, many human geographers and phenomenologists in the 1970s focused on the significance of place [10:209]. Phenomenology regards home as an experienceable object, which emphasizes the important role of time and recognizes that special events in people's lives affecting people's experience of home [11:48]. Relph [12] points out place as the center of human existence. Tuan [13] studies the concepts of place, space, and home from a perspective of experience.

For religious believers, the significance of home concentrates on the spiritual dimension surpassing the physical and emotional level. Home is regarded as the goal of pursuing truth, which is inseparable from self-realization. For instance, the Bible reveals: the God and man are each other's dwelling place (Gen.28:10–19). Buddhism also teaches people: the home is the return to our self-nature. Home is symbolized as a destination of spiritual life such as Paradise or Pure Land.

Psychological and Sociological Aspects. The upsurge of psychological exploration on the meaning of home began in the 1970s [10:209]. Early psychologists focused on the emotional connection between people and home. Relative theories include Person-Environment Theory, Place Attachment and Place Identity. Marcus [14, 15] claims that home is interpreted as a symbol of the self. Porteous [16] emphasizes home as one's territory. Hayward [17] categorizes the meaning of home systematically by giving a clear list, including physical structure; territory; locus in space; self and self-identity, and a social and cultural unit. Appleyard [18] points out that home can meet people's psychological, social and physiological needs. Sixsmith [19] identifies three dimensions of home: personal, social and physical. Canter [20] focuses on people's personal experience in the social context. Tognoli [21] argues that home differentiates from a house, by presenting five characteristics: centrality; continuity; privacy; self-expression and personal identity; and social relationships. Després [22] focused on material and societal forces. Benjamin [23] puts forward 'home is that spatially localized, temporally defined, significant and autonomous physical frame and conceptual system'.

In the sociology field, the research on home is mainly about the themes of stratum, gender, economic relationship, family structure and homelessness. For instance, Somerville argues that home refers to shelter; hearth; heart; privacy; roots; abode and Paradise [24:227]. Kenyon (1999) categories four components of home: physical, temporal, social and personal [25].

2.2   A Conceptual Framework

Through the interdisciplinary literature review, we found that there was a lack of agreement on the definition of home. However, there are similar meanings amongst different interpretations. Inspired by Richard Buchanan's four orders of interior design [26], the meaning of home can be summarized into four dimensions: cultural place, physical space, social family and spiritual destination. Meanwhile, they show four types of relations respectively: the 'things-things' communication relationship, the 'people-things' function relationship, the 'people-people' interaction relationship, and 'people-oneself' recognition relationship (Fig. 1).

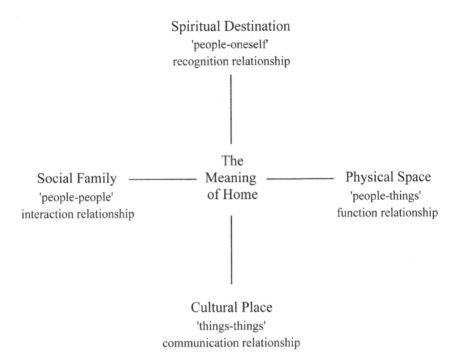

Fig. 1. The conceptual framework of the meaning of home.

'Cultural place' refers to the communication relationship between things and things. As a recognizable place, home contrasting with its surroundings shows its own symbolic characteristics and unique meaning. It has a relatively fixed identity, which depends on the specific geographical coordinates (such as district, street and house number), spatial features, as well as the natural and artificial environment of its residential areas.

'Physical space' refers to the function relationship between people and things. Space is an architectural phenomenon, with the physical structure, roof, four walls, furniture items, decorations, domestic applications, and related services. The physical dimension of the home is functional. It can be reflected only when the space is used by people. The physical space not only provides a shelter for basic activities such as sleeping but also meets the needs of familiarity, security, belonging and ownership.

'Social family' refers to the interaction between people and people. Home is not only a cultural place, a physical house but also a social unit of people. Family is a societal relationship and network of family members. The basic nuclear family usually consists of parents, children, brothers, and sisters. An extended family would include more people relationships, such as grand parents, friends and other relatives.

'Spiritual destination' refers to the recognition relationship between people and themselves. Home is a process of people looking for meanings in their inter-self existence. It can be an idea, a belief or a set of value systems. This kind of awareness and consciousness enables people to integrate all parts of complex life and form unity around a common purpose or goal. People will define the boundary of the home according to their realization. For example, students may view their dormitory as home, and religious believers may regard heaven as their eternal home.

3   The Problematic Areas of the Home

An investigation was undertaken through observations and interviews. Five care homes in Putuo District of Shanghai were visited, and five managers and twenty-seven older people were interviewed. Using the conceptual framework of the meaning of home as a reference, we revealed four existing problems of care homes.

3.1   Sampling

According to the service nature and the charging rate, five care homes were selected (Table 1). Putuo District Social Welfare Institution was organized by the district level government. This type of care home tends to provide the best services and facilities, and the price of accommodation was low. Ai Wan Ting Nursing Home was the only one funded by Putuo Education Bureau. Most of its residents were retired teachers or their relatives. It had small rooms and low cost. New Chang Zheng Welfare Institution and Shi Quan Sha Tian Nursing Home were set up and supported by the local community. They met the basic living needs at reasonable prices. Zhong Huan Yi Xian Nursing Home is a privately funded facility, with good service and high price.

Table 1.   Basic information of five care homes in Putuo District, Shanghai.

Name	Year of establishment	Ownership	Area (m^2)	Beds
1. Putuo District Welfare Institution	1979	Government	5400	244
2. Ai Wan Ting Nursing Home	2007	Government	1300	51
3. New Chang Zheng Welfare Institution	1998	Community	4300	176
4. Shi Quan Sha Tian Nursing Home	2002	Community	3000	200
5. Zhong Huan Yi Xian Nursing Home	2010	Private	12506	290

The criteria for selecting interviewees are: 1) interested in this study, 2) having worked or lived in care homes for more than one month, 3) able to communicate without help. Five managers were interviewed, one of whom had worked for 16 years. Twenty-seven tenants were also interviewed, ranging from ages of 70 to 94, with residential periods in care homes from 10 months to 7 years.

3.2   Data Collection

Data were collected from observation and semi-structured interviews. First of all, the indoor and outdoor environments were investigated and recorded by camera and notes, including public spaces, private rooms, various facilities, as well as people's activities and behaviours. Secondly, five managers and twenty-seven tenants were interviewed. The managers were asked questions about how to help the older residents to experience home. The tenants were asked about whether they had difficulties to adapt in care homes, what the ideal home they desired, and what made them feel the care home as 'home'. The average interview time took around an hour each. The interviews were audio recorded and important information was summarized in notes.

3.3   Data Analysis

The data collected include observation pictures, notes and interview recordings. Firstly, the photos were accurately described in words, and the interview recordings were transcribed into texts. Secondly, the phenomenological analysis method, 'Focus on meaning', was used to process the data, with three steps: meaning coding, meaning condensation and meaning interpretation [27] (Kvale and Brinkmann 2015). 'Meaning coding' provided a basic structure for analysis. According to the conceptual framework of the meaning of home, the problematic issues in care homes raised by the respondents were classified into four categories. 'Meaning condensation' was to extract the text into concise contents. 'Meaning interpretation' was a direct structural interpretation of the text. The literal meaning and hidden meaning were both explored.

3.4   Findings

Based on the conceptual framework of the meaning of home, four problematic areas of care homes were revealed, i.e. cultural symbols, spatial functions, social relationships, and value beliefs. There is a centralized contradiction in every aspect, namely: non-institutionalization and institutionalization, autonomy and constraint, dependence and alienation, aggregation and separation (Fig. 2).

Cultural Symbols: Non-Institutionalization and Institutionalization. The five care homes convey the institutional symbol, which conflicts with older people's desire for a non-institutionalized living environment. Their names and management styles gave an impression of authorities.

Unit Name. Names such as Nursing Home or Welfare Institution represent the nature of an institutional organization. A tenant said: 'some people are afraid of nursing home. It sounds desolate, lonely and disgraceful'. Many people felt moving into care home is 'a helpless choice, with no alternative means to take care of oneself.'

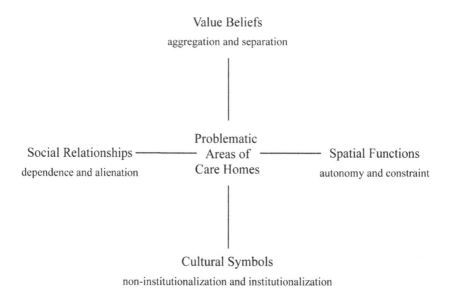

Fig. 2. Problematic areas of care homes.

Management System. Hardware facilities and internal services are manipulated through institutional management. One manager said: 'The older people who live on the first and second floors can take care of themselves, and paralyzed people live on the third floor'. A tenant complained: 'There is no balcony in any rooms, and there are dense railings outside the window'. Some also said: 'Curtains and sheets are white, like those in a hospital. The bed, the door and the furniture are all the same style'.

Spatial Functions: Autonomy and Constraint. There were obstacles between the expected autonomous lifestyle and the actual constrained mechanism. It is very difficult for a unitary functional standard to meet older people's different and diverse needs.

Living Space. Most of the residents were forced to abide the rules and they could not personalize their private space. One manager said: 'the space is too small to put anything. Residents are not allowed to change the layout here, especially in bedrooms for two or four persons to share. The simpler, the better.'

Furniture Facilities. Indoor facilities lacked safety and usability. A tenant mentioned that she had once slipped over the floor, and suggested that 'the floor should be made by non-slippery material, it should be soft, so even if people fall down, it would not be very serious.' Another tenant said: 'the clock hanging on the wall of the corridor once fell down and almost injured the person sitting under it.' A tenant said: 'the cabinet should be accessible, not too high and too deep. Currently we can't get two-thirds of the depth in the cabinet.'

Social Relationships: Dependence and Alienation. There is a certain sense of alienation between the elderly and other residents, caregivers and managers, which is far from the ideal harmonious relationship of family members.

The Relationship Between the Elderly People and Other Residents. If a tenant's living habits differed from others, s/he tended to be alienated from others. A resident said, 'There are other three people in my room, each has different habits. They often have conflicts.' One tenant said, 'I only have one good friend here. Other people don't have common hobbies; they can't talk, and can't fully communicate.'

The Relationship Between Residents and Caregivers. Staffs' attitudes sometimes will lead to residents' negative emotions. A tenant said: 'the attitude of the staff is very important, especially the attitude of the caregivers. If the room is not clean, people get very upset.' One manager said, 'The elderly people are easily affected by caregivers and managers. They worry about whether we care about them or not.'

Value Beliefs: Aggregation and Separation. Active ageing needs the support of value belief, while many older people do not have substantial spiritual life. It results in weak self-identity and vague life goals.

Identity Recognition. The tenants' self-recognition and their attitude to care home were not unified. If elderly people do not accept the care home environment, it is difficult to integrate into it. A manager said, 'It's hard for older people to adapt if they have a fixed and stubborn mind and think they have to maintain their past lifestyle.'

Life Goals. If tenants do not consider the meaning of life and pursue life goals, their participation and perception will be very low in care homes. One manager said, 'If there are few activities, people will feel inadequate.' A tenant complained, 'I feel like I have nothing to do every day.'

4   Experience: A Method of Being-at-Home

John Dewey, an American philosopher and educator, developed the experience theory. He argues that an experience has a structure with four characteristics: purpose, form, manner and material [28] (Buchanan, 2007:15). Each complete experience is guided by a specific purpose, supporting human action and reception [29] (Dewey, 1980:50). The manner of experience is the interaction between people and the environment, 'every experience is the result of interaction between a live creature and some aspect of the world in which he lives' [29] (Dewey, 1980:44). In the interaction, people not only have to adapt to the environment, but their initiatives will change the environment. People play the role of both doing and receiving, supporting each other and maintaining a balance. The whole experience has a dynamic and continuous form. It is a temporal process, which embodies three stages with 'inception-development-fulfillment' [29] (Dewey, 1980:55). Materials of experience include aesthetic, intellectual (thinking) and practical (overt doings) dimensions [29] (Dewey, 1980:55). Emotion has a cohesive effect in integrating the scattered parts of the experience as a whole [29] (Dewey, 1980:42).

Residents have experienced in the care home, but do not have an experience. Creating a homey experience by design can make use of four characteristics of the experience theory: purpose, form, manner and material. The purpose is to transform care home into home. The manner is residents' interaction within the care home environment. Older people participate in the creation of the environment, which provides the sources to promote the occurrence of experience, and at the same time affects and changes residents' physical and psychological perception. The concrete methods of interaction are embodied in four action behaviors: to identify cultural symbols, to use physical spaces, to build social relations, and to discover value believes (Fig. 3).

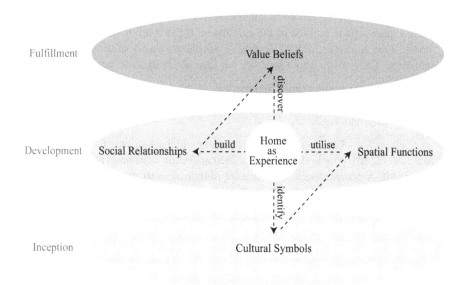

Fig. 3. Design suggestions on experiencing home.

Suggestion 1: Identifying cultural symbols. To enhance the affinity of care homes, cultural symbols can be designed to construct a visual or emotional impression. There are many symbols, including names, location, architectural design, aesthetic decoration, private items (e.g. souvenirs), etc. It is the expression of individual personality or social imagination, through communicational signs to create a place called home.

Suggestion 2: Utilising physical spaces. In order to meet the diverse needs, physical space design should be guided by the concept of inclusive design, taking into account older people's various impaired abilities (such as reduced mobility, vision and hearing loss, cognitive impairment). There is a need to consider how to provide a safer, more comfortable and flexible design in terms of space function layout, furniture design, and material selection. Besides, facilities must be installed securely and repaired in time.

Suggestion 3: Building social relations. Maintaining harmonious people-people relationships in care homes can be achieved by design. This relies on the social interaction of the elderly with other residents, staff, family, friends and people living nearby (neighbors and community). These relationships represent trust and support. Opportunities for interaction can be realized through a series of collective activities. These activities can go beyond the boundaries of the house and are organized outdoors. For example, providing a special space for the elderly to communicate with relatives and friends; increasing learning or entertainment events to encourage people to participate actively and enhance mutual understanding with their peers; improving caregivers' responsible attitude to increase residents' satisfaction.

Suggestion 4: Discovering value believes. Designers can attempt to understand residents' spiritual needs and improve their value beliefs, so as to stimulate older people to find the meaning of life. People have a way of knowing themselves and perceiving care home environment. They can be promoted to achieve self-realization by a designerly way, thereby expanding the understanding boundaries of the home and integrate it into the extended home environment actively. It is an opening to one's own recognition, and returning to one's inner-self home.

The form of experience consists of three stages: inception, development and fulfillment. This is a continuous process of being-at-home. At the inception stage, we could improve the cultural symbols of care home to help older people to have a sense of identity. In the development stage, we may construct tenants' social relationships and make space function inclusive. In the fulfillment stage, with the accumulation of daily life, we can help older people gradually find the meaning of life and spiritual support, so that they and the environment integrate into a harmonious unity. The integration requires people to devote aesthetic, intellectual and practical efforts. Additionally, experiencing home is a circulative course. A satisfying experience will further conduce older people to identify the cultural symbols of care home, and then a new round form of experience will be evolved over time (Fig. 3).

The key to creating a homey experience is to deepen the understanding of the meaning of home. The deeper the research on the connotation of home, the easier it is to find the right direction of care home design. If we pay attention to the culture and physical dimensions, then people tend to design a material place and space. If we view home from the social dimension, care home design will pay more attention to the social relationship. If we understand the meaning of home at the spiritual level, then care home design will pursue value beliefs.

Once residents pursue the self-realization and expand the boundary of home, they will find their real home, an inner-self. They will break away from the shackles of defining their identity with external materials. Home could be everywhere and become portable. The transformation from home into care home can be understood as a 'leaving home - seeking home - returning home' process. The older people leave their own home, and then try to establish a new home in the care facility environment, and finally can return to his/her real home: 'inner-self' (Fig. 4).

Leaving Home   Seeking Home   Returning Home

Fig. 4. A journey of residents' relationship with home.

5 Conclusion

In order to resolve the confusion of living in care homes, this study proposes the idea of 'home as experience', to explore how design can help older people to regain the sense of home in a new environment. The complex meaning of home was discussed through interdisciplinary literature review, and a conceptual framework of home was built, with four dimensions: cultural, physical, social and spiritual. Through visiting five care homes in the Putuo District of Shanghai, we identified four problematic aspects based on the conceptual framework. According to Dewey's experience theory, we proposed the method of transforming a care home into home through identifying cultural symbols, utilizing physical spaces, building social relations, and discovering value believes. On the theoretical side, this study produces a conceptual framework to help designers understand the meaning of home. On the practical side, the existing problematic areas in care homes were identified and suggestions for designers' future practice provided. Different stakeholders: designers, managers, caregivers, residents, family members and social groups, need to cooperate in order to realize 'home as experience'.

References

1. Lundgren, E.: Homelike housing for elderly people-materialized ideology. Hous. Theory Soc. **17**, 109–120 (2000)
2. Zhan, H.J., Feng, Z., Chen, Z., Feng, X.: The role of the family in institutional long-term care: cultural management of filial piety in China. Int. J. Soc. Welfare **20**, S121–S134 (2011). https://doi.org/10.1111/j.1468-2397.2011.00808.x
3. Gaugler, J.E., Leitsch, S.A., Zarit, S.H., Pearlin, L.I.: Caregiver involvement following institutionalization: effects of preplacement stress. Res. Aging **22**(4), 337–359 (2000)
4. Hooyman, N.R., Kiyak, H.A.: Social Gerontology: A Multidisciplinary Perspective, 10th edn. Pearson, Hoboken (2017)
5. Hollander, J.: It all depends. In: Mack, A. (ed.) Home: A Place in the World. New York University Press, New York (1993)
6. Janeway, E.: Man's World, Women's Place. Bell, New York (1971)
7. Rybczynski, W.: Home: A Short History of an Idea. Penguin, New York (1986)
8. Heidegger, M.: Poetry, Language, Thought. Harper and Row, London (1971)
9. Bachelard, G.: The Poetics of Space. Orion Press, New York (1964)
10. Moore, J.: Placing home in context. J. Environ. Psychol. **20**(3), 207–217 (2000). https://doi.org/10.1006/jevp.2000.0178
11. Bai, K., Fu, G.Q.: The concept of 'home': concept, perspective and analysis dimension. Thinking **39**(1), 46–51 (2013). 白凯,符国群."家"的观念:概念, 视角与分析维度.思想战线 **39**(1), 46–51 (2013)
12. Relph, E.: Place and Placelessness. Pion, London (1976)
13. Tuan, Y.: Rootedness versus sense of place. Landscape **24**, 38 (1980)
14. Marcus, C.C.: The house as symbol of self. In: Lang, J., Burnette, C., Moleski, W., Vachon, D. (eds.) Designing for Human Behaviour: Architecture and the Behavioural Sciences. Dowden, Hutchinson and Ross, Stroudsberg (1974)
15. Marcus, C.C.: House as a Mirror of Self: Exploring the Deeper Meaning of Home. Conari Press, Berkeley (1995)
16. Porteous, D.: Home: The Territorial Core. Geogr. Rev. **66**, 383–390 (1976)

17. Hayward, G.: Home as an environmental and psychological concept. Landscape **20**, 2–9 (1975)
18. Appleyard, D.: Home. Arch. Assoc. Q. **2**, 2–20 (1979)
19. Sixsmith, J.: The meaning of home: an exploratory study of environmental experience. J. Environ. Psychol. **6**, 281–298 (1986)
20. Canter, D.V.: The Psychology of Place. Architectural Press, London (1977)
21. Tognoli, J.: Residential environments. In: Stokols, D., Altman, I. (eds.) Handbook of Environmental Psychology. Wiley Interscience, New York (1987)
22. Després, C.: The Form, Experience and Meaning of Home in Shared Housing. University of Wisconsin-Milwaukee, Milwaukee (1991)
23. Benjamin, D.: Afterword. In: Benjamin, D., Stea, D. (eds.) The Home: Words, Interpretations, Meanings and Environments. Ethnoscapes: Current Challenges in the Environmental Social Sciences. Avebury, Aldershot (1995)
24. Somerville, P.: The social construction of home. J. Arch. Plann. Res. **14**(3), 226–245 (1997)
25. Kenyon, L.: A home from home: students' transitional experience of home. In: Chapman, T., Hockey, J. (eds.) Ideal Homes? Social Change and Domestic Life, pp. 84–95. Routledge, New York (1999)
26. Buchanan, R.: Surroundings and environments in fourth order design. Des. Issues **35**(1), 4–22 (2019). https://doi.org/10.1162/desi_a_00517
27. Kvale, S., Brinkmann, S.: InterViews: Learning the Craft of Qualitative Research Interviewing. Sage Publications, Los Angeles (2015)
28. Buchanan, K.: Toward a Poetics of Fibre Art and Design. Göteborg University, Gothenburg (2007)
29. Dewey, J.: Art as an Experience. Perigee Books, New York (1980)

Towards Lively Surveillance?
The Domestication of Companion Robots

Constance Lafontaine[(✉)]

Concordia University, Montreal, Canada
`constance.lafontaine@concordia.ca`

Abstract. Robot pets of varying degrees of sophistication are advertised as ideal companions for older adults, with claims that they support their emotional and cognitive needs. A new generation of companion robot pets is emerging equipped with internet connections, recognition software, and AI platforms to mimic desired aspects of animal-human relationships and to provide surveillance features. These enhanced technological capacities are twinned with the promise that these robots make the "perfect pet". This paper draws upon fieldwork undertaken at the Consumer Electronics Show (CES) 2019 in Las Vegas, especially focussing on the much-hyped Lovot: a zoomorphic companion robot developed by the company Groove X "to be loved by you". By examining the technological affordances of the Lovot, the paper considers what the robotization of human-animal relationships tells us about shifting notions of companionship through the life course, and the relational worlds of older adults. The paper further considers how a rhetoric of pethood, love and companionship, and a construction of liveliness can be used to usher new technologies of surveillance into the domestic spaces and quotidian lives of older adults.

Keywords: Companion robots · Pets · Surveillance · Older adults · Collaborative machine assistance and robotics · Persuasive technology and the elderly · Robotic technology and the elderly · Surveillance and alert system for the elderly

1 Introduction

CES, previously known as the Consumer Electronics Show, is the largest show of its kind in the world. Colossal showrooms in Las Vegas hotels and convention halls set the stage for a dizzying assemblage of people, lights and tech gadgets of all sorts. In 2019, "more than 4,500 exhibitors showcased the latest tech innovations to some 180,000 attendees" [1]. A team of researchers from the Ageing + Communication + Technologies (ACT) project conducted fieldwork over the course of CES 2019. We sought to better understand emerging consumer-oriented innovations and the discourses that frame them, focussing especially on the technologies designed for older adults. In true techno-utopian [2] fashion, many of the products presented at CES are contextualized by grand promises about a bright, exciting, healthy and wealthy future. Some products will solve our health woes and allow us to live longer, others will enrich our experiences of being in the world by connecting us like never before.

© Springer Nature Switzerland AG 2020
Q. Gao and J. Zhou (Eds.): HCII 2020, LNCS 12208, pp. 486–496, 2020.
https://doi.org/10.1007/978-3-030-50249-2_35

With each iteration of CES, the media decrees certain products to be the "highlights" of the show, the "best of CES", or its "coolest gadgets". During both CES 2019 and 2020, a companion robot from the Japanese company Groove X was plucked from the products on display to receive notable media 'buzz' worldwide [e.g., 3–5]. The Lovot, as it is called, is a small zoomorphic companion robot. A Lovot retails for some 3,000 American dollars and a monthly subscription fee. It is newly available on the Japanese market and is expected to be released in the United States in 2020. In the company's words, "Lovot was born for just one reason – to be loved by you" [6]. Its name, as readers might have guessed, is a *portmanteau* for the words "love" and "robot".

In this paper, I discuss fieldwork undertaken at CES in Las Vegas in early January 2019. I draw more specifically from two interviews I conducted with the CEO and founder of Groove X, Kaname Hayashi, as well as the media and promotional materials on the Lovot. I focus on this particular robot by virtue of the bold claim that it will bring about a "new relationship between human beings and robots" [6]. I also consider, more broadly, the rise of social robots that use sensors, artificial intelligence and 'Internet of things' technology, and that are targeted and marketed to older adults. I home in on the overlap of these advanced robots and a category of social robots that has been called 'companion robots', which are designed to enhance the health or wellbeing of older adults chiefly by providing companionship [7]. Companion robots that offer features similar to that of the Lovot have been imbued in popular media with a salvationist rhetoric and promises of helping "solve" what are perceived as large-scale social problems [8], like a spreading "loneliness epidemic" in the Western world [9], and social isolation among older adults that is supposedly intensified by aging populations [10]. These discourses juxtapose a pessimistic reading of the present and an optimistic vision for the future, and they make a case for resolving societal woes through corporatism and capitalism.

What are the implications of these zoomorphic companion robots, which are kitted with advanced surveillance capacities, and what are the implications of drawing on a discourse of pethood, love and companionship to contextualize their adoption into the lifeworlds of older adults? I approach this topic from an age, media and animal studies perspective, and seek to introduce and explore some critical questions within human-animal-machine entanglements that are subsumed by zoomorphic robots.

2   The Lovot

2.1   Introducing a Love Robot

When I spoke to Hayashi in January 2019, he pointed out that the Lovot is the most sophisticated companion robot on the market, and the older adult population is its primary target. Hayashi reported that, in limited testing undertaken by the company before that point, the Lovot was shown to improve sociability of older adults, and he hoped the robot would allow them to live in their homes for longer periods of time. Contrary to other companion robots designed for older adults living in care facilities, including those living with dementia, the Lovot showed to be an especially promising option for older adults who live at home autonomously, offering them steady, 24-h companionship.

Zoomorphic robots, as I further discuss in the next section of this paper, are understood to be robots with recognizably animal characteristics and features. The Lovot stands in contrast with other zoomorphic robots designed for older adults like Paro the seal or the Joy for All cats and dogs. The Lovot is primarily innovative as a companion robot because of its assemblage of advanced technological functions. It is the first companion robot to have a combination of a 360-degree camera, a heat sensor that tells humans apart from other animals and objects, microphones, some fifty sensors on its body, and cloud computing capacity with artificial intelligence functions [6]. These technologies allow the Lovot to recognize its primary owner and other individuals by identifying voice and facial features. It can maintain unique relationships with up to 1,000 different people over its life, including with 100 people simultaneously.

It exhibits various levels of 'love' for each person it knows. It can discern human moods and behaviors and adapt its actions accordingly, showing recognizable signs of affection and even jealousy. When I first encountered a Lovot at CES it came over to see me, seeming curious. I pet it on the side of its head, but it backed away quickly. Hayashi picked up the Lovot and explained its rejection of me: it had been "shy" throughout CES because there were too many new people—or strangers—around. It was quickly adapting to new faces and such a large public forum proved to be a challenge. But the robot's trepidation, and the need to build a connection, is a feature, not a bug. With this robot, just as with a companion animal, a relationship must be built. The expression of love is not a given and must be earned through regular and positive interactions with the robot, foregrounding reciprocity in the relationship and defining mutual attachment as a rewarding experience (Fig. 1).

Fig. 1. A Lovot at CES 2019. Photo by author.

2.2 The Promise of Companion Robots

The goal of this paper is to explore some considerations at the heart of the domestication of zoomorphic robots, and not to ascertain the efficacy of companion robots, or to put into question the idea that some people, including older adults, might enjoy or otherwise gain something from interacting with them. Sarrica, Brondi and Fortunati point to the fact that there does not exist a single definition for social robots and there is a notable lack of consensus, in both scientific and popular discourses, with regards to the level of sociality and autonomy that should be expected from them [11]. It is worth noting that published research points to the benefits tied to older adults' interactions with robot pets [e.g., 12, 13]. One such benefit might lie in robots' ability to generate social connections, as Wada and Shibata suggest, and to mediate relationships [14].

Yet, both Pu et al.'s [15] and Broekens, Heerink, and Rosendal's [7] reviews of research conducted on social robots point to some of the flaws in existing studies and highlight the need for more research. First, there is dearth of high-quality studies; second, there is a lack of rigorous design in the research undertaken or unclear methodologies; third, the samples are too small or findings too anecdotal to be reliable; and fourth, there is a need for more long-term research to know if positive signs wear off after the novelty of the new robot fades [7]. Sharkey and Sharkey [16] issue a warning as researchers continue to assess the efficacy or impact of companion robots. When findings are indicative of benefits, specifically in terms of isolation and loneliness, researchers should wonder whether an alternative to a robot might be better. In other words, an older adult with few social connections might gain something from a robot companion, but could they gain more from an enriched social environment? [16]

There is also a remarkable cleavage between even the most positive research findings, and the claims of private companies, which frame their technologies as life altering, without offering any reliable evidence. For instance, the popular Joy for All companion pets by Ageless Innovation (formerly produced by the Hasbro toy company) were displayed at the AARP kiosk at CES 2019. They are described by the company as lifechanging technologies for older adults. The same animatronic dog that was branded as a toy for kids less than a decade ago is now described as a health robot that reduces isolation and loneliness and can even replace medication. It is also insinuated to slow cognitive decline and the progression of dementia [17].

3 Zoomorphic Designs

3.1 The Best Parts of an Animal

Many of the emerging robots–especially those designed for companionship for older adults–do not have a slick futuristic design or a humanoid appearance, meaning that they do not have the appearance of a human. Indeed, research like the focus groups conducted by Wu, Fassert and Rigaud [18] suggests that older adults tended to dislike robots that were humanoid in design. Instead, soft fur tends to cover hard, mechanical bodies and miniature technologies are used to maintain their small size, giving them a decidedly zoomorphic appearance. But a robot cat or dog that simulates convincingly a pet relationship is no easy feat, because many older adults know exactly what it feels like to interact with a cat or dog. Many of them have had their own pets, and an animatronic robot easily fails to replicate the nuances of this form of companionship. This points to a challenge of authenticity in the design of robot pets.

Then, there are robots like Paro the seal, especially designed to interact with older adults living in care facilities, including older adults living with dementia. The seal was chosen by the makers of Paro because of the raging debate about the seal hunt in Canada at the time, when seals stood out as cute, helpless, exotic and threatened wilderness. Crucially, for the people who handle Paro, there is no known haptic connection to replicate, no pet seal behavior to recognize as either familiar or as deficient.

The Lovot is similar in its reliance on a fictionalized or exotic rendering of an animal to avoid the authenticity trap of robot pets, circumventing the need to replicate any known encounter. Yet, it replicates some cherished elements of pethood. One media article explained: "a little like a penguin, a little like a sloth, Lovot is a companion robot with big googly eyes and an even bigger AI-powered heart" [9]. This observation points to a rendering of animality that is exotic and amorphous, yet tailored to the human's predilections within the human-animal relationship.

The Lovot has been designed to be an optimal techno-companion species: it is small and light, and it has flippers that are designed to make it easy to pick up and hug. The Lovot rolls around on wheels that retract when it is picked up, so that handling and hugging it is comfortable. Its temperature is just a bit higher than that of a human, and it has "a sensitive body that encourages 'skinship' (the closeness between a mother and a child)" [19]. Its round face is animated with LCD screen eyes that seem to express emotion. It makes endearing sounds, though there is a handy mute function. Its "voices, as you hear them from the speaker, simulate the sound echoing inside an oral cavity, generating a sense of life and vitality" [19].

Its technological affordances are recast to mimic some of the biological features of pet life. For instance, it has a 10-year life span, and it "sleeps" at night (i.e., it recharges and downloads software updates). It is designed to be pleasantly unruly, and shows some pet behaviors like fear and jealousy that deepen the engagement, yet signal the independence of the robot. As Hayashi pointed out, one of the issues with furry robots like Paro (a usually white or light-colored furry seal) is its propensity to get dirty from being repeatedly handled. Yet the practices of technological care required to keep the Lovot clean—like frequently changing its clothes to wash them—are rewarded by a deepened affection towards the human, thus instilling mutual care as a feature of the relationship. The Lovot conforms to a narrow notion of what a non-human companion should be for an older adult: idealized and sanitized. In the companies' marketing, zoomorphic robots are said to offer all the joys of pethood and none of its responsibilities [17, 19].

3.2   Liveliness

We are constantly being readied by science fiction (and tech journalism) for the imminent arrival of the technology *par excellence* that will live up to the challenge of confounding our ability to discern real from simulated life, and that will be capable of eliciting human love. Media articles about the Lovot echo these tropes, with authors suggesting that the Lovot challenges the boundaries between machine and animal. As one points out, the Lovot "is the first robot I can see myself getting emotionally attached to" [20]. Another states "I could already feel myself starting to succumb to Lovot's charms" [9].

The promise of falling in love with your robot is explored in the growing field of lovotics, within which love is considered a "contingent process of attraction, affection and attachment from humans towards robots and the belief of vice versa from robots to humans" [21]. Yet, much of the research into lovotics has tended to emphasize love more narrowly as an attachment that is inspired by romantic love or sexual attachment between humans [22]. Lovotics and technologies specifically oriented towards human sexuality (especially those geared towards women's sexuality) have been marginalized from such mass consumer showcases as CES, which opened itself to sex technologies on a trial basis in 2020 [23]. This absence has carved out a space for other—perhaps more socially palatable—forms of robot love to be celebrated as novel consumer technologies.

As Kahn et al. argue, a new technological genre of autonomous, adaptive, personified and embodied objects is emerging that defies the traditional distinction between animate and inanimate. This is where language is unable to articulate what these new ontologies mean to human life [24]. The Lovot conjures an alternative lifeform that navigates a delicate balance between mimicking the experience of pethood on one hand, and creating a new, unfamiliar encounter on the other. There is an important distinction to make, as robot pets are gaining in capacity and becoming tailored and adapted to older adults, they are not becoming increasingly lifelike; they are not replicating known forms of life like a human or another species. Yet, these technologies are becoming increasingly *lively*.

The construction of liveliness is far from being a new development, and Chow points to the longstanding human tradition of pursuing liveliness by generating an illusion of life via mechanical means [25]. Here, I also use the term liveliness in the sense that has been theorized by Collard and Dempsey [26] and Barua [27], in the context of animal studies. The authors underscore the relational conditions under which the liveliness of certain non-humans becomes crucial to their existence as desirable commodities. In some cases—as with pets, or animals in safaris—liveliness is imperative to an animal's 'encounter value'. Understanding liveliness in these terms helps to map how some features of life become recognized and valued within certain contexts and economies. It also illuminates how a robot pet, itself a technological rendering of the idealized non-human companion, is inspired by the characteristics, forms and behaviors of life that are selectively valued as encounterable in our existing relationships with animals. Technologies like the Lovot do not mimic life but they capture the elements that subtend companion animals' encounter value. Liveliness is interpreted through mechanical means, and curated by adopting and adapting the desired characteristics of pethood.

4   Companion Robots as Technologies of Surveillance?

4.1   The All-Seeing Lovot

The apparatus of sensors that make Lovot lively in its relationship with the human encompasses the same features that make it double as a technology of surveillance. This operates in a similar way to the increasingly perceptive and invasive devices of convenience or entertainment that infiltrate the 'smart' home without meaningful or transparent provisions for data protection [28]. The Lovot's 360-degree camera, its heat sensors, its microphones, its people recognition capacities are, by default, all connected to the cloud, and data about the users is saved in the robot's Nest or charging station. The sensory capacities of the Lovot are promoted to be used by caregivers to monitor an older person and their environment. As Hayashi explained, the Lovot can give love and companionship to an older person, but "it also can offer peace of mind to their loved ones". Caregivers could opt to turn on the camera or microphone remotely and tap into the Lovot's sensory apparatus to check in on the older adult and the older adult's environment to detect signs of out-of-bound behavior. "It is a soothing robot… for everyone" Hayashi explains. As the Lovot gets released in the Japanese and—soon—other markets, health-related applications are being devised and researched. Here, Soshana Zuboff's warning about the rise of 'surveillance capitalism,' and the familiar ark of technologies that can seem innocuous when we first encounter them, is worth highlighting. She explains that "insights and techniques once intended to illuminate and enrich quickly disappear into the magnetic field of the commercial surveillance project, only to reappear later as ever more cunning methods of supply, manufacture and sales" [28].

The surveillance function of the Lovot makes it fit within other major trends that our research team observed when conducting fieldwork at CES 2019. First, there is an assumption that older adults' only stake to the digital world lies in being the recipients of technologies that rectify age-related physical, cognitive or social decline [29]. In this way, much of the innovations that concern themselves with later life treat aging as an ailment to overcome through consumerism, feeding into and strengthening a successful aging discourse according to which one's aging boils down to individual choice and action [30]. Second, there is an alarming generalized disregard for questions related to privacy or consent in the design, development, testing and deployment of technologies, especially as they relate to older people. We asked developers to discuss if or how older adults would consent to these technologies entering their lives. These questions were often met with hesitation about how to navigate the boundaries of private, domestic life and an uncertainty about exactly who (companies, institutions, caregivers, families or older adults themselves) should determine these boundaries. Third, through the first two points, we ultimately see the construction of older people as subjects to be controlled, surveilled and sometimes infantilized through increasingly invasive technologies that are meant to be appended to their bodies or embedded their homes.

4.2   The Domestication of Animals and the Domestication of Technologies

The theory of media domestication brought forth by Silverstone and his colleagues suggests that when new technologies progressively push into the boundaries of our private lives, they can elicit a panic, or a reluctance. Domestication thus emphasizes the dynamic relationships between users and innovations, and refers to the process by which new technologies become accepted and incorporated into the home or into the everyday [31]. The domestication theory of media suggests that technologies can be 'tamed' through various processes, and that the panic that they might have brought about when they first emerged gets minimized over time. Technologies come to have a physical and symbolic place in the home [33]. Domestication theory, as Haddon points out, originated from the metaphor of animal domestication, and the taming of animals [32]. As more advanced AI-based systems that monitor and track older adults are poised to enter the market, we should be attuned to the forces that mediate domestication, and to the rhetorical and other strategies employed to tame technologies that have surveillance capacities, to favor adoption among an older public, and quell even the most justified gestures of social resistance or reluctance.

I suggest that emphasizing the animal referent of the domestication metaphor helps us to understanding one of such strategies. The language used is important, and processes of 'naming' and 'classifying' serve to position an object within a semantic field, and help individuals orient themselves towards objects in specific ways [34]. It may be the case that a category of 'companion robot' (a term that mirrors the 'companion animal'), a rhetoric of love, and a construction of liveliness are used to shape a path that ushers technologies of surveillance into the domestic spaces and quotidian lives of older adults. The design of the Lovot renders a technology of surveillance into a zoomorphic form that is animated with a liveliness that humans recognize and value. The human's attachment to the robot and the robot's responses are consistently characterized as expressions of love. In doing this, the Lovot harnesses one of domestication's most established institutions: the place of the companion animal and more specifically pethood, as well as the bonds of love that are understood by humans to underpin their relationship with pets.

The uneven relationship of power between humans and animals is at the heart of the enterprise of animal domestication. Domestication, as it relates to the construction of pethood, has entailed making certain species fundamentally dependent on humans for their survival [35]. It has also called for far-reaching efforts to shape species and breeds according to the physical and behavioral traits deemed by humans to be desirable [35] or encounterable. These features of domestication help us understand the double function of pets as commodities and companions, and as fixtures in humans' most intimate social worlds. Zoomorphic robots' appeal as technologies that easily append themselves to domestic spaces might lie in their ability to harness the socially-entrenched contours of the pet-human relationship, and the fantasy of a totally controllable and moldable companion. Lively surveillance technologies ask us to entertain relationships of love with the devices that monitor us, and animals may represent a mediative force in the domestication of new technologies.

5 Conclusions and Implications for Future Research

In discourses of innovation and techno-utopianism, there is an assumption that digital technologies can offer idealized solutions to perceived problems related to age. However, the development of these technologies often happens without asking older adults what they want. This paper began by inquiring about the implications of zoomorphic companion robots that are outfitted with advanced surveillance capacities and that borrow from the discourse of pethood, love and companionship to contextualize their adoption by older adults. By probing the Lovot as an entanglement between the categories of human, animal and machine, I have highlighted zoomorphic robots' ability to harness a liveliness constructed from our relationships with pets in order to instantiate a sanitized and idealized version of companionship. I have also pointed to the double meaning of domestication as a means of exploring the potential for zoomorphic robots to bind themselves to the institution of pethood so as to claim a growing place in the older adults' homes.

It may be tempting to approach the domestication of advanced technologies with an assumption that these devices will narrowly serve a population that has the financial means to afford the latest innovation. Certainly, few of us can afford to pay thousands for a robot pet for ourselves, or for a loved one. But as Virginia Eubanks points out, when technologies of surveillance become popularized or domesticated, they tend to be used to assert existing social orders and to exert control over marginalized populations [36]. Many companion and other social robots are being marketed precisely for older adult populations that are deemed vulnerable because of social isolation. As care robots, therapeutic robots or companion robots become more affordable, more popularized, more entrenched within the norms of health and insurance provision, we might wonder if interacting with robots will remain a privilege, or even a choice. Will growing older without robot companions, and with live humans and live animals instead, become the position of privilege? Can valuing robot companions as a substitution or proxy for embodied, reciprocal relations between living creatures of all sorts create a justification for further isolating some older adults and further constricting their networks? Who deserves to live with other life forms, and what does the enthusiasm for companion robots for older adults say about our expectations of their social worlds?

Further, as interspecies relationships get recast as human-robot relationships, how is our notion of companionship altered, and do non-humans suffer from our continued efforts to sanitize and idealize pethood and our struggles to render it into robot form? Human-pet relationships can be messy in all senses of the word, and indeed the messiness of interspecies relationships can become heightened with the old age of either party (sometimes, one needs to downsize to a dwelling that does not allow pets; sometime one's bladder begins to fail and one has accidents on the floor). Donna Haraway emphasizes the messy co-constitution of beings through companionship and relationships of mutual response-ability over the course of species' lives [37, 38].

The Lovot betrays our society's anthropocentric and instrumental view of animals with the idea that life is not necessary to the formation of pethood. As technologies like the Lovot instantiate Descartes' figuration of animality as 'automata' [39], how does this impact our treatment of real animals, and the expectations that we have of our relationships with them? In which circumstances and for whom does embodied life stop being a pre-requisite to companionship? Companionship in later life seems to be reduced to its instrumental function to such an extent that reciprocal life is no longer a necessary feature, and liveliness suffices.

Acknowledgements. This research is supported by Ageing + Communication + Technologies (ACT, www.actproject.ca), a research project based at Concordia University and funded by the Social Sciences and Humanities Research Council (SSHRC).

References

1. CES Press Release: CES 2019 Proves AI and 5G Will Transform the Future. https://www.ces.tech/News/Press-Releases/CES-Press-Release.aspx?NodeID=d7f8b183-398e-4f32-ac14-21c9d35ac996. Accessed 13 Jan 2020
2. Segal, H.: Technological Utopianism in American Culture. University of Chicago Press, Chicago (1985)
3. Taulli, T.: Cool AI Highlights At CES. https://www.forbes.com/sites/tomtaulli/2019/01/13/cool-ai-highlights-at-ces/#75cfc77bf94a. Accessed 12 Jan 2020
4. Bayern, M.: The 8 coolest robots spotted at CES 2020. https://www.techrepublic.com/article/the-8-coolest-robots-spotted-at-ces-2020/. Accessed 12 Jan 2020
5. Gallarate, S.: CES 2020 innovations prove that robots will soon become our new best friends. Screenshot Magazine. https://screenshot-magazine.com/the-future/ces-2020-robots-friends/. Accessed 12 Jan 2020
6. Groove, X.: Lovot Concept Book (2018)
7. Broekens, J., Heerink, M., Rosendal, H.: Assistive social robots in elderly care: a review. Gerontechnology **8**(2), 94–103 (2009)
8. Volti, R.: Society and Technological Change. Macmillan, London (2006)
9. Collins, K.: At CES 2019, I met a robot that showed me a future where we're not so lonely. https://www.cnet.com/news/at-ces-2019-i-met-a-robot-that-showed-me-a-future-where-were-not-so-lonely/. Accessed 12 Jan 2020
10. Kelly, H.: Technology is changing how we grow old and die. https://www.cnn.com/2019/01/18/tech/technology-elderly/index.html. Accessed 12 Jan 2020
11. Sarrica, M., Brondi, S., Fortunati, L.: How many facets does a "social robot" have? A review of scientific and popular definitions online. Inf. Technol. People (2019). https://doi.org/10.1108/ITP-04-2018-0203
12. Kanamori, M., et al.: Pilot study on improvement of quality of life among elderly using a pettype robot. In: IEEE International Symposium on Computational Intelligence in Robotics and Automation (2003)
13. Hutson, S., Lim, S.L., Bentley, P.J., Bianchi-Berthouze, N., Bowling, A.: Investigating the suitability of social robots for the wellbeing of the elderly. In: D'Mello, S., Graesser, A., Schuller, B., Martin, J.C. (eds.) ACII 2011. LNCS, vol. 6974, pp. 578–587. Springer, Heidelberg (2011). https://doi.org/10.1007/978-3-642-24600-5_61
14. Wada, K., Shibata, T.: Social effects of robot therapy in a care house: change of social network of the residents for one year. J. Adv. Comput. Intell. Intell. Inform. **13**(4), 386–392 (2009)

15. Pu, L., Moyle, W., Jones, C., Todorovic, M.: The effectiveness of social robots for older adults: a systematic review and meta-analysis of randomized controlled studies. Gerontologist **59**(1), 37–51 (2019)
16. Sharkey, A., Sharkey, N.: Granny and the robots: ethical issues in robot care for the elderly. Ethics Inf. Technol. **14**, 27–40 (2010). https://doi.org/10.1007/s10676-010-9234-6
17. Joy for All Companion Pets. https://joyforall.com/. Accessed 12 Jan 2020
18. Wu, Y., Fassert, C., Rigaud, A.: Designing robots for the elderly: appearance issue and beyond. Arch. Gerontol. Geriatr. **54**(1), 121–126 (2012)
19. Lovot. https://lovot.life/en/technology/. Accessed 12 Jan 2020
20. Lee, D.: Lovot is the first robot I can see myself getting emotionally attached to. https://www.theverge.com/2019/1/10/18176002/lovot-groovex-robot-emotional-attachment-ces-2019. Accessed 12 Jan 2020
21. Samani, H.A.: Lovotics: Loving robots. LAP Lambert, Saarbrücken (2012)
22. Cheok, A.D., Devlin, K., Levy, D.: Love and Sex with Robots. Springer, Cham (2016). https://doi.org/10.1007/978-3-319-57738-8
23. Lerman, R.: Sex Tech Might Just Be the Biggest New Thing at CES 2020. https://time.com/5760692/ces-gadget-show-2020/. Accessed 12 Jan 2020
24. Kahn P.H., et al.: In: 6th ACM/IEEE International Conference on Human-Robot Interaction (HRI)
25. Chow, K.: Animation, Embodiment and Digital Media, p. 14. Palgrave MacMillan, New York (2013)
26. Collard, R., Dempsey, J.: Life for sale? The politics of lively commodities. Environ. Plan. A **45**(11), 2682–2699 (2013)
27. Barua, M.: Lively commodities and encounter value. Environ. Plan. D: Soc. Space. **34**(4), 725–744 (2016)
28. Zuboff, S.: The Age of Surveillance Capitalism: The Fight for a Human Future at the New Frontier of Power. Public Affairs, New York (2019)
29. Gullette, M.M.: Agewise: Fighting the New Ageism in America. The University of Chicago Press, Chicago and London (2011)
30. Katz, S., Calasanti, T.: Critical perspectives on successful aging: does it "appeal more than it illuminates"? Gerontologist **55**(1), 26–33 (2015)
31. Silverstone, R., Haddon, L.: Design and the domestication of information and communication technologies: technical change and everyday life. In: Silverstone, R., Mansell, R. (eds.) Communication by Design: The Politics of Information and Communication Technologies. Oxford University Press, Oxford (1996)
32. Haddon, L.: Domestication analysis, objects of study, and the centrality of technologies in everyday life. Can. J. Commun. **36**(2), 311 (2011)
33. Haddon, L.: Roger Silverstone's legacies: domestication. New Media Soc. **9**(1), 25–32 (2007)
34. de Rosa, A.S.: Social Representations in the "Social Arena". Routledge, New York (2013)
35. DeMello, M.: Animals and Society: An Introduction to Human-Animal Studies. Columbia University Press, New York (2012)
36. Eubanks, V.: Automating Inequality: How High-Tech Tools Profile, Police, and Punish the Poor. St. Martin's Press, New York (2018)
37. Haraway, D.: The Companion Species Manifesto: Dogs, People, and Significant Otherness. Prickly Paradigm Press, Chicago (2003)
38. Haraway, D.: Staying with the Trouble: Making Kin in the Chthulucene. Duke University Press, Durham (2016)
39. Descartes R.: Oeuvres de Descartes. In: Adam, C., Tannery, P. (eds.) Vrin/CNRS, Paris (1964–1976)

Explore the Demands of the Elderly by Integrating QFD and Scenario-Based Design

Shuo-Fang Liu, Chun-Han Tsai[✉], and Ching-Fen Chang

Department of Industrial Design, National Cheng-Kung University,
No. 1, University Road, Tainan City 701, Taiwan, R.O.C.
masaomi980266@gmail.com

Abstract. Cooking is an important behavior in daily life, but it is very easy to be dangerous in the kitchen. With the increase of age, the deterioration of physical functions causes many difficulties in cooking. The purpose of this study was to understand the difficulties of older people in the kitchen. In response to limited resources, identify the most urgent problems that need improvement, reduce the risks in the lives of the elderly, and achieve independent living and healthy aging. This study uses Quality function deployment combined with the participants' and experts' opinions to find the demand and physiological functions that need to be assisted and improved most, and provides a reference for future research, assistive devices and smart home development. Use Scenario-Based Design to discover more ideas for participants and gain a deeper understanding of the problems encountered by the elderly. In the end, the problem that needs to be improved is "Forgot cooking something and do something else". The physiological functions that need to be assisted most are hand stability, attention and memory. In the future, the development of assistive products for the elderly can be carried out in the direction of tactile feedback and vibration reminders. It can be used on hand devices in conjunction with other sensory functions.

Keywords: Quality function deployment · Scenario-Based Design · Sensory system · Elderly · Ageing · Ageing in place

1 Introduction

According to the United Nations report, the decline in fertility, coupled with longer lifespans, has led to global ageing population. The population over 65 years old has risen from 120 million in 1950 to 650 million in 2017 in the world. East Asia and Southeast Asia have the largest population of 261 million. It is estimated that the elderly population will increase to 1.5 billion by 2050 [1].

The demographic structure of society is rapidly changing because of the ageing population. The impact on society is comprehensive, Including politics, economy, finance, culture, education and family [2]. Ageing is a common problem in the world, is an inevitable process in life. The time, speed, and results that occur in each person are different.

© Springer Nature Switzerland AG 2020
Q. Gao and J. Zhou (Eds.): HCII 2020, LNCS 12208, pp. 497–509, 2020.
https://doi.org/10.1007/978-3-030-50249-2_36

The literature points out that the ageing phenomenon of the elderly is roughly divided into five aspects, Physical function, Physiological function, Sensory systems, Psychological characteristics, Living structure [3]. The Sensory systems of the human body is important for receiving messages and dealing with environmental information. Hands are a significant tool for interacting with devices and the environment [4]. Degradation of sensory systems and Physical function have a great impact on life.

1.1 The Effect of Aging

Aging causes the deterioration of sight, hearing and touch. Due to the aging of the visual system, turbidity of the crystalline lens, yellowing of the crystalline lens, and reduction of pupil light adjustment, vision begins to decline at the age of 40–50 years old, resulting in reduced vision, reduced color, fear of glare, and adaptation time to light and dark becomes longer [5, 6]. Due to the degradation of the hearing system, the ability to hear and perceive information began to decline at the age of 40–45, the speech recognition ability decreased, and it was difficult to distinguish high-frequency chirping and low-vibration sounds, leading to hearing loss and even deafness. The ability to communicate with others is limited, causing social withdrawal [5]. The skin will also gradually become rough, the number of sensory cells will decrease, the feeling of cold and heat, light touch, pain will decrease, and the touch will be dull, which will cause problems such as difficult operation, trauma and burns, and agility decline [5, 7].

With the increase of age, the body function gradually deteriorates, the body size becomes smaller, Skeletal and joints weaken, and the ability to exercise is poor [3, 5]. After 65 years old, the function of the hand gradually declines [8]. The adverse effects of aging on hand function, including grip force, finger pinch force, and tactile sensation, have significantly decreased, leading to a decrease in the quality of life and independence of the elderly. Increasingly difficult to perform daily tasks [9, 10].

1.2 User Environment Demand

With the development of technology, there are many product-oriented design in the market, which is developed from the aspects of function and cost control. User-Oriented Design (UOD) emphasizes that users should be deeply understood, based on users' demand and expectations, using functions and technologies to turn requirements into products or services [11].

The literature refers to the "environmental docility hypothesis", that stronger people are less susceptible to the environment, and those with lower ability are more dependent on external conditions and more susceptible to environmental impact. When the environment is in line with the ability, people can be more capable and independent [12]. Because the elderly needs an environmental suitable for their activity patterns and deteriorating sensory system [13]. Therefore, we should reduce the obstacles and difficulties for the elderly in the environment. Improve the satisfaction of life experience and the environment for users, rather than let users adapt to the under-designed environment [14]. For example, because the ability to receive light has dropped,

Lighting should be installed in the darker and where is easy to fall. For the elderly who is weak of hearing, the equipment used should be boosted [5]. In order to accurately change the living environment of the elderly and improve the satisfaction and pleasure of the elderly, understanding their environmental needs is the primary goal.

1.3   Quality Function Deployment (QFD)

Quality function deployment is a process of planning and communication. Use the House of Quality (HOQ) matrix to quantify the relationship between design decisions and product quality. Transform customer requests and technical elements into design criteria, identify priorities that affect design, and facilitate the integration of different positions within the company. identify priorities that affect design. Facilitate the integration of different positions within the company. HOQ manages the process of product development, improves product quality, reduces the number of design changes, and thus shortens time to market and lowers costs, making products easier to produce and closer to customer needs [15–17].

QFD has been widely used in manufacturing, in addition to developing products can also be used in development services [17]. Some literatures use QFD combined with FMEA method to explore service requirements [18]. There are also studies that provide improved and innovative priorities for medical processes by using QFD [19]. There are many physical functions caused by aging, but resources are limited. QFD can find out the important order of needs and improve the environment of the elderly in the most suitable and effective way [18].

1.4   Scenario-Based Design

Scenario-Based Design is a HCD (Human-Centered Design) perspective design method that uses situational description or script to expose user needs. By observing or collecting data such as photos, constructing one or more characters from the data to represent users can help better express behavior or feelings. Create a scenario that allows character activities to achieve goals, describe or visualize the process of character activities, and the feelings and decisions of each stage of the process. This method allows designers to better understand the characteristics of users and explore the relationship between the product itself and the context of use [20, 21].

Memory is a strange ability. The less information hidden in an image, the more memories you can recall. Black and white photos are more likely to inspire memories than color photos. Simple images may be more instructive than complex images. Because of the special representation of images, photo inspiration can evoke memories, feelings and messages. Compared to words, images evoke deeper elements of human consciousness [22, 23]. On the other hand, when the experimental environment is limited, it is impossible to conduct interviews in real places. Image Elicitation can help the participants to recall, and can evoke memories that are not remembered by verbal protocol.

1.5   Summary

Cooking is a very important behavior in life, and the kitchen is a very important room in the family [24]. Some studies point out that cooking improves survival in Taiwan's elderly [25]. In order to make the elderly successful ageing, "Active participation in life" and "healthy aging" are important [26]. However, the kitchen is usually the most vulnerable place for people in the home, because improper use of equipment or kitchen activities can cause injury and danger [27].

According to the above literature, we can understand that aging is an irresistible factor, and aging population is a global problem. There will be more and more elderly people in the future, but the current research on the needs of elderly people is insufficient. Although product-oriented can promote the development of new products, but user-oriented is closer to user needs. Aging in Place is promoted all over the world [12]. Safe and comfortable living at home is considered to be more beneficial to physical and mental state of the elderly [13]. However, when you are young, you can adapt to a environment easily, but may have problems in old age. This study uses QFD in combination with Scenario-Based Design to explore the problems and demands of the elderly and to improve the environment of the elderly. Image Elicitation was used for interviews to stimulate participants' perceptions of life and to explore problems. The field simulated by the visual card was set in the kitchen in the home environment. Although familiar but dangerous. QFD starts from user needs and turns requirements into design criteria. In response to limited resources, we can find the most urgent improvement needs and problems. It also provides a reference for the development of assistive devices for the elderly and the development of smart homes and kitchens.

2   Method

Aging causes the decline of human physiological functions. To improve the difficulties of the elderly, this study uses QFD and Scenario-Based Design to discuss the needs that elderly people will encounter in the kitchen to achieve the following goals:

1. Understand the difficulties of the elderly in the kitchen, provide more in-depth and comprehensive research reference
2. Identify the most urgent problems that need improvement and reduce the risks in the lives of older people
3. Promote the independence and quality of life of the elderly and make them healthy aging.
4. Provide references for future assistive devices and smart home development.

2.1   Participant

Some scholars distinguish elderly by age; "young old" is 65–74 years old, "mid old" is 75–84 years old; "old old" is over 85 years old. The aging can be divided into three stages according to the Activities of Daily Living (ADLs): The "primary aging" elderly people have some aging characteristics, such as white hair, spots on the skin, loss of vision, hearing loss, etc. Although there are some degradations, they are healthy and comfortable; The "secondary aging" of the elderly is affected by diseases and bad habits, leading to a decline in physical function, mental and cognitive function, and requires help from others; "tertiary aging" because of the rapid decline of various functions, the elderly are sick in bed or unable to act on their own [28]. From the above literature, we know the differences in the aging stage of elderly people. Most elderly-related studies have set the age to be over 65. But for the Participant who is about to enter old age, participant conditions for this experiment were limited to 55 years old and above, and the "primary aging" elderly with cooking habits.

2.2   Experiment Setup

This experiment mainly uses QFD as the experimental method, as shown in Fig. 1. The following will be described separately according to the experimental process:

1. Demand element (DE)
   Use QFD to find hand problems in the life of elderly people. Prepare kitchen simulation cards in advance, including common cabinets, counters, refrigerators, gas stoves, sinks, dining tables and chairs, and draw corresponding windows, walls and doors on site. Through Image Elicitation, participants were simulated to reproduce the kitchen scene and interviewed, as shown in Fig. 1. Finally, the final DEs are obtained through coding in Grounded Theory.

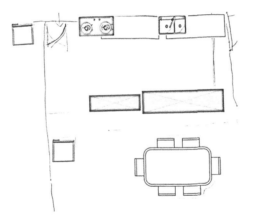

Fig. 1. Example of kitchen simulation card

2. Physiological function element (PFE)
   Derive PFE using DE.
3. Demand function matrix
   Explore the relationship between DE and PFE, add expert opinions, and grade the degree of correlation between each demand and function, 0–5 points, the higher the score, the stronger the relationship between the elements, and finally get the average of the degree of correlation, then converted into a pattern and filled into the demand

function matrix to complete the relationship matrix. Irrelevant is 0 points, do not fill in the matrix; very uncorrelated is 1 point, expressed as Δ; moderate correlation is 3 points, expressed as ○; extreme correlation is 5 points, expressed as ◎ complete the relation matrix.

4. Problem importance

   Through the questionnaire, the importance of DE to the participants was obtained. DE is used as a questionnaire item, and each item uses a 5-point Likert scale for importance ranking, with 1 being the least important and 5 being the most important. Questionnaire items include age, gender, frequency of cooking, occupation, hand disease, operational difficulties, DE importance, frequency of encountering DE problems.

5. Weight to complete HOQ

   The DE importance is converted to the PFE importance. The Experiment setup of this study is shown in Fig. 2.

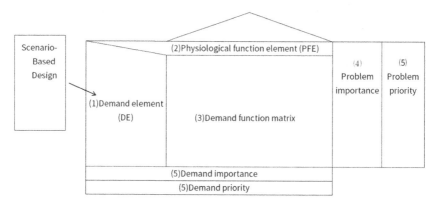

Fig. 2. Experiment setup

3   Result

3.1   Demand Element (DE)

In response to the problems encountered in the home environment, interviews were conducted with 6 participants participating in observation and Image Elicitation. Analyze and encode the collected data, using three coding methods of Grounded Theory: open coding, axial coding, selective coding. During the coding process, different modes can be repeated [29, 30]. First, the transcript obtained from the interview is segmented line by line in open coding, and the sentences are subdivided and named to obtain 53 sentences. The similar concepts are roughly classified into 24 sub-categories, and the sentences in each sub-category are classified as: Unresolved problems and dilemmas, Resolved problems or alternatives, Descriptive statements. From the sub-category, 14 categories are integrated, and the common problems and unresolved problems of the participants can be seen. Finally, the four common kitchen problems are summarized, which means that the problem elements of the elderly are derived. They are "Get scald when cleaning the gas stove and countertop and moving the pan", "Cut the hand while using a knife", "Feel burdened when using the pan", "Forgot cooking something and do something else." The DE of this research is on the left side of Fig. 4.

3.2 Physiological Function Element (PFE)

Based on previous literature, interviews, and observations, we summarized all the physiological functions related to the DE. In the end, we got six PFEs, which are "Temperature sensitivity", "Attention", "Memory", "Vision", "Tactile acuity", "Hand stability". PFE is shown at the top of Fig. 4.

3.3 Demand Function Matrix

The questionnaire was used to collect the opinions of 5 experts, including 4 medical background experts, with an average experience of 18 years, and 1 expert with relevant medical knowledge and design development experience, 4 years. Explore the relationship between DE and PFE, and finally get 5 unrelated, 9 low correlation, 5 moderate correlation, 5 highly correlated items. The Demand function matrix for this study is shown in Fig. 4.

3.4 Problem Importance

Data Analysis

A total of 39 questionnaires were returned, including 32 valid samples and 7 invalid responses. The response rate is 82.05%. Most of participant cook every day, and the samples are divided into three groups by age, 55–64, 65–74, above 65 years old. Women are the majority of all participants. Data of demographical as shown in Table 1. The average value of DE importance is shown on the right side of Fig. 4.

Table 1. Data of demographical

Items		No	Percentage
Age	55–64	11	34.4
	65–74	7	21.9
	75+	14	43.8
Cooking frequency (days/times)	1	21	65.6
	2	6	18.7
	3	3	9.4
	20	1	3.1
	26	1	3.1

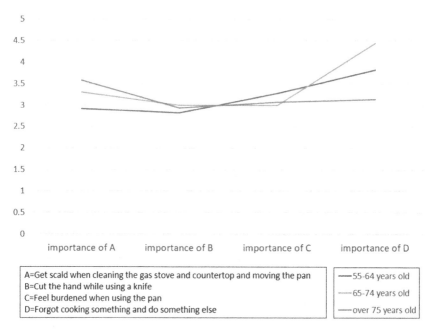

Fig. 3. Line chart of the average of the importance in each age group to the DEs

We performed Analysis of Variance (ANOVA) for the importance and age of each DE. The homogeneity is 0.238, 0.323, 0.271, 0.075, which are all greater than 0.05, indicating that the sample is homogeneous. The importance of the four questions is not significant between the three age groups, which means that the importance of the questions to the subjects does not differ significantly with age. A line chart of the average of the importance in each age group to the DEs is shown in Fig. 3.

The frequency of occurrence of DE is converted into a score, 4 points for sorting 1, 3 points for sorting 2, 2 points for sorting 3, and 1 point for sorting 4. Calculating the average number can be found in the order of high to low frequency: "Get scald when cleaning the gas stove and countertop and moving the pan", "Feel burdened when using the pan", "Forgot cooking something and do something else", "Cut the hand while using a knife". The average number of DE occurrence frequencies is shown in Table 2.

Table 2. The average numbers of DE occurrence frequencies

DE	Frequency of occurrence
Get scald when cleaning the gas stove and countertop and moving the pan	2.84
Cut the hand while using a knife	2.25
Feel burdened when using the pan	2.50
Forgot cooking something and do something else	2.41

3.5   Weight to Complete HOQ

After filling in the DE importance and relationship matrix, use the independent collocation method to multiply the DE importance by the correlation degree in the corresponding relationship matrix (1 point, 3 points, 5 points), and add up to get the total score of the PFE. Prioritize the PFEs to complete HOQ. The PFE of this study is shown in Fig. 4.

Physiological function element (PFE) / Demand element (DE)	Temperature sensitivity	Attention	Memory	Tactile acuity	Vision	Hand stability	Problem importance	Problem priority
Get scald when cleaning the gas stove and countertop and moving the pan	○/ 9.84	○/ 9.84	△/ 3.28	○/9.84	◎/16.4	◎/16.4	3.28	2
Cut the hand while using a knife		○/ 8.73	0	△/2.91	△/2.91	◎/14.55	2.91	4
Feel burdened when using the pan	△/ 3.13	△/ 3.13	△/ 3.13	△/3.13	△/3.13	◎/15.65	3.13	3
Forgot cooking something and do something else	△/ 3.66	○/ 10.98	○/ 18.3				3.66	1
Demand importance	16.63	32.68	24.71	15.88	22.44	46.6		
Demand priority	5	2	3	6	4	1		

Fig. 4. HOQ

We can know the priority level of DE from HOQ, list in sequence: "Forgot cooking something and do something else", "Get scald when cleaning the gas stove and countertop and moving the pan", "Feel burdened when using the pan", "Cut the hand while using a knife". After weighting with the relationship matrix, the priority levels of PFE are obtained, list in sequence: "Hand stability", "Attention", "Memory", "Vision", "Temperature sensitivity", and "Tactile acuity".

4   Discussion

In order to better grasp the difficulties and problems of the elderly in the kitchen, from the data obtained from interviews and Scenario-Based Design, we can roughly see the tendencies of the needs of the elderly. After coding, find out the context of the problem, and get DE and PFE. Discuss the deduction with experts, and get the relationship between DE and PFE. According to the questionnaire, it is found that among these kitchen problems, the most urgent problem is "Forgot cooking something and do something else". The more relevant PFE is attention and memory. "Get scald when cleaning the gas stove and countertop and moving the pan" is a secondary issue. The more relevant PFE is hand stability and vision. The third most important issue is "Feel burdened when using the pan". The most relevant PFE is hand stability, and the last question is "Cut the hand while using a knife", and the more relevant PFE is hand stability and attention. Older people think that the most important problem is different from the most frequently encountered problem. The most important problem is "Forgot cooking something and do something else" The most frequently and common problem is "Get scald when cleaning the gas stove and countertop and moving the pan". From the interviews, we can know that the elderly people think that the higher-risk problems are more important. Their own injuries are secondary. Forgetting the gas stove may cause fire. Although the burns are most often encountered, the results are relatively minor.

After constructing HOQ and weighting, the elderly's functions in hand stability, attention and memory need to be assisted and resolved. The following discusses hand stability, attention and memory.

In activities of daily living (ADLs), hand functions and skills are a big part of performing work and tasks. The work of the hand is extremely subtle and sensitive, and it also requires a lot of strength. It is the most important part of the upper limbs. Decreased hand function reduces the quality of life and independence of the elderly. Hand degradation includes grip and pinch, hand dexterity, posture maintenance, and speed [8, 9]. It may be due to decreased muscle coordination, finger agility, and hand sensation and degeneration of the central nervous system [9]. It is closely related to the degradation of skeleton, blood vessels and nervous system. It can be subdivided into joints, muscles, tendons, skeletons, nerves and receptors, blood supply, skin and nails, and distance changes controlled by nerves, etc. [8]. The hand function of the elderly decreases with age after age 65, and the age difference becomes more pronounced after age 75 [8, 10]. As women age, they degenerate more severely than men [9]. Consistent with the results in this study that women encountered "Feel burdened when using the pan" frequently. It varies with pathological conditions (osteoporosis, osteoarthritis, rheumatoid arthritis, and Parkinson's disease) [8].

The cognitive process of older people changes with age, and certain types of memory decline. Cognitive control may be worsened by damage to the prefrontal brain area [31]. Distractions have an adverse effect on memory function. The increased attention load reduces the ability to participate in fine coding by the left prefrontal cortex [32]. The decline in memory and attention may cause many inconveniences and dangers in life. Our memories are networks of interconnected cortical neurons, formed by association, that contain our experiences in their connectional structure. The composition of cognition and working memory comes from the activation and association of experience. Internal and external stimuli can reactivate memory [33].

5   Conclusion

Everyone gradually gets older, in the age when the average life expectancy is getting longer and the fertility rate is declining. The problem of the elderly has been highly valued, but the difficulties derived from the older society are still a big challenge. In the interview, we can learn that many elderly people will find ways to adapt to the problem, ignore the problem, or simply give up the task completely, resulting in injury, illness, or limited life. Such a vicious cycle ultimately leads to the elderly's restricted lives, physical and mental health, and loss of independence. In the declining physiological functions and limited resources, how to accurately find the problem points, the most effective assistance and improvement of the elderly's life is very important work.

Scenario-Based Design can explore more ideas of Participant and let everyone know more about the problems that elderly people will encounter in the kitchen. QFD can combine the opinions of Participant and experts to unify the needs of the problems to improve, and find out the most requires auxiliary physiological functions. The problems that need to be improved most are "Forgot cooking something and do something else", and the most important physiological functions are hand stability, attention and memory.

5.1 Limitations of the Study

The field of this study was set in the kitchen, but the majority of the households responsible for cooking were women, resulting in more women participants than men. The results are more suitable for women than men, but the problem of men in the kitchen also needs attention. Compared to eating outside, cooking by yourself can better control your diet and health, so cooking is an important activity for both men and women. During the interview, it was found that most of the participants did not have a specific concept of tactile sensation, and were less active in improving the degradation of tactile sensation, or even failed to detect the tactile-related degradation, which may cause deviations in importance and affect the research results.

5.2 Support and Improvement

Inspired by interviews and literature, here are a few ways to provide assistance with hand stability, memory, and attention.

- Stimulation enhances muscle coordination and the nervous system. Peripheral nerve stimulation can affect functional measures of motor performance. Some scholars have used median nerve stimulation to increase the muscle strength of patients with chronic stroke. Two hours after stimulation, the pinch of the hand increased [34]. Another study pointed out that an imperceptible, random frequency vibration was simultaneously applied to the wrist during hand movements. This sensory stimulus has an effect on the sensorimotor cortex and can also be used for neurological rehabilitation [35].
- Aids memory and attention through information stimulation. Human sensory systems are channels for receiving information, and can be used to assist attention and memory through vision, hearing, and tactile channels. According to previous research by the team, four different materials of mobile phone screen protectors were used to evaluate the usability of elderly people over 50 years of age. The results showed that the touch protectors with matte texture are more beneficial to the elderly using mobile phones [36]. Another study by the team explored the application of vibration feedback, and the results showed that vibration feedback is a good supplement for the elderly [37]. Haptic feedback is a good way to receive messages. Tactile messages can be sensed without special attention, which can effectively improve the use and operation of elderly people.

In the future, the development of assistive products for the elderly can be carried out in the direction of tactile feedback and vibration reminders. Combined with feedback from other sensory system, it can be used on hand devices. Vibration can also stimulate nerves, strengthen muscle strength, reduce problems encountered in kitchen operations, improve the independence and quality of life of elderly people, and achieve healthy aging. In the future, this research framework can be used for other demand. The field can be set at different locations, and different auxiliary devices are made for different situations and objects. It can also be used to explore the needs of people with disabilities, intelligent home, and solve daily environmental difficulties. Reduce the risk of facing danger, and improve the quality and satisfaction of life experience.

Acknowledgements. We are thankful for the financial support from The Ministry of Science and Technology (MOST), Taiwan. The grant MOST 107-2221-E-006-169 & MOST 108-2221-E-006-048.

References

1. United Nations, Department of Economic and Social Affairs, Population Division. World Population Prospects 2019: Highlights (ST/ESA/SER.A/423) (2019)
2. Huang, F-S.: Aged Society and Elder Education. Adult and Lifelong Education Bimonthly. Lucky Bookstore, Taipei (2004)
3. Shih, C.-H.: A Study of Smart Life Industry Development- An Example of Aging-in-Place for the Elderly. Unpublished master's thesis, National Cheng Kung University, Place, Taiwan (2008)
4. Chiu, Y.-J.: Planning of Urban Senior Center by Studing Behavior of The Elderlys: Taipei City for An Instance. Unpublished master's thesis, National Taipei University of Technology, Taiwan (2013)
5. Liao, C.-C.: Study on Current Living Environment Usage of the elderly in Public Housing of Tainan City. Unpublished doctoral dissertation, National Cheng Kung University, Place, Taiwan (2007)
6. Saxon, S.V., Etten, M.J., Perkins, E.A.: Physical change and aging: a guide for the helping professions. Springer Publishing Company (2014)
7. Harte, R.P., et al.: Human centred design considerations for connected health devices for the older adult. J. Pers. Med. **4**(2), 245–281 (2014)
8. Carmeli, E., Patish, H., Coleman, R.: The aging hand. J. Gerontol. Ser. A: Biol. Sci. Med. Sci. **58**(2), M146–M152 (2003)
9. Ranganathan, V.K., Siemionow, V., Sahgal, V., Yue, G.H.: Effects of aging on hand function. J. Am. Geriatr. Soc. **49**(11), 1478–1484 (2001)
10. Shiffman, L.M.: Effects of aging on adult hand function. Am. J. Occup. Ther. **46**(9), 785–792 (1992)
11. Veryzer, R.W., Borja de Mozota, B.: The impact of user-oriented design on new product development: an examination of fundamental relationships. J. Prod. Innov. Manag. **22**(2), 128–143 (2005)
12. Lawton, M.P., Simon, B.: The ecology of social relationships in housing for the elderly. Gerontologist **8**(2), 108–115 (1968)
13. Lawton, M.P.: The elderly in context: perspectives from environmental psychology and gerontology. Environ. Behav. **17**(4), 501–519 (1985)
14. Crews, D.E., Zavotka, S.: Aging, disability, and frailty: implications for universal design. J. Physiol. Anthropol. **25**(1), 113–118 (2006)
15. Hauser, J.R., Clausing, D.: The House of Quality (1988)
16. Hsu, T.S., Pan, C.H., Yang, C.L.: A QFD based approach for product positioning. J. Chin. Inst. Ind. Eng. **14**(2), 209–216 (1997)

17. Leary, M., Burvill, C.: Enhancing the Quality Function Deployment Conceptual Design Tool (2007)
18. Chen, S.H.: Determining the service demands of an aging population by integrating QFD and FMEA method. Qual. Quant. **50**(1), 283–298 (2016)
19. Luo, C.M., Chang, H.F.: Safety process innovation in medical service industry. Qual. Quant. **47**(5), 2915–2931 (2013)
20. Yanagida, K., Ueda, Y., Go, K., Takahashi, K., Hayakawa, S., Yamazaki, K.: Structured scenario-based design method. In: International Conference on Human Centered Design, pp. 374–380. Springer, Heidelberg (July, 2009)
21. Rosson, M.B., Carroll, J.M.: Scenario-based design. In: Human-Computer Interaction, pp. 161–180. CRC Press (2009)
22. Ellis, J., Hetherington, R., Lovell, M., McConaghy, J., Viczko, M.: Draw me a picture, tell me a story: evoking memory and supporting analysis through pre-interview drawing activities. Alberta J. Educ. Res. **58**(4), 488–508 (2012)
23. Harper, D.: Talking about pictures: a case for photo elicitation. Vis. Stud. **17**(1), 13–26 (2002)
24. Taha, Z., Sulaiman, R.: Perceived kitchen environment among Malaysian elderly. Am. J. Eng. Appl. Sci. **3**(2), 270–276 (2010)
25. Chen, R.C.Y., Lee, M.S., Chang, Y.H., Wahlqvist, M.L.: Cooking frequency may enhance survival in Taiwanese elderly. Public Health Nutr. **15**(7), 1142–1149 (2012)
26. Abdulrazak, B., Yared, R., Tessier, T., Mabilleau, P.: Toward pervasive computing system to enhance safety of ageing people in smart kitchen. In: ICT4 Ageing Well, pp. 17–28, 2015 May
27. Wai, A.A.P., Devi, S.S., Biswas, J., Panda, S.K.: Pervasive intelligence system to enable safety and assistance in kitchen for home-alone elderly. In: International Conference on Smart Homes and Health Telematics, pp. 276–280. Springer, Heidelberg, June 2011
28. Chen, C.-H.: The concept of total planning for senior housing. Taiwan Geriatr. Gerontol. **1**(3), 122–137 (2006)
29. Charmaz, K.: Constructing Grounded Theory. SAGE, Thousand Oaks (2014)
30. Wang, S.-Yu., Windsor, C., Yates, P.: Introduction to grounded theory. J. Nurs. **59**(1), 91–95 (2012)
31. Mather, M., Carstensen, L.L.: Aging and motivated cognition: the positivity effect in attention and memory. Trends cogn. Sci. **9**(10), 496–502 (2005)
32. Grady, C.L., Craik, F.I.: Changes in memory processing with age. Curr. Opin. Neurobiol. **10**(2), 224–231 (2000)
33. Fuster, J.M.: Network memory. Trends Neurosci. **20**(10), 451–459 (1997)
34. Conforto, A.B., Kaelin-Lang, A., Cohen, L.G.: Increase in hand muscle strength of stroke patients after somatosensory stimulation. Ann. Neurol.: Off. J. Am. Neurol. Assoc. Child Neurol. Soc. **51**(1), 122–125 (2002)
35. Seo, N.J., et al.: Use of imperceptible wrist vibration to modulate sensorimotor cortical activity. Exp. Brain Res. **237**(3), 805–816 (2019)
36. Liu, S.-F., Chang, C.-F., Wang, M.-H., Lai, H.-H.: A study of the factors affecting the usability of smart phone screen protectors for the elderly. In: Zhou, J., Salvendy, G. (eds.) ITAP 2016. LNCS, vol. 9754, pp. 457–465. Springer, Cham (2016). https://doi.org/10.1007/978-3-319-39943-0_44
37. Liu, S.-F., Cheng, H.-S., Chang, C.-F., Lin, P.-Y.: A study of perception using mobile device for multi-haptic feedback. In: Yamamoto, S., Mori, H. (eds.) HIMI 2018. LNCS, vol. 10904, pp. 218–226. Springer, Cham (2018). https://doi.org/10.1007/978-3-319-92043-6_19

How to Handle Data Management
of Assisting Lifelogging Technologies
from a User's Point of View

Julia Offermann-van Heek$^{(\boxtimes)}$ ⓘ, Wiktoria Wilkowska ⓘ,
and Martina Ziefle ⓘ

Human-Computer Interaction Center, RWTH Aachen University,
Campus-Boulevard 57, 52074 Aachen, Germany
{vanheek,wilkowska,ziefle}@comm.rwth-aachen.com

Abstract. A shift to higher proportions of older people and people in need of care requires new solutions and technologies with the potential to assist people in their everyday activities and to support them in being as independent and self-determined as possible. Lifelogging technologies have this potential by the collection, storage, and evaluation of personal data. Despite their potential, the users' acceptance of such technologies is of great importance, in particular with regard to the technology's handling of data security and privacy. For this reason, a quantitative study was carried out using an online questionnaire (N = 182), investigating two different application contexts of lifelogging technologies: a preventive context (frailty monitoring) and an assisting context related to patients suffering from dementia. Based on a preceding qualitative study, data access, purpose of data processing, duration as well as location of data storage were chosen as factors which were investigated, applying a conjoint analysis approach. The results revealed that the purpose of data processing and data access were the most decisive factors when users decide about the data management of lifelogging technologies and comparing the two contexts, contradicting decision patterns were found in particular for data access. Beyond these insights, user group specific decision patterns were identified for each of the application contexts. This study provides relevant insights into the users' perspectives and requirements with regard to data management of lifelogging technologies, which should be taken into account for technology development and communication.

Keywords: Data handling · Data management · Privacy · Data security · Data storage · User perception · Acceptance · Lifelogging technology

1 Introduction

Demographic change causing increasing proportions of older people and people in need of care will challenge the society and policy even more within the next years [1, 2]. Thereby, a growing number of people in need of care and support are confronted with a shortage of skilled workers in the field of health and nursing care [3, 4]. As one solution, the development of assisting technologies, also called ambient assisted living, smart

© Springer Nature Switzerland AG 2020
Q. Gao and J. Zhou (Eds.): HCII 2020, LNCS 12208, pp. 510–530, 2020.
https://doi.org/10.1007/978-3-030-50249-2_37

home, or lifelogging technologies, gains in importance, because these technologies have the potential to assist people and to relieve their everyday life [5, 6]. In the field of assisting lifelogging technologies, it is tried to support healthy aging as well as a largely independent life within the own home environment for older and also frail people by collecting, storing, and evaluating personal data from lifelogging devices or systems [7]. By using e.g. smart watches or in-home lifelogging systems, it is possible to identify unhealthy behavior [8], to enable a prevention of diseases [7], or to support family or professional caregivers in caring for older people in need of care applying functions such as a detection of falls and emergencies [6, 9]. Despite their potential and functionality, assisting lifelogging technologies have not broadly been used in health-related contexts so far [10]. A possible explanation lies in a missing or not sufficient acceptance of these technologies due to data security and privacy-relevant aspects related to the management of personal data when lifelogging technologies are used. Therefore, the current study aimed for an investigation of how personal data from using assisting lifelogging technologies should be managed from the (future) user's point of view. For this purpose, on online survey was conducted applying a conjoint analysis approach in order to identify which data management issues are most decisive for the acceptance of lifelogging technologies.

2 Acceptance and Handling of Lifelogging Technology

This section presents the current state on lifelogging technology acceptance as well as relevant findings with regard to data management, data security, and privacy. Afterwards, this study's research aim and respective research questions are introduced.

2.1 Research on Lifelogging Technology Acceptance

In the last years, some studies investigated the acceptance of assisting lifelogging technologies. Existing work has shown that assistance systems in a health specific context are overall evaluated positively and the technologies are considered to be beneficial and useful [11–13]. Thereby, the technologies' potential to enable a longer and independent life at home as well as a relief of burdens of caring persons was especially acknowledged. In addition, an increase in felt safety as well as enhanced independence and autonomy represent perceived benefits and motives to use assisting lifelogging technology [14]. Contrary to that, some disadvantages or barriers are also associated with using assisting lifelogging devices and systems. As the collected data represent personal health data and lifelogging data technologies are closely integrated into the everyday life of people, using these technologies in health-related contexts also raises privacy concerns or a perceived loss of control among users [14–17]. In this connection, the fear of unauthorized disclosure of data to third parties was also considered as a relevant barrier and disadvantage of using lifelogging technology. Further, the use of assistive technologies in care has also been associated with the social isolation of older people. To sum up, previous research has shown that there are many different beneficial and impeding factors that can influence the acceptance of lifelogging technologies.

2.2   Data Management, Data Security, and Privacy

As it has already been pointed out that data security and privacy regarding personal data from using lifelogging technology represent essential factors for the acceptance of lifelogging technology, relevant aspects referring to the handling and management of lifelogging data are detailed in the following.

Data protection or privacy of one's own data is linked to the control of an individual with regard to its data and the further use of the data [18]. Privacy in the context of data, especially online data, is a widely discussed topic and is protected in the EU by the General Data Protection Regulation GDPR. According to the GPDR, the basic principle is that people should be in charge of the handling of their data [19]. Depending on the type of technology and the respective lifelogging application, a large amount of user data is collected and stored. According to Selke [7], all data are important that can be collected about the user, because a wider range of data allows more detailed analyses. Thereby, the question where and how long large amounts of data are stored represents aspects of major relevance. For example, Gurrin et al. [8] discussed the advantages and disadvantages of local storage (at the lifelogger's home) on the one hand, and storage of data on a cloud storage-based platform, on the other hand. Local storage has the advantage, that the lifelogger has control over the data, but limited access to the data, as it is only possible at home. Furthermore, it is assumed that this type of storage is less secure than storage in a cloud and it is questioned if the users are really able to maintain their data themselves. For this reason, it is assumed that storage in a cloud is the best option for lifelogging data, whereas this type of storage involves security and privacy concerns from the user side [8]. Besides location and duration of data storage, it also plays a role who is allowed to have access to the lifelogging technology data, as this is also perceived as a limitation of individual privacy and can impact the acceptance of a technology [20, 21]. In summary, this section shows that privacy and data security are multi-faceted aspects and have to be considered when data management regarding lifelogging technologies is investigated from a user's point of view.

2.3   Research Aim and Questions

So far, research has found that data security and privacy are relevant barriers of using lifelogging technology. In contrast, it has not been investigated how data management regarding personal data of using lifelogging technologies should concretely be handled from a user's point of view. Therefore, this study aims at an investigation of concrete data management scenarios, integrating relevant data security and privacy aspects from a user's point of view. Based on a previous interview study, four factors were selected for the applied conjoint analysis (see Sect. 3.2) in order to identify the users' preferred way of data management. Thereby, two different application contexts of lifelogging technology usage were investigated in order to find out if the preferred way of data management depends on the respective lifelogging technology application. In more detail, the respective research questions were the following:

1. RQ1: Which aspect of data management is most decisive for the acceptance of lifelogging technologies: data access, purpose of data processing, duration, or location of data storage?
2. RQ2: Are there differences in the decision patterns related to the both investigated lifelogging application contexts?
3. RQ3: Are there user specific decision patterns related to the both contexts and can they additionally be characterized by demographics or individual user factors?

3   Empirical Approach

This section presents the empirical approach of the present study, starting with a description of the applied conjoint analysis approach as well as the research design and conceptualized online survey. Afterwards, data analysis procedures and this study's sample are introduced.

3.1   Conjoint Analysis Approach

Conjoint analysis is a statistical method for estimating preferences and was developed in 1964 by Luce and Tukey [22]. It allows to measure preferences and enables a holistic examination of decision-making situations, in which different attributes are weighed against each other. Since 1971, this method has been used in market research to develop marketing strategies for product launches [23]. In the last decades, the potential of this method went beyond market research and has started to be increasingly used for acceptance research [24]. Thereby, it is applied in diverse areas in order to understand decision processes of users or customers [25]. For the conjoint analysis approach, a set of attributes and characteristics of a product has to be defined, that could influence the users' decisions. The selection of these attributes and their characteristics presents the most important task within the conceptualization and implementation of a conjoint analysis approach. In contrast to common methods in social science, such as surveys, conjoint analysis is based on a de-compositional procedure, determining overall assessments of holistic concepts, related to (final) products or (psychological) decision scenarios. For this purpose, different alternatives or configurations (so-called "choice sets") are presented to the participants. These choice sets usually consist of three to five different attributes (e.g., product color or product price) and vary in the specific characteristics of the attributes – so-called attribute levels (e.g., yellow vs. red or 100$ vs. 110$). Then, the participants are asked to select several times the combination of attributes levels which matches their preferences most closel Taking these preferences as a basis [26], the relative importance of each attribute as well as the part-worth utility values of each attribute level are calculated. Thereby, the relative importance indicates the relevance of an attribute for the participants' decisions compared to the other included attributes. The part-worth utilities indicate whether an attribute level had a rather positive or a negative contribution to the final decisions of the participants in comparison to the other included levels of an attribute [26]. Out of a variety of different conjoint analysis types, this study applied a choice-based-conjoint analysis (CBC) approach, because it is widely used and imitates complex decision processes, and thus, comes closest to real purchase and decision situations. These complex decisions are characterized by the fact that several attributes influence the final decision and that they all appear together in different scenario configurations [27].

3.2   Research Design

As mentioned before, the study aimed at an investigation of preferred ways of data management related to the usage of lifelogging technologies. For this purpose, two different lifelogging application contexts were selected in order to get broader insights and to be able to compare different lifelogging opportunities and the respective preferences of the future users. The first context referred to a preventive lifelogging application, enabling a **frailty monitoring** of older users. In more detail, the frailty monitoring system contained different technologies, such as a wearable activity tracker to measure walking speed and activity levels, a bathroom scale to track weight loss, or a grip ball to measure upper extremity muscle strength. Collecting the information of this system, it is then possible to identify changes in health and behavior in order to assess frailty early and accurately. The other application referred to a **support of dementia patients** using computer vision and environmental sensors. This lifelogging application aimed at a monitoring of actions of an older patient with dementia during common activities of the everyday life, and at the provision of (automated) reminders of the activities and tasks that should be done (e.g., hand washing, medicine intake). In order to compare those two examples of lifelogging applications, each application context was introduced to the participants in detail and separately. In addition, the evaluation of both applications was randomized.

Based on a preceding qualitative interview study and in line with results within the existing research on lifelogging acceptance, four different factors (i.e., attributes) were selected which were integrated in the data management scenarios (see Table 1): data access, purpose of data processing, duration of data storage, and location of data storage. With regard to *Data Access*, the participants of the interview study as well as previous research [20, 21] have highlighted that the definition of people having access to processed data is of utmost importance for the users' individual privacy. Therefore, data access represented one attribute within the conjoint analysis study and it was differentiated between three different entities who are (not) allowed to have access to the lifelogging data: 1) *For Me* (as the user of the lifelogging technology), 2) *For (my) Family* and 3) *For (my) Doctor(s)*. These three options were evaluated quite differently, and it was mentioned that data access should be adapted to the respective application. As a second aspect, it turned out within the interview study that the *Purpose of Data Processing* is relevant for the future users and they wished to differ between the options 1) *Self-Interest* (as typical motive for sportive lifelogging) and 2) *Scientific Research* (being beneficial for diverse research areas). As a third opportunity, several interviewees mentioned several times that some health insurance companies started with rewarding insured persons, when they would use lifelogging technologies (such as smart watches or wristbands) and reach defined targets with regard to physical activity and health (3. *Receiving a Bonus*). Hence, these three different purposes of processing lifelogging data were investigated. In line with previous results, the interview study revealed that the **Location of Data Storage** is also of relevance for future users. Within the interviews and in line with current research [e.g., 8], the participants differentiated between 1) *Local Storage (at my home)* and 2) *Cloud Storage*. As a third option, it was discussed to store the data in the (family) doctor's office (3. *Doctor(s)*). Hence, these three location options were integrated in the conjoint analysis approach. With regard to **Duration of Storage,** the interview participants, discussed the benefits and barriers of different storage durations. As they thought that a too short duration of data storage will aggravate a data comparison in case of diseases, a duration of 1 week was defined as the shortest duration of data storage 1) *Short-term (max. 1 week))*. Further, a 2) *Middle-term (max. 3 months)* and a 3) *Long-term (permanent)* duration was determined in order to investigate differences in the perception of a range of storage durations.

An overview of all attributes, their levels, and their visualizations are presented in Table 1. For each of the two applications, the participants had to complete 8 decision tasks, in which they had to choose their most preferred scenario constellation out of three different alternatives. Thereby, the order of the two applications was randomized. To avoid a loss of information, the conjoint tasks were executed in a forced choice format, which means that a "none-option" was not included. In order to increase the comprehensibility of the attributes and their levels, the levels were displayed both verbally and visually in the selection tasks. The uniqueness of the pictograms and semantic equivalence to the terms were confirmed in pretests before the study was

Table 1. Attribute levels and their visualizations (red box marks an exemplary scenario).

Attribute	*Attribute levels*		
Data Access	For Doctor(s)	For Family	For Me
Purpose of Data Processing	Receiving Bonus	Scientific Research	Self-Interest
Location of Data Storage	Doctor	Cloud	Local
Duration of Data Storage	Short-term (max. 1 week)	Middle-term (max. 3 months)	Long-term (permanent)

started. The number of decision tasks was limited to 8 randomized selection tasks, since the combination of all attribute levels would have led to 81 ($3 \times 3 \times 3 \times 3$) possible alternatives. This reduction of decision tasks required a test of the design's efficiency. This test ensured validity of the conjoint design although the possible effect that probably some attribute levels might not appear together in a set of scenario decisions. For the present study, a median efficiency of 99% and a standard error below .05 confirmed the validity of the current design (8 choice tasks), indicating that it was comparable to the hypothetical orthogonal design [30].

3.3 Online Survey

The online survey consisted of three main parts. Within the first part, the participants indicated demographic information, such as their age, gender, highest educational level, and living area. In addition, they also indicated health-related aspects (answer options: yes/no) in terms of their health status (i.e. if they suffer from a chronic disease) and if they are currently in need of care. Further, it was also asked (answer options: yes/no) if the participants are experienced in care. Here, it was differentiated between professional care experience, passive care experience (a person within the personal environment is in need of care), and active care experience (to be or have been the caregiver of a person in need of care).

Within the second part of the survey, the described attributes and levels of the conjoint analysis were introduced to the participants. Thereby, each level and its visualization were explained briefly to the participants and they were asked to select each time the most preferred data management scenario out of different alternatives within the subsequent choice tasks.

The third part represented the main part of the survey and contained the conjoint choice tasks. In a randomized order, the participants were either first introduced to the "frailty monitoring"- or the "support of dementia patients" -lifelogging application. Then, the participants selected their most preferred scenario in each of the eight randomized choice tasks. Subsequently, they did the same eight choice tasks being previously introduced to the respective second lifelogging application (either "frailty monitoring" or the "support of dementia patients"). At the end, the participants had the opportunity to leave feedback or comments on the survey, the applied methodology, or the topic of the study on an optional basis.

3.4 Data Analysis

Sawtooth Software was used in order to conduct different analysis types of the conjoint analysis (i.e., calculation of relative important scores, estimation of part-worth utilities, and latent class analysis). First of all, the attributes' relative importance for the decisions in addition to the part-worth utilities of all attribute levels were calculated based on the Hierarchical Bayes analysis and respective algorithms [24, 27]. This type of analysis enables to understand and identify decision patterns and preferences regarding data management related to the whole sample of participants. As we assumed that the decision patterns might not be the same for all participants, we aimed at an understanding of user group specific decision patterns, and therefore, a so-called latent-class analysis was necessary in a second step [28, 29]. This data-driven analysis method was used for an identification of user profiles, being characterized by similar decision and preference patterns. In addition, these identified user profiles can then be analyzed for similarities and differences with regard to user diversity factors (i.e., demographics, individual attitudes). During the latent class analysis process, the study's sample was post-hoc divided into groups based on similar preferences in the decisions. The number of groups as well as their characteristics are presented in detail in Sect. 4.2.

3.5 Description of the Sample

Data was collected in Germany in summer 2019 by distributing a link to the online survey and the completion of the survey took approximately 20 min. Overall, N = 231 participants took part in the study. For the analysis, dropouts as well as dubious answers (e.g., responses with a processing time under five minutes) were removed from the data set and after the data cleaning, the sample contained n = 182 participants.

The participants' age ranged from 16 to 88 years (M = 34.80; SD = 14.68) and 61.00% (n = 111) of them were female and 38.50% (n = 70) were male. Asked for their highest educational level, the majority indicated to have a university degree (54.90%, n = 100), while 15.90% (n = 29) indicated to have a university entrance degree (qualification). Further, 20.90% (n = 38) reported a completed apprenticeship, 3.80% (n = 7) a secondary school degree, and also 3.80% (n = 7) a PhD degree. Thus, the sample turned out to be highly educated. In addition, the participants were also asked for their living area and the majority indicated to live in city centers (61.50%, n = 112), while less participants indicated to live in suburban (12.60%; n = 23) and rural areas (25.80%; n = 47). Asked for their health status, 16.5% of the sample (n = 30) indicated to suffer from a chronic disease, while only 0.5% (n = 1) indicated to depend on support and care. Asked for previous experiences with health and care, about 14.80% (n = 27) indicated to have professional experience as a caregiver. Further, almost a third of the participants reported that a person in their environment is in need of care (29.70%, n = 54, "passive care experience"), while 10.4% (n = 19) indicated to have already been the caregiver for a family member in need of care ("active care experience").

4 Results

In the following, the results of the study are presented, starting with the results for the whole sample and for both contexts. Afterwards, the results are analyzed for user-specific decision patterns and are described for each context separately.

4.1 Data Handling from the Users' Perspective (RQ1 & RQ2)

In a first step, the relative importance of the attributes, which were selected for the conjoint analysis approach, are reported for both investigated contexts (see Fig. 1). Overall, it can be seen that the order of all attributes' importance was the same for both contexts. Thereby, the *Purpose of Data Processing* represented the most important decision criterion and was even more important for the "Frailty Monitoring" context (41.32%; SD = 16.90) compared to the context of the "Support for Dementia Patients" (35.94%; SD = 14.54). In contrast, the second important attribute *Data Access* was more relevant for the decisions in the "Support for Dementia Patients" (33.64%; SD = 14.51) context than for "Frailty Monitoring" (28.11%; SD = 14.29). *Location of Storage* was of third importance and almost equally relevant for both contexts: "Frailty Monitoring" (18.63%; SD = 10.35) and "Support for Dementia Patients" (19.87%; SD = 10.61). Finally, the *Duration of Data Storage* represented the least relevant decision criterion for both lifelogging contexts ("Frailty Monitoring": 11.94%; SD = 8.51; "Support for Dementia Patients": 10.55%; SD = 6.31).

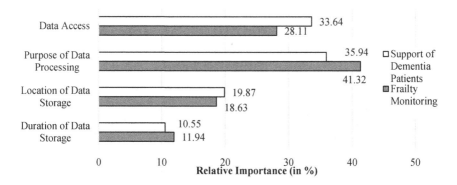

Fig. 1. Relative importance of attributes for both application contexts.

To analyze the decision patterns in more detail, the part-worth utilities of all attribute levels were investigated (see Fig. 2). Starting with the most relevant attribute for both contexts, *Purpose of Data Processing*, similar decision patterns resulted for both contexts: *Receiving Bonus* clearly presented the least preferred option for both, the "Frailty Monitoring" (−79.15) and the "Support for Dementia Patients" (−72.40) context, while benefits for *Scientific Research* ("Frailty Monitoring": +27.86; "Support for Dementia Patients": +30.21) and in particular the purpose of *Self-Interest* ("Frailty Monitoring": +51.29; "Support for Dementia Patients": +42.19) were comparably more preferred and received positive utility values.

Within the second important decision criterion, *Data Access*, the most striking differences with regard to the participants' decision patterns were found. For the "Frailty Monitoring" context, data should be accessible *For Me* (+12.82) represented the most preferred option, whereas in tendency data access *For Family* (−0.58) was of almost neutral preference and data access *For Doctors* (−12.64) was comparably least desired. In contrast, data access *For Family* (+34.26) represented the most preferred option for the "Support of Dementia Patients" context. Here, data access *For Doctors* (−6.33) was rather not preferred and data access *For Me* (as a patient) (−27.93) represented the least preferred option.

With regard to the attribute *Location of Data Storage*, a rather similar decision pattern resulted for both groups again: a *Local* ("Frailty Monitoring": +25.50; "Support for Dementia Patients": +18.21) data storage presented the most preferred option, followed by data storage at the *Doctor* ("Frailty Monitoring": +2.81; "Support for Dementia Patients": +12.48), whereas data storage in a *Cloud* ("Frailty Monitoring": −28.31; "Support for Dementia Patients": −30.68) represented clearly the least preferred option.

Further, also a very similar decision pattern resulted for the *Duration of Data Storage*: a *Middle-term* storage ("Frailty Monitoring": +6.86; "Support for Dementia Patients": +7.50) was preferred most, whereas a *Short-term* storage ("Frailty Monitoring": −2.32; "Support for Dementia Patients": +0.41) was of almost neutral preference and *Long-term* storage ("Frailty Monitoring": −4.54; "Support for Dementia Patients": −7.92) represented the comparably least preferred alternative.

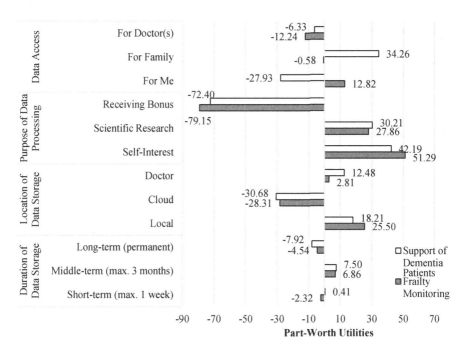

Fig. 2. Part-worth utilities of all attribute levels for both application contexts.

Finally, an overview of the most and least preferred ways of data management is given for the both lifelogging contexts. For the "Frailty monitoring" context, data management should serve the purpose of *Self-Interest*, data should be accessible *For Me* (as affected person), stored *Locally* and *Middle-term*. In contrast, the least preferred alternative of data management would serve the purpose of Receiving a bonus from an insurance institution, where data would be stored *Long-Term* in a Cloud, and would be accessible for the doctor(s).

For the "Support of Dementia Patients" context, the ways of data management would be actually the same, except of the *Data Access*: the most preferred way of data management contained data access *For Family* (in addition to the purpose of *Self-Interest*, a *Middle-term* and *Local* storage of data), while the least preferred option of data management included data access *For Me* (as dementia patient) in addition to the purpose of *Receiving a Bonus* as well as *Long-term* data storage in a *Cloud*.

4.2   User Group Specific Data Handling Patterns (RQ3)

The comparably high standard deviations of the relative importance scores as well as of the attribute levels' utility values indicated the existence of different user-specific decision patterns. Therefore, a latent class analysis approach was pursued in order to identify underlying decision patterns of different groups of participants. For both contexts, a two-group segmentation showed the best data fit (according to the relevant parameters: criteria percentage certainty, consistent Akaike information criterion (CAIC), and relative chi square). In the following, the user-specific results are presented for each context separately, starting each with a description of the identified user groups and their characteristics, followed by a presentation of the user group-specific decision patterns.

Table 2. Characteristics and inference statistical results regarding segmented groups for the "Frailty Monitoring"-context.

Variables	Group 1 (n = 77)	Group 2 (n = 105)	P
Age (M (SD))	36.53 (15.94)	33.52 (13.62)	n.s.
Gender	67.5% female (n = 52) 31.2% male (n = 24) 1.3% diverse (n = 1)	56.2% female (n = 59) 53.8% male (n = 46)	<.10
Education	57.1% university degree (n = 44) 39.0% university quali. (n = 30) 3.9% secondary school (n = 3)	60.9% university degree (n = 64) 35.2% university quali. (n = 37) 3.9% secondary school (n = 4)	n.s.
Living area	57.1% city center (n = 44) 19.5% suburban area (n = 15) 23.4% rural area (n = 18)	64.8% city center (n = 68) 7.6% suburban area (n = 8) 27.6% rural area (n = 29)	n.s.
Health status	20.8% chronic illness (n = 16)	13.3% chronic illness (n = 14)	n.s.
Prof. care experience	19.5% yes (n = 15) 80.5% no (n = 62)	11.4% yes (n = 12) 88.6% no (n = 93)	n.s.
Passive care experience	19.5% yes (n = 15) 80.5% no (n = 62)	37.1% yes (n = 39) 62.9% no (n = 66)	<.01
Active care experience	9.1% yes (n = 7) 90.9% no (n = 70)	11.4% yes (n = 12) 88.6% no (n = 93)	n.s.

Frailty Monitoring: Two groups were identified differing with regard to the decisions in their data management preferences. In a first step, it is necessary to analyze whether both groups differ with regard to demographic and individual characteristics as well.

As presented in Table 2, inference statistical analyses did not reveal significant differences with regard to age, the participants' highest level of education, their living area, or their health status. However, both groups tend to show differences (<.10) with regard to their gender distribution: Group 1 was characterized by a slightly higher percentage of female participants than Group 2. With regard to previous experiences in care, the analysis did not reveal significant differences regarding professional or active care experience. However, both groups differed significantly with regard to private passive care experience, which means that a higher percentage of Group 2 (37.1%) reported to have a person in need of care within their personal environments compared to Group 1 (19.5%). In summary, Group 1 was characterized by a slightly higher proportion of women and less passive care experience, while Group 2 contained a comparably balanced gender distribution and was characterized by a comparably higher passive care experience.

The user group specific differences with regard to the relative importance of attributes are presented in Fig. 3. In the context of "Frailty Monitoring", the two groups differed enormously with regard to the relevant decision criteria in data management preferences. For Group 1, *Data Access* (37.51%) and *Location of Data Storage* (34.12%) represented the most important decision criteria, followed by the *Purpose of Data Processing* (19.19%). In comparison, the *Duration of Data Storage* (9.18%) was least relevant for the decisions. In contrast, the *Purpose of Data Processing* (81.40%) represented the central decision criterion for Group 2. *Location of Data Storage* (10.00%), *Duration of Data Storage* (4.31%), and also *Data Access* (4.28%) were unimportant for this group's decisions.

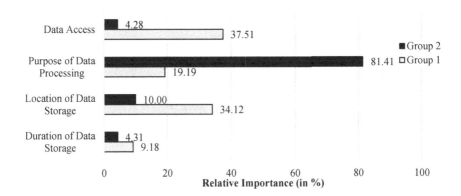

Fig. 3. Relative importance for two groups within the "Frailty Monitoring" - context.

A closer look at the preferences regarding the attribute levels reveals the underlying decision patterns of both groups (see Fig. 4). Considering the most important attribute for the Group 1, *Data Access*, a clear decision pattern was visible: The data access *For Me* (+83.31) represented the most preferred alternative, whereas the data access *For Family* (−16.58) and even more *For Doctor(s)* (−66.73) resulted both in a negative contribution to this groups' decisions. According to the low relative importance of this attribute for the Group 2, the utility values should not be overinterpreted. In tendency, *For Family* (+9.89) seemed to be the most preferred alternative of data access in this group.

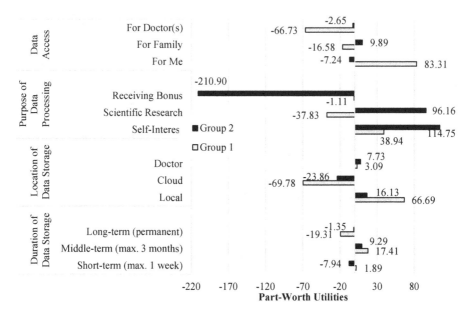

Fig. 4. Part-worth utilities for all attribute levels for two groups within the "Frailty Monitoring" - context.

Table 3. Characteristics and inference statistical results regarding segmented groups for the "Support for Dementia Patients"-context.

Variables	Group 1 (n = 62)	Group 2 (n = 120)	P
Age (M (SD))	38.77 (17.53)	32.74 (12.55)	<.01
Gender	67.7% female (n = 42) 30.6% male (n = 19) 1.6% diverse (n = 1)	57.5% female (n = 69) 42.5% male (n = 51)	<.10
Education	56.5% university degree (n = 35) 40.3% university qualification (n = 25) 3.2% secondary school degree (n = 2)	60.8% university degree (n = 73) 35.0% university qualification (n = 42) 4.2% secondary school degree (n = 5)	n.s.
Living area	54.8% city center (n = 34) 14.6% suburban area (n = 9) 30.6% rural area (n = 19)	65.0% city center (n = 78) 11.7% suburban area (n = 14) 23.3% rural area (n = 28)	<.10
Health status	17.7% chronic illness (n = 11)	15.8% chronic illness (n = 19)	n.s.
Prof. care experience	22.6% yes (n = 14) 77.4% no (n = 48)	10.8% yes (n = 13) 89.2% no (n = 107)	<.05
Passive care experience	22.6% yes (n = 14) 77.4% no (n = 48)	33.3% yes (n = 40) 66.7% no (n = 80)	n.s.
Active care experience	11.3% yes (n = 7) 88.7% no (n = 55)	10.0% yes (n = 12) 90.0% no (n = 108)	n.s.

Looking at the main relevant attribute for Group 2, *Purpose of Data Processing*, *Self-Interest* (+114.75) and *Scientific Research* (+96.16) represented both preferred options. In contrast, *Receiving a Bonus* (−210.90) obviously was the rejected option and represented a knockout criterion for data management in this group. In contrast, a different decision pattern was found for Group 1. This group in tendency preferred *Self-Interest* (+38.94) as purpose of data processing, however, *Receiving a Bonus* (−1.11) had a comparably neutral relevance for the decisions and benefits for *Scientific Research* (−37.83) represented the least preferred option.

The preferences with regard to the attribute *Location of Data* Storage were in tendency similar for both groups, although the range of values was clearly higher for Group 1 in line with the higher relative importance of the attribute. Hence, a *Local* data storage was even more preferred by Group 1 than Group 2 and a data storage in a *Cloud* was less preferred by Group 1 than Group 2. Finally, the utility values of the comparably least important attribute for both groups, *Duration of Data Storage*, were not interpreted in detail due to the rather low importance of this attribute for both groups.

Support for Dementia Patients: In a second step, also the decision patterns with regard to the "Support of Dementia Patients" context were analyzed for user group specific insights. Again, the analysis identified two groups, differing in their decision behaviors. Analyzed for the potential differences with regard to demographic and attitudinal characteristics, the inference statistical results are presented in Table 3. Considering demographic characteristics, the analysis did not reveal significant group differences with regard to the participants' education or health status. Instead, the two groups differed significantly in their age, and in tendency also with regard to gender and the participants' living area. With regard to the previous care experience, both groups did not differ with regard to the active or passive private care experience. Instead, Group 1 was characterized by a slightly higher percentage of people having professional care experience compared to Group 2. To summarize the main group differences, Group 1 was a little older than Group 2 and contained slightly higher proportions of females as well as lower percentages of people living in the city center.

Besides these differences, the group-related decision patterns related to the attributes' relative importance are shown in Fig. 5. It can be taken from the figure that the decision patterns clearly differed. For Group 1, *Data Access* (53.25%) represented the most relevant decision criterion, followed by *Location of Data Storage* (17.35%), *Purpose of Data Processing* (17.03%), and *Duration of Data Storage* (12.37%) as least important decision criterion. In contrast, *Purpose of Data Processing* (50.77%) represented the most important decision criterion for Group 2, followed by *Data Access* (28.12%), *Location of Data Storage* (17.91%), and *Duration of Data Storage* (3.19%) as clearly least relevant decision criterion.

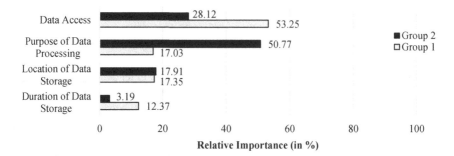

Fig. 5. Relative importance for two groups within the "Support of Dementia Patients"- context.

The underlying decision patterns of all attribute levels related to the relative importance of attributes for both groups are presented in Fig. 6. In line with the results regarding the "Frailty Monitoring" context, the main differences for the "Support of Dementia Patients" context are connected with the *Data Access* and *Purpose of Data Processing*.

Starting with the most relevant attribute for Group 1, *Data Access*, a completely contradicting decision pattern can be observed: The data access *For Family* (+82.35) and *For Me* (as patient) (+48.29) represented both preferred options, whereas the data access *For Doctor(s)* (−130.64) clearly negatively contributed to this group's decisions; For Group 2, however, data access *For Doctor(s)* (+40.37) and *For Family* (+31.74) represented positively contributing options, while the data access *For Me* (−72.12) represented the least preferred alternative.

Looking at the most relevant decision criterion for the Group 2, *Purpose of Data Processing*, benefits for *Scientific Research* (70.14) as well as *Self-Interest* (62.82) were the preferred options, while *Receiving a Bonus* (−132.95) contributed negatively to the decisions of this group. In contrast, *Self-Interest* (+42.73) represented the only preferred option in the decision patterns of Group 1, while the other options, *Scientific Research* (−25.39) and *Receiving a Bonus* (−17.34), represented less preferred and negatively contributing alternatives.

Considering the decision patterns regarding *Location of Data Storage*, both groups preferred least the storage of the data in a *Cloud*. For Group 1, *Local* data storage represented the most preferred option (+33.98), while Group 2 favorized data storage by the *Doctor* (+27.89). With regard to the least important attribute for both groups, *Duration of Data Storage*, the results were also not described in detail.

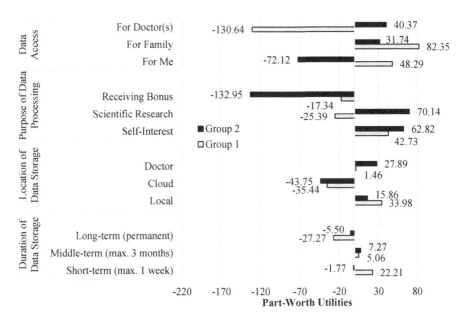

Fig. 6. Part-worth utilities for all attribute levels for two groups within the "Support of Dementia Patients"- context.

5   Discussion

The current study represented a first approach to analyze decision patterns with regard to the data management preferences of the described lifelogging applications. In the following, the results are discussed and limitations as well as suggestions for future work are given.

5.1   Context-Specific Acceptance of Lifelogging Technologies

Overall, the results showed differences with regard to the data management aspects depending on the lifelogging application, revealing that the purpose of the data processing was even more important for the frailty monitoring application, whereas data access was more important for the lifelogging application supporting dementia patients. However, the order of the attributes' relevance remained the same for both applications. A possible explanation of the differences lies in the diverse sincerity of both applications. The participants' feedback showed that they were more interested in knowing the purpose of the data processing when the preventing lifelogging application was focused.

In a more severe situation, such as the support of dementia patients application – in which risks for the patient's safety and well-being are present – the questions of who is being able to access data and who is probably alerted in case of emergency become more relevant [31]. This is in line with previous research in the field which also identified data access as a relevant and important factor in case of caring for dementia patients and for older people in general [13, 21]. The most striking differences with regard to the diverse opportunities of data management were thereby found for the data access. The results showed that – depending on the different lifelogging applications – the data access is permitted for different entities: for the frailty monitoring application, the lifelogger him- or herself should be the only person being allowed to have access to the lifelogging data, whereas data access for the family and, in particular, for the doctor(s) is not desired and contributes neutrally to negatively to the scenario decisions. Instead, the data access is allowed for the family when using lifelogging application that supports dementia patients, while it is not desired for the patient him- or herself and neither for the doctors. Starting with the preventing frailty monitoring application, a possible explanation for the participants' desire to have the control about data access themselves is that they judge themselves to be still capable of dealing with the lifelogging technology's processed data. In contrast, in case of dementia patients, it seems to be more suitable and adequate for the participants to hand over the responsibility of data management to the family (presumably as caring persons).

Considering the opportunities of the other data management aspects, the two lifelogging applications did not differ significantly. For both applications, the purpose of receiving a bonus represented a knockout criterion, which is therefore clearly not desired as an alternative within the management of lifelogging data, independent from the lifelogging context. With regard to the location and duration of data storage, a local and middle-term storage represented the comparably most desired alternative, also independent from the lifelogging application.

In a second step, also user-specific evaluations of data management preferences were analyzed. Overall, the results revealed that several user characteristics have the potential to shape the preferences with regard to the data management of lifelogging technologies. In particular, and in line with research in the field, the decision patterns are influenced by the participants experience in care, but also by their age and, in tendency, by gender [14, 32, 33]. In both examined examples of lifelogging applications, a two-group segmentation resulted, showing one group, which overall perceives the use of lifelogging more pragmatically giving attention to the important details of the data management, such as access and location of the stored information. As opposed to that, the other group seems first to theoretically analyze the reason for the intended use, searching firstly for the actual purpose of the use and only then to decide how to handle the other aspects of the data management.

For the preventing lifelogging application, participants differing in particular in their experience in care showed diverse decision patterns. Here, the purpose of the data processing was much more important for the more care experienced people, whereas data access and location of the data storage were more relevant for the less experienced participants. Thereby, the less experienced participants clearly stated that they prefer data access only for the lifelogging user and local data storage, while these aspects were not evaluated unambiguously differently by the more experienced persons. Instead, the decisions of the more experienced persons clearly showed a rejection of receiving a bonus as purpose to process the data (in relation to the other alternatives), while this decision pattern was not observable for the less experienced participants. A possible explanation for these patterns could be that care experienced people scrutinize the reason of processing and storage of data (in not acutely serious health situations) more strongly than less care experienced persons. Hence, this criterion could serve as a main decision criterion for this group, while the other parameters (data access and location of storage) represent the relevant decision criteria for the less experienced persons.

For the application supporting dementia patients, data access represented the most important decision criterion for older, (professionally and/or privately) more care experienced persons, while the purpose of data processing was most relevant for the decisions of younger participants being (professionally and/or privately) less experienced in care. In particular, the diverse decision patterns with regard to the data access were striking: Older persons preferred data access for family and the dementia patient, while they rejected data access for doctors; instead, the younger group denied data access for the dementia patient but allowed it for the doctors and family. Here, we assume that different factors come into play. Younger, comparably less experienced people seem to think that dementia patients were not capable to take the responsibility and control for their own lifelogging data. Therefore, they want to handover the responsibility and data access to the doctors and families of the dementia patients. In contrast, older, more care experienced participants want to keep the dementia patients in control over their lifelogging data (supporting them in being independent as long as possible) in addition to the data access for their (caring) families. A further interesting result is that these participants do not prefer data access for the doctors: This decision pattern could be reasoned by a more reality-driven knowledge of the older respondents about the lack of skilled workers and specialists in the nursing and care. Therefore, this group desires and requires the management of data by families and the patients themselves.

In conclusion, the identified influences of user characteristics on the preferences in lifelogging data management highlight the importance to carefully tailor these technologies and their data handling specifically to the respective application and group of users, who will finally interact with the technologies and systems.

5.2 Limitations and Future Work

The present approach provided insights into the users' perspectives and preferences with regard to data management when lifelogging technologies are used. However, there are some limitations of the current approach which should be considered for future research on lifelogging technologies and respective data management procedures.

As a specific characteristic of the scenario-based approach in this study, it cannot be guaranteed that the estimated preferences predict the actual behavior of the participants and, therefore, the participants' real preferences with regard to the data management of applied lifelogging technologies could be different when lifelogging technologies are actually used [34]. A further methodological limitation refers to the limited number of attributes being used in the conjoint analysis approach. In order to limit the complexity for the participants, we decided to reduce the number of attributes to four relevant aspects which were previously identified in a preceding study and within literature. Nevertheless, it should be considered that the results obviously depend on the integrated factors and could be completely different when other relevant factors are integrated into the study. For future studies, other topically relevant aspects (e.g., type of the processed data, perceived intimacy of the data) should be additionally integrated in the conjoint analysis approach. Then, the attributes' relevance and potential changes could at least in tendency be compared to the present results. For this purpose, it could be considered to use either a choice-based conjoint analysis approach again (then some factors should be left out) or another approach such as an adaptive conjoint analysis approach could be used (allowing for a higher number of attributes) [35].

With regard to the study's sample, future studies should try to reach even larger and, in particular with regard to gender, more balanced samples, as the current study contained a higher proportion of female compared to the male participants. Although the study also reached older participants, the mean age of the participants was rather young. In particular with regard to the lifelogging application "Support of Dementia Patients", future studies should try to reach higher proportions of older participants and, ideally, also participants suffering from dementia and age-related diseases, in order to integrate their perspectives and whishes with regard to data management into the development and design of lifelogging applications.

Acknowledgements. The authors would like to thank all participants for sharing their opinions on assisting lifelogging technologies. Further, thanks go to Katharina Merkel for research support. This work resulted from the project PAAL – "Privacy Aware and Acceptable Lifelogging services for older and frail people" and was funded by the German Federal Ministry of Education and Research (16SV7955).

References

1. Börsch-Supan, A., Bucher-Koenen, T., Coppola, M., Lamla, B.: Savings in times of demographic change: lessons from the german experience. J. Econ. Surv. **29**, 807–829 (2015). https://doi.org/10.1111/joes.12116
2. Fekete, A.: Social vulnerability change assessment: monitoring longitudinal demographic indicators of disaster risk in Germany from 2005 to 2015. Nat. Hazard **95**, 585–614 (2019). https://doi.org/10.1007/s11069-018-3506-6
3. Haustein, T., Mischke, J., Schönfeld, F., Willand, I.: Older people in germany and the EU. Statistisches Bundesamt, Wiesbaden, Germany, February 2016
4. Greve, B.: Long-term Care for the Elderly in Europe: Development and Prospects. Taylor & Francis, Routledge (2016)
5. Bouma, H., Fozard, J.L., Bouwhuis, D.G., Taipale, V.: Gerontechnology in perspective. Gerontechnology **6**, 190–216 (2007)
6. Rashidi, P., Mihailidis, A.: A survey on ambient-assisted living tools for older adults. IEEE J. Biomed. Health Inf. **17**, 579–590 (2012). https://doi.org/10.1109/JBHI.2012.2234129
7. Selke, S.: Lifelogging: Digital Self-tracking and Lifelogging-Between Disruptive Technology and Cultural Transformation. Springer, Wiesbaden (2016). https://doi.org/10.1007/978-3-658-13137-1
8. Gurrin, C., Smeaton, A.F., Doherty, A.R.: Lifelogging: personal big data. Found. Trends® Inf. Retrieval **8**, 1–125 (2014). https://doi.org/10.1561/1500000033

9. Mubashir, M., Shao, L., Seed, L.: A survey on fall detection: principles and approaches. Neurocomputing **100**, 144–152 (2013)
10. Ernsting, C., et al.: Using smartphones and health apps to change and manage health behaviors: a population-based survey. J. Med. Internet Res. **19**(4), e101 (2017)
11. Gövercin, M., et al.: Smartsenior@ home: acceptance of an integrated ambient assisted living system. results of a clinical field trial in 35 households. Inf. Health Soc. Care **41**, 430–447 (2016). https://doi.org/10.3109/17538157.2015.1064425
12. Wild, K., Boise, L., Lundell, J., Foucek, A.: Unobtrusive in-home monitoring of cognitive and physical health: reactions and perceptions of older adults. J. Appl. Gerontol. **27**(2), 181–200 (2008)
13. Lorenzen-Huber, L., Boutain, M., Camp, L.J., Shankar, K., Connelly, K.H.: Privacy, technology, and aging: a proposed framework. Ageing Int. **36**(2), 232–252 (2011)
14. Peek, S.T., Wouters, E.J., Van Hoof, J., Luijkx, K.G., Boeije, H.R., Vrijhoef, H.J.: Factors influencing acceptance of technology for aging in place: a systematic review. Int. J. Med. Inf. **83**, 235–248 (2014). https://doi.org/10.1016/j.ijmedinf.2014.01.004
15. Padilla-Lopez, J., Chaaraoui, A., Gu, F., Florez-Revuelta, F.: Visual privacy by context: proposal and evaluation of a level-based visualisation scheme. Sensors **15**, 12959–12982 (2015)
16. Ferdous, M.S., Chowdhury, S., Jose, J.M.: Analysing privacy in visual lifelogging. Pervasive Mob. Comput. **40**, 430–449 (2017)
17. Gelonch, O., et al.: Acceptability of a lifelogging wearable camera in older adults with mild cognitive impairment: a mixed-method study. BMC Geriatr. **19**(1), 110 (2019)
18. Bélanger, F., Crossler, R.E.: Privacy in the digital age: a review of information privacy research in information systems. MIS Q. **35**(4), 1017–1042 (2011)
19. Voigt, P., von dem Bussche, A.: The Eu General Data Protection Regulation (GDPR). A Practical Guide, 1st edn. Springer, Cham (2017)
20. Steggell, C.D., Hooker, K., Bowman, S., Choun, S., Kim, S.J.: The role of technology for healthy aging among Korean and Hispanic women in the United States: a pilot study. Gerontechnology **9**, 433–449 (2010). https://doi.org/10.4017/gt.2010.09.04.007.00
21. Joe, J., Chaudhuri, S., Chung, J., Thompson, H., Demiris, G.: Older adults' attitudes and preferences regarding a multifunctional wellness tool: a pilot study. Inf. Health Soc. Care **41**, 143–158 (2016). https://doi.org/10.3109/17538157.2014.965305
22. Luce, R.D., Tukey, J.W.: Simultaneous conjoint measurement: a new type of fundamental measurement. J. Math. Psychol. **1**(1), 1–27 (1964)
23. Green, P.E., Srinivasan, V.: Conjoint analysis in consumer research: issues and outlook. J. Consum. Res. **5**(2), 103–123 (1978)
24. Arning, K.: Conjoint measurement. In: Matthes, J., Davis, C.S., Potter, R.F. (eds.) International Encyclopedia of Communication Research Methods, pp. 1–10. Wiley-Blackwell, Wiley (2017). https://doi.org/10.1002/9781118901731
25. Rao, V.R.: Applied Conjoint Analysis, 1st edn. Springer, New York (2014)
26. Orme, B.: Interpreting the Results of Conjoint Analysis, Getting Started with Conjoint Analysis: Strategies for Product Design and Pricing Research. pp. 77–89, Research Publications LLC, Madison (2010)
27. Sawtooth Software: The CBC System for Choice-Based Conjoint Analysis. Technical Paper Series (2009). https://www.sawtoothsoftware.com/download/techpap/cbctech.pdf
28. Sawtooth Software. Survey Software & Conjoint Analysis—CBC Latent Class Technical Paper. Sawtooth Technical Paper Series (2014). https://www.sawtoothsoftwarecom/support/technical-papers/sawtooth-software-products/cbc-latent-class-technical-paper-2004
29. Green, P.E., Krieger, A.M.: Segmenting markets with conjoint analysis. J. Mark. **55**, 20–31 (1991). https://doi.org/10.2307/1251954

30. Sawtooth Software: Testing the CBC Design. Technical Paper Series (2019). http://www.sawtooth-software.com/help/lighthouse-studio/manual/index.html?hidweb_cbc_designs_6.html

31. Holmberg, M., Valmari, G., Lundgren, S.M.: Patient' experiences of homecare nursing: balancing the duality between obtaining care and to maintain dignity and self-determination. Scand. J. Caring Sci. **26**(4), 705–712 (2012)

32. Lai, C.K., Chung, J.C., Leung, N.K., Wong, J.C., Mak, D.P.: A survey of older Hong Kong people's perceptions of telecommunication technologies and telecare devices. J. Telemed. Telecare **16**, 441–446 (2010)

33. Zimmer, Z., Chappell, N.L.: Receptivity to new technology among older adults. Disabil. Rehabil. **21**, 222–230 (1999)

34. Ajzen, I., Fishbein, M.: Understanding Attitudes and Predicting Social Behavior, 1st edn. Prentice-Hall, Englewood Cliffs (1980)

35. Green, P.E., Krieger, A.M., Agarwal, M.K.: Adaptive conjoint analysis: some caveats and suggestions. J. Mark. Res. **28**, 215–222 (1991)

Contextual Design of Intergenerational Innovative Service for Aging in Place

Suphichaya Suppipat[1], Wei-Ming Cheng[2],
and Sheng-Ming Wang[2(✉)]

[1] Institute of Environmental Engineering and Management,
National Taipei University of Technology, Taipei, Taiwan
[2] Department of Interaction Design, National Taipei University
of Technology, Taipei, Taiwan
ryan5885@mail.ntut.edu.tw

Abstract. Traditionally, government agencies tend to deploy many resources on aging people with incapacitation or dementia. However, the promotion of the idea of "aging in place" is more and more popular and doable that it has been. Aging in place becomes a big challenge in the coming century. Smart home devices could facilitate senior citizens to stay safer and healthier in their houses. A service-oriented business such as co-living service, focusing on building socialization and maintaining privacy, could also drive a housing market and develop more sharing economy platforms. The objective of this service design project is to create a symbiotic relationship between two different generations to exchange knowledge and skills, and also live with and learn from each other. Various design thinking tools were applied, including Personas, User Journey Map, PEST Analysis, Business Model Canvas, etc. A new service system diagram has been proposed. The application of merging smart home devices, such as Chatbot into seniors' houses and an intercultural co-living environment could benefit three aspects, including supporting age-in-place, mastering new skills, and driving economic growth.

Keywords: Aging-in-place · Kano Model · Co-living · Chatbot · Sharing economy

1 Introduction

Taiwan is currently considered an aged society, with 14.35% of senior citizens aged over 65 compared with the total population in 2018 [1]. Referring to data from the Ministry of the Interior (MOI), there were about 527,380 households in Taiwan that had an older adult. Those include those living alone and living with a spouse. The figure rocketed more than 50% compared with the number in 2009 [1]. When people live longer and healthier, some severe consequences emerged, including a decrease in income, increased loneliness due to loss of usual cycle of friends and family members, loss of social role and status, and appearance of free time [2, 3]. Older people want to use those free time available in their retirement for the benefit of themselves and their loved ones [2].

© Springer Nature Switzerland AG 2020
Q. Gao and J. Zhou (Eds.): HCII 2020, LNCS 12208, pp. 531–544, 2020.
https://doi.org/10.1007/978-3-030-50249-2_38

All of those losses directly affect seniors' self-esteem as well as mental health. The statistics of the Department of Mental and Oral Health under the Minister of Health and Welfare show that senior citizens are likely to attempt suicide because of poor health, loneliness, poverty, and lack social life [4]. The other problem would be a hard time finding accommodation. Merely one percent of Taiwan's landlords accept a single senior citizen as their tenant, even though he or she has a monthly income of 14,000 Taiwanese dollars ($460) [5]. The problem is not about the rent money but, instead, the worry of an unnatural death would drive down the value of their property by around 30% depending on the location [5]. The average house in Taiwan's capital Taipei costs more than 15 times the average annual household income due to a real estate investment boom driven by wealthy China-based expatriates, and many low and middle-income Taiwanese even cannot afford the price [5].

Similar problems about loneliness and difficulty in finding an affordable place to stay have also occurred among international students. According to a new report released by the Ministry of Education (MOE), the number of foreign students choosing to study in Taiwan has continued to climb over the years [6]. The highest number of international students in 2018 hailed from China, Malaysia, Vietnam, and Indonesia, respectively [6]. Besides China and Southeast Asian countries, the students from Germany were recorded as the second-highest among European countries that registered to study in Taiwan [7]. Taiwan's MOE has announced plans to double the country's international student enrolment by 2019 and promote Taipei to be a hub for Mandarin language learning [8]. Moreover, Taipei City ranked seventh out of 102 cities in the IMD Smart City Index 2019 [9]. Developing the innovative technologies and strategies necessary for a smart city is not only improve residents' quality of life but also attract international students to come to Taiwan for a new study abroad destination.

This design research project aims to solve social problems by applying the concept of Sharing Economy with smart home technology and drive economic growth by making use of the non-performing asset and vacant properties. The main immediate objective is to help international students and single senior citizens in Taipei finding safe and affordable accommodation, as well as getting additional knowledge and skills. Associate with this objective, and the key results are a platform where international students can search for an affordable accommodation, a place where international students can give and take additional knowledge and skills to and from Taiwanese senior citizens while staying with them, and an extra source of income for Taiwanese senior citizens who have a lot of free time available and are still healthy.

2 Literature Review and Related Works

Aging in place trend is likely to continue its pattern in the coming era. There are several reasons why seniors tend to remain in their homes longer, including better health and higher levels of education than previous generations, healthcare, and technology improvements that facilitate aging in place more convenient [10]. Moreover, satisfaction with their quality of life, a secure attachment to their homes, neighborhood, and communities, Economy, and mental pressure, as well as fear of losing continuity of habits and routines, are also one of the not-to-move reasons [3, 10]. On the other hand, the reasons for relocation or moving into retirement communities reflected push and pull factors, such as health conditions, maintaining independence, staying in control, avoiding loneliness, needs of security, and familiarity with the facility [3]. Referring to the study of Löfqvist et al. [3], "moving to a nursing home was expressed as the final frontier and constituted negative and distressing thoughts that evoked strong feelings". The need for "in-between housing" could make a minor step for seniors to relocate toward more suitable housing, with the possibility of receiving care and support [3].

In the care of elders, the most common experiences are fear of falling, urinary incontinence, sight and hearing loss, reduced mobility and strength, social isolation, cognitive impairment, and difficulty managing medications [11]. The critical concept of aging in place is to create a well-designed housing environment that supports seniors' independence. This concept will help seniors stay healthier and active longer, avoid expensive and debilitating hospitalizations, and avoid relocation to a nursing home [11]. Recently, there are various services offering seniors acquire additional knowledge and skills as well as encourage socialization and smart home devices, helping seniors stay safer and healthier in their homes for longer. Those smart home features usually include motion-sensing devices for automatic lighting control, motorized locks, door and window openers, motorized blinds and curtains, smoke and gas detectors, and temperature control devices, etc. [11, 12]. There are various devices and technologies available in the market. Here we focus on ten technologies as follows:

1. **Motion sensors and smart sensors:** Sensors are tiny, low-powered devices that can be placed anywhere in a house. These devices have the most significant impact on aging in place since sensors can capture the patterns of seniors' daily living and flag anomalies to caregivers. Monitoring activities, such as a motion sensor camera, work unobtrusively in the background without the intrusive noise or lights [12]. Smart sensors can learn social routines. For example, a contact sensor on a medicine cabinet can let a caregiver know when it has been accessed and how many times. As a result, caretakers can monitor activity from the sensors and receive alerts about any issues such as lack of activity, a parent forgetting to take medication, or a fall [12]. The Walabot Home, a sensor system designed to be placed on a bathroom wall, scans continuously for movement and detects if a person has fallen and automatically placing a call for help [12]. Smartbox and PROSAFE have designed to solve the neurological and cognitive problems of seniors. It utilizes a set of infrared motion sensors connected to either a wireless or wired network to support automatic recognition of resident activity to accommodate seniors with Alzheimer's disease [11].

2. **Smart home hub:** Smart home automation can shut the lights off, lock the front door, and turn down the thermostat when someone gets into bed. The ability to connect to smart lights, sensors, switches, door locks, and many other gadgets allows a senior to control their home by voice easily. Voice control is the key to make the smart home suitable for seniors. It virtually eliminates the learning curve found in most technology that can be a significant barrier to seniors [12]. A smart home hub that is popular in the market, such as the Echo Plus and Echo Show. Sensors like Fibaro motion sensors can monitor for intruders, but when connected to a smart home hub, they can also do useful things like turn on lights when someone walks past them [12].

3. **Smart security systems:** Smart security systems can be installed to monitor doors, windows, and motion. If there is a problem, the system can trigger an alarm notifying authorities and caregivers. This type of system also works with smoke alarms, flood sensors, and freeze/temperature sensors [12]. For example, Abode's smart home security system recently announced a professional installation program. Also, this Abode door sensor can be configured to send alerts to a trusted caregiver when the door is opened [12].

4. **Mesh WiFi system:** The mesh WiFi system uses multiple routers working together to channel high-speed Internet to extend the WiFi signal to every corner and connect all the devices in a house [12]. This system has made aging in place technology much more viable. It doubles as a smart home hub, which supports a wide range of connected devices, including sensors that can help monitor movement in the house to alert a family member or caregiver if there is a problem [12].

5. **Voice-activated virtual assistants:** A smart speaker with a voice-activated virtual assistant, such as Amazon's Alexa, can be beneficial to seniors living alone both as a tool and a digital companion [12]. Also, Alexa can work as a smart home hub. This type of automation devices are not a substitute for social interaction with real people; however, they can be used to augment real social interaction and provide useful services [11]. For example, LifePod, this type of virtual assistant can also take the pressure off a caregiver [12].

6. **Energy monitoring:** It is a whole home electrical monitoring system designed to track energy usage and connect to the electrical panel in a house. It can also tell what devices are on or off in the house and let a user turn them off remotely via an application [12]. The monitoring device, such as Sense, will be installed in an electrical panel and learn different devices working in the house. Also, this system can be set to send alerts when specific home devices are in use or not in use and allow caregivers or family members to monitor regular activity and notice when something works differently.

7. **Smart appliances:** A smart countertop kitchen appliance can facilitate seniors living alone to cook simpler, healthier, and safer. June Oven, for example, is an all-in-one cooking function oven, including a toaster oven, convection oven, air fryer, and slow cooker. This smart appliance also includes simple touchscreen controls, a built-in camera for checking on the food via a smartphone screen, and sending a notification to a smartphone when the food is almost ready [12]. Moreover, this oven can be set a command through Alexa's voice control, making it possible for visually impaired users to cook by themselves. Caregivers can also check on the oven and make sure it is not turn on when it is not in use and can turn it off remotely [12].

8. **Medicine dispensing machine:** The dispensing machines have been designed and constructed with a microprocessor system that will identify the times at which medicines are taken from a standard medication box. Moreover, the machines have a voice recording to remind seniors to take their medication [11]. With these advanced and computerized functions, the nurse can detect seniors who are having difficulty taking medications according to the plan [11].

9. **Robotic pets:** People become increasingly comfortable with artificially intelligent entities [11]. In the field of robotics and automation, robotic pets have been developed. Tiger Buddy is envisioned as a friendly, information kiosk that is

available on-demand, without seniors or family members feeling like they are a bother to a caregiver [11]. These robotic devices have been examined in the way of providing information to elders warmly and positively [11]. The Tiger Buddy will help bring the seniors together and also tackle social isolation to some degree by helping to encourage group activities and even providing something to talk about among the seniors [11].

10. **Telecare technologies:** Telecare is as known as remotely caregiver when patients no longer have to visit the hospital or the general practitioner's consulting rooms frequently. Furthermore, physicians do not have to pay patients a regular visit to their houses for diagnosing and monitoring chronic diseases due to mediated interactions by ICTs [13]. Telecare technologies currently change the landscape of healthcare services not only by distributing care work to familiar places such as patients' homes but also by introducing the new spaces of telemedical centers [13]. Telecare professionals are expected to act as intermediaries among patients, telecare devices, and healthcare professionals. Although telecare technologies introduce virtual interactions between healthcare providers and patients, these technology-mediated care practices are always positioned somewhere [13]. This kind of technology makes aging in place much more comfortable.

3 Assumptions and Methodologies

In the first phase of this intergenerational and intercultural co-living service design project, primary and secondary data collection of the living lifestyle of international students and senior citizens in Taipei City, Taiwan, were conducted. International students at the National Taipei University of Technology (NTUT) were the focus group for this study. We design seven steps of data collection and analysis to deploy a new business model as follows:

Step 1: Web-based Questionnaire: The web-based questionnaire was designed based on multiple choices and a rating scale. First, seven questions asking international students' personal information and opinion of the possibility of intergenerational and intercultural co-living services in Taiwan were constructed with multiple choices and optional short answers. The last question, self-evaluating of smart devices acceptance, was constructed with a Likert-type scale. This type of scale is one of the most practical methods to examine the quality quantitatively, and a ten-point scale was used in this study, ranging from amateur to professional (1 = Amateur and 10 = Professional). Those eight questions were presented in the web-based questionnaire, such as:

1. Where are you from?
2. What is your current status in Taiwan?
3. What type of accommodation you are living in?
4. How much the rental price per month you can afford or prefer?
5. If you need or want to share the place with others, what kind or which group of people you prefer?
6. If you have a roommate, what kind or which group of people you prefer?

7. What kinds of Taiwanese, either modern or traditional skills, do you want to learn?
8. Please rate your acceptance level on smart devices.

Step 2: Personas Analysis: In order to present different user types in this service design, personas were created to understand target users' needs, experiences, behaviors, and goals. Personas are fictional characters [20]; the role-based personas were selected to represent the user's role of senior landlords and foreign tenants in this intergenerational and intercultural co-living service design project. Using personas is one of the various methods to help designers escalate to the third phase of the design thinking, the ideation phase [20].

Step 3: User Journey Map: A user journey map is a visualization of an individual's relationship with a product or service over time and across different channels [21]. There are different shapes and formats to make a user journey map, however, the map commonly represents in a timeline of all touchpoints between a user and a product or service. This timeline contains information about all channels that users use to interact with a product and services. The most important thing is to identify all main touchpoints and all channels associated with each touchpoint and understand four aspects are 1) Motivation: Why are they trying to do it? 2) Channels: Where interaction takes place. 3) Actions. Users took the actual behaviors and steps. 4) Pain points: What are the challenges users are facing?

Step 4: PEST Analysis: A PEST analysis is a strategic business tool used by organizations to discover, evaluate, organize, and track macro-economic factors which can impact on their business now and in the future. The framework examines opportunities and threats due to Political, Economic, Social, and Technological forces [22]. Outputs from the analysis inform strategic planning processes and contribute to market research.

Step 5: Product Opportunity Gap (POG): A product opportunity exists when there is a gap between what is currently on the market and the possibility for new or significantly improved products that result from emerging trends [23]. The identification of a Product Opportunity Gap (POG) is the core force that drives companies that manufacture products, supply services, and process information. Successfully identifying a POG is a combination of art and science [23]. It requires constant cyclical consideration of several factors in three major areas: Social trends (S), Economic forces (E), and Technological advances (T), see Fig. 1. In this study, three different case studies related to seniors and co-living services were analyzed together with SET factors in order to define POG and propose a new business model.

Step 6: Business Model Canvas: Smart cities project ideas template and business model canvas derived from Osterwalder and Pigneur [24] was applied to follow design thinking stages (e.g., empathize, define, and ideate) and find value propositions of new service design. The Business Model Canvas is a strategic management and entrepreneurial tool that allows designers to describe, design, challenge, invent, and pivot a business model [24]. In this study, we focused on the value of additional knowledge and skills that two different generations can give and take, also live with and learn from each other.

Step 7: Service System Diagram: Service design is the activity of planning and organizing people, infrastructure, communication, media, and components of a service in order to improve its quality, the interaction between a service provider and customers, and the customers' experience [25]. The service system diagram is a data flow diagram that shows actions and channels where users experience while engaging in a service design context. A service system diagram of the proposed co-living service was drawn to understand service flows, touchpoints, and significant sources of income from the service offering.

4 Results and Discussions

After spreading out the web-based questionnaire publicly for two weeks, solely 27 international students responded. 85% were students from Asian countries, and the rest was from European and South American countries. 63% were graduate students, while 22% and 15% were exchange students and Mandarin Chinese language learning students, respectively. Over 60% of them are living in a dormitory (four students shared one room) and a shared apartment. A majority of the students could afford the rental price per month, less than 15,000 NTD. If they needed to share the place with others, there were four kinds of people they prefer: people who can speak the same language, Taiwanese, and people who come from either the same of different countries. It was not necessary who a roommate was; their preferences were someone who can get along, share something in common, keep clean, and respect others' privacy. The most popular additional skills that they would like to learn while staying in Taiwan are language learning, traditional food cooking, and Taiwanese arts and crafts. Over one-third of the students rated themselves on a professional level as smart device users.

After applying Personas, the target users of this service design would be a senior landlord and foreign student tenants who plan to stay in Taiwan for short- and long-term (see Fig. 1).

Mrs. Wang: A 65-year-old retired university professor

She is specialized in Chinese literature. Her husband passed away 5 years ago. She doesn't have any children. She is still healthy and would like to age-in-place. She would love to learn new skills and spend her free time for the benefit of herself. She can speak Chinese, Japanese and English well. Also, she has her own apartment with 2-3 rooms available and would like to earn some extra money for traveling abroad with her friends.

Lucy: An exchange student from Malaysia (22)

Her major is in Electrical Engineering and Computer Science. She is planning to study in Taipei for 6 months and would like to learn the Chinese language and Taiwanese culture during staying in Taiwan. She is looking for an affordable price (less than 10,000 NTD per month) and a clean room available close to the university and has a small kitchen for her to cook Malaysian food sometimes.

Steffan: A Chinese language school student from Germany (18)

He has just finished his senior high school in Berlin and would like to come to Taiwan for Chinese language learning. He is planning to study the Chinese language in Taipei for 3 months and travel around the island before he goes back to his home country. Also, he would love to learn about Taiwanese culture during staying in Taiwan. He is looking for an affordable price shared apartment (less than 15,000 NTD per month) closed to the language school or some other attraction places in the city.

Fig. 1. Personas

A user journey map of senior landlords and foreign student tenants was drawn, see Fig. 2. Bad experiences with unknown roommate

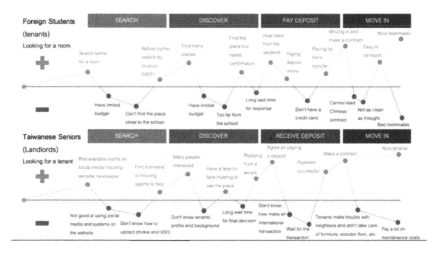

Fig. 2. User journey map

The pain points of senior landlords are:

- Do Not familiar with system on the housing website
- Do not know about tenants' background
- Difficulty on international transaction
- High maintenance costs due to bad tenants

The pain points of Tenants are:

- Limited budget
- Not sure about a room condition/cannot see the real place
- Too young to have a credit card
- Cannot read Chinese contract

By using PEST Analysis (see Table 1), political factors that could impact the service provider would be government subsidies for social entrepreneurs and startups, tax rebates from using energy-saving home appliances, and consumer protection laws. Overall economic forces would be an increasing number of international students and senior citizens in Taiwan, an aging workforce and labor market, a boom of property value, and the housing market. The social trend that significantly impacts on the target market was an age-in-place trend. Technology that can affect the way of creating products and services were smart home devices and emerging technologies related to healthcare service.

Table 1. PEST analysis

Political	Economic
Political or politically motivated factors that could impact the organization	Overall economic forces that could impact on your success
Government subsidies and donations to social enterprises, tax rebates for energy-saving home appliances, labor/environmental/consumer protection laws, Taiwan government award, grant, and loan is helping new startups and SMEs	Smart city trend, Taiwan's aging rate, property values, and housing market, an aging workforce and labor market, labor costs, an increasing number of international students studying in Taiwan
Social	**Technological**
Social attitudes, behaviors, and trends that impact your organization and target market	Technology that can affect the way you make, distribute, and market your products and services
Aged society, Age-in-place trend, justification of fearing emergencies, cultural issues/taboos, loneliness and depression, life consult, going solo, international migration trend	5G, technology and communication infrastructure, Telehealth, Telecare, Robot, IoT, smart home devices, eco/energy-saving home appliances

After comparing the pros and cons of three service design case studies related to older adults and co-living ideas, the common pain points of Rent-a-granny, Ossan Rental, and Senior co-housing services are a high level of trust, an issue of privacy, and personal information disclosure. To find a POG, SET factors are shown in Table 2:

Table 2. SET analysis

Social trends	Economic	Technological
• Age-in-place • Increasing in the aging workforce • Aged society in Taiwan • Increasing of international migration • Single adults/childless couples	• Seniors have disposable income and non-profitable asset • Buying aids, products or services for a better quality of life • The boom of healthcare products and services • The demand for available living spaces in a big city to study or work	• Internet of Things (IoT) • Robot and machine learning • Artificial Intelligence (AI) • Telehealth and Telecare • Smart home devices

A business model canvas under the umbrella of smart city development was shown in Table 3.

Table 3. Business model canvas

Smart cities project business model canvas

Who will help you? Key partners	How do you do it? Key activities	What do you do? Value proposition	How do you Interact? Audience relationships	Who do you help? Audience segments
1. Smart home devices & systems provider 2. Real estate/housing agency 3. University/school	1. Register all seniors with their available properties 2. Modify the apartment 3. Train the seniors to use home smart devices	1. Offer affordable co-living space for foreign students in Taiwanese seniors' residence 2. A platform where foreign students can give and take additional knowledge and skills to and from Taiwanese senior citizens 3. Provide extra sources of income for the senior citizens	1. Brothers/sisters 2. Friends 3. Life consultant	1. Senior citizens 65+ 2. Foreign students 3. Housing market
	What do you need? Key resources		**How do you reach them?** Distribution channels	
	1. House monitoring system 2. Payment system 3. Cleaning and maintenance services		1. Website 2. LINE 3. Home smart devices	
What will It cost? Cost structure			**How much will It make?** Revenue stream	
1. Modification and renovation costs 2. Training costs 3. Maintenance costs			1. 7,000 NTD per month (for staying at least 6 months) and 12,000 NTD per month (for staying less than 6 months) 2. 3–5% service fee 3. Eco-label appliances tax rebate and government funding and grants for startups and social entrepreneurs	

The value propositions of this new business model are:

1. Offer affordable co-living space for international students in Taiwanese seniors' residence.
2. A platform where international students can give and take additional knowledge and skills to and from Taiwanese senior citizens
3. Provide additional sources of income for senior citizens.

A service system diagram was shown in Fig. 3. According to the diagram, the significant income would come from three different sources:

1. Pay more for private info
2. Tax rebates and government subsidies for house modification
3. Service fee for monthly online payment system

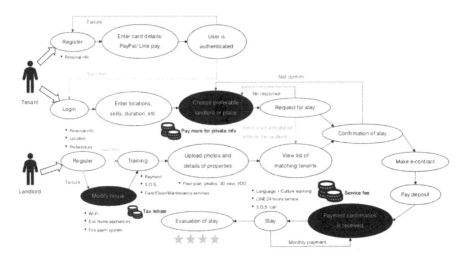

Fig. 3. Service system diagram

The above proposing results are presented in a workshop for discussing and reviewing both limitations and core values. The following are the outline from the workshop.

1. **Barriers:** The house modification phase tends to increase the investment cost during start a business up. If the project has not got government support and subsidies, this issue will need to be considered more. Also, a survey of the rental prices in a housing market among competitors is needed. The project should focus more on cultural aspects and how to connect people in different generations since these are the core values of this service design.

   Moreover, the most critical issue is how to encourage younger generations to live with older generations. Finding a way to communicate and promote this service to raise their attention is necessary. Similarly, finding a way to encourage senior citizens joining the program is also tricky since most of older adults still receive the news and find the rental place through conventional media like newspapers [2, 5].

2. **Benefits:** This co-living service system is designed to solve various problems of an aging or aged society. Relocation after retirement is known as a stressful major life event of seniors, and this involves the complex processes during moving [3]. Firstly, it offers a freeway for seniors who would like to follow the steps of aging in place easier. The seniors who own an apartment that might be too big for them to cope with [3] can make use of this service to get an extra income. Secondly, a house will be modified with necessary smart home devices to be ready for an age-in-place

lifestyle. Lastly, seniors can acquire additional knowledge and skills through living with the younger generation and living in a smart home. Referring to the study of Nikitina and Vorontsova [2], skills related to computer programs and the Internet are the top wish list among seniors to master. The associated key results of this service providing would reduce the suicide rate among seniors in Taiwan due to loneliness and stress.

3. **The Prototype Development and Evaluation Plan:** In the next phase of the study, a pilot study should be implemented among seniors who will be a target user of the service. In-depth interviews and the willingness to learn new technologies among those seniors are required to justify a chance of survival for this service in the future market. The next step is to consider other potential target users, such as expatriates and single senior citizens, without their own house. Also, the issue is about how to sustain the business and make a profit out of this service is the most critical area to work on for this kind of social business operation. The evaluation system of the service taker's satisfaction should be set in order to improve the service and be a data source for further development.

4. **The Chatbot Innovation Service:** Nowadays, Chatbots are already holding everyday conversations with the elderly. However, despite playing a significant part in successful interventions, the adoption of these technologies has been limited. One key barrier to broader adoption has been the traditional "top-down" design process that uses in creating technology for older adults. This process focuses on technology-oriented but not human-centered design with little consideration of user perspectives and preferences or their real-world constraints. Thus, this research proposes a contextual design framework to investigate the Innovative Chatbot applications that can use to support aging in place in Taiwan. Contextual Design is a user-centered design process that composes a variety of research methods that enable the designer to understand the users and their context. It provides a rich and qualitative understanding of who the users are and how they engage in activities or tasks daily.

According to the workshop results, we implemented this research into three-phases. The first phase begins with exploring the current Chatbot mechanism available in the market, such as Amazon Alexa, Google Assistant, and Apple Siri. Then outline the functions that can provide for developing innovative applications to support aging in place as well as their limitations. Afterward, this research recruits two groups of people: 10 elderly (60–65 years old) and 10 middle age (50–59 years old); to implement focus group interview and make the comparison of these two groups in the aspect of technology acceptance, interactive voice operation, the needs of technology to support aging in place, persona and user scenarios. The second phase of this research integrates the results collected from the first phase into contextual design processes and proposes the innovative applications of Chatbot that will use to support aging in place. We use the quality function deployment (QFD) matrix to show the design results and then outline the macro and micro factors of the innovative Chatbot applications. The final phase of this research begins with the Kano Model questionnaire design of then dispatch it to the target audiences and receive 25 effective responses for further analysis.

5 Conclusion and Future Works

By applying the concept of Sharing Economy with smart home technologies, this service design project could solve social problems in a certain way. Firstly, this service can facilitate seniors to cope with the upcoming age-in-place lifestyle. Secondly, a well-designed co-living environment can encourage international students and senior citizens to acquire and master their additional knowledge and skills. Thirdly, this business model proposal can drive economic growth by making use of seniors' vacant properties and promoting the employment of those seniors. Moreover, this research results shall follow the policy of achieving and sustaining good health and well-being, and create the values of equality in different generations, racism, and inclusive design to access the smart and emerging technologies. In the future, it will fulfill the sustainable development goal of sustainable cities and communities.

Furthermore, the results of the implementation of this research show that the middle age group is more enthusiastic about using innovative Chatbot applications than the elderly group. The middle age group also shows they are more willing to accept aging in place when they are getting old and independent living with the help of innovative technology than the elderly group. The Kano Model analysis perform in this research shows that the fundamental attributes of innovative Chatbot applications should include the application to integrate with the smart home devices and control the devices using voice command. The one-dimensional attributes should consist of a deep learning mechanism to record daily activities and remind them of their regular schedule. However, they do not like the design that integrates the Chatbot application with wearable devices to detect their physiological information and deliver to their doctor directly. The interview results show that they prefer to have individual privacy while they are doing aging in place. The excite-attributes of the contextual design include the innovative Chatbot applications that can talk to them. At the same time, they are home alone and provide an automatic connection to social media networks to review the update of their friends and input their updates by voice. The future studies of this research will focus on creating a prototype of the innovative Chatbot applications proposed by using the contextual design in this research and evaluate through user testing.

References

1. Liang, Y.: Taiwan now considered an 'aged society'. Xinhua, 15 October 2018
2. Nikitina, O., Vorontsova, G.: Aging population and tourism: socially determined model of consumer behavior in the "senior tourism" segment. Procedia-Soc. Behav. Sci. **214**, 845–851 (2015)
3. Löfqvist, C., Granbom, M., Himmelsbach, I., Iwarsson, S., Oswald, F., Haak, M.: Voices on relocation and aging in place in very old age—a complex and ambivalent matter. Gerontol. **53**(6), 919–927 (2013)
4. Chen, W., Hou, E.: 25 percent of suicides in 2016 in Taiwan involved seniors: center. Focus Taiwan, 23 June 2017
5. Kastner, J.: Taiwan's elderly vs. ghost-fearing landlords. Alijazeera, 08 October 2014

6. DeAeth, D.: Foreign students in Taiwan 10% of total university and college students in 2018. Taiwan News, 03 February 2019
7. Ministry of Foreign Affairs: Taiwan-Germany higher education policy forum wraps up. Taiwan Today, 06 November 2019
8. ICEF: Taiwan aims to double international student numbers by 2019. ICEF Monitor, 08 November 2016
9. Ministry of Foreign Affairs: Taipei ranked 7th in IMD Smart City Index. Taiwan Today, 08 November 2019
10. Lerner, M.: More seniors 'aging in place' mean fewer homes on the market to buy. The Washington Post (2019)
11. Rantz, M.J., et al.: A technology and nursing collaboration to help older adults age in place. Nurs. Outlook **53**(1), 40–45 (2005)
12. Tuohy, J.P.: 9 smart home devices for aging in place (2019). https://www.dwell.com/article/9-smart-home-devices-for-aging-in-place-5528881a. Accessed 30 Dec 2019
13. Oudshoorn, N.: Telecare Technologies and the Transformation of Healthcare, vol. 53, no. 9. Palgrave MacMillan (2019)
14. Oltermann, P.: Germany's 'multigeneration houses' could solve two problems for Britain. The Guardian, 02 May 2014
15. Reuters: 'Rent-a-granny': German pensioners answer the call, CNN, 04 December 2000
16. Lim, S.: You can now rent middle-aged 'uncles' in Japan for $12 an hour to do chores or offer life advice. Business Insider Singapore, September 2018
17. Balistrieri, E.: Rent a dude for ¥1,000: an interview with Takanobu Nishimoto of Ossan Rental. The Japan Times, 18 September 2013
18. Kropf, N.P., Cummings, S.: Here is how senior cohousing differs from an over-55 community, Marketwatch, September 2019
19. Robinson, M.: Millennials are paying thousands of dollars a month for maid service and instant friends in modern 'hacker houses'. Business Insider, March 2017
20. Dam, R.F., Teo, Y.S.: Personas – A Simple Introduction. Interaction design foundation (2019). https://www.interaction-design.org/literature/article/personas-why-and-how-you-should-use-them. Accessed 04 Jan 2020
21. Babich, N.: A beginner's guide to user journey mapping. UX Planet (2019). https://uxplanet.org/a-beginners-guide-to-user-journey-mapping-bd914f4c517c. Accessed 28 Oct 2019
22. GroupMap: "PEST Analysis". https://www.groupmap.com/map-templates/pest-analysis/. Accessed 23 Dec 2019
23. Cagan, J., Vogel, C.M.: What drives new product development. In: Creating Breakthrough Products: Revealing the Secrets That Drive Global Innovation, pp. 2–31. FT Press Financial Times (2012)
24. Osterwalder, A., Pigneur, Y.: Business model generation. Strategyzer AG (2010). https://www.strategyzer.com/canvas. Accessed 12 Dec 2019
25. Aalborg University: Service systems design. The Danish Agency for Higher Education (2019). https://studyindenmark.dk/portal/aalborg-university-aau/copenhagen/service-systems-design?filters=SearchableText%3D

Two Faces of Privacy: Legal and Human-Centered Perspectives of Lifelogging Applications in Home Environments

Wiktoria Wilkowska[1]([✉]) [iD], Julia Offermann-van Heek[1] [iD],
Liane Colonna[2], and Martina Ziefle[1] [iD]

[1] Human-Computer Interaction Center, RWTH Aachen University,
Campus-Boulevard 57, 52074 Aachen, Germany
wilkowska@comm.rwth-aachen.de
[2] Department of Law, Stockholm University,
Universitetvägen 10C, 10691 Stockholm, Sweden

Abstract. In view of the consequences resulting from the demographic change, using assisting lifelogging technologies in domestic environments represents one potential approach to support elderly and people in need of care to stay longer within their own home. Yet, the handling of personal data poses a considerable challenge to the perceptions of privacy and data security, and therefore for an accepted use in this regard. The present study focuses on aspects of data management in the context of two different lifelogging applications, considering a legal and a human-centered perspective. In a two-step empirical process, consisting of qualitative interviews and an online survey, these aspects were explored and evaluated by a representative German sample of adult participants (N = 209). Findings show positive attitudes towards using lifelogging, but there are also high requirements on privacy and data security as well as anonymization of the data. In addition, the study allows deep insights into preferred duration and location of the data storage, and permissions to access the personal information from third parties. Knowledge of preferences and requirements in the area of data management from the legal and human-centered perspectives is crucial for lifelogging and must be considered in applications that support people in their daily living at home. Outcomes of the present study considerably contribute to the understanding of an optimal infrastructure of the accepted and willingly utilized lifelogging applications.

Keywords: Lifelogging technology · Privacy · Data security · Anonymization · Data management

1 Introduction

An aging society characterized by rising numbers of people in need of assistance and care pose tremendous challenges for the whole society. Using lifelogging technologies in domestic environments represents one potential approach to support elderly and people in need of care to stay longer within their own home. Meanwhile the spectrum

Q. Gao and J. Zhou (Eds.): HCII 2020, LNCS 12208, pp. 545–564, 2020.
https://doi.org/10.1007/978-3-030-50249-2_39

of technologies in this area is extremely broad and includes wearable and non-wearable technologies, single devices and complex smart home systems, or camera- as well as sensor-based systems likewise [1]. On the one hand, all these technologies have multiple advantages, such as facilitating everyday life, relieving (caring) persons, increasing safety, supporting autonomy and independence, and motivating a healthier and more active lifestyle. On the other hand, there are barriers regarding handling of personal data from the legal and the human-centered point of view [2].

The legal framework safeguarding lifelogging is highly fragmented, consisting of a complex patchwork of laws that relate to everything from medical-device regulation to the management of health records. One area of particular legal concern is that of privacy and data protection. Here, laws vary significantly, depending on jurisdiction and, even where the use and development of a lifelogging device falls squarely within a particular region, there is still significant confusion concerning the scope of applicable laws. This paper will examine how legal conceptions concerning data storage and anonymization apply within the context of lifelogging technologies and, more concretely, it will address whether there are gaps or inconsistencies in the law that may hinder the further development of these important societal tools.

From the human-centered perspective, despite various advantages of lifelogging, existing concerns, especially data protection and privacy issues impede the user's acceptance. An empirical study examined, therefore, aspects which are perceived as relevant for the management of the personal data in technology assisting people in their private environments. This means, among others, opinions about storage duration and location of the logged data as well as anonymization and permissions of access to the personal information.

2   State of the Art

Using lifelogging applications in home environments involves different aspects which are assumed to be important to the users. As such technologies capture a great amount of private information that people may not want to share to others or only to selected individuals (e.g., family physician), privacy poses the main aspect, and the greatest concern at the same time. This paper refers to such privacy concerns from two perspectives: Firstly, it considers the current legal framework, and secondly, it focuses on the human-centered perspective of using lifelogging and the resulting data management. In this section the current state of the art in respect thereof is given.

2.1   The Legal Framework for Data Management of Lifelogging Applications

Data Storage. Article 5(1)(e) of the GDPR states that personal data shall be "kept in a form which permits identification of data subjects for no longer than is necessary for the purposes for which the personal data are processed…" [3]. It further sets forth narrow exceptions where storage is permissible without a link to a specific processing purpose when data "will be processed solely for archiving purposes in the public interest, scientific or historical research purposes or statistical purposes" [3]. In the event one of these limited exceptions is applicable, a data controller is nevertheless under a strict obligation to take appropriate safeguards, including technical and organizational measures, in order to protect the rights and freedoms of the data subject [3] (Article 5(1)(e), Article 89).

Essentially, the storage limitation seeks to ensure that personal data are kept only for as long as is necessary for the specific purpose for which it was obtained. In other words, even where a data controller collects and uses personal data in a fair and lawful manner, it cannot keep it for a period longer than it actually needs it: once the purpose has been fulfilled, the data should be erased or anonymized. Here, the close links that this principle has to data minimization and accuracy are apparent. The GDPR does not explicitly define time limits and, as such, they must be decided on a case-by-case basis.

There is a serious tension between lifelogging technologies and the storage limitation principle. By design, lifelogging technologies are ambient and turned on 24/7, seeking to create a perpetual record of an individual's life. Here, Allen describes lifelogs as a kind of "memory machine" that "enable unprecedented accurate retention and recall of personal life" [4]. The idea is to collect and store data for long periods of time in order to understand important aspects about an individual's life and health. When data is deleted the possibilities to recall and draw insight about an individual's life disappear [4]. Another problem with the storage limitation principle concerns the practical difficulties that exist with implementing it on the ground. While the law requires that data is deleted when no longer necessary to fulfill the purposes for which it was processed, it is often the case that there are many copies of data that can be easily overlooked [3] (Article 5(1)(e)). For example, these copies may exist in backups or other distributed copies. It is further worth mentioning that even if storage could somehow be limited by the inclusion of a "stop recording" functionality into a lifelogging device, the reality is that lifelogging devices are embedded into the fabric of everyday life as well as into the human body itself making this function largely infeasible [5].

Despite the challenges to the storage limitation principle, technical solutions may provide a mechanism to manage legal concerns in line with the principle of Privacy by Design set forth in Article 25 of the GDPR [3]. For example, Hippocratic Databases (HDB) are being developed which provide granular and selective access to data based on their privacy and sensitivity [6, 7]. Furthermore, fog computing [8] is being explored as a means to permit system developers to enforce privacy controls at the point of collection (i.e. at the device itself) and thus permit privacy management systems guided by the principle of data minimization [8].

Anonymization. While anonymization is not defined in the GDPR, the Article 29 Working Party has explained it as "a technique applied to personal data in order to achieve irreversible de-identification" [9]. Recital 26 of the GDPR further adds that anonymized data is "data rendered anonymous in such a way that the data subject is not or no longer identifiable" [3]. Here, it is important to mention that it is not clear what is meant precisely by "irreversible de-identification" and more specifically, whether data is only considered anonymized where there is zero probability of reidentification or whether some kind of "reasonableness" standard applies [9]. Nevertheless, if data are rendered anonymous then the GDPR is not applicable since the law only applies to the processing of personal data [3] (Article 2).

In addition to the concepts of "personal data" and "anonymized data", the GDPR introduces a third category of data: pseudonymized data [3] (Article 4(5)). According to the GDPR, the process of pseudonymization involves the conversion of data about an identified person into data about a merely "identifiable" person [10]. That said, it is important to remember that data will not be considered to be pseudonymized unless the additional data necessary for re-identification, are kept safely inaccessible for the users of pseudonymized data [3] (Article 4(5)). While pseudonymous data is not exempt from the GDPR, the law offers several key incentives to apply the technique such as the explicit satisfaction of the "data protection by design" requirement [3] (Article 25(1)) and the chance to repurpose data for another compatible use [3] (Article 6(3)(e)).

Data anonymization techniques can be used on all different types of personal data collected by a lifelogging technology such as data about an individual's appearance (video), health status (physiological signals), communications (audio) and behavior [11]. There are a variety of anonymization techniques such as noise addition, permutation, differential privacy, aggregation, k-anonymity, l-diversity and t-closeness [9]. Currently, however, there is a significant legal debate about the strengths of these various techniques and whether any of them can guarantee anonymity [12–15].

Anonymization in the context of lifelogging devices raises serious challenges insofar as the true value of lifelogging lies in the analysis of personal data. This dilemma is often framed as the data-utility problem where the concern is that anonymization may limit the benefits of the data or even completely ruin the total value of the data set. For example, if a lifelogging technology stores images in order to permit and individual with mild dementia to recall events or persons, de-identifying those persons will likely have a negative effect on the service provided [16]. Here, it is essential that a privacy-by-context approach is taken with respect to the specific device and application.

2.2   The Human-Centered Perspective on Lifelogging Technology

From the human-centered perspective, research has investigated the acceptance of assisting lifelogging technologies for different applications, taking specific user-relevant parameters into account. Several studies in this regard have shown that assistive lifelogging technologies applied in health-related contexts are overall positively perceived, and most of the specific applications are considered to be beneficial and useful, in particular when applied to support and assist individuals in older age (e.g., [17–19]).

Most of all, the advantages of enabling a longer and independent life at home as well as relieving the burdens of caring persons were acknowledged by potential users. Increase in felt safety and also enhanced independence represented further relevant motives to use assisting lifelogging technology [2].

In contrast to these perceived benefits of using assisting lifelogging applications, barriers and concerns are also associated with the use of such devices and systems. Based on the fact that lifelogging technologies collect personal health data and closely intervene in people's everyday lives, concerns with regard to privacy and data security as well as the fear of losing control represent central barriers of using the lifelogging applications [2, 20–22]. In this connection, the fear of unauthorized disclosure of the personal data to third parties was also considered as a relevant disadvantage of using lifelogging technology. In more detail, research found that it is of utmost importance for future users who are allowed to have access to the lifelogging technology data, as this is also perceived as a limitation of individual privacy and can significantly impact the acceptance of the technology [23, 24]. In general, it is an important aspect that a large amount of user data is collected and stored when lifelogging technologies are applied, differing in the extent depending on the specific application and technology. From a rather technical point of view [25], it is preferred to collect as much information as possible about the user, as more detailed analyses are enabled by larger amounts of data. In contrast, users are often not willing to share and collect large amounts of data, scrutinizing in particular the location and duration of storing large amounts of data. Related to this, research has discussed [26] different opportunities of data storage and their respective (dis)advantages, highlighting storage in a cloud as technologically best option for lifelogging data, whereas this type of storage involves security and privacy concerns from a user-centered perspective.

Overall, privacy and data security represent complex parameters which have to be considered when a user-centered development and design of lifelogging applications is targeted. Here, it is necessary to integrate the users' wishes and requirements with regard to the data management of lifelogging technologies in order to reach a broad and sustainable adoption of lifelogging devices and systems.

2.3   The Research Objectives

Considering the legal and human-centered framework, in the next step it is essential to empirically examine aspects associated with handling of personal information when using lifelogging technologies, integrating the real users. Given the great number of different applications in this area, the present study evaluated aspects of data management based on two exemplary applications. Choosing these, the context-dependency and the comparability of findings should be investigated.

The specific aim of the empirical approach was to evaluate perceptions of the individual privacy, data security, and anonymization as well as data storage and access in the context of lifelogging. The research addressed the following main questions (RQ):

- RQ1: Do requirements of privacy depend on the context of use the lifelogging?
- RQ2: Do concerns regarding the general data security significantly change depending on the nature of the data ("my data" vs. "data of someone else")?
- RQ3: Is anonymization of data necessary when using lifelogging?
- RQ4: Do preferences of data storage (location and period of time) change depending on the usage context?
- RQ5: Who is allowed to access the personal lifelogging data?

In the next section, we first describe the used method of the empirical study before the statistical findings, analyzing these research questions, are presented.

3   Method

The empirical study examined the relevant aspects for management of personal data when using lifelogging technology in a private context. Besides the main aspects of privacy and data security, the focus lay on opinions about the storage duration and location of the logged data as well as about anonymization, and permissions for accessing personal information were examined.

In order to address the phenomenon of contextual dependency, two applications have been studied so that comparisons can be made regarding the mentioned aspects. Comparing the two different lifelogging applications, the study aimed at reaching different future users. For this purpose, we firstly used a scenario which aimed for healthy (older) adults, describing a preventive health application meant to be used for activities of daily living (i.e., for basic activities like personal care, mobility, dietary intake, etc. and for instrumental activities: medicine intake, food preparation, money management, etc.). Secondly, we introduced the participants to a scenario of an assisting lifelogging application for persons suffering from dementia.

The study used a mixed-method approach to empirically investigate the research questions. First, interviews were conducted in order to explore the general knowledge of already existing lifelogging technologies. The findings from the qualitative method served then as the basis for the following online questionnaire, which aimed at validating the outcomes. In this paper, we primarily concentrate on the quantitative findings.

3.1   Data Collection

Qualitative Study. In order to enable the quantitative investigation of the empirical questions, the initial step was an exploratory approach to generate sufficient knowledge and understanding of perceptions of, and attitudes towards, lifelogging technologies – not only for activities of daily living (i.e., mobility behavior, nutrition, personal care and hygiene) but also in the field of dementia care (i.e., sleeping behavior). For this purpose, we interviewed N = 14 participants by means of a semi-standardized interview. In some cases, efforts were made to find interview partners who already have professional or private experience with people with dementia.

The method of qualitative content analysis according to [27] was used to analyze the guided interviews and the resulting key outcomes were fully incorporated in the conceptualization of the quantitative data collection.

Quantitative Study. In the second step, a standardized online questionnaire was used to validate the previously obtained results in a larger sample. As this method allows for more representative statements, the main focus in this paper was laid on this part of the presented empirical research. The survey was structured in four main parts.

We started with collection of the demographic data from the participants, such as age, gender, education, and place of residence. In this part, also their self-assessed health status was queried and the respondents' experience with persons suffering from dementia in a private as well as professional context.

The following part referred to the knowledge of, and experience with, lifelogging technologies in everyday life. In advance, the survey shortly explained the term lifelogging and different contexts of possible application fields were given as examples, among others health monitoring, location and presence detection, performance measurement at work, consumption tracking, outsourcing of memory (i.e. data collection in the form of images and data to create a life archive). Here, participants also evaluated the use of lifelogging in their everyday life.

The two last parts of the questionnaire addressed the same lifelogging applications that had already been focused on in the qualitative method: activities of daily living and application of lifelogging for people suffering from dementia (the applications are described in more detail in Sect. 3.2), and the structure of the two was comparable. At the beginning, a short scenario described the particular application and the relevant human activity as well as the types of sensors used to collect the logging data. Participants were firstly asked to share their opinions regarding technology acceptance, including aspects like the perceived ease of use, perceived usefulness, and benefits and barriers related to the particular lifelogging application. After that, participants evaluated

Table 1. Item examples for assessments of required privacy and handling of lifelogging data used in the online survey.

Construct	Item description	Scale
Privacy	"Respect for privacy should be a top priority in lifelogging." (ADL) "I have greater privacy concerns when using cameras to record everyday activities than when using sensors in mobile phones and smart wristbands." (ADL) "The use of lifelogging technologies in dementia care is similar to monitoring, which limits the right of self-determination of the person with dementia." (PwD) "The privacy of dementia patients can no longer come first, as they need care." (PwD)	Likert-scale from 1 ("I strongly disagree") to 6 points ("I strongly agree")
Data security	"The security of the data I have collected through lifelogging about my daily activities is important to me." (ADL) "Any misuse of the data collected, which could harm people suffering from dementia, must be prevented by appropriate security measures."(PwD)	
Anonymization	"I have less privacy concerns if my lifelogging data is stored anonymously." (ADL) "I have less privacy concerns if the lifelogging data of the demented person is stored anonymously."	

questions regarding attitudes referring to privacy issues and data management (i.e., data security, permitted retention/storage period of the personal data, location of the data storage, access to the personal data, and the requirement of anonymization). In this paper, outcomes of the latter – of privacy and data management – are reported. In order to align the scales for privacy and data security in the two applications for later statistical analysis, we scaled them to 100 points. Item examples of the relevant constructs are given in Table 1.

At the end of the questionnaire, authors expressed their gratitude to the participants for sharing their personal opinions on the topic and participants were given the possibility to voice criticism, ask questions, and make comments.

3.2   Two Lifelogging Applications

In order to better understand the data management of lifelogging technologies, the results of the present study apply to two different cases. These applications enable gaining deep insights into the opinions of all age groups of adults the lifelogging applications address, among them healthy individuals as well as persons suffering from a geriatric condition of dementia and their caregivers. At the same time, the questions regarding handling of private data in the two applications allow for a 'me'-perspective and the perspective for other people concerned, like relatives, family members or friends.

The first application addressed activities of daily living (*ADL*) aiming at a recognition of such, using wearable cameras, cameras located in the environment, sensors embedded in mobile phones and smart wristbands. ADLs can be divided into basic and instrumental. Basic ADLs consist of self-care tasks that include, among others, bathing and showering, personal hygiene (including brushing, combing, and styling hair), dressing, toilet hygiene (getting to the toilet, cleaning oneself, and getting back up), functional mobility (ability to walk, get in and out of bed), and self-feeding. Instrumental ADLs, although not necessary for fundamental functioning, but they let an individual live independently in a community. These include cleaning and maintaining the house, managing money, moving within the community, preparing meals, shopping for groceries and necessities, taking prescribed medications, and using the telephone or other form of communication.

The second application focused on supporting people suffering from dementia (*PwD*) and their caregivers, using environmental sensors at home for behavioral analysis. For this purpose, data generated from environmental sensors located in the monitored subjects are collected in a remote platform and used to generate sensible and usable information for the caregivers. As the application deals with behavioral analysis, the data analysis aims at detecting anomalies. The application makes use of a simple sensor, a so-called bed presence sensor located under the subject's mattress, that makes possible to check when and how many times during a day the subject goes to or gets off bed, the time he/she gets up in the morning and goes to sleep in the evening, etc. By collecting these data over a given amount of time, it is possible to derive a kind of average behavior. On that basis, the average data can be used to check if anomalous events or trends take place.

3.3   Research Design

The empirical study aimed at an investigation of the users' preferences regarding privacy and handling of data when using lifelogging technologies in the private environment. These topics were explored and evaluated in a two-step method procedure, which focused on the two lifelogging applications described above: ADL and PwD.

In the first step, a qualitative approach in terms of semi-structured interviews explored the participants' knowledge about, and use of, lifelogging technologies in their everyday lives and aimed at getting first insights into opinions and evaluations on privacy and data management. Based on the results, in a second step a quantitative study was conceptualized in order to validate the findings in an online questionnaire.

Taking the German population as an example, this study intended to provide an overview of opinions referring to privacy and desired handling of personal data resulting from using lifelogging applications in private environments. Using a scenario-based method, after introductions to the particular applications participants evaluated following variables, which were considered for the later statistical analyses:

- *Privacy* (i.e., 7 items in the context of ADL, Cronbach's $\alpha = .72$; 6 items in the context of PwD, Cronbach's $\alpha = .73$; for the statistical mean comparisons scaled to 100 points);
- *Data security* (i.e., 3 items in the context of ADL, Cronbach's $\alpha = .71$; 3 items in the context of PwD, Cronbach's $\alpha = .62$; min = 3 and max = 18 points);
- *Anonymization* (anonymization vs. no anonymization);
- *Storage duration* of the logged data (no storage – one month – three months – one year – unlimited);
- *Storage location* of the logged data [local vs. cloud (direct access possible) vs. server of the provider (no direct access possible)];
- *Access permission* to the personal information (myself – family members – friends – authorized provider – health insurance company – nursing staff – family doctor).

In general, the used scales for privacy and data security achieved a satisfactory internal consistency ($\alpha > .7$). Only in one case, i.e., for the items assessing data security in the application meant to support people with dementia, the scale slightly missed the required α-level. Though, for the statistical comparison we decided to use this scale anyway, on the condition that we will carefully consider this shortcoming in the interpretation of the findings. The research design of the study is depicted in Fig. 1.

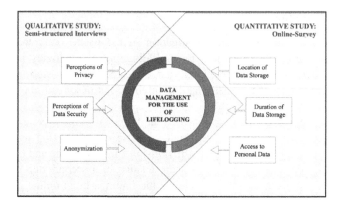

Fig. 1. Research model for the present study.

3.4 Description of the Participants

The empirical study was conducted in German language. In the following, the interviewees of the qualitative interviews and the respondents of the quantitative online survey are described in more detail.

Participants of the Qualitative Study. The interviewees (N = 14), which were aged between 23–74 years (*M* = 41.3, *SD* = 16.8; 64% female), differed with regard to their experience with lifelogging and reported various levels of experience in the area of care of people with dementia. A large majority of the interviewees (71.4%) reported to have experience with lifelogging technology. Far fewer of them reported professional experience (28.6%) with dementia care, but half of the interviewed persons (50%) mentioned to support people with dementia in their private lives. Thus, different knowledge constellations could be achieved in the sample, resulting in a balanced relationship between "laypersons" and "experts" with regard to the technology and healthcare.

Participants of the Quantitative Study. Overall, N = 209 participants aged between 18–79 years (*M* = 37, *SD* = 15.1) completed the questionnaire. The genders of the sample were balanced with 53.6% women and 46.4% men, and the education level was overall quite high (50% held a university degree, 21.5% completed vocational training, 20% reported a general higher education entrance qualification).

The responses came from a very mixed sample of German adults: Almost half of the respondents (49.3%) rated their general state of health as 'good' and around 19% stated that they had at least one form of a chronic illness. More than half of the participants (56%) reported lifelogging experience, whereby they mostly used lifelogging for health monitoring, attendance recordings, and performance measurement at the workplace. Regarding contact with dementia, almost half of all respondents (47%) indicated to have contact points with people suffering from dementia in their private lives; additional 10% of the respondents were involved in the care of persons with dementia in their private surroundings. Moreover, the majority of the participants reported to be married (35%) or to live in a solid relationship (41%) and 22% of the sample indicated to live alone. Regarding the current living location, most of the respondents reported to live in a (big) city (55%) and suburbs (12%), and more than a third of the sample (33%) reported to live in the countryside.

In the following, based on this representative sample statistical analyses referring to preferences in data management when using lifelogging are described in more detail.

4 Results

In this study, aspects perceived as necessary for handling of the personal data resulting from the use of the lifelogging technologies are reported by means of descriptive statistics like means (M) and standard deviations (SD) and percentages (%) of the examined sample are given to describe proportions. To statistically compare the means for the sample on two different occasions, i.e., for the two applications (ADL and PwD) paired-samples t-tests were used and effect sizes were calculated by eta squared (η^2). The level of statistical significance (p) is set at the conventional level of 5%.

The result section describes first the general perceptions of lifelogging technology evaluated by real users. Second, the users' requirements regarding privacy and data security are analyzed, comparing lifelogging applications supporting older people in the activities of daily living as well as persons suffering from dementia. Next subsections refer to the anonymization and storage – therein the preferred location and duration – of the personal data for the two lifelogging applications. And, in the final part of the result section evaluations referring to the persons being allowed to have access to these data are described.

4.1 A General Perception of Lifelogging Technologies

In order to provide an overview of the general opinions regarding available lifelogging technologies, the online survey used the method of a semantic differential [28]. This method is designed to measure connotative meanings of a concept or object and it allowed in this study to derive attitudes of the respondents, who already use lifelogging in different contexts. For this purpose, participants assessed series of bipolar pairs of adjectives defined by verbal opposites (e.g., simple–complicated, supporting–restricting) on a six-steps rating scale. Figure 2 depicts the resulting polarity profile.

Overall, more than half of the respondents (56%; n = 117) declared to use lifelogging technologies (e.g., for health monitoring, tracking of consumption of different kind, measurement of performance, etc.) and evaluated the bipolar dimensions. The profile resulting from the means of the particular dimensions shows that users predominantly assessed lifelogging in a positive way. The connotations describe the evaluations of the technology as rather simple [to use], supporting, convenient, useful and helpful. Yet, the outcomes regarding its relevance resulted in a negative tendency, which means that users perceive the technology rather as irrelevant than life-changing.

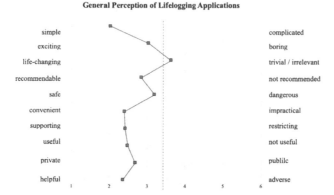

Fig. 2. Mean values resulting for the adjective pairs describing characteristics of the general perceptions and use of lifelogging technologies; N = 117.

4.2 Requirements for Privacy and Data Security

Considering the topic of the data management in the context of lifelogging technology, perceptions of privacy and data security account for the most crucial parts of its acceptance and are decisive for decisions to use or not use the technology. The present study evaluated the opinions of the participants using diverse items referring to the part-aspects of the perceived individual privacy (ADL: 7 items, PwD: 6 items) and data security (ADL: 3 items, PwD: 3 items).

To compare the results with regard to the requirements of *privacy*, a paired-sample t-test was used and revealed statistically significant differences [$t(208) = 14.3, p \leq 0.001$; $\eta^2 = 0.5$] in the perceptions of using lifelogging for activities of daily living ($M = 80.2$, $SD = 13.8$) in comparison to the use for the support of people with dementia ($M = 65.9$, $SD = 13.7$). The resulting eta squared value of .50 lets conclude that there was a large effect with a substantial difference between the privacy requirements for the two lifelogging applications. This effect is depicted in Fig. 3 on the left.

The same statistical analysis was applied for the assessments of *data security* and exposed statistically significant effect [$t(208) = 7.6$, $p \leq 0.001$; $\eta^2 = 0.2$] likewise. However, considering the effect size the differences between security of data for ADL ($M = 14.4$, $SD = 2.8$) and PwD ($M = 12.9$, $SD = 2.8$) were small. Figure 3 on the right presents the differences.

Summing up, as for requirements of privacy and security in the management of personal data, results uncovered that people have higher demands for the use of lifelogging applications concerning their daily activities as for the technology that monitors behavioral pattern of dementia patients.

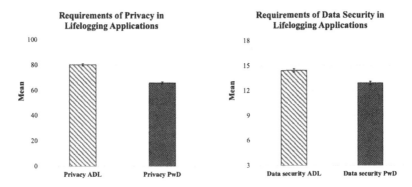

Fig. 3. Mean differences for requirements of privacy (left) and data security (right) in lifelogging applications: activities of daily living (ADL) and for people with dementia (PwD); N = 209.

4.3 Anonymization

In the next step, we statistically analyzed what role does anonymization play in the two lifelogging applications and whether the evaluations differ for the two investigated lifelogging applications. The resulting means reached 4.2 of maximum 6 points (ADL: $SD = 1.5$; PwD: $SD = 1.3$) and the t-Test for paired samples accordingly revealed no significant differences for the both application examples [$t(208) = -0.4, n.s$]. Thus, according to this finding, participants clearly required anonymization of the personal data, independently of the type of the used lifelogging technology.

Later in the questionnaire, participants were asked to assess the importance of the data anonymization for the storage of the personal data on different storage platforms (local vs. cloud vs. provider storage). The resulting percentages for the required anonymization are presented in Fig. 4 below.

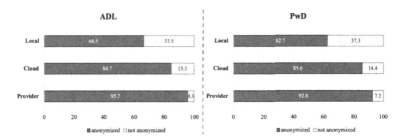

Fig. 4. Percentage (%) of persons who wish anonymization when using lifelogging for activities of daily living (left) and for support of people with dementia (right); N = 209.

The patterns on the different storage platforms are very similar for both applications. Especially when personal data are supposed to be stored on the sever of the provider almost all of the participants demanded anonymization. Also, when using cloud data storage, the vast majority desired to anonymize the data. Solely when lifelogging data are stored locally, respondents perceived less necessity to anonymize their data. Still, two third of them indicated the wish to protect themselves by making their personal data anonymous.

In sum, anonymization of the personal data seems to play an important role in the perceptions of the (potential) users for lifelogging technologies, regardless of the particular context of use.

4.4   Storage of Data: Preferred Location and Period of Time

With regard to the storage of the personal data, the study evaluated preferences of two further aspects. The first referred to the location of the data storage (local vs. cloud vs. provider) and the second investigated the preferred period of time for the storage (no storage vs. one month vs. three months vs. one year vs. unlimited). The resulting percentages for the particular categories are presented in Fig. 5 for the ADL-application and in Fig. 6 for the PwD-application.

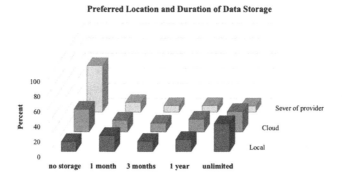

Fig. 5. Percentages (%) of preferred options for the duration and location of data storage when using lifelogging application for the activities of daily living: local server (left), cloud (middle) and server of the provider (right); N = 209.

Looking at the graph for the ADL-application, it becomes clear that local storage, which means the use of for instance smartphone, personal computer or fitness wristband, is the most accepted way for the respondents to keep their personal data for an unlimited period of time (37%). Another 27% of the participants can imagine to store the data without time limitations in the cloud. On the other side, considering the cloud even more respondents (30%) opted in favor of no storage, whereas this option was clearly preferred for the storage on the server of the provider (62%).

For the lifelogging application concerning support for people with dementia, for the most respondents the least trusted and, therefore, popular option for data storage was likewise the server of the provider (53%). And also, similar to the other application, the highest consent for unlimited data storage was given for the local storage possibilities (27%), however, according to the only slightly differing bars in the graph, the opinions regarding the storage preferences in this context were quite different.

Preferred Location and Duration of Data Storage

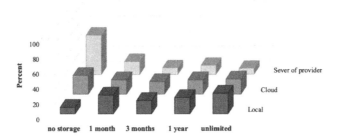

Fig. 6. Percentages (%) of preferred options for the duration and location of data storage when using lifelogging application for the support of people with dementia: local server (left), cloud (middle) and server of the provider (right); N = 209.

All in all, it can be stated that the local storage was perceived as the most favorable, and the server of the provider was the least preferred option for the storage of the personal data resulting from using lifelogging technology.

4.5   Permissions of the Data Access

In the last step of the result section, findings referring to permissions of personal data access are thematized. Figure 7 depicts these for the both focused applications.

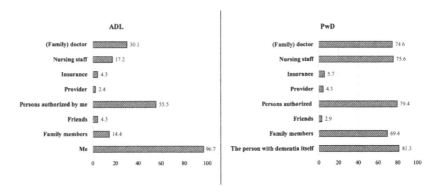

Fig. 7. Percentages (%) of permissions for the access to personal data resulting from using lifelogging application for the activities of daily living (left) and for the support of people with dementia (right); N = 209.

Considering the use of lifelogging for activities of daily living, almost all respondents (97%) required to have access to their personal data, more than half of them (55%) would allow the access for authorized persons and around 30% would permit their family doctor to have insight into the data. In this context, the data access was the least granted to the provider, friends, and insurance.

For permissions in the PwD-application, differing access pattern emerged. Here, additionally to the permissions for the persons with dementia (81%), doctors (75%), and authorized persons (79%), very much accepted was also the access for family members (69%) and the nursing staff (76%). Whereas, similarly to the ADL-application, insurances, the provider, and friends were generally rather refused to have access to the personal data of people with dementia.

5 Discussion

The use of assisting lifelogging technologies in private environments offers a wide range of opportunities for the increasingly ageing societies. Health monitoring, preventive parameter measurements, dietary habits, or mobility tracking represent only some of the possible lifelogging application fields, which have the potential to assist and facilitate the everyday life, support the autonomy, and motivate an active lifestyle of the users. On the other side, such technologies generate a large amount of personal data, the management of which must be thoughtfully executed, or it results in considerable barriers that make the use difficult for the potential users. Especially in the health-related area, invasion of privacy and defective data security are crucial obstacles on the way to a successful implementation of lifelogging [29].

But what does it mean to manage the personal information well or thoroughly, and, is the legal framework for data privacy in line with the requirements of the real users? These questions disclose two faces of privacy which were addressed in this paper. The empirical research presented above examined aspects associated with data management in the context of two different lifelogging applications and we first sum up the outcomes, discussing them in terms of the research questions formulated at the beginning.

5.1 Summary of the Results

Using a two-step approach, we studied aspects perceived as important part of data management and evaluated them within a representative German sample. Findings showed that users of current lifelogging technologies assess them mostly in a positive way. However, they also consider lifelogging as a nice technical addition rather than a life-changing innovation.

In terms of the research objectives, the first one referred to the question whether privacy concerns significantly differ depending on context of use and therefore of the nature of the lifelogging data. As for requirements of privacy, the study results revealed that people have higher demands for the use of applications concerning logging of their daily activities contrary to the technology that monitors behavioral pattern of dementia patients. The same pattern was found for opinions regarding perceptions of security in the management of personal data. These findings can have different reasons: One could be the degree of involvement ('am I involved?' vs. 'are others involved?') which – according to the outcomes – implies that when individuals themselves are affected, the relevance of privacy and data security are considered significantly higher than in case when third parties are involved. Another reason can refer to the complexity of the application and, at the same time, the amount of the collected data: According to that, people would feel less invaded in their privacy when only one activity is tracked (in our example: the sleeping behavior of a specific group of people) as compared to the one that logs diverse activities of the daily life, such as personal hygiene, functional mobility, eating behavior, communication, shopping behavior, cleaning, etc. Based on these findings, it stands to reason that from the users' point of view the requirements on privacy and data security regarding lifelogging applications are guided by their perceived involvement and are higher the more complex are the resulting logging data. Overall, the evaluations resulted in high mean values for the two scales (all in the upper quarter of the overall scale), which suggests that both privacy and data security are very important aspects of the data handling.

Moreover, anonymization of the personal data was perceived as an inevitable part of the data management. According to the reached means for its importance, anonymization plays in opinion of the (potential) users an important role for lifelogging technologies, regardless of the particular context of use – there were no significant differences found in the study for the different applications. In addition, the relevance increased the more 'further away' the data were kept, i.e., for the local storage the necessity of data anonymization was perceived as less important than when data storage was performed by a third-party supplier. In this regard we can therefore clearly answer our research question insofar as that the anonymization of logging data is perceived as a necessary requirement of an accepted use.

Sticking to the subject of storing the personal data, the location and duration of the data storage were identified as relevant aspects for the use of lifelogging, regardless of the use context. The participants perceived the local storage as the most favorable option, and the server of provider/third-party supplier was the least preferred alternative for keeping the personal information. In addition, the study found out that the more local the storage, the greater was the preference for timely unlimited storage.

The results regarding access to logged data records are, in turn, context-dependent: The proportion of those who would allow access to their data for different groups of people is significantly higher for the application in dementia care than for the example of ADL tracking. Overall, people are quite willing to share their logged data with doctors as well as authorized persons, independently from the used application. In case of a health condition like dementia, the allowance of data sharing is even expanded to the nursing staff and family members, as these persons are highly involved in the everyday support and care of the diseased individuals.

In sum, the presented results lead to the conclusion, that privacy and data security are inherent parts and highly required aspects of the use of lifelogging applications. People mostly prefer the local storing of their logged information and the less local the storage takes place and the greater the restrictions on the access to the one's own data, the greater is the users' desire for anonymization.

With respect to the legal framework, the rules concerning privacy largely overlap with the requirements of individual users. The law recognizes contextual factors, for example, it places much stricter requirements on the processing of sensitive personal data than that of non-sensitive data [3] (Article 6, Article 9). While the law does not distinguish between the amount of data collected *per se* (so long as personal data is being processed then a data controller is obligated to comply with the GDPR), it does require that risker processing activities, for example, those that involve huge amounts of health data collected from a multiplicity of different sensors, must meet additional requirements such as the completion of a Data Protection Impact Assessment [3] (Article 35). The idea that data should be stored as locally as possible is entirely consistent with the data minimization principle which requires that data be deleted or anonymized when it is no longer necessary to meet the purposes of the processing. The law is also consistent with user perceptions about access requirements, providing greater access to doctors and caregivers. In order to "access" or process data, a data controller must have a lawful ground [3] (Article 6, Article 9). While individual consent is a major ground to process personal data, it is nevertheless possible to process personal data where it is necessary to protect the vital interests of the data subject [3] (Article 6(d), Article 9(c)) or the processing is necessary for the purposes of preventive or occupational medicine [3] (Article 9(h)).

5.2   Limitations and Future Research Directions

The present approach provided insights into legal and human-centered perspectives on data security and privacy in the context of using lifelogging technologies and services. Both perspectives should be considered when lifelogging technologies are developed, designed, and communicated to (future) users. Nevertheless, there are some limitations and recommendations which should be considered for further research and developments.

A first methodological limitation refers to the scenario-based approach applied in this study. As the participants evaluated aspects like duration of data storage or anonymization of data based on scenarios (describing two different lifelogging applications), it cannot be ensured that their reported preferences predict their actual behavior: therefore, it could be that the participants' evaluations are different when they actively use the described lifelogging applications [30]. Hence, future studies should address the participants' evaluations after an active usage, enabling hands-on experience within experiments and usability tests. Additionally, for future studies it would be very interesting to investigate other relevant aspects, such as diverse types of processed data differing for example in their (perceived) intimacy.

As a further limitation, it should be considered that this study's sample contained German participants of almost all ages (18–79 years) and was balanced with regard to gender. Future studies should validate the results in further countries in order to compare the requirements of data management, depending on the participants' origins. In particular, with regard to lifelogging technologies being applied for supporting dementia patients and their caregivers, future studies should try to integrate even more the professional caregivers, the dementia patients themselves as well as the technical development of such specific lifelogging applications into empirical studies.

As a final remark and related to the fact that this study showed meaningful connections between the legal and the human-centered perspective on data security and privacy issues in the context of lifelogging technologies, future studies should aim at a closer interlocking of these perspectives in terms of directly joint empirical studies.

6 Conclusion

Lifelogging technologies pose tremendous promise and possibility for improving the lives of an aging population. Having said that, they also present serious concerns that require careful legal attention and scrutiny. The current legal framework is not up to the task of managing the threats posed by lifelogging technologies as it lacks both comprehensiveness and coherence.

Acknowledgements. The authors thank all participants for kindly sharing their opinions on assisting lifelogging technologies. We also thank Linda Engelmann for the research support. This work resulted from the project PAAL – "Privacy Aware and Acceptable Lifelogging services for older and frail people" and was funded by the German Federal Ministry of Education and Research (16SV7955). In addition, the support of the JPI More Years, Better Lives and the Swedish Research Council for Health, Working Life, and Welfare (2017-02302) is gratefully acknowledged.

References

1. Rashidi, P., Mihailidis, A.: A survey on ambient-assisted living tools for older adults. IEEE J. Biomed. Health Inform. **17**, 579–590 (2012)
2. Peek, S.T., Wouters, E.J., Van Hoof, J., Luijkx, K.G., Boeije, H.R., Vrijhoef, H.J.: Factors influencing acceptance of technology for aging in place: a systematic review. Int. J. Med. Inform. **83**, 235–248 (2014). https://doi.org/10.1016/j.ijmedinf.2014.01.004
3. General Data Protection Regulation: Regulation (EU) 2016/679 General Data Protection Regulation (GDPR), O.J. (2016)
4. Allen, A.L.: Dredging up the past: lifelogging, memory, and surveillance. Univ. Chicago Law Rev. **75**(1), 47–74 (2008)
5. Colonna, L.: Legal and regulatory challenges to utilizing lifelogging technologies for the frail and sick. Int. J. Law Inf. Technol. **27**(1), 50–74 (2019)
6. Agrawal, R., Kiernan, J., Srikant, R., Xu, Y.: Hippocratic databases. In: Proceedings of the 28th International Conference on Very Large Data Bases, VLDB 2002, Hong Kong, China, pp. 143–154 (2002)
7. Grandison, T., Johnson, C., Kiernan, J.: Hippocratic databases: current capabilities and future trends. In: Gertz, M., Jajodia, S. (eds.) Handbook of Database Security, pp. 409–429. Springer, Boston (2008). https://doi.org/10.1007/978-0-387-48533-1_17
8. Makker, S.R.: Overcoming "Foggy" notions of privacy: how data minimization will enable privacy in the internet of things. Univ. Missouri-Kansas Law Rev. **85**, 895 (2017)
9. Data Protection Working Party: Opinion of the Article 29. Data Protection Working Party on Anonymisation Techniques, 0829/14/EN WP 216, 10 April 2014
10. Kotschy, W.: The New General – Is There Sufficient Pay-off for Taking the Trouble to Anonymize or Pseudonymize Data? Ludwig Boltzmann Institute for Human Rights, Vienna (2016)
11. Flórez-Revuelta, F., Mihailidis, A., Ziefle, M., Colonna, L., Spinsante, S.: Privacy-aware and acceptable lifelogging services for older and frail people: the PAAL project. Presentation at the IEEE 8th International Conference on Consumer Electronics, Berlin (ICCE-Berlin) (2018)

12. Ohm, P.: Broken promises of privacy: responding to the surprising failure of anonymization. UCLA Law Rev. **57**, 1701 (2010)
13. Yakowitz, J.: Tragedy of the data commons. Harvard J. Law Technol. **25**, 1 (2011)
14. Schwartz, P.M., Solove, D.J.: The PII problem: privacy and a new concept of personally identifiable information. New York Univ. Law Rev. **86**, 1814 (2011)
15. Rubinstein, I., Hartzog, W.: Anonymization and risk. Wash. Law Rev. **91**, 703 (2016)
16. Colonna, L., Mihailidis, A.: A methodological approach to privacy by design within the context of lifelogging technologies. Rutgers Comput. Technol. Law J. (Rutgers Newark) (2020, forthcoming)
17. Gövercin, M., Meyer, S., Schellenbach, M., Steinhagen-Thiessen, E., Weiss, B., Haesner, M.: SmartSenior@home: acceptance of an integrated ambient assisted living system. Results of a clinical field trial in 35 households. Inform. Health Soc. Care **41**, 430–447 (2016). https://doi.org/10.3109/17538157. 2015.1064425
18. Wild, K., Boise, L., Lundell, J., Foucek, A.: Unobtrusive in-home monitoring of cognitive and physical health: reactions and perceptions of older adults. J. Appl. Gerontol. **27**(2), 181–200 (2008)
19. Lorenzen-Huber, L., Boutain, M., Camp, L.J., Shankar, K., Connelly, K.H.: Privacy, technology, and aging: a proposed framework. Ageing Int. **36**(2), 232–252 (2011). https://doi.org/10.1007/s12126-010-9083-y
20. Padilla-Lopez, J., Chaaraoui, A., Gu, F., Florez-Revuelta, F.: Visual privacy by context: proposal and evaluation of a level-based visualisation scheme. Sensors **15**, 12959–12982 (2015)
21. Ferdous, M.S., Chowdhury, S., Jose, J.M.: Analysing privacy in visual lifelogging. Pervasive Mob. Comput. **40**, 430–449 (2017)
22. Gelonch, O., et al.: Acceptability of a lifelogging wearable camera in older adults with mild cognitive impairment: a mixed-method study. BMC Geriatr. **19**(1), 110 (2019)
23. Steggell, C.D., Hooker, K., Bowman, S., Choun, S., Kim, S.J.: The role of technology for healthy aging among Korean and Hispanic women in the United States: a pilot study. Gerontechnology **9**, 433–449 (2010). https://doi.org/10.4017/gt.2010.09.04.007.00
24. Joe, J., Chaudhuri, S., Chung, J., Thompson, H., Demiris, G.: Older adults' attitudes and preferences regarding a multifunctional wellness tool: a pilot study. Inform Health Soc Care **41**, 143–158 (2016). https://doi.org/10.3109/17538157.2014.965305
25. Selke, S.: Lifelogging: Digital Self-Tracking and Lifelogging-Between Disruptive Technology and Cultural Transformation. Springer, Wiesbaden (2016). https://doi.org/10.1007/978-3-658-13137-1
26. Gurrin, C., Smeaton, A.F., Doherty, A.R.: Lifelogging: personal big data. Found. Trends® Inf. Retrieval **8**, 1–125 (2014). https://doi.org/10.1561/1500000033
27. Mayring, P.: Qualitative content analysis: theoretical background and procedures. In: Bikner-Ahsbahs, A., Knipping, C., Presmeg, N. (eds.) Approaches to Qualitative Research in Mathematics Education. AME, pp. 365–380. Springer, Dordrecht (2015). https://doi.org/10.1007/978-94-017-9181-6_13
28. Osgood, C.E.: Semantic differential technique in the comparative study of cultures. Am. Anthropol. **66**(3), 171–200 (1964)
29. Abouelmehdi, K., Beni-Hssane, A., Khaloufi, H., Saadi, M.: Big data security and privacy in healthcare: a review. Proc. Comput. Sci. **113**, 73–80 (2017)
30. Ajzen, I., Fishbein, M.: Understanding Attitudes and Predicting Social Behavior, 1st edn. Prentice-Hall, Englewood Cliffs (1980)

Cultural and Entertainment Experiences for Older Adults

Media, Generations, and the Platform Society

Piermarco Aroldi[(⊠)] and Fausto Colombo

Università Cattolica del Sacro Cuore, Milan, Italy
{piermarco.aroldi,fausto.colombo}@unicatt.it

Abstract. In the last decades, many studies investigated the relations between media and generations. Two issues dominated the debate on this topic. The first one was the digitization of the media system as a discontinuity (often emphasized as a revolution) capable of supporting the formation of a new "digital" generation. The second one was the global scope of the main socio-cultural processes connected to the worldwide diffusion of the Internet, and the consequent birth of a "global" generation. This article looks at the present mediascape as just a part of that structures of opportunities and constraints contributing to shape the collective identity of the new generations, together with new political movements and global issues. As far as the mediascape is concerned, networked individualism and platformization of the society are highlighted as the most significant features of discontinuity; in such perspective, particular attention should be given to the programmability of the media contents shared through social media platforms and to the scope of collective memory. At the same time, youth political movements and the climate change emergency push in directions not yet predictable.

Keywords: Media and generations · Platform society · Collective memory

1 Introduction

Over the last two decades, the concept of "generation" has been assuming an increasing relevance in very different domains such as the political, technological, demographical, marketing discourses. In media and audience studies, generational identity has also become a key socio-cultural variable affecting audiences in two main aspects.

The first one entails the focus on age groups as segments of the audience in order to understand their specific media uses and preferences as well as the way different generational features affect media practices, with a special attention given to selection and uses of technologies, contents, genres, and languages and to media texts interpretations. In this perspective, especially after the so called digital revolution, marketing discourses often framed the young generations on the basis of their preferred media technologies, e.g. the "digital natives" vs. "digital immigrants" debate (and its popularization as "digital"/"e"/"bit"/"mobile"/"iPod"/"Nintendo"/"Facebook"/"Social media", and-so-on, *generations*).

The second one focuses on the role played by the media in shaping generations: their values, tastes, habitus and behaviors, as a part of the relevant experiences characterizing the formative years of their members. Sometimes, the stressing of said role

Q. Gao and J. Zhou (Eds.): HCII 2020, LNCS 12208, pp. 567–578, 2020.
https://doi.org/10.1007/978-3-030-50249-2_40

refers to a theoretical model that sounds more like a sort of individual technological "imprinting" that took place once and for all, than like an explanation of a wider diachronic, cultural, and collective process such as the "making" of a generation, or *generationing* [1, 2].

"Generation" in itself is a very common concept but, in the same time, a very controversial one. In his seminal work on generations [3], Mannheim proposes – in analogy with the Marxian concept of "class" – the well-known distinction between "generation in itself", as a social formation comprising people born in the same years (age-cohort) that in the same life stage experience the same historical events in the same structure of opportunity (a generational *location* or status), and the "generation for itself", equipped with the consciousness of participating a "common destiny" (generation as an *actuality* or more generational *units*). Generation *in itself* or *for itself* thus differs for a matter of self-consciousness [4].

After Mannheim, other authors described generations based of their common "structure of feeling" [5], "habitus" [6], "generational semantic" or "we-sense" [7, 8] or "cultural identity" [9]. Following Scherger, it is probably useful distinguish between "generations as social formations" and "generations as discursive constructs" [10]. In such a constructivist approach, the concept of generation relies on interpretive processes aimed at understanding similarities and differences between cohorts; striving to "make sense of the contemporaneity of, and conflicts between, people born at different historical times" [10]. Therefore, generations are also the consequence of the features attributed to their members via a plurality of social discourses. Zizi Papacharissi calls them "structures of storytelling" [11]. These discourses may be produced through narratives, rhetoric, political ideology or even mythology, marketing strategies, and obviously academic research too.

There is a strong and mutual relationship between social formations and discursive constructs: on one hand, social discourse contributes to shape social formations, even when they are resisted and contested; on the other, generations as social formations help to produce generational discourses about both themselves and the other generations, in a very co-constructing way.

Furthermore, we can differentiate between exogenous forces and endogenous forces shaping the generations: the former are represented by all the elements previously *ascribed* to a shared identity (such as socio-demographics) and to "structure of opportunity" (such as historical events, formative conditions, level of technological development, and so on), but also by the social discourses produced by the other generations often engaged in a conflicting way. The latter are represented by all the *acquisitive* elements of generational identity and its social agency (values and habitus, acknowledged leaderships, life-styles and tastes), but also the mass of social discourses celebrating one's own generation (self-representations, self-narratives, meaningful rituals, and so on).

2 Generations and Media

A generation is a collective entity based on both objective and subjective features, "an age cohort that comes to have social significance by virtue of constituting itself as a cultural identity" [8]. It is composed by people who were born in the same period of time, have the same age, share a common world of formative (sometime traumatic) past experiences in their early years, and are nowadays in the same position in terms of life course or in the family chain. These individuals share, in a reflexive dimension, a particular "generational semantic", a sort of common "we sense", and some kinds of "habitus".

We can now describe, from a phenomenological point of view, the complex processes of generational identity-making and how they are affected by media. First of all, media (hardware/technologies as well as software/contents) have a part in defining the formative experiences of a generation because they are so deeply embedded in everyday practices to become a "natural" element of its social landscape and its common sense; they however become obsolete and alien to next generations. Furthermore, historical events as well as cultural values and their symbolic forms are often mediated by the media (e.g. the landing of the first man on the moon seen on black-and-white Tv set on a hot summer night). Media also provide a great part of the material and the tools used in the making of the generational semantic and repertoires [12, 13]: characters, stories, songs, linguistic jokes shared by a generation, and especially the "edifying" contents children are provided with by the adults.

Secondly, media are resources that articulates the public spaces of the generational discourses and reflexivity, as is evident in the example of rock music during the Sixties: they allow people to get connected to each other, to have a mutual social visibility, to build a mythical self-narrative and to develop some meaningful rituals (case in point: the big mass-event of Woodstock). They are used to create one or more self-representations (like the song "My generation" by The Who was), entitling some people to speak "on behalf of" and "in front of" their coevals or the members of other generations.

Finally, media, as a part of the present experiences of a defined generation, interact and cope with its stratified memories: in other words, they act as "catalysts" and "hooks" for personal and collective memories, producing new forms and feeling (such as fandom, cultism, revival, nostalgic moods etc.). All this considered, nostalgia is a keyword, since "the nostalgic relationships to past media experiences, the bitter-sweet remembrances of media habits connected to earlier points in life" act strongly in generating a "passionate" engagement with the media [14].

This process could be developed in an exogenous way, i.e. when a generation is nostalgically repositioned by the media, or in a more endogenous way, i.e. when a generation contributes to position itself in this kind of nostalgic perspective or in some other ways of empathic moods, and the media just sustain and habilitate the social discourses of its members (like in an online forum for Boomer Women [15]).

Following the sociological tradition started with Mannheim to the present, a "social generation" can be seen as the outcome of both exogenous or 'objective' forces and endogenous or 'subjective' forces. Among the former there are historical events, material conditions of existence, and a certain cultural environment; amongst the latter there are evaluation criteria, narratives, rituals, and discursive forms that celebrate the sharing of such experiences as qualifying elements shared by all those who are born in that time.

Media and communication technologies participate in this "generational identity building" by simultaneously being part of both exogenous and endogenous forces, and by contributing to articulate each other through their contents and discourses. On one hand, media technologies and their contents form part of the historical moment experienced by the members of a same generation, at the same time and at the same age. On the other hand, they contribute to shape a similar "stratified consciousness" and its inclinations by providing peers with a thematic and expressive repertoire, feeding a common collective memory, and offering a public stage for generational identifications and celebrations.

3   Generations, Mass Media, and Digital Media

Two issues have entered last decade's debate on the relationship between media and generations: the first one is the discontinuity introduced by the new digital media with respect to the legacy mass media, and the possible consequent birth of a "digital generation". The second one is the global scope of the main socio-cultural processes connected to the worldwide diffusion of the Internet, and therefore the possible manifestation of a "global generation".

As far as the first instance is concerned, we have already hypothesized that the novelty of ICT concerns above all the generationing processes connected with the dimensions of "memory", "reflectivity", and "space" [16].

The dimension of memory concerns the survival of the same media experiences in the individual memory and in the collective awareness of the members of a generation. It is a shared repertoire of textual, iconographic, musical and technological references that allow mutual recognition and support communication as a set of common, and sometimes exclusive, codes. In the analogical and mass mediascape [17], these common repertoires could be formed almost exclusively on the basis of having shared their ephemeral "contemporaneity" and significance with members of a given age group; on the other hand, the internet is now a repository of texts and media products, therefore always accessible to members of different generations, regardless of their age. Memory, once externalized through the web, would deprive the media of their function of reference and comparison [18] and would free the sharing of their texts from the necessary -historical and biographical, and therefore generational- contemporaneity.

As far as reflectivity is concerned, the novelty of digital media lies in the possibility of creating a "public sphere" more easily accessible than traditional mass media. While the latter required the overcoming of some "bottlenecks" such as the achievement of professional skills or leadership positions in order to allow the members of a generation to "give voice" to their peers, the Internet would let people to more easily give a "public speech" in front of the members of their own generation, thus making easier the production of a generational "we sense" as opposed to the "we sense" of other generations.

Few years after, Antonella Napoli [19] investigated how peer-to-peer and cross-generational web-based communicative practices could affect the same three main sociological categories of reflectivity, space and memory. In her work, the novelty is constituted by the social media platforms, which play an important role in supporting both inter-generational communication and generational identity building, or re-configuration. Since the social web allows "meta-communicative" potentialities and the awareness to be part of a public and to be in public, they foster a re-configuration of generational identity. Social media therefore offer the opportunity to amplify cohesion and solidarity, resurface old ties and friendships and renew customs, habits and repertoires. While depositing sediment in the collective memory and strengthening peer-to-peer cohesion, social media platform also open "the possibility to assert a new self-history […] within that generation sphere" [19].

As regards space, the global spread of the Internet and the main digital-content-sharing platforms would make it possible to go beyond the national dimension that characterized the expression of cultural industries during the twentieth century. Since the "generational semantics" produced by the media have been linked to this national dimension, as demonstrated by several cross-national researches on this subject [20, 21], overcoming this national territoriality could therefore facilitate the emergence and development of world-wide generations.

This brings us back to the second issue, which concerns the "global generation". A few years ago, by questioning this concept and its narrative, we already challenged its oversimplification due to an excess of technological determinism and marketing rhetoric [22]. As historical realities generational identities are indeed characterized by structures of opportunities and constraints; media are only a part of this structures contributing to shape the semantics and memory of a generation. When globalizing forces hit the entire structure of constraints and opportunities and by doing so also transform the global media system: the processes of generational identity supported by the media do not remain confined within national boundaries, and their complexity proves to be strengthened, not reduced, by this globalization. Thus, getting back to the model of relationship between media and generations, our point is that we need both a less (technologically) deterministic and a less (media-centric) reductionist model [23]: a model less focused on exogenous forces and more attentive towards endogenous, or "reflexive", forces of a generation as they develop not only in the "formative years" but more comprehensively during the whole lifespan.

4   Networked Individualism and Platform Society as a Discontinuity

We will now try to describe the current media ecosystem, imagining it as the mediascape that the Millennials (those born between the early 80s and the late '90s) and especially the Generation Z (those born from the late '90s onward) live in as their taken-for-granted setting. This ecosystem is the provisional result of a series of waves that - as happened with the industrial revolution - are characterizing the long digital revolution.

We can describe this ecosystem today as characterized by three fundamental elements:

1) The new objects/terminals (smartphones, tablets, smart watches and smart assistants): they have common characteristics of mobility, personalization, increasing relevance of voice interaction. They also allow the use of any type of content: written, iconic, audio-visual, sound; and therefore tend to encourage a rather high consumption of time by the user.

2) The strong centrality of social platforms. These platforms have now reached a leading position in the diffusion among users around the world, thus facilitating the connection between users and orienting it thanks to the algorithmic management of interactions, and promoting new forms of communication (such as stories). In addition, they partly disseminate content originated from other media, such as news, video, advertising, music and so on [24, 25].

3) The now complete digitization and convergence of legacy media: all the great media that have characterized the history of the twentieth century, from discography to cinema, from radio to television, from journalism to book publishing are or have been converted to digital form. Moreover, the Web on one hand and the apps on the other allow the fruition of contents that until a decade ago were still the prerogative of the large legacy media supply chains. So not only newspapers, cinema, television, music and radio have digitized, but their typical products are now also available for use on new mobile devices.

More in-depth and extensive analyses can be added to this phenomenological description. As far as the everyday experience of this new mediascape is concerned, the three revolutions described by Rainie and Wellman (that of social networks, that of the Internet and that of mobile telephony) contributed to shape to the so-called *networked individualism* [26]. The social network revolution has offered individuals the possibility of not necessarily depending on cohesive groups and stable community-based affiliations. It has diversified relations and made it possible to bridge between non-contiguous social circles. The Internet revolution has given individuals a new communicative power, in terms of both access to information and speaking. Lastly, the mobile telephony revolution has converted ICT into an appendix to the human body, allowing anyone to connect anytime and anywhere, and further weakening spatial constraints as a consequence. From this point of view, the Internet and the social web are not the cause of networked individualism, but an enabling factor and at the same time a symptom of the profound transformations affecting our advanced societies [27].

As regards the companies' structure, it should be noted that the large digital platforms (Amazon, Alphabet, Facebook, Apple and Microsoft) occupy the first place in terms of turnover among all the companies in the world and, following a monopsony model, they tend to constantly expand, limiting or absorbing the competitors with a force never before known on a global scale [28–30]. This is a novelty, given the fact that legacy media could also have significant dimensions, and perhaps incorporate different elements of the supply chain, from the conception and production of content to its distribution. However, their economic size has always been somewhat limited compared to the large industrial giants (for example, the oil industry). This phenomenon is explained by the very functioning of the platforms, which exist without assets (YouTube does not need to produce video, but rather host videos produced by others), are based on the centrality of algorithms and transform collaboration between users into economic value, leading to the conception of cultural production by users (especially young age) according to a completely new way.

A very classic example of this is sharing: the typical form of exchange, fruition and production on platforms. Sharing, in a certain phase of the Net's diffusion, had a properly collaborative nature and often opposed the legality of copyright (e.g. the dramatic case of music at the time of peer-to-peer exchange) enhancing the value of sharing from below. Today instead it is mainly a model of value production for platforms that realize profit starting from the sharing of content by users, who are indeed allowed and encouraged to do so (think of the business models of YouTube, Facebook, Instagram and so on) [31].

Today we can talk about an economy of performativity. Compared to traditional media, whose economy is based on the passive attention of the viewer, digital media tend to require also the concrete action of users, via a post, a comment, a click, thanks to which they:

a) Give value to the host platform and/or the available for fruition or for a purchase
b) Provide data on themselves and sometimes on their social network
c) Allow platform algorithms to customize the offer addressed to them or their network.

It is no coincidence that this particular value mechanism is now referred to as datacapitalism or capitalism of surveillance [32, 33], since all on-line behavior is monitored and used to have a better knowledge of the identity and habits of the users.

The elements we have mentioned constitute a key to understanding the diversity of the media ecosystem, especially for today's young people. This context cannot be compared with other previous ecosystems, such as the generations of present parents (baby boomers) or older siblings (X and Y generations). We are therefore faced with a deep fracture, which objectively make us foresee for this last generation future forms of identity construction that are substantially different from those marking previous generations.

5   Generationing in the New Mediascape

Networked individualism and *platformization* of the Web [34] are, therefore, the traits assumed by the new mediascape, especially in the last decade; questioning the possible transformations occurred in the process of generationing during the transition from mass media to social media is easier when focusing the attention on said traits.

First of all, the amount of global media contents made available by the Internet, spread through social media and customized by the algorithms alongside with an increasing amount of user- generated contents may result in a fragmentation of communication flows and a pulverization of audiences. These audiences do not necessarily share the few media content available, as was the case in the era of scarcity or availability [35]. As far as content is concerned, the enormous growth of content on an ever-increasing number of media has led to a fragmentation of consumption, so that today it is difficult to imagine which films, series, novels and so on will sport the traits of a typical generational content. In addition, in the era of abundance, audiences are no longer homogeneous on a national basis, but are structured as niches that resemble each other on a transnational level when it comes to tastes and styles of consumption. The indifference to the spatial location of the global network, accentuated by mobile devices, leads to the redefinition of in-group boundaries, urging the emergence of a plurality of new collective cross-national identities.

At the same time, however, the accentuation of the individualistic dimension of social networks can act as an element of contrast to the building of strong shared identities, favoring more instrumental, multiple and ephemeral associations. In a general context in which the intermediate social bodies suffer the erosion of networked individualism, it is not difficult to hypothesize that even generational identity can be weakened by the same processes that are eroding the ideas of community based on family, trade union or religious nature.

On the other hand, the algorithms act both as new drivers of access to shared content and as potential activators of new social bonds between users. Advice on cultural consumption provided by the algorithms on the basis of previous data, or connection with individuals who may be part of the user's social network based on shared contacts or common interests, are two examples of how the "programmability" [36] of social media platforms works. Such programmability can therefore play a role in fostering visibility, popularity and sharing of media contents and social discourse around which new cultural identities are consolidated, regardless of the generational identity of users and of the mutual recognition of same-generation members in such cultural practices. In a way similar to the "outsourcing" of individual and social memory operated by Web archives, social media algorithms can outsource the processes of association, both favoring and weakening the generational basis of this connection. For example, while some phenomena of filter bubbles or homophily may coincide with the generational boundaries of a cohort, others may end up straddling them in an intergenerational perspective or - more simply - indifferent to any generational affinity.

Any unidirectional reading of the relationship between the new mediascape and generationing processes must, in fact, take into account the increasing complexity of the mediascape itself.

a) The first consideration concerns the increasing fragmentation of platforms and contents. Platforms are not universal, but cover precise geopolitical areas, as shown by the figure below (see Fig. 1):

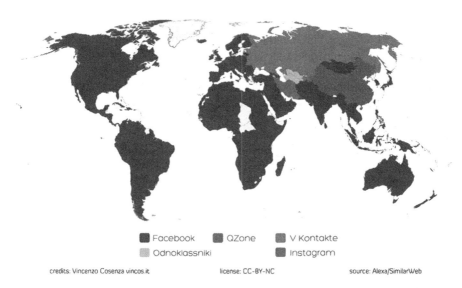

credits: Vincenzo Cosenza vincos.it   license: CC-BY-NC   source: Alexa/SimilarWeb

Fig. 1. Global diffusion of social network platforms (Source Alexa/SimilarWeb, by vincos.it)

Moreover, as we have already mentioned, there is a life cycle in which the most consolidated platforms see their users grow old (in the sense that older users gradually enter and young people leave), to the detriment of the new platforms, which collect youth users [37].

In particular, this last element causes the generational typecasting of the single platform to shatter. In twenty years' time, today's sixteen-year-olds will be able to remember their use of Instagram, while people two years younger may have a nostalgic memory of Tik Tok. The rapid obsolescence of technologies and platforms could pose some obstacles to the generationing process.

Another important aspect of the cultural effect of platforms is the complex role they play in building social memory. On one hand, they are very powerful archival agents, capable of storing large amounts of information for very long periods; on the other hand, this memory capacity encounters two types of difficulty. Firstly, the liquidity of the network, which can see content disappear without it being more recoverable. Secondly, the geopolitical reasons at play, which lead some countries to build real memories as opposed to those of other countries. These two instances ensure that the memory of generations is still infiltrated by national cultures and policies, thus generating faults in the processes of sharing memories and events and, more generally, that the generational structure of memory is configured in a different way from the past [38].

b) The second consideration derives from a more holistic and social approach to generational composition. For the first time in many decades, today adolescents and young people show aspects - not strictly media-related but rather linked to their agency - that hint the construction of a possible collective identity of a generational type.

There are two elements in this sense: the first being the large number of political movements, protests and claims, which in 2019 saw young people protagonists. Think of the on-going movements that span from Chile to Sudan, from Algeria to Haiti, from

Hong Kong to Iraq and Iran, from Ecuador to Lebanon, but also to the complex and very extensive Friday for Future movement, whose icon is Greta Thunberg. A recent photo of sixteen-year-old Greta alongside eight-year-old Indian activist Licypriya Kangujam at the Cop25 climate conference in Madrid (2–13 December 2019) can, in this optic, well exemplify a new generation's ability to publicly speak out and organize itself on a global scale through social media, bypassing the bottlenecks posed by traditional media.

As second element, these movements' inception lies in two global demands that seemingly will represent the core issues of the political debate over the next decades: the growth of inequalities and the environmental issue. If, as we can imagine, the future debate will indeed still resolve around these themes, we can perhaps foresee that the generation currently behind the movements - as already happened in 1968 – will identify itself not so much in the media landscape and in the memory provided by the media (contents and devices), but rather in a new political will oriented towards the solution of global problems [9].

6 Conclusion

The era of platforms undoubtedly constitutes the ecosystem in which the next generations all over the world are forming. The cultural and symbolic strength of this ecosystem is undeniable, and, at least in part, can be described in global terms. At the same time, the major economic and political issues of the present see the societies of the planet face at least two global challenges, such as the growth of inequalities and the environmental issue. However, the observation of the geopolitical nature of the platforms with their heterogeneous diffusion by cultural and linguistic areas and the different cultures and memory practices that they favor, once again warn us against the utopia of simply defining the generations currently undergoing a global phase of formation. That said, we can testify to the reappearance in very different areas of the globe of youth centrality, motivated by the great issues just mentioned and characterized by literacy in the currently available communication technologies. This authorizes us to think that – even given their local diversity - the processes of generational construction can present at least one common and shared feature, namely the rediscovering of a unified agency such is the ability to reoccupy the streets and the squares, to claim the right to a voice and a future. Only the years to come will be able to confirm (or deny) this working hypothesis.

References

1. Alanen, L.: Childhood as generational condition: children's daily life in central finland town. In: Alanen, L., Berry, M. (eds.) Conceptualizing Child-Adult Relations, pp. 129–143. Routledge, London (2001)
2. Siibak, A., Vittadini, N.: Editorial: Introducing four empirical examples of the "generationing" process. Cyberpsychol. J. Psychosoc. Res. Cyberspace, 6(2) (2012). article 1

3. Mannheim, K.: The Problem of Generations. Essays on the Sociology of Knowledge. Routledge & Keegan Paul, London (1952)
4. Hart-Brinson, P., Yang, G., Aroldi, P.: Techno-social generations and communication research. In: Nussbaum, J.F. (ed.) Communication across the Life Span, pp. 91–106. Peter Lang, New York (2016)
5. Williams, R.: The Long Revolution. Chatto & Windus, London (1961)
6. Bourdieu, P.: La Distinction. Minuit, Paris (1979)
7. Corsten, M.: The Time of Generations. Time and Society 8(2), 249–272 (1999)
8. Corsten, M.: Media as the Historical New for Young Generations. In: Colombo, F., Fortunati, L. (eds.) Broadband Society and Generational Changes, pp. 37–49. Peter Lang, Frankfurt am Main (2011)
9. Edmunds, J., Turner, B.S.: Generations, Culture and Society. Buckingham and Philadelphia. Open University Press, London (2002)
10. Scherger, S.: Concepts of generation and their empirical application: From social formations to narratives – a critical appraisal and some suggestions. University of Manchester: CRESC Working Paper no. 117 (2012)
11. Papacharissi, Z.: Technologies, Generations, and Structures of Storytelling. In: Nussbaum, J. F. (ed.) Communication Across the Life Span, pp. 27–33. Peter Lang, New York (2016)
12. Aroldi, P., Colombo, F. (eds.): Le età della Tv. Indagine su quattro generazioni di spettatori italiani. Vita e Pensiero, Milano (2003)
13. Bolin, G.: Media Generations: Experience, Identity and Mediatised Social Change. Routledge, London-New York (2016)
14. Bolin, G.: Media generations: objective and subjective media landscapes and nostalgia among generations of media users. Participations 11(2), 108–131 (2014)
15. Tommaso, L.: The construction of age identity in an online discourse community: the case of boomer women speak. In Baliarno, G., Nisco, M.C. (eds.) Languaging Diversity. Identities, Genres, Discourses. pp. 163–175. Cambridge Scholars Publishing, Newcastle-upon-Tyne (2015)
16. Aroldi, P.: Generational belonging between media audiences and ICT users. In: Colombo, F., Fortunati, L. (eds.) Broadband Society and Generational Changes, pp. 51–67. Peter Lang, Frankfurt am Main (2011)
17. Appadurai, A.: Disjuncture and Difference in the Global Cultural Economy. Public Cult. 2 (2), 1–24 (1990)
18. Ruchatz, J.: Externalisierung. In: Pethes, N., Ruchatz, J.: Gedächtnis und Erinnerung: ein interdisziplinäres Lexikon, pp. 160–163. Rowohlt Taschenbuch, Reinbek (2001)
19. Napoli, A.: Social media use and generational identity: Issues and consequences on peer-to-peer and cross-generational relationships – an empirical study. Participations 11(2), 182–206 (2014)
20. Aroldi, P., Ponte, C.: Adolescents of the 1960s and 1970s: an Italian-Portuguese comparison between two generations of audiences. Cyberpsychol. J. Psychosoc. Res. Cyberspace 6(2), 1–11 (2012)
21. Bolin, G.: Media Times. The Rhythm of Ages: analyzing mediatization through the lens of generations across cultures. Int. J. Commun. 10, 5252–5269 (2016)
22. Aroldi, P., Colombo, F.: Questioning 'Digital Global Generations'. A critical approach. Northern Lights: Film and Media Studies Yearbook, pp. 175–190 (2013)
23. Wachelder, J.: Regeneration: generations remediated. Time Soc. 28(3), 883–903 (2019)
24. Van Dijk, J., Poell, T., De Waal, M.: The Platform Society. Public Values in a Connecting World. Oxford University Press, New York (2018)
25. Cusumano, M.A., Gawer, A., Yoffie, D.B.: The Business of Platforms: Strategy in the Age of Digital Competition, Innovation, and Power. HarperCollins, New York (2019)

26. Rainie, L., Wellman, B.: Networked: the new social operating system. MIT Press, Boston (2012)
27. Marinelli, A.: Prefazione all'edizione italiana. In: Rainie, L., Wellman, B.: Networked. Il nuovo sistema operative sociale. Guerini, Milano (2012)
28. Fuchs, C.: Culture and Economy in the Age of Social Media. Routledge, London (2015)
29. McChesney, R.H.: Digital Disconnect. How Capitalism is Turning the Internet Against Democracy. New Press, New York (2013)
30. Taplin, J.: Move Fast and Break Things How Facebook, Google and Amazon Have Cornered Culture and What it Means for All of Us. MacMillan, London (2017)
31. Meikle, G.: Social Media. Communication. Sharing and Visibility. Routledge, London (2016)
32. Mayer-Schönberger, V., Range, T.: Reinventing Capitalism in the Age of Big Data. Basic Books, New York (2018)
33. Zuboff, S.: The Age of Surveillance Capitalism: The Fight for a Human Future at the New Frontier of Power. Public Affairs, New York (2019)
34. Helmond, A.: The platformization of the web: making web data platform ready. Soc. Media Soc. 1(2), 1–11 (2015)
35. Ellis, J.: Seeing Things: Television in the Age of Uncertainty. Tauris, London (2000)
36. Van Dijck, J., Poell, T.: Understanding Social Media Logic. Media and Communication 1 (1), 2–14 (2013)
37. World Economic Forum Homepage, https://www.weforum.org/agenda/2019/10/social-media-use-by-generation/, last accessed 2019/12/19
38. Colombo, F.: The generational role of media and social memory: a research agenda. Comunicazioni Sociali 2, 215–231 (2019)

Intergenerational Perspectives on Audiences Studies: From Youth to Senior Representations

Maria José Brites[1(✉)], Inês Amaral[2,3], and Sofia José Santos[4,5]

[1] Universidade Lusófona/CICANT, Porto, Portugal
mariajosebrites@ulp.pt
[2] Faculdade de Letras da Universidade de Coimbra, Coimbra, Portugal
ines.amaral@uc.pt
[3] Centro de Estudos de Comunicação e Sociedade da,
Universidade do Minho, Braga, Portugal
[4] Faculdade de Economia da, Universidade de Coimbra, Coimbra, Portugal
sjs@ces.uc.pt
[5] Centro de Estudos Sociais da, Universidade de Coimbra, Coimbra, Portugal

Abstract. This paper aims to theoretically explore and discuss intergenerational perspectives on audience studies, shedding light on trends and invisibilities. Literature on the topic has been especially concerned either with interactions between children and young people, or among themselves and with other age groups, or with elders' engagement. This paper reviewed studies to identify contexts of research focused on the point of view of children and young people, and also gaps that the audience studies should address particularly concerning the case of senior citizens.

Keywords: Intergeneration · Children · Young people · Senior citizens

1 Introduction: Generations and Intergenerations

According to Bolin and Skogerbø "from a life course perspective, age is also a dynamic of its own, with different stages that have their own specific characteristics, and that influence media behaviour in conjunction with other social circumstances that make up phases of life" [1]. Intergenerational media research is constituted as an important, already established and recently very fruitful field of work, with a prevalent focus on children, young people and adults. Whereas children and young children have been approached taking into account their role as digital leaders, adults have been particularly considered in their role as parents and teachers. An especially complex and still less developed subarea is the intergenerational audience research, which implies a preoccupation with the interrelationship between different generations, challenging the research contexts, objectives and fieldwork.

The digital era is contributing to reinforcing ties between generations [1]. In fact, "generational inter-learning processes can be of great relevance to increase different generations relations with the digital" [2]. Compared to the analogue media era, the digital age encourages "the blurring of barriers between different age groups that interact through and with technologies" [2]. This technologically-based interaction across different generations may enable generation gaps to be overcome and, most of all may promote "the sharing of knowledge and forms of sociability anchored in different generational contexts" [2], enriching each generations' both digital experiences and practices. As digital media experience is increasingly inter-generational and technology evolves at a quick pace, critical media literacies involving an intergenerational approach are pivotal within today's mediascape.

In this regard, it can be considered that "as the media also contribute to the construction of the identity of the generations and therefore to the perception that other age groups make of them, it is imperative to empower citizens for unmediated media experiences. In the digital environment in which these experiences take place, there is a constant social construction of reality. The promotion of critical media literacies and digital competences in the media education plans implies understanding the central role that digital has in the multiplicity of screens that today fill the media ecosystem. However, media education cannot be focused exclusively on one generation and must be addressed in lifelong learning as well as an intergenerational approach" [2].

2   Method

The literature on media and audiences studies stemming from an intergenerational perspective has been gaining relevance, although it still remains underdeveloped. This paper intends to contribute to an exploratory mapping of this field by means of an interpretative review of existing literature on this specific area. To guide our map and analysis, we used the following research question to guide our study: which trends can be identified in the literature on intergeneration from the perspective of children and young people and also from seniors media and audience studies?

To put our interpretative literature review forward, and inspired by similar previous works, we used a two-step complementary approach. First, and given our expertise, we selected the most relevant studies in the field [55] in the perspective of an interpretative review [56]. Afterwards, we followed Martyn Hammersley [57] suggestions and considered that this proposal was meant to "stand-alone" as "'interpretive' reviews", meaning that the exact aim was to reflect on what was done before and systematize, in order to establish trends and gaps. "[I]nterpretive reviewing involves application of a qualitative methodological approach. Here, the emphasis is on the interpretative role of the reviewer in making sense of the findings of different studies to construct a holistic picture of the field (…). This is a development out of the traditional or narrative review" [57].

3   Interpretative Literature Review

3.1   Children and Young People's Perspectives: From Legal Definitions to Sociological and Media Contexts

The definition of children and young people within academia and in media studies is a challenging endeavour. When attempting to clearly define what represents to be a "young" human being, there are some difficulties. By default, youth is usually associated with a particular age [3] that can be legally and biologically identified, often interconnecting these two dimensions. Nevertheless, from the point of view of sociology and media studies, these cohorts have consistent differences, regardless we are considering them as children or as young people [3].

Several countries establish legal age at 18, the time one can start to exist as a voting citizen, and thus as adult or young people. Another view is supported by relevant international documents, such as the Convention on the Rights of the Child [4], that considers that a human being until 18 is a child. So, until 18, and depending on the context, one can be considered as a child or young people, even if each one of the definitions and perspectives has differentiated points of view and implication in the research. Different authors point to the need to bear in mind distinct circumstances when defining which groups of youngsters should be included in the category of "youth", namely the specific situation and context where the youngsters live, and their own perspective on the world and on themselves. Often youngsters with more than 14/15 years old prefer, for instance, news and media related to adults and not with children [5, 6]. Statistically, the UN also considers that youth is categorized from 15 to 24 years old [7].

To draw the dividing analytical line that establishes who is or is not "young" is not easy. One constructive way is to involve the children and young people's own perspectives and try to get close to their own definitions and self-identification [5]. Specifically, for example, when undertaking research with participants that consider themselves to be "young people" instead of "children" it might be problematic to classify them as "children". They often consider themselves rather with an eye on adulthood than on childhood. Young people can be staged between childhood and adulthood and to be considered only as citizens in the process before they have legal age to vote, a standpoint that challenges the citizenship of young people [8].

3.2 Children/Young People and Their Parents: From Traditional Media to Digital Media

Another important intergenerational perspective is related to the children/young people and their parents, the form they live in the family and also how family influences their media environment's options. Decades of research on how these contexts are relevant and how they influence media options to certify the importance of considering it. This intergenerational environmental is pivotal in relation to media options, as considerable research in the field of audience's studies states. In this sense, the contexts where families live should be greatly considered [9–12] since socioeconomic background makes a difference in the role that media play in the lives of family members. Likewise, education, job positions, and family relationships should be examined [13–15]. "Social disadvantage is in most cases strongly connected to lower formal education and worse future prospects. This goes hand-in-hand with a lack of participation opportunities within society. As regards processes of technological and societal change—framed as the meta-process of mediatization—we have to consider that socially disadvantaged people, in particular children and adolescents, are at risk of falling further and further behind. Therefore, we need to investigate how socially disadvantaged children and adolescents grow up in their specific life situation." [16]

This is still important in times of digital media and corresponding digital skills [17]. The digital era has moved us from a particular unidirectional power relation with parents influencing their child's life to a complexified interconnection of power relationships on both sides in the digital era. The passage from traditional to digital ensures new opportunities: "although economically disadvantaged families experience the digital generation gap with particular intensity, their strategies reveal that they and their teenage children are able to deal with these challenges in creative and effective ways" [13]. Also, youngsters for the first time in history have, until a certain point, better skills than adults in matters of great relevance in society. This challenges the traditional role of adults as actors who take care, educate, and create rules for younger generations [18]. In turn, young people might consider that adults don't have the knowledge to "impose authoritarian practices on them", particularly as they seem to lack "the knowledge that might allow them to operate authoritatively" [13].

Children and youth cultures in the context of home and family gained analytical relevance in the last decades [14, 16, 19–22]. "Whereas 'screen media' such as television, video games, and movies are viewed with greater suspicion, personal computers are viewed as at least potentially beneficial for educational goals, and cell phone use is seen as necessary for safety and connection, but also a potential nuisance" [13]. Parents, in spite of trying to establish rules (including time management) they usually end up trusting the ways in which their teenage children "chose to engage in practices in the digital realm [13] ".

Despite the different (potential) problems that digital contexts entail, they express and constitute a realm of the new media environment, where both youngsters and adults use technology to stay connected. Social media "changed everyday life in families, drawing attention to the increased contact and connectivity that digital media allow" [1]. There is a real possibility of connection where it wasn't before. There is a "web-based media as the connecting link between family members of different generations, where they help in 'maintaining emotional bonds and enhancing connectedness', thus overcoming the geographical separation of family members of different generations" [1]. Specially in qualitative and participatory research there is the need to address very carefully all the dimensions, in order to respect the research participants.

3.3 Children/Young People and Teachers

The field of children/Young people and teachers is mostly concentrated in the media literacy field with an eye on the context of life at school, especially in relation to digital environments and support preoccupations on media competences [23]. In this case, as it happens with family environment, children and young people digital knowledge are upturning the roles of adults and youngsters. This challenges existing roles and makes students' voices in need of increasing consistency [24].

Teachers are often overwhelmed with diverse activities in schools, so they don't always have time for new tasks. The UNESCO curriculum [24] offers some suggestions for trainers to consider when they think of activities in schools. Among them there is the need to encourage students to read and discuss information in different media formats, also in their own expressions. A central aspect that relays on generational differences and knowledge, and also with questions of adjustments on educational paradigms, is the fact that the educational strategies of teachers sometimes need a more complex exchange of knowledge and collaboration between students and teachers [25]. "In reality, it is difficult to ignore the differences and generational gaps, which actually may not be so large but are perceived as such by the teachers' negative self-representations" [26]. Teachers are aware of these differences [25, 26]. Technology, however, is not enough to ensure digital competences to the usually labelled "Technology Generation" or "Generation Z" [25]. In fact, teachers' skills concerning both technology and pedagogy are pivotal in the "development of learning processes to introduce technologies as tools in the service of education" [25].

As such, researchers on youth and media can play a very relevant role in shutting the gap between teachers and young students through shedding light on the need to disrupt what is usually called "static knowledge in schools", ethics concerning technology usage and marginalisation [27] of specific groups, rendering themselves and their experiences invisible. In fact, "in unambiguous material terms, not all young people are on equal footing in negotiating the developmental orthodoxies imposed in schools. Around the globe, society's most vulnerable student populations-poor students, indigenous students, students deemed to have divergent exceptionalities, students from racial groups long discriminated against-suffer most from the impositions of these orthodoxies. A central reason for this is that the institutional definitions put forth in schools always necessarily reflect and interact with the social spheres that encircle them" [27].

A possible and important framework that can and should be adopted at school is to implement and improve participatory approach [27–29], that can place children, youth and adults in a collaborative environment. This is not always an easy task: "the ideological space of schooling often structures teacher-student interactions in ways not conducive to engaging what's most important about young people's online work. Attempts at addressing this work under the ideological weight of school systems often imbue the values of new forms of online interaction that young people appreciate - sharing, collaboration, community, openness" [27].

As it happens with adults as parents, teacher's authority was challenged by the realm of the digital age.

3.4   Seniors' Perspectives

If the implications in regard to children and young people, and generational and intergenerational are complex, sometimes even influenced by commercial interests, to consider the perspective of older adults, we have to be even more careful in the form we address the definitions in the field. So we will now detail some grounding aspects that were previously mentioned in this paper. Corsten [30] presents the concept of 'political generations' as opposed to 'historical generations', which refers to 'collective memory' and 'social times'. It follows that there is a 'generational belonging' [31]. Mannheim [32] argues that the collective cohesion of the generations depends on the 'generational site' and how they are interpreted ('generational context'), promoting 'generational units' with similar experiences and that position themselves in the same way. Mannheim [32] argues that the continuing character of generational changes amplifies the notion of a 'generational situation'. The notion of "we-sense" [30] summarizes historical and social experiences, individual or collective, which allow identification with groups. Therefore, different generations experience social and technological changes in the perspective of coexistence. The media experience stems from sociocultural environments [33]. Thus, "generational media identities are culturally, socially and historically shaped" [2]. Considering that the media promotes 'generational identity' and 'generational belonging', Aroldi [31] argues that media play a central role in the dynamics of generation-building processes. The intergenerational dimension, as noted before, has been little explored in media studies [34], mainly concerning the older population. The precursory works of Bolin and Skogerbø [1], Aroldi [31], Colombo and Fortunati [33], and Loos, Haddon and Mante-Meijer [35] emphasize that the media find in intergenerational relations a path that can surpass the labels of 'digital natives' [36], 'net generation' [37] or 'digital generation' [38]. Since the definition of generation is not static [30, 32], audiences tend to be increasingly intergenerational. As Lim [39] argues "distinct 'media generations' are identified through the association of successive generations of youths with the most prevalent media of their time". The simplification of the concept of generation derives from a technological determinism [40] that seems to define that only the younger generations dominate the media and technologies. This argument perpetuates generational gaps. Lim states that "prior research has also amply demonstrated that the generational approach had been used to productively map different generations in terms of their initial introduction to media, media use patterns, exposure to media content, attitudes towards media and technology, and media literacy skills" [39]. The generational approach was used to map different generations on media usage patterns, exposure to media content, media and technology attitudes, and media literacy skills [40]. However, the introduction of technology into everyday life has brought about profound changes in audience use and consumption. The generational perspective tends to be intergenerational due to social relations and practices, as well as the production of media content designed for cross-generational audiences.

The family dimension reflects many intergenerational relationships. In the last years, research focused on children/youth and older people have been burgeoning. Accordingly, traditional generational gaps have been positively managed within each family's life, specifically concerning grandsons and grandparents relationships, at times geographically distant. The definition of older people does not refer to a homogeneous [41] nor to an invisible group [42]. The traditional definition of the relationship 'grandchildren-grandparents' has been changing as "new communication technologies, and social media have produced 'networked families' or new relational families" [43]. Several studies show that mobile and network communication acts as an 'umbilical cord' between children and parents [44] while at the same time ensuring greater autonomy [43, 45]. Web-based communication environments and social media apps offer families the possibility of a more significant connection [46]. The domestic realm of media use is often based on asymmetries in the skills of different generations. However, these intergenerational differences reflect the way technologies and media are used by people in different contexts and situations [39], contributing to mutual (inter generational) learning.

Finally, a persistent relational gap is the one between adults and older adults. It is an intergenerational relationship that needs to be addressed in the near future within audiences' studies. Although frequently rendered invisible [42] and perceived as a homogeneous group [41], older adults (and also adults, we would add) should be considered taking into account specificities, challenges, multidimensions and idiosyncrasies of these groups. For example, even if these two generations are the ones which can afford media access, financial conditions also vary among adults and older adults - some might actually be unable to buy said access. Another missing link concerning research on this topic is that adults and older adults are also parents and sons but to most of the research they are not seen as relevant as the family connections including younger generations.

Vittadini argues that "media generations are constructed as collectively produced, shared and processed responses to the availability and pervasiveness of a particular technology, which then becomes an element of generational identity" [47]. The self-identification and the 'generational belonging' [31] rely on this perspective. However, the dynamics of media and audiences refer to 'generational situation' [32]. Therefore, the appropriation that different generations make of technologies and their uses, as well as media consumption, are intertwined within family relationships [2]. Napoli argues that "the online environment facilitates strengthening of ties, including cross-generational ones, and a re-configuration of the generational identity" [48]. In this sense, "intergenerational relationships that narrow in digital can overcome the so-called generation gaps, fostering intergenerational interaction, which allows the sharing of knowledge and forms of sociability anchored in different generational contexts. This idea implies the coexistence of generational experiences and technological changes that occur in the digital environment" [2].

The domestication of technologies [49] is often considered unlikely by older generations. The domain of digital skills is, by definition, presented as a guarantee of the younger generations born without knowing the analogue. However, this is a static generation analysis that ignores its multidimensionality and particularly stereotypes older adults [50, 51]. Generations follow the evolution of digital and media, especially in their working life.

Media experiences of generations intersect with the notion of memory. As media may disrupt memory [52], media nostalgia emerges as a trend within cross-generational audiences. Magladry argues that "mainstream nostalgia is invested in intertwining individual and group identities together, effectively guiding subjects to conflate their personal identities with their own specific cultural and social contexts, and vice versa" [53]. The trend is to create redesigned content consistently and appealing to all generations [54].

4 Conclusions and Implications for Future Research

This article seeks to answer the following research question: What trends can be identified in the literature review on intergeneration from the perspective of children and young people and also from seniors media and audience studies?

Based upon our analysis, we identified within research on children and young people's perspectives: 1) a general/disseminated concern with legal definitions, 2) a detailed analysis on sociological and media studied contexts, 3) discussions on the relation between children/young people and their parents and connections between children/young people and teachers concerning their media practices. In turn, when looking at studies on audiences concerning senior citizens, we identified a gap in the research focusing on elders and adults.

This interpretative literature review on intergeneration and audience studies offered us insight into interconnections that can be established between children/young people and adults concerning media practices. In this regard, we would highlight the complexities in the definition of children and young *people*. In fact, although the subjects and processes that both concepts intend to synthetise may overlap and sometimes be conflated as a single concept, each of them express nuances that should be further explored and taken into account. In addition, *children* and *young people* are often times considered when analysing or reflecting on *parenthood,* making adults that relate to them to be often and mainly identified merely as *parents* and *teachers,* excluding or dismissing as less important the social roles adults might perform when interacting with *children* and *young people*. It is, thus, essential to enlarge and in-depth the research on adults, including the intergenerational roles they perform, besides the ones of being parents or teachers.

Conversely, older adults are far less represented in existing, a creating a research gap that needs to be filled in the future. In fact, older adults are mostly characterized considering their relation to the family and the family media routines. In this regard, enhanced research on this field needs to be undertaken as senior citizens are some of the most fragile generations concerning media uses and appropriations, a research agenda which includes older people in the research puzzle will be socially relevant towards a more equal intergenerational media practices in society.

References

1. Bolin, G., kogerbø, E.S.: Age, generation and the media. Northern Lights **11**, 3–14 (2013)
2. Amaral, I., Brites, M.J.: Trends on the digital uses and generations. In: Proceedings of INTED2019 Conference. Valencia (2019)
3. Pais, J.M.: Culturas juvenis. Imprensa Nacional-Casa da Moeda, Lisboa (2003)
4. Nations, U.: Convention on the Rights of the Child, U. Nations, Editor. United Nations (1989)
5. Brites, M.J.: Jovens e culturas cívicas: Por entre formas de consumo noticioso e de participação. LabCom Books, Covilhã (2015)
6. Meirinho, D.: Olhares em Foco: Fotografia participativa e empoderamento juvenil. LabCom, Covilhã (2016)
7. Nations, U.: Definition of youth. https://www.un.org/esa/socdev/documents/youth/factsheets/youth-definition.pdf. (n/a)
8. Buckingham, D.: The Making of Citizens: Young People, News and Politics. Taylor & Francis e-Library, Londres e Nova Iorque (2006)
9. Bourdieu, P.: Los tres estados del capital cultural (trad. De Mónica. Landesmann). Sociológica **5**, 11–17 (1987)
10. Ponte, C.: Uma geração digital? A influência familiar na experiência mediática de adolescentes. Sociologia - Problemas e práticas **65**, 31–50 (2011)
11. Mascheroni, G., et al.: Learning versus play or learning through play? How parents' imaginaries, discourses and practices around icts shape children's (digital) literacy practices. Media Educ. **7**(2), 261–280 (2016)

12. Clark, L.S.: The Parent App: Understanding Families in the Digital Age. Oxford University Press, Oxford (2014)
13. Clark, L.S.: Digital media and the generation gap: qualitative research on US teens and their parents. Inf. Commun. Soc. **12**(3), 388–407 (2009)
14. Hasebrink, U., et al.: Comparing children's online opportunities and risks across Europe: Cross-national comparisons for EU Kids Online (Deliverable D3.2, 2nd edition). LSE, London (2019)
15. Opermann, S.: Generational use of news media in Estonia: media access, spatial orientations and discursive characteristics of the news media. Södertörn, Södertörns högskola, p. 335 (2014)
16. Paus-Hasebrink, I., Kulterer, J., Sinner, P.: Social Inequality, Childhood and the Media: A Longitudinal Study of the Mediatization of Socialisation. Palgrave Macmillan, Cham (2019)
17. van Deursen, A.J.A.M., van Dijk, J.A.: Digital Skills: Unlocking the Information Society (2014)
18. Fleming, M.J., et al.: Safety in cyberspace: Adolescents' safety and exposure online. Youth Soc. **38**(2), 135–154 (2006)
19. Bovill, M., Livingstone, S.: Bedroom culture and the privatization of media use. In: Bovill, M., Livingstone, S. (Eds.) Children and their Changing Media Environment: A European Comparative Study, Lawrence Erlbaum Associates, Mahwah (2001)
20. Livingstone, S., Helsper, E.: Gradations in digital inclusion: children, young people and the digital divide. New Media Soc. **9**(4), 671–696 (2007)
21. Livingstone, S., et al.: How Parents of Young Children Manage Digital Devices at Home: The Role of Income, Education and Parental Style. EU Kids Online, LSE, Londres (2015)
22. Livingstone, S.: Young People and New Media: childhood and the changing media environment. SAGE Publications, London (2002)
23. García-Ruiz, R., Matos, A., Borges, G.: Media Literacy as a responsibility of families and teachers. J. Media Literacy **63**(1&2), 82–91 (2016)
24. Scheibe, C.: "Sounds Great, But I Don't Have Time!": helping teachers meet their goals and needs with media literacy education. J Media Literacy Educ. **1**, 68–71 (2009)
25. Fernández-Cruz, F.-J., Fernández-Díaz, M.-J.: Generation Z's Teachers and their Digital Skills. Comunicar. **46**(XXIV), 97–105 (2016)
26. Brites, M.J.: "We don't know how to work with the media or develop it with students": Discourses and fears from the teachers. In: Gómez Chova, L., Martínez, A.L., Torres, I.C. (Eds.) EDULEARN19 Proceedings: 11th International Conference on Education and New Learning Technologies. IATED Academy, Palma (2019)
27. Saul, R.: Education and the mediated subject: what today's teachers need most from researchers of youth and media. J. Child. Media **10**(2), 156–163 (2016)
28. Hobbs, R., Coiro, J.: Everyone learns from everyone: collaborative and interdisciplinary professional development in digital literacy. J. Adolesc. Adult Lit., 1–7 (2016)
29. Hobbs, R.: Digital and Media Literacy: Connecting Culture and Classroom. Corwin, California (2011)
30. Corsten, M.: The time of generations. Time Soc. **8**(2–3), 249–272 (1999)
31. Aroldi, P.: Generational belonging between media audiences and ICT users. In: Colombo, F., Fortunati, L. (eds.) Broadband Society and Generational Changes, pp. 51–68. Peter Lang, Frankfurt am Main (2011)
32. Mannheim, K.: The problem of generation. In: Mannheim, K. (ed.) Essays on the Sociology of Knowledge, pp. 276–320. Routledge & Kegan Paul, London (1952)
33. Colombo, F., Fortunati, F.: Broadband Society and Generational Changes. Peter Lang, Frankfurt am Main (2011)
34. Ponte, C.: Generational uses of new media - a review. Eur. J. Commun. **28**(2), 338–342 (2013)

35. Loos, E., Haddon, L., Mante-Meijer, E.: Generational Use of New Media. Routledge, Farnham (2012)
36. Prensky, M.: Digital natives, digital immigrants. Horizon **9**(5), 1–6 (2011)
37. Tapscott, D.: Growing up Digital: The Rise of the Net Generation. McGraw-Hill, New York (1998)
38. Papert, S.: The Connected Family: Bridging the Digital Generation Gap. Longstreet, Atlanta (1996)
39. Lim, S.S.: Young people and communication technologies: emerging challenges in generational analysis. In: Nussbaum, J. (ed.) Communication Across the Lifespan, pp. 5–19. Peter Lang, New York (2016)
40. Buckingham, D.: Is there a digital generation? In: Buckingham, D., Willett, R. (eds.) Digital Generations: Children, Young People and New Media, pp. 1–13. Erlbaum, Mahwah (2006)
41. Daniel, F., Antunes, A., Amaral, I.: Representações sociais da velhice. Análise. Psicológica **33**(3), 291–301 (2015)
42. Amaral, I., Santos, S.J., Daniel, F., Filipe, F.: (In)visibilities of men and aging in the media: discourses from Germany and Portugal. In: Zhou, J., Salvendy, G. (eds.) HCII 2019. LNCS, vol. 11593, pp. 20–32. Springer, Cham (2019). https://doi.org/10.1007/978-3-030-22015-0_2
43. Taipale, S., Farinosi, M.: The big meaning of small messages: the use of WhatsApp in intergenerational family communication. In: Zhou, J., Salvendy, G. (eds.) ITAP 2018. LNCS, vol. 10926, pp. 532–546. Springer, Cham (2018). https://doi.org/10.1007/978-3-319-92034-4_40
44. Ribak, R.: Remote control, umbilical cord and beyond: the mobile phone as a transitional object. Br. J. Dev. Psychol. **27**(1), 183–196 (2009)
45. Ling, R.: Children, youth, and mobile communication. J. Child. Media **1**, 60–67 (2007)
46. Siibak, A., Tamme, V.: "Who introduced granny to Facebook?": an exploration of everyday family interactions in web-based communication environments. Northern Lights Film Media Stud. Yearbook **11**, 71–89 (2013)
47. Vittadini, N.: Generations and media: the social construction of generational identity and differences. In: Carpentier, N., Schrøder, K., Hallett, L. (eds.) Audience Transformations. Shifting audience positions in late modernity, pp. 65–81. Routledge, New York (2014)
48. Napoli, A.: Social media use and generational identity: issues and consequences on peer-to-peer and cross-generational relationships - An empirical study. Participations J. Audience Reception Stud. **11**(2), 182–206 (2014)
49. Silverstone, R.: Consuming Technologies. Media and Information in Domestic Spaces. Routledge, London (1992)
50. Loos, E.: Generational use of new media and the (ir)relevance of age. In: Colombo, F., Fortunati, L. (eds.) Broadband Society and Generational Changes, pp. 259–273. Peter Lang, Berlin (2011)
51. Loos, E.: Senior citizens: digital immigrants in their own country? Observatorio (OBS*) **6**(1), 1–23 (2012)
52. Nora, P.: L'événement monstre. Communications **18**(1), 162–172 (1972)
53. Magladry, M.: Mediated nostalgia: individual memory and contemporary mass media. Continuum **30**(2), 268–271 (2016)
54. Lizardi, R.: Mediated Nostalgia: Individual Memory and Contemporary Mass Media. Lexington Books, Lanham (2014)
55. Mathieu, D., et al.: Methodological challenges in the transition towards online audience research. Participations **13**(1), 289–320 (2016)
56. Eisenhart, M.: On the subject of interpretive reviews. Rev. Educ. Res. **68**(4), 391–399 (1998)
57. Hammersley, M.: Literature review. In: Lewis-Beck, A.B., Liao, T.F. (Eds.) The SAGE Encyclopedia of Social Science Research Methods, vol. I, pp. 577–579. SAGE Publications, Thousand Oaks (2004)

Designing an Online Escape Game for Older Adults: The Implications of Playability Testing Sessions with a Variety of Dutch Players

Amir Doroudian[1(✉)], Eugène Loos[2(✉)], Anne Ter Vrugt[2(✉)],
and David Kaufman[1(✉)]

[1] Simon Fraser University, 8888 University Dr., Burnaby, B.C., Canada
{adoroudi,kaufman}@sfu.ca
[2] Utrecht University School of Governance,
Bijlhouwerstraat 6, 3511 ZC Utrecht, The Netherlands
e.f.loos@uu.nl, annetervrugt@gmail.com

Abstract. This study evaluated the playability of an online escape game designed using a User-Centred Design (UCD) process for older adult players aged 65 and older. The participants were 30 Dutch older adults who played the game in pairs on tablets over 15 game sessions. The data were collected through surveys, interviews, and observation field notes. The results indicated that, overall, the players enjoyed the game. They enjoyed the collaborative nature of the game and the game challenges the most. They also thought that the game story is engaging. However, the evaluation revealed that the game controller was a source of frustration and that the goals of several of the game tasks were not clear for the players. Moreover, it seems that the game needs to be customizable so that each pair of players could determine the pace and difficulty level of the game.

Keywords: Older adults · Playability testing · User-centered design · Online escape game

1 Introduction

A transition in the demographic patterns of western societies has resulted in a significant increase of the older adult population. They are consumers of many leisure activities offered by digital technologies. The growing ownership of digital devices by older adults has resulted in an increase in older adults who play digital games (https://www.pewresearch.org/internet/2017/05/17/tech-adoption-climbs-among-older-adults/ and https://ec.europa.eu/eurostat/statistics-explained/ index.php/people_in_the_EU_-_statistics_ on_an_ageing_society). However, older adults (65+), especially non-gamers, still play digital games far less frequently than older adult gamers and younger generations [1]. However, it is unlikely that this is only due to a lack of interest or openness to play digital games. Other factors, such as lack of perceived benefits and shortage of such games explicitly designed to meet older adults' needs, might be some other, more plausible, factors [2].

© Springer Nature Switzerland AG 2020
Q. Gao and J. Zhou (Eds.): HCII 2020, LNCS 12208, pp. 589–608, 2020.
https://doi.org/10.1007/978-3-030-50249-2_42

Digital games are powerful tools that could help older adults' well-being by engaging them cognitively, emotionally, and socially [1, 3]. The use of digital games by older adults deserves commercial and academic attention, similar to the use of digital games by children [4]. During the past two decades, numerous empirical studies have been conducted on the preferences and motivations of older adults for playing digital games, [e.g. 2–11], but empirical studies on digital games designed for an older adult audience are rare and there are several barriers to the adoption and use of digital technologies, including digital games, by older adults [12]. Mattke, Klautzer, Mengistu, Garnett, Hu, and Wu [12] found that a lack of comprehensive instructions, little incentives to invest their time, and a low value of digital technology in their lives are among these barriers. By including older adults in the design and evaluation of digital games targeted at them, some of these barriers could be addressed. Moreover, understanding the preferences and needs of older adults, as well as acknowledging their limitations and capabilities may result in more enjoyable games that will be used by more people for longer terms [13].

One type of games that may be of interest to older adult game players may be escape games. Escape games, also known as escape rooms, are defined as "live-action team-based games where players discover clues, solve puzzles, and accomplish tasks in one or more rooms in order to accomplish a specific goal (usually escaping from the room) in a limited amount of time" [14, p.1]. Over the past few years, escape games have grown in popularity around the world. Escape rooms first appeared in Japan in 2007 and, in about five years, expanded to other parts of Asia, as well as Europe, North America, and Australia [14]. Escape games are collaborative and require communication, teamwork, delegation, observation, and critical thinking. Often, the rooms are themed and follow a storyline and the puzzles are of different types, including logic, mechanical, spatial, word, and math puzzles [15].

There are several reasons why an online escape game was chosen for this study. First, escape games have grown in popularity around the world, particularly in Europe and North America, attracting diverse players from various age groups. Second, the gameplay of escape games offers opportunities for cognitive and social engagement (see [1, 3] for more information about the impact of digital games on the physical, cognitive and social well-being of older adults). Collaboration and interaction with other players are necessary for completing game tasks in most real-life and virtual escape games. Since one of the main motivations of older adults for playing digital games is social interaction [e.g., 13], it seems that escape games seem may be an appropriate game that would be enjoyable for them to play. Finally, an online escape game would offer opportunities to interact with digital interfaces, use electronic communication, and perform game tasks using a digital device through a enjoyable, collaborative activity.

The purpose of this study was to evaluate the playability of an online escape game designed for older adults with a Dutch audience. The game was created using a User-Centred Design (UCD) process in Vancouver, BC, Canada. The game is based on real-life-escape rooms. Evaluating the playability of the game is important because this is an essential element of player-centered game design. Playability is basically the concept of usability in the context of game design. It is an important quality characteristic of a product or system. Usable systems are efficient, easy to learn, satisfactory in actual use, and not prone to errors [16].

According to Rubin and Chisnell [17], "[u]sability testing employs techniques to collect empirical data while observing representative end-users using the product to perform realistic tasks" (p. 19). In the context of game design and evaluation, playability goes beyond the basic user interface to include other elements of the game experience, such as game play, game story, and mechanics. In this empirical study, we used a qualitative method to observe the players playing the game, administered a questionnaire based on validated heuristics, and interviewed the players about their experience to learn about the extent to which our game is playable by its target audience. We used an iterative process, as we refined the game based on the feedback from the players.

This study aimed to answer the following question: How playable is the online escape game prototype, "A Tale of Tales," for older adults?

2 Literature Review

Globally, the population of adults aged 60 and older has risen from 382 million in 1980 to 962 million in 2017 [18]. Due to the significant social and economic implications of this demographic change, support needs to be provided to seniors to help them age successfully. Digital games have shown several benefits for older adults, including cognitive, psychological, and social benefits [1, 3]. However, older adult non-gamers – that is, people aged 60 years old and older who do not play digital games on a regular basis – have several characteristics that need to be address in game design. For example, many of such players have limited knowledge of game platform technology and are far less motivated to play digital games to the perceived value they associate with it [2]. Furthermore, older adult non-gamers find it difficult to interact with many digital games, due to perceptual, cognitive, and motor limitations [2, 19, 20]. Therefore, games that are specifically designed for this group of players might be more engaging and, thus, successful [21]. Brown and De Schutter [5], among other researchers [e.g. 20, 22, 23] suggested some design considerations for designing games for older adults that emphasize the importance of the players' past as a source of insight to create meaningful games and also their future to ensure the game would be accessible and usable [5]. These findings suggest that the older adult, as the end user, should be included in the design.

2.1 Designing Digital Games for Older Adults

Previous research on game design for older players has focused on the development of enjoyable game playing experiences and motivating older adults to engage in healthy physical, cognitive and social activities through engagement in play [1–11, 22]. During the past decades, various game design guidelines and recommendations have been developed for creating digital games for older players. For example, Gamberini et al. [22] and IJsselsteijn et al. [24], who focused on digital games for entertainment and cognitive enhancement, offered several recommendations for game challenges and complexity suited for older players, as well as game interface and visual adaptability. Similarly, Vasconcelos et al. [25] focused on the interface design for older adults.

Moreover, Awad et al. [26] offered an affordance-based approach, based on which, it is important that the game adapts to the players' action capability. Finally, De la Hera et al. [27] and Loos et al. [28] reviewed empirical studies on (co)design of intergenerational digital games. The former distinguishing two types of factors are important to take into consideration while designing digital games: player-centric and game-centric factors. The latter concluding that involving older and younger players in the co-design process is a logical condition to foster meaningful play, gaming being a shared play activity for which the players need each other. Brown and De Schutter [5] suggested some design considerations, including the importance of identifying the types of play older adults engaged in in childhood, accommodating for age-related changes, and accommodating for gamily gaming.

2.2 User-Centred Design and the Concept of Usability

Karat [29], defined UCD as "an iterative process whose goal is the development of usable systems, achieved through the involvement of potential users of a system in system design" (p. 38). Similarly, there are several methods to adapt UCD for a given design based on the way the designer involves the end-users, such as focus groups, usability testing, and participatory design [30]. How to adapt a particular UCD method depends on the goals of the developers, the available resources and the context of the development.

The International Organization for Standardization [31] defined UCD as an "approach to systems design and development that aims to make interactive systems more usable by focusing on the use of the system and applying human factors/ergonomics and usability knowledge and techniques" (p. 2). A user-centred design is especially crucial for a game targeted at an underrepresented audience, such as older adults, whose needs and points of view might be drastically different from those of the developers and researchers. An integral element of UCD is usability testing. Usability is defined as "…a quality attribute that assesses how easy user interfaces are to use, making it possible for the customers to develop tasks in a clear, transparent, agile and useful way" [32, para. 1]. The International Organization for Standardization [32] defined usability as "the extent to which a product can be used by specified users to achieve specified goals with effectiveness, efficiency and satisfaction in a specified context of use" (para. 11). The most suitable method of testing could be ensured when the test involves representative users who interact with representative scenarios. The conductor of the usability test collects data on the user's success, speed of performance, and satisfaction. As for iterativeness, the more iteration on the testing, the better the product-system [33].

2.3 Evaluating Playability

Several game design scholars (e.g., [34–36]) advocate for an iterative design method that relies on collecting feedback from the players. Iterativeness in this context means designing, testing, evaluating, and redesigning the game throughout the development process. Fullerton et al. [35] encourage designers to create a playable version of the game immediately after brainstorming ideas to receive feedback early in the design process; otherwise, anticipating *play* would be nearly impossible. Today, "playtesting," which is an integral part of iterative design, is one of the most established ways to include players in the design.

An accepted and widely used method of usability evaluation is heuristics which are design guidelines that serve as evaluation tools for game designers. Heuristics are typically used to evaluate interface usability, but, as mentioned earlier, to evaluate playability, other components should be addressed, as well. These components are game play, game story, and game mechanics. A validated set of heuristics for evaluating playability is *Heuristics for Evaluating Playability* (HEP), created by Desurvire et al. [37]. HEP contains 43 heuristics on four categories. *Game Play* is related to challenges and tasks the player face to win the game. *Game Story* has to do with the story and character development. *Game Mechanics* is related to the structure of the game, i.e., how the game units interact with the environment. *Game Usability* has to do with the interface and the controls the player uses when interacting with the game.

Another validated questionnaire is the Core Elements of the Gaming Experience Questionnaire (CEGEQ) [38]. The authors assert that in order for the gaming experience to not be negative, the Core Elements of the Gaming Experience (CEGE) must be present in a digital game. It should be noted that the CEGE do not determine whether a player will have a positive experience. However, if the CEGE are present, the player will not have a negative experience [38]. In other words, the CEGE questionnaire can give confidence to the designers that their game has the core elements of gaming experience and is, thus, playable and engaging. Two main areas of the CEGE are puppetry – consisting of control, ownership, and facilitators – and the actual video game details, including game play, rules, scenario, environment, graphics, and sound. CEGEQ helps determine the presence of the CEGE during the gaming experience.

In this study, we used both HEP and CEGE items to create our playability questionnaire based on our needs and what were most relevant to our purpose and to the elements of our online escape game prototype.

3 Escape Game Presentation

Adopting a UCD process that was discussed in details by Doroudian et al. [39], an online escape game was created in Vancouver, BC, Canada, called "A Tale of Tales." "A Tale of Tales" is a cooperative puzzle game based on real-life escape rooms. Real-life escape rooms are "live-action team-based games where players discover clues, solve puzzles, and accomplish tasks in one or more rooms in order to accomplish a specific goal (usually escaping from the room) in a limited amount of time" [40, p. 1].

"A Tale of Tales" is primarily intended for older adult players to engage them through elements of real-life escape rooms and the affordances of digital games. It is a two-player game that is played on two screens. The game was designed for multiple platforms, including PC, Mac, and Android operating systems. The theme of the game borrows elements from the story of Alice in Wonderland by Lewis Carroll. The storyline follows a character called "Ink Monster" who lives in a library. The Ink Monster takes the players into the world of the book and the game starts from there. The players must first escape the book, and they encounter the first game environment is a maze with three portals to different rooms. The players should find these portals, enter them, and solve the puzzles to escape each room. There is no time limit in the game. Once the players are in the maze, one of them is a navigator with a bird's-eye view of the maze and the other player moves inside the maze (see Fig. 1).

Fig. 1. Player One's view of the maze (left) and Player Two's view of the maze (right)

There are three portals in the rooms that lead to three different rooms. Room One is crossword puzzle with questions directly related to Alice in Wonderland. There are hints on the walls. Player One is inside the room and can explore it and Player Two sees the crossword puzzle's table (see Fig. 2).

Fig. 2. Room One: Player One's View (Left) and Player Two's view (right)

The second room is a two-part puzzle consisting of a color-ordering puzzle and a clock-setting puzzle based on the tea party passage of Alice in Wonderland. Completing the color-ordering puzzle unlocks the second puzzle (see Fig. 3).

Fig. 3. Room Two: Player One's view (left) and Player Two's view (right)

Finally, the third room involves a matching puzzle in which the players must find the missing words of a short poem by looking at a series of pictures and then find a code to get out of the room (see Fig. 4).

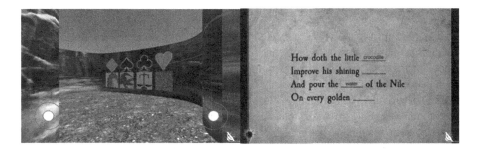

Fig. 4. Player One's view (left) and Player Two's view (right)

In all three rooms, there are code machines that the players must use to get out of the rooms. The codes are letters, numbers, and symbols that are discovered by completing the puzzles in the rooms.

4   Method

An exploratory case study approach was employed in this playability testing study. We relied on multiple sources of data – survey, interview, and observation – to explore the inquiry in its complexity and entirety. This reliance on multiple sources of data facilitated the evaluation within its context, so that the problem was explored through multiple perspectives. Further, multiple sources of data rendered a rich description of the inquiry and strengthened the trustworthiness of this qualitative research. In this project, there were two researchers present at the research site observing and collecting data through multiple methods, including surveys, interviews, and observation. The digital game was translated into Dutch for this empirical study that we conducted in the Netherlands. We used Android tablets in the game sessions. Initially, the controllers in the Android version were two virtual joysticks: one for direction and the other for movement. We merged the joysticks into one during the playability testing based on the players' feedback and half of the players played the game with a single virtual joystick that performed all the movements.

4.1 Participants

In this study, 30 older adults of 65 years of age and older were recruited from churches senior community centres, partly through the social network of the researcher, and a call in a magazine of an association for older people in the Netherlands (purposive sampling). The 65 age marker was used because of the methodological practicality and the fact that it is the standard retirement age in most countries. There were 16 men and 14 women. The participants were physically mobile and cognitively normal and the participants' demographic information was collected.

4.2 Data Collection Instruments

Survey
Demographic information was collected through a background survey that included items on the participants' age, sex, education, digital skills, and experience with digital games. Moreover, the participants completed a playability questionnaire that was adapted from the Core Elements of the Gaming Experience Questionnaire (CEGEQ) [38] and Heuristics for Evaluating Playability (HEP) [37]. We chose the items from these tools according to their relevance to our escape game and what was most important to us for this particular prototype. Our playability questionnaire included 23 Likert-scale items that were applicable to our game (see Table 2 in Sect. 5.2). These items were divided into three main categories: the design, the control, and the experience of playing the game. The questionnaire also included four open-ended questions about what the players liked most and least about the game, whether they think the game is appropriate for older adults, and if they have any other comments about the game or their experience (see Sect. 5.2).

Observation Protocol
An observation protocol was used to collect field notes on several aspects of the older adults' play, including the ease with which players start the game and operate in it, how they navigate in the game, when they get frustrated and excited during their play, and any relevant comments on the participants' game play (see Sect. 5.4).

Interview
The interviews were carried out after each game session with the pairs of players who played the game together and were guided by an interview protocol with the following questions:

1. Are you going to play these games again? Why?
2. What did you like best about the games?
3. Which elements of the game did you find the most engaging? Why?
4. Describe what worked well for you and what didn't in the game?

5. Which aspects of the games didn't you like?
6. What could have been improved in the game?
7. Do you have any other comments?

All interview sessions were audio-recorded and they lasted an average of 15 min. The interviewer also took notes during the interviews.

4.3   Data Collection Procedure

Most of the game sessions were held in study rooms at Utrecht University but some of them were held in the participants' homes in other places in The Netherlands. The digital game sessions were held one at a time, except for two parallel sessions. The participants played the online escape game in pairs using Android tablets in the same room. There were two research assistants present during the game sessions. A Dutch-speaking person was in charge of most of the communications with the participants, including conducting the interviews and providing help to the participants. The other research assistant was in charge of setting up the escape game, resolving technical glitches, and supervising the game sessions. Both persons observed the digital game sessions and wrote field notes guided by the observation protocol.

The data collection started with the participants' signing a consent form, and they completed the background questionnaire (see Table 1 in Sect. 5.1) and were then briefed by one of the research assistants about what to expect in the game and the session. The participants played the game for an average of approximately 60 min. However, each digital game session lasted approximately 100 min with the survey (see Sect. 5.2) and interview (see Sect. 5.3). Participants were assigned the roles of Player One and Player Two, and they changed roles half-way through the game in order for them to experience both roles in the online escape game. The main difference in these roles was that Player One had to do more game actions and, therefore, used the controllers more often, whereas Player Two was mostly a navigator who had to verbally communicate the routes and other information necessary to complete the puzzles. Once they finished the game, the participants completed the playability survey (see Table 2 in Sect. 5.2) and then each pair sat for an interview that lasted approximately 15 min.

4.4   Data Analysis

The quantitative data collected from the participants through the background survey and the Likert-scale items of the playability survey were entered into separate spreadsheets in a Microsoft Excel. After cleaning and checking for any irregularities, these data were analyzed for descriptives using Microsoft Excel.

The qualitative data collected through the open-ended questions of the questionnaire and the interviews (see Sects. 5.2 and 5.3) were analyzed qualitatively by coding the responses and finding themes. Before the coding process, the responses from the questionnaire were translated from Dutch into English and were entered in a spreadsheet. The Dutch-speaking research assistant who conducted the interviews translated the responses and entered them into a separate spreadsheet. Similarly, the field notes during the testing were categorized and were entered into spreadsheets.

The first step in the coding process was to do a close reading of all the responses. During this process, several categories of codes emerged. Second, these categories were organized in columns with the following headings: "collaboration," "navigation," "controller challenge," "puzzle challenge," "puzzle preferences," "fun highlights," and "other barriers." These were further divided into the themes that emerged in those columns. Whenever a new theme emerged, a corresponding column was added. The categories were then ranked based on their frequency in the responses (see Table 1). The main reason this approach was deemed practical was that the responses were short.

Table 1. The ranking of the categorized responses

Rank	Category
1	Controller challenges
2	Fun highlights
3	Enjoying collaboration
4	Navigation
5	Puzzle challenges
6	Other barriers

5 Results

5.1 Participants Demographics

Table 2 shows the demographic data of the 30 participants. 16 of the participants were men and 14 were women. There were 14 players between 65 to 69 years old, 11 players between 70 to 74, four players between 75 to 79 and 1 player was 80 to 84 years old. Twenty-two players (73.4%) were married or partnered and eight of them (26.6%) were single. Almost half of the players had higher professional education, seven players (23.4%) had secondary education or a lower certificate, five players (16.6%) had vocational education, and four of them (13.4%) had a university degree. Most of the players (76.6%) were living with someone else. As for digital skills, the majority of the players (63.4%) indicated that they are intermediate, 30% were advanced, and 6.6% believed they were beginner. However, it should be noted that most of them did not have a clear assessment about their digital skills. Therefore, their self-assessments were not definitive. Nineteen players (63.4%) had played digital games before, of whom 37% would play once a day, 21% once a month, 16% once a week, and 5% a few times a week.

Table 2. Demographics of the players

Characteristics	Category	Frequency (n)	Valid percent (%)
Sex	Female	6	20.0
	Male	24	80.0
	Total	30	100.0
Age	65–69	14	46.6
	70–74	11	36.6
	75–79	4	13.4
	80–84	1	3.4
Relationship status	Married/Partnered	22	73.4
	Single/Divorced	8	26.6
Education level	Lower than secondary school	3	10.0
	Secondary school	4	13.4
	Vocational education	5	16.6
	Higher professional education	14	46.6
	University	4	13.4
Do you live alone?	Yes	7	23.4
	No	23	76.6
Digital skills	Beginner	2	6.6
	Intermediate	19	63.4
	Advanced	9	30.0
Have you played digital games before?	Yes	19	63.4
	No	11	36.6
Frequency of playing digital games	Once a month	4	21.0
	Once a week	3	15.7
	A few times a week	1	5.3
	Once a day	7	37
	Other	4	21.0
	Total	19	100.0

5.2 The Playability Survey

The Likert-Scale Items
Table 3 below shows the results of the Likert-scale items from the usability questionnaire. With regard to the design of the game, most respondents (80%) liked the visuals of the game; however, most of them thought the art design was not appropriate for them. Moreover, almost all of them agreed that the graphics are appropriate for this kind of game, but they didn't like the animations in the game. As for the instructions and hints, most respondents found the instructions in the game difficult to follow, but most of them indicated that the help offered in the game was helpful. Finally, most respondents reported that they had difficulty understanding the rules of the game.

Table 3. The Likert-Scale Items from the playability questionnaire

Category	Item	Strongly disagree	Disagree	Neutral	Agree	Strongly agree
Design of the game	I liked the way the game looked	0	2	3	11	13
	I did not understand the rules of the game	0	3	6	14	7
	The graphics were appropriate for the type of the game	0	1	1	16	12
	I didn't like the animations of the game	0	1	1	12	16
	The art design was not appropriate for me	0	1	8	12	10
	The game display was optimal with respect to the size of the screen	0	0	4	10	15
	I couldn't follow the instructions of the game	0	5	4	16	5
	The help offered in the game was useful	0	0	1	11	17
The Control of the Game	The game was easy to play	0	0	12	11	1
	I did not have a strategy to win the game	2	10	10	5	1
	It was easy to navigate the interface of the game	3	8	11	5	2
	The learning content was too difficult for me	12	11	5	2	0
	The feedback was useful to me	0	1	2	18	9
	The game required quick response, which was a challenge for me	4	9	11	6	0
Overall Experience	I enjoyed playing the game	0	1	2	15	11
	I would like this game to be more competitive	1	5	21	2	1
	The learning content was interesting to me	1	2	10	16	1
	I got bored playing this game	11	11	9	1	9
	I would play this game again	1	5	3	14	8
	I was frustrated while playing this game	12	11	5	2	0
	I learned something new while playing this game	4	3	9	10	5
	The game tasks were complicated for me	7	17	4	1	0
	The game motivated me to keep playing	1	3	5	17	5

As for the control of the game, half of the respondents couldn't decide if the game was easy to play but the other half found it easy to play. Most respondents either didn't have a strategy to "win" the game or were undecided about it. Some respondents found the interface of the game easy to navigate, but a larger number found it difficult. Almost all of them found the game feedback useful. Finally, the majority of the respondents reported that the game required actions that were too quick for them.

In terms of overall experience, most respondents enjoyed playing the game and only a few of them were bored with it. The majority of them said they would play the game again; however, they wanted it to be more competitive. Only two players reported frustration during the game. Half of the respondents believed they learned something new. Almost all of them thought the game tasks were not too complicated for them. Finally, most of them believed that the game motivated them to keep playing.

The Open-Ended Items

The usability questionnaire included four open-ended questions that were intended to complement the Likert-scale items. The responses to these questions were entered in a spreadsheet and categories were given to issues in the responses. Here are the main issues the players wrote about in the questionnaire.

- *Collaboration to achieve a shared goal was the most enjoyable element of the game play for the players.*

The word "collaboration" stood out in the responses. Most respondents indicated that they enjoyed the collaborative nature of the game and "playing together" was the best thing they liked about this game. One player said, "I liked the playing together. It was original and challenging." Moreover, some respondents reported that they liked the challenges in the game tasks and that solving the puzzles was very engaging.

- *The virtual controllers and, thus, moving in the game was a source of frustration.*

The players referred to the difficulty of moving in the game, mainly due to the two virtual joysticks. One player said, "navigating was difficult. Going to different directions was very inconvenient with two joysticks." It seems that the players had the most difficulty with movement inside the maze. The same difficulty was reported, to a lesser extent, in the rooms, too. Some other players indicated that the speed of movements was too fast for them.

- *The players believed that the game is appropriate for their age.*

The players believed that the game is appropriate for their age, as it mostly kept them engaged and the game tasks had the right amount of challenge in most cases. But they also referred to the speed of the game and the controllers as factors that could be modified to better tailor the game to older adults. Some of them also asked for more diverse puzzles in the rooms.

- *The players voiced a need for more instructions and hints.*

The players believed that the instructions in the game were not sufficient. They thought their play experience could be improved if there had been more hints and instructions throughout the game. Some of them thought the goals of each puzzle should be made clear from the beginning. Others believed that it was almost impossible to finish the game without physical help from someone who knows the game.

5.3   Results of the Interviews

After they were finished playing the game, each pair sat for an interview to respond to ten questions regarding their experiences in the game. The responses were coded and organized in a spreadsheet and then themes emerged from the categories of codes. In this section, these four themes are presented.

- *The Players Would Play the Game Again, if There Are More Themes and Puzzles*

The players liked the game and most of them said they would play the game again. However, they requested more diverse game stories and puzzles. Also, they wanted different levels of difficulties to choose from. Some of the players said that it is important that both players be engaged throughout the game, rather than one player having fewer tasks to do and the other player being overloaded.

- *Finding solutions for the puzzles with a partner was the most fun element of the game play.*

Almost all participants believed that the collaborative nature of the game and striving for a shared goal was the most enjoyable part of their play experience. This in line with the finding of the survey. From their elaborations on this, it can be inferred that they liked the verbal interaction and the trial-and-error process to find codes and figure out the goals of the puzzles.

- *The Difficulty with Navigation Negatively Affected the Players' Play Experience*

As they indicated in the survey, the participants also expressed their dissatisfaction with the two virtual joysticks, even with the single virtual joystick. Most of the complaints regarded the fact that using both hands at the same times for direction and movement was difficult. Some players believed that the difficulty was due to lack of experience and it could be resolved with practice, while others thought that this kind of controller didn't work for them due to their motor skill limitations. Some other participants thought that the problem was mostly the fast speed rather than the controllers.

- *The Multiple Objectives of the Game Tasks Were not Clear to the Players*

The respondents believed that they couldn't figure out the purpose of the puzzle on their own without the research assistant's help when they were "stuck." What they mean was that when they were encountered with a new task, they looked for assistance. Overall, it seems that the players did not engage with the "clue finding" part of the rooms very much. Their comments suggest that they preferred to skip the exploratory stage in each room and get to solving the puzzles.

5.4   Results of the Observation

During the game sessions in this phase, the research assistants collected field notes guided by an observation protocol that focused on several aspects of the players' interaction with the game. The protocol focused on the ease with which players start the game and operate in it, instances of frustration, instances of excitement, difficulty navigating the game, and any relevant observation that could be important for improving the game.

According to the observers' notes, the players didn't have difficulty starting the game, except in one case. However, the players seemed frustrated on several occasions during the game. Most prominently, they were frustrated when trying to use the virtual joysticks to move in the maze. This is in line with the results of the usability survey and the interviews. Another source of frustration was making mistakes inside the rooms. This was especially the case in the second room when they would get the color order wrong. The third source of frustration was when the navigator made mistake in finding the correct route to the rooms. Finally, the design of the third room seemed to have frustrated the players, since they had to move between two places often to figure out the final code.

A difficulty that was observed frequently during the game session was identifying the portals in the birds-eye view of the maze. It seemed that the portals, which were in star and ball shapes, were not conspicuous enough for older adults. Moreover, when they were done with one room and wanted to find the next room, they had difficulty identifying the correct room.

The observation data shows that, at some point in any of the three rooms, the players did not know what to do. In the first room, some players did not know how to access the code after solving the crossword puzzle. The code was visible by pressing on a light switch. In the second room, most players did not know what the purpose of the puzzle is, so a research assistant had to explain it to them. In the same room, half of the players did not know they can, and should, move the clock handles. In the third room, where there are four pictures on the wall that correspond to card suits above them, most players did not know how to figure out the code based on the suits and the order of the pictures.

6   Discussion

This study aimed to evaluate the playability of an online escape game designed with, and targeted at, older adults. Following the recommendations in the literature (e.g., [24, 41]), we decided to use direct input devices for the playability testing of the game. Direct input devices, such as tablets, allow older adults with mobility issues to place the tablet in a position that is comfortable for them. They also provide a more intuitive way of interaction with a digital device compared to indirect input devices like laptops.

The participants of this study were all Dutch and most of them were between 65 to 69 years old. However, they were quite diverse in terms of education level and their experience with digital games.

The results of the evaluation suggest that the players were satisfied with the overall interface design of the game. They also found the game feedback useful, and enjoyed playing the game in general. The game seemed to have kept them motivated to keep playing. Most of them indicated that they would play the game again. However, it should be noted that many respondents might not have been able to keep playing the game during sessions without the help given by the research assistants, including hints and sometimes even helping them with the controllers. An interesting finding was that, although the players found the game tasks not too complicated, the majority of them reported that they did not understand the rules of the game. Based on the interview responses, it seems that what they described as "not understanding the rules" was in fact a game task: finding clues. The players were reluctant to spend an extended amount of time figuring out what to do and find clues with their partner.

This is in line with Gamberini et al.'s [23] observation that older adult players need more help using materials throughout the game. Overall, these findings suggest that the players did not engage in the clue finding part of the rooms. Perhaps in an untimed game session happening in the players' natural play context (e.g., their homes), this could be different. After all, the game is designed to be played at leisure and without a time limit. Moreover, the presence of the research assistants could have made the players rely too much on their help. Therefore, the decision to put more hints in the game is a difficult one because discovery and trying out different possibilities is a core element of escape room gameplay that fosters collaboration and social interaction between the players.

The results also indicate that the players found it difficult to move in the game, mostly due to the controllers, the pace of the game, and inefficient communication with the game partner. Using the virtual joysticks turned out to be the most significant source of frustration for players. This finding is in line with that of Aison et al. [9], who found that older adults had difficulty using controllers and joysticks and they cited it as the most common factor distracting them from game enjoyment. Inefficient communication could be another reason for the failure to navigate the game with ease. Since the players see different views of the game, communicating what they see and what information to give is essential to navigating the game with ease. However, the observational data shows that some players were not efficient in this regard. It should be noted that the double virtual joysticks were replaced by a single joystick after holding half of the game sessions. This refinement was helpful, as we observed less frustration in the players. However, it seemed that the problem still persisted to some extent.

The results of this evaluation suggests that the players enjoyed the collaborative nature of the game more than succeeding in it. This finding confirms Altmeyer and Lessel's [42] statement that socializing is a core motivator for older adults. It seems that older adults play digital games more to communicate and maintain social contact than to succeed in the game. They are also more inclined to help each other and promote positive relations than to compete with each other [42]. The players followed up on their response by indicating that achieving a shared goal with their game partner was something they liked the most in their experience.

Another finding was that, although the players indicated they would play the game again, they had some conditions to be motivated to do so. Specifically, they said they would play the game again if they know they will encounter something new each time. They also expressed their preference for being able to customize the speed and difficulty level of the game. Finally, it is worth noting that the results of the survey and interview results contradicted our observation in some cases. Most notably, it seems that some players were frustrated with different aspects of the play; however, they did not reflect this frustration in their survey and the interview responses.

Based on these findings, this evaluation provided sufficient data to conclude that the game is playable in terms of interface design and fostering collaboration to achieve shared goals. However, it still needs improvements in some areas, including game control, providing cues as to what the player needs to do next, and more clear objectives for the game tasks, such as the puzzle in room two.

7   Conclusion and Limitations

This evaluation aimed to answer the research question on how playable our online escape game is. The findings revealed that the game requires refinements and further playability testing and field testing before publication. Our findings suggest that older adults prefer puzzles with clear goals that are explicitly stated at each stage in the game. They would also like to know all the actions they have to do in their roles in the game. The players also prefer to be able to customize the game to match their pace and abilities. They respond better to direct-input devices and need controllers that require simple actions. The evaluation also showed where the game needs further improvement for it to be ready for distribution to a broader audience. Despite these issues, they greatly appreciated the social and collaborative aspects of playing this game. Most older adults enjoyed the game and stated that they would play it again.

Furthermore, although we did not empirically measure the impact of the game on social interaction in this evaluation, the game was designed with emphasis on facilitating social interaction for older adults. Our observation suggests that the game did facilitate social interaction among our players, since navigating and solving puzzles depended on verbal communication. It also seems that they enjoyed this interaction because, first, the interview responses tell us that the collaborativeness of the game was a positive highlight of the players' experience and, second, based on our observation, they had a good time chatting with each other during and after the game sessions. That being said, it is necessary to empirically evaluate the impact of the game on promoting social connectedness in older adults, as well as in intergenerational players.

A limitation of this study was the contrived context of our game sessions. The players played the game in the same room in presence of two research assistants who provided hints and guidance during the game. In addition, the fact that some of the respondents personally knew one of the research assistants who was present during the game sessions might have affected their behavior or their responses. These are important factors that could have affected the results significantly. Therefore, further field-testing of the game is required to validate these findings and make sure the game could achieve its goals.

References

1. Zhang, F., Kaufman, D.: Physical and cognitive impacts of digital games on older adults: a meta-analytic review. J. Appl. Gerontol. **35**(11), 1189–1210 (2015)
2. Brown, J.A.: Digital gaming perceptions among older adult non-gamers. In: Zhou, J., Salvendy, G. (eds.) ITAP 2017. LNCS, vol. 10298, pp. 217–227. Springer, Cham (2017). https://doi.org/10.1007/978-3-319-58536-9_18
3. Loos, E., Kaufman, D.: Positive impact of exergaming on older adults' mental and social well-being: in search of evidence. In: Zhou, J., Salvendy, G. (eds.) ITAP 2018. LNCS, vol. 10927, pp. 101–112. Springer, Cham (2018). https://doi.org/10.1007/978-3-319-92037-5_9
4. De Schutter, B.: Never too old to play: The appeal of digital games to an older audience. Games and Culture **6**(2), 155–170 (2011)
5. Brown, J.A., De Schutter, B.: Game design for older adults: lessons from a life course perspective. Int. J. Gaming Comput. Med. Simul. (IJGCMS) **8**(1), 1–12 (2016). https://doi.org/10.1177/1555412010364978
6. Nap, H., Kort, Y., IJsselsteijn, W.: Senior gamers: preferences, motivations and needs. Gerontechnology **8**(4), 247–262 (2009)
7. Brown, J.A.: Let's play: understanding the role and meaning of digital games in the lives of older adults. In: Proceedings of the International Conference on the Foundations of Digital Games, pp. 273–275. ACM (2012)
8. Loos, E., Zonneveld, A.: Silver gaming: serious fun for seniors? In: Zhou, J., Salvendy, G. (eds.) ITAP 2016. LNCS, vol. 9755, pp. 330–341. Springer, Cham (2016). https://doi.org/10.1007/978-3-319-39949-2_32
9. Aison, C., Davis, G., Milner, J., Targum, E.: Appeal and interest of video game use among the elderly (2002). http://www.booizzy.com/jrmilner/portfolio/harvard/gameselderly.pdf
10. Aarhus, R., Grönvall, E., Larsen, S.B., Wollsen, S.: Turning training into play: embodied gaming, seniors, physical training and motivation. Gerontechnology **10**(2), 110–120 (2011)
11. Loos, E.: Exergaming: meaningful play for older adults? In: Zhou, J., Salvendy, G. (eds.) ITAP 2017. LNCS, vol. 10298, pp. 254–265. Springer, Cham (2017). https://doi.org/10.1007/978-3-319-58536-9_21
12. Mattke, S., Klautzer L., Mengistu T., Garnett J., Hu J., Wu, H.: Health and well-being in the home: a global analysis of needs, expectations, and priorities for home health care technology. Rand Corporation Pittsburgh (2010). http://www.rand.org/pubs/occasional_papers/OP323.html
13. Marston, H.: Older adults as 21st century game designers. Comput. Games J. Whitsun **1**(1), 90–102 (2012)
14. Nicholson, S.: Peeking behind the locked door: a survey of escape room facilities (2015). White Paper. http://scottnicholson.com/pubs/erfacwhite.pdf
15. Pan, R., Lo, H., Neustaedter, C.: Collaboration, awareness, and communication in real-life escape rooms. In: Proceedings of the 2017 Conference on Designing Interactive Systems, pp. 1353–1364 (2017)
16. Nielsen, J.: Usability Engineering. Academic Press, Boston (1993)
17. Rubin, J., Chisnell, D.: Handbook of Usability Testing, 2nd edn. Wiley Publishing, Indianapolis (2008)
18. Department of Economic and Social Affairs Population Division, United Nations. World Population Ageing 2017. United Nations, New York (2017). https://www.un.org/en/development/desa/population/publications/pdf/ageing/WPA2017_Highlights.pdf

19. Astell, A.: Technology and fun for a happy old age. In: Sixsmith, A., Gutman, G. (eds.) Technologies for Active Aging: International Perspectives on Aging (Book 9), vol. 9, pp. 169–187. Springer, New York (2013). https://doi.org/10.1007/978-1-4419-8348-0_10

20. Loos, E.F., Bergstrom, J.R.: Older adults. In: Bergstrom, J.R., Schall, A.J. (Eds.) Eye Tracking in User Experience Design, pp. 313–329. Elsevier, Amsterdam (2014)

21. Loos, E.F.: Designing meaningful intergenerational digital games. In: Proceedings of the International Conference on Communication, Media, Technology and Design, Istanbul, 24–26 April 2014, pp. 46–51 (2014)

22. Gerling, K.M., Schulte, F.P., Masuch, M.: Designing and evaluating digital games for frail elderly persons. In: Proceedings of the 8th International Conference on Advances in Computer Entertainment Technology. Association for Computing Machinery, New York, NY (2011)

23. Gamberini, L., Alcaniz, M., Barresi, G., Fabregat, M., Prontu, L., Seraglia, B.: Playing for a real bonus: videogames to empower elderly people. J. Cyber Therapy Rehabil. 1(1), 37–48 (2008)

24. IJsselsteijn, W., Nap, H.H., de Kort, Y., Poels, K.: Digital game design for elderly users. In: Proceedings of 2007 conference on Future Play, pp. 17–22. ACM and Wiley, New York (2007)

25. Vasconcelos, A., Silva, P., Caseiro, J., Nunes, F., Teixeira, L.: Designing tablet-based games for seniors: the example of CogniPlay, a cognitive gaming platform. In: Proceedings of the 4th International Conference on Fun and Games, pp. 1–10 (2012)

26. Awad, M., Ferguson, S., Craig, C.: Designing games for older adults: an affordable based approach. In: 2014 IEEE 3rd International Conference on Serious Games and Applications for Health (SeGAH), pp. 1–7 (2014)

27. De la Hera, T., Loos, E.F., Simons, M., Blom, J.: Benefits and factors influencing the design of intergenerational digital games: a systematic literature review. Societies 7(3), 18 (2017)

28. Loos, E., de la Hera, T., Simons, M., Gevers, D.: Setting up and conducting the co-design of an intergenerational digital game: a state-of-the-art literature review. In: Zhou, J., Salvendy, G. (eds.) HCII 2019. LNCS, vol. 11592, pp. 56–69. Springer, Cham (2019). https://doi.org/10.1007/978-3-030-22012-9_5

29. Karat, J.: User centered design: quality or quackery? Interactions 3(4), 18–20 (1996)

30. Gulliksen, J., Boivie, I.G.B., Persson, J., Blomkvist S., Cajander A.: Key principles for user-centred systems design. In: Seffah, A., Gulliksen, J., Desmarais, M.C. (eds.) Human-Centred Software Engineering - Integrating Usability in the Software Development Lifecycle, pp. 17–37. Springer, Dordrecht (2005). https://doi.org/10.1007/1-4020-4113-6_2

31. International Organization for Standardization: ISO 9241- 210: Ergonomics of Human-centred System Interaction – Part 210: Human-centred Design for Interactive Systems. International Organization for Standardization, Geneva (2010)

32. International Organization for Standardization: ISO/TS 20282-2:2013 Usability of Consumer Products and Products for Public Use — Part 2: Summative Test Method. International Organization for Standardization, Geneva (2013)

33. Diah, N., Ismail, M., Ahmad, S., Dahari, M.: Usability testing for educational computer game using observation method. In: Proceedings of the 2010 International Conference on Information Retrieval & Knowledge Management (CAMP), pp. 157–161 (2010)

34. Sykes, J.: A Player-centred approach to digital game design. In: Rutter, J., Bryce, J. (eds.) Understanding Digital Games, pp. 75–92. Sage, London (2006)

35. Fullerton, T., Swain, C., Hoffman, S.: Game Design Workshop: Designing, Prototyping, and Playtesting Games. CMP Books, Gilroy (2004)

36. Pagulayan, R.J., Keeker, K., Wixon, D., Romero, R., Fuller, T.: User-centered design in games. In: Jacko, J., Sears, A. (eds.) Handbook for Human–Computer Interaction in Interactive Systems, pp. 883–906. Erlbaum, Mahwah (2003)

37. Desurvire, H., Caplan, M., Toth, J.: Using heuristics to evaluate the playability of games. In: CHI 2004 Extended Abstracts on Human Factors in Computing Systems, pp. 1509–1512 (2004)

38. Calvillo-Gámez, E.H., Cairns, P., Cox, A.L.: Assessing the core elements of the gaming experience. In: Bernhaupt, R. (ed.) Evaluating User Experience in Games. HIS, pp. 47–71. Springer, Cham (2010). https://doi.org/10.1007/978-1-84882-963-3_4

39. Doroudian, A., Hausknecht, S., Kaufman, D.: Creating an online escape room game for older adults: needs assessment, design process, and usability testing. In: Zhou, J., Salvendy, G. (eds.) ITAP 2018. LNCS, vol. 10927, pp. 516–525. Springer, Cham (2018). https://doi.org/10.1007/978-3-319-92037-5_36

40. Nicholson, S.: Peeking behind the locked door: a survey of escape room facilities. White Paper. (2015). http://scottnicholson.com/pubs/erfacwhite.pdf

41. Wood, E., Willoughby, T., Rushing, A., Bechtel, L., Gilbert, J.: Use of computer input devices by older adults. J. Appl. Gerontol. **24**(5), 419–438 (2005)

42. Altmeyer, M., Lessel, P.: The Importance of social relations for well-being change in old age – do game preferences change as well? In: Positive Gaming: Workshop on Gamification and Games for Wellbeing (2017). http://ceurws.org/Vol-2055/paper2.pdf

Evaluating Seniors' Virtual Reality Experience Performed at a Local Community Event in Japan

Kenichiro Ito[1]([✉])(iD), Ryogo Ogino[1], Atsushi Hiyama[2], and Michitaka Hirose[3]

[1] Institute of Gerontology, The University of Tokyo,
7-3-1 Hongo, Bunkyo-ku, Tokyo 113-8656, Japan
k.ito@iog.u-tokyo.ac.jp
[2] Research Center for Advanced Science and Technology, The University of Tokyo,
4-6-1 Komaba, Meguro-ku, Tokyo 153-8904, Japan
[3] Graduate School of Information Science and Technology, The University of Tokyo,
7-3-1 Hongo, Bunkyo-ku, Tokyo 113-8656, Japan

Abstract. Head-mounted display has become one of the most known hardware and best practice experience for virtual reality. However, it still lacks of opportunities for many people who may not have much interest in gaming such as seniors. While many seniors have some interest to virtual reality through watching television program, the opportunity to actually experience is still limited. Therefore, this paper focused first to provide an opportunity for seniors to experience virtual reality, and then investigate about their impression and acceptance. An event booth to experience virtual reality contents was provided at a local community event held for senior. Voluntary participants were asked to answer questionnaires after the virtual reality experience. The questionnaire was gathered from 11 seniors over the age 65. Evaluation of acceptance was done using the System Usability Scale, indicated not so high acceptance of usability though positive outcomes delivering higher satisfaction than anticipated.

Keywords: Senior · Head-mounted display · Acceptance · Virtual Reality

1 Introduction

HMD has become the flagship device for the Virtual Reality (VR) industry. It has been well commercialized and accepted within the entertainment market. However, initial setup of the system still requires high technological knowledge which is barrier to those who lack of required knowledge. Although, many of the potential users without enough technological knowledge are interested in VR which also includes the seniors. Many seniors have basic knowledge of what an HMD is from watching broadcast on televisions, though many do not have any VR experience.

Considering the aspects of the aging society, seniors' plays an important role in terms of affecting the whole society from all kinds of views. As it does

Q. Gao and J. Zhou (Eds.): HCII 2020, LNCS 12208, pp. 609–621, 2020.
https://doi.org/10.1007/978-3-030-50249-2_43

affect the consumer electronic market, the products which are on the market also affects the seniors' life. Therefore, consideration of seniors' wants, needs and or requirements and their acceptance towards the products are important considering seniors' daily life and care. Many considerations with VR technology and senior have been explored though consideration from a system level are not yet fully known, especially from a local community system level. Hence, this paper explores how seniors' may accept the HMD through local community events providing HMD experience.

2 Head-Mounted Display in Japan: The Market and the Seniors

Many people in Japan without high knowledge about the field of VR, often recognizes "VR" and "HMD" as an equal concept, moreover, "HMD" is the physical representation of "VR". Since this is clearly a misunderstanding from an academic point of view, this paper will first organize the correct term of "VR", and the relationship with "HMD". Firstly, "VR" has several well-known definitions or principles such as, the $I = 3$ [1] which is composed of *Immersion, Interaction, Imagination*, and AIP cube [2] which is composed of *Autonomy, Interaction, Presence*. While the definitions are explained and expressed in high abstract level, one of the most simple and well known reference is called a Reality-virtuality Continuum [3,4]. Within these concepts, the physical device of "HMD" may provide functions of MR/AR device [5] configured from whether it has non see-through monitor or a see-through display, or configured with a video see-through system.

Allocating the concepts to actual products released on the VR market, non see-through monitor type HMD are for example, PlayStation VR (made by Sony) [6], Oculus Rift CV (made by Facebook) [7], HTC Vive (made by HTC) [8] and Valve Index VR (made by Valve) [9]. These type of HMD has become very popular to provide entertainment, although, many of the device cost around 50.000 JPY to 200.000 JPY (500 USD to 2.000 USD) also requiring additional hardware such as a game console or computer with good graphic processor. Also a smartphone-based type HMD has been released such as, Google Cardboard [10], Hacosco [11], GearVR [12] and free companion HMD featured at CardboardClub [13]. The smartphone-based type are normally cheap (1 USD to 50 USD) since almost all functions are realized divert from the smartphone.

Although the HMD consumer market is rapidly growing, the adoption rate is obviously not as high compared to laptops or smartphone. This is because HMD is still an emerging technology where the main consumers are still innovators and early adapters [14–16]. The issues with motion sickness [17,18] also dangles while some guidelines are proposed [19–21], however, it is yet still not well known how to prevent motion sickness. Some works reports that 20%–80% VR users experience some kind of classical motion sickness [22]. Therefore, even the users that are strongly interested in state-of-art technologies adopting VR are feeling sickness while using, it leaves a question of whether the majorities and laggards will act the same. However, user experience of motion sickness cannot be predicted since it relies on individual difference and the VR contents the user is experiencing. Hence, providing user experience opportunities without or minimized sickness for non-innovator and non-early adapters are important for further expansion of the VR consumer market.

Seniors are considered to be close to laggards since their priority in changing their life is small. However, the attitude in changing their life do depend on the individual, and many seniors watch many television programs which has featured VR and HMD many times. Although, television programs only introduce the scenery, which lacks in providing actual opportunities to experience the HMD. Therefore, firstly, providing the opportunity of HMD experience to seniors, and secondly, hopefully giving positive experience to the seniors are necessary approaches to expand the HMD industry in Japan, and well as proving better daily life to the seniors.

There are many research providing various reports about adaptation of VR for seniors [23]. While there are huge affect of individual difference, the physical decline of spatial cognition ability due to aging are especially a fact to consider. Some report about the decline of capability to recognize 3D environment [24], sickness in a very simple environment composed of one CRT monitor [25,26], as well as serious sickness leading the senior participants dropping out from experiments [27,28]. Therefore, adoption of HMD for majority or laggard seniors will need to overcome many issues, including how to provide positive experience even with some expected motion sickness.

While consideration of VR sickness are important, moreover, consideration of seniors' wants, needs and or requirements shall also be well considered in terms of providing positive experiences. Especially, while VR sickness and user experience are being explored [29], investigation of the system acceptance towards the products are important considering seniors' daily life and care, though not yet been well explored. Within seniors' daily life and care, the role of local community are considered to be important in terms of prevention of frailty. Previous research [30] indicates from a content point of view, user-centered designed serious games using "mixed reality" with therapeutic regimens could effect their motivations, engagement and adherence to rehabilitation programmes resulting a better health outcome [31,32]. Therefore, this paper explores how seniors' may accept the VR experience through local community events providing HMD experience.

3   Virtual Reality Experience in a Local Community Event

To explore the virtual reality experience in a certain local community, Toyoshikidai area of Kashiwa city located in Chiba prefecture was chosen as a field for research. This area has been chosen because the Institute of Gerontology has been cooperating with the Kashiwa city as a model city for aging society for the past years. Within the area of Toyoshikidai, two local events were

Table 1. Event schedule of the luncheon meeting.

11:00	Open
11:30–11:50	Opening speech and greetings
Session 1	
11:50–12:20	Quiz of movies and music from the old days
12:20–12:50	Lunch time
12:50–13:20	Concert and sing-along by the local senior harmonic band
Session 2	
13:30–15:00	Booth activity time(*)
15:00	Close

(*) The opportunity to experience HMD was provided in this session.

Fig. 1. Scenery picture during Session 1 at the luncheon meeting.

chosen for setup opportunities to experience VR. First, a regional community event named the "luncheon meeting" for senior people living alone and second, a small cafe event opened at the local community center named Toyoshikidai Community Activity Center.

3.1 Regional Community Event: Luncheon Meeting for Senior People Living Alone

At the Toyoshikidai area of Kashiwa City located in Chiba Prefecture, an local community event called "Luncheon meeting for senior people living alone" is organized annually. More or less 200 local seniors attend this event, with some session within the event is organized by the Institute of Gerontology, the University of Tokyo. The Institute of Gerontology has been significantly cooperating with the local community to develop a successful community and social participation for seniors [33]. The 10th annual event was held on the 14th, October 2019 at a facility within the Toyoshikidai area. The event schedule is shown in Table 1.

2019-10-14 Luncheon meeting
Part 2 (13:30 – 15:00)
7 booth area

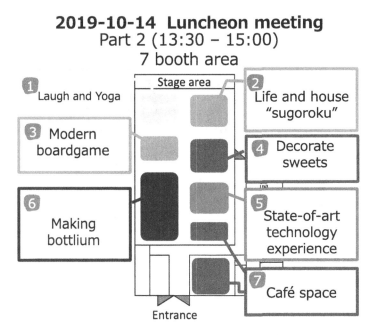

Fig. 2. Overview of the booth areas at the luncheon meeting Session 2. The opportunity to experience HMD was provided at the booth "State-of-art technology experience" area.

Fig. 3. Scenery of a senior experiencing a HMD contents at the booth.

As shown in Table 1, the luncheon meeting starts at 11:30 with an opening speech for the event, and consists from 2 major session. Session 1 is composed of quiz time, lunch time, and concert and sing-along time preformed by the local

Fig. 4. Scenery of a staff checking the system setup at the booth.

senior harmonic band (Fig. 1). Session 2 is composed of six parallel session, each done withing the booth area (Fig. 2). Within the booth *State-of-art technology experience*, a HMD experience area was prepared (Fig. 3). Other state-of-art technology showed a demonstration of a new human-interface to setup a Internet of Things system.

3.2   Cafe and VR Experience at Toyoshikidai Community Activity Center

At the same Toyoshikidai area of Luncheon meeting, there is a community activity center which runs several programs for local seniors mainly provided also from the local seniors. Normal events like drinking tea or coffee, practicing music and singing and all kinds of workshop and activities are held. Withing one of the cafe events, a small booth to experience the virtual reality environment was provided. The event was held on the 27th, December 2019 from 13:00 to 16:00. The booth was prepared at a corner of the room (Fig. 4) to avoid inconvenience with people relaxing at the cafe.

3.3   Procedure of the Virtual Reality Experience

Since this research aim is to investigate the seniors' current acceptance level of VR environment through providing the opportunities, current leading consumer HMD, the Oculus Quest was chosen for the device to be in use. The application to experience was mainly focused for the tutorial application "First Steps" which the Oculus Quest provides. For the experiment participants which did not wish to move around a lot, the participant watched 360° video from "Oculus Video". The seniors were informed with the following precautions before starting the application. The informed precautions are as follows (original sentences are written in Japanese).

Table 2. List of the 15 questionnaire to evaluate the seniors HMD experience.

List of questionnaire	
Q01	I enjoyed using the VR system
Q02	I think that I would like to use the VR system daily
Q03	I think I would like to take the VR system to my home
Q04	I think that I would like to introduce VR device to my friends
Q05	I think that I would like to use this VR system frequently
Q06	I found the VR system unnecessarily complex
Q07	I thought the VR system was easy to use
Q08	I think that I would need the support of a technical person to be able to use this VR system
Q09	I found the various functions in this VR system were well integrated
Q10	I thought there was too much inconsistency in this VR system
Q11	I would imagine that most people would learn to use this VR system very quickly
Q12	I found the VR system very cumbersome to use
Q13	I felt very confident using the VR system
Q14	I needed to learn a lot of things before I could get going with this VR system
Q15	I would like to attend similar event to experience VR systems

– Experience time may be limited in case of crowded situation.
– We have carefully selected the VR contents from among the contents publicly released by production companies, although, some people may feel VR sickness similar to car sickness by experiencing VR contents.
– The experience can be stopped at any time. Please do note hesitate to tell us if you are not feeling well.

After the VR experience the participants were asked to answer the questionnaire consists of fifteen questions shown in Table 2. The questionnaire was designed based on usability scale named System Usability Scale (SUS) [34]. The questions Q05 to Q14 was taken from the SUS, and from Q01, Q02, Q03, Q04, Q15 was prepared to evaluate the satisfaction of the VR experience.

4   Results

The questionnaire was gathered from 4 seniors from the "Luncheon meeting" and 7 seniors, 1 young from the "Cafe" events. However, one senior participant from the "Cafe" felt extreme sickness complaining when writing the questionnaire. Therefore, the participant's questionnaire was excluded from the results since it is a strong bias in terms of usability; whereas such results shall be analyzed to explore to prevent sickness. Hence, the number of participants for the "Cafe"

Table 3. Questionnaire results of senior participants from the "Luncheon meeting" means and standard deviations on the age, Q01 to Q04, Q15 and SUS score.

Group: Luncheon meeting		
Statistic	Mean	SD
Age	79.250	4.031
Q01	5.000	0.000
Q02	3.000	1.633
Q03	2.250	0.957
Q04	3.500	1.000
Q15	4.250	0.957
SUS	30.625	9.214

($n = 4$, Male $= 0$, Female $= 4$)

Table 4. Questionnaire results of senior participants from the "Cafe" means and standard deviations on the age, Q01 to Q04, Q15 and SUS score.

Group: Cafe		
Statistic	Mean	SD
Age	78.667	5.574
Q01	4.667	0.516
Q02	2.333	0.816
Q03	2.667	1.211
Q04	3.833	0.753
Q15	4.333	0.516
SUS	43.333	8.898

($n = 6$, Male $= 0$, Female $= 6$)

Table 5. One-way analysis of variance of *SUS* by *Location*.

	SS	df	F	p
Location	387.604	1	4.767	0.061*
Residuals	650.521	8		

($*p < .1$)

Table 6. Statistical summary of both events combined.

Seniors (Luncheon meeting + Cafe)		
Statistic	Mean	SD
Age	78.900	4.771
Q01	4.800	0.422
Q02	2.600	1.174
Q03	2.500	1.080
Q04	3.700	0.823
Q15	4.300	0.675
SUS	38.250	10.740

($n = 10$, Male $= 0$, Female $= 10$)

is 6 seniors. The means and standard deviations of the age of participants and the questionnaire results with SUS score is shown in Table 3 and Table 4, for the "Luncheon meeting" and "Cafe", respectively. It has also been checked if there are any significant difference between the events using a one-way analysis of variance, no significant difference were found. However it shall be noted that a weak significant difference (p $= 0.061$) in SUS score was observed from the comparison between the event (Table 5). The summary of both results are shown in Table 6.

4.1   Comparison with Previous Results

A similar experiment has been done in the past to seniors and young [35]. Similar questionnaire based on SUS was also delivered in the previous experiment, which makes it possible to compare the SUS results. Although there are several different condition to be noted. Firstly, previous research used an Oculus Go as the device for the participants to experience, which has many differences such as resolutions, sensors and application. Secondly, the previous research compared the results between 10 young participants and 5 senior participants. Third, previous research only gathered data at the "Luncheon meeting" hold at the date 2018-10-14. Fourth, although there shall be no affect to the SUS score, question Q02 asked a different question *I think that today's VR experience was easy to understand*, rather than the question asked for this research *I think that I would like to use the VR system daily*.

Considering the differences, a three-way analysis of variance was done for comparable questions; Q01, Q03, Q04, and the SUS score. The means and standard deviations of the age of participants and the questionnaire results with SUS score is shown in Table 7 and Table 8, for the young and senior, respectively. The young/senior were labeled as *Group*, the difference of device as *Device*, whether the participant is living alone or with someone else as *Family*, a three-way analysis of variance was conducted for Q01, Q03, Q04, and the SUS score (Table 9, Table 10, Table 11 and Table 12).

5   Discussion

From Table 9, comparison between the young and senior had significant difference at SUS. The difference in device also showed significance, though this is likely to be biased because there was only one participant who are young and experienced Oculus Quest. Interestingly there were also some significant difference at *Q03*, which may imply that seniors may feel not confident in using the device at home,

Table 7. Questionnaire results of young participants means and standard deviations for Q01, Q03, Q04, SUS score.

Group: Young		
Statistic	Mean	SD
Age	34.417	13.365
Q01	4.917	0.289
Q03	3.833	1.528
Q04	4.417	0.793
SUS	70.000	20.057
($n = 12$, Male $= 6$, Female $= 6$)		

Table 8. Questionnaire results of senior participants means and standard deviations for Q01, Q03, Q04, SUS score.

Group: Senior		
Statistic	Mean	SD
Age	77.357	5.799
Q01	4.786	0.426
Q03	2.571	1.342
Q04	3.786	0.802
SUS	41.786	12.988
($n = 14$, Male $= 1$, Female $= 13$)		

Table 9. Three-way analysis of variance of *SUS*.

	SS	df	F	p
Group	1	5144	25.939	0.000*
Device	1	1505	7.588	0.013*
Family	1	202	1.021	0.325
Group:Device	1	849	4.284	0.052
Group:Family	1	249	1.254	0.274
Device:Family	1	45	0.226	0.640
Residuals	19	3768		

($*p < .05$)

Table 10. Three-way analysis of variance of *Q01*.

	SS	df	F	p
Group	1	0.1108	0.902	0.354
Device	1	0.0136	0.110	0.743
Family	1	0.1189	0.968	0.338
Group:Device	1	0.0098	0.080	0.781
Group:Family	1	0.0004	0.003	0.955
Device:Family	1	0.7979	6.497	0.020*
Residuals	19	2.3333		

($*p < .05$)

Table 11. Three-way analysis of variance of *Q03*.

	SS	df	F	p
Group	1	10.29	4.792	0.041*
Device	1	0.05	0.025	0.875
Family	1	0.38	0.179	0.677
Group:Device	1	1.38	0.643	0.433
Group:Family	1	6.39	2.975	0.101
Device:Family	1	0.09	0.041	0.841
Residuals	19	40.80		

($*p < .05$)

Table 12. Three-way analysis of variance of *Q04*.

	SS	df	F	p
Group	1	2.572	3.818	0.066
Device	1	0.020	0.029	0.866
Family	1	0.967	1.435	0.247
Group:Device	1	0.954	1.417	0.249
Group:Family	1	0.501	0.743	0.399
Device:Family	1	0.032	0.047	0.830
Residuals	19	12.800		

($*p < .05$)

regarding the value of mean is 2.571. Since this research scope is within the field of *Consumer Electronics*, the results provides insights about that there are possibilities that HMD may not suite current seniors. This can also be observed from the result of SUS score, whereas the seniors have a generally low score with the mean as 41.786, which some early research suggest as an unacceptable level of usability [36].

On the other hand, the mean for young SUS score was 70 whereas it indicates that the HMD experience is in an acceptable range, fairly good but not excellent. However, it is to be noted that it indicates the HMD experience was "not unacceptable", rather than "acceptable" since it is easier to show how "unacceptable" it is rather that to show how "acceptable" it is [37]. Also, it also shall take an account on this "acceptance" can be argued as that it is only an subjective score which lacks of objective point of view. Although, it can be discussed that once a product becomes well popularized, it may overall may not need to be strictly assessed considering that people get used to it. For example, highly advanced products such as television and smartphones have already become popularized even within the seniors. Even with some known issues such as the remote television controller becoming complex, or the smartphone becoming a very complex system.

Last but not least, VR sickness needs to be considered affecting the results. While only one participant actually complained about the sickness, it is widely known that even with the young generation feels VR sickness. It is necessary to consider how the sickness affects some subjective scoring for further research, using one or more appropriate scales [29].

6   Conclusion

This paper explored whether the consumer based HMD can be acceptable to the seniors within some limited time at an local community event. While it is known that HMD or state-of-art technologies to be challenging to the seniors, it is yet unclear how it may be accepted by the seniors. To explore this issue, this paper conducted a field research at a regional event for seniors in Japan. An opportunity to experience HMD booth has been prepared with an questionnaire asking several questions including SUS. Based on statistical analysis, we obtained several results also by comparison of last year event including insights that seniors are feeling the current HMD may be hard to use at their own home. For further analysis, consideration of how VR sickness may affect the SUS shall be explored, as well as providing more opportunities within similar events for further experimental analysis, and moreover, providing entertainment to the seniors.

Acknowledgement. The authors are grateful to the elder citizens in Kashiwa city, to the voluntary students and voluntary staffs attending the regional event. The research was partially supported from the following funds: JSPS Program for Leading Graduate Schools (Graduate Program in Gerontology, Global Leadership Initiative for an Age Friendly Society, The University of Tokyo), The University of Tokyo Virtual Reality Education Research Center Project No.15, JSPS Early-Career Scientists No. 19K14028, JSPS Grant-in-Aid for Scientific Research B No. 19H03956. Conflict of Interest: The authors confirm that there is no conflict of interest related to the content of this research.

References

1. Burdea, G.C., Coiffet, P.: Virtual Reality Technology. Wiley-Interscience, London (1994)
2. Zeltzer, D.: Autonomy, interaction, and presence. Presence Teleop. Virtual Environ. **1**, 127–132 (1992)
3. Milgram, P., Kishino, F.: A taxonomy of mixed reality visual displays. IEICE Trans. Inf. Syst. **12**, 282–292 (1994)
4. Milgram, P., Takemura, H., Utsumi, A., Kishino, F.: Augmented reality: a class of displays on the reality-virtuality continuum. In: Proceedings of Telemanipulator and Telepresence Technologies, vol. 2351, pp. 282–292 (1995)

5. Kiyokawa, K.: Trends and vision of head mounted display in augmented reality. In: International Symposium on Ubiquitous Virtual Reality, pp. 14–17 (2012)
6. Playstation VR. https://www.playstation.com/en-us/explore/playstation-vr/. Accessed 23 Feb 2020
7. Oculus Rift. https://www.oculus.com/rift/. Accessed 23 Feb 2020
8. VIVE. https://www.vive.com/us/product/vive-virtual-reality-system/. Accessed 23 Feb 2020
9. Valve Index VR. https://steamvr.jp/. Accessed 23 Feb 2020
10. Google Cardboard - Google VR. https://vr.google.com/cardboard/. Accessed 23 Feb 2020
11. Hacosco. https://hacosco.com/. Accessed 23 Feb 2020. (in Japanese)
12. Samsung Gear VR. https://www.samsung.com/global/galaxy/gear-vr/. Accessed 23 Feb 2020
13. Cardboardclub. http://cardboardclub.jp/get/giftkit/. Accessed 23 Feb 2020. (in Japanese)
14. Rogers, E.M.: Categorizing the adopters of agricultural practices. Rural Sociol. **23**, 346–354 (1958)
15. Moore, G.: Crossing the Chasm: Marketing and Selling Technology Products to Mainstream Customers. Harper Business, New York (1991)
16. Plouffe, C., Vandenbosch, M., Hulland, J.: Why smart cards have failed: looking to consumer and merchant reactions to a new payment technology. Int. J. Bank Market. **18**, 112–123 (2000)
17. Merhi, O., Faugloire, E., Flanagan, M., Stoffregen, T.A.: Motion sickness, console video games, and head-mounted displays. Hum. Factors **49**, 920–934 (2007)
18. Munafo, J., Diedrick, M., Stoffregen, T.A.: The virtual reality head-mounted display Oculus Rift induces motion sickness and is sexist in its effects. Exp. Brain Res. **235**(3), 889–901 (2016). https://doi.org/10.1007/s00221-016-4846-7
19. So, R.H., Lo, W., Ho, A.T.: Effects of navigation speed on motion sickness caused by an immersive virtual environment. Hum. Factors J. Hum. Factors Ergon. Soc. **43**, 52–461 (2001)
20. Lin, J.J., Abi-Rached, H., Lahav, M.: Virtual guiding avatar: an effective procedure to reduce simulator sickness in virtual environments. In: Proceedings of the SIGCHI Conference on Human Factors in Computing Systems, pp. 719–726. ACM (2004)
21. Porcino, T.M., Clua, E., Trevisan, D., Vasconcelos, C.N., Valente, L.: Minimizing cyber sickness in head mounted display systems: design guidelines and applications. In: IEEE 5th International Conference on Serious Games and Applications for Health (SeGAH), pp. 1–6 (2017)
22. Gallagher, M., Ferré, E.R.: Cybersickness: a multisensory integration perspective. Multisens. Res. **31**, 645–674 (2018)
23. McGee, J.S., et al.: Issues for the assessment of visuospatial skills in older adults using virtual environment technology. Cyber Psychol. Behav. **3**, 469–482 (2000)
24. Yetka, A.A., Pickwell, L.D., Jenkins, T.C.: Binocular vision: age and symptoms. Ophthal. Physiol. Opt. **9**, 115–120 (1998)
25. Lee, H.C.: The validity of driving simulator to measure on-road driving performance of older drivers. In: 24th Conference of Australian Institutes of Transport Research, pp. 1–14 (2002)
26. Mouloua, M., Rinalducci, E., Smither, J., Brill, J.C.: Effect of aging on driving performance. In: Proceedings of the Human Factors and Ergonomics Society 48th Annual Meeting, vol. 48, pp. 253–257 (2004)

27. Park, G.D., Allen, R.W., Fiorentino, D., Rosenthal, T.J., Cook, M. L.: Simulator sickness scores according to symptom susceptibility, age, and gender for an older driver assessment study. In: Proceedings of the Human Factors and Ergonomics Society 50th Annual Meeting, vol. 50, pp. 2702–2706 (2006)

28. Allen, R.W., Park, G.D., Fiorentino, D., Rosenthal, T.J., Cook, L.M.: Analysis of simulator sickness as a function of age and gender. In: 9th Annual Driving Simulation Conference Europe (2006)

29. Somrak, A., Humar, I., Hossaim, M.S., Alhamid, M.F., Hossain, M.A., Guna, J.: Estimating VR Sickness and user experience using different HMD technologies: an evaluation study. Future Gener. Comput. Syst. **94**, 302–316 (2019)

30. Couceiro, M.S., Dias, G.N.F.: Technology for the active senior. In: Active Ageing and Physical Activity. SWQLR, pp. 105–118. Springer, Cham (2017). https://doi.org/10.1007/978-3-319-52063-6_4

31. Laut, J., Cappa, F., Nov, O., Porfiri, M.: Increasing patient engagement in rehabilitation exercises using computer-based citizen science. Plos One **10**, 1–17 (2015)

32. Li, C., Rusák, Z., Horváth, I., Hou, Y., Ji, L.: Optimizing patients' engagement by a cyber-physical rehabilitation system. In: GI-Jahrestagung, pp. 1971–1976 (2014)

33. Ogino, R.: Role for higher education institutions in supporting lifelong learning and social participation (1) creation of learning site for seniors. Mombu Kagaku Kyoiku Tsushin (Commun. Educ. Cult. Sports Sci. Technol.) **370**, 20–22 (2015). (in Japanese)

34. Brooke, J.: SUS: a "quick and dirty" usability scale. In: Jordan, P.W., Thomas, B., Weerdmeester, B.A., McClelland, I.L. (eds.) Usability Evaluation in Industry, pp. 189–194 (1996)

35. Ito, K., Ogino, R., Hiyama, A., Hirose, M.: Senior's acceptance of head-mounted display using consumer based virtual reality contents. In: Zhou, J., Salvendy, G. (eds.) HCII 2019. LNCS, vol. 11592, pp. 170–180. Springer, Cham (2019). https://doi.org/10.1007/978-3-030-22012-9_13

36. Bangor, A., Kortum, P.T., Miller, J.T.: An empirical evaluation of the system usability scale. J. Hum. Comput. Interact. **6**, 574–594 (2008)

37. Lewis, J.: Binomial confidence intervals for small sample usability studies. In: Ozok, A.F., Salvendy, G. (eds.) Advances in Applied Ergonomics: Proceedings of the 1st International Conference on Applied Ergonomics, pp. 732–737 (1996)

Computer-Based Foreign Language Learning Programs for the Elderly – A Review Study

Blanka Klimova$^{(\boxtimes)}$

University of Hradec Kralove,
Rokitanskeho 62, 500 03 Hradec Kralove 3, Czech Republic
blanka.klimova@uhk.cz

Abstract. Technologies among elderly people are now increasing on their popularity of use. Older people use them to communicate with their relatives and friends, making appointments with a doctor, or doing shopping. The purpose of this article is to discuss the use of computer-based foreign language learning programs for healthy elderly with special focus on English language learning. More specifically, the author aims to explore benefits and limitations of the use of these computer-based foreign language learning programs for the well-being of the elderly. The methodology is based on a literature review conducted in two databases: Web of science and Scopus. The findings of this review article reveal that the use of technologies among elderly people is rising. Moreover, these technologies might be utilized in cognitive training of these people, for instance, in foreign language learning, which also has a positive impact on the plasticity of their brain and thus on the maintenance and/or enhancement of their cognitive functions. However, there is an urgent need of research in this area, as well as fast implementation of cognitive trainings, such as computer-based foreign language learning, among healthy older individuals.

Keywords: Computer-based foreign language programs · Older people · Well-being · Benefits · Constraints

1 Introduction

Although elderly people appear to be less technologically savvy than the general public, this group is more digitally connected than ever. Technologies are nowadays becoming part of seniors' lives. 82% of elderly people use the Internet and two thirds of them at the age of 65–69 years use the high-speed Internet at home [1]. This number is expected to steadily grow since active seniors (i.e., still working people) at the age of 60 years at present use the Internet on a daily basis [2]. 59% of seniors at this age also own a smartphone [1].

Technologies may help older people with the tasks of their daily living. For example, seniors use them to communicate with their relatives and friends, making appointments with a doctor, or doing shopping [3]. In this way, technologies enable them to stay independent and socially inclusive. Thus, technologies can also prevent the loneliness and social isolation of older adults [4].

In addition, technologies seem to play an important role in cognitive training, which can help older people to fight against aging diseases such as dementia. Nowadays, there

© Springer Nature Switzerland AG 2020
Q. Gao and J. Zhou (Eds.): HCII 2020, LNCS 12208, pp. 622–629, 2020.
https://doi.org/10.1007/978-3-030-50249-2_44

exist many computer-based cognitive training programs, which can improve older people's reasoning skills, short-term memory, working memory, processing speed and visual working memory [5–8].

Apart from that, older people use technologies for learning a foreign language, which can also help them improve or maintain their cognitive skills, increase their self-esteem, or enlarge their opportunities of socializing [9–12]. For instance, a US initiative, called the Speaking Exchange, uses Skype to connect seniors living in care homes with students learning English. Thus, older people feel socially needed and young people from Brazil can master English. A similar project runs in the United Kingdom. It is called Cloud Grannies and connects retired people with children in India [13].

Moreover, the study by Bubbico et al. [9] revealed how a 4-month long second language learning program (16 weeks, 2 h sessions per week) lead to functional changes in the brain of healthy older people. The results showed a significant improvement in global cognition together with an increased functional connectivity in the right inferior frontal gyrus (rIFG), right superior frontal gyrus (rSFG) and left superior parietal lobule (lSPL). Similarly, Valis et al. [12] in their study with 42 cognitively unimpaired older individuals showed that subjects in the experimental group studying English three hours per week for 12 weeks slightly improved their cognitive functions in comparison with those in the passive control group (not studying English). Generally, research indicates that regular foreign language learning may contribute to the maintenance of older people's cognitive skills, specifically working memory skills [14, 15].

The purpose of this article is to discuss the use of computer-based foreign language learning programs for healthy elderly with special focus on English language learning. More specifically, the author aims to explore benefits and limitations of the use of these computer-based foreign language learning programs for the well-being of the elderly.

2 Methods

The author searched for available studies on this topic in the world's databases Web of Science and Scopus. The search covered the period of 2010 till 31 July 2019. The search period starts with the year 2010 because at this time older people started to be involved in using technologies [16, 17]. The author analyzed and evaluated the findings of the selected studies in order to perform a comparison of the findings of the research studies detected on the basis of the following keywords: technologies AND English learning AND older people, technologies AND English learning AND elderly, technologies AND foreign language learning AND older people, technologies AND foreign language learning AND elderly, foreign language learning AND elderly, foreign language learning AND older people.

Altogether 129 articles were generated from both databases. Most of the articles were found in the Web of Science (90). After a thorough review of the titles and abstracts (67) and their duplication (18) of the selected studies, 34 studies were screened and after that, 14 studies remained for the full-text analysis.

These full-text articles were then analyzed and evaluated on the basis of the following inclusion and exclusion criteria. The inclusion criteria were as follows:

- The articles had to be published between January 1, 2010 and July 31, 2019.
- Only peer-reviewed journal articles written in English were included.

- The articles, which included only healthy older individuals were considered.
- Only original studies, i.e., empirical studies, were involved.
- The primary outcome concentrated on the use of technologies in foreign language learning by older individuals.

The exclusion criteria were as follows:

- The studies, which focused on a different target group and research topic were excluded such as [4, 9, 10, 18–22].
- Descriptive studies and reviews, e.g. [7, 23–25].

In addition, a backward search was also performed, i.e., references of the detected studies were evaluated for relevant research studies that authors might have missed during their search. Thus, only two studies were eventually analyzed and evaluated.

Figure 1 below then describes the selection procedure of the detected studies.

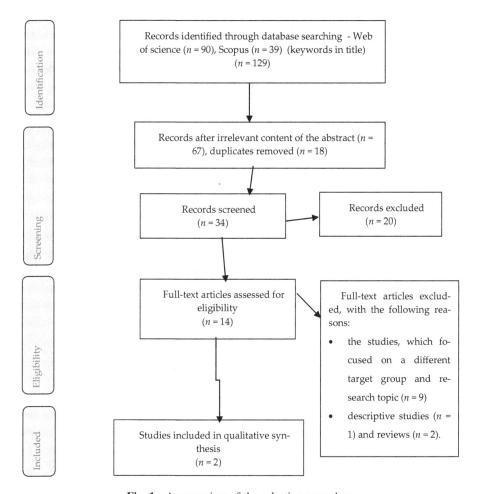

Fig. 1. An overview of the selection procedure

3   Findings and Discussion

The findings reveal that research on the use of technologies in foreign language learning by healthy older individuals is very rare. After a very thorough review of the detected studies, the author found only two studies on the research topic. It was a pilot study by Ware et al. [11], which was of French origin, and Wong et al. [26], which is a joint article of Chinese and Australian researchers. The main topic was learning a foreign language by older healthy individuals and the use of technologies. The study used standardized outcome measures, i.e., standardized tests for measuring cognitive functions, questionnaires, post-intervention, semi-directive interviews, and a content/ theme analysis.

Ware et al. [11] developed a technology-based English training program for 14 older French adults. The program was based on the assumptions provided by Antoniou et al. [23]. These assumptions involved various factors, such as that computer-based language training can be administered anywhere and at any time to suit learner's needs, the content can be adjusted and items can be repeated. In addition, learners can socialize. The average age of the participants was 75 years. The course lasted for four months and consisted of 16 two-hour sessions. The participants found the program feasible, stimulating, amusing, and enjoyable, although some of them had difficulties with English. Overall, it seems that learning a foreign language can be a good thera-peutic and cognitive intervention. Nevertheless, the results also showed the need for computer training and the importance of social ties.

Wong et al. [26] in their prospective randomized controlled study worked with 153 cognitively unimpaired older individuals at the age between 60 and 85 years who were recruited from community centers for older adults in Hong Kong. The subjects were divided into three groups: 1. foreign language group, in which they learned basic English (experimental group); 2. games, in which subjects played cognitively stimu-lating activities, for example, puzzles (active control group); and 3. music appreciation group, in which subjects watched traditional and contemporary Chinese music videos (passive control group). All these intervention trainings lasted up to five hours per week for six months. In the experimental group, subjects used a computer-based language training software called Rosetta Stone, which helps learners speak English in con-versations with bite-sized lessons that focus on delivering spoken words alongside visual and audio cues [27]. Figure 2 below provides an illustration of one of the tasks.

In addition, subjects within each training group met for regular social activities, on average twice a month. The findings of this study show that computer-based foreign language learning and games, but not music appreciation, improved overall cognitive abilities that were maintained at 3 months after training.

The results of the studies described above are in line with the results of other research studies on foreign language learning, such as [9, 12, 28, 29] whose authors also emphasize the role of foreign language studies on the enhancement or maintenance of cognitive functions among healthy elderly people. Research also shows that healthy elderly people' *performance on cognitive tests reflects the predictable consequences of learning on information-processing, and not cognitive decline* [30].

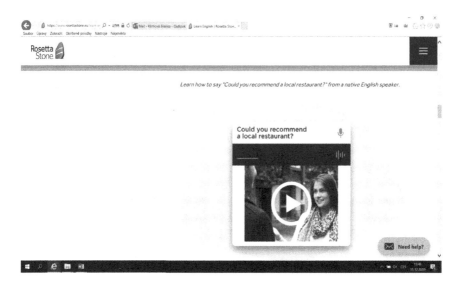

Fig. 2. An example of one of the tasks of Rosetta Stone computer-based language program [27]

Moreover, the use of modern technologies can enable them to escape from their daily routine, as well as to experience challenge and fun [31] and thus, suppress feelings of depression, which is one of the most serious comorbidities in the aging process [32, 33].

Furthermore, social ties among older people are very important [25]. Therefore, technologies should be used as support to face-to-face foreign language classes during which elderly people can get acquainted with their peers and make new social ties. For further related research into the use of mobile technologies in educational process and learning foreign languages see Pikhart [35–37].

The limitations of this article consist in a very small number of studies on the research studies, which indicates that there is an urgent need of research in this area, as well as the fast implementation of cognitive training, such as foreign language learning, among healthy older individuals.

4   Conclusion

Generally, the findings of this review study reveal that the use of computer-based foreign language learning programs among elderly is not common. However, the results of the selected studies show that these computer-based foreign language learning program trainings may generate a lot of benefits for the elderly, especially as far as the enhancement of their cognitive functions and broadened social contacts are concerned. However, more research with larger subject samples needs to be conducted in this area.

Table 1 below then summarizes the main benefits and limitations of the use of computer-based foreign language learning programs by the elderly people.

Table 1. Main benefits and limitations of the use of computer-based foreign language learning programs by the elderly people for their well-being

Benefits	Limitations
• positive impact on human psyche • improvement and/or maintenance of cognitive functions • reduction of anxiety and depression • finding new friends, new social ties • gaining self-confidence • stimulation to learn and practice a foreign language even in an older age	• resistance to work with a computer • worse coordination of movements • difficulties to react fast • vision and hearing constraints • difficulties to remember new words

As Pfenninger and Singleton [34] claim, *L2 acquisition in the third age needs to be regarded not just as a goal in itself but as a means of promoting social interaction and integration, and that it is partly through the stimulation of social well-being that its cognitive effects may potentially be observed.*

Acknowledgements. This study is supported by the SPEV project 2020, run at the Faculty of Informatics and Management, University of Hradec Kralove, Czech Republic. The author thanks Josef Toman for his help with the data collection.

References

1. Interesting New Statistics Reveal Elderly Internet Usage is on the Rise (2019). https://www.stellartransport.com/interesting-new-statistics-reveal-elderly-internet-usage-rise/
2. Klimova, B., Simonova, I., Poulova, P., Truhlarova, Z., Kuca, K.: Older people and their attitude to the use of information and communication technologies – a review study with special focus on the Czech Republic (older people and their attitude to ICT). Educ. Gerontol. **42**(5), 361–369 (2016)
3. Klimova, B., Poulova, P.: Older people and technology acceptance. In: Zhou, J., Salvendy, G. (eds.) ITAP 2018. LNCS, vol. 10926, pp. 85–94. Springer, Cham (2018). https://doi.org/10.1007/978-3-319-92034-4_7
4. Fan, Q.Y.: Utilizing ICT to prevent loneliness and social isolation of the elderly. A literature review. Cuad. Trabajo Soc. **29**(2), 185–200 (2016)
5. Corbett, A., Owen, A., Hampshire, A., Grahn, J., Stenton, R., Dajani, S., et al.: The effect of an online cognitive training package in healthy older adults: an online randomized controlled trial. JAMDA **16**(11), 990–997 (2015)

6. Hyer, L., Scott, C., Atkinson, M.M., Mullen, C.M., Lee, A., Johnson, A., et al.: Cognitive training program to improve working memory in older adults with MCI. Clin. Gerontol. (2016). https://doi.org/10.1080/07317115.2015.1120257

7. McAvinue, L.P., Golemme, M., Castorina, M., Tatti, E., Pigni, F.M., Salomone, S., et al.: An evaluation of a working memory training scheme in older adults. Front. Aging Neurosci. **5**, 20 (2013)

8. Walton, C., Kavanagh, A., Downey, L.A., Lomas, J., Camfield, D.A., Stough, C.: Online cognitive training in healthy older adults: a preliminary study on the effects of single versus multi-domain training. Transl. Neurosci. **6**, 13–19 (2015)

9. Bubbico, G., et al.: Effects of second language learning on the plastic aging brain: functional connectivity, cognitive decline, and reorganization. Front. Neurosci. **13**, 423 (2019)

10. Klimova, B.: Learning a foreign language: a review on recent findings about its effect on the enhancement of cognitive functions among healthy older individuals. Front. Hum. Neurosci. **12**, 305 (2018)

11. Ware, C., Damnee, S., Djabelkhir, L., Cristancho, V., Wu, Y.H., Benovici, J., et al.: Maintaining cognitive functioning in healthy seniors with a technology-based foreign language program: a pilot feasibility study. Front. Aging Neurosci. **9**, 42 (2017)

12. Valis, M., Slaninova, G., Prazak, P., Poulova, P., Kacetl, J., Klimova, B.: Impact of learning a foreign language on the enhancement of cognitive functions among healthy older population. J. Psycholinguist. Res. **48**(6), 1311–1318 (2019)

13. Wakefield, J.: The Generation that Tech Forgot (2015). https://www.bbc.com/news/technology-32511489

14. Borella, E., Carretti, B., Zanoni, G., Zavagnin, M., De Beni, R.: Working memory training in old age: an examination of transfer and maintenance effects. Arch. Clin. Neuropsychol. **28**, 1–17 (2013)

15. Karbach, J., Schubert, T.: Training-induced cognitive and neural plasticity. Front. Hum. Neurosci. **7**, 48 (2013)

16. Sayago, S., Sloan, D., Blat, J.: Everyday use of computer-mediated communication tools and its evolution over time: an ethnographical study with older people. Interact. Comput. **23**, 543–554 (2011)

17. Heart, T., Kalderon, E.: Older adults: are they ready to adopt health-related ICT? Int. J. Med. Inf. **82**, e209–e231 (2013)

18. Colibaba, C.A., Gardikiotis, R., Gheorghiu, I., Colibaba, L.C.: The intergenerational bilfam project and its therapeutical effects on elderly people. In: Proceedings of 2013 E-Health and Bioengineering Conference (EHB) (2013). https://doi.org/10.1109/ehb.2013.6707372

19. Aramendia-Muneta, M.E., Galarza-Lanz, J.R., Mañas-Larraz, M.: e-Bridge to mobility: a non-formal online learning european platform. In: Cases on Informal and Formal E-learning Environments, pp. 81–100 (2013)

20. Yates, L., Kozar, O.: Expanding the horizons of age-related research: a response to the special issue 'complexities and interactions of age in second language learning: broadening the research agenda'. Appl. Linguisti. **38**(2), 258–262 (2017)

21. Tong, C., Sims-Gould, J., McKay, H.: InterACTIVE interpreted interviews (I3): a multi-lingual, mobile method to examine the neighbourhood environment with older adults. Soc. Sci. Med. **168**, 207–213 (2016)

22. Rasskazova, T., Glukhanyuk, N.: Listening as a cognitive age-related resource for foreign language learning. In: Proceedings of INTED 2017: 11th International Technology, Education and Development Conference, pp. 4586–4592 (2017)

23. Antoniou, M., Gunasekera, G., Wong, P.C.M.: Foreign language training as cognitive therapy for age-related cognitive decline: a hypothesis for future research. Neurosci. Biobehav. Rev. **37**(1002), 2689–2698 (2013)

24. Pokrovskaya, E.M., Lychkovskaya, L.E., Molodtsova, V.A.: E-learning course in a foreign language as a means of improving well-being environment for active agers. In: Anikina, Z. (ed.) GGSSH 2019. AISC, vol. 907, pp. 219–223. Springer, Cham (2019). https://doi.org/10. 1007/978-3-030-11473-2_24

25. Liyanagunawardena, T.R., Williams, S.A.: Elderly learners and massive open online courses: a review. Interact. J. Med. Res. **5**(1), e1 (2016)

26. Wong, P.C.M., et al.: Language training leads to global cognitive improvement in older adults: a preliminary study. J. Speech Lang. Hear. Res. **62**(7), 2411–2424 (2019)

27. Roseta Stone (2019). https://www.rosettastone.eu/learn-english/

28. Kliesch, M., Giroud, N., Phenninger, S., Meyer, M.: Research on second language acquisition in old adulthood: what we have and what we need. In: Gabrys-Barker, D. (ed.) Third Age Learners of Foreign Languages. Multilingual Matters, Bristol (2017)

29. Bak, T.H., Long, M.R., Vega-Mendoza, M., Sorace, A.: Novelty, challenge, and practice: the impact of intensive language learning on attentional functions. PLoS ONE **11**(4), e0153485 (2016)

30. Ramscar, M., Hendrix, P., Shaoul, C., Milin, P., Baayen, H.: The myth of cognitive decline: non-linear dynamics of lifelong learning. Top. Cogn. Sci. **6**, 5–42 (2014)

31. Diaz-Orueta, U., Facal, D., Nap, H.H., Ranga, M.M.: What is the key for older people to show interest in playing digital learning games? Initial qualitative findings from the LEAGE project on a multicultural european sample. Games Health J. **1**(2), 115–123 (2012)

32. Popa-Wagner, A., Buga, A.M., Tica, A.A., Albu, C.V.: Perfusion deficits, inflammation and aging precipitate depressive behaviour. Biogerontology **15**(5), 439–448 (2014)

33. Sandu, R.E., Buga, A.M., Uzoni, A., Petcu, E.B., Popa-Wagner, A.: Neuroinflammation and comorbidities are frequently ignored factors in CNS pathology. Neural Regen. Res. **10**(9), 1349–1355 (2015)

34. Phenninger, S.E., Singleton, D.: A critical review of research relating to the learning, use and effects of additional and multiple languages in later life. Lang. Teach. **52**(4), 419–449 (2019)

35. Pikhart, M.: Interculturality in blended learning: challenges of electronic communication. In: Uskov, V.L., Howlett, R.J., Jain, L.C. (eds.) Smart Education and e-Learning 2019. SIST, vol. 144, pp. 97–106. Springer, Singapore (2019). https://doi.org/10.1007/978-981-13-8260-4_9

36. Pikhart, M.: Technology enhanced learning experience in intercultural business communication course: a case study. In: Hao, T., Chen, W., Xie, H., Nadee, W., Lau, R. (eds.) SETE 2018. LNCS, vol. 11284, pp. 41–45. Springer, Cham (2018). https://doi.org/10.1007/978-3-030-03580-8_5

37. Pikhart, M.: Computational linguistics and its implementation in e-learning platforms. In: Pappas, I.O., Mikalef, P., Dwivedi, Y.K., Jaccheri, L., Krogstie, J., Mäntymäki, M. (eds.) I3E 2019. LNCS, vol. 11701, pp. 634–640. Springer, Cham (2019). https://doi.org/10.1007/978-3-030-29374-1_51

Virtual Kayaking: A Local Culture-Based Virtual Reality Paddling Experience

Kao-Hua Liu[1,2(✉)], Tomoya Sasaki[3], Hiroyuki Kajihara[2],
Atsushi Hiyama[3], Masahiko Inami[3], and Chien-Hsu Chen[1,2]

[1] Industrial Design Department, National Cheng Kung University,
Tainan 70101, Taiwan
maarkliu@ide.ncku.edu.tw, chenhsu@mail.ncku.edu.tw
[2] Hierarchical Green-Energy Materials Research Center,
National Cheng Kung University, Tainan 70101, Taiwan
tanibito@gmail.com
[3] Research Center for Advanced Science and Technology,
The University of Tokyo, Tokyo 153-8904, Japan
{tomoya,hiyama,inami}@star.rcast.u-tokyo.ac.jp

Abstract. An activity in a well-designed virtual environment can provide both a short-term emotional impression and an immersive experience related to personal and cultural experience. In this study, we dissect the "Coming-of-Sixteen" (COS) ritual, a local rite of passage that derives from the Tainan city of Taiwan, and meticulously select kayaking activity as the theme among other related activities. Next, we propose a virtual kayaking experience (VKE) system that includes the physical movement of users using virtual reality (VR) techniques. We adopt real scenes of tradition-based culture as the vision of VR to evoke the motivation of the elderly, and also engage bystanders in the experience through these familiar scenes. To evaluate the feasibility of applying the VKE system to the rehabilitation of elderly people, we conduct two formative user-studies. The results suggest that virtual reality technology provides an opportunity to leverage culturally relevant activities, which can enhance the engagement of the elderly rehabilitation.

Keywords: Culture-based VR · Rehabilitation · Physical activity · Research through design

1 Introduction

Over the last few years, the emerging technologies for full-body interactive experiences and games have grown. Technologies that support full-body interaction can generally categorized based on our sensations such as vision, audio, and haptic. In addition to technologies for vision or audio, new mechanisms have been proposed to achieve different types of haptic feedback. Therefore, the integration of technologies for full-body interaction requires various types of hardware and software. These range from HTC Vive [8] for immersive experience to the Nintendo Switch [9], which displays vision on screen for multiplayer, and include systems that aim at providing specific exergames, enabling the engagement of friends, and instructing a group of elders to execute simple movements to maintain their health or rehabilitate them.

© Springer Nature Switzerland AG 2020
Q. Gao and J. Zhou (Eds.): HCII 2020, LNCS 12208, pp. 630–642, 2020.
https://doi.org/10.1007/978-3-030-50249-2_45

A well-designed virtual environment is capable of providing users with not only the short-term emotional impression, but also an immersive experience related to personal [6] and cultural experience as well, even when they only receive feedback in vision [2]. In this study, we propose virtual kayaking experience (VKE), an effort-saving and safe system that provides an immersive first-person kayaking experience (Fig. 1). VKE enhances the sense of presence of virtual kayaking experience by importing real scenes in the vision of users, and it augments the sense of immersion by applying a haptic device that can provide full-body force feedback. Although there are several kayaking games and arcade games nowadays, we aim to realize an advanced virtual kayaking experience by augmenting multimodal feedback and evoking emotional connection by linking traditional spirit. Hence, we designed a visual and haptic feedback system focusing on the essential elements of kayaking activity within the" coming-of-sixteen" (COS) ritual, a local rite of passage that derives from the Tainan city of Taiwan [17].

In this study, we provide three main contributions: (1) a proposed design process to enable kayaking experience in a virtual environment, called VKE; (2) a description of the implementation of the VKE system; and (3) two formative user studies to evaluate the potential of the VKE system for the rehabilitation of elders or as a COS archive approach.

Fig. 1. Virtual kayaking experience (VKE) allows user paddling in virtual environment.

2   Related Work

2.1   Full-Body Interaction in Games and VR Experience

Previous works show that the use of full-body interaction in games and VR experience undeniably benefits many aspects of rehabilitation. First, full-body interaction in games is incipiently proved to allow users to have an advanced experience in the virtual environment [10], effectively enhancing the sense of immersion and increasing the motivation of patients to perform rehabilitation exercise [7, 11]. Second, one of the advantages of employing virtual reality related technologies is that they can accurately instruct users to perform correct movements of health promotion related exercise [12], and moreover visualize the skeleton of users to remind them to maintain specific postures for core muscle training [1]. Last, through positioning technology, it takes no effort to collect the movement data of users [13], and even physical and cognitive hybrid activities data when they are playing games [14]. Consequently, there is great potential in applying full-body interaction to elderly rehabilitation.

Multimodal feedback is a critical factor within full-body interaction. Apart from visual feedback, haptic feedback plays an important role in enhancing the sense of immersion. As a unique approach of providing haptic feedback, some research use propellers or rotors to generate force. Thor's Hammer [19] consists of six motors and propellers in a cube to generate 3-DOF force feedback. LevioPole [4] allows users to sense full-body scale kinesthesia by connecting two rotor units using a rod. These approaches can be integrated into full-body interaction in VR. For example, the virtual super-leaping [3] experience, an immersive virtual experience that provides the feeling of extreme jumping in the sky, uses the method used in LevioPole.

2.2   VR for Culture-Based Experience

VR has great potential for comprehensively presenting nonverbal elements within a scenario, and hence, it is an appropriate story-telling technology to realize experience with abundant contexts, such as sightseeing [21] and museum visits [22]. In addition, a virtual environment provides opportunities to make mistakes without taking any risk in some situations. One such scenario is surgical education [23]. Furthermore, the competence of users can be automatically recorded and measured as data using the VR software [24] for further evaluation. According to these cases, attractive elements exist in high-risk cultural activities, and extreme sports can be abstracted and recompose into safer VR games.

3   Crystallized in Virtual Kayaking Experience

In this section, we thoroughly explain how kayaking is selected as the representative activity of the COS tradition of the Tainan city, and, how we map our sensations to decide the architecture of the VKE system. Finally, appropriate technologies are used to implement the system.

3.1   Cultural Elements Analysis

We applied a cultural design model [5] to decompose the COS culture of the Tainan city. Figure 2 shows the results of our analysis.

The harbor lifestyle of Tainan in the past is believed to give impetus to the COS ritual [18]. Because of the prosperity of the harbor business in the past, child labor was recruited with half pay. Nevertheless, the employer should provide full pay to children once they are 16 years old. Hence, this ritual is important with respect to both spiritual meaning and reality aspects. There are many social expectations within the COS ritual, such as one should pursue their goals with perseverance. Thus, the Tainan government is highly proactive to integrate different activities with this ritual to enrich the cultural deposit. For instance, finishing kayaking in the Tainan canal of 10 km [15, 16] can prove that participants are tough enough to conquer challenges in the future.

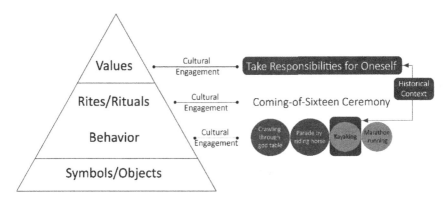

Fig. 2. Analysis of coming-of-sixteen (COS) culture

3.2   Design of Virtual Kayaking Experience System

At the first stage, we aim at realizing kayaking activity in a virtual environment. Therefore, the main challenge is how to kayak while still escaping from limitations of weather and canal conditions. Thus, because of the development of advanced technologies to augment our perceptions in a virtual environment, we decided to adopt VR related techniques to build a VKE system. Furthermore, to provide this multimodality somatic experience into virtual reality, we focus on three key perceptions: vision, haptic, and sense of balance as shown in Fig. 3.

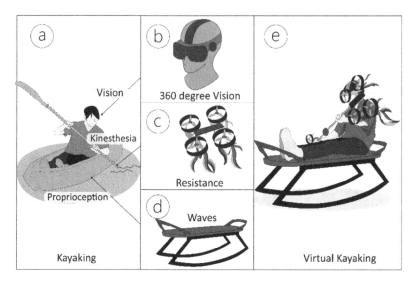

Fig. 3. (a) Some key sensations from real kayaking, and mapping each sensation to feedback elements such as (b) 360-degree vision, (c) resistance of water, and (d) waves of the boat. (e) VKE includes these elements and provides feedback to users using VR techniques.

3.3 Implementation

As shown in Fig. 4, the overall architecture of the proposed VKE system can be generally categorized into hardware and software sections.

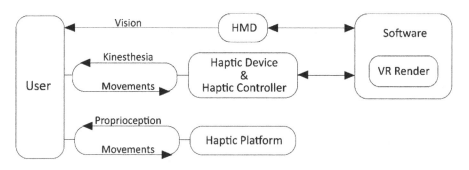

Fig. 4. Components of VKE system

To allow users to intuitively manipulate the rod-like controller and engage bystanders in the VKE system, we utilize the form variation approach to explore the feasible structure of the physical device after sorting critical parameters of the kayaking activity. The vision while kayaking is implemented via the Unity program. Next, a linear force feedback device and a rocking chair are applied as somatic props to increase the sense of immersion, and eventually integrated into the Unity program.

Vision Making. First, to present the real canal scene of Tainan to users, a drone (DJI Mavic Pro) and a 360-degree camera (Insta360 ONE X) were applied to video shooting. Figure 5(a) shows the actual setup of video shooting. The reason why we did not use a remote control boat for shooting is because of the consistency of perceptions. Because the effects of rippling and splashing while paddling must be consistent with the movements of users, we prefer a still water surface rather than a waving surface for easier adjustment of the consistency of vision and movement (Fig. 5(b)). For haptic feedback, a handheld device is employed to provide full-body linear force feedback and interaction in the virtual kayaking activity. We shot 360-degree videos that are arranged and handled using the Unity software, as shown in Fig. 5(c).

Fig. 5. (a) 360-degree camera attached above the drone for video shooting. (b) Drone flying 80 cm above the surface of the river. (c) Unity software handling 360-degree videos for the content

Haptic Devices. This rod-like device consists of two units Fig. 6(a) shows the device components such as propellers, motors, and speed controllers, which are the same as previous work [3]. Benefited from this mechanical design, the handheld device serves as a paddle-like controller in this virtual kayaking experience and provides linear forces to simulate force feedback of paddling. Among the sense of balance, proprioception is the sensation of awareness about an ambient environment, which means the simulation of the unstable surface of the canal is needed for an immersive experience. Therefore, a human-scale interaction rocking chair was designed to create the feeling of unstable waves.

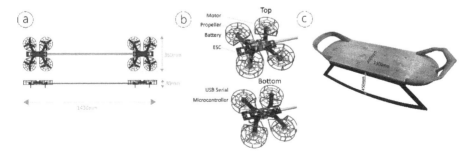

Fig. 6. (a) Size of haptic device. (b) Electric components. (c) Size of rocking chair

4   Formative User Study

The research group has conducted two informal user studies to record and observe how people interact with VKE system (Fig. 7). The first is a public demonstration that is open to any participant to experience it. Next, 9 elderly people with an average age of 72.5 years are recruited to join the second user testing.

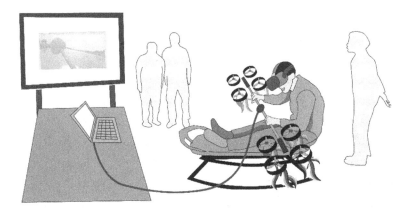

Fig. 7. Setup overview of VKE system for user study

4.1   Public Demonstration

We demonstrated the VKE system at a Taiwan domestic exhibition for a day and had 30 participants experienced it, as shown in Fig. 8. In this event, users were briefly instructed about the experiencing sequences and how to manipulate the haptic device before starting the VKE system. At the beginning stage, the users were explicitly informed to start the experience after the propellers were activated. Next, user should make sure that the paddle is inserted into water to push the water backward to move forward. Based on the on-site observations, three noteworthy behavior patterns were summarized: (1) users from the Tainan city curiously look around from the viewpoint on virtual canoe although they are familiar with this area; (2) some users try to move backwards by reverse stroke; (3) bystanders can interact with user through appropriate human-scale hardware design.

Fig. 8. Bystanders interact with user through human-scale hardware.

4.2   User Study of Elderly People

Participants. Nine participants with an average age of 72.5 years were recruited through friends (three males aged 72–86 years, and six females aged 66–73 years). All of these participants had no experience of using VR and had not previously used force feedback devices. Furthermore, all participants were born residents of the Tainan city, but never attended any kayak activity that was held by the local government. Moreover, all the elderly participants were first timers of paddling or kayaking.

Procedure. Before starting to experience the VKE system, a staff member demonstrates the whole process from wearing the head mounted display to kayaking till the end of experience. Next, the participants are guided one after the other to go through the whole virtual kayaking experience. Finally, a semi-structured interview is conducted to gather feedback from them (Fig. 9).

Fig. 9. (a) Explaining experiment process before conducting formative user study. (b) A researcher demonstrating the whole experience process. (c) Guiding participant to adjust grip width and correcting her posture.

Findings. Three interesting findings were observed from the user study of the elderly people: (1) Cultural Engagement from Local Scene. It was an active atmosphere of discussing the history of the real scene in Tainan while one experienced VKE (Fig. 10(c)). Participants shared their personal memories related to what they saw with others; (2) Priorities of Multimodal Feedback. We found that all participants were focused on what they saw rather than how long they repeatedly paddled; (3) Various Types of Paddling Behavior. An important issue in the VKE interaction process is how a user paddles using a hand-held haptic device. To observe the real behavior patterns of the user, we do not restrict the frequency of paddling, direction, and any other way of using the haptic device (Fig. 10(a)). Therefore, we found that most of the elderly participants had incoordination problem while paddling (Fig. 10(b)). Therefore, it is necessary to fix the hand-held device if the users are required to complete a certain movement perfectly in the rehabilitation scenario.

Fig. 10. (a) Participant kayaking slowly. (b) Participant having incoordination problem while paddling. (c) Bystanders discussing the historical context of this scene.

5   Discussion and Implications

5.1   Virtual Kayaking vs. Kayaking

The focus of our first prototype was not only to simulate real kayaking movements as much the same as possible, but also to explore the feasibility of applying immersive exergames to enhance the motivation of doing exercise with repeated movements. Hence, there is still scope of improvement in the paddling movements design. For example, the proposed VKE system only offers forward paddling feedback, but real kayaking is composed of various movements.

5.2   VKE for Rehabilitation

Our findings from user study indicate some further issues in three aspects of the VKE system, which are usability, engagement, and feasibility of applying VKE in the rehabilitation scenario.

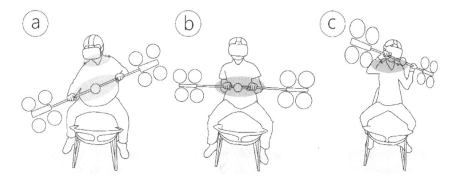

Fig. 11. (a) Standard posture of paddling. (b) Gripping of the narrow width. (c) Shrugging posture of the participant

In terms of usability, first, we designed a standard posture for VKE, as shown in Fig. 11(a). However, users often rotate the haptic device in the wrong direction or grip an inappropriate width of the rod because they are not familiar with kayaking (Fig. 11(b)). Although we already showed users hints in their vision, the results suggest that we need to restrict the way they hold the haptic device by adding a tangible handle on the rod.

In terms of the user engagement, we found that participants paid almost all of their attention to experiencing content, and hence, they often forgot how long they were experiencing it. The elderly participants engaging in our user study showed high acceptability and interests towards our VKE system, which is a positive response to feasibility evaluation. On the other hand, some elders had vision problems, and different types of media to represent vision content are necessary.

In terms of the feasibility of the application, we considered the nature posture of users during the experience. Apart from gripping the rod in wrong direction, participants also shrug while kayaking, which affected the posture and has to be avoided during the experience, as shown in Fig. 11(c). The shrug problem could be solved by placing a stand to support the center of mass of the haptic device. As for the rocking chair, it could not swing naturally because users are used to step on the ground while sitting on the chair. Hence, in future, a pair of the pedal is necessary to better present sense of proprioception.

5.3   Extendibility of the VKE System

One of the purposes of our study was to explore how bystanders interact with users through the design of the VKE system. Hence, we decided to film a well-known local scene as the visual content of the VKE system in an attempt to evoke a cultural connection between users and bystanders. Furthermore, the handle of the rocking chair is designed for bystanders to shake the chair (Fig. 12). Through the experiencing process, a culture-related discussion continuously popped up, which is a good phenomenon for occupational therapists while doing reminiscence therapy with a group of elders. We optimistically anticipate the somatic experience with cultural contents, and exergames can further improve the qualities of both physical rehabilitation and fulfill social needs of the elderly. Moreover, based on our user study, we found that compared to the traditional archiving approaches, such as sound and video files, the integration of surround vision and behavior patterns shifts from passive preservation to active promotion of intangible culture.

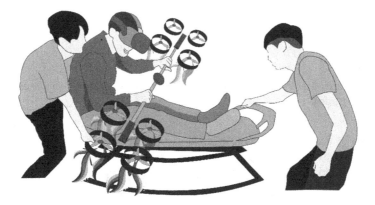

Fig. 12. Rocking chair of VKE system creating another interaction pattern between bystanders and a user.

6   Conclusion

In this study, we proposed VKE that allows users to experience immersive kayaking activity in VR. To abstract the determining factors of real kayaking experience, we decomposed our body feedback of kayaking based on different sensations. We then integrated different technologies in a virtual environment according to selected multimodal feedback, including vision, hearing, haptics, and proprioception. Therefore, this VKE system was accomplished. The VKE system consists of an HMD-based visual feedback and a haptic device that is constructed using two rotor units and a rod to provide full-body scale kinesthesia. Besides, a rocking chair serves as a simulator of waves to provide the sense of proprioception. We described the reasons behind the decision making of the representative activities within the COS tradition to fit properly in the historic context. Furthermore, the technical details of the system were reported to articulate how we achieved our system design. We conducted two formative user studies to evaluate the feedback of users after experiencing the VKE system and observe the behavior pattern of elderly people who are the future target group of the VKE system. The findings were reported and some phenomena from observation were discussed. In future work, we propose some perspectives for improvements: (1) utilize computer graphics-related techniques to enrich the visual content for the historical perspective to evoke more emotional connections; (2) to simplify the manipulation process, the haptic device and rocking chair can be integrated into an arcade game machine form. On the other hand, as for the elderly people, the fixed position of the seat and handle of the haptic device help them to maintain the correct posture while experiencing, such that they can perform the designed rehabilitation movements much more precisely; (3) some elders have vision or hearing problems. Hence, different medias of presenting vision and hearing content are necessary.

Acknowledgments. This work was supported by JST Japan-Taiwan Collaborative Research Program, Grant Number JPMJKB1603, Japan.

References

1. Kojima, T.: Frailty prevention exercise for middle-aged and aged female using motion instruction system in virtual environment. TVPSJ **21**(2), 273–281 (2016)
2. Transforming Elder Care through VR: Nursing Tech Pioneer - Kenta Toshima. https://www3.nhk.or.jp/nhkworld/en/tv/rising/20191128/2042090/. Accessed 28 Nov 2019
3. Sasaki, T., Liu, K.H., Hasegawa, T., Hiyama, A., Inami, M.: Virtual super-leaping: immersive extreme jumping in VR. In: Proceedings of the 10th Augmented Human International Conference on Proceedings, pp. 1–8 (2019)
4. Sasaki, T., Hartanto, R.S., Liu, K.H., Tsuchiya, K., Hiyama, A., Inami, M.: Leviopole: mid-air haptic interactions using multirotor. In: ACM SIGGRAPH 2018 Emerging Technologies on Proceedings, pp. 1–2 (2018)
5. Hung, Y.-H., Li, W.-T., Goh, Y.S.: Integration of characteristics of culture into product design: a perspective from symbolic interactions. In: Rau, P.L.P. (ed.) CCD 2013. LNCS, vol. 8023, pp. 208–217. Springer, Heidelberg (2013). https://doi.org/10.1007/978-3-642-39143-9_23
6. Donahoe, J., Moon, L., VanCleave, K.: Increasing student empathy toward older adults using the virtual dementia tour. J. Bac. Soc. Work **19**(1), S-23 (2014)
7. Tageldeen, M.K., Elamvazuthi, I., Perumal, N., Ganesan, T.: A virtual reality based serious games for rehabilitation of arm. In: 2017 IEEE 3rd International Symposium in Robotics and Manufacturing Automation (ROMA) on Proceedings, pp. 1–6 (2017)
8. HTC, VIVE. https://www.vive.com/. Accessed 10 Feb 2020
9. Nintendo, Nintendo Switch. https://www.nintendo.com/switch/. Accessed 10 Feb 2020
10. Amir, M.H., Quek, A., Sulaiman, N.R.B., See, J.: Duke: enhancing virtual reality-based fps game with full-body interactions. In: Proceedings of 13th International Conference on Advances in Computer Entertainment Technology on Proceedings, pp. 1–6 (2016)
11. Trombetta, M., Henrique, P.P.B., Brum, M.R., Colussi, E.L., De Marchi, A.C.B., Rieder, R.: Motion rehab AVE 3D: a VR-based exergame for post-stroke rehabilitation. Comput. Methods Programs Biomed. **151**, 15–20 (2017)
12. Göbel, S., Hardy, S., Wendel, V., Mehm, F., Steinmetz, R.: Serious games for health: personalized exergames. In: Proceedings of the 18th ACM International Conference on Multimedia on Proceedings, pp. 1663–1666 (2010)
13. Hemmi, K., Kondo, Y., Tobina, T., Nishimura, T.: Floor projection type serious game system for lower limb rehabilitation using image processing. In: Boonyopakorn, P., Meesad, P., Sodsee, S., Unger, H. (eds.) IC2IT 2019. AISC, vol. 936, pp. 119–128. Springer, Cham (2020). https://doi.org/10.1007/978-3-030-19861-9_12
14. Lin, Y.H., Mao, H.F., Tsai, Y.C., Chou, J.J.: Developing a serious game for the elderly to do physical and cognitive hybrid activities. In: Proceedings of 6th International Conference on Serious Games and Applications for Health (SeGAH) on Proceedings, pp. 1–8. IEEE (2018)

15. Bureau of Civil Affairs Tainan City Government, 2013 Kayaking activity News release on official website. https://bca.tainan.gov.tw/News_Content.aspx?n=1056&s=142991. Accessed 19 Feb 2020

16. 2019 Facebook Fanpage of Kayaking activity. https://www.facebook.com/TAINANSIXTEEN/. Accessed 19 Feb 2020

17. Cultural Affairs Bureau Tainan City Government, Tainan's Coming-of-Age Tradition. https://culture.tainan.gov.tw/english/news/index-1.php?m2=93&id=28605. Accessed 19 Feb 2020

18. Kailong Temple, Main Organizer of Coming-of-Sixteen Tradition. http://7mothers.vrbyby.com.tw/scenerys.php. Accessed 19 Feb 2020

19. Heo, S., Chung, C., Lee, G., Wigdor, D.: Thor's hammer: an ungrounded force feedback device utilizing propeller-induced propulsive force. In: Proceedings of the 2018 CHI Conference on Human Factors in Computing Systems on Proceedings, pp. 1–11, April 2018

20. Cheng, A., Yang, L., Andersen, E.: Teaching language and culture with a virtual reality game. In: Proceedings of the 2017 CHI Conference on Human Factors in Computing Systems on Proceedings, pp. 541–549 (2017)

21. Guttentag, D.A.: Virtual reality: applications and implications for tourism. Tourism Manag. 31(5), 637–651 (2010)

22. British Museum offers virtual reality tour of Bronze Age, BBC News. https://www.bbc.com/news/technology-33772694. Accessed 19 Feb 2020

23. Haluck, R.S., Krummel, T.M.: Computers and virtual reality for surgical education in the 21st century. Arch. Surg. 135(7), 786–792 (2000)

24. Ota, D., Loftin, B., Saito, T., Lea, R., Keller, J.: Virtual reality in surgical education. Comput. Biol. Med. 25(2), 127–137 (1995)

Online Cultural Participation in Italy.
The Role of Digital Media Across Generations

Paola Panarese[(⊠)] and Vittoria Azzarita

Sapienza University of Rome, Rome, Italy
{paola.panarese,vittoria.azzarita}@uniromal.it

Abstract. The growing usage of digital technologies is reshaping the way individuals interact with culture, increasing the volume, accessibility and diversity of cultural participation. Although the Internet and digital media make cultural participation easier and more direct, there is also evidence that digital technologies reproduce existing inequalities characteristic of offline cultural participation, which tends to vary considerably with people's education, social position, geographic location and age cohort. Indeed, we cannot deny a certain correspondence between age cohorts and media usage practices.

Adopting a generational cohort approach, the present chapter intends to investigate online cultural practices of members of different cohorts co-present in Italy in order to focus on inter-generational and intra-generational relationships. To explore this topic, we examine data on online cultural participation collected by the Italian National Statistical Institute (ISTAT) within the 2015 edition of *Leisure Time Survey-LTS* (I cittadini e il tempo libero). We use multiple correspondence analysis (MCA) to provide key insights on relationships between categories. Our findings suggest that in Italy, digital media are vehicles of a wider, more diverse and democratic cultural participation among generation cohorts under certain conditions. While the results confirm that digital media open up access to, and participation in a number of cultural activities, they also show that engagement with online cultural practices remains mostly limited to individuals with the motivations and abilities to enjoy the opportunities provided by a digitized society.

Keywords: Cultural participation · Generational cohort · Digital media

1 Introduction

The concept of generation is linked to the idea that sharing a certain 'time' leaves a mark on the ways individuals feel, think and act [16]. At the heart of this idea is the conviction that the events of the historical period in which youth is lived can create a peculiar common conscience [36]. From this perspective, a generation is the product of sharing both the same temporal collocation and a framework in which a set of social actors lives the events and represents itself in a recognizable way [33].

Common social and intellectual changes are necessary to promote the formation of a *unity of generation* [33] or a *we sense* [13]. Shared memory and narratives distinguish one generation from the others, more than contexts or events, which can be common to several generations at the same time [44]. Thus, the members of a generation «not only

© Springer Nature Switzerland AG 2020
Q. Gao and J. Zhou (Eds.): HCII 2020, LNCS 12208, pp. 643–660, 2020.
https://doi.org/10.1007/978-3-030-50249-2_46

have something in common, they have also a (common) sense for the fact that they have something in common» [19, p. 258]. In particular, the sharing of a cultural identity derives from *generational glues* [3], such as:

- generational semantics, i.e. the set of topics, themes, interpretative models, linguistic tools through which it is possible to transform a shared experience into a generational discourse;
- generational *we sense*, that is, having something in common and sharing the awareness of having something in common;
- habitus, as Bourdieu [7] intended it, as a constant system of dispositions to act in a certain way, a collection of social practices through which the experiences, identity and taste of a generation are manifested, marking the 'differences' between generations [1];
- a set of choices that depends on belonging to a generation rather than having common socio-demographic attributes [44].

These glues have strong links with the culture industry and the media, which offer resources to draw on in the process of building identity and generational belonging [12] and in the spread of common narratives [11, 19, 24, 43]. The digital media, in particular, have a dual interactional and representational nature: on the one hand, they connect people within their communicative practices; on the other, they foster narratives and objectification of personal everyday life [39].

This relationship with the media, however, must not be understood deterministically; such a perspective fails to consider the multiple forces that act on a social level, does not take into account the convergence and integration of different communication channels [5, 29], fails to evaluate pitfalls and risks related to an unconscious use of the media [30], and also neglects those reflections on the digital divide [48], affordances [10, 37] and the less expert use of technologies by the youngest which emerge from many studies [12, 30, 31].

Whilst avoiding determinism, we cannot deny a certain correspondence between age cohorts and media usage practices. The media can, with the opportunities and risks they afford, promote social change - in the form of technological change - and characterize a generational shift inherent in other social phenomena. Indeed, the generational approach can help us resist deterministic readings by identifying the mutual influences between media and generations. Thus, generational belonging can produce different cultural appropriations and practices, while the Web can foster new intergenerational communication and cultural forms.

Although in recent years the generational approach has been adopted by many scholars, theoretical assumptions and methodology used to analyze generations appear 'strangely underdeveloped' [22] and there is some difficulty in operationalizing the concept of generational belonging. For example, there is no agreement on the boundaries of different generations [19, 22, 34, 51] and the concepts of cohort and generation are often confused. While cohort refers to (conventional) tools to conduct social studies [14, 41], the idea of generation recalls a temporal sharing and an awareness of belonging [16]. A cohort is a group of people who live the same event at the same time. If this event is birth, we talk about a birth cohort formed by all those who were born within the same time frame (a year or a longer period of time) and who consequently age together [4]. Generational belonging is, instead, self-attributed by members of the generation itself or assigned by members of other generations; its boundaries are mobile [11].

Among social scientists, the use of the terms *generation* and *cohort* as overlapping concepts has prevailed. Moreover, there remains the problem of defining valid criteria for the subdivision of cohorts. Since each cohort is always the result of the interrelation between *agency* and *structure* [14], it is necessary to identify how much a generation depends on its location and how much on its 'actualization', that is, its becoming a generation.

On this basis, the present chapter intends to reconstruct online cultural practices of members of different cohorts co-present in Italy, to focus on inter-generational and intra-generational relationships, in the belief that 'generationality' emerges mainly from comparison with other coexisting generations [36]. We focus on three cohorts: the 'Baby Boomer Generation' (aged 55 to 74 years), 'Generation X' (aged 35 to 54 years), and 'Generation Y' (aged 14 to 34 years). We conceptualize generation from a sociological point of view as "a multi-dimensional concept, where biographical traits shall coexist alongside historical, biographical and cultural ones," including social and economic changes brought by the proliferation of digital technology [2, p. 53]. To this extent, we prefer not to use generation labels like 'Internet Generation' or 'Net Generation', to avoid emphasizing ICTs' role in shaping a generational identity.

We consider people's involvement in online cultural activities as recorded by the Italian National Statistical Institute (ISTAT)'s survey *Leisure Time Survey-LTS* (I cittadini e il tempo libero) and continue with a multiple correspondence analysis (MCA) and a cluster analysis (CA). The aim of the work is to explore patterns of digital media use for cultural purposes (such as creating, downloading and sharing cultural content, watching films and videos online, streaming music, and so on) across generational cohorts in order to address the following research question: are digital technologies enablers of a wider and more diverse online cultural participation, or do they reproduce existing inequalities characteristic of offline cultural participation which tends to vary considerably according to education, social position, geographical location and age cohort?

2   Online Cultural Participation in Europe and Italy: An Overview

Before examining the data, this section summarizes some of the evidence available on the use of ICT in participating in online cultural activities, such as creating, downloading and sharing cultural content, watching films and videos online, streaming music, etc., in Europe and Italy. A key problem in assessing the extent of online cultural engagement is the difficulty in defining the term participation. As Carpentier [15] states, the signifier participation is characterized by a wide variety of meanings. Indeed, in the cultural field, the concept of participation remains an ambiguous umbrella term deployed to cover a multitude of heterogeneous activities and practices [50]. The lack of a common definition puts cultural participation "in a problematic state of flux" [9, p. 4], a situation that is further complicated by the fact that the boundaries of participation change constantly over time [38]. To this extent, the growing usage of digital technologies is reshaping the way individuals interact with culture, increasing the volume, accessibility and diversity of cultural participation [35].

According to the *Indicator Framework on Culture and Democracy* (IFCD), developed by the Council of Europe and the Hertie School of Governance [20], people who participate in culture online do so as consumers and/or producers, often over-lapping (see, for example, the hybrid case of 'prosumer'). In particular, the IFCD distinguishes between 'online cultural participation' and 'online creativity'. The former refers to 'individual online engagement with cultural creations' and includes activities such as reading online newspapers, searching for cultural information, purchasing cultural products, listening to music, watching films and videos online, streaming live concerts, and so on. The latter indicates how people use digital media for distributing their own cultural creations and takes into consideration activities such as producing, uploading and sharing online creative content, editing photos, videos, articles, etc. [20]. Going beyond this distinction, we consider online cultural participation (or engage-ment) as a multi-faceted concept incorporating various kinds of online participation in cultural life that cover both consumption and production behavior.

Although the belief in the capacity of digital media to enhance cultural participation represents a key justification for public investment and cultural policies aiming at building and maintaining inclusive and democratic societies [35], there is also evidence that digital technologies generate "new opportunities for cultural distinction, segmen-tation, and hence inequality" [35, p. 2]. Therefore, on the one hand, the Internet and digital media make cultural participation easier and more direct [6], whilst on the other they "are likely to exacerbate rather than ameliorate existing inequalities in access to culture" [35, p. 2], thereby showing that the ability to use the Internet implies specific skills and knowledge. Consequently, the concept of the so-called 'digital divide' [47–49] has arisen through research that has shown that what people do online increasingly reflects (and exacerbates) offline economic, social, and cultural disparities [25]. As Mihelj, Leguina and Downey [35] pointed out, it is possible to identify three phases of research on 'digital inequality'. In summary, the first level of digital inequality pays significant heed to access to hardware, software and/or the Internet; the second level refers to a skill or knowledge gap in terms of use; while the third level is linked to the previous digital divides and focuses on the consequences of having more or less access, asking which socio-demographic groups are able to benefit more from digital tech-nologies. Similar concerns have been highlighted by the Council of Europe [20], which has included unequal access or participation in online cultural life among the chal-lenges related to digitization. Following the perspective of Brake [8], the Council of Europe [20] defines digital divides not only in terms of 'material' and 'skills access', but also in terms of 'motivational access', in the sense of the desire to use digital tools and 'usage access', which indicates the scope of the use of digital tools in general.

According to the last edition of Eurostat's *Culture statistics*, "new forms of online cultural participation have emerged with the development of digital technologies and the spread of the Internet" [23] Based on information gathered from the annual

Community survey on ICT usage in households and by individuals,[1] data elaborated by Eurostat show that, in 2018, some 72% of EU-28 Internet users (aged 16 to 74 years) watched Internet streamed TV or videos. A similar pattern was observed in 2017 when analyzing the use of the Internet for reading online news sites, newspapers and news magazines (72%). These were considerably higher than the corresponding shares registered for listening to music over the Internet (56%) or playing or downloading games over the Internet (33%). An analysis by age group indicates that there was a relatively wide 'generation gap' in terms of online cultural participation in the EU, revealing that online cultural activities seem to be less attractive for older generations. Indeed, "aside from reading online news sites, newspapers and news magazines, young people (aged 16 to 24 years) in the EU-28 were more likely than older people to make use of the Internet for a wide range of cultural purposes" [23] Thus, in 2018, some 90% of the Internet users in this age group watched streamed TV or videos (compared with 54% of Internet users aged 55 to 74 years), 86% listened to music online (compared with 30%), while 58% played or downloaded games (compared with 20%). Analyzing the data by socio-economic characteristics, it is possible to note that reading online news (2017 data), streaming TV or videos, or listening to online music were more common among Internet users with a tertiary level of educational attainment and with a higher level of household income. By contrast, the share of Internet users playing or downloading games was higher among people with no more than a lower secondary level of educational attainment and was relatively similar across all four income quartiles. In addition, findings about Internet users' involvement in online cultural activities point out a clear gender gap – in favor of men – for all four cultural purposes (i.e. reading online news sites/newspapers/news magazines; watching internet streamed TV channels or videos; listening to music; playing or downloading games) analyzed by Eurostat (with the largest difference recorded for playing or downloading games).

In Italy, this trend is generally confirmed by data collected by the National Statistical Institute (ISTAT) through the survey *Aspects of Daily Life ADL* (Aspetti della vita quotidiana).[2] In general, data indicate that in 2017 young people (aged 15 to 19 years) and men were more likely than average to make use of the Internet and personal computer. Moreover, people living in the Northern and Central regions and in metropolitan areas were more inclined to make use of the Internet and personal computer than individuals living in the South of Italy and in smaller towns [28]. Using the classification developed by ISTAT in its *Annual Report – 2016 Edition*, the study *Internet@Italia 2018*, jointly realized by ISTAT and Fondazione Ugo Bordoni (FUB), provides an overview of the use of the Internet across five different generation groups, named as follows: Reconstruction Generation (including people born in the period

---

[1] As reported by Eurostat's website [23], the data concerning the use of the Internet by individuals cover the adult population within the age range of 16 to 74 years and are focused on the frequency with which the population of those who had used the Internet within the previous three months carried out various activities.

[2] As stated by Cicerchia [17], "started in 1993, this sample survey is a part of an integrated system of social surveys (The Multipurpose Surveys on Household, MSH) and collects fundamental information on the daily life of individuals and their households" (p. 39).

1926–1945), Baby Boomer Generation (including people born in the period 1946–1965), Transition Generation (including people born during the period 1966–1980), Millennium Generation (including people born in the period 1981–1995), and Net Generation (including young people born during the period 1996–2010).[3] Taking into consideration the findings published in that research, it is interesting to note that in Italy, in 2016, the share of population who regularly used the Internet[4] varied widely between generations: 10.4% of individuals belonging to the Reconstruction Generation, 51.9% of Baby-boomers, 76.9% of those from the Transition Generation, 86.1% of Millennials, and 73.6% of young people belonging to the Net Generation [27]. Focusing on regular Internet users, the report registers that, in 2016, the share of Italians who used the Internet for cultural and ludic activities[5] had increased exponentially when compared with 2006, growing from 53% to 81.4%. An analysis by generation group indicates that, in 2016, a growing share of regular Internet users belonging to the Baby Boomer Generation (74.9%) and the Transition Generation (79.6%) used the Internet for cultural purposes, partially bridging the initial gap with the Millennium Generation and registering an increase of 33 and 28 percentage points respectively over the period 2006–2016. In addition, the study highlights a clear relationship between generation group, level of educational attainment, and level of online cultural participation: higher education and younger age tend to be associated with more frequent online cultural participation. In particular, the higher an individual's educational attainments, the more frequently they are likely to engage with culture online. Indeed, in 2016, Baby-boomers with a tertiary level of educational attainment were generally more likely to make use of the Internet for cultural purposes than the average of the same generation group's regular Internet users (84.1% compared with 74.9%). According to this research, it is possible to conclude that education plays a crucial role in bridging the divides across generations [27]. However, at the same time, these findings confirm that level of education and student status are the most important variables in determining the probability of taking part in online cultural activities. In other words, cultural capital is also an important driver of cultural distinction in the online sphere [35].

---

[3] The cohorts are grouped according to having experienced entry into adult life at times that represented a critical change in the *continuum* of the history of Italy [27]. Specifically, 'Reconstruction Generation' is the main protagonist of the post-war period; 'Baby Boomer Generation' includes people who were born during the baby boom following the Second World War and is divided into two sub-groups: the 'commitment group' related to the social battles of the 1970s and the 'identity group' characterised by a strong political affiliation or a vision based on the fulfilment of personal achievements; 'Transition Generation' is the generation that marks the shift from the previous millennium to the actual one; 'Millennium Generation' is the Euro generation; and 'Net Generation' includes people who were born and grew up during the Internet age (*ibidem*).

[4] According to the study, regular Internet users indicates those who had used the Internet within the previous three months [27].

[5] These include activities such as listening to web radios, watching streamed TV, reading online newspapers and magazines, reading or downloading books or e-books, playing games or downloading games, images, books, music, etc. [27].

To provide an in-depth analysis of the reasons for not using the Internet and the perception of the Internet across generations, the study conducted by ISTAT and FUB [27] uses information gathered from the *Leisure Time Survey-LTS* (I cittadini e il tempo libero) – run by ISTAT – which takes into account reasons, interests and passions for a number of activities. By distinguishing 'material reasons' (linked to the cost and availability of digital devices) and 'motivational reasons' (linked to skills, time and interest), the report points out that the highest proportion of people citing material reasons as the principal grounds for not using the Internet was recorded among young people between 6 and 24 years, while motivational reasons (especially, lack of skills and interest) was frequently cited by people aged 45–64 years. Highlighting the presence of digital divides in terms of skills and the desire to use digital tools across generations, the study also indicates the presence of two diametrically opposed perspectives on the Internet. The negative position is summarized by agreement to such concepts of the Internet as a danger; a risk to personal security; a threat to social interactions. In contrast, the positive perspective is characterized by agreement with such ideas as the Internet being useful, pleasant and fun; facilitating people's lives; allowing for better knowledge, etc. From this point of view, it is not surprising to note that students, those with a tertiary level of educational attainment, Millennials and members of the Net Generation tend to stress the positives of digital life, while Internet non-users, those with no more than a primary level of educational qualification and the Reconstruction Generation emphasize the negative aspects of the Internet. The idea of the Web as an essential and vital element of our lives, as expressed by young people, seems to reflect the viewpoint of the Millennium and the Net Generations as the first generations to grow up surrounded by digital media and ubiquitous connections.

3   Methodology

Based on this empirical and theoretical background, and adopting a generational cohort approach, the main question we will attempt to answer is the following: is online cultural participation able to reach and involve wider and more diverse audiences, or does it replicate the same limits of offline cultural participation in terms of education, social position and age?

To explore this topic, we use information gathered by the Italian National Statistical Institute (ISTAT), the only national public organization that collects data on the cultural participation of a representative sample of the Italian population on a regular basis [17]. Specifically, we use quantitative data from the 2015 edition of *Leisure Time Survey-LTS* (I cittadini e il tempo libero), a part of an integrated system of social surveys (The Multipurpose Surveys on Household, MSH) that collects important information on leisure time use and cultural habits and practices of individuals and their households (Ibid.). This is a thematic survey, run by ISTAT, whose first wave took place in 1995 and which was carried out every 5 years until 2006. The 2015 edition focuses on notions, attitudes and behaviors related to the leisure time sphere and investigates in more detail several online cultural practices such as using personal computers and the Internet, watching Internet streamed TV or videos, listening to music over the Internet, reading online newspapers and news magazines, and so on (Ibid.). The information presented throughout this paper is focused on involvement in online cultural activities during the 12 months prior to the survey. The online cultural activities investigated by the survey and covered by our analysis include: using the Internet; using a personal computer; using the PC for creative purposes; watching videos on YouTube or other digital platforms; sharing your own videos or other people's videos; sharing your own photos or other people's photos; editing photos; tagging photos on social media; watching Internet streamed TV; watching movies on a personal computer or smartphone; listening to radio stations over the Internet; listening to music over the Internet; sharing music online; downloading music onto a personal computer or smartphone; reading online newspapers or weekly magazines.

Using a generational cohort approach, we chose to refer our analysis to a subsample ($n = 30,542$) composed of three main generation cohorts in order to avoid an extreme polarization between the oldest respondents and the youngest. Without intending to explore the formation of generation cohorts in Italy, and given the prevalent use of the US segmentation labels widely adopted by many countries [46], the three groups included in our analysis are: the Baby Boomer Generation (born between 1941 and 1960), Generation X (born between 1961 and 1980), and Generation Y (born between 1981 and 2001). As mentioned before, following Aroldi [2], we have preferred not to use generational labels such as the 'Internet Generation' or 'Web Generation' in order to avoid the risk of technological determinism.

For the purpose of reducing the many survey questions about online cultural participation, we used multiple correspondence analysis (MCA), followed by cluster analysis (CA).[6] MCA provides a useful tool to explore data, covering multiple and diverse variables. Specifically, MCA is part of a family of descriptive methods (e.g., clustering, factor analysis, and principal component analysis [PCA]) that reveal patterning in complex datasets, providing key insights on relationships between categories [21]. We selected the aforementioned online cultural activities, generation cohort and educational attainment as active categories. To be more specific, we selected 20 activities, covering a wide range of online cultural and recreational activities, some very popular, like watching videos on YouTube, others minority activities, like watching movies on a smartphone or downloading music to a personal computer. Other socio-demographic characteristics (for example, sex, occupational position, geographic location, degree of urbanization), the self-perception of digital competencies and questions about how respondents learned to use the Internet and the PC had been chosen as supplementary categories, indicating modalities that do not intervene in the determination of axes but are useful for interpreting them.

---

[6] In order to conduct multiple correspondence analysis, we used the software SPAD, which allows us to carry out MCA combined with CA, performed on the factors produced by factor analysis (in our case, we used the first two factors).

4   Findings

Generally, when speaking about digital engagement in Italy, the data show that, in 2015, the share of Generation Y using the Internet within the previous three months was over 90%. This share was over 76% for Generation X and at its lowest for the Baby Boomer Generation (41.1%). A similar pattern was observed when analyzing the use of the personal computer. In 2015, 82.5% of Generation Y had used a personal computer within the previous three months, 68.8% of Generation X and 37.5% of Baby-boomers. The questions asked respondents to self-evaluate their digital competencies from 'very well' to 'with a lot of difficulties', allowing us to differentiate between those that perceive themselves to be skilled digital users and those seeing themselves as insufficiently skilled (with low or no digital competencies at all). Looking at generation cohort, it is possible to note that 36.8% of respondents belonging to Generation Y had a high level of confidence in using the Internet. In comparison, this share was 16.2% for Generation X and only 4.8% for the Baby Boomer Generation. Similarly, high skills in using a personal computer were reported by 28.3% of Generation Y, 13.8% of Generation X and only 4.6% of Baby-boomers, indicating that ageist (self-)stereotypes might occur when we consider ICT use across generations [18]. In addition, the self-perception of having advanced skills in using the Internet and personal computer, although far from exclusively male across generations, might be considered 'masculine', highlighting also the presence of sexist (self-)stereotypes when referring to skills [18, 32, 42]. In this regard, we can define sexist and ageist (self-)stereotypes as inaccurate and biased beliefs about alleged uses of digital devices that homogenize and stigmatize women and older people to the extent that they perceive themselves as insufficiently skilled despite their real level of competences [18, 26, 45]. Although the gender gap in skills was registered across all generation groups, it significantly affected Generation X where male users were noticeably more likely than women to see themselves as advanced ICTs users: 17.6% *vs* 10% (in the case of PC usage) and 20% *vs* 12.6% (in the case of Web usage) (see Tables 1 and 2). Put in these terms, we can see the power of a generation-related digital divide, where Generation Y reveals not only a higher level of engagement in digital activities but also a more balanced usage and perceived level of competence by sex, when compared with Generation X and Baby-boomers.

As mentioned before, our focus in this paper is the generation-digital media-online cultural participation nexus. In conducting multiple correspondence analysis we were interested in observing whether digital media might enable online cultural participation across generations. In our MCA, we interpreted two factors, the first of which accounts for 35.03% of the variance, and the second of which accounts for 7.51%. The total cumulative variance of the first two dimensions was 42.54%.

Figure 1 reveals that on the first factor, arranged from left to right, it is possible to observe the level of online cultural activity across generations. To be more specific, the first factor is composed of a negative semi-axis (on the left) which indicates the online activism of Generation Y, and a positive semi-axis (on the right) which represents the online inactivity of the Baby Boomer Generation, with Generation X in a middle position. This suggests a primary tension between the 'engaged' and 'disengaged' with online culture. The second factor (from top to bottom of Fig. 1) highlights a link between education and forms of online cultural engagement.

Taking into consideration supplementary categories related to the first factor, we can note that members of Generation Y engaged in a large variety of online cultural activities are students, those reporting high digital competencies, people who learned to use the Internet and personal computer at school or with the help of friends. It is interesting to note that most of the forms of online cultural participation on the left of the first axis are forms of engagement which involve people both as consumers and as producers: they include sharing your own videos and photos, editing photos, tagging photos on social media, watching movies on a personal computer or smartphone, listening to music over the Internet, sharing music online and downloading music to a personal computer or smartphone. On the other hand, Baby-boomers, who do not have any sort of engagement with online cultural life, tend to declare as having no digital competencies, retired or housewives. Therefore, data seem to confirm that those who perceive themselves as more digitally literate show the willingness and ability to engage widely with culture through digital communication channels.

Table 1. Contingency table: self-perception of competence level (use of personal computer) * sex * generation cohort (column percentage)

Generation cohort	Self-perception of competence level	Sex		
		Man	Woman	Total
Generation Y	High level	**30.8%**	25.7%	28.4%
	Medium level	50.7%	54.2%	52.4%
	Low level	8.8%	10.5%	9.6%
	No competence	9.7%	9.6%	9.6%
	Total	100.0 (n = 4,228)	100.0 (n = 4,050)	100.0 (n = 8,278)
Generation X	High level	**17.6%**	10.0%	13.8%
	Medium level	40.7%	39.5%	40.0%
	Low level	20.9%	26.5%	23.8%
	No competence	20.8%	24.0%	22.4%
	Total	100.0 (n = 5,878)	100.0 (n = 6,154)	100.0 (n = 12,032)
Baby Boomer Generation	High level	**6.6%**	2.7%	4.6%
	Medium level	**25.2%**	16.9%	20.9%
	Low level	21.1%	18.9%	20.0%
	No competence	47.1%	**61.5%**	54.5%
	Total	100.0 (n = 4,959)	100.0 (n = 5,273)	100.0 (n = 10,232)

Data: Istat, Leisure Time Survey-LTS (I cittadini e il tempo libero), 2015

Table 2. Contingency table: self-perception of competence level (use of the Internet) * sex * generation cohort (column percentage)

Generation cohort	Self-perception of competence level	Sex		
		Man	Woman	Total
Generation Y	High level	**38.6%**	34.9%	*36.8%*
	Medium level	49.2%	51.6%	*50.4%*
	Low level	6.5%	7.7%	*7.1%*
	No competence	5.7%	5.8%	*5.7%*
	Total	*100.0*	*100.0*	*100.0*
		(n = 4,228)	*(n = 4,050)*	*(n = 8,278)*
Generation X	High level	**20.0%**	12.6%	*16.2%*
	Medium level	44.4%	43.2%	*43.8%*
	Low level	19.0%	24.3%	*21.7%*
	No competence	16.6%	19.9%	*18.3%*
	Total	*100.0*	*100.0*	*100.0*
		(n = 5,878)	*(n = 6,154)*	*(n = 12,032)*
Baby Boomer Generation	High level	**6.7%**	3.1%	*4.8%*
	Medium level	**26.7%**	18.8%	*22.6%*
	Low level	19.8%	17.9%	*18.8%*
	No competence	46.8%	**60.2%**	*53.8%*
	Total	*100.0*	*100.0*	*100.0*
		(n = 4,959)	*(n = 5,273)*	*(n = 10,232)*

Data: Istat, Leisure Time Survey-LTS (I cittadini e il tempo libero), 2015

Looking at the second factor, our MCA shows that education affects types of online cultural participation. We find that people with a tertiary level of educational attainment are more likely to read online newspapers or magazines, especially when considering members of Generation X. According to supplementary categories, we can see two opposite conditions: on the one hand, we find people with higher economic and cultural capital in managerial and professional occupations, those living in the North of Italy and in metropolitan areas; on the other hand, there are retired or working-class people, women, people living in the Southern part of the country and in small towns. In this regard, education matters. The effect of education is to determine not only whether individuals participate in online cultural activities but also the types of practice they choose. In general, data suggest that the combination of education and generational membership seems to have very significant impacts on online cultural participation.

Further investigation using cluster analysis gave some additional insights. Table 3 shows four different groups; their characteristics indicate that generational membership and the ability to access and use digital media "are not just occurring side by side; they are likely to interact in their effects" [25, p. 2]. To this extent, we can see that the first cluster is mostly composed of the 'voracious online cultural participants' from Generation Y. They are young people with high levels of confidence in using the Internet and personal computer, who are involved in all forms of online cultural participation considered by our MCA. For this generation, online cultural participation is an everyday activity that implies not only consuming other people's contents but also

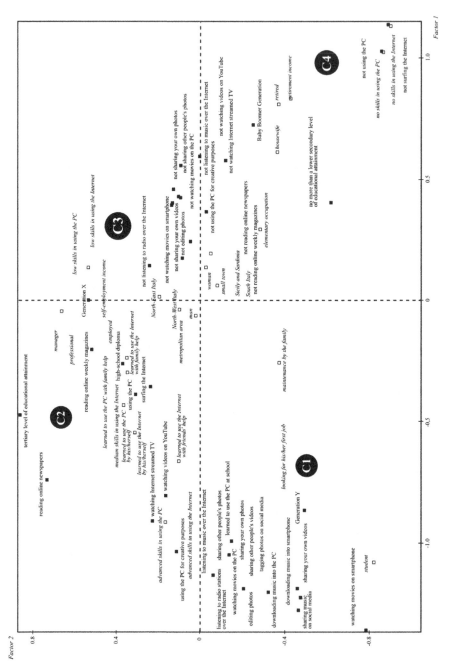

Fig. 1. Multiple correspondence analysis: factors 1 and 2

playing an active and creative role, using digital media to produce and disseminate their own creations.

The second cluster, which represents the 'interested online cultural participants', consists mainly of individuals from Generation X in higher-professional occupations, with university degrees and intermediate or advanced self-reported skills in using digital technologies. These digitalized members of Generation X show great enthusiasm and interest in online cultural activities; they demonstrate an intense involvement very similar to that of Generation Y.

The third and largest cluster (almost one-third of the sample) includes mostly members of Generation X who tend to use the Internet and personal computer but are not involved in any other forms of online cultural engagement. These 'parsimonious online cultural participants' are mainly people with an intermediate level of education (high-school diploma) and with low or medium self-reported digital skills, who seem to interact with digital technologies more frequently for work purposes, showing a very modest degree of online cultural participation.

Finally, the fourth cluster represents the 'digital disengaged'. This cluster is found more in the South of Italy and is characterized by a negative self-assessment of digital skills and a gender gap at the expense of women. It consists mainly of Baby-boomers – be they housewives, retired people or individuals in blue-collar occupations – with low educational attainment, who seem to be at higher risk of digital exclusion. To sum up in the Council of Europe's terms [20], the Italian non-participant remains "disproportionately female, elderly, lower income [and educated] and rural" (pp. 13–14) also in the digital environment. Although in Italy there has been a remarkable reduction in the share of people who have never used the Internet, dropping to 32.7% from 63% of the population over the period 2006–2016 [27], our findings indicate that conditions for online cultural participation are not as simple as Internet access [40].

Table 3. Cluster characteristics: significantly associated categories (arranged in descending order by T-value; supplementary categories in italics)

Cluster
1. Voracious online cultural participants (20.42%)
Downloading music; downloading music to a smartphone; sharing music on social media; listening to music over the Internet; watching movies on a personal computer; sharing your own photos; watching videos on YouTube or other digital platforms; tagging photos on social media; watching Internet streamed TV; watching movies on a smartphone; Generation Y; using a personal computer for creative purposes; sharing other people's videos; editing photos; sharing other people's photos; sharing your own videos; listening to radio stations over the Internet; surfing the Internet; using a personal computer; reading online newspapers; high-school diploma; tertiary level of educational attainment; reading online weekly magazines; *learned to use the Internet by him/herself; self-reported advanced skills in using the Internet; student; learned to use personal computer at school; learned to use personal computer by him/herself; self-reported advanced skills in using personal computer; maintenance by the family; self-reported medium skills in using personal computer; learned to use the Internet with friends' help; self-reported medium skills in using the Internet; looking for his/her first job; learned to use personal computer with family and relatives' help; man; looking for a new job; Central Italy; learned to use the Internet with family and relatives' help; metropolitan area*

(continued)

Table 3. (*continued*)

Cluster

2. Interested online cultural participants (21.15%)

Sharing other people's photos; sharing your own photos; surfing the Internet; sharing other people's videos; watching videos on YouTube or other digital platforms; using personal computer; tagging photos on social media; watching Internet streamed TV; sharing your own videos; listening to music over the Internet; reading online newspapers; Generation X; tertiary level of educational attainment; not watching movies on smartphone; using personal computer for creative purposes; high-school diploma; not listening to radio stations over the Internet; sharing music online; reading online weekly magazines; Generation Y; editing photos; watching movies on personal computer; *learned to use personal computer by him/herself; self-reported medium skills in using the Internet; learned to use personal computer by him/herself; self-reported medium skills in using personal computer; employed; employee income; learned to use the Internet with friends' help; professional; learned to use the Internet with family and relatives' help; self-reported advanced skills in using the Internet; self-reported advanced skills in using personal computer; learned to use personal computer at school; manager; self-employment income; low skills in using personal computer; metropolitan area; North-West Italy; looking for a new job; Central Italy*

3. Parsimonious online cultural participants (31.06%)

Surfing the Internet; not sharing your own photos; not sharing other people's videos; using personal computer; not sharing music on social media; not sharing other people's photos; not tagging photos; not sharing your own videos; not downloading music into personal computer or smartphone; not listening to music over the Internet; not editing photos; not watching movies on personal computer; not watching movies on smartphone; not using personal computer for creative purposes; not listening to radio stations over the Internet; not watching videos on YouTube or other digital platforms; Generation X; high-school diploma; not watching Internet streamed TV; tertiary level of educational attainment; reading online weekly magazines; not reading online newspapers; *self-reported low skills in using the Internet; self-reported low skills in using personal computer; learned to use the Internet with family and relatives' help; employed; professional; self-reported medium skills in using the Web; learned to use personal computer with family and relatives' help; learned to use the Internet by him/herself; employee income; learned to use personal computer by him/herself; self-reported medium skills in using personal computer; not learned to use personal computer at school; manager; self-employment income; North-East Italy; man; North-West Italy*

4. Online culturally disengaged (27.37%)

Not surfing the Internet; Not using personal computer; not watching videos on YouTube or other digital platforms; not listening to music over the Internet; not watching Internet streamed TV; with no more than a lower secondary level of educational attainment; not sharing your own photos; not watching movies on personal computer; not using personal computer for creative purposes; not downloading music into personal computer; Baby Boomer Generation; not sharing other people's photos; not downloading music into smartphone; not sharing music online; not tagging photos on social media; not reading online newspapers; not sharing other people's videos; not sharing your own videos; not watching movies on smartphone; not editing photos; not reading online weekly magazines; *self-reported no skills in using the Internet; self-reported no skills in using personal computer; retirement income; retired; housewife; elementary occupation; South Italy; woman; self-employed; small town; Sicily and Sardinia*

5 Conclusion

Our work represents an attempt to address the question whether digital media are vehicles of wider, more diverse and democratic cultural participation, providing new opportunities of online cultural engagement across generation cohorts and stimulating growing levels of participation across all socio-demographic groups. Although our analysis does not allow us to take into account the latest developments in the field of online cultural participation as it draws on data gathered in 2015 (that is, the most recent version available of ISTAT's *Leisure Time Survey)*, the significant variety of activities provided by the *Leisure Time Survey* dataset offers us the possibility to obtain an overview of how different generational cohorts engage with culture online.

Overall, our findings suggest that in Italy, online cultural participation highlights a polarization between those 'engaged' and 'disengaged' with culture, also in the digital environment. This 'participation gap' [8] reflects the presence of a digital divide among generational cohorts in terms of skills and knowledge at the expense of the lower educated and the elders. While it is not possible to determine respondents' real ability to use the Internet and personal computer, as data are based on a self-assessment of digital skills, our MCA shows that generational cohorts with a higher digital confidence are likely to engage in and with culture online more frequently. To this extent, two general conclusions concerning the role that digital media currently play in stimulating online cultural participation can be drawn. Firstly, the online cultural vitality of Generation Y as well of a significant proportion of Generation X seems to be the effect of familiarity with ICTs and interest in the realm of digital devices, rather than the sole consequence of the ubiquitous presence of digital media. Thus, "instead of cutting dramatically one generation from another, [digital media] are likely to link them" [2, p. 64] when people can develop their capabilities to enjoy the opportunities provided by a growing digital society. These observations reflect the general tendency that older generations seem to be less interested in online cultural activities [23] mainly for 'motivational reasons' [27], revealing that there are several obstacles and struggles with everyday digital interfaces older cohorts still face [40]. Secondly, education emerges as an enabler of online cultural engagement. This is particularly evident when comparing the second cluster with the third one, showing different styles of online cultural participation within the same generational cohort (i.e. Generation X). From this perspective, our analysis suggests that digital media act as a catalyst for individuals to engage in cultural life under certain conditions.

It might be interesting to note that the dataset deployed to conduct our analysis did not allow us to investigate cultural tastes and preferences of respondents more deeply, not asking for example what kinds of videos individuals watch on YouTube, what kinds of photos they share, for what creative purposes they use the PC, or for what reasons people use the Internet. Without being able to capture cultural tastes and appropriations among different cohorts co-present in Italy, analysis is restricted to whether or not people are involved in online cultural activities; yet the fact that most of the culturally engaged indicate a number of activities might imply that digital media seem to foster a greater interest in different types of online creative and artistic activities with the condition of being young, able to use digital technologies or higher educated.

In contrast, this lack of information prevents us from investigating more in detail the participation gap in terms of 'usage divides' among different generational cohorts. As Brake [8] notes, most available statistical datasets consider usage a binary variable and do not break down digital tool usage further into groupings by type or intensity of use. From a cross-generational perspective, it would be useful to know more precisely what kinds of online cultural forms distinguish one generational cohort from the others.

Although our analysis has its limits, our conclusions align with the results of existing studies on the potential negative effects of digital technologies on cultural participation [35]. Indeed, the digital exclusion of Baby-boomers and the partial cultural disengagement of the less privileged members of Generation X confirm that traditionally disadvantaged groups have less capacity to benefit from the increase in the volume and choice of cultural content provided through digital media (Ibid.), reproducing the existing disparities that characterized offline cultural participation. In a digitized society, it is extremely important to keep in mind that digital exclusion puts marginalized and older people at a higher risk of online cultural exclusion, especially in a context defined by increasing socio-economic inequalities and the inevitable process of population ageing due to increased life expectancies, combined with a falling birth rate [25]. To conclude, in Reneland-Forsman's [40] terms, "access to technology is obviously not enough" in order to stimulate online cultural participation, especially "when non-users fail to see the need for or benefit from digital solutions and those still not included are at risk of being further behind" (p. 341).

References

1. Aroldi, P. (ed.): Media + generations. identità generazionali e processi di mediatizzazione. Vita & Pensiero, Milano (2011)
2. Aroldi, P.: Generational belonging between media audiences and ICT users. In: Colombo, F., Fortunati, L. (eds.) Broadband Society and Generational Changes, pp. 51–67. Peter Lang, Frankfurt am Main (2011)
3. Aroldi, P., Ponte, C.: Adolescents of the 1960s and 1970s: an Italian-Portuguese comparison between two generations of audiences. Cyberpsychol. J. Psychosoc. Res. Cyberspace 6(2) (2012). https://cyberpsychology.eu/article/view/4268/3307. Accessed 15 Dec 2019
4. Bagnasco, A., Barbagli, M., Cavalli, A.: Corso di sociologia. Il Mulino, Bologna (1997)
5. Bolter, J.D., Grusin, R.: Remediation. Understanding New Media. The MIT Press, Cambridge (1999)
6. Bonet, L., Négrier, E. (eds.): Breaking the Fourth Wall: Proactive Audiences in the Performing Arts. Kunnskapsverket, Elverum (2018)
7. Bourdieu, P.: Le Sens pratique. Minuit, Paris (1980)
8. Brake, D.R.: Are we all online content creators now? Web 2.0 and digital divides. J. Comput. Mediated Commun. 19(3), 591–609 (2014)
9. Brown, A.S., Novak-Leonard, J.L., Gilbride, S.: Getting in on the Act: How Arts Groups are Creating Opportunities for Active Participation. The James Irvine Foundation, San Francisco (2011)
10. Bucher, T., Helmond, A.: The affordances of social media platforms. In: Burgess, J., Poell, T., Marwick, A. (eds.) The SAGE Handbook of Social Media, pp. 233–253. SAGE Publications, London (2018)

11. Buckingham, D.: Is there a digital generation? In: Buckingham, D., Willett, R. (eds.) Digital Generations: Children, Young People, and New Media, pp. 1–13. Routledge, Abingdon (2013)

12. Buckingham, D.: Youth, Identity, and Digital Media. The MIT Press, Cambridge (2008)

13. Bude, H.: Die Wir-Schicht der Generation. Berliner Journal für Soziologie **7**, 197–204 (1997)

14. Burnett, J.: Generations. The Time Machine in Theory and Practice. Ashgate Publishing Limited, Farnham and Burlington (2010)

15. Carpentier, N.: Media and Participation. A Site of Ideological-Democratic Struggle. Intellect, Bristol (2011)

16. Cavalli, A.: Generazioni. In: AIS (ed.) Mosaico Italia. Lo stato del Paese agli inizi del XXI secolo, pp. 76–78. FrancoAngeli, Milano (2010)

17. Cicerchia, A.: Measuring participation in the arts in Italy. In: Ateca-Amestoy, V.M., Ginsburgh, V., Mazza, I., O'Hagan, J., Prieto-Rodriguez, J. (eds.) Enhancing Participation in the Arts in the EU, pp. 35–49. Springer, Cham (2017). https://doi.org/10.1007/978-3-319-09096-2_3

18. Comunello, F., et al.: Women, youth and everything else: age-based and gendered stereotypes in relation to digital technology among elderly Italian mobile phone users. Media Cult. Soc. **39**(6), 798–815 (2017)

19. Corsten, M.: The time of generations. Time Soc. **8**(2), 249–272 (1999)

20. Council of Europe: Online Participation in Culture And Politics: Towards More Democratic Societies? Printed at the Council of Europe (2018)

21. Di Franco, G.: Corrispondenze multiple e altre tecniche multivariate per variabili categoriali. FrancoAngeli, Milano (2006)

22. Edmunds, J., Turner, B.S.: Global generations: social change in the twentieth century. Br. J. Sociol. **56**(4), 559–577 (2005)

23. Eurostat: culture statistics: 2019 edition. Online publication (2019). https://ec.europa.eu/eurostat/statistics-explained/index.php?title=Culture_statistics_-_use_of_ICT_for_cultural_purposes. Accessed 16 Dec 2019

24. Fanchi, M.G.: Identità mediatiche. Televisione e cinema nelle storie di vita di due generazioni di spettatori. FrancoAngeli, Milano (2002)

25. Fleming, A., Mason, C., Paxton, G.: Discourses of technology, ageing and participation. Palgrave Commun. **4**(54), 1–9 (2018)

26. Iclaves: Women in the digital age: final report. European Union. Iclaves, Universitat Oberta de Catalunya (2018)

27. ISTAT-FUB: Internet@Italia 2018. Domanda e offerta di servizi online e scenari di digitalizzazione. Fondazione Ugo Bordoni, Roma (2018)

28. ISTAT: Annuario Statistico Italiano 2018. Istituto nazionale di statistica, Roma (2018)

29. Jenkins, H.: Fan, Bloggers and Gamers. Exploring the Participatory Culture. New York University Press, New York (2006)

30. Livingstone, S.: Audiences and Publics: When Cultural Engagement Matters for the Public Sphere. Rowe Ltd, Bristol (2005)

31. Livingstone, S., Lievrouw, L.A. (eds.): Handbook of New Media. SAGE, Thousands Oak (2002)

32. López-Sáez, M., et al.: Why don't girls choose technological studies? adolescents' stereotypes and attitudes towards studies related to medicine or engineering. Span. J. Psychol. **14**(1), 74–87 (2011)

33. Mannheim, K.: Das Problem der Generationen. Kölner Vierteljahres Hefte für Soziologie **7** (2), 323–371 (1928)

34. Markert, J.: Demographics of age: generational and cohort confusion. J. Current Issues Res. Advertising **2**(2), 11–25 (2004)
35. Mihelj, S., Leguina, A., Downey, J.: Culture is digital: cultural participation, diversity and the digital divide. New Med. Soc. **21**(7), 1465–1485 (2019)
36. Napoli, A.: Generazioni online. Processi di ri-mediazione identitaria e relazionale nelle pratiche comunicative web-based. FrancoAngeli, Milano (2015)
37. Norman, D.A.: The Design of Everyday Things, 3rd edn. Basic Books, New York (2013)
38. O'Hagan, J.: European statistics on participation in the arts and their international comparability. In: Ateca-Amestoy, V.M., Ginsburgh, V., Mazza, I., O'Hagan, J., Prieto-Rodriguez, J. (eds.) Enhancing Participation in the Arts in the EU, pp. 3–17. Springer, Cham (2017). https://doi.org/10.1007/978-3-319-09096-2_1
39. Pasquali, F., Scifo, B., Vittadini, N. (eds.): Crossmedia Cultures. Giovani e pratiche di consumo digitali. Vita & Pensiero, Milano (2010)
40. Reneland-Forsman, L.: 'Borrowed access' – the struggle of older persons for digital participation. Int. J. Lifelong Educ. **37**(3), 333–344 (2018)
41. Ryder, N.: The cohort as a concept in the study of social change. Am. Soc. Rev. **30**, 843–861 (1997)
42. Sáinz, M., Eccles, J.: Self-concept of computer and math ability: gender implications across time and within ICT studies. J. Vocat. Behav. **80**, 486–499 (2012)
43. Siibak, A., Tamme, V.: Who introduced granny to Facebook? an exploration of everyday family interaction in web-based communication environments. Northern Lights **11**(1), 71–89 (2013)
44. Siibak, A., Vittadini, N.: Editorial: introducing four empirical examples of the "generationing" process. Cyberpsychol. J. Psychosoc. Res. Cyberspace **6**(2) (2012). Article 1
45. StC: Che genere di tecnologie? Ragazze e digitale tra opportunità e rischi. Save the Children Italia, Roma (2018)
46. Ting, H., Lim, T-Y., Cyril de Runb, E., Kohb, H., Sahdan, M.: Are we baby boomers, Gen X and Gen Y? a qualitative inquiry into generation cohorts in Malaysia. Kasetsart J. Soc. Sci. **39**(1), 109–115 (2018)
47. Van Deursen, A., Van Dijk, J.: The digital divide shifts to differences in usage. New Med. Soc. **16**(3), 507–526 (2014)
48. Van Dijk, J., Hacker, K.: The digital divide as a complex and dynamic phenomenon. Inf. Soc. **19**(4), 315–326 (2003)
49. Van Dijk, J.: Digital divide: impact of access. In: Rössler, P. (ed.) The International Encyclopedia of Media Effects. Wiley, London (2017)
50. Walmsley, B.: Audience Engagement in the Performing Arts. A Critical Analysis. Palgrave Macmillan, Switzerland (2019)
51. Wohl, R.: The Generation of 1914. Harvard University Press, Cambridge (1979)

Gameful Tale-Telling and Place-Making from Tourists' Generation to Generation: A Review

Liliana Vale Costa$^{(\boxtimes)}$ ⓘ and Ana Isabel Veloso$^{(\boxtimes)}$ ⓘ

DigiMedia, Department of Communication and Art, University of Aveiro,
Aveiro, Portugal
{lilianavale,aiv}@ua.pt

Abstract. The ageing population and current changes in family structures have led to an increasing interest in forging strong relationships between different generations through leisure travel activities. Despite the popularity of digitally-mediated interventions in the tourism sector, there remains a lack of its use in uniting different generations through tale-telling, place-making and eliciting sustainability with a 'slow tourism' attitude. The aim of this paper is to review the potential use of game storytelling to foster family tourism and unite different generations while in a leisure-travel context. Twenty peer-reviewed papers published between 2000 and 2019 in English-language publications met inclusion criteria. The review presents the potential benefits and requirements for encouraging intergenerational interactions through game storytelling in a tourism setting.

Keywords: Game storytelling · Place-making · Family tourism ·
Intergenerational interactions

1 Introduction

The demographic changes observed over the past few years in society [1], the decline in multigenerational households [2] and the increasing growth of the tourism sector [3] have highlighted the importance of literature on the use of digitally-mediated solutions to foster family togetherness towards oriented-goal leisure activities and memorable experiences [4].

According to the Statistical Office of the European Union (Eurostat) [5], 48.8% of 65+ EU inhabitants adhered to tourism activities in 2015, being a growing market. Furthermore, family travel involving grandparents, adults and children is also estimated to increase, in comparison with other leisure travel forms [6]. If, on the one hand, this type of tourism is motivated by a sense of escapism from daily routines [7], on the other hand, such need to create family memories, encourage family togetherness and transmit some legacy from older to young generations [6] may be unravelled.

Considering that communication between older and younger generations (especially whether there is a familial bond) relies heavily on the use of storytelling [8] and that location-based and alternate reality games may reconfigure the way gamers relate

© Springer Nature Switzerland AG 2020
Q. Gao and J. Zhou (Eds.): HCII 2020, LNCS 12208, pp. 661–672, 2020.
https://doi.org/10.1007/978-3-030-50249-2_47

with the places/environment and technology through context-aware challenges, there is expected potential of games to unite generations in tale-telling and place-making in a slow tourism principle, which may consist of challenges in unexplored places, sustainable consumption and increasing length of stays in order to augment the experience and interaction within the environment.

The aim of this study is to review the potential use of game storytelling to foster family tourism and unite different generations in a tourism setting.

The paper is structured as follows: Section 'Intergenerational Interactions mediated through games' provides a brief overview of the use of games to foster intergenerational interactions. Section 'Games and Tourism' discusses the use of game design applied to the Tourism sector. The Method section covers the purpose and scope of the review, search strategy and data analysis. Finally, the potential benefits and requirements for encouraging intergenerational interactions through game storytelling in a tourism setting are presented.

2 Intergenerational Interactions Mediated Through Games

The past few years have seen a remarkable growth in the cottage industry of brain-training and exergames targeted to all family members [9, 10]; and, subsequently, the evolving strategies adopted by Nintendo and Microsoft to widen their audience with the introduction of both gesture-based and natural interfaces and simplified versions of game controllers [11]. These changes seem to be very promising in order to shorten the gap between young and older generations in terms of their use of technology devices, language, and level of connectedness and intimacy through the use of communal goals, shared challenges, computer-mediated communication and proxemic design.

Given that intergenerational interactions may bring some benefits related to emotional well-being [12, 13], reduction of ageism and change in the representation of age in media [14], discussing the role of digitally-mediated tools in providing communal activities and appealing different age groups is a timely topic in that it may reinforce affiliation, pride and exchange of different knowledge basis [14].

Furthermore, a convergence of interests between different generations – e.g. play age (aged between 3 and 6) or school age (aged between 6 and 12) and old age (aged 65 and over) is likely to occur [15]. According to Erickson's Eight stages of Development [15], narratives may stimulate imagination, initiative and curiosity in play or school ages whereas wisdom and storytelling are valued during the ageing process.

Grandparents often use storytelling in order to communicate family and cultural identity, values, history and traditions [8] to younger generations and with the spread of digital technologies in domestic spaces, merging both physical and digital environments may incite episodic playful interaction and dialogue between different generations, beyond facilitating different types of playing [8: 170]:

- Social Play: This type of playing is social, relative with the interaction with others;
- Fantasy Play: This type of playing is related to the pretended games that are used while playing.

Intergenerational play is commonly intertwined with learning and, therefore, these intergenerational game-mediated interactions are often characterized by the link established between learning and leisure needs [14], personal growth with the transmission of family values, past stories and previous experiences [7] and shared knowledge between different generations [16].

Some examples of Intergenerational Games are QQFarm [7], Age Invaders [17], Save Amaze Princess [18], and Blast from the Past [19], which present the following characteristics: (a) enable social interactions, shared contexts and meeting places; (b) allow computer-mediated communication, peer-to-peer mentoring and scaffolding; (c) Simulate real-life problems with role-playing; (d) Co-design with both generations; (e) Provide easy-to-use interfaces and adaptable game controllers; and (f) Enable passive/watching play.

In general, games can foster intergenerational interactions by meeting the following design features: (a) provide a communal activity that encourages social interactions between different generations; (b) change intergroup anxiety/attitudes through the representation of different generations in the media; (c) act as reminders of the status of family members and close intergenerational gaps through collaborative challenges and negotiations between different generations; (d) enable interaction that involves body language through the use of mimesis and gesture-based interfaces; and (e) balance the users' skills and challenges.

3   Games and Tourism

In the ever-expanding market of tourism, there is an increasing need to find innovative solutions for improving the tourist experience [4], perceived wellbeing [20] and catering for the tourism and leisure needs of different age groups.

In recent years, more attention has been devoted to family travel involving grandparents, adults and children owing to the increase in longevity [6] and the use of digital tools seem to be have the potential to serve theme-park based routes, prolong the sense of the place tourists are visiting, augment the tourists' historical and cultural experiences and facilitate both outdoor activities and sense of attachment with the visited place.

The use of games in non-leisure contexts, specifically in learning and training - e.g. [21, 22] and its importance in behavioral design [23] have been widely discussed, however, its use in such an internally motivated activity as tourism has not been sufficiently clarified in terms of the rationale.

According to Bulencea and Egger [4], the application of game elements and techniques in the tourism context enable the creation of memorable experiences. Although other literature [21, 23, 24] acknowledged its potential and its connection with motivation and behavioral theories, there is no reference to the changes in behavior that may be encouraged with a taken-for-granted internal-rewarding activity. In this research, the use of games in tourism are hypothesized to be a media that can foster a sustainable and slow form of tourism consumption by unravelling unknown places, strengthen the connection with local communities, places, traditions and own identity, and increase the trip length.

Being play and games part of Human nature and important to the individuals' intellectual, physical and social capabilities, the use of games to mediate the interaction of Humans with different places, time (past, present and perceived future) and other identities (cultures, values, traditions), the following characteristics of the Human Species [25, 26] (Fig. 1) may be explored:

Fig. 1. Interlink between 'Homo Ludens' proposed by Huizinga [27] and other characteristics of Human beings that can be encouraged through different game elements

- *Homo faber* refers to the Human capacity to craft and act upon the environment. Action-oriented games (*i.e.* crafting, acquiring and training new skills) can elicit this characteristic;
- *Homo creator* refers to the nature of Humans as God's creation [28]. The tourist-player capacity to reconfigure the place (world-building/place-making) and *modding* (modification) of the digital environment is explored;
- *Homo riddens* is relative to the Human capacity to laugh and games can stimulate fun with animations and pattern-discovering challenges that may pleasure the Human brain [29];
- *Homo curious* refers to the Human capacity to inquire, inform and search information. Problem-solving in games, searching for clues and interpreting the information presented in different points-of-interest (POIs) have the potential of stimulating tourists' curiosity;
- *Homo socius* is relative to the Human capacity to be socially engaged in groups. Social games can bring players together and strengthen the sense of belonging to communities;
- *Homo duplex* refers to the Human capacity to double face that is often explored with role-playing and game avatars;
- *Homo imitans* or the Human capacity to imitate others' behaviors is encouraged through mimetic interfaces, with the use of natural interfaces [11, 25];
- *Homo mendax* refers to the Human capacity to lie – *e.g.* make a bluff, whereas *Homo discerns* is related to the Human capacity to learn and, through games, experiential learning can be created;

- *Homo oeconomics* refers to the Human desire to acquire and maximize wealth and game activities often deal with outcomes and management of resources;
- *Pan narrans and Homo aestheticus* are relative to the Human capacity to tell stories [30] and express emotions. Game narrative and aesthetics engage players in these types of Human species.

The following games are some of the examples that may reinforce the mentioned end-users' identities connection with the environment [31]: (a) Treasure hunts; (b) Mystery games; (c) Living-Action Role Playing (LARPS); (d) Smart Street Sports; (e) Playful Public Performance; and (f) Urban Adventure games. Regarding the application of these games in tourism and place-making, some of the examples are:

- *Hello Lamp Post* [32] and *Urbanimals* [31] use mobile devices in order to forge citizens' interactions with city objects or/and virtual elements 'hidden' in such places and revealed with the use of Augmented Reality, which are associated with a certain piece of information/text message. The interaction with daily-life objects is done through the use of micronarratives;
- *Trip4All* [33] is a virtual assistant addressed to older adults during the tourist experience, using location-based challenges, storytelling and maps;
- *FI-WARE* [34] is a game that uses Point of Insterest (POIs), curiosities, stories and history-based characters (*e.g.* Antoni Gaudi, Joan Miró, Pablo Picasso) in order to offer historical tours about Barcelona.

Other games and gamification apps (e.g. Foursquare and Destination Marketing Organisation - DMO, Brazil Quest Game, Tourism Australia, Jet Off to Geneva or Ski Jump by Visit Norway), in which the tourists' daily lives and own rhythm act as playground.

Overall, games and storytelling may congregate physical and digital environments, gathering pieces of the city stories and 'retell them to pedestrians' [35], inviting communication in the physical space [36], promoting exploration of the places through clue-solving and cryptograms [37]; and creating awareness to the city values (*e.g.* urban governance, sociability, sustainability) and challenges (*e.g.* access to communal facilities, pollution levels) [38].

4   Method

4.1   Purpose and Scope of the Review

The main purpose of this study is to understand the potential of storytelling, games and gamification to foster intergenerational interactions in tourism. The specific goals are to: (a) identify the benefits of game design and storytelling to foster family tourism; and (b) provide examples of the way games can encourage sustainable tourism consumption and tale-telling with local communities and communication between older and younger generations.

4.2   Search Strategy

We searched from March to May 2019 in Scopus, Web of Science and ACM databases for publications in English. We used the search terms "storytelling" AND "tourism" AND ("family" OR "young" OR "old") and the search yielded 151 potentially eligible articles. We excluded those that did not address games or storytelling in an intergenerational tourism setting and with no access- 131 articles - leaving 20.

The inclusion criteria were: (a) being published between 2000 and 2019; and covering (b) the use of games and/or storytelling in a generational and tourism setting.

4.3   Article Coding

We coded the articles according to how game storytelling can foster family tourism and unite different generations while in a leisure-travel context. The following codes were used: (a) benefits and (b) requirements for encouraging intergenerational interactions through game storytelling in a tourism setting.

5   Results

Analysis of the twenty peer-reviewed papers focused on the use of game storytelling to foster family tourism and unite different generations in a tourism setting. Two categories were found: (a) Benefits of using games in multigenerational tourism; and (b) Design requirements.

5.1   Benefits of Using Games in Multigenerational Tourism

A number of benefits that games in multigenerational tourism can ensue have been claimed in the literature review based on pilot projects and user studies. These are:

- Increase the length of visits to a place during off-peak seasons and the distribution of tourists over destinations [39] in order to ensure novelty and sustainable tourism;
- Reinforce the sense of belonging to a community and meet tourists with common interests through computer-mediated communication (CMC), shared information and cooperative challenges;
- Encourage heritage preservation [7, 40] – not only the material one but also the immaterial that is related to ancestral knowledge, often transmitted by older generations via traditions, legends, rituals, practices and lived experiences [41] as a legacy to the next generations;
- Improve the brand image of a destination and ease the tourist's decision-making process by complementing the information provided by Destination Marketing Organizations (DMOs) [39];
- Motivate tourists to explore and learn about the history, geography and identity of different places [42] through the use of stories and contact with locals [42]. The process of storytelling towards a place does not only constitute a way to understand the place but also to identify oneself to it [43] and remembering [42]; and

- Enrich and prolong the travel experience with pre-knowledge about a place [42], stories from multiple visits [42], dissemination of cultural knowledge [44] and shared visibility of a point of interest [45].

5.2 Design Requirements

In terms of the design requirements for encouraging intergenerational interactions through game storytelling in a tourism setting, these are:

- Provide pre-trip marketing campaigns for destinations [39] and routes with certified information – e-guidebooks [39, 44, 46–49] These campaigns can be delivered by social games that are played before arriving at the destination [39];
- Enable access information about the place and planning activities [39, 43, 46] – know the weather forecast, the DMO' s contact information, game tutorials [39], attractions, events, distances [43], opening times, prices, traffic and accessibility [43];
- Compile historical, cultural and entertainment information at a particular Point of Interest [46], recommend places and show POIs contents relative to the tourists' location, context, personality trait and motivation (e.g. curiosity, adventurous) [46];
- Engage tourists in mobile tale-telling about the places in order to make connections with locals [42] and progress in the solution of quests [43] through the use of QR codes, follow the story, online information [39], scanned travel books, guidebooks, travel blogs [39, 44, 46–49]; and/or augmented reality to solve puzzles and riddles related to historical sites [43, 50, 51];
- Enable automatic check-ins [48], clues about sightseeing, history, everyday life in a specific place [45–47, 52], culture and award with special gifts, trophies, stamps of a tour [39] or city keys [45];
- Create awareness towards local resources and suppliers during travel-related activities and walking tours [7, 39];
- Allow gamers' participation, competition and spectatorship [53]. Accessible tourism is an additional concern in order to ensure access to attractions, day tours and commodities [54]; and
- Find pieces of a puzzle, hidden symbols or items, located GPS objects – photos, maps, historical events and characters, creating a sense of 'being there' [55, 56], multiple narrative versions and navigation- challenge-rewards [43].

Overall, there are a number of lessons that can be learned from experiences in those papers, i.e. direct social games to pre-trip marketing trips and routes with certified information; inform about the place and planning activities and context-aware information and recommendations to certain points of interest, activities or events; connect mobile tale-telling to the places to be explored and automatic check-ins; create awareness towards local resources and suppliers; allow passive game-playing; and find pieces of a puzzle, hidden symbols or items, located GPS objects. These recommendations may have an impact on the following: (a) length of visits to a place; (b) sense of belonging to a community through the use of cooperative challenges; (c) heritage preservation; (d) brand image of Destination Marketing Organizations (DMOs); and (e) tourist's motivation to explore, learn and re-visit the place history, geography and identity.

6 Discussion

This review identified 20 papers published between 2000 and 2019, related to the potential benefits and requirements for encouraging intergenerational interactions through game storytelling in a tourism setting.

Most of the reviewed publications highlight its potential to increase the length of visits and the distribution of tourists over destinations and the transmission of traditions and knowledge from older generations and locals to younger generations and tourists.

In fact, (re-) connecting generations and enabling local tourism experiences through communal challenges that rely on a 'hands-on' and 'do-it-yourself' approach (e.g. outdoor activities or pick-your-own food) can, for example, be a way to combine the principles of *Homo faber*, *Homo creator* and *Homo socius*.

Older and younger generations tend to communicate through storytelling, especially whether there is a familial bond. Consequently, the narrative space (*e.g.* location, characters), the timing of the platform (*e.g.* sequential, parallel, non-linear) and level of involvement (*e.g.* passive, active, collaborative) [57] are crucial in deploying media in this tale-telling process with local communities and different generations.

In general, one should take account pre-trip marketing campaigns and tourist's decision making, context-aware information that occur in loco, engage in mobile tale-telling about places and progress in the solutions of quests, enable automatic check-ins and create awareness towards local resources, and find pieces of a puzzle, hidden objects and navigation-challenge-rewards [43].

The review, however, has some limitations considering the fact that the majority of studies that claimed the benefits of their approaches and design recommendations substantiated those claims by conducting user studies with pilot projects and a small number of user studies. Other studies would be needed in order to address concrete ways to engage the different generations through games and digitally-mediated storytelling.

Further work is being carried out to develop games addressed to senior tourism in an online community-based context, under the research project FCT SEDUCE 2.0 – Use of Communication and Information in the miOne online community by senior citizens, POCI-01-0145-FEDER-031696.

Acknowledgements. This work was supported by the research project SEDUCE 2.0 - Use of Communication and Information in the miOne online community by senior citizens. This project is funded by FCT – Fundação para a Ciência e a Tecnologia, I.P., COMPETE 2020, Portugal 2020 and European Union, under the European Regional Development Fund, POCI-01-0145-FEDER-031696 SEDUCE 2.0.

References

1. United Nations, Population. Division of the Department of Economic and Social Affairs of the UN Secretariat. Report of the World Population Prospects: the 2006 Revision (2007). http://pcsi.pa.go.kr/files/wpp2006_highlights.pdf. Accessed 20 May 2019
2. Hakoyama, M., MaloneBeach, E.: Predictors of grandparent–grandchild closeness: an ecological perspective. J. Intergenerational Relat. **11**(1), 32–49 (2013). https://doi.org/10. 1080/15350770.2013.753834
3. Rita, P.: Tourism in the European Union. Int. J. Contemp. Hospitality Manage. **12**(7), 434–436 (2000). https://doi.org/10.1108/09596110010347374
4. Bulencea, P., Egger, R.: Gamification in Tourism: Designing Memorable Experiences. GmbH: Books on Demand (2015)
5. Statistical Office of the European Communities: EUROSTAT: People in EU–Statistics on an Ageing Society. Eurostat, Luxembourg (1990)
6. Schanzel, H., Schänzel, H., Yeoman, I., Backer, E.: Introduction: families in tourism research. In: Schanzel, H., Schänzel, H., Yeoman, I., Backer, E. (eds.) Family Tourism: Multidisciplinary Perspectives, vol. 56. Channel View Publications, Bristol (2012)
7. Che, Y., Lehto, X.Y., Cai, L.A.: Activity pattern of family travelers in a rural area—A case in Southern Indiana. J. Qual. Assur. Hospitality Tourism **13**(2), 103–122 (2012). https://doi. org/10.1080/1528008x.2012.643183
8. Kornhaber, A., Woodward, K.L.: Grandparents, Grandchildren: The Vital Connection. Transaction Publishers, Nova Jersey (1981)
9. Leinonen, M., Koivisto, A., Sirkka, A., Kiili, K.: Designing games for well-being; exergames for elderly people. In: European Conference on Games Based Learning, p. 635. Academic Conferences International Limited, Reading, October 2012
10. Nouchi, R., et al.: Brain training game improves executive functions and processing speed in the elderly: a randomized controlled trial. PLoS ONE **7**(1), e29676 (2012)
11. Juul, J.: A Casual Revolution: Reinventing Video Games and Their Players. Wiley, MIT press, Cambridge (2010)
12. Loos, E.: Designing meaningful intergenerational digital games. In: International Conference on Communication, Media, Technology and Design, pp. 46–51 (2014)
13. Park, A.L.: Do intergenerational activities do any good for older adults well-being? a brief review. J. Gerontol. Geriatr. Res. **3**(5), 181 (2014). https://doi.org/10.4172/2167-7182. 1000181
14. Harwood, J.: Understanding Communication and Aging: Developing Knowledge and Awareness. Sage Publications Ltd, Thousand Oaks (2007)
15. Zastrow, C., Kirst-Ashman, K.: Understanding Human Behavior and the Social Environment. Cengage Learning, Massachussets (2006)
16. Voida, A., Greenberg, S.: Wii all play: the console game as a computational meeting place. In: Human Factors in Computing Systems, pp. 1559–1568. ACM, New York (2009). https:// doi.org/10.1145/1518701.1518940
17. Khoo, E.T., Cheok, D.A.: Designing physical and social intergenerational family entertainment. Interact. Comput. **21**(1), 76–87 (2009). https://doi.org/10.1016/j.intcom. 2008.10.009
18. Al Mahmud, A., Mubin, O., Shahid, S., Martens, J.B.: Designing social games for children and older adults: two related case studies. Entertainment Comput. **1**(3), 147–156 (2010). https://doi.org/10.1016/j.entcom.2010.09.001

19. Vanden Abeele, V., De Schutter, B.: Designing intergenerational play via enactive interaction, competition and acceleration. Pers. Ubiquit. Comput. **14**(5), 425–433 (2010). https://doi.org/10.1007/s00779-009-0262-3
20. Fullagar, S., Markwell, K., Wilson, E.: Starting slow: thinking slow mobilities and experiences. In: Fullagar, S., Markwell, K., Wilson, E. (eds.) Slow Tourism: Experiences and Mobilities, vol. 54. Channel View Publications, Bristol (2012)
21. Kapp, K.M.: The Gamification of Learning and Instruction: Game-Based Methods and Strategies for Training and Education. Wiley, New Jersey (2012)
22. Van Staalduinen, J.P., De Freitas, S.: A game-based learning framework: linking game design and learning. In: Khine, M. (ed.) Learning to Play: Exploring the Future of Education with Video Games, vol. 53, p. 29 (2011)
23. Elias, P., Rajan, N.O., McArthur, K., Dacso, C.C.: InSpire to promote lung assessment in youth: evolving the self-management paradigms of young people with asthma. Medicine 2.0 **2**(1) (2013). http://doi.org/10.2196/med20.2014
24. Werbach, K., Hunter, D.: For the Win: How Game Thinking can Revolutionize Your Business. Wharton Digital Press, Philadelphia (2012)
25. Herrero, L.: Homo Imitans: The Art of Social Infection: Viral Change in Action. MeetingMinds, UK (2011)
26. Romeo, L.: Ecce Homo! A Lexicon of Man. John Benjamins Publishing, Amsterdam (1979)
27. Huizinga, J.: Homo Ludens. Edições 70, Lisboa (2015)
28. Watts, P.M.: Nicolaus Cusanus: A Fifteenth-Century Vision of Man. Studies in the History of Christian Tradition, vol. 30. Brill, Leiden (1982)
29. Koster, R.: Theory of Fun for Game Design. O'Reilly Media Inc., Sebastopol (2013)
30. Benade, R.: Pan Narrans: architecture and 21st century storytelling [Master's Thesis]. University of the Witwatersrand, South Africa (2011). http://wiredspace.wits.ac.za/handle/10539/10657. Accessed 8 Jan 2020
31. Montola, M., Stenros, J., Waern, A.: Pervasive Games: Theory and Design, 1st edn., pp. 1–303. Morgan Kaufmann Publishers, Burlington (2009)
32. Nijholt, A.: Mischief humor in smart and playable cities. In: Nijholt, A. (ed.) Playable Cities. GMSE, pp. 235–253. Springer, Singapore (2017). https://doi.org/10.1007/978-981-10-1962-3_11
33. Signoretti, A., et al.: Trip 4 all: a gamified app to provide a new way to elderly people to travel. Procedia Comput. Sci. **67**, 301–311 (2015). https://doi.org/10.1016/j.procs.2015.09.274
34. Gordillo, A., Gallego, D., Barra, E., Quemada, J.: The city as a learning gamified platform. In: 2013 IEEE Frontiers in Education Conference (FIE), pp. 372–378, October 2013. https://doi.org/10.1109/fie.2013.6684850
35. Bedö, V.: Size and shape of the playing field: research through game design approach. In: Nijholt, A. (ed.) Playable Cities. GMSE, pp. 67–86. Springer, Singapore (2017). https://doi.org/10.1007/978-981-10-1962-3_4
36. Cristie, V., Berger, M.: Game engines for urban exploration: bridging science narrative for broader participants. In: Nijholt, A. (ed.) Playable Cities. GMSE, pp. 87–107. Springer, Singapore (2017). https://doi.org/10.1007/978-981-10-1962-3_5
37. Wolff, A., et al.: Engaging with the smart city through urban data games. In: Nijholt, A. (ed.) Playable Cities. GMSE, pp. 47–66. Springer, Singapore (2017). https://doi.org/10.1007/978-981-10-1962-3_3
38. Schouten, B., Ferri, G., de Lange, M., Millenaar, K.: Games as strong concepts for city-making. In: Nijholt, A. (ed.) Playable Cities. GMSE, pp. 23–45. Springer, Singapore (2017). https://doi.org/10.1007/978-981-10-1962-3_2

39. Garcia, A., Linaza, M.T., Gutierrez, A., Garcia, E.: Gamified mobile experiences: smart technologies for tourism destinations. Tourism Rev. **74**(1), 30–49 (2019). https://doi.org/10.1108/TR-08-2017-0131
40. Cipolla-Ficarra, F.V., Cipolla-Ficarra, M., Harder, T.: Realism and cultural layout in tourism and video games multimedia systems. In: Proceedings of the 1st ACM International Workshop on Communicability Design and Evaluation in Cultural and Ecological Multimedia System, pp. 15–22. ACM, New York, October 2008. https://doi.org/10.1145/1462039.1462043
41. Cunha, C.R., Mendonça, V., Morais, E.P., Carvalho, A.: The role of gamification in material and immaterial cultural heritage. In: Proceedings of the 31st International Business Information Management Association Conference (IBIMA), pp. 6121–6129. International Business Information Management Association (IBIMA), Milan (2018)
42. Bilous, R.H.: Making connections: hearing and sharing M acassan-Y olŋu stories. Asia Pac. Viewpoint **56**(3), 365–379 (2015). https://doi.org/10.1111/apv.12092
43. Díaz, M.G.A., Toftedahl, M., Svensson, T.: The mystery of Elin. Incorporating a city cultural program on history and heritage into a pervasive game. In: Proceedings of the 2014 Conference on Interactive Entertainment, pp. 1–10. ACM, December 2014. https://doi.org/10.1145/2677758.2677768
44. Yu, J., Wang, Q., Chen, H.: Application of kinect-based motion recognition algorithm in cultural tourism. In: Proceedings of the 2018 VII International Conference on Network, Communication and Computing, pp. 307–311. ACM, New York, December 2018. https://doi.org/10.1145/3301326.3301377
45. Costa, P.J.: Map gaming for local promotion. In: Proceedings of the Workshop on Open Source and Design of Communication, pp. 45–48. ACM, New York, November 2010. https://doi.org/10.1145/1936755.1936769
46. Appel, A.P., Candello, H., de Souza, B.S., Andrade, B.D.: Destiny: a cognitive mobile guide for the Olympics. In: Proceedings of the 25th International Conference Companion on World Wide Web, pp. 155–158. International World Wide Web Conferences Steering Committee, April 2016. https://doi.org/10.1145/2872518.2890531
47. Kozak, M.: Family-based travel narratives: confirmatory personal introspection of children's interpretations of their journey to three destinations. J. Hospitality Tourism Manage. **29**, 119–125 (2016). https://doi.org/10.1016/j.jhtm.2016.06.005
48. Sharma, M.P.: Factors affecting the adoption of ICT in hospitality & tourism industry. In: Proceedings of the Second International Conference on Information and Communication Technology for Competitive Strategies, p. 92. ACM, New York, March 2016. https://doi.org/10.1145/2905055.2905151
49. Swacha, J., Muszynska, K.: Towards a generic eGuide gamification framework for tourist attractions. In: Proceedings of the 2018 Annual Symposium on Computer-Human Interaction in Play Companion Extended Abstracts, pp. 619–625. ACM, New York, October 2018. https://doi.org/10.1145/3270316.3271535
50. Doi, S., Wang, Y., Zhao, C., Utsuro, T.: Design of a trivia game for traveling and domestic enjoyment in Japan. In: IMCOM 2017: Proceedings of the 11th International Conference on Ubiquitous Information Management and Communication, pp. 1–6 (2017)
51. Pyae, A., Potter, L.E.: A player engagement model for an augmented reality game: a case of Pokémon go. In: Proceedings of the 28th Australian Conference on Computer-Human Interaction, pp. 11–15. ACM, New York, November 2016. https://doi.org/10.1145/3010915.3010960

52. Yang, C.C., Sia, W.Y., Tseng, Y.C., Chiu, J.C.: Gamification of learning in tourism industry: a case study of Pokémon go. In: Proceedings of the 2018 2nd International Conference on Education and E-Learning, pp. 191–195. ACM, New York, November 2018. https://doi.org/10.1145/3291078.3291113

53. Cox, T., Carter, M., Velloso, E.: Public DisPLAY: social games on interactive public screens. In: Proceedings of the 28th Australian Conference on Computer-Human Interaction, pp. 371–380. ACM, November 2016. https://doi.org/10.1145/3010915.3010917

54. Wan, Y.K.P.: Equal access to integrated resort amenities for people with disabilities. Int. J. Hospitality Tourism Adm. **16**(3), 251–274 (2015). https://doi.org/10.1080/15256480.2015.1054755

55. Bellarbi, A., Domingues, C., Otmane, S., Benbelkacem, S., Dinis, A.: Underwater augmented reality game using the DOLPHYN. In: Proceedings of the 18th ACM Symposium on Virtual Reality Software and Technology, pp. 187–188. ACM, New York, December 2012. https://doi.org/10.1145/2407336.2407372

56. Jang, S.A., Baik, K., Ko, K.H.: Muru in wonderland: an immersive video tour with gameful character interaction for children. In: Proceedings of the 2016 ACM Conference Companion Publication on Designing Interactive Systems, pp. 173–176. ACM, June 2016. https://doi.org/10.1145/2908805.2909417

57. Pratten, R.: Getting Started in Transmedia Storytelling: A Practical Guide for Beginners. CreateSpace, Seattle (2011)

Footour: Designing and Developing a Location-Based Game for Senior Tourism in the miOne Community

Ana Isabel Veloso$^{(\boxtimes)}$ (iD), Diogo Carvalho (iD), João Sampaio (iD),
Sofia Ribeiro (iD), and Liliana Vale Costa (iD)

DigiMedia, Department of Communication and Art, University of Aveiro,
Aveiro, Portugal
{aiv,diogocarvalho28,aurindo,saribeiro,
lilianavale}@ua.pt

Abstract. In a fast-paced and ageing society, the use of digital platforms to foster senior tourism has become a central issue for finding new strategies to engage senior citizens in retirement, usually an experience period of new sensations and family leisure-travel. In fact, senior citizens are a target group that is growing in terms of domestic tourism with longer overnight stays at a destination, in comparison to younger age groups. This paper describes the process of designing, developing and assessing a Location-based Game for Senior Tourism, entitled Footour. Five participants aged between 59 and 72 (M = 68, SD = 4.82) tested one of the routes proposed in the game relative to the Aveiro City, in a tourism setting. Participant observation and questionnaire surveying were employed. The participants were surveyed about travel planning, criteria for visiting a place and game functionalities. Results indicated that they usually choose places with historical settings and search previously about the place and social activities. The following functionalities were found to affect the whole digitally-mediated experience: (a) Association of historical information to Points-of-Interest; (b) Share of resources, status and social activities; and (c) Interlinking past/present photographs and other content to the visited places and routes.

Keywords: Location-based games · Senior tourism · Games · Experience

1 Introduction

Senior tourism has been an ever-expanding market owing to the increasing ageing society [1], the role of family travelling to strengthen local communities [2], a generational connection towards family values [3], and the availability of time and resources to leisure activities in older age [1]. In fact, 48.8% of 65+ EU inhabitants adhered to tourism activities in 2015 and this number is expected to increase over the next years [4], leading to the need of developing new services and products that accommodate senior citizens' needs.

Furthermore, infrastructure, software and platforms have been regarded as a service (IaaS, PaaS and SaaS) in a mobile and networked society and digital applications have not only been omnipresent in domestic spaces but also pervasive [5] in individual's daily life.

© Springer Nature Switzerland AG 2020
Q. Gao and J. Zhou (Eds.): HCII 2020, LNCS 12208, pp. 673–687, 2020.
https://doi.org/10.1007/978-3-030-50249-2_48

On the one hand, this interconnectedness of information and devices has led to the globalization of many sectors [6], including transports and tourism, subsequently having an impact on one's mobility, knowledge of new cultures, pleasure for travelling and quality of life. On the other hand, far too little attention has been paid to the design and use of digitally-mediated products to foster sustainable and cultural tourism in senior citizens.

Alternate Reality Games (ARGs) based on the end-user's location can positively affect intergenerational relationships [7, 8] and, through the use of game elements, a memorable touristic experience can be created [1]. Indeed, ARGs blend physical and digital spaces in order to present context-aware information and present challenges associated to a certain place, augmenting and prolonging the touristic experience [1, 7, 8] in time – pre-experience, *in loco* and post-experience.

The aim of this paper is to identify the functionalities that may affect the whole digitally-mediated touristic experience, describing the process of designing, developing and assessing a location-based game for senior citizens, entitled Footour.

Section 2 covers the use of digital platforms and storytelling in tourism and examples of games in this context. Section 3 presents a location-based game proposal that addresses Senior Tourism – mobile version, desktop and administration tool. Section 4 provides an overview of the game evaluation process and user study, namely, participants' information, research procedures and ethical issues. Finally, Sect. 5 discusses the results and proposes a set of guidelines for developing a location-based game for senior tourism.

2   Background

Over the past years, the use of Information and Communication Technologies (ICT) in the Tourism sector has been a timely topic given globalization [6] and transition to a post-industrial society [9]. In specific, social networks and Search Engine Optimization (SEO) tools have been relevant to promote individual's status and facilitate decision-making [10, 11].

Georeferenced services have also been essential to disseminate touristic information [1] and, subsequently, may connect the end-users, places and environment through the use of street objects, location-based distributed stories, maps and eventual riddles, game invitations and role-playing [7, 12, 13]. Some examples of games that use some of these tools are [12]: (a) Treasure hunts; (b) Mystery games; (c) Live-action role-playing (LARPs); (d) Smart Street Sports; (e) Playful public performance; and (f) Urban Adventure games. These can be alternate and based on location, *i.e.* merging "virtual reality" and "real virtuality" in the player's brain and consider neighborhoods as the game interface [14]. According to McGonigal [15, p.3], ARGs are "an interactive narrative, or immersive drama played out online and in real-world spaces taking over several weeks or months in which hundreds, thousands, or 10's of thousands of players come together online to real play, not role play forming unusually collaborative social networks and working together to solve a mystery or problem that would be absolutely impossible to solve alone."

Given that these types of games merge both physical and digital spaces and map imagery usually communicate the player's space and their negotiations with the environment [16], ARGs have an enormous potential to engage senior citizens in public spaces and contribute to citizen-environment interactions that are often characterized by (a) scaffolding and levels of progression and skill collection; (b) rewards and citizens' involvement in challenges/missions that can have an impact on society; and (c) improve citizens' wellbeing and quality of life.

Regarding Senior Tourism, literature [17–19] suggests that this target group has longer overnight stays at a destination in comparison to younger age groups and often returns to a destination rather than visit a new place [17]. Their motivations to travel are the following: (a) Travel for pleasure, discovery, and learning – 'Novelty seekers' [17, 18]; (b) Spending time with family – 'family travelers' [17, 18]; (c) Travelling for spiritual and intellectual enrichment – 'Active resters' and 'Learners' [17, 18]; (d) Socialization purpose and escape from routine – 'Escapists, Nostalgic and Friendlies' [19]; (e) Access to historic sights and engage in physical activities [17–19] and (f) Prestige – 'Status seekers' [17–19].

For discovery travelling, storytelling is another game element that should be considered in order to ensure the gamer's participation and transmission of memorable experiences and meaning to a place [1]. Indeed, stories associated to travelling experiences are important to long-term memories [20] and may foster the tourist-prosumer role (content consumer and producer), being the basis of both the gamers' observation and intervention in the environment.

In view of all that has been mentioned so far, one may suppose that storytelling, place routes with entry points to unravel the story, progression levels, rewards and context-aware challenges are some of the strategies, in which digitally-mediated interfaces can augment the whole pre-, during and post-experience.

2.1 Related Work

Although there are many digitally-mediated tools applied to the tourism market, its development for senior citizens within the tourism context is still in its infancy. Table 1 is an account of some examples of games that are applied to the tourism sector.

Table 1. Examples of the use of location-based games or gamified apps in Tourism

Designation	Description
Les voies du patrimoine [21]	This app enables young tourists and senior citizens to follow a pre-defined route in Murbach, France. Based on a geolocation system with an audio guide for young and senior citizens, the app unlocks historical information relative to a set of cultural heritage sites. The main functionalities are: Pre-defined thematic routes (*e.g.* Art, Parks…); Geolocation; Levels; Duration and Audio-description
Musement [22]	This app enables the end-user to search for Points of Interest (POI) and plan the routes to try on the next trip. The main functionalities are: Planning trips; Check information about the place; Buy travelling tickets and access to events; and Share doubts about the trip

(continued)

Table 1. (*continued*)

Designation	Description
TripAdvisor [23]	This travel companion is a rating app with place recommendations that enables the end-users to plan their travelling activities and helps the end-users in the decision-making process. The main functionalities are: Planning tools, Trips, Travel recommendations with Points of Interest; Check information about eating places, hotels, museums, among others; Booking; Maps with popular places and attractions; Reviews; Photos; Articles; and Videos
Q-Hawk Sample [24]	This traveler app is under development and targeted to people who want to visit new Points of Interest and find touristic activities and events, based on the selected places and personal interests. The main functionalities are: Access to the tour; and Provide information about events and festivals according to personal interests; Select activities when travelling solo, with friends, as a couple, family or parents; Personalize tours and travel activities
Granada accessible [25]	This app is specifically addressed to people with mobility difficulties. It presents information about the Granada city, Spain and enables the end-users to create the Points of Interest and select the means of transport and mobility difficulties. The main functionalities are: Provide information about the pavement condition; Create a customized route accordingly with the individual's physical condition and mobility
Mapp4all [26]	This app informs the end-user about the location of WCs, assistance points and emergency contacts in order to ensure the tourists' mobility and accessibility relative to a certain place. The main functionalities are: Step-by-step tutorials; Accessibility options; Audio phone; Report a place; and Access information
Les Bons Plans de Barcelone [27]	This app aims to inform the tourist about the place and enables to book the hotel, access the map, and check principal attractions nearby. The main functionalities are: Access to urgent contacts (*e. g.* health centers, firefighters…); Booking hotels; and Access to Points of Interest and services in the city map
Google trips [28]	In this app, it is possible to create trips and recommend routes with Points of Interest based on the end-user's email with their trip and destination. The main functionalities are: Save Points of Interest; Access to map and activities; Detect routes through travel tickets, and Booking
JiTT. Travel Aveiro [29]	JiTT.travel AVEIRO takes place in Aveiro. The main functionalities are: Pre-defined routes based on time, Offline maps; Information about the POI and monuments; Access to emergent contacts; Save visited POI
Ria Aveiro [30]	Ria Aveiro application enables the end-users to choose a particular route with different POI and routes. The main functionalities are: Plan trips and route locations on the map based on distance

(*continued*)

Table 1. (*continued*)

Designation	Description
TravelPlot Porto [31]	TravelPlot introduces a gamified experience that helps to discover the city of Porto, finding treasures in the Points of Interest mentioned in the application In the itineraries, the tourist can choose to follow a route with: (a) the nearest points; (b) points that are on the same route as the Point of Interest where the user is; and (c) visit Points of Interest in chronological order. Finally, the app allows interaction with the app before, during and after the visit
Pokémon GO [32]	This location-based game uses social resources and geo-reference in order to enable gamers' competition and interaction with other end-users in different places. The main functionalities are: Invite friends; Compete; Collect items; and Ranking
Scavify [33]	This app was designed in order to create end-user's experiences that are centered on a set of challenges, a task-based system, points and reward achievement. It was designed to create better experiences for people to explore, learn and interact with the world around them through challenges with geolocation points
The whole story [34]	This app uses augmented reality in order to display the city statues in its female version and report their story. The mains functionalities are: Augmented-reality; Location-based information; and User-generated content

These applications were found by searching on Google Play and Apple Store using the terms "apps" and "tourism" or/and "Aveiro" between January 2019 and March 2019. In brief, these app highlight some important functionalities to incorporate in Footour: (a) Access to a set of Points of Interest and routes; (b) Access to important and urgent information while visiting a place; (d) Provide a set of pre-determined routes based on distance, attractions and pavement conditions; (e) Award the players with points and resources; and (f) Unlock content based on the end-users' location.

3 Footour: A Game Design Proposal for Senior Tourism

3.1 The Mobile Location-Based Game

Footour is a location-based game that aims to foster senior tourism in Aveiro and other cities, through the use of routes with Points of Interest (POI). Each route has a specific theme and narrative associated to the city and each point of interest has a guiding character, mini-games, photos, texts and the possibility of hearing the story associated to the place.

Based on the literature and previous contact with a group of adult learners at a University of Third Age, the design process took into account the following requirements: representation of Points of Interest in a map; such information and important contacts as police, hospital and taxi nearby end-users' location were included; and font's readability and the contrast between main and complementary colours (Fig. 1).

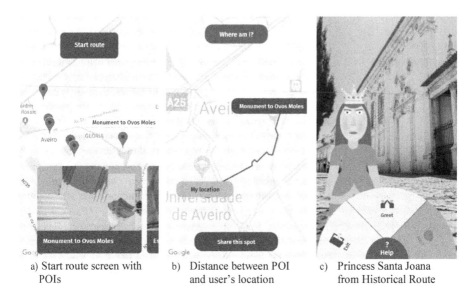

a) Start route screen with   b) Distance between POI   c) Princess Santa Joana
   POIs   and user's location   from Historical Route

Fig. 1. Example of a planning route in Footour

The routes were settled in historical facts and each POI contained information regarding that spot. Additionally, every route had multiple POI near each other given the target audience, who may experience some age-related mobility limitations.

The game was developed in React Native in order to build a cross-platform native game, both available to Android and iOS devices. Figure 2 shows the system architecture.

As shown in Fig. 2, the Expo Software Development Kit (SDK) was used to manage all the assets and simulate the game in own devices. Information about the places, routes and mini-games were stored, using NodeJs and MySQL. Additionally, third party services were accessed via Application Programming Interfaces (APIs) to get the weather, directions (Google Places and Directions API), user's current location through GPS and contacts of specific places in the map. The Desktop game was programmed in React.JS, since this enabled the creation of multiple components to be applied to different web pages. Furthermore, React.JS contains a Virtual DOM, which enabled the creation of fast and scalable web apps.

Relative to the game navigation, a navigation menu was used to access to different game actions. In every game screen, the end-user can go back to the menu and the buttons that are 'call to actions' are highlighted with a different colour. The end-user can also have access to the "Help" menu or, at any time, leave the route.

When the user is moving from one point to another, (s)he can update the current location, using the button "Onde estou?" (Where am I?) and check the distance to the next POI. For each POI, a different character (Fig. 3), who is an ambassador of the chosen route welcomes and guides the player. For example, the historic characters Princess Santa Joana (a), São Gonçalinho (b), João de Aveiro (c), and José Estêvão (d) are the ambassadors of the Historic Route. D. Odília Soares (e) is the ambassador of the Gastronomical Route 'Ovos Moles', whereas Condessa Mumadona (f) guides the player in the Salt Pans Route.

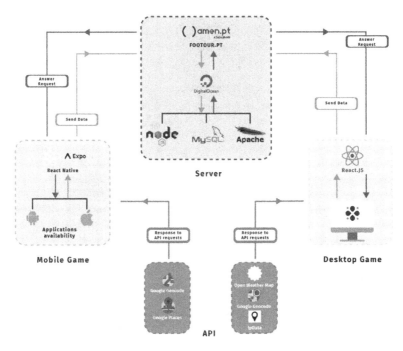

Fig. 2. System Architecture

Fig. 3. Game Characters – Ambassadors of different routes (Princess Santa Joana (a), São Gonçalinho (b), João de Aveiro (c), and José Estêvão (d) – Historical Route; D. Odília Soares (e) – Gastronomical Route 'Ovos Moles'; Condessa Mumadona (f) – Salt Pans Route)

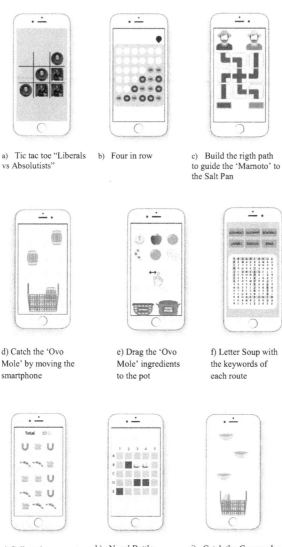

a) Tic tac toe "Liberals vs Absolutists" b) Four in row c) Build the rigth path to guide the 'Marnoto' to the Salt Pan

d) Catch the 'Ovo Mole' by moving the smartphone e) Drag the 'Ovo Mole' ingredients to the pot f) Letter Soup with the keywords of each route

g) Collect the money to Saint Joana offers to the poor people h) Naval Battle i) Catch the *Cavacas* by moving the smartphone

j) Puzzle with Portuguese tiles

Fig. 4. Mini-games

The players' progress in the game is associated with their profile and ranking based on a point and resource-achievement system. Players can, then, use these resources and points achieved during the location-based game experience that occurs *in loco* and reconstruct the place in the Desktop game (post-touristic experience).

Finally, it is worth noting that the game Footour is available with Google Play[1] and each Point of Interest encompasses different mini-games (Fig. 4) – *e.g.* Tic tac toe Absolutism vs Liberalism (Fig. 4-a); Connect Four with pieces allusive to the Aveiro region (Fig. 4-b); Find the way to guide the "Marnoto", a Portuguese name to mean a person who works in salt evaporation (Fig. 4-c); Catch the *Ovo Mole*, traditional candy of Aveiro, moving the smartphone (Fig. 4-d); Drag and drop the ingredients to make the sweet of the city, Ovos Moles (Fig. 4-e); At the end of each route the players are challenge to play a letter soup which contains some keywords of the route that they played (Fig. 4-f); Collect the coins to Saint Joana can help the poor people of Aveiro City (Fig. 4-g); Naval Battle symbolizes the discovery of Congo and Zaire by João Afonso of Aveiro who accompanied Diogo Cão as pilot (Fig. 4-h); Catch the *Cavacas*, another traditional candy of Aveiro which are thrown from the *São Gonçalinho* chapel (Fig. 4-i); Puzzle with Portuguese tiles (Fig. 4-j);

Having presented the mobile location-based game, the following section addresses the desktop game.

3.2   Reconstructing Prior Experiences in a Desktop Game

The desktop game enables players to rebuild the visited city within the mobile game (Fig. 5).[2] It aims to enhance the tourism experience after the player wins the mini-games in a POI.

The resources obtained *in loco* can be used to buy monuments and states of the visited city. In addition, each monument contains different information meant to stimulate a new desire to know.

In a nutshell, this game also contains information about the visited cities, the routes that were performed and the city weather with command voice. The monuments that the player buys can also be customized on certain periods of time - for example, a festive season, Easter, Christmas in order to ensure the players' check-in on the game.

Considering that Tourism entities and other agents are crucial to manage changeable data about the routes, an administration tool was also created. It enables the player to report new Points of Interest, ensuring the game's sustainability and scalability.

---

[1] Footour.   https://play.google.com/store/apps/details?id=com.footour.footour&hl=pt_BR   (Access date: Jan 25, 2019).

[2] Footour Desktop game: www.footour.pt (Access date: Jul 28, 2019).

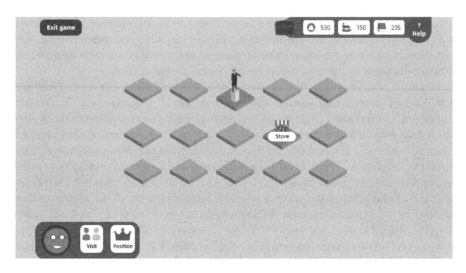

Fig. 5. City reconstruction (Desktop game)

4   Game Evaluation and User Study

Game evaluation was performed using "Heuristic Evaluation" and User Study. In terms of "Heuristic Evaluation", the following principles [35] were used: (a) Match between system and real world by using a language close to the user – *e.g.* feedback; (b) Recognition rather than recall by minimizing players' memory on specific commands to interact with the game and use 'back buttons' to go back to the main menu.

In addition, Footour presents consistency in its identity (*e.g.* colors associated to different actions, typography and iconography). All the icons were designed based on the brand Footour (Fig. 6).

Fig. 6. Iconography and the logo 'Footour'

The procedures undertaken in User Study are addressed in the following subsections.

4.1 The Participants

The initial sample consisted in 10 adult learners, 3 withdrawals due to health reasons, one due to personal reasons and one due to weather conditions, leaving 5 participants aged between 59 and 72 years and old (M = 68, SD = 4,82), who were crucial to detect the game errors [36, 37]. Forty percent are female (N = 2) and sixty percent are male (N = 3). The participants' schooling varies from basic to high school – 40% enrolled High Degree (N = 1), 20% enrolled basic school (N = 1), 20% enrolled High school (N = 1) and 20% other degree (N = 1)

Regarding the daily use of your mobile phone, 60% reported that they use up to 2 h daily (N = 3), 20% answered that they use between 4 to 6 h daily (N = 1) and 20% did not answer (N = 1). They often access the Internet via mobile phone (20% using up to 2 times a day, 20% using 2 to 4 times and 40% between 4 and 6).

4.2 Procedures

The five participants tested the pre-determined gastronomical route 'Ovos Moles', taking into account the distance-time factor. This visit lasted nearly 2 h and involved four Points of Interest (1. Cais da Fonte Nova, 2. Museu da Santa Joana, 3. Confeitaria Peixinho, 4. Praça General Humberto Delgado, and 5. Maria da Apresentação). The activities were the following:

1. Acknowledge the participants' availability to participate in the trip;
2. Help the participants installing and registering the game in their mobile phones;
3. Play the mini-games, win resources and unlock the next POI with additional information about the monuments and local history;
4. Interact with the route ambassador. In this case, D. Odília Soares, who introduced the recipe of the most symbolic sweet in the Aveiro region - 'Ovos Moles';
5. Group discussion and survey about the game-mediated experience. The participants were surveyed about their travel planning activities, criteria used to visit a place, social context when travelling (*e.g.*travel alone, with family, friends…), experience in guided travelling and feedback on the touristic experience, using the game 'Footour.'

Participant observation was also used in order to identify the participants' difficulties when playing the location-based game.

4.3 Ethical Issues

This study is part of the SEDUCE 2.0 research project and it safeguards: (a) The informed consent of the participants aged 55 and over; (b) voluntary participation; (c) involvement of the research team in the process; and (d) that the risks of participating in the study do not outweigh the risks associated with the participants' daily lives.

5 Results

For assessing the participants' game-mediated touristic experience, they were asked about their previous touristic context.

When surveyed about travelling planning, the participants reported that they had the habit of planning their visits by choosing historic sites, trying to anticipate the routes to take, the place events and activities, and group/family and friends' trips. In addition, the participants ascertained that they enjoy group guided tours and most of them seem to have a positive experience with guided tours, in comparison with non-guided ones – e.g. "[...] they are much more interesting"- P03; "They are completely different" – P02; "[...] makes all the difference."- P01.

In response to the participants' criteria for choosing a visiting place, they demonstrated interest in historical routes associated with each POI. These are some of their statements: "I usually search information to know more about the place" – P02; "I look for historical places" – P04; "I visit places with the purpose of visiting friends or family" – P01; and "I search for information before selecting the place to visit."

In general, these pre-touristic experience elements may affect the use of the game Footour *in loco* and justify the relevancy of some game features that were included: Association of POIs to historical micronarratives; Foster social dynamics through the exchange of resources; and Interconnection of places and routes with Past vs Present photos. Relative to the use of the game 'Footour', Table 2 provides a brief overview of the participants' assessment of the game-mediated touristic experience.

As shown in Table 2, most of the participants agree that the game's narrative represented the city history (N = 5, 100%) and that the game connected the present and the past (N = 4, 80%) and invoked memories about Aveiro (N = 4, 80%) with the historical ambassadors of each route.

Table 2. Participants' assessment of the game-mediated touristic experience

	Totally disagree		Disagree		Neutral		Agree		Totally agree		No answer	
	N	%	N	%	N	%	N	%	N	%	N	%
I preferred to visit Aveiro with game than without game	0	0	0	0	1	20	2	40	1	20	1	20
The narrative represented the city's history	0	0	0	0	0	0	3	60	2	40	0	0
The game enabled me to discover new history facts about Aveiro	0	0	0	0	1	20	2	40	2	40	0	0
The game connected the present and the past	0	0	0	0	1	20	4	80	0	0	0	0
The game invoked past memories about Aveiro	0	0	0	0	1	20	2	40	1	20	1	20

(continued)

Table 2. (*continued*)

	Totally disagree		Disagree		Neutral		Agree		Totally agree		No answer	
	N	%	N	%	N	%	N	%	N	%	N	%
The resources "Salt, food and knowledge" encouraged me to check my game performance"	0	0	0	0	1	20	2	40	1	20	1	20
I identified myself with the motivations and the story of D. Odília Soares	0	0	0	0	0	0	5	100	0	0	0	0
I used the 'Help' button when I had doubts	0	0	0	0	1	20	1	20	1	20	1	20
The mini-games motivated me to visit different places in Aveiro	0	0	0	0	1	20	2	40	2	40	1	20
The pre-determined routes enabled me to discover traditional and regional products	0	0	0	0	0	0	2	40	2	40	1	20
I was frustrated when playing the game	0	0	2	20	2	40	0	0	2	40	0	0
I lost the track of time	0	0	1	20	1	20	0	0	0	0	2	40
Arriving to the POIs was easy	0	0	0	0	0	0	1	20	3	60	1	20

6 Discussion and Future Work

The project set out to identify the functionalities that may affect the whole digitally-mediated touristic experience, describing the process of designing, developing and assessing a location-based game for senior citizens, entitled Footour.

Results indicated that senior citizens usually choose places with historical settings and search previously about the place and social activities in a touristic setting. The following functionalities were found to affect the whole digitally-mediated experience: (a) Association of historical information to Points-of-Interest; (b) Share of resources, status and social activities; and (c) Interlinking past/present photographs and other content to the visited places and routes.

A limitation of this study is that a small and convenience sample was used and, therefore, results should be interpreted with caution. Further research is required to determine the game functionalities that are being used in pre-, *in loco*, and post-touristic experience and extend it to other places and contexts.

Acknowledgements. This work was supported by the research project SEDUCE 2.0 - Use of Communication and Information in the miOne online community by senior citizens. This project is funded by FCT – Fundação para a Ciência e a Tecnologia, I.P., COMPETE 2020, Portugal 2020 and European Union, under the European Regional Development Fund, POCI-01-0145-FEDER-031696 SEDUCE 2.0.

References

1. Bulencea, P., Egger, R.: Gamification in Tourism. Books on Demand, Norderstedt (2015)
2. Schänzel, H., Yeoman, I., Backer, E.: Intoduction: families in tourism research. In: Schänzel, H., Yeoman, I., Backer, E. (eds.) Family Tourism: Multidisciplinary Perspectives, pp. 1–10. Channel View Publications, Bristol (2012)
3. Chen, Y., Lehto, X.Y., Cai, L.A.: Activity pattern of family travelers in a rural area—a case in Southern Indiana. J. Qual. Assur. Hospitality Tourism 13(2), 103–122 (2012). https://doi.org/10.1080/1528008x.2012.643183
4. Statistical Office of the European Communities.: EUROSTAT: People in EU–Statistics on an ageing society, Eurostat, Luxembourg (1990)
5. De Schutter, B., Brown, J., Abeele, V.: The domestication of digital games in the lives of older adults. New Med. Soc. 17(7), 1170–1186 (2014). https://doi.org/10.1177/1461444814522945
6. Castells, M.: The Internet Galaxy: Reflections on the Internet, Business, and Society. Oxford University Press, Oxford (2004)
7. Costa, L., Veloso, A.I.: Alternate reality games and intergenerational learning. In: Conferência de Ciências e Artes dos Videojogos, IPCA, Barcelos, Portugal (2014). https://doi.org/10.13140/rg.2.1.4397.8961
8. Hausknecht, S., Neustaedter, C., Kaufman, D.: Blurring the lines of age: intergenerational collaboration in alternate reality games. In: Romero, M., Sawchuk, K., Blat, J., Sayago, S., Ouellet, H. (eds.) Game-Based Learning Across the Lifespan. AGL, pp. 47–64. Springer, Cham (2017). https://doi.org/10.1007/978-3-319-41797-4_4
9. Tofler, A.: The Third Wave. Bantman Books, New York (1984)
10. Bing, P., Zheng, X., Law, R., Fesenmaier, D.: The dynamics of search engine marketing for tourist destinations. J. Travel Res. 50(4), 365–377 (2010). https://doi.org/10.1177/0047287510369558
11. Xiang, Z., Gretzel, U.: Role of social media in online travel information search. Tourism Manage. 31(2), 179–188 (2010). https://doi.org/10.1016/j.tourman.2009.02.016
12. Montola, M., Stenros, J., Waern, A.: Pervasive Games: Theory and Design, 1st edn, pp. 1–303. Morgan Kaufmann Publishers, Burlington (2009)
13. Klausen, M.: Re-enchanting the city: hybrid space, affect and playful performance in geocaching, a location-based mobile game. J. Urban Cult. Stud. 1(2), 193–213 (2014). https://doi.org/10.1386/jucs.1.2.193_1
14. Gallagher, N., et al.: Neighborhood factors relevant for walking in older, urban, African American adults. J. Aging Phys. Act. 18(1), 99–115 (2010). https://doi.org/10.1123/japa.18.1.99
15. McGonigal, J.: Reality is Broken: Why Games Make us Better and How They can Change the World. Penguin Books, London
16. Costa, L.V., Veloso, A.I., Mealha, Ó.: A review of proxemics in 'smart game-playing'. In: Mealha, Ó., Divitini, M., Rehm, M. (eds.) SLERD 2017. SIST, vol. 80, pp. 219–226. Springer, Cham (2018). https://doi.org/10.1007/978-3-319-61322-2_22
17. Lieux, E., Weaver, P., McCleary, W.: Lodging preferences of the senior tourism market. Ann. Tourism Res. 21(4), 712–728 (1994). https://doi.org/10.1016/0160-7383(94)90079-5
18. Shoemaker, S.: Segmentation of the senior pleasure travel market. J. Travel Res. 27(3), 14–21 (1989). https://doi.org/10.1177/004728758902700304
19. Cleaver, M., Muller, T., Ruys, H., Wei, S.: Tourism product development for the senior market, based on travel-motive. Tourism Recreation Res. 24(1), 5–11 (1999). https://doi.org/10.1080/02508281.1999.11014852

20. Tung, V.W.S., Ritchie, J.R.B.: Exploring the essence of memorable tourism experiences. Ann. Tourism Res. **38**(4), 1367–1386 (2011). https://doi.org/10.1016/j.annals.2011.03.009
21. Les voies du patrimoine GooglePlay Homepage. http://bit.do/eMhtz. Accessed 29 July 2019
22. Musement GooglePlay Homepage. http://bit.do/eMhuK. Accessed 29 July 2019
23. TripAdvisor GooglePlay Homepage. http://bit.do/eMhvi. Accessed 29 July 2019
24. Q-Hawk Sample GooglePlay Homepage. http://bit.do/eMhvv. Accessed 29 July 2019
25. Granada Accessible GooglePlay Homepage. http://bit.do/eMhzu. Accessed 29 July 2019
26. Map4all GooglePlay Homepage. http://bit.do/eMhzT. Accessed 29 July 2019
27. Les Bons Plans de Barcelone GooglePlay Homepage. http://bit.do/eMhAe. Accessed 29 July 2019
28. Google Trips GooglePlay Homepage. http://bit.do/eMhAr. Accessed 29 July 2019
29. JiTT.travel AVEIRO GooglePlay Homepage. http://bit.do/eMhAN. Accessed 29 July 2019
30. Ria Aveiro GooglePlay Homepage. http://bit.do/eMhCD. Accessed 29 July 2019
31. TravelPlot Porto GooglePlay Homepage. http://bit.do/eMigq. Accessed 29 July 2019
32. Pokémon GO GooglePlay Homepage. http://bit.do/eMihq. Accessed 29 July 2019
33. Scavify GooglePlay Homepage. http://bit.do/eMihF. Accessed 29 July 2019
34. The Whole Story GooglePlay Homepage. http://bit.do/eMih7. Accessed 29 July 2019
35. Nielsen, J., Molich, R.: Heuristic evaluation of user interfaces. In: Proceedings of the SIGCHI Conference on Human Factors in Computing Systems Empowering People – CHI 1990 (1990). https://doi.org/10.1145/97243.97281
36. Barnum, C., et al.: The "Magic Number 5": is it enough for web testing? In: CHI 2003 Extended Abstracts on Human Factors in Computing Systems - CHI 2003, pp. 698–699, Lauderdale, Florida, 05–10 April 2003. https://doi.org/10.1145/765891.765936
37. Virzi, R.A.: Refining the test phase of usability evaluation: how many subjects is enough? Hum. Factors J. Hum. Factors Ergon. Soc. **34**(4), 457–468 (1992). https://doi.org/10.1177/001872089203400407

Communicating a Scattered Cultural Urban Event: A Survey on User Needs Across Generations

Valentina Volpi[(⊠)], Antonio Opromolla, and Carlo Maria Medaglia

Link Campus University, Via del Casale di San Pio V 44, 00165 Rome, Italy
{v.volpi,a.opromolla,c.medaglia}@unilink.it

Abstract. In public urban spaces different generations meet and eventually end up by sharing the same kind of activities. Nowadays, more occasions of encounter are generated by a widespread push to the re-appropriation of urban spaces for green, social and inclusive aims, so creating sustainable urban ecosystems. Information and Communication Technologies scattered in the urban environment boost these processes by supporting the user experience in different kinds of services. For example, in the transport sector several digital technologies allow the use of shared mobility services and sustain other kinds of more sustainable behaviors for travelers both improving their mobility experience and motivating them towards a common green goal. According to this scenario, the paper examines the physical and digital media and services that might support the user experience during a scattered cultural urban event. Indeed, events that concern different urban spaces at the same times require different kinds of efforts by the attendants, from retrieving information about the available sites, to getting the indication on how to reach them. However, different habits and needs emerge according to the different age of the attendants. The paper shows the results of a survey administered to a group of people from different ages attending a cultural event in Rome. The study analyzes the kind of media and services people used and suggested to retrieve information about the event. Then it envisions some opportunities that emerge in creating services supporting the communication and the user experience of the event, and of the city as well.

Keywords: Generational differences in IT use · Multimedia design for the elderly · Human smart city · Urban user experience · Social innovation

1 Introduction

Cities host and become interfaces for different social and cultural activities which imply the mixed use of urban spaces. The civic mixing [1] generated by the sharing of spaces, especially the public ones, created connections between groups with different backgrounds and ages, feeding a social variety and a thriving public life that is vital for the city itself. This aspect become of very interest because of the renewed attention given to social innovation, and especially to the social inclusion of disadvantaged categories, such as elderly people [2]. In effect, leaving them behind in the creation of a more

© Springer Nature Switzerland AG 2020
Q. Gao and J. Zhou (Eds.): HCII 2020, LNCS 12208, pp. 688–706, 2020.
https://doi.org/10.1007/978-3-030-50249-2_49

desirable urban environment can bring to negative impacts and consequences for the sustainability of the entire system. The increasing impact of ageing population is a big challenge that cannot be ignored, but several solutions and approaches that can contribute to successfully deal with it can be identified [3]. In this regard, nowadays, many occasions of encounter are generated by participatory or sharing processes aiming at creating sustainable urban ecosystems, as the sharing of knowledge, resources and ideas empowers people and contributes to build a sense of belonging and a push to collaboration across different sectors, and generations, too. This brings to presume that the more city users interact with the different urban elements and social groups present in the city, the more they become engaged and possibly become part of a community committed towards the achievement of common goals. Inclusion and openness can trigger empowerment processes that lead to a social change. Of course, culture is a key element in the realization of this ambitious goal, both as mobilizing factor and occasion for professional and civic improvement. Cultural urban events are ideal means to make this happen as festivals influence people's idea of a city and have become central to processes of urban development and revitalization [4]. The use of Information and Communication Technologies (hereafter ICTs) may improve the interaction between people and its environment by providing a better user experience enhancing the fulfillment of personal and collective goals, for example by promoting and supporting sustainable development. This is evident for instance in the mobility field where some important projects have been implemented for moving towards more sustainable behaviors [5, 6].

According to this scenario, the paper focuses on the media and services (especially the digital ones) that can support the user experience during a scattered cultural urban event. Special attention is paid to the communication aspects, as information is the first resource needed to elaborate any type of choice. But, nonetheless, all the situations experienced by the event attendants are considered in the discussion and identification of digital services supporting their activities by looking at their event attendance as a whole with their experience of the city. Indeed, the visit to different cultural sites scattered in different parts of a city requires the use and coordination of different urban services, such as mobility or education, social services, security, etc. In addition, the different age of the attendants is another element to focus on in order to assure a more suitable experience to the event attendants. So, the paper aims to analyze the different needs of people attending a scattered urban event by considering their different age groups and by giving priority to information and communication needs as a basis for the satisfaction of other related needs. In detail, the event taken into analysis is an annual event held in Rome that for just one weekend provides free access and free-guided tours to buildings of architectural interest not normally open to the public. It offers also some special events, including walking tours, performances, workshops, lectures, talks and exhibitions. In this way, it promotes architecture and heritage sites to a wider audience and represents an opportunity to discover new and little-known places in the city of Rome. This format is diffused and replicated in many other cities in Italy and abroad (from which it originates). It adopts and spreads the concept of heritage days, also called doors open day or open doors days, that in the last forty years has been implemented across Europe for promoting heritage as a common value [7]. Similar schemes are being applied also outside Europe in a growing number of countries.

In some cases, such as in the specific one analyzed in this paper, a major focus is put on architecture. The joint effort of the different organizations of the city for providing extra and free entrance to buildings, monuments and sites scattered all over the city and the celebration of this common heritage as a resource to care about all together transform the event in a city festival. By applying this format, the specific event on which the research is focused offers an innovative experience (in respect of that generally experienced by people in traditional museums) in visiting urban cultural heritage and promotes the widespread participation of both Institutions and civic society. In so doing, it connects the social fabric of the city through its urban interface, creating new opportunities for social inclusion and for triggering innovation and citizens engagement. The positive feedback and engaging formula revealed by the event are proved by the number of people attending the event and of opened sites that continues to increase from the first till the last edition of the event. These characteristics made it worth of a further study and highlight the importance of a proper communication and information of the event for creating a more effective dialogue with Institutions and civic society on account of its impact on the city.

So, the paper is organized as follows: after the Introduction, Sect. 2 briefly presents the main related work about cultural urban events and civic engagement in city development. Section 3 shows the survey on communication user needs across generation administered to the attendants at the above-mentioned event held in Rome by describing the purpose, the methodology and the results of the research. Then in Sect. 4 the media and services used and suggested by the survey respondents for enhancing the communication and the participation in the event are discussed, together with the other general information gathered about the respondents to the survey and possible related design solutions for improving UX and creating civic engagement. Some opportunities that emerge in designing digital services and solutions supporting the whole user experience of the event, and of the city as well, are envisioned too in presenting Conclusions and Future Work.

2 Cultural Urban Events and Civic Engagement in City Development

In the academic literature the focus on cultural urban events has been discussed from different points of view. First, the presence of this kind of events is considered as an important tool for urban regeneration. As stated by Smith [8], they are generally considered both as a way of giving new impetus to specific urban areas or to entire undeveloped territories and, consequently, as a way of stimulating economic investments and gaining civic engagement. The central element, in this context, is related to the need of identifying and forecasting real and concrete impacts of this kind of events, not only from the economic point of view but especially from a social point of view. The work of Morales Pérez [9], for example, by carrying out a study which analyses the perception of residents of a specific city on an international event organized by public Institutions, focuses on how cultural urban events contribute to the social and cultural development of the city, by promoting shared social values and by strengthening local identity and culture. The increasing importance given in the academic literature to not only economic, but also social impacts of cultural events is also demonstrated by the elaboration of frameworks and conceptual and methodological models which measure and analyze the social effects of urban cultural events [10]. Among the main possible social impacts of a cultural urban event, the author identifies: the possibility of a shared experience enabled by the event, the revitalization of traditions, the building of community pride, the possibility of creating new cultural skills, the increased interest towards the city, etc. Another work which emphasizes the social dimension below cultural event is the study of Liu [11], which evidences how well organized cultural urban events can not only stimulate citizen participation in the cultural sector, but they can also increase the sense of place, so as to be considered a central element for a urban development strategy.

In any case, in order to register positive impacts on the city, especially from the social perspective, for this type of event it is necessary to invest in improving people experience, which means enhancing the way people can perform the activities related to the fruition of this kind of events. The work of Valli [12], for example, analyses the overall people experience before, during and after specific events, by studying for example the process which conducts to the decision to take part in the event, the people experience in interacting with the mobility services, the activities related to the tickets purchase, etc. In particular, this study, although it only involves young adults, identifies some opportunities of using digital media to improve the overall people experience in this kind of events (digital technologies can be used, for example, for giving information on accommodation and facilities or for providing people tools which help them to better organize the activities). Moreover, about the use of digital media in cultural urban events, the work of Holt [13] focuses on how these tools, and in particular social media, like Facebook and Instagram, increase the possibility of sharing information about the event among people and getting them more engaged not only in the activities of the event, but also in the values of the community which organizes it.

In this context, a central point is that most of the studies that focus on the elements that can improve people experience in the cultural urban events, involve young generations or young adults. However, some works focus also on different targets. The studies that focus on the elderly generally consider them as a source of cultural and identity elements that kick off specific events, focusing in this way on their cultural participation in the urban issues (see, for example, the work of Jakubowska [14]), or as a target that is necessary to involve in cultural activities in order to increase the social inclusion of this category of people (see, for example, the work of Ghenta [15]), by also focusing on the elderly needs in the experience during cultural urban events. In particular, the work of Nollet [16] identifies psychological, psychical, social, material, cultural and existential barriers and motivators that encourage or demotivate their participation in cultural activities.

3   The Survey on Communication User Needs Across Generations

3.1   Purpose of the Research

The survey shown and analyzed in this paper is part of a research on the reception by city users of a new kind of cultural urban event based on openness as a possible means for generating positive impact and creating citizen engagement in the urban environment. Indeed, new forms of using and relating with the city appear thanks to the hybridization of public spaces, mixing physical and digital spaces of interaction [17], and the spreading of social innovations aiming at enhancing urban heritage and urban social networks.

The main objective of the research is the improvement of the experience of all the participants of such event, which are, not only the visitors entering the numerous, different and scattered sites of the city, or the volunteers assisting them and embodying the contact points between front and back end of the event, but also the public and private (for profit or nonprofit) organizations and subjects opening the structures and sites to visit. So, the survey was aimed to gather and analyze their needs, but also to collect their feedbacks and suggestions about the organization and the individual and social impacts deriving from the participation in the event. The results of the survey were expected to help in identifying good practices to adopt and new possible services to offer to participants in order to improve their experience and to increase their level of engagement for bringing new social value at urban level. In this sense, part of the survey was aimed at gathering communication user needs across generations by analyzing the different channels for dissemination and information. In this paper the term "generation" refers to a group of individuals of about the same age (see Subsect. 3.3 for a detailed categorization) within Western society, and especially the Italian one, so having similar experiences, needs and attitudes.

The whole research was conducted jointly with the organizers of the event and it represents a further way to strengthen connections and cultivate relations with their audience, as typically in participatory processes.

3.2   Methodology

The data analyzed and discussed in this paper are collected through an online questionnaire addressed to the participants to a specific event held in Rome letting people freely visit public and private sites of architectural interest. In detail, the questionnaire provides for six categories of respondents: 1) Visitors of the 2018 edition of the event; 2) Volunteers of the 2018 edition of the event; 3) Institutions and nonprofit organizations of the 2018 edition of the event; 4) For profit organizations of the 2018 edition of the event; 5) Attendants at the event that have not taken part in the 2018 edition; 6) People never attending the analyzed event. As the questionnaire has been diffused through the official newsletter of the event, but also through social channels, it has been planned to gather the major amount of prompts and information helping to improve the event, even from who, for any reason, could not take part in it.

The whole survey examines four main categories of queries: 1) General information, including questions about personal data for the general (and anonymized) categorization of respondents; 2) Experience, including questions about the participation of respondents in other similar cultural events and their attitude towards the analyzed event for defining their interest towards cultural initiatives and their level of involvement in the analyzed event; 3) The experience with the 2018 edition, including questions on practical aspects for defining the level of satisfaction of participants and the effects derived from taking part in the event; 4) New perspectives, including questions about attendants priorities and food for thought to take forward in the next editions of the event for defining possible improvements and positive impacts on the urban environment.

However, for the purpose of this paper we have extrapolated from the whole survey only the data referring to the 2018 edition, the last one monitored. Moreover, the participants to the previous editions are excluded because they cannot take into account the possible improvements brought in the last edition (2018). Only the answers of volunteers and visitors are considered for the purpose of this paper because for the organizations the field "age" clearly was not included into the form. The respondents (volunteers and visitors) of the 2018 edition of the analyzed event are 627 overall, in the following paragraph a detailed description of their distribution across the different ages and roles is given. Some specific questions focusing on the communication of the event have been selected from the whole research for a further analysis according to the age group of the respondents. In details, the selected questions are (excluding those used for profiling the respondent that refer to their role in the event; current domicile; age; level of education; operation in the sector of architecture, creativity, design and cultural heritage; participation in some other similar – for themes and modes – cultural urban events):

1. By which channel have you been aware of the 2018 edition of the event?
2. In occasion of the 2018 edition of the event, did you make known the event to someone else that had never heard of it?
3. Where did you found the most part of information on sites and events to visit during the 2018 edition of the event?
4. Do you suggest us to employ new means for enhancing the dissemination of the event? Which ones?
5. Are there other services that could improve the experience with the event (e.g. Wi-Fi hotspots, information desks, etc.)?

From 1 to 3 they are all close-ended questions, but question number 2 is a dichotomous (yes/no) type of question, while number 1 and 3 are checklist type multiple choice questions, including the option "Other" that has to be freely completed. On the contrary, questions number 4 and 5 are made of two distinct parts: a first dichotomous (yes/no) type question, used as a filter question, and a second open-ended type question. Referring to the latter, the different categories of answers were created after the completion of the survey. In detail, the original responses collected have been read and analyzed in depth one by one and associated to different semantic categories that synthesized them, for example the category "traditional advertising" includes suggestions about the use for the dissemination of the event of TV, radio, newscast, print media, billboards, etc. Some answers have been included in more than one category as they gave more than one suggestion.

Most of the responses are presented into this paper without considering the division between visitors and volunteers, as the main characteristic of the respondents that satisfy the requirement of the study is the connection with the event and the awareness of the contents and initiatives spread by it.

3.3   Results from the Online Survey

The respondents considered for the study presented into this paper are distributed as following:

- 28 respondents in the 18–24 age group (of which 22 volunteers and 6 visitors).
- 108 respondents in the 25–34 age group (of which 28 volunteers and 80 visitors).
- 122 respondents in the 35–44 age group (of which 9 volunteers and 113 visitors).
- 151 respondents in the 45–54 age group (of which 6 volunteers and 145 visitors).
- 132 respondents in the 55–64 age group (of which 15 volunteers and 117 visitors).
- 86 respondents in the 65+ age group (of which 22 volunteers and 64 visitors).

Table 1 shows the distribution of visitors and volunteers who participated into the survey according to their age. The most part of visitors is in the age range 35–64, while the most part of volunteers is divided between the 18–34 and 55–65+ age range. 71 respondents participated at the analyzed event for the first time in 2018, mostly as visitors, except for the categories 18–24 and 65+ where they are in most cases volunteers and the category 25–34, where the number of new participants is equally distributed between visitors and volunteers (Table 2).

Table 1. Distribution of the respondents according to their age and role in the analyzed event. Values are reported as percentage and corresponding number of respondents.

	18–24	25–34	35–44	45–54	55–64	65+	TOT.
Visitors	1,1%	15,2%	21,5%	27,6%	22,3%	12,2%	100%
	(6)	(80)	(113)	(145)	(117)	(64)	(525)
Volunteers	21,6%	27,5%	8,8%	5,9%	14,7%	21,6%	100%
	(22)	(28)	(9)	(6)	(15)	(22)	(102)

Table 2. Age and role of the respondents who participated in the analyzed event for the first time in 2018. Values are reported as percentage per age categories and corresponding number of respondents.

	18–24	25–34	35–44	45–54	55–64	65+	TOT.
Visitors	20%	50%	87,5%	95,5%	88,9%	37,5%	67,6%
	(2)	(7)	(7)	(21)	(8)	(3)	(48)
Volunteers	80%	50%	12,5%	4,5%	11,1%	62,5%	32,4%
	(8)	(7)	(1)	(1)	(1)	(5)	(23)

Although most of the respondents in each target group is domiciled in Rome, the 18–24 and 25–34 target groups reveal a higher percentage of respondents coming from other places, mostly in the same region of Rome (Lazio), as shown in the Table 3.

Referring only to the visitors of the 2018 edition of the event (525 respondents), where the 5/7 of respondents are almost equally distributed among the 35–44, 45–54, 55–64 target groups, the 90,9% of the respondents had been living in Rome when attending the event. In respect of this information, the distinction between volunteers and visitors is not relevant as the general base of the participants engaged into the event is clearly on a local scale.

Table 3. Current domicile of the respondents according to their age. Values are reported as percentage per age categories and corresponding number of respondents.

	18–24	25–34	35–44	45–54	55–64	65+
Rome	71,4%	69,4%	89,3%	94%	90,2%	95,3%
	(20)	(75)	(109)	(142)	(119)	(82)
Region of Lazio	14,3%	23,1%	4,1%	4%	5,3%	1,2%
	(4)	(25)	(5)	(6)	(7)	(1)
Other Italian Regions	10,7%	6,5%	5,7%	2%	3%	2,3%
	(3)	(7)	(7)	(3)	(4)	(2)
Abroad	3,6%	0,9%	0,8%	/	1,5%	1,2%
	(1)	(1)	(1)		(2)	(1)

In general, most of the respondents has a high level of education, as shown in the Table 4. The type of interest towards culture and cultural events of the respondents to the questionnaire is measured through their effective activity in the sector of architecture, creativity, design and cultural heritage and their participation in some other similar (for themes or modes) cultural urban events. In general, they seem interested in culture. In fact, in the age group 18–24 the 78,6% (22) of the respondents works in the sector of architecture, creativity, design and cultural heritage; the 65,7% (71) in the age group 25–34; the 33,6% (41) in the age group 35–44; the 31,8% (48) in the age group 45–54; the 23,5% (31) in the age group 55–64; the 18,6% (16) in the age group 65+. On the other hand, who participated in similar cultural urban events is the 60,7% (17) of the respondents in the age group 18–24; the 65,7% (71) in the age group 25–34; the 85,2% (104) in the age group 35–44; the 82,1% (124) in the age group 45–54; the 84,8% (112) in the age group 55–64; the 76,7% (66) in the age group 65+. Referring to the division between visitors and volunteers regardless of their age group, the 68,4% (359 out of 525 respondents) of respondents as visitors did not work in the sector of architecture, creativity, design and cultural heritage, while it is the 38,2% (39 out of 102 respondents) among the respondents as volunteers. Moreover, looking at the participation in other similar cultural urban events, the most part of respondents as visitors (the 72,2%, i.e. 379 out of 525 respondents) and the 37,3% (38 out of 102 respondents) of respondents as volunteers participated in a very similar structured event (i.e. offering open entrance to buildings and places belonging to the public heritage, but at a national level). It is by far the most attended event among those suggested by the questionnaire, as the second most attended event among visitors has been attended only by the 29,9% (157) of respondents, and the most part of respondents as volunteers (the 50%, i.e. 51 out of 102 respondents) did not participated in any of the other similar events suggested by the questionnaire (all the other similar events attended by volunteers are below the 10% of respondents).

Table 4. Level of education of the respondents according to their age. Values are reported as percentage per age categories and corresponding number of respondents.

	18–24	25–34	35–44	45–54	55–64	65+
Doctoral degree or equivalent degree	/	17,6% (19)	27% (33)	17,2% (26)	19,7% (26)	16,3% (14)
Master's degree or equivalent degree	/	48,1% (52)	45,9% (56)	47,7% (72)	41,7% (55)	53,5% (46)
Bachelor's degree or equivalent degree	32,1% (9)	23,1% (25)	11,5% (14)	7,3% (11)	9,1% (12)	3,5% (3)
High school diploma	67,9% (19)	11,1% (12)	14,8% (18)	27,2% (41)	28,8% (38)	23,3% (20)
Middle school diploma	/	/	0,8% (1)	0,7% (1)	0,8% (1)	3,5% (3)
Primary school diploma	/	/	/	/	/	/
None	/	/	/	/	/	/

Focusing the attention on the media and services people used for retrieving information and attending the event, at the question "By which channel have you been aware of the 2018 edition of the event?" all the age groups, except the 18–24 one, put at the first place "Web/Social Network" (33,3% in the 25–34 age group, 65,6% in the 35–44 age group, 57,6% in the 45–54 age group, 49,2% in the 55–64 age group, 32,9% in the 65+ age group). The 18–24 target group put at the first place "Meeting events at University/Institute/School" (50%), and only at the second place "Web/Social Network" (25%), as well as "Word of mouth" (25%). Among the age groups the other channels are divided as shown in Table 5.

Table 5. Channels by which the respondents have been aware of the 2018 edition of the event. Values are reported as percentage per age categories and corresponding number of respondents.

	18–24	25–34	35–44	45–54	55–64	65+
Web/Social network	25% (7)	33,3% (36)	65,6% (80)	57,6% (87)	49,2% (65)	32,9% (28)
Newspapers/TV/Radio	/	3,7% (4)	4,1% (5)	9,3% (14)	14,4% (19)	22,4% (19)
Advertising posters	/	5,6% (6)	1,6% (2)	3,3% (5)	5,3% (7)	/
Word of mouth	25% (7)	25% (27)	18% (22)	17,9% (27)	16,7% (22)	15,3% (13)
Meeting events at University/Institute/School	50% (14)	19,4% (21)	0,8% (1)	1,3% (2)	0,8% (1)	1,2% (1)
By invitation	/	7,4% (8)	4,9% (6)	5,3% (8)	5,3% (7)	9,4% (8)
Other	/	5,6% (6)	4,9% (6)	5,3% (8)	8,3% (11)	18,8% (16)

Referring to this question, a focus on the division between visitors and volunteers makes sense for the target groups 18–24, 25–34, 55–64 and 65+, that are the categories where there is a more substantial number of volunteers in respect to the visitors. In detail, a significant channel for the recruiting of volunteers in the 55–64 and 65+ age groups have been indicated by the respondents (all volunteers) in the field "Other", i.e. a specific project led by a national Club, by respectively 4 and 10 respondents. In the 18–24 and 25–34 age groups the more significant channel for the recruiting of volunteers is "Meeting events at University/Institute/School", indicated by respectively 12 and 11 respondents. Another element to highlight is that in the 18–24 age groups the "Word of mouth" have been used only by the volunteers (7 respondents). In general, regardless of their age group, more than half of the visitors (53,1% out of 525 respondents) have been aware of the 2018 edition of the event by Web/Social Network, immediately followed by the "Word of mouth" (18,7% out of 525 respondents) and "Newspapers/TV/Radio" (10,9% out of 525 respondents). Among volunteers there is equivalence between the "Meeting events at University/Institute/School" (24,5% out of 102 respondents) and "Web/Social Network" (23,5% out of 102 respondents), immediately followed by the "Word of mouth" (19,6% out of 102 respondents).

At the question "In occasion of the 2018 edition of the event, did you make known the event to someone else that had never heard of it?" most of the respondents gave an affirmative answer, with high percentages in all the age groups, and especially in the age range between 18 and 64, as shown in Table 6. The respondents that gave a negative answer are almost all visitors, except for 2 volunteers in the age group 35–44.

Table 6. Answers of the question: "In occasion of the 2018 edition of the event, did you make known the event to someone else that had never heard of it?". Values are reported as percentage per age categories and corresponding number of respondents.

	18–24	25–34	35–44	45–54	55–64	65+
Yes	100%	90,7%	91,8%	90,1%	89,4%	88,4%
	(28)	(98)	(112)	(136)	(118)	(76)
No	/	9,3%	8,2%	9,9%	10,6%	11,6%
		(10)	(10)	(15)	(14)	(10)

In respect of the multimedia means through which participants found most of the information on sites and special events to visit during the 2018 edition of the event ("Where did you found the most part of information on sites and events to visit during the 2018 edition of the event?"), the most used one is the "Web or mobile site of the event": 66,7% (4) in the 18–24 age group, 92,5% (74) in the 25–34 age group, 92,9% (105) in the 35–44 age group, 84,1% (122) in the 45–54 age group, 76,1% (89) in the 55–64 age group, 76,6% (49) in the 65+ age group. The "Facebook page of the event" is equally used by the 18–24 age group (66,7% corresponding to 4 respondents). In the other age groups the gap between the most and the second more used means is greater: In effect, following the "Web or mobile site of the event" there are at the second place: "Paper map of the event" for the 25–34 age group (32,5% corresponding to 26 respondents), "Facebook page of event" for the 35–44 (23% corresponding to 26 respondents) and for the 45–54 (22,8% corresponding to 33 respondents) age groups, "Paper guide of the event" for the 55–64 (23,1% corresponding to 27 respondents) and the 65+ (31,3% corresponding to 20 respondents) age groups (see Table 7). The question was addressed only to the visitors of the 2018 edition of the event, since the volunteers did not plan an itinerary, and the respondents could select more than one option.

Table 7. Answers of the question (only for visitors): "Where did you found the most part of information on sites and events to visit during the 2018 edition of the event?". Values are reported as percentage per age categories and corresponding number of respondents.

	18–24	25–34	35–44	45–54	55–64	65+
Facebook page of the event	66,7% (4)	18,8% (15)	23% (26)	22,8% (33)	12% (14)	7,8% (5)
Web or mobile site of the event	66,7% (4)	92,5% (74)	92,9% (105)	84,1% (122)	76,1% (89)	76,6% (49)
Paper guide of the event (for payment)	/	25% (20)	16,8% (19)	15,9% (23)	23,1% (27)	31,3% (20)
Paper map of the event (for free)	16,7% (1)	32,5% (26)	15% (17)	20% (29)	22,2% (26)	21,9% (14)
Other Social Networks (not of the event)	/	/	/	3,4% (5)	0,9% (1)	/
Other Web or Mobile sites (not of the event)	/	3,8% (3)	7,1% (8)	6,2% (9)	12,8% (15)	6,3% (4)
Traditional media (Newspaper/TV/Radio)	/	/	4,4% (5)	3,4% (5)	4,3% (5)	9,4% (6)
Word-of- mouth	16,7% (1)	1,3% (1)	5,3% (6)	5,5% (8)	6% (7)	9,4% (6)
Other	/	1,3% (1)	/	/	1,7% (2)	1,6% (1)

Also considering the percentage on the whole visitors of the 2018 edition of the event, regardless of their age group, the Web or mobile site of the event was the most used means for gathering information on sites and events to visit during the 2018 edition of the event (the 84,4%, i.e. 443 out of 525 respondents). Paper map of the event (the 21,5%, i.e. 113 out of 525 respondents), paper guide of the event (the 20,8%, i.e. 109 out of 525 respondents) and Facebook page of the event (the 18,5%, i.e. 97 out of 525 respondents) rank well below.

Referring to the means and services needed by attendants at the event, some close and open-ended questions were administered to both visitors and volunteers. In detail, to the questions "Do you suggest us to employ new means for enhancing the dissemination of the event? Which ones?" the most part of respondents in the 18–24 age group (57,1% corresponding to 16 respondents) answered "Yes", while in the 65+ age group there is an equal distribution between who answered "Yes" and who "No" (50% corresponding to 43 respondents). In both cases, are proportionally mostly the volunteers that answered "Yes". On the contrary, the most part of respondents in the 25–34 age group (53,7% corresponding to 58 respondents), in the 35–44 age group (66,4% corresponding to 81 respondents), in the 45–54 age group (64,9% corresponding to 98 respondents) and in the 55–64 age group (56,8% corresponding to 75 respondents) answered "No". Among them, in each age group are proportionally mostly the visitors that answered "No". In the 18–24 age group half (50% corresponding to 8 respondents) of those who answered "Yes" suggested to employ online advertising and to invest more on social channels. In the 25–34 age group the half (52% corresponding to 26 respondents) suggested instead to employ traditional advertising (TV, radio, newscast, print media, billboards, etc.). In the 35–44 age group the most suggested means for dissemination were traditional advertising (TV, radio, newscast, print media, billboards, etc.) (34,1% corresponding to 14 respondents), online advertising and more investments on social channels (26,8% corresponding to 11 respondents) and the realization of public and private partnerships, along with the networking with schools, universities and professionals from every sector (22% corresponding to 9 respondents). Analogously, in the 45–54 age group most of the respondents who answered "Yes" suggested to employ the traditional (32,1% corresponding to 17 respondents) or the online/social network (28,3% corresponding to 15 respondents) advertising, while the 18,9% of the respondents who answered "Yes" (corresponding to 10 respondents) asked in general for getting more information (quantity, timeliness and diffusion, both on paper and online). Also in the 55–64 age group the most suggested means are the traditional ones (the 38,6% corresponding to 22 respondents), then followed by the request for getting more information (quantity, timeliness and diffusion, both on paper and online) (the 28,1% corresponding to 16 respondents) and online/social network advertising (the 15,8% corresponding to 9 respondents). Finally, in the 65+ age group half of those who answered "Yes" (55,8% corresponding to 24 respondents) suggested to employ the traditional advertising (TV, radio, newscast, print media, billboards, etc.) that clearly detaches from the other gathered options in the category. Some means to employ for dissemination that were suggested by a lesser part of respondents, but that are present in all the age groups are the realization of public and private partnerships, along with the networking with schools, universities and professionals from every sector and the request for getting more information (quantity, timeliness and diffusion, both on paper and online). In the different age groups, except for the 18–24 age group, also emerged the suggestion to employ advertising on public transport means and in public spaces and that to employ the newsletter and direct messaging (e.g. WhatsApp). In the 25–64 age range a few people suggested the use of the mobile app or other digital interactive media. Only the 18–24 and 65+ age groups gave the advice of a wider engagement of citizens and a more structured participation and collaboration with the stakeholders.

To the question "Are there other services that could improve the experience with the event (e.g. Wi-Fi hotspots, information desks, etc.)? Which ones?" over half of the respondents in the 18–24 (60,7% corresponding to 17 respondents) and 25–34 (53,7% corresponding to 58 respondents) age groups answered "Yes". In the 65+ age group half of the respondents answered "No" (50% corresponding to 43 respondents). In the rest of the age groups "Yes" is the most chosen answer, but, if considering the sum of "No" and "Don't know" answers, it is slightly below the majority. The distribution of affirmative ("Yes") and negative ("No" and "Don't know") answers is proportionally almost the same between volunteers and visitors in the 18–24, 25–34 and 35–44 age groups, where there is a prevalence of affirmative answers. On the contrary, in the 65+ age group volunteers were definitely more propositional than visitors, while in the 55–64 age group it is the opposite. Finally, in the 45–54 age group there is a prevalence of affirmative answers for both volunteers and visitors, but volunteers were definitely more propositional than visitors. Information desks and Wi-Fi hotspots were by far the more recurrent services suggested by the respondents who answered "Yes" to the question about other services that could improve the experience with the event. Of course, these two options were prompted by the examples given right inside the question. But, at the same time, the great number of people choosing these options, especially for information desks, confirms the supposition made about what kinds of service were needed. In effect, the latter was an option suggested by more than the half of respondents in each age group (58,8% corresponding to 10 respondents in the 18–24 age group; 63,8% corresponding to 37 respondents in the 25–34 age group; 55,6% corresponding to 30 respondents in the 35–44 age group; 64% corresponding to 48 respondents in the 45–54 age group; 58,1% corresponding to 36 respondents in the 55–64 age group; 57,9% corresponding to 22 respondents in the 65+ age group). The request for Wi-Fi hotspots at disposal during the event was less diffused, but always bigger than the other options (41,2% corresponding to 7 respondents in the 18–24 age group; 20,7% corresponding to 12 respondents in the 25–34 age group; 16,7% corresponding to 9 respondents in the 35–44 age group; 22,7% corresponding to 17 respondents in the 45–54 age group; 29% corresponding to 18 respondents in the 55–64 age group; 21,1% corresponding to 8 respondents in the 65+ age group). Some other services that could improve the experience with the event that were suggested by a lesser part of respondents, but that are present in almost all the age groups are: the improvement of the information and communication services about the event, present in all the age groups, especially in the 45–64 age range; the improvement in usability and diffusion of the event guide and map, also present in all the age groups, but mostly in the 25–34 one; the improvement of the mobile app and website of the event, present in the 25–65+ age range, especially in the 45–54 age group; the creation of itineraries for visiting the sites, present in the 18–54 age range, especially in the 25–34 age group; the improvement of the booking system for visiting the sites, suggested by a few people in the 18–54 age range, especially in the 35–44 age group. Finally, a few people in the 25–64 age range, especially in the 55–64 age group, suggested the employment of specific digital and interactive supports to improve the comprehension of the sites while visiting them.

3.4 Discussion and Limitations of the Study

The present paper shows a study about the different communication needs of the participants of a scattered cultural urban event held in Rome that let people freely visit public and private sites of architectural interest. The latter results to be a crosscutting event through different age groups, as the respondents to the questionnaire belong to a wide age range that include from 18 to 65+ years old people. The age group 18–24 is the smallest and it mostly consists of volunteers recruited through academic channels.

Considering their unfamiliarity with management and working life, a more effective communication aiming at attracting more people from this age group should pointing out the capacities and skills-building opportunities offered by the event. At the same time more suiting ways of creating interest, motivation and engagement in this age group should be identified. The other age groups present a higher number of respondents and mostly consist of visitors, even if in the 65+ age group there are several volunteers in respect of the number of visitors. However, the distinction between volunteers and visitors does not really matter, since they use the same media and services for retrieving information about the event and volunteers have a direct knowledge of what could improve the experience of people attending the event. Moreover, volunteers often can visit the site assigned to them or might manage to visit other sites. The only relevant aspect that might be pointed out are the kinds of recruiting channels for volunteers that appear to be especially effective for people of 18–34 and 65+ age groups. In detail, volunteers are recruited mostly through educational organizations, such as Universities, and Clubs that are committed towards the promotion of knowledge and cultural heritage. In this sense, the existence of a community of interest seems to be an incentive for taking part to the event in an active and collaborative way, especially for age categories that generally have a less perceived influence on society.

The provenience is another factor that seems to influence the participation in the event. Indeed, that analyzed is an event that especially engages local people. As it could be expected, the proximity to the location of the event really affects the 65+ age group, but their attitude seems in line with the other age groups. The high level of education of the respondents and their interest towards culture and cultural events despite the fact that they are not effectively active in the sector of architecture, creativity, design and cultural heritage suggest that they might be interested in more specialized and elaborate information supporting their experience during the event. However, the number of people working in the sector of architecture, creativity, design and cultural heritage is higher among the younger people and decreases as the age increases. Consequently, different priorities could motivate the participation into the event according to the specific age group. As mentioned above, the professional opportunities offered by the event, e.g. the improvement of organizational and managing skills, could be a stimulus for younger generations, while other common values and personal goals or interests could move the older generations.

In general, the use of digital means and services does not appear to be a problem, as Web and social networks result to be the most diffused channel through which the respondents entered in contact with the 2018 edition of the analyzed event. Again the 18–24 age group creates an exception, as the main touchpoints for them were the meeting events at University/Institute/School, that confirm the centrality of these Institutions in their participation in the event. An equal influence is exerted on this youngest age group by the Web and social networks and by the word of mouth. This leads to think that they really rely on social relations and communities. This last statement can be generally applied also to the other age groups, especially for visitors. On the contrary, the more aged groups show to still make a higher use of traditional media, such as Newspapers, TV and radio, while the word of mouth seems to be not really determining, maybe for the lesser occasions that usually elderly people have in meeting other people. A similar trend is shown also by the results emerged from the question "In occasion of the 2018 edition of the event, did you make known the event to someone else that had never heard of it?", which highlight how, despite the high percentage of affirmative answers in all the age groups, the 65+ category is slightly lower by comparison. Another important information retrieved is that almost all the volunteers communicated the event to new attendants. This underlines their engagement and satisfaction in spreading their experience. Especially for elderly people, this can represent a way for inclusiveness and self-empowerment. So some interventions in support of the digital literacy of the elderly people should be considered, in order to give to a growing number of them the occasion to take part in this or similar initiatives, even as active players in the dissemination of the event. Indeed, Web and mobile sites were the most used channels by visitors to create a link with the event and get important information allowing the participation in it. However, despite this was the most used channel in all the age groups two observations should be made. The first is that the percentage of people using ICTs generally is lower in the more aged groups, especially in the 65+ category, while in the same groups the use of printed and traditional media tends to increase. The difference among the age groups in not very marked, but still it is worth to be considered. The other observation is that, again, the role of social networks, in detail Facebook, is more standing out for the 18–24 age group, while is almost irrelevant for 65+ age group. However, the 45–54 and 55–64 age groups results to be in comparison to the others, those that used the greater number of channels, both traditional and digital, to retrieve information on sites and events to visit during the 2018 edition of the event. These two observations corroborate the need for interventions in support of elderly ability and awareness in the use of digital technologies and social media. At the same time, an intervention aiming at achieving a better media literacy would be beneficial also for young people. Actually, there is not a serious lack of usage of these means, but more a need for support. What emerged by the answers to the open-ended questions seems to confirm this, as people in the 55–64 age groups appear to consider digital technologies and social media as possible means for enhancing communication and user experience during the event. They particularly recommend the use of digital and interactive devices supporting the comprehension of the visited sites that in effect are less uncomfortable than the paper map to carry around and even more rich in information than the paper guide. However, a careful interaction design of the specific solution and the coherent design of the whole service is needed, in order to really help and satisfy attendants' needs and to include also those people that are less confident or willing in the use of these devices.

By referring to the open-ended questions, they reflect the general picture already described into this paper. First, volunteers appear to be more active and ready to identify possible ways to improve communication and user experience during the event. This is a positive fact, especially for the 65+ age group, where for both questions volunteers results more propositional than visitors, maybe for a greater self-confidence and empowerment gained through a more active participation in the event. Moreover, the 18–24 and the 65+ age groups are those that seem more needing for a bigger engagement into the making of the event. Regarding the kind of media to employ for dissemination, a multimedia strategy remains the best option for attracting as much people as possible. Traditional media (including also some digital media) prevail on online and social network advertising, which are instead the preferred from the 18–24 age group. But what is remarkable is the suggestion for a more widespread dissemination of the event around the city (through billboards and advertising on public transport means and in public spaces) and the creation of partnership, mostly with education organizations, as means for a collective development of the city. Another remarkable finding is the general need for communication, comprising the quantity of available information and its timeliness and diffusion, both on paper and online, that emerge in different parts of the survey. Even the answers regarding the kind of services needed for improving the experience with the event point out this need by asking for more information desks all around the city where to have access to Internet and physically ask for suggestions and directions, for example about itineraries, bookings and waiting times. Information desks can also contribute in making visible the event for both visitors looking for more information and new potential attendants passing through the place. Moreover, their widespread presence could create a network of meeting points connecting the whole city and creating a sense of community at urban level. Except for the Wi-Fi hotspots, the request for digital and social media related services was very low in all the age groups and mostly refer to the already mentioned digital devices supporting the visit and the mobile app and website of the analyzed event. However, despite the fact that it is not a pronounced need, the improvement of the mobile app of the event could be a practical way for supporting and satisfying other information and people needs in joining the event, such as the creation of visit itineraries, the visit booking and management, the multimedia guide for sites, etc.

This big need of information has to be considered in the communication strategy plan and in the user experience design of a scattered cultural urban event. In detail, the need for information, especially for visitors, is primarily targeted to the planning of an itinerary for the visit on the basis of the descriptions of the available sites and of their conditions for the access (visit schedule, number of people per each visit, etc.). It is important that this information was available sufficiently in advance to give people time for selecting the sites of interest and creating a satisfying itinerary. For this reason, also information about mobility or indications on how to reach the opened sites are essential for the planning activity of visitors. In order to support their activities, different requirements are needed. First, timeliness in giving the right and wanted information is essential. Secondly, the suggestion of recommended itineraries or the communication of special services through digital and paper media could help people in finding more satisfying options. This is particularly convenient when using a mobile app, especially for those people that have no time or have to change plans on the moment. Indeed, through a mobile app offering real time information people are able to have a broader sight on the whole event. Moreover, by interacting with it, they could personalize their experience. Indeed, since the event is scattered all over the city and consists in visiting different sites (generally with a limited number of entrances allowed), prior and real time information about mobility and crowded sites could really help visitors in having a great experience in joining the event and volunteers in suggesting the best itinerary. Besides the practical information that are the entry point for the event, other digital services could enhance the user experience by giving people some different goals for enhancing their participation in the event. In this regard digital services might support the user experience during this specific event and promote more sustainable behaviors, such as the use of sharing and green mobility or the preservation of the urban cultural heritage. As already mentioned, great attention and a careful study of the context is needed in the design of such solutions, that can be aggregated by a digital platform of the event, aiming at informing and creating civic engagement and collaboration among the attendants.

Before moving to conclusions and future work some mentions of some flaws and shortcomings affecting the study described in this paper must be done. First, the results showed represent a part of a wider survey that considered altogether gives a clearest picture. Nevertheless, the main limitations of the study consist in the unequal distribution of roles and people in the different age groups and in the limited representativeness of the sample of people who took part into the 2018 edition of the event (small sample size, especially for volunteers). These limitations derive by the self-selection of respondents and by other barriers generally affecting the reliance of web surveys, e.g. the access to the Internet. Furthermore, although the web survey was send by newsletter and email to people effectively involved into the event, it was also freely disseminated through social networks and probably not all the contacted people filled it. Another limitation is the fact that the length of the questionnaire might have discouraged from its compilation or led to a tiredness in the final answers (mostly open-ended questions). Moreover, there are no specific questions about the requirements and needs deriving from belonging to a different age group. Finally, for now the results of the survey cannot be compared to other data on the same event or on other similar events. In conclusion, the online questionnaire was useful to rapidly obtain a large amount of data and information, but the use of other methods could be better for obtaining a more representative sample and for identifying innovative patterns to create social change by considering generational requirements.

4   Conclusions and Future Work

The main focus of this paper is the analysis of the kind of media and services people used for retrieving information and attending a specific event deeply connected to the urban environment. Special attention is given to the comparison among different age groups (from 18 to 65+ years old people), in order to find points of contact and distinctness that should be considered in the design of physical and digital services supporting the communication and the user experience of the event. Most of the identified needs are cross-generational, but there are also requirements for more personalized services, such as the employment of specific digital and interactive devices supporting the comprehension of the visited sites. This suggests the implementation of modular features and services on a shared digital platform of the event, designed for meeting different generational needs, but available to all.

The results discussed in the previous section let emerge several opportunities for enhancing the communication and the user experience of the event, and of the city as well, by creating a more engaging experience. In detail, the communication emerges as a key component for the accomplishment of an event structured as the one described into this paper, i.e. condensed in a couple of days and scattered all over the city. Indeed, it requires a collaborative approach and a great commitment from all the participants:

the volunteers that are physically present on the sites guiding, managing and assisting visitors; the owners and managers of the opened structures and sites that make them available for the event; the visitors that move from one place to another of the city for enjoying as much sites as possible; the organizers that coordinate the whole complex event; and many other stakeholders less visible, but equally important for the realization of the event. In such scenario, designing ad hoc communication and information solutions that support all the participants in their activities and facilitates the collaboration among the different actors and ages groups, not only enhances their user experience, but also creates more value for city and society. In this regard the use of a shared digital platform supported by in-person interactions might really improve the user experience and especially strengthen the engagement and the inclusion of two age groups at the extremes, i.e. the young (18–24) and the older people (65+), that generally remain excluded by an active role in social events or have to face more hindrances, like the lack of autonomy. Indeed, ICTs may help the different generations in different ways (see Subsect. 3.4), but their use is not a central element for any of them. On the contrary, they may help in transforming the event in a participatory process by combining personalization and inclusiveness through the digital platform of the event. Besides being a cultural moment, it could become a touchpoint for activating social and professional connections and for starting a process towards the sustainable development of the urban environment. Of course, this is a complex process and it needs a further analysis of the needs and perspectives of all the stakeholders. In this regard, as a future work, we plan to replicate the survey trying to increase and make more reliable the sample size. Some modifications of the survey are needed, too, such as changing some questions, reducing its length and focusing it on the last edition, in accordance to the gathered feedbacks. In addition to this, we plan to broaden the research by organizing focus groups, in-depth interviews and co-creation workshops open to all the different age groups aiming at building a path towards the identification of innovative solution at social and urban level.

References

1. Gehl Institute: The Public Life Diversity Toolkit 2.0. Toolkit, Gehl Institute (2016). https://issuu.com/gehlinstitute/docs/20160128_toolkit_2.0
2. Harris, M., Aldbury, D.: The Innovation Imperative: Why Radical Innovation Is Needed to Reinvent Public Services for the Recession and Beyond. NESTA, London (2009)
3. Organisation for Economic Co-operation and Development (OECD): Fostering innovation to address social challenges. In: Workshop Proceedings, OECD (2011). https://www.oecd.org/sti/inno/47861327.pdf
4. Richards, G., Palmer, R.: Why cities need to be eventful. In: Richards, G., Palmer, R. (eds.) Eventful cities, pp. 1–37. Butterworth-Heinemann, Oxford (2010). (ch. 1)
5. Lissandrello, E., Morelli, N., Schillaci, D., Di Dio, S.: Urban innovation through co-design scenarios. In: Knoche, H., Popescu, E., Cartelli, A. (eds.) SLERD 2018 2018. SIST, vol. 95, pp. 110–122. Springer, Cham (2019). https://doi.org/10.1007/978-3-319-92022-1_10
6. Forbes, P.J., Wells, S., Masthoff, J.: SUPERHUB: integrating behaviour change theories into a sustainable urban-mobility platform. In: Using Technology to Facilitate Behaviour Change and Support Healthy, Sustainable Living Workshop at BHCI (2012)

7. Council of Europe. https://www.coe.int/en/web/culture-and-heritage/european-heritage-days
8. Smith, A.: Events and Urban Regeneration. The Strategic Use of Events to Revitalise Cities. Routledge, London (2012)
9. Morales Pérez, S., Pacheco Bernal, C.: Residents' Perception of the Social and Cultural Impacts of a Public Music Festival in Catalonia. Almatourism – J. Tour. Cult. Territ. Dev. **8**(7), 21–36 (2017)
10. Colombo, A.: How to evaluate cultural impacts of events? A model and methodology proposal. Scand. J. Hosp. Tour. **16**(4), 500–511 (2016)
11. Liu, Y.: Cultural event and urban regeneration: lessons from Liverpool as the 2008 European capital of culture. Eur. Rev. **24**(1), 159–176 (2016)
12. Valli, J.: What was your last event experience? City discovered what kind is a holistic event experience for young urban adults. Project deliverable, "Next Media. A tivit Programme" (2011)
13. Holt, F., Lapenta, F.: The social experience of cultural events: conceptual foundations and analytical strategies. In: Sundbo, J., Sorensen, F. (eds.) Handbook on the Experience Economy, pp. 363–380. Edward Elgar Publishing, Cheltenham (2013). (ch. 19)
14. Jakubowska, A., Kłosiewicz, E., Mękarski, M.: Changing the image of elderly people in Poland: the senior citizen as an important audience member and creator of culture. ENCATC J. Cult. Manag. Policy **5**(1), 53–66 (2015)
15. Ghenta, M., Bobarnat, E.: Engagement of older persons in cultural activities: importance and barriers. J. Econ. Dev. Environ. People **8**(4), 6–12 (2019)
16. Nollet, F.: Elderly and cultural participation in society. Presentation for the Annual Meeting of ENOTHE (2012). http://www.enothe.eu/activities/meet/ac12/Appendix5.4.3.pdf
17. Frith, J.: Splintered space: hybrid spaces and differential mobility. Mobilities **7**(1), 131–149 (2012)

Acceptance Level of Older Chinese People Towards Video Shooting Games

Rita W. L. Yu[✉], Wai Hung Yuen, Lu Peng, and Alan H. S. Chan

Department of Systems Engineering and Engineering Management,
City University of Hong Kong, Kowloon, Hong Kong
{winglamyu7-c,waihyuen6-c}@my.cityu.edu.hk,
{lupeng2-c,alan.chan}@cityu.edu.hk

Abstract. This study aimed to explore the acceptance level of older Chinese individuals in Hong Kong towards video shooting games (VSGs). Factors that influenced older adults to play VSGs were examined using qualitative research methods. A modified technology acceptance model (TAM) was used to explain and predict why older adults accept or reject VSGs. Experiments with three types of VSGs (mild violence, moderate violence and sports related) and face-to-face interviews were conducted with 47 adults above the age of 65 years. Six factors that affected the acceptance level of older adults towards VSGs were examined. These factors included physical and cognitive abilities, facilitating conditions, social influence, challenge, enjoyment and experience. Physical and cognitive abilities were respectively defined as general physical capabilities, such as balance and flexibility, and mental capabilities, such as reasoning and problem solving. Facilitating conditions were related to accessibility of VSGs, such as financial resources and technical support from others. Social influence denoted the effect of other people on older adults' thoughts, behaviours and acceptance of VSGs to meet the expectations of the social environment. Challenge represented the perceived difficulty of older adults regarding VSGs, which influenced their willingness to play such games. Enjoyment was the state of taking pleasure in VSGs, and experience included the knowledge and skills that players can acquire from similar or related games.

Results showed a negative correlation between age and acceptance level of VSGs. Participants between the ages of 65 and 75 years had a higher behavioural intention towards playing VSGs than those between the ages of 76 and 85 years and above. However, 96% of the participants had never played VSGs prior to the experiments, which showed that shooting games may not be a preferred video game genre among older adults. Physical and cognitive abilities and facilitating conditions were the most significant factors that influenced the older gamers' acceptance of VSGs. This finding suggested that improvements in physical and cognitive abilities and encouragement from peers and family members could lead to a significantly high willingness in older adults to play VSGs. Results also showed that the effects of social influence and challenge on the acceptance level of older adults towards VSGs were insignificant. Interestingly, enjoyment had a neutral or no relationship with VSG acceptance of older gamers, and older adults preferred sports-related VSGs over violence-related VSGs. These findings were important for understanding the factors that affected game acceptance of older individuals.

© Springer Nature Switzerland AG 2020
Q. Gao and J. Zhou (Eds.): HCII 2020, LNCS 12208, pp. 707–718, 2020.
https://doi.org/10.1007/978-3-030-50249-2_50

Keywords: Technology acceptance model (TAM) · Video shooting game (VSG) · Older Chinese people · Qualitative research

1 Introduction

In 2019, the United Nations stated that 1.02 billion people in the world were 60 years old or over, which is nearly three times the total number in 1980 (382 million older adults). Moreover, the population of older adults is estimated to reach nearly 2.08 billion by 2050 (United Nations 2019). Multiple age-related changes in older adults affect their acceptance and perception of as well as ability to use digital technology (e.g. Chen et al. 2014; Ma et al. 2016; Yu et al. 2018). These changes interact with one another and present special challenges for older people to overcome (Johnson and Finn 2017). The rapid increase in the use of technology in daily life creates serious challenges for most older adults, as they must interact with technological products and entertainment to stay healthy, independent and active (Teh et al. 2017). Commercial video games are designed to be enjoyable, challenging and capable of fostering sustained player engagement, and players can gain cognitive benefits from playing video games (Anguera and Gazzaley 2015).

Older adults tend to choose puzzle and stimulating games over other genres, such as multiplayer online games and first-person shooting games (Blocker et al. 2014). In 2019, racing games were reported as the favourite of male (61%) and female (76%) millennial gamers (between the ages of 18 and 34 years; International Software Association, 2019). By contrast, card and casino games were the favourite of male (58%) and female (59%) boomer gamers (between the ages of 55 and 64 years). Older adults preferred genres such as card, puzzle and virtual board games over other game genres owing to their simplicity and familiarity; moreover, they are easy to learn, play and control (Salmon et al. 2017). Such genres suit older adults' lifestyle, as they do not require much commitment and discipline from the gamers (Cota et al. 2015).

Video game playing can minimise age-related declines in cognition and mobility in older adults and improve or maintain daily functions (Salmon et al. 2017). Nevertheless, most studies on video game training have used action video games (especially first-person shooter games), rather than puzzle, card and virtual board games, to demonstrate improvements in age-associated declines in the perceptual and cognitive abilities of older adults (Green and Bavelier 2015). Playing action video games can provide numerous benefits to older adults; however, older individuals are reluctant to play such games owing to the presence of various barriers. Although several recent studies have addressed the benefits of playing action video games to the cognitive abilities of older adults, research on factors affecting the acceptance of video shooting games (VSGs) among older Chinese individuals remains scarce.

2   Research Framework

The technology acceptance model (TAM) has been widely used to investigate the acceptance and usage of technological products and services (Davis et al. 1989). The TAM states that technology usage can be predicted by behavioural intention (BI), which is dependent on perceived usefulness (PU) and perceived ease of use (PEOU). PU is defined as the degree to which a person believes that using a particular system would enhance his or her job performance, whilst PEOU is defined as the degree to which a person believes that using a particular system would be effortless. The TAM has been widely used to investigate older adults' adoption of gerontechnology (e.g. Chen et al. 2012, Joseph et al. 2016). Perceived gaming benefits to the cognitive functions of older adults have been shown as the factors affecting their acceptance of gaming (e.g. Kaufman et al. 2016; Duplàa et al. 2017). In the present study, the TAM is used to determine the factors affecting the acceptance of VSGs among older Chinese people.

Current action video games are mainly targeted at adolescents and young adults and present barriers to older adults with age-related declines in physical and cognitive abilities. Action video games are generally fast paced and feature violent content, which discourage and demotivate older adults from playing VSGs (Deng et al. 2017; Chesham et al. 2017). Social influence may also play an important role in the acceptance of older adults of video games (Chen and Chan 2013). A few older adults consider video games as childish and meaningless; moreover, such individuals are concerned that other people might perceive them as immature for playing such games (De Schutter and Vanden Abeele, 2010). Furthermore, older adults believe that they cannot or should not enjoy gaming owing to stereotypes on the social perception of aging and gamers (McLaughlin et al. 2012). In addition, the complexity of games affects older adults' acceptance of video games. Older adults have expressed that they do not want to waste time engaging in gameplays that are too challenging (Brown 2017). Enjoyment, which is an important aspect for maintaining connections with family members, has been shown as a prominent reason among older adults for playing video games (Osmanovic and Pecchioni 2016). Facilitating conditions refer to the extent to which an individual believes that an existing technical infrastructure could support his or her use of a system (Venkatesh et al. 2003). In general, older adults' perception of facilitating conditions, such as cost, access and availability of game support, significantly affects their intention to play video games (Pan and Jordan-Marsh 2010).

Five factors that may have direct impacts on PEOU and PU of VSGs are included in the proposed research model (Fig. 1). These factors include physical and cognitive abilities (PCA), facilitating conditions (FC), social influence (SI), challenge (CH) and enjoyment (EN) from playing VSGs.

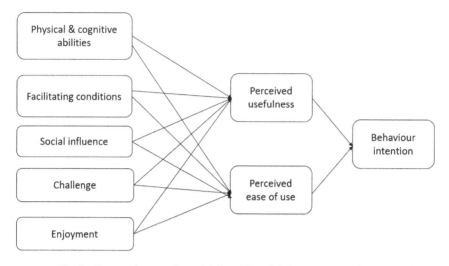

Fig. 1. Proposed research model for older adults' acceptance of VSGs

3 Methodology

3.1 Participants

The population of this study was Chinese individuals in Hong Kong between the ages of 65 years and above. The respondents were identified and approached in public parks, university areas and elderly centres in Hong Kong. All the participants were required to sign a consent form to ensure that they fully understood the study purpose, procedure, risks and benefits as well as their rights. A total of 47 respondents comprised of 26 men and 21 women participated in the study. The age (between 65 and 75 years: 36%; between 76 and 85 years: 32%; 85 years and above: 32%) and gender (male: 55%; female: 45%) of the respondents were evenly distributed. The majority of the respondents were married (81%), living with family members (72%) and attained secondary education (60%). Interestingly, 96% of the participants had never played VSGs. Table 1 summarises the demographic characteristics of the respondents.

Table 1. Demographic information (N = 47)

Demographic characteristics	Frequency	Percentage
Age		
65–75	17	36%
76–85	15	32%
>85	15	32%
Gender		
Male	26	55%
Female	21	45%

(*continued*)

Table 1. (*continued*)

Demographic characteristics	Frequency	Percentage
Education Level		
Primary or below	17	36%
Secondary	28	60%
Associate degree/diploma	2	4%
Bachelor's degree or above	0	0%
Living arrangement		
Alone	8	17%
With family	34	72%
With relatives	5	11%
With friends	0	0%
Elderly home	0	0%
Primary source of income		
Salary	0	0%
Retirement wages	6	13%
Savings	14	30%
Family	17	36%
Social subsidy	10	21%
Others	0	0%
Marital status		
Single	3	6%
Married	38	81%
Divorced	1	2%
Widowed	5	11%
VSG experience		
Yes	2	4%
No	45	96%

3.2   Procedure

This study used playtesting sessions that combined questionnaires with hands-on video-game playing to quantify the older adults' acceptance of VSGs. This approach is well suited for individuals with no previous game experience and is more informative than interviews and surveys (Khoo et al. 2007). Each respondent participated in a 10-min introduction session, followed by a 15-min playtesting session with three shooting games and a 20-min interview session. A 10-min break was given to the participants between the playtesting and interview sessions.

In the introduction session, the participants were asked to watch a short video clip explaining how the three VSGs are played. Afterwards, the experimenter briefly repeated the instructions to ensure that the participants understood the game rules. For the playtesting session, the participants were asked to play the three games (5 min each). Finally, in the interview session, the participants were asked to evaluate their acceptance of VSGs using a questionnaire.

3.3   Shooting Games

This study presented the participants with three single-player VSGs, namely Kill Shot Virus, Skeet Shooting 3D and Destroy Office: Stress Buster FPS Shooting Game. Kill Shot Virus is a zombie-killing first-person shooting game. The participants had to utilise a large set of weapons to protect survivors, kill undead zombies and stop a virus from spreading. Skeet Shooting 3D is a clay pigeon shooting game. The participants needed to control a gun to shoot down clay targets, which are automatically flung in the air from fixed stations. Meanwhile, Destroy Office: Stress Buster FPS Shooting Game is an office-destruction first-person shooting game. The participants had to destroy a modern office using multiple weapons and machine guns.

3.4   Questionnaire

The participants' acceptance of VSGs was measured using a questionnaire. The questionnaire measurements consisted of factors affecting the acceptance of shooting games. It consisted of 41 items written in Chinese, with closed 10-point Likert-type scales, ranging from 1 (strongly disagree) to 10 (strongly agree).

Behaviour Intention (BI), Perceived Usefulness (PU) and Perceived Ease of Use (PEOU). Behaviour intention is defined as the extent to which an individual intends to perform a specific behaviour (Davis et al. 1989). In this study, BI to play was defined as a participant's willingness to play VSGs. PU is defined as the degree to which a person believes that playing VSGs could enhance his or her game performance (Davis et al. 1989). Meanwhile, PEOU was defined as the degree to which the participants feel that playing a VSG does not require physical or mental effort (Davis et al. 1989).

Social Influence (SI). Social influence is defined as the degree to which an individual perceives that significant individuals believe that he or she should use a new system (Venkatesh et al. 2003). SI leads to technology adoption, which incorporates two essential elements, namely, the adoption of VSGs by individuals and the embedment of VSGs in society (Vannoy and Palvia 2010). Social influence may affect older adults' attitudes and acceptance of VSGs (Dwivedi et al. 2019).

Enjoyment (EN). Enjoyment is the extent to which the act of using a system is perceived as personally enjoyable in its own right apart from having instrumental value (Davis et al. 1992). EN has been proposed in previous studies as a determinant of ease of use (Venkatesh et al. 2002; Mun and Hwang 2003). EN was expected to positively affect older adults' acceptance of VSGs.

Physical and Cognitive Abilities (PCA). Age-related changes in cognitive, perceptual and motor systems are important considerations in designing technology for older adults (Czaja et al. 2019). Older adults may perceive games differently compared with young adults. Age-related changes in motor control, such increased difficulties with fine motor control and coordination, and the onset of disease processes, such as arthritis, can change the way older adults interact with games (Charness and Boot 2009). Aging is also associated with the general slowing of cognitive processes, decreased memory capacity, difficulty in goal maintenance and decreased attentional control (Charness and Boot 2009). These changes in functions can slow performance and result in a high number of errors when older adults interact with games that are not targeted at them.

Facilitating Conditions (FC). Facilitating conditions refer to conditions associated with the perception of environmental objective factors that support the use of geron-technology (Venkatesh et al. 2003). These objective factors focus on accessibility of technology and support from the environment. In this study, indicators of FC included the financial resources of the participants and available help from others.

Challenge (CH). Challenge refers to perceived difficulty in understanding and playing VSGs. It is also related to older adults' PU and PEOU of playing VSGs. When older adults perceive games as challenging, they are likely to believe that the games would boost their cognition (Boot et al. 2018).

3.5 Measures

TAM factors in the research model were measured with items adapted from prior related studies. PU, PEOU, BI, physical and cognitive abilities and facilitating conditions each consisted of five factors (Davis 1989; Yi and Davis 2001; Ryu et al. 2009; Griffith et al. 2011). Four items comprised social influence, and enjoyment and challenge consisted of three items each (Leung et al. 2005; McDowell 2006). The items for each factor are summarised in Table 2.

Table 2. Summary of factor items

Perceived usefulness PU
"I think my physical performance (health and reaction time) can be improved by VSGs"
"I think playing VSGs effectively consumes my leisure time"
"I think playing VSGs would make my life fun and enjoyable"
"I think playing VSGs can improve my social relationships"
"I think playing VSGs is generally beneficial to me"
Perceived ease of use PEOU
"I feel easy to use the mobile phone for VSG"
"I feel easy to perform the game control as I want"
"I can master mobile phone controls for VSGs"
"I do not need any more instructions for the VSGs"
"I can play VSGs alone without the help of others"
Behaviour intention (BI)
"I believe that my health status is good enough to play VSGs"
"I believe that playing VSGs is entertaining"
"I believe that playing VSGs improves my quality of life"

(continued)

Table 2. (*continued*)

"I believe that the benefits of playing VSGs outweigh the costs of playing VSGs (e.g. money, time, harm to body, opportunity cost and so on)"

"I am willing to play VSGs if I have spare time and sufficient resources prepared"

Physical and cognitive abilities (PCA)

"I can promptly react in my daily life"

"I can read clearly in my daily life"

"I can learn fast in my daily life"

"I feel that playing VSGs can enhance my reaction time"

"I feel that playing VSGs can make me learn faster"

Facilitating conditions (FC)

"I can easily seek technical support from my friends/family in playing VSGs"

"I can easily access gaming devices (mobile) for playing VSGs"

"My living environment allows me to play VSGs (adequate network and charging locations)"

"My financial status allows me to play VSGs"

"My friends/family encourage me to play VSGs"

Social influence (SI)

"The public thinks that VSGs are a form of healthy entertainment"

"The public thinks that VSGs are a luxury product/activity"

"The public shows no discrimination towards VSGs"

"I think that playing VSGs encourages me to integrate with others"

Enjoyment (EN)

"I enjoy playing VSGs"

"I think that playing VSGs is a good form of entertainment"

"I feel that time passes quickly when I play VSGs"

Challenge (CH)

"I think VSGs are challenging"

"I am proud when I achieve certain missions in VSGs"

"Playing VSGs involves my muscles and reaction practice"

4 Findings

The proposed model was assessed by examining the internal consistency of each factor and the correlations between each factor. Stepwise regression analyses were performed to check the effects of the various factors. SPSS 23 and AMOS 26 were used to perform all statistical analyses.

Analysis of the Research Model

A series of stepwise regression analyses were performed to examine the effects of five factors, namely, physical and cognitive abilities social influence, challenge, facilitating conditions and enjoyment, on PEOU and PU. The effects of PEOU and PU on BI were also examined. The results are summarised in Fig. 2.

The results indicated that only physical and cognitive abilities, facilitating conditions, social influence and challenge could predict PU. Analysis of variance showed that the model was significant [$F_{(4, 42)} = 133.835$, $p = 0.000$]. The coefficient of determination (R^2) was 0.927, and the adjusted R^2 was 0.920, thereby indicating that the regression model accounted for 92% of the total variance in PU.

Furthermore, the findings indicated that only physical and cognitive abilities, challenge, facilitating conditions and social influence could predict PEOU. Analysis of variance showed that the model was significant [F (4, 42) = 58.055, p = 0.000]. The coefficient of determination (R^2) was 0.847, and the adjusted R^2 was 0.832, thereby indicating that the regression model accounted for 83.2% of the total variance in PEOU.

In addition, PU and PEOU could predict BI. Analysis of variance demonstrated that the model was significant [F (2,44) = 72.930, p = 0.000]. The coefficient of determination (R^2) was 0.768, and the adjusted R^2 was 0.758, thereby indicating that the regression model accounted for 75.8% of the total variance in BI.

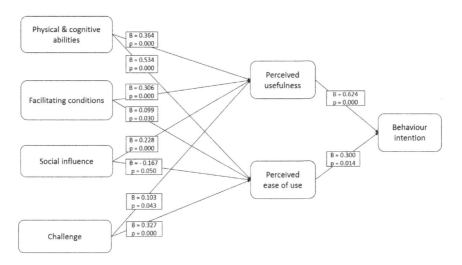

Fig. 2. Model for older adults' acceptance of VSGs

5   Discussion and Conclusion

In this study, the TAM was modified to incorporate older adult-related factors. Using the modified model, factors that contributed to the acceptance of VSGs among older adults in Hong Kong were investigated. A total of 47 respondents, 65 years old and above, participated in this study. Four factors, namely physical and cognitive abilities, challenge, facilitating conditions and social influence, were satisfactory predictors of acceptance of VSGs among older adults. In agreement with the expectations from the TAM, PU and PEOU were predictors of BI to play VSGs. The adoption of video games was related to how older adults perceived the usefulness of the games (McCreadie and Tinker 2005). Older adults accepted and played new games if they believed and realised that VSGs could improve their lives and satisfy their needs. PEOU, which is also an indicator of BI, indicated that older adults were likely to accept VSGs that are easy to play and have a simple interface design.

Physical and cognitive abilities were positively associated with PEOU and PU. Age-related declines in perception, psychosocial functioning, cognition and movement influenced older adults' need and ability to play video games (Erber 2013). People with poor physical and cognitive health might find interacting with games difficult. Age-related hearing and visual impairments may also influence the ease of playing action games, such as fast-paced VSGs. Challenge was shown to exert a significant effect in predicting PEOU and PU. High technologies have lower adoption rates compared with survival and basic technologies (Chen et al. 2012). High technologies are defined as those that involve innovation, and users generally need to exert considerable effort to learn to use these new products or services. As VSGs do not belong under survival or basic technologies, older adults may find learning to play them challenging.

Facilitating conditions were directly associated with PEOU and PU. The acceptance of older adults of VSGs was influenced by facilitating conditions, thereby indicating that obtaining environmental support (e.g. game teaching and gaming opportunities) was very important in helping older people overcome barriers to playing VSGs. Social influence also influenced the acceptance of VSGs among older adults. Social influence indicated that the adoption of video games by individuals and society influenced older adults' acceptance of VSGs. Nevertheless, the influence of enjoyment on PEOU and PU was not found, which contradicts the findings of previous studies (Wang et al. 2011). This result may be due to the participants' lack of experience in playing VSGs. Without experience in playing VSGs, older adults may not be aware of the enjoyment that such games could provide.

The results of the study pointed out the important role of physical and cognitive abilities, challenge, facilitating conditions and social influence in positively influencing older adults' decision to play VSGs. The model illuminated the underlying relationships between the acceptance factors and existing TAM variables, thereby providing insights into how the acceptance and design of VSGs can be further improved and facilitated for older gamers. These findings can significantly extend prior research on older adults' acceptance of VSGs by linking older adult-related factors to well-known TAM variables and empirically validating their relationships.

Acknowledgement.   The authors would like to thank for the support of Strategic Research Grant 7004906 of City University of Hong Kong.

References

Anguera, J.A., Gazzaley, A.: Video games, cognitive exercises, and the enhancement of cognitive abilities. Curr. Opin. Behav. Sci. **4**, 160–165 (2015)

Blocker, K.A., Wright, T.J., Boot, W.R.: Gaming preferences of aging generations. Gerontechnol.: Int. J. Fund. Aspects Technol. Serve Ageing Soc. **12**(3), 174 (2014)

Boot, W.R., et al.: Exploring older adults' video game use in the PRISM computer system. Innov. Aging **2**(1), igy009 (2018)

Brown, J.A.: Digital gaming perceptions among older adult non-gamers. In: Zhou, J., Salvendy, G. (eds.) ITAP 2017. LNCS, vol. 10298, pp. 217–227. Springer, Cham (2017). https://doi.org/10.1007/978-3-319-58536-9_18

Charness, N., Boot, W.R.: Aging and information technology use: Potential and barriers. Curr. Dir. Psychol. Sci. **18**(5), 253–258 (2009)

Chen, K., Chan, A.H.S.: Use or non-use of gerontechnology—a qualitative study. Int. J. Environ. Res. Public Health **10**(10), 4645–4666 (2013)

Chen, K., Chan, A.H.S., Chan, S.C.: Gerontechnology acceptance by older Hong Kong people. Gerontechnology **11**(2), 102–103 (2012)

Chen, K., Chan, A.H.S., Ma, Q.: Cell phone feature preferences among older adults: a paired comparison study. Gerontechnology **13**(2) (2014)

Chesham, A., Wyss, P., Müri, R.M., Mosimann, U.P., Nef, T.: What older people like to play: genre preferences and acceptance of casual games. JMIR Serious Games **5**(2), e8 (2017)

Cota, T.T., Ishitani, L., Vieira Jr., N.: Mobile game design for the elderly: a study with focus on the motivation to play. Comput. Hum. Behav. **51**, 96–105 (2015)

Czaja, S.J., Boot, W.R., Charness, N., Rogers, W.A.: Designing for Older Adults: Principles and Creative Human Factors Approaches. CRC Press (2019)

Davis, F.D.: Perceived usefulness, perceived ease of use, and user acceptance of information technology. MIS Q. **13**, 319–340 (1989)

Davis, F.D., Bagozzi, R.P., Warshaw, P.R.: User acceptance of computer technology: a comparison of two theoretical models. Manag. Sci. **35**(8), 982–1003 (1989)

Davis, F.D., Bagozzi, R.P., Warshaw, P.R.: Extrinsic and intrinsic motivation to use computers in the workplace 1. J. Appl. Soc. Psychol. **22**(14), 1111–1132 (1992)

De Schutter, B., Vanden Abeele, V.: Designing meaningful play within the psycho-social context of older adults. In: Proceedings of the 3rd International Conference on Fun and Games, pp. 84–93. ACM, September 2010

Deng, M., Chan, A.H.S., Wu, F., Liu, S.: Effects of the contextual variables of racing games on risky driving behavior. Games Health J. **6**(4), 249–254 (2017)

Duplàa, E., Kaufman, D., Sauvé, L., Renaud, L.: A questionnaire-based study on the perceptions of Canadian seniors about cognitive, social, and psychological benefits of digital games. Games Health J. **6**(3), 171–178 (2017)

Dwivedi, Y.K., Rana, N.P., Jeyaraj, A., Clement, M., Williams, M.D.: Re-examining the unified theory of acceptance and use of technology (UTAUT): towards a revised theoretical model. Inf. Syst. Front. **21**(3), 719–734 (2019). https://doi.org/10.1007/s10796-017-9774-y

Entertainment Software Association: Essential facts about the computer and video game industry (2019). https://www.theesa.com/wp-content/uploads/2019/05/ESA_Essential_facts_2019_final.pdf

Erber, J.T.: Aging and Older Adulthood. Wiley, Hoboken (2013)

Green, C.S., Bavelier, D.: Action video game training for cognitive enhancement. Curr. Opin. Behav. Sci. **4**, 103–108 (2015)

Griffith, J.F., Yeung, D.K., Leung, J.C.S., Kwok, T.C., Leung, P.C.: Prediction of bone loss in elderly female subjects by MR perfusion imaging and spectroscopy. Eur. Radiol. **21**(6), 1160–1169 (2011). https://doi.org/10.1007/s00330-010-2054-6

Johnson, J., Finn, K.: Designing User Interfaces for an Aging Population: Towards Universal Design. Morgan Kaufmann, Burlington (2017)

Joseph, S., Teh, P.L., Chan, A.H.S., Ahmed, P.K., Cheong, S.N., Yap, W.J.: Gerontechnology usage and acceptance model (GUAM): a qualitative study of Chinese older adults in Malaysia. Gerontechnology **14**(4), 224–238 (2016)

Kaufman, D., Sauvé, L., Renaud, L., Sixsmith, A., Mortenson, B.: Older adults' digital gameplay: Patterns, benefits, and challenges. Simul. Gaming **47**(4), 465–489 (2016)

Khoo, E.T., Merritt, T., Cheok, A., Lian, M., Yeo, K.: Age invaders: user studies of intergenerational computer entertainment. In: Ma, L., Rauterberg, M., Nakatsu, R. (eds.) ICEC 2007. LNCS, vol. 4740, pp. 231–242. Springer, Heidelberg (2007). https://doi.org/10.1007/978-3-540-74873-1_28

Leung, K., Bhagat, R.S., Buchan, N.R., Erez, M., Gibson, C.B.: Culture and international business: recent advances and their implications for future research. J. Int. Bus. Stud. **36**(4), 357–378 (2005). https://doi.org/10.1057/palgrave.jibs.8400150

Ma, Q., Chan, A.H.S., Chen, K.: Personal and other factors affecting acceptance of smartphone technology by older Chinese adults. Appl. Ergon. **54**, 62–71 (2016)

McCreadie, C., Tinker, A.: The acceptability of assistive technology to older people. Ageing Soc. **25**(1), 91–110 (2005)

McDowell, I.: Measuring Health: A Guide to Rating Scales and Questionnaires. Oxford University Press, Oxford (2006)

McLaughlin, A., Gandy, M., Allaire, J., Whitlock, L.: Putting fun into video games for older adults. Ergon. Des. **20**(2), 13–22 (2012)

Mun, Y.Y., Hwang, Y.: Predicting the use of web-based information systems: self-efficacy, enjoyment, learning goal orientation, and the technology acceptance model. Int. J. Hum.-Comput. Stud. **59**(4), 431–449 (2003)

Nunnally, J.C.: Psychometric Theory 3E. Tata McGraw-Hill Education, New York (1994)

Osmanovic, S., Pecchioni, L.: Beyond entertainment: motivations and outcomes of video game playing by older adults and their younger family members. Games Cult. **11**(1–2), 130–149 (2016)

Pan, S., Jordan-Marsh, M.: Internet use intention and adoption among Chinese older adults: from the expanded technology acceptance model perspective. Comput. Hum. Behav. **26**(5), 1111–1119 (2010)

Yu, R.W.L., Peng, L., Chan, A.H.S., Teh, P.L., Lam, L.Y.C.: Attitudes and perceptions of older chinese people in hong kong towards silver gaming. In: Zhou, J., Salvendy, G. (eds.) ITAP 2018. LNCS, vol. 10927, pp. 571–586. Springer, Cham (2018). https://doi.org/10.1007/978-3-319-92037-5_40

Ryu, M.H., Kim, S., Lee, E.: Understanding the factors affecting online elderly user's participation in video UCC services. Comput. Hum. Behav. **25**(3), 619–632 (2009)

Salmon, J.P., Dolan, S.M., Drake, R.S., Wilson, G.C., Klein, R.M., Eskes, G.A.: A survey of video game preferences in adults: building better games for older adults. Entertain. Comput. **21**, 45–64 (2017)

Teh, P.L., et al.: Does power posing affect gerontechnology adoption among older adults? Behav. Inf. Technol. **36**(1), 33–42 (2017)

United Nations, Department of Economic and Social Affairs, Population Division: World Population Prospects (2019). https://population.un.org/wpp/

Vannoy, S.A., Palvia, P.: The social influence model of technology adoption. Commun. ACM **53**(6), 149–153 (2010)

Venkatesh, V., Morris, M.G., Davis, G.B., Davis, F.D.: User acceptance of information technology: toward a unified view. MIS Q. **27**, 425–478 (2003)

Venkatesh, V., Speier, C., Morris, M.G.: User acceptance enablers in individual decision making about technology: toward an integrated model. Decis. Sci. **33**(2), 297–316 (2002)

Wang, L., Rau, P.L.P., Salvendy, G.: Older adults' acceptance of information technology. Educ. Gerontol. **37**(12), 1081–1099 (2011)

Yi, M.Y., Davis, F.D.: Improving computer training effectiveness for decision technologies: behavior modeling and retention enhancement. Decis. Sci. **32**(3), 521–544 (2001)

Author Index